WRITING UNDER TYRANNY

..

Writing Under Tyranny

*English Literature and
the Henrician Reformation*

GREG WALKER

OXFORD
UNIVERSITY PRESS

OXFORD
UNIVERSITY PRESS

Great Clarendon Street, Oxford OX2 6DP

Oxford University Press is a department of the University of Oxford.
It furthers the University's objective of excellence in research, scholarship,
and education by publishing worldwide

Oxford New York

Auckland Cape Town Dar es Salaam Hong Kong Karachi
Kuala Lumpur Madrid Melbourne Mexico City Nairobi
New Delhi Shanghai Taipei Toronto

With offices in

Argentina Austria Brazil Chile Czech Republic France Greece
Guatemala Hungary Italy Japan Poland Portugal Singapore
South Korea Switzerland Thailand Turkey Ukraine Vietnam

Oxford is a registered trade mark of Oxford University Press
in the UK and in certain other countries

Published in the United States by Oxford University Press Inc., New York

British Library Cataloguing in Publication Data

Data available

Library of Congress Cataloging in Publication Data

Data available
Typeset in 10.5pt/12pt AGaramond
by SPI Publisher Services, Pondicherrty, India

Printed in Great Britain on acid-free paper by
Biddles Ltd, King's Lynn, Norfolk

ISBN 0-19-928333-8   978-0-19-928333-0

1 3 5 7 9 10 8 6 4 2

'Tyranny is, so to speak, a nervous breakdown of the body politic.'
(Maurice Latey, *Tyranny: A Study in the Abuse of Power*)

Acknowledgements

This book was written thanks to the award of a three-year Major Research Fellowship from the Leverhulme Trust. Without this award I would not have had the time to begin, let alone to complete, so substantial a project. I should like to place on record my very sincere gratitude to the Trustees for their support and encouragement of my work.

While writing this book I have also enjoyed the generous, informed criticism and advice of numerous friends and colleagues who have read draft chapters, answered arcane queries, and suggested new avenues and ideas that I might pursue. Again, without such help this volume would never have seen the light of day. Many of my detailed debts are recorded in the notes to what follows, but I should like to offer more general thanks here to all of those people who gave of their time and expertise so generously. David Salter, John J. McGavin, Claire Jowitt, John Scattergood, and G.W. Bernard read various sections of the book in draft, offered invaluable advice, and in many cases kindly allowed me to read unpublished articles and chapters of their own. Anne Marie D'Arcy both read draft chapters and offered invaluable information and suggestions that sharpened my thinking and improved the text at numerous points. Elaine Treharne was an unflaggingly supportive friend and Head of Department throughout the project. Michael Davis, Vince Newey, Dave Postles, Tony Kushner, Kevin Sharpe, Pete Smith, Kevin Jacklin, Kevin Anthony, Alex Moseley, Janette Dillon, Bob Godfrey, Richard Foulkes, Michael and Andrew Hagiioannu, Bella Millett, Martin Stannard, Mark Rawlinson, Gordon Campbell, and Pat and Dennis Joynt, were variously exemplary friends, advisers, and colleagues. Andre Lascombes, Michel Bitot, Marie-Helene Besnault, and Richard Hilman offered me the chance to try out some of these ideas in a congenial atmosphere at the International Colloquium on Tudor Theatre at Tours, and similar hospitality was offered by the convenors of the research seminars at the Universities of Nottingham, Exeter, Leeds, Oxford, and Queen Mary, London. I am grateful to them, and to the librarians at the Huntington Library, San Marino, California, and the Harry Ransom Humanities Research Library at the University of Austin, Texas, for allowing me to consult texts in their care, and to the British Academy, the Arts and Humanities Research Board, and the Research Committee of the University of Leicester for financial support for research trips and study leave. I should also like to record my thanks to the two anonymous press readers whose generous, detailed reports both helped me to tighten the arguments in a number of places and encouraged me that there was a topic here to be pursued. Andrew McNeillie was, once more, the paragon of commissioning editors.

As ever, my greatest personal debts are to my family, to Sharon, Matt, David, and Tessa the dog, for keeping me busy when I was not pondering the fate of Tudor poets, and to Nottingham Forest Football Club for giving me other things to worry about.

Contents

List of Abbreviations

Acts and Monuments	The Rev. Josiah Pratt, ed., *The Acts and Monuments of John Foxe* (8 vols., London, 1870)
BL	The British Library
EHD v	C. H. Williams, ed., *English Historical Documents, volume V: 1485–1558* (London, 1967)
EHR	*The English Historical Review*
EETS	The Early English Text Society
Hall, *Chronicle*	Edward Hall, *The Union of the Two Noble and Illustrious Houses of Lancaster and York*, ed. H. Ellis (London, 1809)
HJ	*The Historical Journal*
JEH	*The Journal of Ecclesiastical History*
LP	J. S. Brewer, *et al.*, eds., *Letters and Papers, Foreign and Domestic, of the Reign of Henry VIII* (21 vols. in 36, London, 1862–1932)
METh	*Medieval English Theatre*
PRO	The Public Record Office
Spanish Calendar	G. A. Bergenroth, *et al.*, eds., *Calendar of State Papers Spanish* (13 vols., London, 1862–1954)
State Papers	*State Papers Published Under the Authority of His Majesty's Commission, King Henry VIII, Public Record Office* (11 vols., London, 1830–52)
STC	A. W. Pollard and G. R. Redgrave, eds., *The Short Title Catalogue of Books Printed in England, Scotland, and Ireland, 1475–1640*, 2nd edition, revised and enlarged by W. A. Jackson, F. S. Ferguson, and K. F. Pantzer (London, 1976)
TRHS	*The Transactions of the Royal Historical Society*
Venetian Calendar	R. Brown, *et al.*, eds., *Calendar of State Papers Venetian* (9 vols., 1864–98)

A Note on the Texts

In what follows I have modernized the spelling of all prose texts and documents, leaving only problematic or enigmatic words in their original spelling. All verse quotations remain in the original.

Introduction

By no stretch of the available definitions was the England of 1509, or even of 1527, tyrannically governed. At his accession in 1509 Henry VIII was hailed as an ideal prince. He was, the poets and scholars declared, the perfect combination of admirable personal qualities and virtuous aspirations; the 'good king' who would put an end to the era of political repression and economic retrenchment overseen by his father, Henry VII, inaugurating a new age of magnanimous, open kingship. Such was, of course, often the way with new kings. Optimism is virtually compulsory when it comes to coronations. But, remarkably, as we shall see, Henry seemed to believe the pious sentiments that he and his scholarly advisers voiced for the occasion, and strove for almost two decades to put them into practice. Only the explosion of the divorce crisis of 1527–32: the King's aptly named 'Great Matter', signalled the end of this unprecedented period of stability and optimism. In the interim the realm had enjoyed a long period of internal peace, its political institutions had proved themselves robust and, by the standards of the time, effective, its people largely prosperous and free to speak their minds, and its king seemingly determined to fulfil the obligations of his office according to the conventional models of virtuous lordship.

By the time of Henry's death in 1547, however, all this had changed. There was a widespread perception that England had fallen under a despotic regime, and that Henry himself was a monster whose death was a blessing to his subjects. Again, to call a king a tyrant after his death was not unprecedented. Decrying the old in order to welcome the new was precisely what Henry's advisers had done in 1509. But Henry was accused of tyranny while he was still alive, not once but many times, not merely by his rivals and enemies abroad but by his own subjects, and despite novel and savage legislation that made it a specific capital offence for anyone to do so. This too was remarkable in contemporary experience. How such a situation came about is a compelling narrative in its own right, and it is the backdrop to the story of this book. But to describe the general trajectory of the reign as the King's fall from a vigorous, virtuous prince to a bloated old tyrant is to tell a relatively familiar story.[1] I want to tell a less familiar and in many ways

more intriguing one. I will examine what people—and particularly articulate
people at the heart of the political nation—*did* about the unprecedented changes
of the 1530s and 1540s. How did well-informed individuals react to the growing
realization that they were living through something previously unthinkable: the
slide into an English tyranny?

Previous studies of reactions and resistance to the Henrician Reformation have
looked at the responses of prominent dissenters, at well-known victims of the
break with Rome such as Thomas More and John Fisher, or have examined the
obvious instances of concerted opposition such as the Lincolnshire Rising and
the Pilgrimage of Grace of 1536–7. In perhaps the best-researched and most
compelling discussion of opposition to the Henrician Reformation to date, *Policy
and Police*, Sir Geoffrey Elton scoured trial records, local archives, and governmental correspondence for any scrap of evidence of how people in the localities
responded to government demands, unearthing numerous, if often incomplete,
accounts of popular grumbling against the regime and the Crown's reaction to it,
of the kinds of spontaneous protests and complaints expressed by men and
women in the parishes against the royal divorce or the direction of religious
policy.[2] Curiously, however, he largely ignored the testimonies of those individuals who have left copious, coherent written evidence of their responses to
government policy in this period, and who explored the most sensitive issues
of public policy and private emotion both in detail and at length. Indeed, the
evidence left by these individuals has rarely been explored from a political
perspective, and never in a comprehensive attempt to chart their reactions to
political change. This book seeks to make good that failure. It focuses on the
articulate and calculated form of engagement with Henrician governance and
policy expressed by those English subjects whose chosen medium was the written
word: the poets, prose-writers, scholars, and dramatists who wrote, revised,
edited, or printed works of fiction and advice during the 1530s. The reactions
of these men, working in and around the royal court, provide a uniquely valuable
test case for the reception of the Henrician Reformation, as such men were both
in a position to witness the king's actions close to, and felt able—indeed often
compelled—to reflect upon what they witnessed in their writings. They were also
intensely implicated in and compromised by the political events they witnessed.
As writers who were in one way or another licensed by the Crown and reliant for
their survival upon royal patronage or protection, they experienced the pressures
of Henry's regime on an intensely personal level. How did they respond to those
pressures? In a culture in which the conventional course for an author wishing to
protest about the state of the nation was to offer a work of supplication or counsel
to the monarch (in the form of a complaint or *speculum principis*: a 'mirror' for
the prince), how did they react to the realization that the King was not simply
unsympathetic to such complaints but was actually the source of the problem?

As we shall see, most of these writers took the only route available to loyal,
articulate subjects in a culture that allowed for no direct opposition to the Crown

but which tolerated a range of other forms of expression. For as long as they felt able they deployed all of the conventional forms: handbooks of moral, spiritual, or political counsel, hypothetical discussions, didactic and speculative writing of many kinds, to register their protests and offer alternative views of what they believed was in the best interests of the commonweal. This book is the story of their struggle to reclaim Henry from tyranny, and of their gradual realization of the fruitlessness of that endeavour. It is an account of how a generation of writers educated to believe in the power of eloquence to move minds and shape events reacted to the realization that it could no longer do so in conventional ways;[3] that the ground rules had changed, and that the King, who had hitherto seemed to listen to the words of his scholars and counsellors however awkward their advice had been, was no longer willing to do so. Ultimately it is the story of how some at least of those writers adapted their work in the light of that realization, and found other forms of literary and political expression more appropriate to the experience of writing under tyranny. In doing so they revolutionized writing in English, laying the foundations of much of what we now see as central to the English literary tradition.

The chapters that follow offer four detailed case studies of writers who in one way or another tried to come to terms with the experience of writing under a despotic monarch. Each author was a courtier or a royal servant directly employed by the King in the implementation or explanation of royal policy, and so well placed both to comment on political events and to feel the pressures and dangers of such commentary on an immediate and personal level. Each has left a lengthy testament to his anxieties about royal policy and his attempts to influence it in the form of one or more substantial literary texts. The stories surrounding the creation of those texts, the issues that they address, and the responses that they elicited are told in the course of this book interweaved with the narrative of the break with Rome, the Royal Supremacy, and the Henrician Reformation.

In the first part of the book I will examine the efforts of three of the King's household servants: William Thynne, Sir Brian Tuke, and John Heywood, each of whom was in his own way wedded to the conventions of the literature of royal advice. When confronted with the dramatic events of the early years of the King's Great Matter and the break with Rome they deployed the traditional remedy of the *speculum principis*, offering books of often sharply critical advice to their sovereign in an attempt to heal the violent social and religious divisions that had been exposed and exacerbated by his actions. In the second part I will focus on a single individual whose work spanned the period of the Henrician Reformation, the scholar and diplomat Sir Thomas Elyot. The dialogues, treatises, and narratives that poured from his pen in the course of the 1530s and early 1540s clearly reflect the stresses and pressures of writing public, political literature in the midst of Henry VIII's Reformation. Probably no better example can be found of the gradual disillusionment and loss of confidence in the traditional forms and processes of political writing brought on by that Reformation than the movement from Elyot's bold, assertive *speculum principis*, *The Book Named the Governor*, written in 1530–1, to the savage satire of his last major work, the bitter, fiercely contemporary reworking of Roman history, *The Image of Governance* (1540). In that movement the disenchantment of an entire generation of English humanists with the claims of their government is presented with an unprecedented and passionate intensity. In the third and final part I will look at two writers who, rather than striving to adapt old literary forms to rapidly changing conditions, sought new forms and new ways to engage with questions of government and policy in their writings: Sir Thomas Wyatt and Henry Howard, Earl of Surrey. Driven by the same disenchantment that prompted Elyot to abandon the *speculum principis*, Wyatt, and still more obviously Surrey, embodied it in new, radically personalized forms of lyrical and narrative verse, and in the process initiated what contemporaries recognized was a revolution in English poetry.

These men did not share a single political or religious perspective. Tuke, Heywood, and Elyot were conservative catholics, alarmed at the doctrinal and institutional innovations heralded by the first session of the Reformation Parliament in 1529. Thynne and Surrey were men of a more reformist stamp, content to criticize many of the abuses of the established church; and Wyatt was somewhere in between. What united them was not a shared faith but their mounting alarm at the direction of Henrician policy and the manner of its implementation. What makes them interesting are the ways in which they responded to that alarm, and sought both to reflect it and to remedy a national crisis through their writing.

The various parts of the book are designed so that they can be read independently as well as sequentially. They tell three distinct stories of individuals whose lives and careers were played out against the inexorable degeneration of English political and public culture in the 1530s and 40s. These stories are intriguing in themselves, and each is told afresh, drawing on new evidence or new analysis of familiar evidence, allowing its subjects to emerge in often very different ways to that presented in earlier accounts. But, taken together these sections add up to a story greater than the sum of its parts: a collective biography of a group of writers who were schooled in a long tradition of literary endeavour and had to learn quickly and painfully to come to terms with the new and violent pressures placed upon them and the beliefs they embodied by the actions of their king. It is the story of how they came to terms with living and writing under tyranny.

1

The Long Divorce of Steel

Tyranny and Political Culture in Henry VIII's England

Sitting by the fire after supper in the house of a rich Bologna merchant, the Welsh evangelical scholar William Thomas was drawn into conversation with a group of his fellow guests. They talked politely, as strangers will, of the differences of climate and culture between Italy and England, and exchanged information about the agricultural and industrial produce of their respective homelands. But their talk soon turned to politics. It was February 1547, and news of the death of Henry VIII had just reached Italy, so the local gentlemen asked their visitor for an account of the late King's personality and history.[1] Thomas happily obliged; but he had hardly got into his elegiac stride when one of the Italians interrupted him with a blunt challenge. 'You are earnest in your king's favour', he said, 'but you consider not that Cicero his eloquence should not suffice to defend him [Henry] of his tyranny, since he hath been known and noted over all to be the greatest tyrant that ever was in England.'[2] Warming to his theme, the unnamed Italian observed that,

I wot [know] not what Nero, what Dionysius, or what Mahomet may be compared unto him, in whom towards God rested no reverence of religion, nor towards man no kind of compassion; whose sword, inflamed by continual heat of innocent blood and whose bottomless belly could never be satisfied through the throat of extreme avarice and rapine; whose inconstant mind, occupied with occasion of continual war, permitted not his quiet neighbours to live in peace; and, in conclusion, whose unreasonable will had place alway[s] and in all things, against equity and reason.[3]

The circumstances may have been contrived, and the conversation, to some degree at least, imaginary, but the issue broached so forcefully by Thomas's interlocutor was all too real. That Henry VIII, the prince who had ascended the throne as the darling of the humanists, the seeming embodiment of royal idealism, had degenerated into tyranny was, by 1547, a commonplace of opinion both at home and abroad. And even during his lifetime, a number of observers offered unflattering comparisons with tyrants from biblical or classical history. The Spanish Ambassador, Eustace Chapuys called Henry's treatment of the church 'tyrannical', and a priest named 'Sir Davy' of Detling in Kent reputedly claimed that he was no prince but 'a tyrant more cruel than Nero, for Nero destroyed but a part of Rome, but this tyrant [Henry] destroyed the whole realm. And as Egeus did pursue the Apostles of Christ, much more doth this tiger persecute Holy Church, and not only the church and the goods of the same, but also he destroyeth the ministers of the same'.[4] William Peto, provincial minister of the Franciscan Observant friary at Greenwich, preached a sermon before the King himself tacitly comparing him to the Old Testament king Ahab (the adulterous murderer of Naboth).[5] In his *Dialogue Against Tribulation*, written while he was a prisoner in the Tower of London, Thomas More offered the examples of King Herod (bewitched by Salome into beheading John the Baptist) and Suleiman the Magnificent (a Muslim ruler, and therefore in medieval catholic eyes, axiomatically tyrannical) as a role-model for Henry VIII, and Cardinal Reginald Pole compared him to Nero, Domitian, and Richard III. At the other end of the religious spectrum, the reformer John Rivius spoke of 'that monstrous and bloody tyrant' Henry, while Philipp Melanchthon called him an English Nero and prayed for his early death.[6]

On what basis were such charges made? The execution of critics such as More and Cardinal John Fisher inevitably loomed large in the portfolio of Henry's crimes. In his lifetime, the Abbot of Colchester allegedly described the deaths of More and Fisher as the acts of 'tyrants and bloodsuckers'.[7] Subsequently, the Elizabethan antiquary William Camden talked of Henry 'meditating blood and slaughter', noting that 'at one and the same time he raged against the papists, by hanging, drawing, and quartering, and against the protestants, by burning them alive', whereby he grew terrible at home and was taken for a tyrant abroad.[8] In the preface to his *History of the World*, Sir Walter Raleigh widened the allegation, concluding that,

If all the pictures and patterns of a merciless prince were lost in the world, they might all again be printed to the life out of the story of this king. For how many servants did he advance in haste (but for what virtue no man could suspect) and with the change of his fancy ruined again; no man knowing for what offence? To how many others of more desert gave he abundant flowers from whence to gather honey, and in the end of harvest burnt them in the hive? How many wives did he cut off, and cast off, as his fancy and affection changed? How many princes of the blood (whereof some of them for age could hardly crawl towards the block) with a world of others of all degrees (of whom our common chronicles have kept the account) did he execute?[9]

Modern scholarship has also cited the brutal treatment of his wives, of critics such as More and Fisher, and of discarded ministers such as Wolsey and Cromwell as prime evidence of Henry's cruelty. And a good deal of the debate has concerned whether or not legislation such as the Statute of Proclamations of 1539 was tyrannical in intention.[10] But early sixteenth-century definitions of tyranny had as much to do with the character of the sovereign and the processes of political participation he favoured as with the operation of his judicial system. For Henry's contemporaries his persecution of his critics was a symptom of tyranny rather than its essence.

William Thomas's Italian adversary offered a definition of the tyrant based upon the self-indulgent and unrestrained nature of his character and his 'unconstant mind'. 'The principal token of a tyrant', he argued, 'is the immoderate satisfaction of an unlawful appetite, when the person, whether by right or wrong, hath power to achieve his sensual will, and that person, also, who by force draweth unto him that which of right is not his, in the unlawful usurping commiteth express tyranny.' In this he echoed a long tradition of discussions of the nature of kingship and tyranny and of virtuous conduct generally in which the stoical principles of constancy and self-sufficiency were the central characteristics of the 'good' man and the good king alike.[11]

The medieval theologian Thomas Aquinas observed in *On the Government of Rulers*, that kingship is the best form of government, and tyranny the worst;[12] and in many ways the good king and the tyrant were simply mirror images of each other.[13] Where the good king put the common good above his own personal desires, the tyrant did the reverse. Thomas More's epigram on the difference between the two suggested that 'A king who respects the law differs from a cruel tyrant thus: a tyrant rules his subjects as slaves, a king thinks of his subjects as his own children.'[14] Erasmus' *The Education of a Christian Prince* (1516), a copy of which was sent to Henry VIII by the author in 1517, argued that 'whoever wants to bestow on himself the title of prince and wants to escape the hated name of tyrant must win it for himself by benevolent actions and not through fear and threats'. 'The tyrant brings it about that everyone is under his thumb, either in law or through informers; the king delights in the freedom of his people.'[15] Where the good king was open and honest in his dealings, the tyrant was covert and corrupt. Where the good king followed convention and stayed within the law, the tyrant paid no regard to due process and perverted justice in his own interests. 'What is a good king?', asked More in another epigram, 'he is the watchdog, guardian of his flock, who by barking keeps the wolves from the sheep. What is the bad king? He is the wolf.'[16] Most crucial of all, where the good king took advice from the best and wisest of his subjects, and listened to the views of everyone, the tyrant surrounded himself with sycophants and listened to them alone. In the courtly environment, in which every action of the true subject had to be focused on keeping the volatile will of the prince on the straight and narrow, the man most to be feared was that irresponsible creature who turned his back on morality and the good of the many in favour of self-interest, telling the prince that he could, indeed should, do exactly as he liked. Such a man had a name as hated in its own way as that of the tyrant himself: he was the flatterer, the figure against whom the good counsellor set himself in an unceasing struggle for the heart and mind of the prince.[17] Hence, when Stephen Vaughan, a servant and informer of Thomas Cromwell's, wrote to his employer concerning the perils of bad government in November 1531, he reserved his strongest condemnation for the flattering evil counsellor.

Who seeth not that he that is an evil counsellor to a prince is an evil counsellor to a realm? If it be sin to be an evil counsellor to one man, what abomination, what devilish and horrible sin is it to be an evil counsellor to a prince?[18]

As John Guy has demonstrated, Tudor notions of good kingship harked back in part to the classical models of Tacitus and Cicero, and concerned the need to surround the king with reliable counsellors who, analogous to the senators of ancient Rome, could speak boldly for the common good and curb the prince's natural tendencies toward self-interest and wilfulness.[19] The 'uncounselled king' was, almost by definition, a tyrant. Castiglione's hugely influential handbook, *The Courtier*, outlined the central importance of good counsel to its subject's vocation.

The end of the perfect courtier . . . [is] so to win for himself the mind and favour of the prince he serves that he can and always will tell him the truth about all he needs to know, without fear or risk of displeasing him.[20]

Similarly, Erasmus advised the good prince that he must 'accustom his friends to the knowledge that they find favour by giving frank advice'.[21] The diplomat and political theorist Thomas Elyot, who will feature prominently in this book, also stressed the importance of the good counsellor's capacity to speak boldly to the king, regardless of the time or place, in order to dissuade him from vice and entice him to virtue,[22] while Thomas More gave Cromwell a practical warning of the need to be such a counsellor when he entered royal service. 'If you will follow my poor advice', More said, 'you shall, in your counsel-giving unto his Grace, ever tell him what he ought to do, but never what he is able to do . . . For, if [a] lion knew his own strength, hard were it for any man to rule him.'[23] Counsellors were, in this respect the king's surrogate conscience, stepping in when his own failed him.

These models of tyranny were very familiar to Henry VIII. As a child he had learned the lessons of good and bad kingship from his tutors, and the same message was reinforced in the books he read as a youth. Erasmus declared that,

the prince's tutor shall see to it that a hatred of the very words 'despotism' and 'tyranny' are implanted in the future prince by frequent diatribes against those names which are an abomination to the whole human race—Phalaris, Mezentius, Dionysius of Syracuse, Nero, Caligula, and Domitian . . . On the other hand, any examples of good princes should be put forward with frequent praise and commendation.[24]

Henry's tutors seem to have done precisely that. The most notable of them, John Skelton, had cautioned the young prince in the *Speculum Principis* written for his instruction, not to yield to his every whim, but to 'listen to the other point of view. Be easy to talk to. Pursue flatterers with hatred. Content yourself with wise counsel.'[25] Thomas More's *History of King Richard III*, written in the 1510s when he and Henry were close companions, had offered a warning from recent history, recast in the mould of Tacitus's *Annals*, of the need to avoid tyranny.[26] Erasmus presented Henry with a paraphrase of Plutarch's essay, 'How to Distinguish a Friend from a Flatterer', which the King promptly asked to be translated into English.[27]

When Henry had ascended the throne in 1509 he had proclaimed his intention to offer his subjects a new start, a golden age of good lordship, of open hands and open minds, free from the exactions and impositions of the past. The Coronation was greeted by an almost ecstatic outpouring of tributes in verse and prose. In a justly famous public letter to Erasmus, Henry's schoolroom companion Lord Mountjoy could scarcely contain his excitement.

I have no fear, but when you heard that our prince, now Henry the Eighth, whom we may call our Octavius, had succeeded to his father's throne, all your melancholy left you at once. For what may you not promise yourself from a prince with whose extraordinary and almost divine character you are well acquainted . . . But when you know what a hero he now shows himself, how wisely he behaves, what a lover he is of justice and goodness, what affection he bears to the learned, I will venture to swear that you will need wings to make you fly to behold this new and auspicious star . . . If you could see how all the world here is rejoicing in the possession of so great a prince, how his life is all their desire, you could not contain your tears for joy. The heavens laugh, the earth exults, all things are full of milk, of honey and nectar! Avarice is expelled the country.[28]

John Skelton presented Henry with verses celebrating the fact that 'now the years of grace / And wealth are come again'.[29] Thomas More in his *Carmen gratulatorium* ('Poetical expression of good wishes') announced,

This day is the limit of our slavery, the beginning of our freedom, the end of sadness, the source of joy, for this day consecrates a young man who is the everlasting glory of our time and makes him our King—a King who is worthy not merely to govern a single people but singly to rule the whole world—such a King as will wipe the tears from every eye, and put joy in the place of our long distress.

'In your reign, Sire', he concluded, 'the golden age has returned.'[30]

It is important, of course, to look beyond the hyperbole, to seek the substance beneath the aureate froth. There was clearly a good deal of self-interest involved in these scholarly eulogies. When Skelton compared Henry to 'Alexis [Alexander the Great] young of age', for example, the commendation carried with it the implicit suggestion that, if Henry was another Alexander, then his former tutor Skelton must be another Aristotle, and should be treated with similar respect. When Mountjoy observed that 'Liberality scatters wealth with a bounteous hand. Our king does not desire gold or gems or precious metals, but virtue, glory, immortality', it was with more than a hint that he expected some of that liberality to be scattered in his direction and towards those writers whose work might ensure the King's immortality. Moreover, Mountjoy was viewing his world through the filters of his scholarly reading, and presenting it to Erasmus in a vocabulary drawn from the Classics which he knew that his fellow scholar would understand and appreciate. The stances that he and the poets adopted and the language they employed were as stylized and conventional as the coronation ceremony itself. Ascribing to a new prince the sum of all intellectual and physical excellence was a commonplace of political eulogy. Shakespeare was to parody the mode delightfully in *Henry V,* having the Archbishop of Canterbury present its eponymous hero as a virtuoso in every field of human endeavour:

> Hear him but reason in divinity,
> And, all-admiring, with an inward wish,
> You would desire the King were made a prelate;
> Hear him debate of commonwealth affairs,
> You would say it hath been all in all his study;
> List him discourse of war, and you shall hear
> A fearful battle rend'red you in music . . .
> Turn him to any discourse of policy,
> The Gordian knot of it he will unloose,
> Familiar as his garter; that, when he speaks,
> The air, a chartered libertine, is still.
>
> (*Henry V,* i.i.38–57)[31]

It was equally conventional to contrast the joys promised by the new reign with the rigours of the old, as Skelton did when he claimed that, under Henry's stewardship, there would be no more trouble from 'The wolves, the bears also, / That wrought have much care, / And brought England in woe.'[32] More's *Carmen* similarly made much of the immediate changes for the better instituted in all areas of policy-making by the new king,

Our prince opened the seas for trade. If any over-harsh duties were required of the merchants, he lightened their load. And the long-scorned nobility recovered on our Prince's first day the ancient rights of nobles. He now gives good men the honours and public offices which used to be sold to evil men. By a happy reversal of circumstances, learned men now have the prerogatives which ignoramuses carried off in the past. Our prince without delay has restored to the laws their ancient force and dignity (for they had been perverted so as to subvert the realm).[33]

The great model of encomium-writing in this respect was the panegyric in honour of the Emperor Trajan written by Pliny the Younger (the son of Pliny the Encyclopaedist) which systematically used what is called the '*prius et nunc*' ('before and now') topos to celebrate its subject's virtues: *before* he came to the throne there was misery, but *now* there is peace and plenty.[34]

But the nature of the contrasts drawn between Henry and his father, and the venom with which the latter was vilified go well beyond the formalities of the *prius et nunc* convention. There is too much specific denunciation of individual policies in texts such as More's eulogy for this to be dismissed as merely conventional eulogizing:

Laws, heretofore powerless—yes, even laws put to unjust ends—now happily have regained their proper authority . . . No longer is it a criminal offence to own property that was honestly acquired (formerly it was a serious offence). No longer does fear hiss whispered secrets in one's ear, for no one has secrets either to keep or to whisper. Now it is a delight to ignore informers. Only ex-informers fear informers now.

The whole people used to be, on many counts, in debt to the King, and this in particular was the evil they feared. But our King, though he could have inspired fear in this way and could have gathered from this source immense riches if he had wished to do so, has forgiven the debts of all, and rendered all secure... Hence it is that, while other kings have been feared by their subjects, this King is loved, since now through his action they have no cause for fear.[35]

The reference to the strict taxes, bonds, and impositions of Henry VII's later years is open and obvious.

The fact that these attacks came from writers who were, or had been, closest to the new king (his former tutor Skelton and school-fellow Mountjoy) and men like More who were acutely sensitive to the political climate, and came in texts dedicated to the King himself and destined for the public arena, demonstrates clearly that this was no spontaneous or unregulated outpouring of resentment. Such men were not taking risks in speaking out in this way; this was something that Henry himself wanted to hear. It was, in effect, a mission statement for the new reign, voiced by those men whom Henry knew could speak to the political nation, and to a wider European audience, with conviction and authority.

A king who, according to the Venetian ambassador, was schooled in grammar, philosophy, and theology, and spoke five languages fluently, inevitably excited considerable expectations among scholars and intellectuals.[36] And for the first eighteen years of his reign he did, by and large, deliver on that early promise. He seems to have conspicuously modelled his conduct on the conventional examples of good kingship in his school textbooks and the *speculum principis* tradition: King Arthur, Alexander the Great, and his own forebear and namesake, Henry V. And the nation had prospered. France had been defeated in 1513; the Christian world had beaten a path to London in 1518 to subscribe to a Treaty of Universal Peace brokered by Henry and Cardinal Wolsey, and thereafter England had effectively played third man in the ongoing hostilities between France and the Empire, switching between the roles of mediator and militant ally for one side or the other as the opportunities for advantage dictated.[37]

At this early stage, avoiding tyranny was mainly a matter of not oppressing his people with unnecessary financial demands, of being pious, affable, and successful on the battlefield, and, of course, in taking counsel: things which a young, popular king with no contentious legislative aims had little difficulty in doing. When problems had arisen they were readily accommodated within the accepted paradigms of political conduct. Conventionally, good kings did not need to be perfect, only to be willing to listen to the criticism that would reveal and correct their shortcomings. In 1519 a group of Henry's councillors came to him with complaints about the behaviour of some of the officers and companions of his privy chamber. These young men, known informally as the King's minions, were said to have become so 'familiar and homely' with Henry that they 'played light touches with him', sullying his honour and bringing his household into disrepute. Moreover, they dispraised everything about the court and commended nothing that was not in the latest French fashion, damaging the reputation of the Crown abroad.[38] Faced with what could have been interpreted as implicit criticism of his capacity to order his household and choose his friends, the King reacted with studied regard for propriety and responsibility. He had, he said, appointed his councillors 'both for the maintenance of his honour, and for the defence of all thing that might blemish the same; wherefore if they saw any[one] about him misuse themselves, he committed it to their reformation'.[39] The minions were given a dressing down and dismissed from the court for a period to sober up and learn some responsibility (to 'leave those remnants / Of fool and feather that they got in France / ... And understand again like honest men' as Shakespeare was to put it),[40] and Henry replaced them with four 'sad [i.e. sober and wise] and ancient knights' from his Chamber. What could have become a slur on the King's honour was turned into a demonstration of his royal virtue. Mindful of the salutary examples of those kings, from Rehoboam in the Old Testament to his own predecessors Edward II and Richard II, who had allowed young flatterers to lead them into tyranny, Henry reaffirmed the need for sound and mature counsel, and gained the plaudits of writers like the chronicler Edward Hall as a result.[41] Did he also, perhaps, recall the example of Henry V, who had before his coronation expelled from his court those young gentlemen 'of light conscience and of more light virtue' who would not conform to his new and virtuous life as a king? It is highly likely, for Henry, when he ascended the throne, had specifically commissioned the first biography of Henry V in English, and had modelled his behaviour during the 1513 French campaign on his forebear's conduct at Agincourt.[42] Whatever the precise analogy in his mind, however, the young Henry here and elsewhere showed a commendable capacity to respond to events flexibly, combining the teachings of the conduct books with a pragmatic political sense.

When, in 1525, Francis I suffered a catastrophic defeat at the Battle of Pavia, Henry sought to take advantage of his old enemy's weakness. He asked his subjects for a voluntary donation, the so-called Amicable Grant, to finance an invasion.[43] But the commissioners for what was, in effect, an unprecedented, non-parliamentary tax, quickly ran into widespread and seemingly intractable popular resistance.[44] Again Henry responded flexibly. Claiming to be horrified that such an unreasonable imposition had been placed upon his subjects without his knowledge, he heard the petitions of his people, sought the counsel of his closest advisers, and backed down. The demand was withdrawn and Cardinal Wolsey, cast in the role of the political lightning conductor deflecting criticism from the King, admitted publicly to having made the demand on his own initiative. Henry was able to appear as the good king, stepping in to right the manifest unfairness.[45] He would not get his war with France, but he could content himself that he had been seen to act justly: and in that too there was honour.

While Henry acted in this carefully studied, 'virtuous' way, a generation of politically active individuals grew to maturity secure in the knowledge that England was indeed a stable polity in safe royal hands. The state that the jurist Sir John Fortescue had described in the mid-fifteenth century as the '*dominium politicum et regale*' (dominion political and royal), an ideal, 'mixed', participatory monarchy infinitely superior to the despotism practised in France,[46] had become a political reality. Hence the terrible sense of disillusionment and dislocation that set in when the King began to break the accepted rules of good lordship and to use increasingly obvious forms of intimidation and coercion to impose his will on his subjects.

When Henry, by launching his Great Matter, embarked upon a political journey that a sizeable proportion (probably the majority) of his advisers did not approve of, and which was evidently against the wishes of the mass of his people, he was forced to abandon (albeit at first only gradually) those models of behaviour that gave his rule cultural legitimacy. His counsellors started to tell him things that he did not want to hear, and on issues of such importance that he was not prepared to accept what they were saying. The results were wide-ranging and catastrophic. People were subjected to far more unwelcome demands, and many died if they did not acquiesce. Yet, even in the later 1530s, the old ideals of virtuous kingship had a place in official discourse, however sullied and compromised they had become in practice. Mindful of the potent suggestion that he was acting without heed to good counsel, Henry sought on numerous occasions to demonstrate that he was not. The proclamation prescribing erroneous books and biblical translations, issued on 22 June 1530 stressed that the King was acting, not on his own initiative but after widespread consultation. He had gathered his primates and divines from the universities and elsewhere, 'giving unto them liberty to speak and declare plainly their advices, judgement and determination'. Only when all these individuals 'by all their free assents, consents, and agreements, concluded, resolved, and determined' to support the case for suppression was the proclamation drawn up and promulgated.[47] In a circular letter sent out to Justices of the Peace on 25 June 1535, he stressed that the royal Supremacy and rejection of papal authority were based, not only upon the teachings of Scripture, but also on 'the deliberate advice, consultation, consent, and agreement as well of the bishops and clergy as by the nobles and commons temporal of this our realm, assembled in our high court of Parliament'.[48] In defending his religious policy against the criticisms of the Pilgrims of Grace, Henry asserted that he 'hath done nothing but the whole clergy of that province of York, as well as the province of Canterbury, hath determined the same to be conformable to God's holy Word and Testament'.[49] But, by 1536, few, if any, of those who experienced the process at first hand would have been convinced by such claims.

English Intellectual Culture and the Impact of the King's Great Matter

The executions of internationally renowned scholars such as More and Fisher and the mass of less well-known men who also died from 1535 onwards, whether on the scaffold or through ill-treatment in prison, convulsed the realm and were received with incomprehension and horror throughout Europe. But English society had, as the following chapter will suggest, been in a state of extended shock ever since the first session of the Reformation Parliament began in November 1529. The deaths of such prominent men, who had until so recently been pillars of ecclesiastical and civil society, and for beliefs that only four years earlier had been the bedrock of religious orthodoxy, were only the most dramatic of a series of shocks to the system received by English culture in the years 1529–34.

The tendency among scholars has been to play down the extent of opposition or resistance to Henry's policies; to discuss the obvious, high-profile cases of Thomas More, John Fisher, or Thomas Abel, who wrote expressly 'against' the evangelicals, the divorce, or the Supremacy, but to assume that they were isolated voices. What needs to be explained, it is assumed, is why more people did not resist. And, indeed, there is some contemporary support for such assumptions. Katherine of Aragon herself was scathing in her criticism of the men whom Henry had assigned to represent her during the Blackfriars divorce trial. Mocking 'such pretty counsellors as these', she dismissed them all as cowards and royal yes-men.

For if I ask Canterbury's advice, he answers me that he will have nothing to do with such affairs, and keeps repeating to me the words '*ira principis mors est*' [the wrath of the prince is death]. The bishop of Durham [Cuthbert Tunstal] answers that he dares not, because he is the King's subject and vassal. Rochester [Bishop John Fisher] tells me to have good heart and hope for the best. All the others have made similar answers, so that I have been obliged to send to Flanders for lawyers, as no one here would or dared draw an appeal in my favour.[50]

Such criticism, understandable though it was, was unfair. Almost all of the men named by the Queen subsequently took considerable risks to further her cause, or to oppose the demands of Henry's Reformation. Fisher's consistent literary advocacy is well known, and was to cost him his life.[51] But Tunstal also protested over the King's claim to supremacy in ecclesiastical affairs, and wrote directly to Henry warning him of the dangers of schism.[52] Even the arch-conformist, Archbishop Warham finally screwed his courage to the sticking place, refusing to use his authority as primate of England to grant the King his divorce, and, prior to his death in August 1532, he prepared a defiant justification of ecclesiastical independence, comparing Henry VIII's demands to those of Henry II at Clarendon, 'which St Thomas [Beckett] died a martyr to oppose'. The liberties of the Church are guaranteed by Magna Carta, he warned, and several kings who had violated them, such as Henry II, Richard II and Henry IV had come to an ill end.[53] Stephen Gardiner also wrote to warn Henry against the Supremacy. His letter was couched in conventionally humble terms, but it nonetheless made the bold point that the clergy exercised God's authority, and 'though we cannot use it condignly, yet we cannot give it away; and it is no less danger to the receiver than to the giver, as your highness of your wisdom can consider'.[54] There were other acts of dissent or non-compliance from a number of Henry's ministers and agents, of which Thomas More's resignation of the Great Seal in 1532 was only the most obvious. Reginald Pole, seemingly destined for a high position in the church, withdrew from royal service and wrote against the divorce and the Supremacy.[55] George Talbot, fourth earl of Shrewsbury, pointedly absented himself from Anne Boleyn's coronation, sending his son to perform the ceremonial functions of his office as Lord Steward in his stead. He had previously told Chapuys in February 1531 that he would never dishonour himself and his family by placing the crown on any other head than Queen Katherine's.[56] In a political culture based upon loyalty to the Crown, the difficulty of such defections and their political impact should not be underestimated. When More resigned, for example, it was the talk of Europe.

Others conformed publicly, but privately recorded their misgivings. William Benet, who was acting to further the divorce in Rome, told Queen Katherine that he favoured her cause. The Duke of Norfolk declared, in conversation with the Marquis of Dorset, that 'it was the devil and no one else who was the originator and promoter of this wretched scheme [for a divorce]'. The Duchess of Norfolk sent the Queen a message of encouragement in January 1531. And the Duke of Suffolk and his wife were reported to be completely opposed to Henry's intention to marry Anne Boleyn, and were considering with Norfolk how to dissuade him from his folly.[57] When Anne threatened Sir Henry Guildford that she would dismiss him from the controllership of the Household once she was queen, he is said to have replied that she would have no need as he would resign, and it was rumoured that he had already attempted to do so, but had his request turned down by the King.[58]

As we shall see, this is not the whole picture of 'loyal' resistance. There was an entire cadre of English scholars and intellectuals who were not in favour of the divorce or the pace or direction of religious reform, or both, who nonetheless remained in royal service, working for King and government to the best of their abilities. It is not sufficient to see such men as cowed or quiescent. They were not inactive. They used their writings, and the various forms of license that their culture allowed them, to argue the conservative case, and as far as they were able, sought to influence government policy through the medium of eloquence. For such activities the words 'opposition' or 'resistance' are, perhaps, inappropriate; certainly they are inadequate to describe the nuances of the essentially supportive, loyalist position that most of them took towards the person of the King and the promotion of his interests. Rather, what these writers attempted to do was to *influence* the direction of policy, to persuade the King and his ministers to avoid what they saw as the dangerous implications of what he was doing, and steer policy towards more positive outcomes.

One reason for the willingness of these men to speak out in this way was precisely that for thirty years or more, the English had enjoyed a relatively stable domestic political culture. There had been no overwhelmingly serious threat to the Crown, no invasions, no major religious or political ferment, allowing room for the development of a relatively open and unregulated debate within elite culture. Life had, as we have seen, been good in England in the first two decades of Henry's reign. In particular it had been good for the scholarly elite, prompting a conspicuous flowering of intellectual freedom and debate. English elite culture had thus grown used to the conventions of good lordship and good counsel, and enjoyed the stability that such a comfortable polity brought with it to exercise their inclinations towards discursiveness and disputation. Theirs was a culture in which debate, point-scoring, and wit were highly valued and widely practised in both formal and informal situations, and this had an inevitable impact on the conduct of politics. Far from being subservient, the political and social elites of the 1520s were an opinionated, quarrelsome, intellectually active bunch of men and women.

Men who had been educated in the humanist grammar schools or their scholastic predecessors, in the Inns of Court or the universities, and the many boys and few girls who enjoyed a private humanist education in aristocratic households, were alike trained in the disciplines of rhetorical argument and debate. The curriculum in each of these institutions was based upon medieval educational principles that made the *Trivium* of grammar, rhetoric, and logic the bedrock of the learning process, the essential intellectual apparatus of the complete human being. Students of all kinds sharpened their wits and learned their trades in rhetorical exercises and mock disputations centred on 'the putting of cases'—the consideration of universal principles by analogy to specific examples, and the arguing on either side (*in utramque partem*) of hypothetical theses: 'What if...?', 'Suppose that...'.[59]

In the grammar schools boys learned by memorizing, repeating, translating, and finally imitating the examples of the best classical authors, discovering how to write and speak elegantly and to argue their way through carefully selected dilemmas and situations. Erasmus enjoined tutors regularly to set their pupils 'a memorable historical story' to consider and debate with their fellows. Among the examples that he suggested were the claim that 'the headlong heat of Marcellus overthrew the Roman cause, the prudent delaying of Fabius restored it'. Consideration of this case would, he asserted, not only allow the boys to exercise their skills in eloquence and logic, but also teach the moral and political lesson that 'too precipitate plans usually turn out unhappily'. Alternatively, pupils might be asked to vituperate the tyrant Julius Caesar or praise the good counsellor Socrates in order both to practise the set forms of oration and to internalize a healthy contempt for despotism and a due regard for truth.[60] The examples of wisdom or folly that they encountered in their reading should be noted down in specially prepared notebooks for commonplaces, divided under separated headings, to provide raw material to be recycled in future exercises or conversations. As Erasmus observed in his dialogue on schoolroom practice, *The Right Way of Speaking Latin and Greek* (1528), 'the sayings of famous men, good pithy aphorisms, proverbs, *bon mots*, all these can serve the purpose [of teaching vocabulary], and moreover, provide extremely useful ammunition for the future speaker on all sorts of occasions'.[61] 'The whole past', as Cicero put it, was thus 'a storehouse of examples and precedents' for contemporary use.[62]

What was common practice in the established schools was also followed by private tutors in royal palaces and the households of the aristocracy. Juan Luis Vives advocated a similar regime when he drew up a syllabus for Princess Mary, daughter of Henry VIII and Katherine of Aragon. She was to spend her early years in the memorization, repetition, and imitation of classical examples that taught morality as well as language skills. 'The verses which are assigned for imitation', Vives wrote, 'let them contain some grave little sentiment, which it will profit to have learned'. From an early age the Princess was intended to learn both the portability and the usefulness of the anecdotes and *sententiae* learned from her books, and to become proficient in passing on such nuggets of instruction to her fellows: 'she will be delighted, meantime with little tales which teach life, which she herself can tell to others'. Vives cited among others, the stories of Joseph in the Old Testament, Lucrece in Livy, and that archetype of virtuous womanhood, patient Grisselda. In the syllabus he designed in 1523 for Charles Mountjoy, the son of Henry's schoolfellow William, Lord Mountjoy, Vives also recommended the keeping of a commonplace book of stories and sayings on 'subjects of daily converse' which the boy was to memorize and refer to daily in his thought and conversation.[63] Such material would form the founda-tions of that part of logic formally termed 'Invention' which Thomas Wilson described as the faculty 'whereby we may find arguments, and reasons, mete to prove every matter where upon question may rise. This part is the store house of places wherein arguments rest.' Sir Thomas Elyot in his *Book Named the Governor*, argued that from the age of fourteen onwards the children of the aristocracy should be exercised in 'the art of the orator', using Quintilian as the basis for a grounding in rhetoric, 'principally which concerneth persuasion; for as much as it is most apt for consultation'. For those pupils who did not desire to become 'an exquisite orator', Erasmus's *Copia* might be used instead.[64] Either way, the ability to speak well and to turn old stories and maxims to contemporary use across the whole gamut of social situations, from the public audience at court to a private conversation with friends, was seen as the crucial attribute of the well-rounded gentleman. Primarily, however, the fruits of this training were political, for, as Elyot, declared, 'the utility that a noble man shall have by reading these orators [Isocrates, Demosthenes, Cicero, Quintilian] is that, when he shall hap to reason in counsel, or shall speak in a great audience, or to strange ambassadors of great princes, he shall not be constrained to speak words sudden, and disordered, but should bestow them aptly, and in their places'.[65] Rhetoric, like wisdom, was learned in order to be applied, chiefly in the exercise of political action for the betterment of the commonweal. And the forum for that action was the royal court.

In the universities and Inns of Court the skills and attributes learned in the schoolroom were sharpened through the application of similar but more advanced skills. At Oxford, undergraduates in Arts and Theology engaged in regular public 'exercises' and disputations, arguing with each other and with their masters (without recourse to notes) on questions of moral and natural philosophy, metaphysics, and logic. There were also exercises known as Variations (*Variatio*) in which a single student would offer arguments for or against a given thesis. In the Faculty of Law students were encouraged, in addition to attending their formal lectures, disputations, and exercises, to engage in the 'putting of cases' over dinner. A similar syllabus existed at Cambridge, and at the Inns the essentially scholastic regime of oral exercises, case-putting, moots and disputations, in which, as Wilfrid Prest has described it, the student 'sought to justify his interpretation of the law by citing the maxims, precedents, and principles which were the authorities of his craft', were to dominate practice until well into the seventeenth century.[66]

Joel T. Altman, drawing on the earlier work of T.W. Baldwin, has demonstrated the importance of this rhetorical training for the development of the debate-laden drama of the period, and of a humanist poetics that thrived on the putting and exploration of hypothetical cases. One need cite only the works of Henry Medwall or John Heywood, whose plays are on one level at least, extended disputations over the kind of hypothetical cases set in the classroom to see the truth of this assertion. The comic servant 'B' in Medwall's interlude *Fulgens and Lucres* makes the debt to the schoolroom case-putting obvious when he begins a part of his argument with the heroine with the phrase, 'Than I put case that a gentilman bore / Have godely maners to his birth according....'[67] More obvious still is the influence upon the thought and writings of Thomas More, whose education took in, not only the rhetorical lessons of the schoolroom, but the legal training of the Inns of Court. His *Utopia* is in essence an extended exercise in the putting of cases. Book I proceeds by a number of such hypothetical arguments, as Hythlodaeus leads his interrogators through a series of 'supposes': 'suppose I was with the French king, and there sitting in his Council...'; 'suppose that some king and his Council were together whetting their wits...' And the whole of Book II is, of course, one long putting of a hypothetical case: suppose there was a realm designed upon purely rational grounds...[68]

More's *Dialogue Concerning Heresies* (1529), his first literary response to the English evangelicals, also employs a series of hypothetical scenarios and cases: 'I...put case that there came [ten] diverse honest men of good substance out of [ten] diverse parts of the realm, each of them with an offering at the pilgrimage...'; 'I put you...another case, that [ten] young women, not very specially known for go[o]d, but taken at adventure, dwelling all in one town . . .'; 'I put case . . . that God himself say to you; "I have showed the truth of this matter to such a man" . . .'; 'Let me put you another case . . . If it were so that Wilken had laid a wager with Simken . . .'. More's fictional interlocutor, the Messenger, illustrates his objections to current ecclesiastical practice with a number of exemplary stories and 'merry tales'. He offers the case of the poor man who 'found [the] priest over familiar with his wife', and a more pointed remark of a merchant to a penitent priest. More responds with generous appreciation of the wit and eloquence behind the Messenger's stories, and offers in return a series of tales of his own, including that of 'a good old idolater' who was given the Bible for the first time, and the clownish behaviour of a series of witnesses at the inquest on the death of the convicted heretic, Richard Hunne. The last of the Messenger's tales offers a succinct example of the sort of playful yet serious exchange characteristic of this mode of argument.

'Mary', quod he, 'it happed that a young priest very devoutly in a procession, bore a candle before the cross for lying with a wench, and bore it light all the long way. Wherein the people took such spiritual pleasure and inward solace, that they laughed apace. And one merry merchant said unto the priests that followed him, "*sic luceat lux vestra coram hominibus*". "Thus let your light shine afore the people" '.

More's persona, taking the anticlerical force of the witticism, can only offer in reply the thought that 'good is it for them [i.e. the clergy] to look on their faults, but for us were it better to look less to theirs and more unto our own'.[69]

An insight into how this culture of 'putting cases' operated in happier times can also be gained from another part of More's *Dialogue*, where the Messenger relates in passing a brief exchange between Henry VII and his Almoner, 'Dr Mayo'. During dinner in the royal household,

It happed that there was fallen in communication the [biblical] story of Joseph, how his master Potipher's wife, a great man with the king of Egypt, would have pulled him to bed, and he fled away.

'Now, Master Mayo', (quod the King's grace), 'ye be a tall, strong man on the one side, and a cunning doctor on the other side; what would ye have done if ye had been not Joseph, but in Joseph's stead?'

'By my troth, sir', quod he, 'and it like your grace, I cannot tell you what I would have done, but I can tell you well what I should have done.'

'By my troth', quod the King, 'that was very well answered.'[70]

That, by 1528, More was unashamedly associating intellectual freedom with the reign of Henry VII—the period he had so fiercely condemned as a time of repression in his coronation eulogy of 1509—suggests how quickly writers sensed the implications for political culture of Henry's Great Matter and his apparent support for religious radicalism.

Much of this book will be taken up with the discussion of formal texts and arguments created by this culture. It will look at the lives and work of a group of men schooled in the system that commended the free association of literary and historical precedents, stories and cases with current events, and the use of literature as a political tool, as they sought to come to terms with the implications of Henry's Reformation, both for themselves and for the country they served. But the rhetorical training, and the sententious, tendentious, habits of mind that it generated, were not restricted to those few individuals who went on to make a living as authors and educationalists. They permeated and influenced a whole generation of educated men and women that grew up in the early sixteenth century, and can be seen to have influenced informal discussions and improvised speech quite as much as the formal orations of sermons and drama or arguments on the printed or manuscript page. The schoolboys and students of the early sixteenth century were naturally disputatious (far more so than the graduates of today), willing to argue, to use exemplary stories to justify their claims, to put counter cases, and seek contrary examples to those offered to them in conversation, from the pulpit, or from figures of authority. They were adept at moralizing and extrapolating arguments from both classical texts and examples from everyday experience, extracting from them general principles and lessons, and applying them to contemporary political and social situations. The ease and readiness with which they reached for literary examples to illustrate their own experience is perhaps nowhere better illustrated than in a brief aside in a letter of 7 March 1528 written to William Edwards, a member of Cardinal Wolsey's household by his friend Richard Watkins. Referring to an earlier letter from Edwards, Watkins declared that he was so delighted by it that he had almost died of joy on the spot, 'like the Roman woman mentioned by Valerius Maximus'.[71] The stories of the past were indeed a living storehouse of examples for Tudor Englishmen to cite on every occasion. And no one seems to have felt themselves so experienced as to be above the need to produce commonplace books and cribs of worthy axioms. Even that most pragmatic of politicians Thomas Cromwell had among his possessions in 1533 an anthology of the speeches made when addressing kings by the prophets of the Old Testament.

In elite circles, at court, in the Inns of Court and the universities, in schools and religious houses up and down the country there was a willingness to discuss and explore ideas, to challenge orthodoxies (within set limits), using the resources of eloquence, reason, and example. What enabled this culture to operate was confidence in the stability and coherence of the framework that underpinned it. The stability of the institutional framework of the schools and colleges, of the intellectual framework of religious and political ideas, and of the framework of personal relationships between the educated and political elite and a king who was open to counsel and instruction, all these things were the bedrock on which intellectual life was founded. Take away or unsettle these foundations, as Henry VIII was to do from 1528 onwards, and the entire culture of enquiry and counsel, and the elegant, eloquent polity it sustained, became unfixed, unnerved, and ultimately dysfunctional.

Curious as it may seem in retrospect, then, it is clear that Henry's subjects had to be taught how to be cowed. While it had always been accepted that the King was to be obeyed and feared, that obedience had generally been unforced and thus the fear more theoretical than real. It was widely accepted that, as one priest, Peter Bentley, put it in 1538, 'a man may say what he will in his own home': and in other places too.[72] Only with the coming of the Supremacy did the bulk of Henry's law-abiding subjects have to learn that his wrath might be turned upon them for merely speaking their mind or exercising their conscience. They had to learn for themselves that, like the heretics, traitors, and criminals who formed the traditional pantheon of victims of royal justice, they too might suffer at his hands merely for speaking out of turn, and so should learn to fear the King's motives. Suddenly the habit of the putting of cases became a highly dangerous activity.

In February 1536, George Rowlands, a Crutched Friar of London, got into a dispute with a layman, John Stanton, whose confession he was hearing. As the discussion turned to the reverence due to the Saints, Rowlands had recourse (not for the first time in their conversation) to an exemplary story. 'I put the case', he said,

> that I know that a thief came to me and asked his alms for God's sake, then would I give him alms, not because he is a thief, but because he asked it of me for God's sake; and so in like manner, whatsoever you give in the honour of God or for any good saint, God shall reward you for it, though it be given to an image of stock or stone.[73]

To talk independently of religious policy and the use of images, however hypothetically, was a dangerous matter in the later 1530s. Rowlands was denounced to Cromwell by Stanton and investigated by the Secretary, before, apparently, being released without charge.

The suddenly dangerous implications of this tendency to debate and moralize the affairs of the great is even better illustrated by another conversation that took place at the priory of the London Crutched Friars, this time on the vigil of St James the Apostle in 1532.[74] The Prior of the house, John Driver, having just returned from Convocation, was clearly exercised by what he had witnessed there. Over dinner his conversation turned from the reporting of colourful court gossip to potentially seditious political provocation. One of the King's fools, he reported, had recently been roughly handled by a group of courtiers to the extent that he finally fell from his horse. The story may have been intended merely to elicit a laugh, or was, perhaps, offered as an illustration of the proverbially fractious, combative nature of court life. But it quickly took on a moralizing, political edge as the Prior began to turn it in his mind into an instance of 'what if . . . ?'. He began to put a case. What happened next? Driver did not say; but what *should have* happened, in order to turn the incident into a satisfying exemplary story, was that the Fool should have said that, just as *he* had now had a fall, so the King too would soon have one, and by implication a far greater one. Warming to his tale, the Prior said that what should have followed *that* is that a learned man of religion who was standing by—perhaps in his imagination it was Driver himself—should have added that, although the King now bore the title *Defensor Fidei* (the Defender of the Faith), so he would soon become known, because of his putting down of the religious houses, as the *Destructor Fidei*.

This story is entirely characteristic of the kind of political culture prevalent in early Henrician England. A group of educated men, meeting over dinner, were exchanging news, and quickly turned to matters occurring at the centre of English political life, the royal court: the source of all the tidings worth relating. The bearer of the news not only passed on a lively narrative of what he had seen there, spiced with entertaining titbits of gossip, but he also extemporized and moralized an analysis of that narrative as he told it, turning it into the rudiments of a didactic tale in precisely the way Erasmus and Vives recommended. Driver was using his learning and his knowledge of a potentially useful story to inform and instruct his fellow diners. In his hands the raw material of news took on something of the quality of a literary anecdote, the sort of short narrative with a pointed, 'moral' ending that filled the printed collections of 'merry tales' so popular in the period. A story of matters low and ignominious: a cruel joke at the expense of the lowest of men, a court fool falling from a horse, became culturally transubstantiated beyond these accidents into a comment on the high mysteries of state. What had begun in the vernacular, a brief comic scene without dialogue, ended in the elevated language of scholarship via a neat if somewhat obvious Latin quibble.

But the story is exemplary in another sense too; for it speaks simultaneously of the political dangers that this kind of playful putting of cases might involve in the increasingly fraught political climate of the 1530s. We know of Prior Driver's anecdote, again, only because it was reported to Thomas Cromwell and led to an investigation and a series of interrogations. One of the men around Driver's table that night was William Crochun, another friar and an informant of Cromwell's. He repeated what he had heard to the Secretary, and was summoned to an inquisitorial interview, presided over by Cromwell and with a London Alderman, John Allen, and Cromwell's secretary, Thomas Wriothesley in attendance. Here Crochun repeated the Prior's words, and Wriothesley recorded them. Another witness, a third friar, Robert Ball, was also interviewed, and admitted that he too had heard the Prior's story, and that it had been told as Crochun had related it. Finally, Driver himself was questioned, and admitted having spoken the words alleged against him, signing his name at the foot of the page as a token of his confession. What had begun as dinner-table banter, the kind of imaginative *jeu d'esprit* that probably graced college common rooms and gatherings of educated men throughout the country, had ended as a formal confession of subversive activity. What finally happened to the garrulous prior is unclear, as we lose sight of the case at this point, but it nonetheless provides a valuable glimpse of the kind of thing that I am discussing here. It is a good example of both what Henry and his ministers were up against in the 1530s when they attempted to regulate potentially dangerous talk (the problem of enforcement as Professor Elton termed it) and equally, of the kind of thing that Henry's educated subjects began increasingly to experience in the same period—a coming to terms with the need to speak—and to write—very differently under the tyranny of Henry's Reformation.[75]

Yet the habit of speaking boldly on issues of principle and practice and the capacity to cite hypothetical cases and apply biblical and classical examples to illuminate contemporary politics were ingrained in elite English culture. They provided a model and a license for subjects to speak critically of their governors, and so were highly resistant to attempts to suppress them from above. As late as spring 1538 the Abbot of Woburn was deploying biblical *examplae* to inform his understanding—and his criticism—of the dissolution of the monasteries. Discussing events with the diplomat and gentleman of the privy chamber Sir Francis Bryan, a man close to the King himself, the Abbot suggested that, just as God had steered King Nebuchadnezzar as his minister to destroy the Temple in Jerusalem and later King Cyrus to rebuild it again, so 'if we repeal and amend our ill living, God at length shall put it in the King's mind to set up these monasteries as fast again as they been put down, *qui cor Regis in manu dei est* [for the heart of the King is in God's hands]'.[76] Although the Abbot discretely suggested that Henry himself might be the one, after a suitable Damascene conversion, to restore again the abbeys that he had first pulled down, the logic of the analogy makes clear the more subversive nature of his real aspirations. For Nebuchadnezzar had been punished for his sacrilege by God in the most dramatic and savage way, bereft of his wits, thrown down on all fours like a beast, and cast out into the wilderness literally to ruminate upon his sins while another subsequently made good the damage he had done. The Abbot was thus being rather more critical of his sovereign than the modest, hopeful slant to his final observation might initially suggest.

In a political environment in which it was treason simply to imagine the death or deposition of the King, such recourse to biblical or classical analogy, and to the hypothetical 'put case', gave well-read English men and women a vocabulary in which they might discuss the failings of their sovereign and contemplate the redress of grievances, thereby engaging critically with national political issues from which they were otherwise excluded.[77] So, more provocatively, the declaration of the Pilgrims of Grace, drawn up at Pontefract in 1536, probably by Sir Thomas Tempest, warned Henry directly that, if he persisted in taking advice from a narrow coterie of evangelical counsellors such as Cromwell and Cranmer, he would share the fate of Rehoboam, who caused the division of the Kingdom of Israel through heeding of such 'young foolish counsel'. They also cited analogues nearer to home. 'And in this noble realm, who read the chronicles of Edward the II, what jeopardy he was in for Peres de Gavestun, Spenseres, and such like counsellors, and . . . Richard the II was deposed for following the counsel of such like'.[78] Such citation of authoritative precedents in turn bestowed authority on speakers who had no other formal claim to political credibility. By drawing upon the fruits of his education, a learned man like Tempest might thus claim not only the privilege of addressing his King, but also the right to instruct him. The possession of authoritative stories, even imaginative, hypothetical ones, might thus allow individuals to take liberties with their governors.

What Henry VIII did in the course of the 1530s was to outlaw such powerful acts of imagining, and the recourse to analogy that underpinned them. The various Acts of Succession of the 1530s, and the 1534 Treason Act, as we shall see, combined to make it an offence merely to suggest that the King was a tyrant, usurper, or heretic; while the inquisitorial apparatus of the Privy Council and Thomas Cromwell's secretariat investigated any hint that reached them of seditious gossip or case-putting. While it was famously said of Henry's daughter Elizabeth that, once she was Queen, she did not like to make windows into men's hearts and secret thoughts:[79] provided they were outwardly loyal what they held in their consciences was their own affair; Henry himself took a much more interventionist line. From 1533 onwards he demanded not merely his subjects' outward obedience, but also their inward approval for all that he did. Through the oaths attached to the Acts of Supremacy and Succession he specifically stated that outward subscription to his claims was not enough: English men and women must swear the oaths without inward grudge or scruple, and they should not grumble or qualify their statements afterwards. As the 1534 Act of Succession put it, his subjects must subscribe 'that they shall truly, firmly, and constantly, without fraud or guile, observe, fulfil, maintain, defend, and keep to their cunning wit and uttermost of their powers, the whole effect of this present Act'.[80] By the same Act, merely speaking against the Boleyn marriage, 'without writing or any exterior deed or act', was made misprision of treason, and the offender subjected to an indefinite period of imprisonment and loss of lands and goods at the King's pleasure. As Thomas More, Fisher, and many others were quickly to discover, a man's conscience as well as his body was now the King's property, to manipulate as he wished, and it was subject to the same harsh demands and penalties.

Such demands were unprecedented in contemporary experience, and startling in their presumption. It would be a strange world indeed, Lord Mountjoy had reputedly asserted, if words were to be made treason.[81] But Henry seemingly saw no strangeness, and no limits to his prerogative in this respect. He instructed Sir Thomas Wyatt, then ambassador to the Imperial court of Charles V, to demand that the Emperor rebuke a number of preachers in Spain who had been criticizing him personally and denouncing his religious policies as heretical. Wyatt received short shrift from Charles in response. 'Preachers will speak against my self when there is cause', he said:

That cannot be let…I will tell you, monsieur l'ambassador, kings be not kings of tongues, and if men give cause to be spoken off, there is no remedy.[82]

But Henry's will was precisely to be the King of his subjects' tongues, and of others' too. As late as 9 January 1539, he was instructing Cromwell to remonstrate with the French ambassador over allegations circulating in France that he was a tyrant, not merely among the vulgar, but even in the King's council.[83]

Each of the authors studied in this book, when confronted with the unprecedented demands that accompanied Henry's Reformation, reacted to them initially at least in time-honoured ways. They looked to the past, as their education and training had taught them to do, for authentic models through which they could seek to redress the ills of the present. They put cases and they told stories. They each co-opted the authoritative voices and traditions of previous generations in order to speak truth to the increasingly irresponsible and unheeding power of Henry's 'imperial' sovereignty. William Thynne and Sir Brian Tuke looked to the late fourteenth century and resurrected the 'father' of English poetry, Geoffrey Chaucer, as their spokesman for the kind of moderate, reforming catholicism and stable, mature, polity that they sought to argue back into being in the England of 1530–1. In their hands Chaucer's poetry came to speak for the traditional virtues of wholeness, fellowship, and community in a period of profound cultural fragmentation. Two years later, John Heywood would look back still further, to high medieval notions of licensed folly, and to classical precedents: the dialogues of the satirist Lucian and the conventions of the Roman theatre, in order to fashion a vehicle for criticism of the excesses of the Royal Supremacy. The drama that he produced, chiefly in *The Play of the Weather* but also in other interludes produced at roughly the same time, observed contemporary politics through a glass that he himself termed 'merry', a mode in which folly and wisdom are mingled in a wry, mischievous form of truth telling designed both to tickle the wit and prick the conscience of the King. Thomas Elyot, conversely, fashioned his literary mirrors for Henry VIII from more serious stuff. He co-opted whole libraries of biblical wisdom and classical scholarship to shed light and reason upon the problems of royal dysfunction and political disorder. Finally, Thomas Wyatt and Henry Howard, Earl of Surrey, stepped beyond the mirror for princes tradition, borrowing the voices of classical satire and invective, and biblical complaint and prophecy, to speak to the gathering crisis of Henry's latter years, and, in Surrey's case, to stake a claim for a role in what came after it, once the great tyrant was dead and men of good will strove to restore the commonweal to virtue again in the reign of his son, the infant Edward VI.

Despite the disparate materials that they used, each writer was similarly determined to fashion from them the tools with which they could diagnose and correct the sickness afflicting their own society. And each, in the process, would adapt their chosen forms: the poetry anthology, the interlude, the dialogue, treatise, lyric, or verse paraphrase, into something new and potent. Like their fellow English men and women who put cases and told stories to each other up and down the country, they used literary forms and narrative frameworks to discuss the behaviour of the King and his ministers, to set that behaviour into wider contexts that made sense of it, and empowered them to judge and seek to influence it for the better. While Henry sought to change the ground-rules of political conduct fundamentally, outlawing previous orthodoxies and replacing them with novel impositions dressed up as 'ancient' truths, these writers tried to reassert the collective values of their class, and exercised the learned traditions of their humanist training in the attempt to bridle and correct a tyrannical ruler.

At the end of More's *History of King Richard III*, the narrator offers an allegorical account of the effects of tyranny upon the lives and assumptions of its subjects. Recalling a fable of Aesop's, he cites the story of the lion who decreed that no horned beast might thereafter reside in his wood upon pain of death. When a peaceable beast 'that had in his forehead a bunch of flesh' made to flee away from the wood, the fox stopped him and asked why he was running, seeing that everyone knew that what he had on his head was not a horn, but flesh. '*I* know that', responded the beast, 'but what if *he* call it a horn, where am I then?'[84] In the course of the 1530s Henry decided to call horns many things that had previously been taken for flesh, and many peaceable creatures would die as a result. In doing so he assuredly joined the ranks of the tyrants, however much he appealed to the theories of good kingship in the attempt to deny the fact.

In *The Education of a Christian Prince*, the book that he sent to Henry in 1517, Erasmus had declared that domestic division and conflict were the hallmarks of a despotic regime:

Tyrants are happy to stir up party conflicts and disputes between their subjects and carefully feed and foster such animosities as happen to arise, improperly trading on such situations to reinforce their tyranny. But a [good] king has the one interest of fostering harmony among his subjects and resolving straight away such dissensions as happen to grow among them—not surprisingly because he understands that they are a most serious disease in the state.[85]

In the 1530s, as the following chapters will show, that definition would return to haunt Henry's England.

PART I

POETRY AND THE CULTURE
OF COUNSEL

The 1532 *Workes of Geffray Chaucer Newly Printed*
and John Heywood's *Play of the Weather*

2

A Gift for King Henry VIII

At some point in 1532, very probably in the late summer, William Thynne, clerk of the kitchen to Henry VIII, presented his sovereign with a handsome gift. It was a folio volume, fresh from the presses of the London printer Thomas Godfray: the first single-volume printed edition of the 'Complete Works' of England's most celebrated poet, Geoffrey Chaucer.[1] The work was the product of a literary passion as well as considerable scholarly endeavour. Thynne's son Francis later claimed that his father had obtained 'some five and twenty' manuscript or printed copies of Chaucer's works, 'whereof some had more and some fewer tales', and, using a commission from the King, had 'made great search' of all the secular and monastic libraries of England in pursuit of the best exemplars of the texts he was to publish: 'So that out of all the Abbeys of this Realm (which reserved any monuments thereof) he was fully furnished with multitude of Books'.[2] According to his son, Thynne produced from this multitude collated versions superior to any that had previously appeared.

One might suspect a degree of hyperbole from the younger Thynne where his father's work was concerned; but the favourable verdict on the volume was not his alone. The scholar and antiquary John Leland wrote in his *Commentarie de Scriptoribus Britannicis* (c. 1540) of how Thynne had 'exercised great labour, diligence, and care in seeking out ancient copies', and had added 'many things' to the earlier Chaucer publications of William Caxton and his successors.[3] The result of this zealous activity was, critics have concurred, a significant contribution to Chaucer scholarship, the first real 'edition' of the poet rather than simply a collection of his writings. It added a number of authentic pieces, amounting to around 15,000 words, to the canon: notably *The Romaunt of the Rose*, *The Legend of Good Women*, *Boece*, *The Book of the Duchess*, and *The Treatise of the Astrolabe* among the longer works, and the shorter poems 'Pity' and 'Lack of Steadfastness', as well as a good deal of apocrypha.[4] But the 1532 *Chaucer* did more than gather together new and superior examples of the poet's writings; it placed those writings confidently in the context of a wider history of English literature. The poet had long enjoyed a reputation among his successors as the 'father'

of vernacular verse—indeed of the English language itself as a poetic medium—
the man who enriched and made respectable a tongue conventionally dismissed
as vulgar and 'primitive'. This edition gave that reputation a definitive status,
monumentalizing it in the authoritative, classical form of a *Complete Works*
in folio (echoing the Continental humanist editions of the *Opera* of Virgil)
and giving it in addition a distinct political agenda.[5] In a bold, declamatory
preface, Thynne—or rather, as we shall see, another courtier, Sir Brian
Tuke, writing in Thynne's name—established the poet's credentials as the crucial
figure in a project to establish an elevated, 'civil' English literary culture on
the model of classical Greek and Latin letters.[6] The Preface then—in an act
designed to ensure the success of that project—placed responsibility for
Chaucer's legacy symbolically and literally in the hands of the book's royal
dedicatee, Henry VIII.

Addressing itself 'to the King's highness, my most gracious sovereign lord
Henry the eight, by the grace of God King of England and of France, Defensor of
the Faith, and Lord of Ireland, etc.', the Preface describes 'speech or language' as
among the greatest of those 'excellencies' that make human-beings akin to angels
and superior to brute beasts.[7] Further, it describes an ongoing process, central to
human civilization, 'to compone and adorn the rudeness and barbarity of speech,
and to form it to an eloquent and ordinate perfection'. First the Phoenicians
devised writing, 'so as the conceit of man's mind' might be 'sensibly and vively
[vividly] expressed'. Next the Greeks established their cultural superiority
through excellence 'in all kinds of sciences' and the 'ornateness' of their tongue.
Then came the Romans who, 'by example of the Greeks, have gotten or won to
them no small glories, in the forming, order, and uttering of [their Latin]...
tongue'. Among modern nations, all civilized vernaculars are merely corruptions
of these earlier languages, but they may achieve their own perfection through a
process of 'aureation' and 'melioration'. Hence the beautification of the native
language, the enriching of it with 'copious' synonyms and alternatives, and the
process of rendering it 'dulce' or sweet on the tongue, became a competition
between states for political and cultural respectability, a conscious claim for the
inheritance of the political and scholarly legacy of the classical past (the,
so-called, *translatio studii* and *translatio imperii*) in which all the significant
European powers played a part.[8] The Italians and Spaniards, Thynne continues,
have languages 'which most approach to the Latinate', but have struggled
against corruption by barbarian and Moorish vernaculars. The French language,
'next unto them in similitude to the Latin', has 'by diligence of people of
the same... in few years passed so amended, as well in pronunciation as in
writing, that an Englishman by a small time exercised in that tongue hath not
lacked ground to make a grammar or rule ordinary thereof'. While, 'the
Germans have so formed the order of their language, that in the same, is both
as much plenty and as near concordance to the phrase of the Latin as the French
tongue hath'.[9]

To this company of aureate languages, English has come relatively late. Indeed, the process of enrichment and 'dulcification' is still in train, and England's status as a linguistic and cultural superpower, her pitch for the *translatio studii*, is still to be argued for by men such as Thynne himself. There has, the Preface asserts,

not lacked amongst us English men which have right well and notably endeavoured and employed themselves to the beautifying and bettering of the English tongue. Amongst whom, most excellent prince, my most redoubted and gracious sovereign lord, I, your most humble vassal, subject, and servant, William Thynne, chief clerk of your kitchen, moved by a certain inclination and zeal which I have to hear of any thing sounding to the laude and honour of this your noble realm, have taken great delectation, as the times and leisures might suffer, to read and hear the books of that noble and famous clerk Geffray Chaucer, in whose works is so manifest comprobation of his excellent learning in all kinds of doctrines and sciences.

(*Works*, fol. Aii(v))

In Chaucer's works, Thynne's text suggests, lie all those qualities necessary to establish the English tongue as equal to those other vernacular languages he cites. In particular, the Preface commends the poet's excellent style and his choice of elevated subject matter, aspects of his writing that are all the more remarkable as they appeared at a time 'when doubtless all good letters were laid asleep throughout the world'.

Just as Chaucer was to refine and polish English letters, so the Thynne of the Preface declares his task as editor to be to clean and polish the Chaucerian text, removing its fifteenth-century scribal accretions and restoring it to its original glory. Hence, motivated by patriotism and loyalty ('in manner appertinent unto my duty, and that of very honesty and love to my country'), he began heroically to recover the lost glories of Chaucerian English, and of English history itself.

As the Preface retells it, the story of the loss and recovery of Chaucer's works merges into that of the loss and recovery of national culture and pride, and both blur into the life-story of Thynne himself as an avid collector and reader of books.

Wherefore, gracious sovereign lord, taking such delight and pleasure in the works of this noble clerk . . . I have of a long season much used to read and visit the same: and as books of diverse imprints came unto my hands, easily and without great study, might and have deprehended in them many errors, falsities, and deprivations, which evidently appeared by the contrarieties and alterations found by collation of the one with the other, whereby I was moved and stirred to make diligent search where I might find or recover any true copies or exemplaries of the said books, whereunto in process of time, not without cost and pain, I attained, and not only unto such as seem to be very true copies of those works of Geffray Chaucer which before had been put in print, but also to diverse other never till now imprinted, but remaining almost unknown and in oblivion, whereupon, lamenting with myself the negligence of the people that have been in this realm who doubtless were very remiss in the setting forth or advancement either of the histories thereof, to the great hindrance of the renown of such noble princes and valiant conquerors and captains as have been in the same, or also of the works or memory of the famous and excellent clerks in all kinds of sciences that have flourished therein, of which both sorts it hath pleased God as highly to nobilitate this isle as any other region of Christendom.

(*Works*, fols. Aii(v)–Aiii)

The final task of the editor, having restored the gems of Chaucer's wisdom and eloquence to their former perfection, was to select a fitting recipient for so precious a treasure. Again the Preface gives a highly personalized inflection to Thynne's account of this process, describing how he, 'devising with myself, who of all other were most worthy to whom a thing so excellent and notable should be dedicate', finally hit upon the perfect (and politically inevitable) patron: the King himself. The implication is that Henry shared with Thynne, and thus with Chaucer, the same qualities of learning, zeal for truth, and realization of the need for refinement and 'aureation' (in all its forms) that would allow him to appreciate the value of the gift. As the latter was, Thynne noted,

a pure and fine tried precious or polished jewel out of a rude or indigest mass or matter, none could to my thinking occur, that since, or in the time of Chaucer, was or is sufficient, but only your majesty royal, which by discretion and judgement, as most absolute in wisdom and all kinds of doctrine, could and of his innate clemency and goodness, would add or give any authority hereunto.

(*Works*, fol. Aiii)

Henry's task was not simply to receive the book, still less to gain the sort of pleasure and delight from it that Thynne earlier described as central to his own enjoyment of the poet's work. The King had instead to take on the more active role of defending the edition in a potentially hostile environment. In taking the *Works* into his hands, Thynne claims, Henry would be acknowledging his role as custodian of centuries of English cultural history, a claim of no little significance in the light of the volume's political agenda, as we shall see. Beginning as a modest and conventional claim to the patron's protection, the Preface builds to a crescendo of highly emotive and specific statements about the volume's likely reception and Henry's responsibility to defend it. The *Works* have by this point taken on the status of a 'precious and necessary... ornament of the tongue of this your realm' in need of vigilant safeguarding from its detractors,

so that under the shield of your most royal protection and defence it may go forth in public and prevail over those that would blemish, deface, and in many things clearly abolish the laude, renown, and glory heretofore compared, and meritoriously acquired by diverse princes and other of this said most noble isle, whereunto not only strangers under pretext of high learning and knowledge of their malicious and perverse minds, but also some of your own subjects, blinded in folly and ignorance, do with great study contend. Most gracious, victorious, and of God most elect and worthy prince, my most dread sovereign lord, in whom of very merit, duty, and succession, is renewed the glorious title of Defensor of the Christian faith, which by your noble progenitor, the great Constantine, sometime king of this realm, and emperor of Rome was, next God and his Apostles, chiefly maintained, corroborate, and defended, almighty Jesu send to your Highness the continual and everlasting abundance of his infinite grace. Amen.

(*Works*, fol. ʌiii)

Prefaces and envoys that sought pre-emptively to protect their authors from scholarly criticism or detraction were relatively commonplace in the early Tudor period. But the extent of this statement, and both the vehemence of tone and the terms it employs, seem excessive even within an inherently combative literary tradition. How might we account for the striking intensity of Thynne's statement? What made this edition of Chaucer's *Works* so potentially contentious?

The 1532 text has frequently been read in the context of Henry VIII's political Reformation. A number of scholars have seen it—or at least its Preface and the general *idea* of a monumental edition of the works of England's 'national' poet— as a contribution to royal propaganda and to the government's campaign to establish the idea of England as an 'empire', independent of Rome and sufficient unto itself in religious as well as secular politics.[10] Just as Henry established himself as Supreme Head of the Church of England, the argument runs, so Thynne offered the King a vision of a self-sufficient and dignified English language and literature, independent of and equal to Italian, French and the other European vernaculars, whose point of origin and supreme head was Geoffrey Chaucer, father of English poets.[11] There is some merit in the idea. But it is crucial to realize precisely how the poet was presented in Thynne's text, and how that presentation in turn related to the kind of Reformation that was underway in England at the time. For Thynne's Chaucer, as we shall see, was a moderate, consensual, figure, not a radical one.

The 1532 edition was a crucial contribution to both the establishment of the Chaucerian canon and the sense of what that canon *meant* to English readers. And the language and logic of Henry VIII's struggle with Rome resonates loudly through the Preface. This theme will be explored in more detail in the pages that follow. It is sufficient here, perhaps, to note the striking sense of a nation and culture embattled in Thynne's commendation of the *Works* to Henry VIII, the sense of the need to protect English—and specifically royal—rights against unjust encroachment from both envious foreigners and disloyal English subjects. These were precisely the terms in which Henry fought his ongoing war of attrition with the papal courts over the right to try his 'divorce' from Katherine of Aragon within England. English princes, Henry claimed, had the right to determine spiritual cases within their own kingdom rather than having to sue to foreign courts for judgement (hence, perhaps, Thynne's allusion to 'strangers under pretext of high learning and knowledge' seeking to 'blemish, deface, and...abolish' the renown of English princes; for it was the King's assertion that the Roman claim to supreme authority was a usurpation of royal prerogatives, and based on both bad law and bad history). On 13 January 1531, for example, Thomas Howard, Duke of Norfolk, Henry's chief minister, had told the imperial ambassador, Eustace Chapuys that popes had, in former times, 'attempted to usurp in England certain authorities and prerogatives. The King's predecessors . . . had never consented to it, and it was not to be expected that King Henry should suffer it at the present moment'. As Chapuys reported the conversation to his master Charles V, Norfolk went on to say 'that kings were before popes, the King was absolute master in his own kingdom and acknowledged no superior', citing the conquest of Rome by the mythical English king Brennius as his precedent and adding that the emperor Constantine, who had reputedly endowed the Roman church with its temporal possessions and authority, had reigned in England, and his mother, Helen, had been English by birth. Hence, Norfolk concluded, only the Archbishop of Canterbury had the authority to settle the matter of the King's marriage, and the Pope had no power or right to intervene.[12]

The politics of Henry's break with Rome seem equally to colour the striking move from secular to religious authority in the final commendation of the 1532 Preface, which praises the monarch in whom the title of Defender of the Faith and the legacy of the Emperor Constantine are renewed, and an authority 'next God and his Apostles' is 'corroborate and defended'. Again, it is fruitful to read this in the context of the King's claim that he enjoyed an 'imperial' authority within his own realm, and was, in Convocation's famous formulation, under God the 'only sovereign lord and protector of the Church of England, and, as far as the law of Christ allows [*quantum per Christi legem licit*], supreme head of the same'. In the light of Norfolk's use of the same example, Thynne's allusion to the Emperor Constantine also seems more telling. As the secular ruler supposedly responsible for the establishment of the institutional church in its current form, Constantine's governance was a crucial test case for the relationship between secular and spiritual authority in a realm—what we might anachronistically think of as the relationship between church and state. Any 'historical' evidence, however anecdotal or apocryphal, concerning Constantine's attitude towards the church that he had reputedly established in its temporal power was thus valuable ammunition in Henry's struggle to convince the Papal courts and his own bench of bishops that the authority to try his divorce lay in England not Rome. Hence the '*Collectanea satis copiosa*' (the 'sufficiently large collection' of arguments and authorities supportive of Henry's imperial claims gathered by a think-tank of royal scholars led by Edward Foxe and presented to the King in 1531) made a good deal of Constantine's example. Rather than question the authenticity of his Donation, as had been done so effectively by the humanist Lorenzo Valla, the *Collectanea* accepted its validity, claiming that it offered documentary proof that the Emperor (and hence all 'imperial' princes) was the original source of ecclesiastical power and authority. What had once been lent to Rome, Foxe and his team argued, might thus be called back again, should the prince require it.[13]

But Constantine's name was also deployed, and to good effect, by critics of the divorce. In April 1531 a preacher, delivering a sermon before the King, claimed that the Emperor had refused to judge in a dispute between two bishops, as he said that it did not belong to a secular prince so to do—the implication being that if Constantine had clearly not attempted to interfere in the jurisdiction of 'his' clergy, neither should Henry. The King, seeing the significance of the allusion, lost his temper, and, opening the window of his oratory, interrupted the preacher, telling him in a loud voice not to tell such falsehoods. The preacher, however, reverently stood his ground, replying that he was not repeating false-hoods, as the story could be found in a number of chronicles. At this, Henry turned his back and stalked off, highly displeased.[14] In citing Constantine as a precursor of Henry's royal authority, then, Thynne's Preface was hitting on no chance or insignificant example of imperial rule, but alluding directly to a figure central to the debates about the nature and scope of the Henrician Supremacy.

It is clear, then, that in order to appreciate fully the impact of the 1532 *Chaucer* upon its first readers, it is important to read the text in the context of the Henrician Reformation. But it is vital also to go beyond the general issues of its form and the language of its Preface if we are to see the full significance of the volume. For, on closer inspection it is clear that the edition was not an uncritical contribution to that Reformation, still less the kind of semi-authorized royal propaganda that some critics have suggested. Rather it was a precise and carefully constructed intervention in the political debates of the moment of its production in 1532—the year of Henry's declaration of the Supreme Headship and the House of Commons' Supplication Against the Ordinaries—the Lower House's rebarbative assault upon the liberties and prerogatives of the English clergy. The political resonances of the *Works* thus go well beyond the representation of Chaucer as a model and source for a new and self-confident view of English vernacular poesy. To understand fully how the volume deployed Chaucer in the arena of courtly and national politics, it is important to read the edition, and in particular the apparatus with which it surrounded the poet's works, with care. For the selection and organization of the prefatory and concluding verses that 'packaged' the poet represented him as a particular sort of writer, and the decisions concerning which texts to include and which to exclude from the volume, and what appears at first glance to be the curious decision to have Brian Tuke ventriloquize Thynne's voice in the Preface, each contributed sign-ificantly to the nature and impact of the text that appeared under William Thynne's name.

But before we turn to the details of the volume, however, it is important to orient ourselves in the political context of 1532, and the extraordinary events that preceded the book's publication.

3

The Signs of the World

The 'Wondrous' Divisions of the Early 1530s

The period from the opening of the Reformation Parliament in October 1529 to the autumn of 1532 when the Chaucer edition appeared, seemed to contemporaries a time of unprecedented social and cultural turbulence. People who were, as the previous chapter suggested, used to a fair amount of robust political debate, and to voicing their opinions if they thought that a situation warranted it, experienced changes that they found both difficult to comprehend, and almost impossible to resist effectively. As we shall see, even educated, articulate members of the political elite were to find the normal mechanisms of expression and engagement with political events increasingly ineffective. The result was something that it is legitimate to call a crisis of cultural confidence. Everywhere people spoke of unprecedented divisions, of schism, and rancorous conflict within the body politic—and even those who had lived through the brief, turbulent reign of Richard III declared themselves unprepared for what they witnessed. The divorce campaign, and Henry's need to pressurize the church at home and in Rome into granting a domestic solution to his 'Great Matter', led to an increasingly bitter religious debate at the political centre, and the sense of a new and alarming social rift throughout the nation: a 'division' (as a treatise published in 1532 by the common lawyer Christopher St German was to call it) 'between the spirituality and the temporality'.[1]

The first session of the Reformation Parliament, which met following the failure of the Blackfriars' 'divorce' court and the fall of Cardinal Wolsey, was notoriously 'anticlerical' in its tone and direction. The government itself had encouraged criticism of the clergy when the Lord Chancellor, Sir Thomas More, in his opening speech declared virtual open season on Wolsey's administrative record, announcing Henry's willingness to hear the grievances of his subjects and his desire to promote laws to suppress 'diverse new enormities...sprung up amongst the people'.[2] The session that followed witnessed a vociferous assault in the House of Commons upon the alleged abuses of the clergy and an equally assertive rebuttal of those accusations from the spiritual peers in the Lords. The chronicler Edward Hall, himself a member of the lower house, described how,

When the Commons were assembled in the nether house, they began to commune of the griefs wherewith the spirituality had before time grievously oppressed them, both contrary to the law of the realm, and contrary to all right.

(*Chronicle*, p. 765)

In particular they complained of what Hall called six 'great causes': excessive probate fees and mortuary fines, clerics acting as stewards of lands to the detriment of poor husbandmen and trading in goods to the ruin of merchants, clerical absenteeism, and pluralism of benefices.

That these debates were unprecedented in the experience of those present is clear from Hall's account.

These things before this time might in no wise be touched nor yet talked of by no man except he would be an heretic, or lose all that he had, for the bishops were [hitherto] chancellors and had all the rule about the King... But now when God had illumined the eyes of the King, and that their subtle doings was once espied; then men began charitably to desire a reformation, and so at this Parliament men began to show their grudges.

(*Chronicle*, pp. 765–6)

That the discussion was actually far from charitable is clear from what followed. The Mortuaries bill met with little opposition in the Lords, perhaps because, as Hall acerbically claimed, 'it touched them little', being a matter for parish priests rather than bishops. But, when the bill to reform probate fees reached the upper house, Archbishop Warham of Canterbury and other spiritual peers 'both frowned and grunted, for that touched their profit'. Indeed,

Dr John Fisher, bishop of Rochester, said openly in the Parliament chamber these words: 'My lords, you see daily what bills come hither from the Common House, and all is to the destruction of the Church. For God's sake see what a realm the kingdom of Bohemia was, and when the Church went down, then fell the glory of the kingdom. Now with the Commons is nothing but 'down with the Church!' And all this, me seemeth, is for lack of faith only'.

(*Chronicle*, p. 766)

Infuriated by the comparison to heretical Bohemia, the Commons protested to the King and secured a measure of apology from Fisher. But the tone had been set, and the arguments continued. Later the clergy were, in their turn 'sorely offended' by words spoken in the Commons. A gentleman of Gray's Inn attacked the clerics' continual resort to the claim of 'prescription and usage' as a justification for their prerogatives. 'The usage hath ever been of thieves to rob on Shooters' Hill', he declared, 'ergo, is it lawful?' The abbots and bishops were as outraged at being compared to thieves as the Commons had been by the allusion to heretics. And when a composite bill concerning pluralism and non-residence, trading, and landowning by the clergy reached the Lords, it 'so displeased the spirituality that the priests railed on the Commons... and called them heretics and schismatics, for which divers priests were punished'.[3]

The legislation that finally emerged from the session was a pale shadow of the issues debated in 1529–30. There were rumours in London in October 1529 that all the temporal possessions of the church would be seized; and on the opening day of the Parliament, 3 November, copies of Simon Fish's fiercely anticlerical tract *The Supplication for the Beggars* were scattered in the streets. It proposed a very radical solution to what it identified as a pernicious clerical hegemony: advising Henry to,

tie these holy idle thieves [i.e. the 'blood-supping' regular clergy] to the carts to be whipped naked about every market place till they will fall to labour... Then shall these great yearly exactions cease... Then shall the gospel be preached... Then shall we daily pray to God for your most noble estate long to endure.[4]

Petitions to Parliament that were not acted upon proposed less bloodthirsty but nevertheless dramatic assaults upon clerical prerogatives and independence, including the restoration of monastic lands to the heirs of their original donors, and (prophetically) the subjugation of ecclesiastical jurisdiction to royal control for a period of seven years. A memorandum on 'Parliament matters', drawn up by Thomas lord Darcy made a number of brutally simple points: 'Item, that never legate nor cardinal be in England. Item, their legacies and faculties clearly annulled and made frustrate... Item, that it be tried whether the putting down of the abbeys be lawful and good or no, for great things hang thereupon'. In early 1530 a prominent London cleric, Dr Miles of St Bride's parish, was murdered by unknown assailants; and such was the furore generated in the capital, that Chapuys thought in December 1530 that 'nearly all the people here hate the priests'.[5]

In the months that followed the disputes spilled out beyond Parliament, finding expression in pulpits and public gatherings across England, as the church's evangelical critics voiced their grievances and the ecclesiastical authorities reacted in kind. At one extreme there were a number of high-profile heresy trials and investigations conducted under the inspiration if not the jurisdiction of More, the new Lord Chancellor. In May 1530 Bishop Stokesley of London presided over a public bonfire in St Paul's churchyard of copies of William Tyndale's translation of the New Testament, while on 22 June a Proclamation banned all books printed in English concerning the Holy Scripture that had not been examined and approved by a bishop. On 19 November four men were paraded through London on horseback bearing copies of Tyndale's works on their bodies as punishment for distributing *The Practice of Prelates* through the City. One among them, however, pranced on a haughty gelding, showing a lofty contempt for the solemn proceedings and threatening to turn them into a mockery. By 1531, however, it was men and not books being burned. During the autumn, More held the bookseller George Constantine in the stocks in the porter's lodge of his house in Chelsea until he broke free and escaped. But Constantine had revealed enough information under interrogation to implicate the Benedictine monk Richard Bayfield in his heresies. Bayfield was arrested, tried, and burned at Smithfield on 4 December. On 9 November a young and well-respected scholar, Thomas Bilney had been publicly burned as a lapsed heretic in Norwich. On 20 December John Tewkesbury, a leather-seller, suffered the same fate at Smithfield. On 15 December James Bainham was interrogated by Bishop Stokesley and similarly condemned. He was to die on 30 April the following year. Even the dead were not safe. In May 1532, one William Tracy was posthumously condemned in southern Convocation for the allegedly heretical contents of his will, while Edward Crome and Hugh Latimer also had articles issued against them in the same gathering.[6]

Attempts have been made to downplay the impact of these trials and investigations, but contemporaries clearly saw them as a new and deeply troubling development. Those who were sympathetic to Luther's teachings, it was said, were fleeing the country for the less repressive cities of the Low Countries; and even those who were not consciously heterodox feared investigation. In December 1531 Hugh Latimer claimed that even St Paul himself would be condemned for heresy by Bishop Stokesley and his courts.[7] Stephen Vaughan, who was in the Low Countries attempting to persuade the evangelical friar Robert Barnes and a number of other writers to return to England and support the royal divorce, warned Thomas Cromwell of the dangers of the current repressive policy in a series of increasingly anxious letters. 'These sharp inquisitions, stripes, and bitter rewards would make some men's hearts faint towards their prince', he wrote. Instead of punishments, tortures, and killings ridding the realm of erroneous opinions 'and bringing men into such fear that they will not be so hardy as to speak or look', they would rather 'cause the sect in the end to wax the greater and those errors to be more plenteously in this realm'. The worst offenders had already fled abroad, and by driving men away 'they would simply make the company (of heretics) in strange places greater, and four will write where only one wrote before'. While denying that he was either Lutheran or 'Tyndalin', he suggested nonetheless that the King should 'be assured that no policy nor threats can take away the opinions of his people until he fatherly and lovingly reforms the clergy, whence spring both the opinions and the grudges of the people'. The Flemings, he warned, were already spitting out blasphemies everywhere against England, angered by the King's divorce. He finished his letter of 14 November 1531 with an apocalyptic flourish: 'behold the signs of the world, which be wondrous!'[8]

On the other side of the religious divide, conservatives were horrified at the headway being made by what they saw as heresy and its advocates in England. Thomas More offered an equally apocalyptic view of events in his *Dialogue Concerning Heresies* (1529), arguing that,

if the world were not near at an end, and the fervour of devotion so sore cold that it were almost quenched among Christian people, it could never have commen to pass that so many people should fall to the following of such a beastly sect.[9]

Ambassador Chapuys was appalled to see the evangelical convert Robert Barnes walking at large in London in December 1531, flaunting his apostasy in the secular clothes he was wearing. And he reported bitterly that another heretic had been released from prison when the King had noticed that one of the views for which he had been condemned was the claim that the Pope was not the head of the Church. Orthodox merchants were said to be considering emigrating to Spain or (like the Lutherans) the Low Countries, where the religious culture was more congenial.[10] In Rome it was reported that the Furies were at work in the English Parliament assaulting the clergy, and Edward Hall records that 'In this season were divers preachings in the realm, one contrary to another concerning the King's marriage'. In his *Dialogue Between Pole and Lupset*, Thomas Starkey lamented that 'things be here so far out of order, so far out of frame' that the whole realm was overcome with a universal pestilence, 'a common frenzy'.[11] In the prologue to the subsidy bill of February 1531, the members of southern convocation complained of the laity's 'late raging against the [Church] ... and [the] personages of the prelates of the clergy with their famous lies and cursed books and works everywhere dispersed to th'intent to blemish and hurt the estimation of the said prelates and clergy and to bring them into common hatred and contempt'. When, also in February 1531, the household of Bishop Fisher, Katherine of Aragon's staunchest supporter, fell victim to a poisoner, it was suspected that heretics were responsible, perhaps, Chapuys suggested, even Anne Boleyn herself. Fisher was unharmed, having not touched the broth into which the poison had been poured, but two of his household servants who did eat it died, as did a number of paupers to whom it had been given as alms. Such was the public outcry that the culprit, whom Hall named as Fisher's cook, one Richard Roos, was publicly boiled alive at Smithfield under legislation specially drafted in the wake of the affair. In the Autumn, a riot occurred in London, when a crowd of women (and men in women's clothing) reportedly several thousand strong descended upon a riverside palace where Anne Boleyn was thought to be staying, intending to lay violent hands upon her. When they did not find her in residence, however, the motley lynch-party dispersed. No action was taken by the authorities, supposedly because the matter was considered 'a thing done by women', and so of no consequence.[12] Strange events were becoming a commonplace of London politics. As Susan Brigden has noted, when in May 1532 two great fish were brought out of the Thames, people took it for 'a prodigy foreboding evil', especially as there had been fourteen suicides in London in the previous few days.[13] The signs of the world were wondrous indeed.

The idea of a fierce and potentially ruinous division between the laity and spirituality had, by 1530 at the latest, become an acknowledged part of the political climate, lamented in speeches and documents at all levels of society. Even those consciously contributing to the schism felt the need to declare their regret that it existed in what they said and wrote. Playing upon Henry's stated demands for order and obedience from his subjects, conservatives and radicals alike decried the continuation of this schism and voiced their demands (whether for a halt to reforms or for further, more radical action) in the form of suggested remedies for the problems it caused. Thus Thomas More's *Dialogue*, while heaping abuse upon the evangelical critics of the clergy, lamented that 'now they [the clergy] blame us [the laity], and we blame them, and both [are] blameworthy, and either part more ready to find others' faults than to mend their own'.[14] In the legal sphere, Christopher St German made the case for the subjugation of the ecclesiastical law to the common law in the form of the treatise mentioned earlier, lamenting *The Division Between the Spirituality and the Temporality*. St German's book asked rhetorically, 'who may remember the state of this realm now in these days without great heaviness and sorrow of heart?', and presented itself as a prescription for reconciling the divided parties. Its Preface announced: 'This little book declareth diverse causes whereby division hath risen between the spirituality and temporality, and partly showeth how they may be brought to a unity', thus ending the current situation in which 'reigneth now envy, pride, division, and strife'.[15] In Parliament, a draft bill, probably also the work of St German, proposed the stripping away of most of the powers and prerogatives of the ecclesiastical courts, but it again represented itself as an attempt to restore the 'love, amity, and good agreement between the spirituality and the temporality', suggesting as a token of its good intentions, that it should be made illegal for either group to malign or insult the other.[16] Most famously, the House of Commons framed its most forthright attack upon the jurisdiction of those same courts as a petition to the King for an end to the 'uncharitable variances and part-taking' between clergy and the laity.[17]

The latter document, the, so-called, Supplication against the Ordinaries, was introduced into the Commons in May 1532, but it drew upon complaints and grievances against court fees, the citing of laymen outside their diocese by the church courts, and other alleged clerical abuses that had been first raised in Parliament in 1529. What gave the Supplication renewed force and resonance was its insistence that it offered a remedy for, rather than merely a continuation of, the anticlerical debates. Drawing both the spread of heretical literature and the behaviour of the bishops' courts into its purview, it lamented the fact that 'much discord, variance, [and] debate hath risen, and more and more daily is like to increase and ensue amongst the universal sort of your [Majesty's] said subjects, as well spiritual as temporal, either against other, in most uncharitable manner to the great inquietation and breach of your peace within this your most catholic realm'.

Their intention, the drafters of the Supplication insisted, was not 'to take away from the said ordinaries their authority to correct and punish sin, and especially the detestable crime of heresy'. Indeed, if current legislation was insufficient in that respect, they would support the drafting of further 'more dreadful and terrible laws for the repress[ion] of the same than hath been in times past', provided only 'that some reasonable declaration may be known to your people how they may, if they will, eschew the peril of heresy'. But what was needed primarily was firm legislative action against abuses on both sides:

In consideration whereof, most gracious Sovereign Lord, forasmuch as there is at this present time, and by a few years past hath been, much misdemeanour and violence on the one part, and much default and lack of patience, sufferance, charity, and goodwill on the other part, a marvellous discord of the goodly quiet, peace, and tranquillity that this your realm heretofore hath been in, ever hitherto through your politic wisdom in most honourable fame and catholic faith inviolably preserved.

Hence the King should ensure that, with 'all violence and uncharitable demeanours on both sides utterly and clearly set apart', some 'necessary and behoveful remedies, laws and ordinances' should be introduced to make clear the responsibilities of the Crown (and thereby limit the jurisdiction of the church courts) and also to 'reconcile and bring into perpetual unity your said subjects spiritual and temporal'.[18] But, having paid lip-service to the danger posed by heretical books, it turned its sights exclusively upon the ecclesiastical courts as the source of the problem.

The 'chief fountains, occasions, and causes' of the division were, the Supplication suggested, those laws concerning temporal matters made by the clergy in their convocations, many of which were 'repugnant to the laws and statutes of your [Majesty's] realm' and 'against your jurisdiction and prerogative royal'. Poor laymen were liable to be summoned before the church courts *ex officio*, 'for displeasure, without any provable cause, and sometimes at the only promotion and suggestion of their summoners and apparitors, [they] being very light and indiscreet persons'. These laymen might then be imprisoned without bail and forced to answer 'to many subtle questions and interrogatories only invented and exhibited at the pleasure of the said ordinaries, their commissaries and substitutes, by the which a simple unlearned [man], or else a well-witted man without learning . . . may be trapped and induced by an ignorant answer to the peril of open penance, to his shame, or else to redeem the same penance for money, as it is commonly used'.[19]

While the disputes between commons and clergy could be fought out in this way as a matter of conflicting counsels, voiced in petitions from Parliament and Convocation to the King for redress, they remained a manageable affair from Henry's point of view. Indeed, they offered him a useful means of consolidating the Supremacy, which no doubt explains Cromwell's role in the drafting of the Commons' Supplication. Henry might use the radicalism of the Commons as an excuse and justification for the anti-papal measures that he himself was introducing, and pose as the moderate influence holding his lay subjects back from still more radical measures. Hence, having imposed the Annates Act on a reluctant House of Commons (going in person to the Commons chamber and prompting the first recorded division in parliamentary history in order to force the bill through), he was able to announce publicly, for consumption in Rome and the

Imperial court, that it was the members of the Commons themselves 'who hate the Pope most wonderfully'. It was the Commons, he said, who had demanded the measure, and unless the Roman courts quickly gave him what he wanted over the divorce, he would no longer be willing to rein in their excesses.[20]

Consequently, when southern Convocation responded to the Commons' Supplication with an appeal to the King that the Church be allowed to continue to enjoy the liberties granted to it by his forebears, and requested that formal definition be given to the scope of the *praemunire* statute to prevent the clergy once again unwittingly falling under its ill-defined provisions,[21] Henry was able to maintain the pose of the neutral arbiter of their grievances as the good prince should, whilst actually dramatically increasing the pressure on Convocation to capitulate to his demands. In May 1532 he passed Convocation's response to the leaders of the Commons for comments, telling them to 'look circumspectly' on what he called their 'very sophistical' petition, yet promising that he would 'be indifferent [i.e. impartial]' between them.[22] But behind the rhetoric of even-handedness was a determination to bring the Church effectively under royal legislative control. At the same time as he was handing Convocation's petition to the Commons, he told a delegation of eight temporal lords and twelve members of the Commons that he had discovered new and alarming information about his spiritual peers. 'Well-beloved subjects', he announced,

We thought that the clergy of this our realm had been our subjects wholly, but now we have well perceived that they be but half our subjects, yea, and scarce our subjects, for all the prelates at their consecration make an oath to the Pope clean contrary to the oath that they make to us; so that they seem to be his subjects and not ours.

Giving the delegates a copy of each of the oaths, he instructed them to 'invent some order that we be not thus deluded of our spiritual subjects'. The ensuing debate, Hall observed, provided 'one of the occasions why the Pope within two years lost all his jurisdiction in England'.[23]

The late spring of 1532 did indeed see the decisive moves in Henry's jurisdictional battle for control of the Church in England. Under intense personal and institutional pressure, Archbishop Warham persuaded a sparsely attended upper house of Convocation to accept Henry's demands. The clerical parliament agreed that it would no longer meet without royal licence, nor would it make any new canons without submitting them first for royal approval, and all existing canons would be subject to scrutiny and ratification by a body nominated by the Crown. In effect the church had given up its legislative independence and handed it to the Crown. The Supremacy was converted from a theoretical authority deployed in diplomatic arguments into a practical legislative jurisdiction. As Chapuys lamented to the Emperor, churchmen would from now on be of less account than shoemakers in England, for the shoemakers at least had the right to gather together at their own instigation for the regulation of their trade. Hereafter there could be no misunderstanding that Henry intended to make his control of the Church a political reality. On the very next day Thomas More resigned the Chancellorship, citing personal incapacity, but leaving no one in any doubt that he could no longer work for a regime that was effectively removing itself from direct communion with Rome. As if to add symbolic weight to the ominous sense that England was witnessing the end of a long period of continuity in ecclesiastical politics, More's resignation fell on 16 May, the same day as the ceremonial interment of John Islip, the long-serving Abbot of Westminster, and one of the best-known churchmen in the capital, who had died on the previous Sunday. Hence, when Henry prorogued Parliament for the summer, its work for him having been completed, its members went home leaving Westminster draped in funereal black. It might well have seemed to be, as one historian has described it, 'the funeral of the middle ages'.[24] Certainly the symbolism suggested the end of an era.

But if the divisions between clergy and temporality had provided Henry with political opportunities, they also posed a genuine threat to civil order and good government. And there is a strong sense, as the early 1530s progressed, of the King, increasingly alarmed by the hornets' nest that his divorce had stirred up, trying to quieten the worst excesses of the debate. A draft Act of Parliament for spiritual causes, probably drawn up in early 1531, contemplated the creation of a series of committees to consider the case for a vernacular New Testament, to investigate allegations of heresy, and to review the conduct of the clergy, thereby taking the most contentious aspects of the public debate back into royal hands. It enjoined somewhat plaintively, that 'it is further enacted that the laity shall not report ill of the clergy or the reverse'.[25] But the divisions between the temporality and spirituality seemed only to widen. An anticlerical tract distributed in manuscript at this time castigated the luxury and ambition of priests, and claimed that 'the laity are already beginning to cry out "cut them down; why cumber they the ground?" '[26]

What had started as something of a manufactured crisis, then (with the agitation in the Commons being tacitly encouraged by the King in order to provide a weapon against the Church), had quickly grown to the point at which it was no longer capable of direction. In February 1532 Norfolk wrote to William Benet, a royal agent in Rome, blithely assuring him of the government's ability to restrain the agitation in the Commons. 'Though the church in this realm hath many "wringers" at her high authority', he claimed, 'nothing hurtful shall be done unless the fault be in the Pope in proceeding wrongfully against the King. Notwithstanding the infinite clamours of the temporality here in Parliament...the King will stop all evil effects if the Pope does not handle him unkindly:' Yet he added somewhat nervously that 'this realm did never grudge the tenth part against the abuses of the church at no Parliament in my days as they do now'. And events beyond London were still more difficult to control. Over Easter 1533, the mutually hostile preaching in Bristol of the reformer Hugh Latimer and a number of his conservative critics became so contentious that the Chancellor of the diocese was prompted to ban them all from the pulpit. Even one of the combatants conceded that 'our crying one against another is not fruitful', while people talked of 'such divisions and seditions among us as never were seen in this realm'.[27] And Henry's public stance as the disinterested judge willing to listen to the grievances of his subjects increasingly frequently gave way to demands for an immediate end to dissent and a return to obedience and 'quietness'. Such ideas, indeed, were to be the hallmark of the legislation of the later 1530s. At almost the same time as Norfolk was vaunting the King's ability to quell dissent to Benet, Henry himself was telling Chapuys that he was seriously considering new measures in Parliament to ensure the peace and good order of his kingdom.[28]

But opposition to royal policies could not be so readily stilled and took many forms, ranging from honest advice to public disorder and outright subversion. In the Council chamber the Treasurer, Sir William Fitzwilliam and the Comptroller of the royal household, Sir Henry Guildford are said to have spoken 'roundly and in very plain terms' in favour of Queen Katherine, and the Duke of Suffolk (Henry's former jousting partner, Thomas Brandon) supported them, adding that England had great need to live in peace and amity with the Emperor, and warmly extolling the latter's qualities—the implication being that the best way to remain friends with Charles V was to restore good relations with Katherine, his aunt. Henry reportedly remained silent about his old friend's warnings, but told Fitzwilliam and Guildford that they did not know what they were talking about.[29] Suffolk later spoke up again in Katherine's defence, telling Henry that she had always obeyed him in everything, but owed higher obedience to two others. When Henry eagerly asked who these individuals were, Suffolk replied that the first was God and the second her conscience, 'which she would not lose for all the world'.[30]

When, in May 1532, Henry asked Parliament for a subsidy to pay for the fortification of the border with Scotland, a passionate debate ensued, during which two members of the Commons were bold enough to say that there was no need for such military precautions, as, without Continental allies, the Scots would never consider an invasion. The best defence was therefore to restore good relations with the Emperor, which might be effected if Parliament petitioned the King to take back his wife and treat her kindly. Otherwise, they claimed, 'they considered the kingdom as completely ruined and lost'. These sentiments, Chapuys reported, met with the approval of the majority of those present, but only prompted Henry to summon a delegation of members of the lower house for a lecture on the justice of his claim for a divorce, and a warning not to interfere in his private affairs in future.[31] In southern Convocation, the lower house, representing the parish priests and junior clergy, demanded that the bishops attempt to reverse their acknowledgement of the Royal Supremacy when they met in the House of Lords, and in May 1531, northern Convocation protested formally to the King against the terms of the Supremacy.[32] When Parliament reconvened in January 1532 and it was rumoured that an attempt would be made there to settle the divorce in England, Bishop Fisher came to Westminster determined to speak on the Queen's behalf despite having been pointedly left off the list of those summoned to attend.[33]

Opposition also took more subversive forms. In September 1531 a servant of the Marquis of Dorset was arrested for saying that, the way things were going, his master would soon be king, and seeking to recruit others to his service.[34] And in the same month, when Bishop Stokesley convened a meeting of the London clergy at St Paul's to organize the collection of their contribution to the £100,000 granted to the King by Convocation, the gathering turned into a riot. Nearly 500 clerics and sympathetic laymen broke down the doors and forced their way into the chapter house, 'buffeting' and striking down divers of the bishop's servants, and prompting Stokesley himself to placate them with soft words for fear of his life. He pressed the demands for donations no further that day. But, once the crowd had dispersed he reported the matter to the Lord Chancellor who ordered the arrest of the ringleaders. In all, fifteen priests and five laymen were imprisoned in the Tower, the Fleet, and elsewhere, where they were to remain 'long after'.[35] In November 1532 Friar Forest, a Franciscan Observant and a vocal opponent of the divorce and evangelical reform alike, preached at Paul's Cross with Stokesley's licence, 'railing and barking' his critics claimed, at the decay of the realm and the pulling down of the churches.[36]

Literature and the Great Division

We have already noticed some literary reflections of the divisions opened up by Henry's divorce campaign. But the printing presses contributed more significantly still to the sense of social dislocation, producing texts that gave durable form to the cacophony of invective. Henry sought to use the printed word in the promotion of his campaign, producing both the *Determinations of the Universities* (November, 1531) and *A Glass of The Truth* (1532), a more popular résumé of the arguments supporting the divorce, for popular consumption,[37] but these texts were merely drops added to a river of argument and abuse already flowing from print-shops in England and overseas. For much of the 'railing' between conservatives and evangelicals, clergy and laity, was conducted through the medium of the printed book.

Works written by exiled evangelicals and printed overseas brought Lutheran doctrine into England in a highly portable and accessible form. Such works were also particularly aggressive in assaulting the central institutions and assumptions of the established church. But to make claims about the extent and impact of evangelical book production and ownership in this period is inherently contentious. It involves straying into the vexed and still unresolved question of how 'popular' the English Reformation was in its origins. To stress the number of heretical books produced in the period implies sympathies with the school that sees the Reformation as prompted by widespread popular discontent with the late-medieval church. To seek to put the radical texts into the wider context of book-production generally in this period suggests an attempt to minimize the extent of religious dissent. I do not want to be sidetracked into a debate about numbers here. What I am suggesting is not that evangelical beliefs and anticlerical attitudes were widespread in London at this time, still less that large numbers of people were suddenly either writing, printing, or buying heretical books. As Eamon Duffy and others have convincingly argued (and an examination of the *Short Title Catalogue of Books Printed in England, Scotland, and Ireland* confirms) most of the books on religious topics printed in the late 1520s and early 1530s were orthodox in nature, designed to facilitate rather than frustrate traditional forms of worship and acts of piety.[38] There was no sudden and massive increase in the production and ownership of heretical material. My claim here is the more modest one that such evangelically inclined books as were imported into England had a disproportionate and dramatic effect on the culture that received them. It is change and novelty rather than continuity that people notice, especially when that novelty is as abrasive and self-advertising as many of the heretical books of this period were. Hence the small corpus of such works produced in 1528–32 had an effect well beyond their numerical significance—especially as they were circulating simultaneously with the sitting of the Reformation Parliament.

In 1528 William Tyndale's *Wicked Mammon* had appeared in England. In 1529, John Frith's *The Revelation of the Antichrist* (printed in Antwerp by Johann Hoochstraten) offered its readers a comparison between 'Christ's acts and our holy father the Pope's', inevitably greatly to the latter's disadvantage; while the Antwerp presses also produced Simon Fish's *Supplication for the Beggars* and *The Summe of the Holye Scripture*.[39] In 1530, Hoochstraten's shop produced William Tyndale's translation of *The Pentateuch* and his *The Practyse of Prelates*, *A Proper Dyalogue Between a Gentilman and a Husbandman* ('each complaining to other their miserable calamity through the ambition of the clergy') with *An ABC to the Spiritualite*, and *A Compendious Olde Treatyse, shewynge howe that we ought to have ye Scripture in Englysshe*, by the fifteenth-century Lollard, Richard Ullerston, modernized for publication, perhaps by Tyndale himself. George Joye's *The Psalter of David in Englisshe* also appeared in 1530, as did the more moderately reformist text of John Colet's sermon to southern Convocation of 1513, reprinted in translation in London by Berthelet.[40] In 1531 there was Tyndale's *Exposition of the First Epistle of St John*, his translation of *The Prophete Jonas*, and *An Answere Unto Sir Thomas More's Dialogue*, George Joye's *The Prophete Isaye, translated into Englisshe*, and *The Letters which Johan Ashwell, Priour of Newnham Abbey, besid[e]s Bedforde, sent secretly to the Bishope of Lyncolne . . . Where in the said Priour accuseth George Joye..of Fower Opinio[n]s: with the answer of the said George unto the same . . .*, John Frith's, *A Disoputacio[n] of Purgatorye*, and Robert Barnes's *Supplication*.[41]

In addition to the new works printed abroad, a number of medieval anticlerical texts were resurrected and printed for new audiences during the first sessions of the Reformation Parliament. *A Proper Dyaloge* embedded a Lollard treatise on the dispossession of the clergy in a newly written dialogue which drew out its relevance to contemporary debates. While 1530 also saw the printing of the Lollard William Thorpe's account of his own heresy trial (again probably modernized by Tyndale) with the Lollard rebel Sir John Oldcastle's *Testament*. Ullerton's *Compendious olde Treatise* was also reprinted, this time bound with another version of *A Proper Dyaloge*. The *Praier and Complaynte of the Ploweman unto Christe* was published in Antwerp in 1531 and again in London in 1532, and in the same year (or early in the next) Thomas Godfray's presses were to produce the Lollard inflected *Plowman's Tale*. All of these texts provided medieval precedents for Tudor evangelical causes. The *Compendious olde Treatyse* declared boldly, and in terms that resonated powerfully with contemporary debates about scriptural translation, that 'it lieth never in Antichrist's power to destroy all English books, for, as fast as he burneth, other men shall draw, and thus the cause of heresy and of the people that dieth in heresy is the frowardness of bishops that will not suffer men to have open communing and free in the law of God . . . And now they turn His law by their cruel constitutions into damnation of the people'.[42] At roughly the same time Robert Redman printed *The Lantern of Light*, which contained a fierce polemic against the established church, its constitutions and doctrines, including the claim that Rome was the head of the Antichrist, archbishops and bishops his members, and the regular clergy his 'venomous tail'. Even preachers operating with episcopal licences, it claimed, bore 'the mark of the beast'.[43]

The repackaging of these late-medieval texts for Tudor audiences was part of a wider strategic agenda on the part of the reformers. As Anne Hudson has demonstrated, through such publications evangelical scholars and printers sought to provide a credible—indeed an authentically 'antique'—lineage for the kind of evangelical and anticlerical demands that resurfaced during the period of the Reformation Parliament, thereby refuting the charge laid against them by conservatives that the 'new learning' was a recent innovation, dreamed up by Luther and his confreres. This strategy was acknowledged explicitly in *A Proper Dyaloge*, when the Gentleman, one of the disputants in the modern debate that frames the medieval treatise, says of that central text,

> Yf soche auncyent thynges might come to lyght
> That noble men hadde ones of theym a syght,
> The world yet wolde chaunge peraventure.
> For here-agaynst the clergye can not bercke,
> Sayenge as they do, thys is a new wercke
> Of heretykes contrived lately.
> And by thys treatyse it apperyth playne
> That before oure dayes men dyd compleyne,
> Agaynst clerkes ambycyon so stately.[44]

Hence the stress placed upon the antiquity of these texts in their prefatory material and title-pages. *A Proper Dyaloge*, for example, is described as having been written in the 'time of king Richard the second', and being thus 'above an hundred year old', and *A Compendious olde Treatyse* is said to have been compiled 'not long after [1300]'.[45] But it is important to note that the strategy was not simply to set the origins of these works sufficiently 'long ago' to refute the charge of novelty. In all but the case of the *Compendious olde Treatyse*, the supposed origins of these books were in the very late fourteenth or early fifteenth centuries, the one period in history during which English literary and intellectual culture could be said to have been flourishing on a par with those of the best of the Continental monarchies. Hence the England of Chaucer, John Gower, and Thomas Hoccleve, of Richard II and Henry IV, was being deliberately represented as simultaneously an England characterized by evangelical fervour and anti-Roman and anticlerical protest. Indeed, the poetry of the period was itself consciously represented as an essentially evangelical enterprise; hence the resurrection (and in some cases the partial invention) of works in the *Piers Plowman* tradition printed or circulated in manuscript in the early 1530s, including *Piers* itself, *The Praier and Complaynte*, *The Plowman's Tale*, and *Jack Upland*, the last two of which were ascribed to Chaucer himself.[46] It is in the context of this attempt to portray the literary culture of the 'Chaucerian' period—and the work of Chaucer himself in particular—as radically evangelical that we should read the appearance of the 1532 *Works*. But, as we shall see, rather than that volume being an attempt to advance that association, it is clear that it was designed for a very different purpose, being part of an attempt to establish a far more politically moderate image of the poet and of the uses of literature in times of political and religious strife.

The first formal attempt to halt the flow of rancorous literature, the Proclamations against heretical books of 22 June 1530 and 3 December 1531, proscribed a swathe of those protestant and anticlerical texts produced overseas in the previous three years: Simon Fish's *Supplication for the Beggars*, William Roy and Jerome Barlow's *Burial of the Mass* (also known as *Rede Me and Be Not Wrothe*) (1528), an anonymous *Book Against St Thomas of Canterbury*, Tyndale's English *New Testament*, *The Practyse of Prelates*, and *An Answer to Sir Thomas More's Dialogue*, and Frith's *Disputation of Purgatory*.[47] But within months further titles had been added to the anticlerical barrage, including St German's *Treatise Concernynge the Division Between the Spiritualitie and Temporality* (1532) and a text printed by John Skot, that advertised its polemical purpose on its title page: *Here [followeth] diverse Enormities used by the Clergy, and by some writers, their adherents, and specially against the heresy of simony used by the clergy: how some of the clergy and their adherents, causeless, have slanderously spoken against this noble realm of England and against diverse of the King's lay subjects, and have preached and written against small offences, leaving ye greater offences in the law of God untouched* (1532). Bishop Tunstal's register for 1532 listed books by Oecolampadius, Zwingli, Bugenhagen, Bucer, and Luther among those brought into London from the Continent at this time.[48]

Conservative writers responded in kind, adding to the disputatious torrent. William Rastell printed *Two Fuitful Sermons* by John Fisher. Thomas More's *Confutation of Tyndale's Answer* (1532) continued his increasingly brutal single-handed literary campaign against the evangelical cause, and Thomas Abel's pugnacious and self-explanatory *Invicta Veritas* (1532, subtitled 'An Answer that by no manner of law, it may be lawful for the most noble King of England, King Henry the eighth to be divorced from the queen's grace, his lawful and very true wife') added its weight to the divorce debate.[49]

What I am drawing attention to here is the effect that such books would have in seeming to confirm the idea of the division between laity and clergy, between a newly militant minority of laymen in positions of influence in Parliament and the court and aggressively reactionary defenders of the established church. The polemical books of both the evangelicals and the defenders of the church brought a new and aggressively divisive intensity to religious debate in England. That this literature, and the threat to civil society that it seemed to pose was alarming to the vast majority of those who either read it, or who heard about it from others, is apparent from the numerous comments and protests that the 'division' provoked. Tellingly, Robert Redman chose the early 1530s to resurrect and print John Lydgate's rumination on civil strife, whose title-page described it as very much a book for and of the moment, 'a little treatise [that] compendiously declareth the damage and destruction in realms caused by *The Serpent of Division*'.[50]

With Parliament and Convocation seemingly intent upon mortal conflict over jurisdiction, the King discarding his wife of twenty years' standing, denying that he had ever been legally married, and claiming for himself new and hitherto unthinkable powers in spiritual affairs, and everywhere previously unchallenged certainties of belief and practice suddenly subject to criticism and assault, it is no wonder that contemporaries spoke of a realm—indeed a culture—in crisis. It has recently been the habit of historians to downplay the impact of the reforms of the early 1530s, and to stress the continuities in royal policy, the limited nature of the legislation enacted, or the essentially coterie nature of the arguments at court and between the lawyers in Parliament and Convocation.[51] There have even been suggestions that the participants were merely going through the motions, performing roles that the King had designed for them which had little impact in the realm at large. But to take this line is to ignore the wealth of evidence that speaks of widespread and deeply felt anxiety, of a sense of disloca-tion and dysfunction in the instruments of government and the conventional mechanisms of social regulation and redress, amounting almost to hysteria. When contemporaries on either side of the religious divide spoke in apocalyptic terms of the signs of the world being wondrous, of unprecedented grudges, railing, and barking, of a common frenzy loose in the realm, and a 'great inquietation' and breaches of the peace, it is as well to listen to them, and to appreciate the sincerity of what they were saying. Even Thomas More, who was generally anxious to play down the scale of evangelical dissent and heterodoxy, was forced to concede that there was a sense of confusion among 'many good and well learned men' who feared 'that now we make a fashion of Christendom, to seem all turned quite up so down', in which persecutors and heretics could not even be told apart.[52] These were unprecedentedly troubled times in the experience of most English men and women, and there were many who were genuinely terrified by where they seemed to be leading.

Attempts to Heal the Divisions

Against the evidence of widespread and divisive grudges and the torrent of polemic, and in the face of the obvious trends in royal policy, a range of more moderate voices called instead for calm and toleration. Political culture, as we have seen, conventionally licensed a range of channels for political expression, and these moderates utilized them to the full. Like their more radical opponents they appealed to the King directly with a variety of forms of good counsel in petitions, pamphlets, sermons, and plays, and took Henry's own calls for quietness and obedience as the basis of their appeals.

There was, moreover, a more immediate justification for such counsel. As ambassador Chapuys shrewdly observed, Henry had publicly sought the judgement of the learned men of Europe over the legality of his divorce and his criticisms of papal jurisdiction, so he could hardly complain when scholars and writers offered him advice on those topics, even if it was not of the kind he wanted to hear. Thus, to cite an extreme case, when, in 1534, one Dr Gwynbourne, a grey friar of Beverley, wrote a tract against the Boleyn marriage, the first thing he did was to send a copy to the King, despite the fact that what he had written was clearly treasonable under the terms of the Act passed that Spring. He did so, he said, because his conscience would not be clear otherwise.[53] More influentially (and rather less naively), Reginald Pole, previously one of those scholars employed to further the divorce campaign, but now disaffected and living in Italy, wrote an extended criticism of royal claims, lamenting the divisions in English society that they had prompted, couching his work in the form of a petition to the King. His aim, he argued, was not to oppose royal policy but rather to advise the King, as all good counsellors should, in such a way as to restore him to his senses before it was too late. Henry now stood, he claimed, at the edge of the water, and he might still save all, but one step further and all his honour would be drowned.[54]

Not all of the critical counsel was so disingenuous. In England, a number of liberal catholics, many of whom were, or had once been, in the circle of scholars and courtiers around Sir Thomas More, adopted a similar stance. Such men had themselves previously argued for moderate reform of the church along Erasmian lines, but they were becoming increasingly concerned by both the pace and the direction of royal policy—and by the social antagonisms that it was generating. More himself had become ever more forthright in his opposition to the evangelicals, addressing them directly in a series of robust, polemical volumes. But many of his friends and fellow humanists took a softer, more conventional line. Such men, many of whom were articulate and eloquent writers in their own right—the backbone of the court's literary establishment—used their writing as a means of voicing their discomfort with royal policies, hoping to persuade the King back from the brink through their eloquence.

Such men, as we have seen, had been brought up in a humanistic educational environment that assumed that literature mattered: that a treatise could influence the prince—indeed that princes relied upon such texts for their own political and moral education. They consequently believed that educated men such as themselves could contribute to political affairs through their eloquence; that by distilling the fruits of their learning in a treatise, a poem, a sermon, or a moral interlude, they could not only entertain and inform their sovereign, but could also influence him, shaping his mind and by so doing, shaping political events. It was assumptions such as these that prompted two men whom we shall follow in greater depth later in this book; the prose writer Thomas Elyot and the playwright John Heywood, to produce a plethora of didactic texts in the course of the early 1530s. Thomas More, for all the apparent idealism of his *Utopia*, had always been a shrewder, more pragmatic observer of practical politics. He quickly saw that the battle for Henry's soul was lost, that the King would, as he himself put it earlier in his career, take off the head of his most favoured counsellor if it would win him just one castle in France.[55] Hence he came to the view that the only winnable battle to be fought through books was that for the hearts and souls of a wider public.

Men such as Elyot, however, responded to the crisis of the early Reformation by bombarding the King and the court with counsel in the belief that literary eloquence alone might change things—or at least win for its authors the place at the Council table that would enable them to shape policy in more direct and practical ways. They did so because they believed that they might prevail, because it was their duty as the King's learned subjects to try, and also, ultimately, because there was little else for moderate, loyal voices to do. In the early 1530s the prospects for counselling the King seemed good, provided that acceptable forms and attitudes were maintained. So Elyot and Heywood produced a string of works designed for consumption at court and at the political centre that argued for social and religious accommodation: for an end to divisive factional argument, and the reconciliation of personal differences in the wider interest of obedience to the King.[56]

Heywood's interludes, each of them written for performance at court during the years 1529–33, made the case for moderation in times of conflict through wit and good humour. *Witty and Witless* ended with an appeal to 'the hy hed most excelent . . . / . . . owr most loved and drade supreme soferayne' (683–4) and those 'havyng a realme in governall' to 'set forthe theyre governans to God's glory all, / Charytably abydynge subjects in eche kynde' (679–81). *The Pardoner and the Friar* parodied the arguments of incendiary, self-interested reforming preachers and corrupt Roman ecclesiasts alike, suggesting the mischiefs that their contention caused to simple folk in the parishes, while *The Play of Love* and *The Play of The Weather* demonstrated the need for the reconciliation of self-interested variance in the interests of social and religious harmony. The former made the case for Christian reconciliation, perhaps most obviously in its punning exploration of the various kinds of 'love' available to its protagonists.

> Let us seke the love of that lovyng lorde
> Who to suffer passion for love was content.
> Whereby his lovers that love for love assent,
> Shall have in fyne above contentacyon
> The felyng pleasure of eternall salvacyon.
>
> (566–70)[57]

The Play of the Weather, as we shall see in Chapter 6, presented on stage an imperial sovereign very like Henry VIII in the form of Jupiter, king of the gods, and suggested wittily that the only way for him to reconcile the vociferous contradictory demands of all his subjects was to maintain the status quo, while presenting it variously as a concession to each of their demands. Finally in *The Four P's*, Heywood confronted religious divisions directly, presenting a quartet of quarrelsome travellers: a Pardoner, a Palmer (pilgrim), a Pedlar and a Potycary (apothecary)—the four Ps of the title—who argue over their own particular brands of religious devotion, seeking to prove its superiority over all the rest. It is left, finally, to the Pedlar to propose modestly that there might be room in the world for all of their beliefs, if only they could learn to tolerate each other. Thus he tells the Pardoner and the Palmer,

> ...though ye walke nat bothe one waye,
> Yet walkynge thus, This dare I saye:
> That bothe your walkes come to one ende...
>
> Thus every vertue, yf ye lyste to scan,
> Is plesaunt to God and thankfull to man.
> And who that by grace of the holy goste
> To any one vertue is moved moste,
> That man by that grace that one apply,
> And therin serve God most plentyfully.
>
> (1153–5, 1171–6)

> One kynde of vertue to dyspyse another
> Is lyke as the syster myght hange the brother.
>
> (1185–6)

> ...beste in these thynges it semeth to me,
> To make no judgement upon ye.
> For as the churche doth judge or take them.
> So do ye receyve or forsake them.
>
> (1211–14)

There is in Heywood's interludes, as critics have long recognized, a distinctly 'Chaucerian' sensibility at work, colouring the comedy and providing a good deal of the material that the playwright dramatizes. Heywood drew heavily on the Chaucerian tradition of anticlerical satire in his descriptions of corrupt pardoners and credulous pilgrims, in his treatment of specious relics and the excesses of popular piety, and his descents into scatological knockabout. But what has been noticed less frequently is the specific political edge that is given to Chaucer's comic legacy in these plays and other products of 'the More circle' at this time. Heywood's version of Chaucer is of a distinctly contemporary poet, and a distinctly political one too. The 'Chaucerian' comedy of *The Four P's*, for example, while it is critical of clerical abuses, is markedly tolerant and ultimately reconciliatory in its conclusions. If one cannot prove a relic to be false or a pardoner to be fraudulent, the play's final speeches declare, one should not condemn it or him, still less associate the whole class of relics or pardoners with their alleged corruption. Such is the quietist conclusion of Heywood's play, just as it was the conclusion of More's first foray into anti-evangelical polemic, the *Dialogue Concerning Heresies*. Interestingly, More too appropriated Chaucer's voice—and specifically his anticlerical reputation—for reconciliatory ends in this early work. He has his fictional antagonist, the Messenger, assert that 'under the name and opinion of a saint's relic, [honour might inadvertently be given] to some old rotten bone [that] was haply some time, as Chaucer saith, a bone of some holy Jew's sheep'.[58] The allusion is to *The Pardoner's Prologue* from *The Canterbury Tales*, but the conclusion is not anticlerical in its impact. For More's persona retorts that if one, in venerating relics with an honest intent and proper piety, happens to offer mistakenly to a false relic, no great harm is done to the worshipper, and no great injustice to the saint.

What these moderate conservative writers were doing, then, in the first years of the 1530s, was re-examining the Chaucerian legacy in the light of current events, deploying the poet's work and reputation in their own struggles over the state and future of the church, the responsibilities of individual Christians, and the direction of the government's religious policies. As the second section of this book will show, Thomas Elyot would also draw Chaucer into his discussion of contemporary politics. In *Pasquil the Plain* (1533) he put the poet's *Troilus and Criseyde* in the hands of his courtly scholar Gnatho, and noted the glaring contradiction between its values and those of the New Testament, which he also carried under his cloak.[59] Hence the hypocritical evangelical symbolically carries the tokens of his dual identity in the books that he reads, the one representing religious fervour, the other amoral courtly sophistication and literary refinement, and the disjunction between the two reveals the fraudulence of his 'new learning'. But there was a deeper resonance to Elyot's choice of texts, for evangelicals would indeed be using Chaucer's work and reputation as a part of their religious strategy within two years of his writing. What Elyot was mocking as an ill-considered combination of reading matter would soon reflect this new weapon in the reformers' arsenal, albeit they would look to the anticlerical elements of *The Canterbury Tales* rather than the courtly poems such as the *Troilus* for their examples of 'characteristic' Chaucerian texts. Hence when More and Heywood sought to counter the arguments and attitudes of the evangelicals in their own work, they reached deliberately for their Chaucer as well. By incorporating the poet's name and his anticlerical comedy in their own writings, and absorbing them into a wider argument for the retention of the religious status quo, both More and Heywood were countering the evangelicals at their own game, disarming Chaucer of his radical potential before it could be effectively deployed in favour of further religious reform. And in Heywood's plays things were taken further, for there Chaucer's religious satires were actively reinterpreted to reassert his credentials as part of a conservative tradition of English religious writing. It is in the light of this strategy that, as the following chapters will suggest, we should see the far more substantial and overt reinterpretation of the Chaucerian legacy attempted in the 1532 *Works* published under the name of William Thynne.

4

Reading Chaucer in 1532

William Thynne, Brian Tuke, and the Politics of Literary Editing

It is as part of the literature of counsel calling for a return to accommodation at court that we should read the publication of the 1532 edition of Chaucer's *Works*. This might initially seem an unlikely claim. The assumption behind those political readings of the edition cited in the previous chapter has always been that William Thynne was a religious reformer who was anxious to employ Chaucer in the interests of a specifically protestant Reformation.[1] But, this is, I think, mistaken, and leads to a misrepresentation of how the *Works* operate as a political document. Read in the context of the debates of 1531–2, the edition proves to be, not an incendiary contribution to the reforming campaign, but a subtly coded call for religious stability and consensus, part of that concerted attempt by members of the conservative scholarly and literary establishment at court and in London to draw Henry VIII back from the brink of religious and political revolution, and restore a sense of equilibrium to domestic politics and political culture. In this context the question of how Chaucer should be interpreted was fiercely contested between conservative and radical scholars. For the 'Chaucerian legacy' was crucially an equivocal one, open to either radical or conservative religious interpretations, and to many shades of ambivalence in between. For evangelicals there was the seemingly anticlerically inclined satire of *The General Prologue* to *The Canterbury Tales*, the Tales of the Summoner, the Shipman, and the Friar, and the Pardoner's Prologue and Tale; each of which mischievously exposed the alleged sins of the clergy and seemingly mocked the credulity of a naïve laity. For orthodox, conservative believers there was the apparently genuine affective piety of the Second Nun's Tale, the Man of Law's Tale, the Prioress's Prologue and Tale, and the Parson's Tale. And there was the seemingly definitive statement of the 'Retraction', that final coda to *The Canterbury Tales* in which the poet explicitly rejected his secular works, including the *Troilus* and those of the Tales 'that sownen [sound] unto sin', and asked to be remembered in the prayers of his readers only for his translation of Boethius's *Consolation of Philosophy*, and other books of legends of saints, and homilies, and morality, and devotion, that thank I our Lord Jhesu Crist and His blissful Mother, and all the saints of heaven, beseeching them that they from henceforth unto my life's end send me grace to bewail my guilts and to study to the salvation of my soul, and grant me grace of very penitence, confession and satisfaction to do in this present life, through the benign grace of Him that is King of Kings and priest over all priests . . . so that I may been one of them at the Day of Doom that shall be saved.[2]

How the poet would be received by the new generation of readers in the 1530s was thus an open question, dependent upon the ways in which editors chose to represent him, how the existing canon was presented, and how new works of either a radical or a conservative stamp might be added to that canon. Hence the struggle to impose a particular confessional inflection upon the poet was to result in a flurry of Chaucerian and pseudo-Chaucerian publications in the course of the 1530s. On one level it is evident that the notion of the poet as a reforming, anticlerical author, a scourge of the ecclesiastical establishment and follower of Wyclif, gained ground as a number of apocryphal proto-protestant texts (*The Plowman's Tale*, *Jack Upland*, *The Pilgrim's Tale*) were published under his name by editors and printers sympathetic to religious reform. But attempts to see Thynne's edition as the source of this campaign are mistaken. In Thynne (and, as I shall argue, Tuke's) hands 'Chaucer' became a spokesman for moderation in religious policy, a figure around whom religious conservatives such as John Heywood, Thomas Elyot, and others in their circle might unite. It was more plausibly Thynne and Tuke's presentation of Chaucer as a religious moderate that prompted writers and printers more sympathetic to the Reformation to 'redis-cover' a more radical Chaucer to set in opposition to their model: the 'right Wyclifian' (as the martyrologist John Foxe was to call him)[3] whom subsequent generations of reformers would celebrate and popularize.

It might well be objected at this point that, if Thynne had wanted to counsel Henry VIII on what he saw as the folly of pursuing divisive anticlerical legisla-tion, then an edition of Chaucer's *Works* was not the most immediate or practical form that such counsel might take. Indeed, if the intention was to advise the King directly, then was not a printed text, which was, by definition, aimed at a far wider 'public' audience, a singularly inefficient means of doing so? I should, therefore, make clear that my argument here is not that Thynne and Tuke produced the *Works* merely, or even perhaps primarily to advance the political views that the text advanced. The promotion of a distinct political and religious position was only one part of the edition's complex agenda, and it may have emerged as one of the 'aims' of the volume relatively late in the production process. As the Preface suggests, and his son was to confirm, William Thynne was motivated by a love of Chaucer, and an enthusiast's zeal to collect and promote the poet's work. And Tuke may well have shared that enthusiasm. Hence the idea of a comprehensive *Works* was probably broached and put into practice between them as an expression of their shared sense of literary history.

But the idea of a 'complete' edition of Chaucer's writings was, as the Preface also makes clear, never a purely 'literary' endeavour. It was, probably from the outset, bound up with notions of linguistic and cultural identity, of what it meant to speak and to *be* 'English', and of national history and pride. Such questions were inevitably already political. And, while Thynne and Tuke were involved in the later stages of the editorial process, these questions of English identity, of social and religious culture, were profoundly unsettled by Henry VIII's divorce, the debates in Parliament, and the early stages of the Break with Rome. At the very time that the editors were collating their texts and deciding on the selection and ordering of the *Works*, notions of what it meant to be English, to be a subject of a king who was now the Supreme Head of the Church as well as the head of state, and what it might mean in future to be Englishmen, suddenly became intensely uncertain and problematic. Thynne and Tuke's responses to these uncertainties inevitably coloured their choices concerning the arrangement and presentation of their edition, as they used Chaucer to, as it were, think through the crisis of 1531–2, and offer a potential solution to the divisions that it had opened up.

That the edition was printed rather than presented directly to the King in manuscript form does not fundamentally alter its political dynamic. Recent work on early print culture in England has stressed the distinct audiences to which manuscripts and printed texts appealed. A. S. G. Edwards has, for example, argued that,

The most immediate consequence of the shift to a print culture is, of course, a loss of particularity. The markets for printed books in England were largely speculative, commercially driven ones aimed at a generalized public rather than an individual private audience, as would be the case with the audience for manuscript texts.[4]

Am I, then, misunderstanding the nature of early publishing in arguing as I have done above? It is important to discriminate within such broad generalizations as Edwards offers. There were almost certainly different 'publics', different motives and intended audiences for publication even within the broad commercial market for a volume like the 1532 Chaucer. While the printer, Thomas Godfrey may well have had his eye consistently upon the commercial bottom line, and the need to reach and appeal to a wide paying readership, Thynne and Tuke clearly had a more nuanced sense of the 'public' for which they were aiming. Their edition was a textual performance aimed at a range of audiences, and their appeals to these various intended reading communities were interconnected. In dedicating the volume to Henry VIII, and addressing him personally in an extended, justificatory Preface, the editors were offering their work to a very particular 'individual private audience': a single royal recipient whom they hoped would read the text and engage with the ideas it embodied. Beyond that single primary reader there was, it must be assumed, a wider—but still essentially coterie—audience of courtly and educated readers; members of the politically engaged classes who were equipped intellectually and vocationally to appreciate the sentiments promoted in the edition and in a position to advance them in debates at the political centre. And beyond this audience was the wider, more diffuse 'public' readership that might buy the text, and which provided the central commercial and cultural justification for the *Works'* production in print. The appeal to these distinct audiences was mutually reinforcing. That the text was dedicated to the King, and thus signalled itself as a prestigious, courtly production, would no doubt have enhanced its appeal as a desirable commodity to those socially and intellectually ambitious purchasers in the coterie and public markets. That the edition provided for the first time a comprehensive collection of Chaucer's writings in a single printed volume that was available to all English readers in turn provided an additional commendation of the work to the King. Thynne and Tuke's achievement was, as the Preface declared, that they were allowing all Englishmen to appreciate the glories of their national poet and the vernacular language that he had purified. Moreover, in producing a notionally definitive collection of the poet's work, they were also securing his legacy for future generations. In accepting the dedication of the volume, Henry would thus be taking possession of a gift that would benefit not himself alone, but all his subjects and their descendants. The 'public' role of the edition thus enhanced its private appeal to the King, and vice-versa.

The 1532 Chaucer: A Collaborative Text?

At first glance the 1532 *Chaucer* seems a conventional enough document, but as one looks at it more closely a number of curious features suggest themselves. My own interest in the volume stems partly from a desire to answer four seemingly very simple questions about its composition. If (as is always assumed) the edition was put together by William Thynne, why was the Preface actually written by another man, Sir Brian Tuke, writing without acknowledgement as if he were Thynne? Why, if it is indeed a *Complete Works* of Chaucer, does the volume contain so many works by other poets, some explicitly acknowledged to be by other hands in the text itself; and why, if Thynne was, as most critics suggest, an ardent reformer, were so many of the texts that he added to the canon so manifestly conservative in their religious content and so unsympathetic to the thrust of the Reformation? Finally, why are those poems arranged as they are, especially at the beginning of the volume, where three texts with no immediately obvious relevance to the collection are printed, with no mention of their presence or purpose in either the Preface or the table of contents? As we shall see, these apparently straightforward questions prove to have no straightforward answers. But the attempt to answer them takes us to the heart of the edition's contemporary significance, suggesting both the motives behind its construction and the impact that it would have had on the political and religious controversies of the moment of its appearance. What follows will explore each of those questions, and the issues they raise, in turn.

The Role of Sir Brian Tuke in 'Thynne's Chaucer'

That it was Sir Brian Tuke, rather than Thynne himself who penned the Preface, despite its first-person narrative and reference to 'I ... William Thynne', is clear from a number of sources. John Leland, citing personal acquaintance with Tuke, noted that the latter had contributed 'a polished, lucid, and stylish preface' to the 1532 edition.[5] Francis Thynne also attested to Tuke's involvement in his father's work, although, as we shall see in a moment, in rather less specific terms.[6] What was decisive in convincing scholars of the nature and extent of Tuke's contribution was, however, the statement, written in Tuke's own clear, bold hand, at the top of the first page of the Preface in the copy of the *Works* now in the library of Clare College Cambridge. It reads simply:

This preface, I sir Bryan Tuke, knight, wrote at the request of m[aste]r clerk of the kitchen, then being, tarrying for the tide at Greenwich.[7]

The statement of authorship seems incontrovertible; but, how can we account for the fact that Tuke wrote the preface for a work ostensibly edited solely by someone else? Most critics, having noted the fact, pass over the question of why he might have done so in silence. But it is, *prima facie*, an unusual occurrence, calling for further investigation. Writers at this time did not, as far as we know, commonly ghost-write material for each other's works. If they provided a commendatory or editorial introduction to someone's work, they generally did so in their own names, as a personal endorsement of, or advertisement for, the text. Tuke seems to have done something quite different. Why?

On the one hand, if Thynne had been looking for someone at court to write his Preface for him, Tuke would have made a credible choice. He was a more substantial figure, socially and politically, than Thynne himself, and enjoyed a close professional relationship with Henry VIII, to whom the edition was dedicated.[8] Moreover he had, as we shall see, a reputation for eloquence and scholarship of the kind that would commend him for such a task. The nature of Tuke's employment at court gave him particular expertise in drafting elegant epistles such as that prefacing the *Chaucer*. He had begun his court career prior to 1506 as a Clerk of the Spicery, became Clerk of the Signet, the keeper of Henry's personal seal, by 1509, and moved through the roles of Clerk of the Council of Calais (1510), Knight of the Body (1516), Controller of the King's Posts (1517), and secretary to Cardinal Wolsey, before becoming Henry's French Secretary (15 March 1523), Treasurer of the Chamber (13 April 1528), and Clerk of Parliament (in both 1523 and 1529). These posts brought with them a range of pertinent roles and responsibilities. In addition to the record-keeping and drafting of administrative documents that were the lot of the treasurer and Clerk of Parliament, Tuke was regularly employed, as controller of the posts and Henry's French secretary, in receiving, translating, summarizing, and drafting letters, often of considerable importance and diplomatic sensitivity in English, French,

Latin, and a variety of ciphers. He was intimately acquainted with Henry's diplomatic manoeuvres and royal correspondence, and indeed served as a diplomatic representative on at least one occasion in the late 1520s, when he proved himself to be a shrewd and adept negotiator.[9] He might, then, be thought a good judge of the most promising terms and approach to adopt in order to win the King's favour for the volume, and a skilled exponent of the arts needed to put the theory into practice. In addition, if Tuke's involvement did become known at court, the edition could only have gained lustre as a result.

Tuke was also at the sharp end of Henry's divorce campaign, one of those royal servants charged with facilitating the King's case against his first marriage and justifying his actions to the political nation. In 1528, when Henry was first developing the case for an annulment, it was Tuke who acted as his amanuensis, helping him to draft the 'book' of arguments that he would eventually present in court.[10] When, in October 1531, the French envoys John Joachim and the Bishop of Bayonne were at court, it was in Tuke's lodgings that they were billeted, and there that Henry and Anne Boleyn dined with them on 23 October.[11] And when a group of royal councillors, led by Lord Chancellor More, and including the Dukes of Norfolk and Suffolk, descended upon Parliament to justify the divorce, Tuke, as Clerk of the Parliament, was prominent in their number. This formal occasion was an important part of Henry's divorce campaign, part of what he hoped would be a successful charm offensive designed to win parliamentary support for the claim that his Great Matter might be settled in England. Hence the important role allotted to Tuke is a further index of the favour in which Henry held him. After More had (no doubt to his acute discomfort) declared, first to the assembled peers in the upper house then to the Commons, that the King had only entered into the divorce process for 'the discharge of his conscience' and not for any baser motive, it was Tuke who on each occasion 'in a loud voice' read out 'word by word' the formal judgements of those Continental universities which had concurred with Henry's arguments that it was against divine law for a man to marry his brother's wife, and that in no circumstances could the Pope dispense with that prohibition.[12]

Tuke was, then, used to acting as Henry's official mouthpiece, both in his role as a secretary, and on more formal occasions such as the report to Parliament. He would thus have made an appropriate choice as the mouthpiece for a Clerk of the Kitchen anxious to commend his Chaucer edition to the King. But, before we accept the idea of Tuke as simply an appropriate 'hired hand' brought in to perform a role that the editor felt unwilling or unable to perform himself, it is worth re-examining the evidence a little more closely. Would Thynne really have needed someone to do his writing for him, however eminent or close to Henry that someone was? The level of scholarship evident in the edition itself would argue otherwise.[13] And, if Thynne did feel the need for literary assistance, why choose Tuke? The fact that the latter's name is nowhere cited in the edition itself seems to rule out the possibility that Thynne was using the secretary's involvement simply to add weight or lustre to the volume. Furthermore, would Thynne really have employed someone with whom he had no real acquaintance to write so important a text on his behalf? A more plausible hypothesis would be that he asked Tuke to write the Preface because the two were already known to each other, even to the extent of having worked together before, and Thynne could consequently trust him to write as he wished. And, on closer inspection, the available evidence—fragmentary though it is—would seem to support that suggestion.

Let us look again at what exactly those commentators who mentioned Tuke's involvement in the edition said that he did. John Leland, who, as we have already noted, counted Tuke as a close acquaintance, spoke of Thynne's editorial endeavours in the following terms:

Our friend Bertholet [sic],[14] however, has bettered Caxton's edition through the industry of William Thynne, who, having exercised great labour, diligence, and care in seeking out ancient copies, added many things to the first [i.e. Caxton's] edition. But in this respect also, Brian Tuke, my closest associate and a marvel of eloquence in the English tongue, has not lacked his own renown, which is displayed in the polished, lucid, and stylish preface to the last printing.[15]

Francis Thynne talked in similar terms of 'the earnest desire and love my father had to have Chaucer's Works rightly to be published'.

For the performance whereof, my father not only used the help of that learned and eloquent knight and antiquary Sir Brian Tuke, but had also made great search for copies to perfect his works.[16]

The precise meaning is not entirely clear in either case, but both Leland and Thynne seem to be saying rather more than that Tuke simply added a preface to a work with which he otherwise had no acquaintance. In Leland's statement that Tuke 'has not lacked his own renown' 'in this respect', 'this respect' would seem more plausibly to relate to the whole 'great labour, diligence, and care in seeking out ancient copies' that he described in the previous sentence, than the specific instance of the Preface that he relates in the next. Similarly, the fact that the younger Thynne described Tuke as 'learned' as well as eloquent, and an antiquary as well as a knight, suggests that the secretary shared his father's love of Chaucer and that his 'help' extended rather further than the provision of an introductory address. Certainly there is evidence elsewhere of Tuke's antiquarian and scholarly interests to support this suggestion.[17] Moreover, the fact that Francis Thynne nowhere mentioned the Preface, but talked rather of Tuke's 'help' in producing the edition suggests strongly that he was describing a more general collaboration.

Some corroboration for this claim is to be found in the Latin commendatory poems written by Leland to Tuke during the 1530s. In a collection of verses to a diverse cohort of scholarly recipients, there is a short poem '*Ad Briennum Tuccam, Equitem*', which addresses its dedicatee in very interesting terms.

> Tucca delivered Virgil's song that fire might not profane it;
> You give me Bacchus [ivy] wreaths,
> Anyone of the learned would save verses from the flame,
> But it is a prince's prerogative to have awarded the ivy.
> By as much as a private citizen is less than a prince,
> So much greater will the British Tucca than the Roman be![18]

The poem alludes to the story of the saving of the text of Virgil's *Aeneid* on the orders of the Emperor Augustus. According to Suetonius's account,[19] the great Roman poet had, on his deathbed, instructed his executors to destroy his epic poem; but at the Emperor's command his wishes were overruled and the work was instead revised and published posthumously by those same executors. What has this story to do with Tuke? Given the conscious evocation in the 1532 *Chaucer* of the *Opera* of Virgil, the association of Virgil with Tuke's name here is suggestive—and elsewhere in the same volume Leland made explicit the Virgil/ Chaucer connection, referring to the English poet as not less in glory than Virgil.[20] But the allusion is still more specific, and rests upon the way that Leland chose to Latinize Tuke's name: Tucca; for Plotius Tucca was one of the two co-executors of Virgil's will who subsequently edited and published his *Aeneid*. As Suetonius tells the story,

[Virgil] named as his heirs Valerius Proculus, his half-brother, to one half of his estate, Augustus to one-fourth, Maecenas to one-twelfth; the rest he left to Lucius Varius and Plotius Tucca, who revised the *Aeneid* after his death by order of Augustus. With regard to this matter we have the following verses of Sulpicius of Carthage:

> Virgil had bidden these songs by swift flame be turned into ashes,
> Songs which sang of thy fates, Phrygia's leader renowned.
> Varius and Tucca forbade, and thou, greatest of Caesars,
> Adding your veto to theirs, Latium's story preserved.
> All but twice in the flames unhappy Pergamum perished;
> Troy on a second pyre narrowly failed of her doom.[21]

What Leland seems to be doing, then, is comparing the literary and editorial efforts of Plotius Tucca with those of his Tudor successor, Tuke (who appears also to have offered Leland some practical patronage—hence the reference to his bestowing 'Bacchus' wreaths' upon the author). What Tuke's literary efforts were is not stated, but the most plausible suggestion, given the links between Virgil and Chaucer made elsewhere, would seem to be the editing and publication of the great work of Virgil's 'English successor'. Hitting upon the happy coincidence of Tuke's surname, his friend alludes to Tuke's 'rescuing' of Chaucer's works from oblivion as the co-editor and preserver of his legacy in the light of his namesake's more literal rescue of Virgil's work. Thus he praises the 'co-executor' and editor of the English Virgil by association with the co-executor and editor of the original Roman poet.

Rather than follow previous accounts and see Tuke as merely the author of the Preface to 'Thynne's *Chaucer*', then, I would argue that their co-operation probably went much further, and that it might be more accurate to see he and Thynne as co-editors, involved in a genuine scholarly collaboration.[22] As Brian Donaghey has suggested in an important article, Thynne may well have been working on the Chaucer edition throughout the 1520s, searching out and gathering texts from a variety of sources, comparing and collating them ready for publication.[23] When precisely Tuke became involved is less clear, but it was probably only in the last two or three years of the project, as the materials were gathered into their final state ready for the press, and decisions were made about the scope and form of the edition.[24]

Circumstantial evidence would seem to support this view. Tuke and Thynne were colleagues whose roles in the royal household would have brought them into fairly regular contact, at least from the late 1520s onwards. Each had lodgings in Greenwich, and Tuke, as Treasurer of the Chamber, would have received regular requests for payment from Thynne in his capacity as Chief Clerk of the Kitchen, such as those for 'apparalling the galepynes [spits]' in the kitchens, for which Tuke made over £50 in May 1528 and a further £24 in October 1530. When they first became aware of their shared love of scholarship in general and Chaucer in particular is not clear. Significantly, perhaps, in making his entry in the accounts for the payment of May 1528, Tuke mistakenly listed the recipient as 'Richard Thynne, clerk of the kitchen', suggesting that he had only recently made his acquaintance. By October 1530, however, he had got his colleague's name right, and may well have come to know him rather more closely.[25]

We should, then, read the references to Tuke's involvement in the volume, and especially his own marginal acknowledgement, with care. The apparently casual nature of Tuke's reference to his own endeavours has tended to deflect attention from his contribution, and to the carefully constructed nature of the Preface itself. The suggestion that the latter was something he quickly threw together while the tide was changing is a fine example of the art of *sprezzatura*—of making difficult things seem simple and inconsequential—that Castiglione identified as the courtier's chief commending grace.[26] In reality the Preface would have taken a considerable amount of time to compose and to prepare for the printer. It is far more plausible to imagine Thynne and Tuke working on it together as the summation of their collaborative endeavours. Indeed, given the strongly auto-biographical elements in the narrative, it would seem likely that Thynne himself may have dictated the details of the story, and that Tuke found the best terms in which to express them for the King's consumption, with both men collaborating on the overall structure and direction of the piece. For all the casual elegance of Tuke's dismissive remark, the Preface was no throwaway afterthought, but a central element in the edition's political strategy, of a piece with the selection and organization of the works that followed. The fact that he did not otherwise advertise his involvement in the text, except to his closest friends, and later in the 'private' note in his own copy of the book, probably has more to do with the sensitive nature of his employment in the divorce negotiations, and a desire to keep a low profile politically, than with any embarrassment concerning the piece itself.

Thynne and Tuke: Religion and Politics

What more, then, is known about the editors of the 1532 *Chaucer*, and why might they have come together to produce the text in the way that they did? We have seen something of Tuke's career, but what about William Thynne himself? Who was he, and why, if as I hope to demonstrate later, the volume was a moderate, conservative text, arguing against the need for radical reform, has history come to see him as a religious radical?

William Thynne's date and place of birth are unknown, but he is said to have been a native of Shropshire and to have studied at Oxford. By 1524 he was second clerk of the royal kitchens and was beginning to receive a number of lucrative grants of lands and offices from the King.[27] In 1526 he was promoted to Chief Clerk of the kitchens, and gained an official lodging at Greenwich. In July and August 1529 he gained the additional offices of Customer of wools, hides, and fleeces in the port of London, and receiver-general of the earldom of March. In 1533 he served as cofferer to Queen Anne Boleyn at her coronation. By April 1536 he was clerk comptroller of the counting house, and by 1542 he was also clerk of the Green Cloth. He died on 10 August 1546, leaving his estate to his wife Anne and his son, Francis, who was born in 1544 or 1545.

Thynne was, then, like Tuke (albeit on a lesser scale), a long-serving and loyal servant of the Crown, a man whose career was spent in the middle and upper ranks of the royal household bureaucracy, and whose social circle was seemingly also drawn from the King's domestic retinue (his wife, Anne, was the daughter of another Clerk of the Green Cloth, William Bond, and the co-overseer of his will was another household official, Sir Edmund Peckham, Cofferer of the King's household). Was Thynne also a religious radical? Most scholars who mention him have assumed that he was, and that his work on the Chaucer edition was motivated by his hostility to the established church.[28] The evidence for this claim is fragmentary, and largely contained in the posthumous recollections of his son Francis, printed in his *Animadversions* of 1599. That the evidence is so late, and inevitably based upon the accounts of others (Francis Thynne was less than two years old when his father died), need not entirely invalidate it. The younger Thynne claimed to have taken considerable pains to obtain accurate information concerning his father's literary activities. He spoke of getting at least some of his facts from individuals 'now of good worship both in court and country, but then my father's clerks', and from Thynne's cousin, Sir John Thynne, a Member of Parliament in the 1530s.[29]

More problematic is the fact that the younger Thynne was writing, not to provide a comprehensive memoir of his father's life, but specifically to criticize the limitations of Thomas Speght's 1598 edition of Chaucer's *Works*, a volume which he saw as in some ways inferior to (and insufficiently generous in its acknowledgement of) his father's earlier publication.[30] Hence Thynne was anxious to defend his father's reputation as an editor, and to suggest that much of the praise for Speght's text would be better directed towards the earlier work. So it is that we find Francis Thynne retrospectively attributing the 'discovery' of many of the hallmarks of the canonical Chaucer of the 1590s to his father's work. Because it was conventional in evangelical circles by the 1590s to see the poet as a forerunner of the protestant reformation; Foxe's 'right Wyclifian', anxious to reform the church along evangelical lines, Thynne presented his father as the man who uncovered and strove to popularize this aspect of his writings. Consequently, the real agenda behind Thynne's biographical sketch is to establish his father's credentials as an anticlerical reformer as well as a scholar, the sort of man who would recognize and appreciate the radicalism in Chaucer's writings.

The crucial part of Thynne's story tells of an attempt by his father to have a radically anticlerical tale included in his *Works*. This text Francis describes as 'The Pilgrim's Tale, a thing more odious to the clergy than the speech of the Plowman', in which 'Chaucer most bitterly [did] inveigh against the pride, state, covetousness, and extortion of the Bishops, their officials, Archdeacons, Vicars general, commissaries, and other officers of the spiritual court'.[31] The story of how Thynne senior was initially thwarted in his attempt to publish the work, but subsequently succeeded in incorporating it in a later edition, gives rise to a number of other statements supporting the idea that he, like the poet he championed, was a tireless critic of the clergy and their abuses. Given its importance, it is worth quoting the passage in full. The King, Francis Thynne claimed, read *The Pilgrim's Tale* in an earlier, single-column edition, produced by Thynne.

This tale, when King Henry the eighth had read, he called my father unto him, saying, 'William Thynne, I doubt this will not be allowed, for I suspect the Bishops will call thee in question for it'. To whom my father, being in great favour with his prince (as many yet living can testify) said, 'If your Grace be not offended, I hope to be protected by you'. Whereupon the King bad him go his way, and fear not. All which notwithstanding, my father was called in question by the Bishops, and heaved at by Cardinal Wolsey, his old enemy for many causes, but mostly for that my father had furthered Skelton to publish his 'Colin Cloute' against the Cardinal, the most part of which Book was compiled in my father's house at Erith in Kent. But for all my father's friends, the Cardinal's persuading authority was so great with the King that, though by the King's favour my father escaped bodily danger, yet the Cardinal caused the King so much to mislike of that tale that Chaucer must be new printed, and that discourse of the pilgrim's tale left out; and so being printed again, some things were forced to be omitted, and the plowman's tale (supposed, but untruly, to be made by old Sir Thomas Wyatt, father to him which was executed in the first year of Queen Mary, and not by Chaucer) with much ado permitted to pass with the rest.[32]

What are we to make of these claims? The account is fraught with difficulty, and cannot be accurate in the detail of many of its assertions. John Skelton's poem

Colin Cloute (one of his, so called, Wolsey satires), was written and circulated in manuscript in 1521–2, at which time Thynne had not yet taken on the lease of the house at Erith in which he was to live from 1531 until his death. The poem was not printed (if this is what is meant by 'publish[ed]') until 1533, by which time both Skelton and Wolsey were dead, and so the 'furthering' could not have occurred and the consequent enmity not been provoked. Thus either the further-ing did not take place at Erith, or it involved a posthumous publication and so did not arouse Wolsey's ire. The idea of an ongoing hatred between Wolsey and Thynne is, then, problematic, to say the least. The account of the *Pilgrim's Tale* is still more difficult to accept. Had Wolsey been instrumental in thwarting the publication of Thynne's *Chaucer*, it would have to have happened prior to 18 October 1529, when the Cardinal resigned the Great Seal and was sent into internal exile. Yet the text that he was supposed to have banned, *The Pilgrim's Tale*, seems clearly to have been written after October 1536, for it lists among a group of rebels against royal authority, 'Captain Cobbler', one of the leaders of the Lincolnshire Rising that began in that month.[33] Thus Thynne could not have attempted to publish the *Tale* either as part of the 1532 *Works* or of some putative lost, single-column edition produced in Wolsey's lifetime.

A number of critics have sought to avoid these difficulties by assuming, more or less explicitly, that Francis Thynne was mistaken merely in confusing *The Pilgrim's Tale* (which was not printed in any surviving edition of his father's *Chaucer*) with *The Plowman's Tale*, another anticlerical piece that did not appear in the 1532 *Works* but was added to the 1542 edition, appearing after *The Parson's Tale*, as a late addition to *The Canterbury Tales*.[34] Could it be, then, that what the younger Thynne was describing was actually his father's difficulties over an attempt to get *The Plowman's Tale* printed in 1532? Again, this seems unlikely. Thynne obviously knew of the existence of *The Plowman's Tale*, and was very clear to distinguish between the two texts in his account. He described *The Pilgrim's Tale* as 'a thing more odious to the clergy than the speech of the Plowman [i.e. *The Plowman's Tale*]', and went on to quote the opening lines of the former accurately, 'that pilgrim's Tale beginning in this sort: In Lincolnshyre fast by a fenne, / Standes a religious howse who dothe yt kenne, etc.'[35] He later described how *The Pilgrim's Tale* was omitted from a reprinted text, while 'the Plowman's tale . . . [was] with much ado permitted to pass with the rest'.[36] It is, then, unlikely that he had confused the two tales in his mind.

As I have argued elsewhere, *The Plowman's Tale* is indeed a radical, anticlerical tract, born out of the controversies of the 1390s and early fifteenth century. It is actually the product of a number of hands, but was printed in 1532 as a Chaucerian text.[37] Hence it is significant that Thynne did not publish it in his *Works* of 1532. It seems likely that he would have known of its existence at that time, as Thomas Godfray, the printer of the *Works*, was to bring out a copy of the poem in the following year (indeed those critics who accept Francis Thynne's story, have assumed that Godfray used a text originally prepared by Thynne for the *Works*). But Thynne and Tuke chose not to print it. If we reject the unlikely idea that opposition from the clergy (led by the dead Cardinal Wolsey) prompted them not to publish it, what might have stopped them, and why did they subsequently print it as part of the later edition of 1542? There are a number of possible explanations. One is offered by Robert Costomiris, who has argued on the strength of certain anomalies in the second edition that Thynne himself (and presumably, if what I have argued above is correct, Tuke also) was not involved in the second edition. The 1542 *Chaucer*, he suggests, was essentially a 'booksellers'' text, produced independently by William Bonham and John Reynes from the text of the 1532 edition.[38] In this scenario it was the booksellers who, whether for commercial or ideological reasons chose to add the *Plowman's Tale* to the text, doing so as cheaply as possible by adding it after the *Parson's Tale*.

An alternative explanation that I would provisionally favour, is that Thynne and Tuke were involved in both editions, but changed their minds about the authenticity of the text. Thynne, as his son affirmed, went to considerable lengths to authenticate the works that he was to print as Chaucer's, and, although he was sometimes misled by scribal attributions or the advice of others, seems to have followed the evidence of his exemplars when he could. In 1532, the editors would have had no strong evidence to substantiate the idea that the *Plowman's Tale* was Chaucer's work. By 1542, however, it had been printed as Chaucer's by a printer whose judgement they presumably respected, and had been in print for almost a decade, apparently without its authenticity being seriously challenged. It may well have been that they simply came to accept either that it was Chaucer's work, or that their edition would not be thought to be comprehensive without it, either way it could no longer be ignored whatever its ideological stance, and so they added it to the revised edition, perhaps signalling a degree of reservation concerning its authenticity by placing it outside *The Canterbury Tales* proper, in the position following *The Parson's Tale*.[39]

A third possible explanation, and one not incompatible with that cited above, is that either Thynne and Tuke's religious views, or the political and ideological situation in which they were working, had changed sufficiently by 1542 that the tale no longer appeared contentious, and so they felt free to add it to their revised edition. The suggestion is not that Thynne and Tuke were arch-conservatives in religion in 1532 and somehow became converted to radicalism in the following decade. Tuke seems, on the evidence cited in the following section, to have remained resolutely orthodox, but Thynne may well have had some degree of moderate reforming sympathy throughout his life. Certainly, by 16 November 1540, when he drew up his will, he was able to commend his soul in conventionally reformed fashion,

to my sweet saviour Jhesus Criste, my only Redeemer and saviour. And to the whole holy company of heaven, of the which, in faith I believe to be one of them, through the merits of Christ's Passion, and no otherwise.[40]

But what is clear from a close reading of the 1532 *Works* is that Thynne was not at that time the sort of radical reformer described by his son, determined to instigate religious change and to attack the clergy whenever and however he could. Far from being a polemicist for the evangelical cause, he seems to have been a moderate figure, whose desires for religious reform were essentially orthodox doctrinally,[41] a man more disturbed by the social and cultural divisions opened up by the Break with Rome and the 'divorce' campaign than exercised by the need to tear down the idols of Antichrist. As we shall see, he seems to have sought through his presentation of Chaucer's poetry to reverse what he saw as the highly divisive events of 1531–2 and to restore an element of stability to English society. By 1542, the apocalyptic overtones of the anticlerical struggles of 1529–32 having passed, and the Royal Supremacy having resulted in a less radical reformed church in England than many conservatives had initially feared, the need to deploy the *Works* in the defence of stability, and keep out such texts as *The Plowman's Tale* might have seemed less pressing.

Certainly it is not reasonable to assume that Thynne and Tuke's choice of texts was driven by a radical religious agenda, and that they added any proto-protestant tale of potentially authentic Chaucerian provenance to their edition as soon as their resources or the political climate permitted. The fate of another pseudo-Chaucerian text, *Jack Upland* provides a valuable corrective to such suggestions. Like *The Plowman's Tale* and *The Pilgrim's Tale*, *Jack Upland* was printed in the 1530s as a work of Chaucer. The printer John Gough offered it for sale with a title-page declaring it to be 'compiled by the Famous Geoffrey Chaucer' around 1536.[42] It did not, however, find its way into the revised 1542 edition of the *Works*, as one might have expected it to have done had Thynne and Tuke wished to radicalize the poet's reputation by adding anything suitable that came to hand. What the printing history of the 1532 and 1542 *Chaucer's* suggests is that Thynne and Tuke were actually very circumspect in accepting into the poet's canon texts that did not suit their political agenda, and where they did print works which they knew were not by Chaucer, they signalled the fact in their editions, whether by labelling them as the work of other writers, or positioning them outside the confines of the *Works* in the prefatory material.

Sir Brian Tuke's Religion

If William Thynne's actions are difficult to square with the image of a religious radical, his collaborator seems an even less likely incendiary evangelical. Indeed, Sir Brian Tuke may have had more direct and pragmatic political motives for favouring a policy of moderation in 1531–2 than his editorial collaborator. Despite the fact that he was, as we have seen, a trusted and loyal royal servant deeply involved in the divorce campaign, he may well have been less sympathetic to the alliances with religious reformers and the diplomatic strategy that accompanied that campaign, with its inevitably anti-Imperial, anti-Spanish complexion, than his official duties would imply. There is some evidence, indeed, to suggest that his diplomatic sympathies lay with an Imperial alliance rather than the pro-French policy that accompanied the break with Rome.

The most striking evidence in this respect is, curiously, personal and domestic. For Tuke, the King's circumspect French secretary, called his first-born sons Maximillian and Charles, the names of the two most recent Holy Roman Emperors (he named his first-born daughters Elizabeth and Mary after the Virgin and her cousin, the mother of John the Baptist). While this need not suggest politically oppositional tendencies—the boys were named at a time when England was allied with the Empire against France—it does suggest a stronger than usual desire to signal his diplomatic affiliations (no other Henrician public servant made so public a declaration of enthusiasm for the Empire), and implies sympathy for the kind of internationalism that was central to Continental Humanist thinking in the earlier 1500s, but was not generally so evident among Henry's counsellors at the time of the break with Rome.[43]

More direct evidence of Tuke's religious position can, perhaps, be gained from the portrait by Holbein, now in the National Gallery of Art in Washington, painted at around the time that the Chaucer edition appeared. Here Tuke wears very prominently on a chain around his neck a crucifix decorated with the Five Wounds of Christ: a devotional item that suggests a very conventional form of affective piety. It may even have been, as Oskar Bätschmann and Pascal Griener have suggested, that the crucifix was 'a magical prophylactic, intended to protect its owner against Ill-health'.[44] If so, then the form of devotion that Tuke so evidently advertises would have been of an impeccably orthodox variety.

And what can be gleaned of Tuke's personal views on politics in general and foreign policy in particular would also suggest a degree of suspicion of French motives on his part, and a lively sense of the importance of the Emperor in securing Christendom against Turkish invasion from without and Lutheran heresy from within.[45] Certainly the Imperial Ambassador, Eustace Chapuys, thought of Tuke as one of the more favourably inclined of Henry's councillors, and the diplomat, like his predecessor Gattinara, remained on friendly terms with him, exchanging news and gossip even when other channels of communication were closed.[46] The ambassador is our source for the story that in February 1534 Tuke declared publicly that it was in the power of the English government to bring about a reconciliation with the Emperor within a couple of hours if they so wished, a striking statement after six years of resolutely pro-French diplomatic strategy.[47] Chapuys is also the source of a story more immediately bearing upon the politics of the 1532 *Chaucer*. In late October 1532, with the *Chaucer* probably ready for sale if not already in circulation, Tuke had spoken up at the Council table for the integrity of Charles V's intentions concerning the threat of a Turkish invasion of central Europe at a time when other councillors were doubting the strength of his commitment.

Writing to the Emperor on 10 November, Chapuys noted that some three weeks earlier the Duke of Norfolk had written to Tuke about the state of affairs in

Europe, with a view to the news being formally conveyed to the other members of the Council. Among the information he reported was a claim that the Emperor had dismissed his army for the winter, while the Turks and their allies still controlled the kingdom of Hungary. As Chapuys complained, the Duke had failed to mention that another army sufficient for the re-conquest of Hungary had been kept in the field at the Emperor's expense under the Prince of Melphi; hence the Council had taken a critical view of Imperial policy based upon partial and misleading information. It was at this point that Tuke intervened to 'alter the Councillors' impression', convincing those whose malice and ignorance had prompted them to be critical to take a more balanced view of the Emperor's intentions.[48]

What Tuke seems to have been trying to do was to ensure that England and the Empire did not fall any further into mutual hostility than was absolutely necessitated by royal policy. Hence he reminded Henry's ministers that Charles was still the best bulwark Christendom possessed against Turkish aggression (while also reminding them, in passing, of the military strength that the Empire could turn against those who opposed it). At the same time, Tuke was also reassuring Chapuys that England was not moving more firmly into alliance with Charles's enemies, the French. No substantial new commitments to the French had been entered into, he reassured the anxious ambassador, in the treaty signed just prior to Henry's trip to Boulogne in November. That Tuke was attempting to build bridges between England and the Empire at the precise time that the Chaucer edition was appearing from Godfray's press, is highly significant. For, as we shall see, a number of the writers who feature in this book, most notably Thomas Elyot and Thomas Wyatt, took a similar stance at key moments in their careers, and precisely the same strategy of peace-making and political moderation underpins the editorial policy of the Chaucer edition.

What Tuke was doing here should not be thought of as oppositional or disloyal in any practical political sense. Both he and Thynne were loyal and committed to the service of the Crown throughout their lives. What Tuke's activities with ambassador Chapuys and at the Council table, and Tuke and Thynne's work on the 1532 *Chaucer* suggest is rather that such diligence and loyalty as they displayed were not incompatible with independence of mind, even over the most sensitive matters of domestic and foreign affairs. What permitted them to express their reservations with current policies, and their hopes and aspirations for change in the future, while remaining actively committed to the service of a policy of which they disapproved, was the notion of good counsel and the freedom that it brought to express their views (if only obliquely) directly to the King. In this way they might make their appeals for change in the spirit of loyal advice, and in the hope that they would ultimately persuade Henry to alter his policies and pursue a line with which they would be more comfortable. Loyalty need not, then, be incompatible with independent, even alternative forms of political engagement, at least not in the political climate of the early 1530s.

In his essay on Tuke in the first edition of the *Dictionary of National Biography*, A. F. Pollard noted somewhat disparagingly, that 'he performed his official duties to the King's satisfaction, avoided all pretence to political independence, and retained his posts to his death'. On the strength of the suggestions made above and his involvement in the 1532 *Chaucer*, this statement needs revision. It seems clear that Tuke performed his duties loyally and to the best of his ability, even down to forwarding a diplomatic policy about which he personally may have had reservations. But behind the scenes he, like his collaborator William Thynne, was working hard to persuade the King to alter his policies, to seek accommodation where he could not find consent, and to heal the wounds that the divorce crisis had opened in the body politic. His proximity to the government and the notion of conciliar 'collective responsibility' may have been the reason for keeping his involvement in the 1532 edition hidden from all but his closest friends until he felt able to acknowledge it himself in the later 1530s, albeit only in the margins of his own edition of the text.

5

Thynne and Tuke's Apocrypha 'Chaucer' and the Poetry of Moderation

If, on closer inspection, the editors of the 1532 *Chaucer* seem to have been more interesting characters, more closely engaged in contemporary politics than is usually assumed, their edition repays such close scrutiny still more fruitfully. And here we can turn to the second of those deceptively simple questions with which the previous chapter began: why does a volume described as the 'Works of Geoffrey Chaucer' contain so many poems written by other writers? The question is prompted by the very first verses that we encounter on opening the edition.

The Preliminary Poems

Following the Preface, the edition prints a curious trio of poems. Unlisted in the table of contents, and placed ambivalently before the title-page of the first of the texts mentioned there (*The Canterbury Tales*), they enjoy a marginal existence, somewhere between the address to the reader and the 'works' themselves. Unattributed to any named author, they might be assumed to be either Chaucerian pieces or commendatory verses from the editors to their royal dedicatee. In fact they are neither. The three are, in order of appearance, the anonymous ballad 'The Eight Goodly Questions / With Their Aunswers', Thomas Hoccleve's 'To the Kynges Most Noble Grace and to the Lordes and Knights of the Garter' (originally two separate poems, written *c.* 1414–16 and addressed to Henry V and his contemporary Garter knights), and an anonymous two-stanza prophecy in the *Prophecies of Merlin* tradition; 'When Faithe Fayleth in Preestes Sawes', sometimes referred to by critics as 'Chaucer's Sayings'.[1] Precisely what these three texts are doing at the beginning of an edition of Chaucer's works is not clear at first glance. As we shall see, they do not discuss the poet or his work in the manner of commendatory verses, nor do they seem, on the face of it, to discuss Chaucerian themes. The editors make no effort to explain the poems' presence, and do nothing to suggest that they attributed them to Chaucer's pen. Faced with such ambiguity, most critics have tended to pass over them in silence.[2] But, they prove to be vitally important to the political impact of the *Works* as a whole.

It is possible that the three were placed in this curiously liminal position for purely pragmatic reasons, being either very late additions to the edition or surplus material for which there was insufficient room in the ballads section at the end of the text.[3] But the arrangement of the volume as a whole and the nature of the pieces themselves suggest they are there by design.[4] As we shall see, the three poems, whether by chance or design, form a single persuasive unit which, placed where it is, develops ideas expressed in the Preface and leads the reader into the main body of the text with certain values and issues foremost in mind. 'The Eight Questions' asserts the need for toleration and moderation on a personal level, elevating the desideratum to avoid vindictiveness and rancour from a question of personality or social etiquette to the status of a timeless verity. Hoccleve's ballad, which follows, calls upon the pillars of the political community, King, lords, and Knights of the Garter, to be resolute in the defence of religious truth, and to suppress rumour and disputation. And, finally, the untitled prophecy warns of the apocalyptic consequences for the whole realm if civil values are not maintained and society is not restored to its proper order and obedience. Taken together these texts address a world newly riven by internal divisions and contention, in which religious faith is crumbling in the face of criticism and hostility, priests are no longer respected or listened to, and the sexual conduct of women is a matter of acute public discussion. It would not be stretching the imagination too far to see the relevance of such a world to readers of the *Works* in 1532 in the wake of the Commons' Supplication and the Royal Supremacy, the collapse of the royal marriage, and attacks upon Anne Boleyn as the most notorious whore in England.

The first of these liminal ballads, 'The Eight Goodly Questions', is an account of how eight 'clerkes of grete science' in Greece strove to show their wisdom by each answering a question concerning human values. These questions address issues of personal moral and spiritual conduct which were conventional enough in late-medieval didactic literature, but they gain a particular resonance and potency in the England of 1532. They begin unexceptionally enough. What, of all earthly things, is best and most commendable to God?: answer: a 'ferme and stable' soul, 'not varyable' (sig. aiv, line 11—my lineation). What is most odious?: a 'dowble man' or deceiver, with a virgin's face and a venomous tale (lines 16–17). What is the best dowry for a wife?: 'A clene lyf . . . without synne, / Chaste and invyolate' (lines 24–25). How can a good reputation be maintained?: 'No fyre make / . . . and no smoke wol aryse' (27–8). The questions dwell momentarily at this point on the question of female morality and the virtue—or otherwise—of spouses. 'What mayden my / Be called clene in chastyte[?]' (lines 29–30): one about whom 'every creature is ashamed on to lye / Of whom every man reporteth great honeste' (lines 32–3).

Having examined female sexual morality, the poem turns to male conduct in the public arena for the subject of the final four questions. 'Who is a poore man, ever ful of wo[e]'?: a rich man who is a niggard and never satisfied ('Sir Guy the bribour is his stewarde' (line 42)). Who is a rich man?: he who is free of all covetousness, whose body is on earth, but whose mind is above ('for God doth him love' (line 49)). Who, then, is a fool?

> He that wolde hurte, and hath no powere,
> Myght he mykel; moche wolde he commaunde.
> His malyce is great; his might nought were.
> He thretteth ful fast; ful lytel may he dere . . .
> God sendeth a shreude cowe a shorte horne.
>
> (lines 51–4, 56)

Finally, who is a wise man? The answer to this question is a veritable manifesto for toleration and self-control.

> He that myght noye, and doth no noyaunce,
> Myght punysshe, and leaveth punyssion,
> A man mercyful, without vengeaunce.
> A wyse man putteth in remembraunce,
> Sayeng, had I venged al myne harme,
> My cloke had nat be furred half so warme.
>
> (lines 59–63)

In other circumstances such statements would be predictable, conventional verities, but in the context of Henry's struggle with Rome, and the assault upon the privileges of the clergy currently underway in Parliament and Convocation, they take on a sharp contemporary edge. Discussions of female virtue and sexual reputation could not but have seemed to touch upon the issues at stake in the King's divorce, discussion of which habitually involved (for conservatives) the assertion of Katherine of Aragon's spotless moral reputation and reference to Anne Boleyn's tarnished one, and (for supporters of the divorce) angry defences of Anne's personal probity. Remarks about the folly of threatening where one cannot harm; and the wisdom of reconciling one's enemies even where one has been slighted in the past, would equally have seemed more than merely personal moral advice in the light of Henry's boasts of his power to unseat the Pope and his complaints concerning the alleged insults to the royal prerogative represented by the clergy's response to the Supremacy. In such circumstances these 'timeless verities' become urgent counsel concerning the current political crisis.

Hoccleve's ballad that follows is written in eight eight-line stanzas, and addresses its royal and aristocratic readers directly, as its title, 'To the Kynge's Most Noble Grace and to the Lordes and Knyghts of the Garter' clearly signals. The first four lines of stanza one and the three following stanzas are aimed at the King, addressing him in terms that would have flattered their original recipient, Henry V, but seem still more strikingly apt as a paean to Henry VIII (himself an admirer of the earlier Henry), the new Supreme Head of the Church and 'imperial' sovereign in England.

> Our Christen Kyng, the heire and successour
> Unto Justinian's devout tendernesse,
> In faith of Jesu our redemptour...
> O liege lorde that have eke the lykenesse
> Of Constantyne, th'ensample and myrrour
> To princes and, in humble buxumnesse,
> To holy churche, o veray sustaynour.
>
> (sig. AIV(v), lines 2–4, 9–12)

Having thus established the King's credentials as a Christian king and heir to the theocratic emperors of old in a way that could not but have won the approval of Henry VIII, however, the poem then turns to describe how he should use his God-given virtues and prerogatives, and here it moves into more contentious territory. The conservative note struck by the allusion to a 'humble' and buxom attitude to 'holy church' is enlarged upon as the King's role as its 'veray' (i.e. true) 'sustaynour' is defined more closely. Henry is, the text asserts, the,

> ...pyller of our faith, and werryour,
> Amonge the heresyes bytter galle.
> Do forthe, do forthe, contynue your socour;
> Holde up Christes baner, lette it nat falle.
>
> (lines 13–16)

The ballad relates a history of the English church and the role of its royal champion clearly distinct from that offered by apologists for further reform.

> This yle or [i.e. ere] this had be[e]n but heth[e]nesse
> Nad be of [i.e. had it not been for] your faith the force and vigour;
> And yet this day the fendes crabbydnesse [fiend's malice]
> Weneth fully to catche a tyme and hour
> To have on us, your lieges, a sharpe shoure,
> And to his servytude us knytte and thralle.
> But aye we trust in you, our protectour,
> On your constaunce we awayte alle.
>
> (lines 17–24)

This is not the vocabulary of the reformers, nor even of Henry's own claims to the Supreme Headship. For the former, England had long *been* a 'hethenesse', a land of unbelief, in the grip of the papal Antichrist and lost in ignorance. Hoccleve's verses, given new life by Thynne and Tuke to address a new King Henry, applaud the King's constancy and faith in the past. They do not talk, as did Henry's own official utterances, of a King newly come to wisdom and insight concerning the extent of clerical and papal usurpation of royal rights.[5] These lines speak of the need to keep a new unholy threat at bay, not to cleanse the land of an old, long-established blight. It is in order to prevent the realm becoming a 'hethenesse' that 'Henry' is called upon to act, not to lead a people out of such a realm into the light of truth. By implication, the King addressed by the verses has always been a stalwart defender of the church, like those paragons of faith Constantine and Justinian whose names the poem invokes. He needs simply to continue in the same vein to prevent disaster. The text does not go so far as to commend loyalty to Rome—in this respect the Supremacy itself is not directly challenged—but its call upon the King to maintain a unified and 'faithful' church implicitly commends the use of the Supremacy to conservative doctrinal ends.

In the following stanza the poet's voice shifts subtly from commendation to instruction, as the King is advised to

> Co[m]maundeth that no wight have hardynesse,
> O worthy Kyng, our Christen emperour,
> Of the faith to dispute more or lesse
> Openly amonge people: her errour
> Springeth al day, engendreth rumour.
> Maketh such lawe, and for ought [that] may befal,
> Observe it wel, there to be ye dettour.
> Dothe so, and God in glorie shal you stal [install].
>
> (lines 25–32)

The call for the King to suppress religious disputation and controversy sets the poem squarely in the context of the debates in Parliament and the wider realm in 1529–32, and Henry VIII's own demands for an end to bickering and division between laity and clergy, papists and heretics. Yet the vocabulary employed in the stanza, and the reference to 'springing' error, as well as the explicit demand that open discussion of matters of religion (a key evangelical demand) be outlawed, set the poem once again firmly on the conservative side of the argument.

Similar sentiments characterize the second half of the ballad, addressed to the nobility and the Knights of the Garter.

> Ye lordes eke, shynyng in noble fame,
> To whiche appropred is the mayntenaunce
> Of Christes cause, in honour of his name,
> Shove on, and put his foes to uttraunce!
> God wolde so, so wolde eke your legiaunce,
> To tho[se] two pricketh you your duite.
> Who so nat kepeth this double observaunce,
> Of meryte and honour naked is he
>
> (lines 33–40)

Again, the vocabulary of maintenance and defence—indeed the very appeal to the nobility itself given the more conservative stance of the House of Lords in relation to the anticlerical demands generated by the Commons)—suggests a markedly conventional social and religious sensibility behind these lines. The final stanzas leave the reader in no doubt on this score.

Our Christen Kyng of Englande and of Frau[n]ce,
And ye, my lordes, with your alyaunce,
And other faithful people that there be,
Trust I to God, shal quenche al this noyau[n]ce,
And this lande sette in highe prosperite.

Conquest of highe prowesse is for to tame
The wylde woodnesse [madness] of these myscreaunce;
Right to the rote repe ye that same,
Slepe nat this, but for Goddes pleasaunce,
And his mother, and in sygnifyaunce
That ye ben of Saynt George's lyvere [livery],
Dothe him servyce and knightly obeysaunce,
For Christe's cause is his, wel knowen ye.
Stiffe stande in that, and ye shal greve and grame
The foe to peace, the norice [nurse] of distaunce.
That nowe is ernest, tourne it in to game.
Nowe kythe of your beleve the constaunce.
Lorde liege, and lordes, have in remembraunce,
Lorde of al is the blyssful Trinyte,
Of whose vertue the mighty habundaunce
You herte and strength in faithful unyte.

(lines 44–64)

The poem thus appeals to the King as Defender of the Faith and Emperor in his own realm, talking to his religious responsibilities, but it does so in terms of the need to end disputes and contention, to close down free discussion of religious issues, not to extend it. There is no call to sweep the church free of abuses, indeed, no acknowledgement that abuses exist; merely a statement of the need to keep a firm hand on the tiller; to maintain a steady course that has already been plotted by previous 'emperors', previous generations, and ultimately by Christ himself.

The final ballad of the three, the brief, untitled prophecy beginning 'When faithe fayleth in preestes sawes [maxims]' completes the sequence of injunction and exhortation with a warning.

Whan faithe fayleth in preestes sawes
And lordes hestes are holden for lawes,
And robbery is holden purchace,
And lechery is holden solace,
Than shal the londe of Albyon
Be brought to great confusyon.

It falleth for every gentylman
To saye the best that he can
In mannes absence,

And the sothe in his presence.
    It cometh by kynde of gentyl blood
To caste away al hevynesse,
And gader togider wordes good;
The werke of wysedome beareth wytnesse.

Again, the question arises: what has all this to do with Chaucer? Did Thynne and Tuke think that this prophecy—and the poems that preceded it—were written by the poet? Their placement, outside the scope of the *Works* proper and their consequently marginal status in the edition, suggest not. The relevance of this short poem, like that of the 'Eight Questions' and Hoccleve's ballad, lies in its relationship to contemporary events rather than to Chaucer's life or the body of his writings. It speaks to the reader's condition, not the poet's, offering him or her a way of reading the works that follow, and a means of applying them to their own circumstances.

From its ambivalent opening line onwards,[6] the poem seems to speak directly to the divisions of the Reformation Parliament, threatening dire consequences if they are not swiftly healed. This short prophecy consequently provides the spur to right the wrongs outlined in the two previous poems. It economically conveys the sense of a realm in which the normal rules of moral, social, and religious decorum are breaking down, and the protocols of good conduct, moral and linguistic integrity, and personal good-will are being swept aside by rancour and self-interest. Hence the anxious appeal in the second stanza is to those guardians of social order, the gentlemen—conventional embodiments of noble speech and conduct—to act before it is too late. As in Hoccleve's ballad, the gentry are conjured into being as the basis of a moral regeneration. And significantly it is again the need to regulate speech, to 'say the best', behave honourably, and gather 'words good' that is posited as the appropriate response to rumour and rancour. Here that need is elevated to the status of an urgent necessity if the corruption that is eating into the social fabric is not to bring about that conventional image of chaos, a world turned upside down.

At face value such concern with the language of political debate might appear a somewhat rarefied, even tangential, response to contemporary events. But it reflects a theme in the debates of the early 1530s. Contemporaries were, as we have seen, concerned at the divisive uses to which liberty of speech was being put, both in Westminster and elsewhere during the first sessions of the Reformation Parliament. Their protests and complaints about the divisions in society are full of references to malign or disreputably motivated uses of language, to marvellous discord and raging, railing and barking, between sections of the political nation. By resurrecting Hoccleve's ballad and the prophecy to lament the loss of decorous speech and the need to return collectively to 'words good', then, Thynne and Tuke were responding to very real contemporary anxieties.

More pointedly and specifically, the address in these verses to gentlemen in particular to take the lead and return to civil language reflects a striking intervention in the Council chamber by George Talbot, the fourth Earl of Shrewsbury. On 6 June 1531 Chapuys reported that the Earl had spoken against Henry VIII's attempts to use the lords of the Council to bully Queen Katherine into acceding to his demands. On two or three occasions when the nobles had gathered to discuss the matter, the ambassador claimed, Shrewsbury had told them 'that they formed almost all the nobility of the kingdom, and that it pertained to them to act as became their name, and not to think or say any villainy nor perversion of justice for any prince or person in the world; and that he thought that he who ruled his actions by right and justice would not do wrong to anyone'. This speech, Chapuys reported, restrained the lords from agreeing to Henry's demands for several days.[7]

Like Hoccleve's ballad and the Prophecy, Shrewsbury's intervention suggested that the need to speak well, to avoid thinking or saying any villainy, was a vital part of noble conduct, and a necessary response to the current political crisis. Like the poems, and like Tuke's Preface that precedes them, Shrewsbury's words conflate the proper uses of language with questions of politics and social rank, claiming for the nobility the responsibility to uphold and regulate correct conduct in both speech and political action. In placing these two poems at the forefront of their edition, then, Thynne and Tuke were drawing attention to precisely these issues, prompting both their aristocratic readers and their royal dedicatee alike to reconsider the dangers implicit in the divisive disputes that the debates of 1529–32 had unleashed, and the responsibilities of the social elite to end them.

Taken together, then, these introductory poems present the reader with a model for interpreting the *Works* to follow. They offer Chaucer's writings, not as texts recovered from a distant past, useful only to antiquarians, but as works of and for the moment of their reception; words of wisdom for readers in the grip of a political and cultural crisis. In this respect the verses carry on the interpretive work begun in Tuke's preface. As we have seen, the Chaucer described and presented to Henry VIII in that brief prose narrative has little in common with the poet who would find favour with future generations in an officially protestant England. Thynne and Tuke's Chaucer is not the radical scourge of clerical abuses celebrated by Foxe and the later sixteenth-century evangelicals. Nor is he the archetypal love-poet, the author of amorous lyrics, biting social satires, and *Troilus and Criseyde*, whom Wyatt and Surrey would adopt as their own. There is nothing in the Preface either that reflects the Chaucer admired in the twentieth century; the wry observer of humanity in all its imperfections, the arch-ironist and experimenter with genres. What the 1532 Preface describes for Henry VIII's benefit is Chaucer the moralist, the scholar and historiographer; the author of a veritable compendium of English learning ('compendiousness' is indeed one of the qualities the Preface principally commends in the poet), a repository of 'doctrines and sciences' that are now to be made available for their royal dedicatee.[8]

The Preface and preliminary poems thus carry a considerable weight in determining how readers will approach the texts to follow. One further example of Thynne and Tuke's editorial method will serve to emphasize the point. As R. F. Yeager has deduced from the foliation, the text of Robert Henryson's *Testament of Creseyde* was added to the edition late in the printing process, once the authentically Chaucerian *Troilus and Criseyde,* which it follows had been set.[9] This suggests two things about Thynne and Tuke's editorial practice. It shows that they were prepared to add material to their collection, even at a very late stage, if they thought it sufficiently important to warrant inclusion. And it implies that what they were doing was very consciously producing a *Works of Chaucer* that contained both Chaucerian texts and pieces by other writers that added to an understanding of the poet's life or writings. Hence the *Testament* was included, despite the declaration in its opening lines that it was the work of a reader of Chaucer's *Troilus* rather than the poet himself ('To cutte the wynter nyght and make it shorte, / I toke a queare, and lefte al other sporte, / Written by worthy Chaucer glorious, / Of fayre Creseyde, and lusty Troylus' (fol. ccxix)). They added it almost certainly because it extended the story of *Troilus and Criseyde* and provided it with an effective moral coda. It was, in short, one of those texts that helped their readers to interpret the edition, glossing and extending the authentic Chaucerian poems they accompany. It is in this light that we should also read the Preface and its attendant verses. These were almost certainly the last section of the *Works* to be drafted and prepared for the press, and hence could reflect most immediately both the events of 1532 and the editors' own responses to them.[10] It may even have been that the three prefatory verses were added after the bulk of the preliminaries had been set in Thomas Godfray's print-shop, hence the fact that they are squeezed into three and a half columns and placed somewhat awkwardly in the space between the end of a list of Contents which does not mention them and the title-page to *The Canterbury Tales.*

The Preface and preliminary verses offer clear guidance on how to approach the works that follow (the former explicitly, the latter tacitly), presenting an image of Chaucer as a particular kind of poet, and thereby influencing the way one approaches his works. Caroline Spurgeon confidently asserted that Tuke's Preface was the first text to cite Chaucer's status as a moral writer as an important part of his claim to literary and cultural importance.[11] This is not strictly true, a number of fifteenth-century authors and scribal collators had similarly appealed to the poet as a moral guide.[12] But Spurgeon is astute in drawing out the novelty of what the Tuke Preface asserts. Where the bulk of previous appreciations of the poet's work, not least those in the earlier printed editions of Caxton, de Worde, and Pynson, had concentrated on the poet's linguistic skills and his role as the enricher of the English tongue that Tuke himself made much of,[13] the 1532 Preface also restored the poet's earlier reputation as a moral force and, still more importantly, gave it a political dimension. Thynne and Tuke constructed their

Chaucer as a political as well as a moral authority, and stressed his function as a guide to princes in troubled times. Theirs was a Chaucer who not only offered sound advice on questions of personal conduct and morality, but counselled his readers consistently on the responsibilities of kings, on the regulation of religion, and even, as we shall see, on the conduct of what one might call an ethical foreign policy. Hence the placement of those texts, both Chaucerian and non-Chaucerian, that are explicitly addressed to princes and governors in prominent positions at the beginning and end of the edition, and hence the fact that the majority of the self-evidently non-Chaucerian material is drawn from the *speculum principis* tradition. Thynne and Tuke's readers—and most obviously their royal dedicatee—are thus presented with a collection of writings that proclaim their value as advice literature: advice literature, moreover, with a proven track record of success with Henry's VIII's royal predecessors. And the advice they offer is implicitly to suppress anticlerical dissention and reconsider current policies.

The success of the editors' endeavours in fashioning a political Chaucer may, perhaps, be judged from the fact that, when Tuke's confidant John Leland came to write a biographical sketch of Chaucer in his *Commentarie de Scriptoribus Britannicis* (c. 1540), he felt justified in describing a poet who would have been almost unrecognizable to his contemporaries, a man who was not only an eloquent moral guide, but the ideal counsellor for princes, schooled in all the liberal arts and political sciences. Leland's Chaucer left Oxford 'an acute logician, a delightful orator, an elegant poet, a profound philosopher, and an able mathematician... Moreover, he left the university a devout theologian', who also 'resorted regularly to the London tribunals and the Inns of Court occupied by the lawyers who were there engaged in interpreting the laws of their country'. As a result, the poet was 'well known to Richard of Bordeaux, the English monarch [i.e. Richard II] and dear to him on account of his virtues, so also for the same reasons he was valued by Henry IV and his son the triumphant victor over the French [Henry V]'.[14] Here indeed was a Chaucer fit to guide Henry VIII through the troubled waters of 1532 and beyond.

The Canon's Tale: Reading the 'Major Works' in 1532

Only once he or she has traversed the orientation course provided by the Preface and prefatory verses, does the reader reach the first of the canonical Chaucerian texts, *The General Prologue* to *The Canterbury Tales*. Suitably primed by the stress in these preliminary texts upon the social, moral, and philosophical aspects of the poet's work, such readers will be more inclined to read *The General Prologue* 'seriously', not as a frivolous social satire, or mischievous anticlerical tract, but as a vision of a diverse and potentially divided society, a vision of the sort of world anatomized in the prefatory material: a poem which was not an end in itself, but a true prologue to and context for the graver *Knight's Tale* to follow.

The choice of *The Canterbury Tales* as the opening text in the *Works* proper is itself an interesting one. Modern readers, conditioned to accept the *Tales* as the poet's best known work, will perhaps need reminding that it was not the text for which he was most celebrated in the early Tudor period. The Chaucer applauded by readers during the century and a half following his death was the poet of courtly romance and dream-vision; as well if not better known for the *Troilus* and *The House of Fame*, and as the translator of Boethius and *The Romance of the Rose* as he was for the unfinished rag-bag of narratives that constitutes *The Canterbury Tales*. One might legitimately have expected the first 'Complete Works' to have begun with the more stately *Troilus* (this was the text with which Richard Pynson began his three volume Chaucer collection of 1526, the nearest thing to a comprehensive edition produced prior to Thynne and Tuke's endeavours), or, if a chronological approach was taken, one of the early dream-visions such as *The Book of The Duchess*. By printing *The Canterbury Tales* as the first substantive item in their edition, Thynne and Tuke were inevitably focusing considerable attention on that work, particularly upon the first and most substantial of the Canterbury narratives, *The Knight's Tale*. And again it is difficult to avoid the conclusion that they were doing so because of the Tale's interest in the 'imperial' figure of Theseus, who stands at the centre of the story, and its concern with the disruption and restoration of social and political order. Such at least might be the aspects of the tale that would commend themselves to readers who had approached it through Thynne and Tuke's prefatory material.[15]

The Knight's Tale, it will be remembered, takes as its central theme the socially and morally disruptive effects created when two young Theban knights, Palamon and Arcite, each fall in love with the same woman: Emilye, the niece of Theseus, Duke of Athens. It is Theseus' role in the Tale to strive to contain the potentially chaotic forces unleashed by the knights' passionate conflict, and to attempt to reconcile the young Thebans both to each other and to the notion of a universe ordered by divine providence. This he eventually does, although only at the cost of Arcite's life, and after the dramatic intervention of the inscrutably malevolent god Saturn. But Theseus' victory, like his creation of the perfectly ordered microcosm of the arena built to house the young men's final combat, is only achieved after he learns afresh the wisdom of restraint and self-control in the face of passionate provocation. As he discovers when he stumbles across the knights fighting an unregulated duel in a forest grove, anger in a prince must give way to reason and compassion if a state is to be governed wisely. Having condemned Palamon and Arcite to death for their misdemeanours, he is prompted to reconsider his verdict by the tearful intervention of his wife, Hyppolita.

> Til at the laste, aslaked was his mode,
> For pyte renneth sone in gentle herte.
> And though he first for yre quoke and sterte,
> He hath consydered shortly in a clause,
> The trespas of hem bothe, and eke the cause,
> And al though his yre her [i.e. their] gylt accused,
> Yet in his reason he hem bothe excused...

> And softe unto hymselfe he sayd: 'fy
> Upon a lorde that woll have no mercy
> But be a lyon, bothe in worde and dede
> To hem that been in repentaunce and drede.[16]

Only when anger has yielded to mercy does Theseus regain the emotional distance and moral authority necessary for him to deliver the Boethian wisdom of his justly famous 'firste mover' speech, in which the chaotic forces of a mutable world, seemingly governed by fortune and mischance are seen to be part of a wider providential scheme. Celebrating 'the fayre chayne of love', the creation of a loving God, that binds the universe together, Theseus offers a moving prospectus for universal harmony, and an argument for reconciling oneself to what one cannot control.

> Than is it Wysedome, as thynketh me,
> To make vertue of necessyte,
> And take it wel, that we may not eschewe,
> And namely that to us al is dewe.
> And who so grutcheth aught, he dothe folye,
> And rebel to Him that al may gye [i.e.govern].
>
> (fol. xiii, lines 3041–6)

'The contrarye of al this', Theseus concludes, 'is wylfulnesse' (3057), the prerogative of the tyrant, the antithesis of obedience, order, and prosperity.

This is the spirit that animated John Heywood's interludes and the other 'Chaucerian' texts emerging from the humanists associated with the More circle in the early 1530s. The arguments for accommodation of differences and contentment with one's lot to be found there echo and gloss the tone and sentiments of Theseus's final injunction to his subjects.

> What may conclude of this longe story,
> But after sorowe, I rede us be mery,
> And thanke Jupiter of al his grace,
> And, er we departen from this place,
> I rede we maken of sorowes two
> One perfyte joye, lastyng ever mo.
>
> (fol. xiii, lines 3067–72)

Hence the sorrowful Palamon and the grieving 'widow' Emilye are united in a marriage that brings happiness to them both and peace to the cities of Athens and Thebes.

If, then, as Seth Lerer has described in his brilliant recovery of what Chaucer meant to his fifteenth-century readers,[17] Chaucer's texts sought to teach their readers how to interpret them, so too does Thynne and Tuke's edition. Just as Chaucer's original poems—and especially *The Canterbury Tales*—offered readers models of readily reproducible attitudes or forms of conduct that they might apply to those texts: the abused Clerk, the boyish Squire, or 'elvish', child-like 'Geffrey Chaucer' himself, so too does the 1532 *Works*. Where fifteenth-century readers of Chaucer's manuscripts might have responded to what they read, 'like the Clerk', 'like a Laureate', and so on, Thynne and Tuke's edition invited Henry VIII, by means of direct address in the Preface and the preliminary verses, to read the narratives that it contains 'like Theseus'; the martial judge and patron of the first and most imposing of *The Canterbury Tales*. They invited their royal reader to find within the volume's pages a model of an 'imperial' peaceweaver and bringer of order, a man who governs regally, with a stern eye and a firm hand, but who nonetheless finds it possible to show mercy and tolerance, and who ultim-ately learns to bring social and political stability to a world of passionate struggle and disorder, through the acceptance—and ultimately the reconciliation—of what had initially seemed intractable differences.

The Additional Poems in the Body of the Text

That Thynne and Tuke seemingly had no difficulties with the idea that Chaucer was a conventional catholic in his beliefs is clear from a number of the texts that they printed among his works. The impeccably orthodox *Lamentatyon of Mary Magdalen* (fos. ccclxi–xv) had been printed as Chaucer's by Pynson in his three volume collection in 1526, so could probably not have been omitted even had the editors been uncomfortable with its sentiments if they wished their edition to have any claim to comprehensiveness. But the *Ballad of Co[m]mendation of Our Lady* (fos. ccclxxiv–iv(v))—in fact a conflation of two poems, both probably written by Lydgate—posed no such problems, and it was introduced into the Chaucer canon by Thynne and Tuke, as was *A Prayse of Women* (fol. cccxi(v)–xii(v)) which also offers a highly orthodox example of Marian devotion. It is possible that the editors believed these to be genuinely Chaucerian pieces. If they did not, then they were consciously striving to increase the number of orthodox religious works in his canon. Whether their inclusion was an error of attribution or more contrived, however, the result was the same; the reinforcement of the *Works'* sense of Chaucer as a doctrinally conventional catholic poet.

Another innovation was the addition of Thomas Usk's semi-autobiographical apologia, *The Testament of Love*, which, as Derek Pearsall has suggested, Thynne and Tuke may well have thought was Chaucer's work on the strength of an apparent allusion to it in Gower's *Confessio Amantis*.[18] This text is often cited in support of the claim that the editors were radicalizing the poet's canon and reputation; but it is difficult to agree with such a claim. *The Testament* is far from radical in its religious or political stances. Its only engagement with anti-clericalism is a short section of highly conventional criticism of worldliness among the clergy, and even this is grouped with lengthier passages attacking 'ungentle' aristocrats and the beguiling ways of lecherous men in such a way as to minimize any specific applications it might suggest.[19] Elsewhere the text is entirely orthodox in its treatment of religious issues, talking approvingly of the

Acts of Mercy, the worship of the Saints, and the teachings of the Church Fathers, and wholeheartedly condemning heresies and erroneous opinions, abusing those who hold such views for living 'bestial' and 'voluptuous' lives.[20]

Rather than approving of anticlericalism and religious reform, the text offers a Boethian strategy for survival in a world (and specifically a City of London) torn by division and rancour. The narrator, who is languishing in prison and close to despair, is, like the narrator of *The Consolation of Philosophy*, visited by a beautiful woman who offers him 'consolation' in the form of spiritual counsel. In Usk's text this allegorical visitor is not Philosophy but Love, and her message concerns the need to reconcile oneself to the apparent disorder of worldly life by keeping one's eyes upon the prospect of salvation and behaving virtuously at all times. The narrator presents himself as a peacemaker, one whose current distress was brought about as a result of his efforts to pacify a turbulent city. He is motivated by a belief that,

Common profit in communalty is nothing but peace and tranquillity, with just govern-ance proceeding from this profit, sythen [since] by counsel of mine inwit [conscience] me thought the first painted things malice and evil meaning, without any good availing to any peoples, and of tyranny purposed.

(fol. cccxxxi(v))

Thus, having taken one side in a civil dispute (the allusion is to the contested London mayoral election of 1383), he later turned against his former allies once he saw that their aim was to disturb rather than to preserve the peace. These enemies, he notes, were

blind and of elde [age] so far-forth beguiled that debate and strife they mainteined and in destruction on that other side, by which cause the peace, that most in communalty should be desired, was in point to be broken and annulled. Also the City of London, that is to me so dear and sweet, in which I was forth grown, and more kindly love have I to that place than to any other in earth . . . thilke [that] peace should thus there have been broken.

(fol. cccxxxi(v))

Knowing that 'peace most is necessary to communalties and cities' (cccxxxi(v)), he admits that he had, prior to his defection, been drawn into the plans of the agitators and evil-doers, 'not witting the privy intent of their meaning'. These agitators had

Drawn also the feeble-witted people, that have none insight of governative prudence, to clamour and to cry on matters that they stirred, and under points for common advantage, they emboldened the passive to take in the actives doing, and also stirred innocents of cunning to cry after things which (quod they) may not stand but we be executors of those matters, and authority of execution by common election to us be delivered, and that must [be] by strength of your maintenance.

(fol. cccxxxi(v))

Once the commons had elected the agitators to high office, however, they proved to 'have no consideration, but only to voluntary [i.e. wilful] lusts, without reason' (cccxxxii). Having spoken out against the ringleaders, however, he had merely been denounced as a liar and betrayer of his masters.

Usk's *Testament* probably commended itself to Thynne and Tuke, whether or not they thought it was Chaucer's, not because of its radicalism, but precisely for its consistent advocacy of peace and civil order. If, indeed, they *did* think that it was Chaucer's own apologia, it would have suited their purposes perfectly, as it seemed to confirm the image of the poet that they were themselves seeking to create in their edition. Here was an author who admitted to having been closely involved in the internecine politics of the City of London, who loved the City dearly, and yet was prepared to abandon his political allegiances in order to oppose what he saw as disruptive factional strife. Here was Chaucer the peace-maker and reconciler writ large, and seemingly with his own pen.

Where the text did stray into more radical politics it was doubly useful to its editors, as it reinforced the idea of the poet as the bold counsellor of princes, who spoke up in the interests of virtue and good government. Drawing upon ideas of 'gentilesse' that Chaucer himself had explored at various points in the legitimate canon (most notably in *The Wife of Bath's Tale* and the short poem entitled 'Gentilesse'), Usk declared that virtue and gentility lay in the personal qualities of the individual rather than in any high office that they held. Indeed, office—or 'dignity'—was not merely neutral but actively malign, in that it tended to magnify any vices or flaws that the incumbent might possess, thereby stimulating 'rancour and debate' in the civil community. In a cruel man, dignity made his tyranny all the greater, by giving him greater scope to exercise his cruelty.

Had Nero never been Emperor, should never his dame have be slain, to make open the privity of his engendering. Herod for his dignity slew many children. The dignity of King John would have destroyed all England. Therefore muckel [much] wisdom and goodness both [is] needed in a person the malice in dignity slyly to bridle, and with a good bit of arrest to withdraw, in case it would prance otherwise than it should.

(fol. cccxli(v))

Again such a text spoke directly to its royal dedicatee in terms he would recognize from a score of other mirrors for princes, of the need to regulate his behaviour, and always to intervene in domestic politics in favour of moderation and good order. The voice of Chaucer the 'good counsellor' created in the preliminary material and solidified in *The Knight's Tale*, *Melibee*, and elsewhere, again seemed to be giving posthumous utterance in favour of stilling the 'anticlerical' disputes of 1532.

The Concluding Ballads

The last section of the *Works* is as important as the preliminary material in 'packaging' the collection as a political document. It brings together a series of

ballads, some more or less authentically Chaucerian, others explicitly attributed
to other writers, that work together to re-establish and corroborate the idea of
Chaucer as a moral authority, a poetic guide for princes, and an advocate of
moderation in all aspects of public and private life.[21]

The verse epistle written by Chaucer's contemporary Henry Scogan, tutor to
the sons of Henry V ('Scogan Unto the Lordes and Gentylmen of the Kynges
House') calls upon Chaucer as a witness to the idea that 'gentilesse' is a product of
deeds not lineage. It sets the poet in the context of courtly counsel, and asks its
readers to take heed of those rulers who fell from grace through personal vice or
tyranny.

> Thynketh . . . howe many a governour,
> Called to estate, hath be set ful lowe
> Through misusyng of right and of errour,
> And therefore I counsaile you vertue to knowe . . .
>
> (fol. ccclxxx(v), lines 93–6)
>
> Rede here ayenst nowe of Nero vertulees [i.e. virtue-less].
> Taketh hede also of proude Balthasare;
> They hated vertue, equyte, and pees.
> And loke howe Antyochus fyl fro his chare,
> That he his skyne and bones al to tare;
> Loke what mischaunce they had for her [i.e. their] vyces.
> Who so wol not by these signes beware,
> I dare wel say infortunate and nyce is.
>
> (fol. ccclxxxi, lines 173–80)

If Thynne and Tuke's aim had been simply to collect and publish as many of
Chaucer's verses as they could find, the presence of Scogan's poem here would be
difficult to explain. The title that they chose for it makes clear they did not think
it was Chaucerian, and its reference to the poet is too fleeting to make it a
valuable addition to knowledge about his life or work.[22] But read in the context
of the editors' political strategy its role in the collection is clearer. By including
the Scogan poem, the editors return to the forefront of their readers' minds the
notion that Chaucer was, despite his interest in amatory lyrics and comic
narratives, a fundamentally serious writer whose work should be read as sound
guidance for governors. Scogan's ballad refocuses attention upon the courtly
context of such counsel (it is, after all, written by a prominent courtier—one
who could address his royal readers as 'my noble sons and eke my lords dear'),
and marks out Chaucer as a writer both well known in courtly circles and
respected there for his wisdom. The poem thus acts as an ideal prologue to
those that follow it, most notably perhaps 'Good Counsayle of Chaucer' (the
poem now known generally as 'Truth'), which appears later on the same page and
offers a series of Boethian aphorisms and injunctions for survival in a world

apparently governed by the caprice of fortune. It, like a number of earlier texts ascribed to the poet's own voice (rather than to a poetic persona such as the Miller or Wife of Bath) is thus identified as a particularly personal address to the reader from the poet *in propria persona*.[23]

Between Scogan's ballad and the 'Good Counsayle' is a short, untitled piece— Chaucer's poem now generally known as 'Lack of Steadfastness'—that revisits many of the themes already identified as central to Thynne and Tuke's editorial and political agenda. The text again calls urgently for the exercise of mercy and pity at all levels of society, in the context of a world suddenly and inexplicably 'turned...up so down' by mutability and 'the lust that men have in dissention' (line 9).

> Somtyme ye world so stedfast was and stable,
> That mannes worde was an oblygacioun,
> And nowe it is so false and disceyvable
> That worde and dede as in conclusyoun
> Is nothyng syke, for turned is up so doun
> Al the worlde, through mede [bribery] and fykelnesse,
> That al is loste for lacke of stedfastnesse...
>
> (fol. ccclxxxi, lines 1–7)

> Trouthe is put downe, reason is holde fable.
> Vertue hath no domynation,
> Pyte is exyled, no man is merciable.
> Through covetyse is blente discretion,
> The worlde hath made a permutation
> Fro right to wrong, fro trouth to fykelnesse;
> Thus al is lost for lacke of stedfastnesse.
>
> (fol. ccclxxxi, lines 15–21)

The brief concluding 'envoi' targets the complaint specifically at the sovereign and makes clear his responsibility for righting the wrongs described.

> Prince, desyre to be honourable;
> Cherisshe thy folke, and hate extorcyon.
> Suffre nothyng that may be reprovable
> To thyne estate done in this regyon.
> Shewe forthe the yerde [i.e. rod] of castygacion;
> Drede God, do lawe, love trouth and worthyness,
> And wedde thy folke agen to stedfastnesse.
>
> (fol. ccclxxxi, lines 22–8)

Such lines would, again, have had especially powerful resonances in the England of 1532. Indeed, more generally the verses gathered in this final section offer a critical mass of material that speaks collectively of a world in chaos, and of strategies for survival in, and the redemption of, that world. Chaucer's 'Ballad to Fortune' (here given the title 'Ballad of the Vyssage withouten Payntyng' (fol. ccclxxxi(v)) follows after 'Good Counsayle', beginning with a complaint to and defiance of a world governed by mutability.

> This wretched worlde's transmutation,
> As wele and wo[e], nowe poor and nowe honour,
> Without order or dewe discretion,
> Governed is by fortune's errour...
>
> (fol. ccclxxxi, lines 1–4)

Against this chaos the poems as a whole assert the need for social stability, loyalty to the established order, and the obligation to know and be happy in one's place.

> But trewly, no force of thy redour [i.e. despite your severity],
> To him that over him selfe hathe maistry,
> My suffysaunce shalbe my socour,
> For, fynally, Fortune I defye.
>
> ('Vyssage', lines 13–16)

'Good Counsayle of Chaucer' offers stoic contentment as the answer to an unstable world.

> That [which] the[e] is sent, receyve in buxomness;
> The wrastlyng of this worlde asketh a fal.
> Here is no home, here is but wyldernesse;
> Forthe pylgrym, forthe beest, out of thy Stal!
> Loke up on high and thanke God of al;
> Weyve thy luste and lette thy gost the[e] lede.
> And trouth the[e] shal delyver, it is no drede.
>
> (fol. ccclxxx1–(v), lines 15–21)

The untitled two-stanza poem (actually Lydgate's 'Go forth King') that follows the envoy to Scogan on the next page extends this injunction to contentedness and the performance of one's allotted role into a universal programme for social and moral stability.

> Go forthe kyng, rule the[e] by sapience;
> Bisshoppe, be able to mynister doctrine.
> Lorde, to trewe counsayle yeve audience;
> Womanhede, to chastyte ever enclyne;
> Knyght, lette thy dedes worship determyne;
> Be rightous, juge, in savyng thy name.
> Rich, do almesse, lest thou lese blysse with shame.
>
> People, obey your kyng and the lawe;
> Age, be thou ruled by good relygion;
> Trewe servant, be dredeful and kepe ye under awe.

And thou poore, fye on presumption!
Inobedience to youth is utter destruction.
Remember you God hath set you so,
And do your parte as ye be ordayned to.

(fol. ccclxxxii, lines 1–14)

The final Chaucerian text before the Latin epitaph for the poet (written by the Italian humanist Stephanus Surigonis, and said to have been hung over his tomb in Westminster), is the ballad 'A Wicked Tongue'. Thynne and Tuke print it with another verse, 'Chaucer Unto the Kynge', as a preface in such a way as to turn the two texts together into yet another *speculum principis*.[24]

O conqueror of Brutes Albyon,
Which that by lyne and free election
Ben very kyng, this to you I sende,
And ye that ay al harmes amende
Have mynde upon my supplycation.

(fol. ccclxxxii(v), lines 1–5)

'A wicked Tongue' itself is a moral meditation upon the vagaries of public opinion and the effects of slander on reputation and honour. Taken alone and in another context it might have read conventionally enough, but redirected through the addition of the introductory stanza to a royal reader, and presented to Henry VIII in the summer of 1532, a number of its stanzas would have had intensely personal implications for its royal dedicatee and political implications for its other courtly readers.

If it befal that thou take a wyfe,
They wol falsly say in their entent
That thou arte lykely ever to lyve in stryfe
Voyde of al rest, without alegement.
Wyves hem maystren, this is their jugement.

(fol. ccclxxxii(v), lines 22–6)

In the face of such wilful and malicious gossip by the unnamed 'they': the world at large, the only strategy is patient sufferance. If one is attractive, 'they' will say one is lecherous, if ugly, then vicious. If one is celibate, they will attribute it to impotence:

Suffre hem speke, and trust wel this:
A wicked tongue wol alwey say amys.

(fol. ccclxxxii(v), lines 41–2)

The final stanza once again makes the now familiar calls to sovereigns for moderation for the suppression of all malicious rumour and the promotion of 'well-speaking'.

> Most noble princes, cherysshers of vertue,
> Remembreth you of high discretyon.
> The first vertue and most plesyng to Jesu
> (By the wrytyng and sentence of Caton)
> Is a good tongue in his opinyon.
> Chastyse the reverse, and of wysedome to this;
> Withdrawe you heryng from al [th]at sayn amys.
>
> (fol. ccclxxxiii, lines 113–19)

Like the Earl of Shrewsbury's intervention in the Council chamber, the poem again seeks to set the ideal of 'right-speaking' against the seemingly more tangible ills of the world that it laments.

Chaucer, War, and Peace

More detailed, and more sustained in its political focus, is another of the texts clearly identified as non-Chaucerian by its title. The ballad usually referred to as 'In Praise of Peace', here entitled 'John Gower Unto King Henry IV', offers another strikingly contemporary appeal to the King to take responsibility for religious affairs, in a way that appears broadly supportive of Henry VIII's 'imperial' claims for headship of the Church.[25] It even asserts the right of princes to take on the Pope's responsibilities and reform the Church if the pontiff is unable to fulfil his spiritual responsibilities.

> But though the heed of holy churche above
> Ne do nat al his hole busynese
> Amonge the people to sette peace and love,
> These kinges oughten of her rightwysenesse
> Her owne cause among hem self redresse.
> Tho Peter's shyp as now hath lost his stere,
> It lyeth in hem the barge to steere.
>
> (fol. ccclxxvi(v), lines 225–31)

But, on closer examination, the text, born out of the experience of the papal schism of the later fourteenth century, argues that the King should use that responsibility to foster moderation and stabilize the status quo rather than promote radical reform. Again, the need to quell rancour and still complaint are paramount among the issues cited.

> If holy churche after the dewte
> Of Christes worde ne be nat avayled
> To make peace, accorde, and unyte
> Among the kynges that be nowe devysed
> Yet natheles the lawe stante affysed
> Of mannes wytte to be so resonable
> Without that to stande him self stable.
>
> (fol. ccclxxvii, lines 232–8)

There is little to comfort advocates of the newly emerging doctrine of Henrician caesaropapism in the text's prescription for royal action and its account of the relationship between church and laity.

> Of holy churche we ben chyldren al
> And every chylde is holde for to bowe
> Unto the mother, howe that ever it fal,
> Or else he must reason disalowe.
> And for that cause a knyght shal first avowe
> The right of holy church to defende
> That no man shal the privylege offende.
>
> Thus were it good to sette al in evyn
> The worldes princes, and the prelates bothe...
>
> (fol. ccclxxvii, lines 239–47)

What had been in the early fifteenth century an appeal for the end of papal schism, becomes in 1532 an eloquent protest at the divisions brought to the surface in the Reformation Parliament.

> Upon three poyntes stant Christes peace oppressed:
> First holy churche in her selfe devyded,
> Whiche ought of reason first to be redressed.
> But yet so high a cause is nat desyded,
> And thus whan humble patience is prided,
> The remenaunt whiche that they shulde rule,
> No wonder is though it stand out of rule.
>
> (fol. ccclxxvii, ll. 253–9)

> The Apostel sayth, there may no lyfe be good
> Whiche is nat grounded upon charyte.
>
> (fol. ccclxxvii(v), lines 353–4)

This text, like the Preface and like the *Collectanea satis copiosa*, cites the crucial test case of Constantine, but deploys him, not as a caesaropapist, but merely as a ruler who showed mercy:

> Whan him was lever [i.e. he would rather] his owne dethe desyre
> Than do the yong chyldren to martyre;
> Of creweltie he left the quarele.
> Pyte he wrought, and pyte was his hele.
>
> (fol. ccclxxvii(v), lines 370–3)[26]

And more strikingly still, the poem talks approvingly of the Emperor's baptism administered by Pope Silvester, whereby 'Rome was sette in thylke honour / Of Christ's fayth' (lines 383–5), before praising the benefits of peacemaking in European affairs once more.

> My worthy liege lorde, Henry by name,
> Which Englande haste to governe and right,
> Men ought wel thy pyte to proclame,
> Which openlyche in al the worldes syght
> Is shewed, with the helpe of God almyght
> To yeve us peace which long hath be debated,
> Whereof thy prise shal never be abated.
>
> (fol. ccclxxvii(v), lines 388–94)

The ballad, as its modern title suggests, is a lengthy statement of the benefits of peace and the adverse consequences of war. Although Gower is willing to concede that a king has a right to wage war in cases of extreme necessity ('to claim and aske his rightful heritage' (line 59)), this is described as always a case of last resort, a temporary aberration in God's scheme for princes.

> But otherwyse, if God him selfe wolde
> Affyrme love and peace bitwene the kynges,
> Peace is the best above al erthly thynges...
>
> (fol. ccclxxv(v), lines 61–3)

> What kyng that wolde be the worthyest
> The more he myght our deedly warre cease,
> The more he shulde his worthynesse encrease.

> Peace is the chefe of al the worldes welth,
> And to the heven it ledeth eke the way.
> Peace is of soule and lyfe the mannes helth,
> [Throw] Of[f] pestylence, and dothe the warre away.
> My liege lorde, take hede of what I say,
> If warre may be lefte, take peace on hande,
> Which may nat be without Goddes sande [instruction].
>
> (fol. ccclxxvi, lines 75–84).

After a brief excursus into the consequences of unchecked warfare ('It sleeth the preest in holy churche at masse, / Forsythe the made, and dothe her flour... to fal / .../Ther is no thing wherof myschefe may growe/ Whiche is nat caused of the warre, I trowe' (lines 107–12)), the poet returns to specifics and the need to purge the royal council of those who would advocate conflict.

> If any man be nowe or ever was
> Ayen the peace thy prevy counsaylour,
> Lette God be of thy counsayle in this caas,
> And put away the crewel warryour...
>
> (fol. ccclxxvi, lines 127–30)

Indeed, even if the entire Council should favour war, the King must reject their advice and, for once, follow his own wisdom in pursuing peace.

> About a kyng good counsayle is to preyse
> Above al other thynges most vaylable.
> But yet a kyng within him selfe shal peyse,
> And seen the thynges that be resonable,
> And therupon he shal his wyttes stable,
> Among the men to sette peace in evyn,
> For love of Him which is the Kyng of Hevyn.
>
> (fol. ccclxxvi, lines 141–7)

The need for peace among Christian princes is set in the context of the threat to Christendom from outside, specifically that from heathen 'paynems' and, by implication, from divisive heretics within.

> To yeve us peace was cause why Christ dyde;
> Without peace may nothing stande avayled.
> But now a man may se on every syde
> Howe Christes faythe is every day assayled,
> With the paynems distroyed and so batayled
> That for defaute of helpe and defence
> Unneth hath Christ his dewe reverence.
>
> (fol. ccclxxvi(v), lines 190–6)

It is in the context of this external threat that the king is enjoined to reunite 'the worldes princes, and the prelates bothe' and re-establish stability in the church, before it is too late.

Again, at first glance, it is hard to recover the precise resonance of such an appeal in the seemingly very different context of 1532. But a closer examination of the political situation of the early 1530s makes it very clear why Thynne and Tuke might have chosen to revive this particular poem of Gower's and add it to their edition. The plea for Christian unity in times of division was clearly as relevant to a kingdom divided by protestant heresies as it was by Lollard dissent and rival claims to papal authority. But the relevance of the text was still more pointed.

For the eighteenth months preceding the publication of Thynne and Tuke's *Chaucer*, the period when the volume would have been collated and prepared for the press, the backdrop to diplomatic activity in Europe was provided by fervent discussion of the possibility of an attack upon Christendom by the 'paynem' Turks. Talk of the need for Christian unity and of the dangers of divisions between princes was common at court and in London throughout this period.[27] Indeed, it was on this very issue that Tuke had spoken out in the Council chamber in October 1532, when he defended the Emperor's good intentions regarding the Kingdom of Hungary.[28] In choosing to print Gower's ballad in praise of peace, then, the editors were reflecting a significant theme in governmental thinking, a theme evident in the pronouncements of both the King and his ministers throughout 1531–2. But, rather than merely echoing the somewhat

hollow royal calls for Christian unity, the ballad, and the edition as a whole, gave
the demand for peace a distinctly critical political edge. For, at precisely the time
that Henry was publicly calling for peace in Europe and seeking to play the role
of champion of Christendom as a means of encouraging the Pope to grant
him what he wanted over the divorce, the divorce campaign itself was adding
significantly to the discord between Christian princes. And Henry, by throwing
in his lot with Francis I, the only monarch who would support him on the issue,
was markedly increasing the chances of England's becoming involved in a war
against Charles V, the most powerful prince in Europe.

In April 1531 it was widely rumoured in Paris that the Emperor intended to
invade England in order to restore his aunt's position and her daughter Mary's
place in the succession.[29] And Henry himself was more than happy to play the
bellicose card in return, threatening the Pope and the Emperor alike, if he could
not get what he wanted on the divorce through fair words and promises. In
January 1531 he visited the Tower of London to inspect the artillery there,
intending, it was said, to demonstrate both to his own subjects and to foreigners
that he was ready to defend himself against all comers.[30] In March 1531 the King
told Chapuys that the Pope could do what he liked, as he cared little about
excommunications, and, while he knew that the Emperor had the power to hurt
him, he doubted that Charles had the will to do so, and in any eventuality he was
able to defend himself and his kingdom.[31] In June he was once more telling
Chapuys that he would never consent to the Pope being judge in his divorce case,
and that he did not care a fig for his excommunications. Warming to his theme
on this occasion, he declared that if the Pope did act unjustly toward him over the
divorce, or do him any injury, he would retaliate, and with his brother and
perpetual ally the King of France, he would lead an army against Rome itself.[32]
Again, in December 1531 he told the Nuncio that he did not care about any
sentence of excommunication the Pope might issue, and in February 1532 he was
declaring that it would be no schism to separate from as venal and corrupt a
church as that of Rome.[33]

On 6 March 1532, the Earl of Wiltshire told a number of Members of
Parliament that he (and by implication the King) was prepared to maintain at
the risk of his life and property that no Pope or prelate could exercise jurisdiction,
promulgate laws, or enforce ordinances in England.[34] In July, Chapuys reported
that Henry himself had recently lost his temper in a most remarkable way over
the Pope's refusal to endorse his intention to marry Anne Boleyn, and had often
said in public that he would tolerate such treatment no longer. On 5 September,
when the Nuncio presented a demand that Henry send a mandate empowering
his agents in Rome to act for him in the courts, he flew into a passion, as he had at
other times, and warned that he would open the eyes of other princes, who were
not as learned as he was, to the extent of the papal usurpation of royal powers.[35]

Such threats, both public and private, were, of course, never realized. The
King had, in practice, little with which he could effectively pressurize the Pope or

Emperor militarily. But they did contribute to a bellicose atmosphere at court and in the capital. Rumours of invasion, or of war, frequently surfaced, and those with political, emotional, or economic ties to the Continent, clearly feared for the future.[36] Hence the appeal for peace contained in Gower's ballad and elsewhere in the 1532 *Chaucer*, addressed real contemporary anxieties in a way that cut across the bows of current royal policy. The injunctions for all Christian princes to unite in peace might then chime with one theme in Henry's public utterances (the sporadic call for unity against the Turks), but it, and still more the warning in Hoccleve's 'To the King...and...the Lords and Knights of the Garter' that the just man was one who never threatened more than he could perform, constituted more generally a far more fundamental call for moderation in the pursuit of the divorce campaign and the direction of foreign policy. Again, the selection of non-Chaucerian material in the *Works* seems designed to address a political agenda that was both very specifically pertinent to the circumstances of 1532, and rather more critical of the Crown than previous accounts have allowed.

The Completeness of the Complete Works: Reading Chaucer in 1532

In stressing the royal and noble addressees of Chaucer's 'Ballads', and in surrounding those texts with those of other writers, the appreciative readers and interpreters of his writings, what Thynne and Tuke were doing was reasserting—even inventing—a community of 'authentic' Chaucer readers, and reaffirming what Chaucer meant to that community. Hence they found room for texts such as the Scogan ballad with its deferential reference to Chaucer's authority, and its obvious provenance within the royal household. In so doing they presented a 'canonical' Chaucer who stood for certain agreed values, and an agreed series of cultural continuities: of faith, of that liberal, reforming catholicism that informed *The Canterbury Tales*, of an aesthetic and political inclusiveness: values that seemed suddenly and dramatically threatened by the events of 1529–32. Moreover, for Thynne and Tuke, as the Preface makes clear, the Chaucer canon represents a profusion of diverse materials, a 'compendiousness in narratioun' of 'doctrynes and sciences' that in itself spoke against the narrowness and exclusivity of the highly vocal evangelical polemicists.[37]

The 'monumentalized' *Chaucer* of 1532 also offered a history lesson to its readers, reinterpreting the period from 1380 to 1420 in a very different light to that currently on offer. At a time when, as we have seen, a number of fiercely anti-clerical, pseudo-Lollard texts in the *Piers Plowman* tradition from this period were being republished (some as Chaucer's own work) as contributions to contemporary debates, threatening to depict the Ricardian age as one character-ized by a deep suspicion of the established church and its doctrines, Thynne and Tuke's edition presented a Chaucer who stood for very different values. They offered a corrective to those vociferous revenants from the medieval past, not, as some scholars have claimed, an adjunct to them. The 1532 *Chaucer* thus co-opted the voices of Hoccleve, Gower, Usk and Scogan, and the anonymous authors of the 'Eight Goodly Questions' and the 'Prophecy' to supplement that of the poet himself, allowing the 'father' of English language and letters to chastise his errant successors in the name of moderation, peace, and social accommodation. Such texts as *The Lantern of Light* and William Thorpe's *Examination*, that were being printed in London and on the Continent at this time as the voice of a buried tradition of English radicalism, were thus tacitly redefined, not as the authentic testimony of Chaucer's contemporaries, but as aberrant texts, precisely the sort of divisive, rancorous, voices that the poet and his true allies had appealed to the King to still in the interests of quiet and prosperity.

Thynne and Tuke were, then, engaged in the opening skirmishes of a struggle over the implications of the Chaucerian legacy that would continue well into the next reign and beyond. In the late 1540s and early 1550s the attempt to claim the poet for the cause of radical reform would take on a new edge, as the 'common-wealth' reformers in the reign of the boy-king Edward VI sought to co-opt the poet, alongside William Langland and other writers of the 'Piers Plowman' tradition (themselves very much more radical than Langland's original text) into their ranks.[38] In the reign of Mary Tudor, 'England's Virgil' was just as determinedly reclaimed for orthodox catholicism. In 1556 the poet's tomb was physically relocated within Westminster Abbey, being moved from its modest position at the entrance to St Benedict's Chapel in the southwest of the aisle to a more central and prestigious position against the east wall of the south transept (where it would eventually form the nucleus of Poet's Corner in the nineteenth century). An arched marble canopy was erected over the new tomb by the antiquarian teller of the Exchequer, Nicholas Brigham, turning it into a fittingly impressive and lasting memorial to the 'English *vates*' (prophetic poet) as a newly commissioned inscription titled him.[39] Chaucer's tomb thus became a physical monument to both his glory and his significance to English literary culture, and at the same time a tacit declaration of his orthodox religious credentials. Not only was the poet taken, literally, from the margins and embraced in the heart of the nation's premier, and newly re-catholicized, ecclesiastical centre, a symbol of his re-adoption by the catholic state, but his tomb itself was presented as a potential shrine and place of literary pilgrimage in the making—a centre for worship for the cult of Geoffrey Chaucer.[40] One imagines that Thynne and Tuke would have approved.

But what it is important to note in the current context is, not so much the longevity of the struggle to identify and possess Chaucer's doctrinal significance that Thynne and Tuke began, but the precise resonances of that struggle in their edition. When Thynne and Tuke deployed the Chaucerian legacy in the interests of political action in 1532 they did so very clearly in the context of the traditional literature of counsel. They crafted their monumental edition as a mirror for Henry VIII and his counsellors, hoping through the persuasive strategies that it voiced to influence the King in the interests of political moderation. In so doing, as I have suggested, they were part of a wider campaign pursued by a number of scholars and civil servants in Henry's service in the early 1530s dedicated to bombarding their sovereign with a variety of forms of literary and dramatic counsel. This counsel aimed to reverse what its authors saw as the adverse consequences of his divorce campaign and the jurisdictional battles with Rome and the English ecclesiastical hierarchy that it provoked. Moreover, given the far more substantial involvement of Sir Brian Tuke in the edition than has previously been allowed, the 1532 *Chaucer* stands as a monument to the extent to which loyal and active government servants involved at the heart of that divorce campaign were prepared to use literature and all the resources at their disposal short of active disloyalty to argue for a change in royal policy.

As the chapters which follow will suggest, the sort of confidence in the literature of counsel that Thynne and Tuke's edition displays would not survive the shocks that the enforcement of Henry VIII's policies were to deliver to English literary and political culture in the later 1530s and 1540s. In this respect the 1532 *Chaucer* represents a monument, not only to the politicized, orthodox Chaucer that its editors constructed, but also to the wider literary culture of counsel and consent that had characterized the first two decades of Henrician rule.

6

Mocking the Thunder

Henry VIII, Jupiter, and John Heywood's Play of the Weather

A still more audacious example of the literature of counsel emerged from the presses of the printer William Rastell in the second half of 1533. John Heywood's 'new and . . . very merry interlude of all manner weathers',[1] now commonly known as *The Play of the Weather*, is a work that, like Thynne and Tuke's *Chaucer*, grew out of the culture of literary scholarship and debate within the Henrician Court. And, like Thynne and Tuke's text, it used literature for political purposes, presenting exemplary material directly to the King in the hope that it would influence his behaviour in the political arena. An examination of the play consequently has a good deal to tell us about the operation of literature (and specifically drama) in the political culture of the court; about the degree to which loyal counsel might be pushed in the direction of implied criticism, even mockery, of the King if carefully handled; and about the aspirations of those moderate scholars and courtiers who sought to limit the damage caused by the King's divorce, the break with Rome, and the Royal supremacy.

John Heywood

John Heywood was a man deeply enmeshed in the literary defence of religious moderation in the early years of Henry's Great Matter. His interludes reveal a consistently conservative position on religious doctrine and the authority of the church. Indeed, he was to be arrested and face execution in 1543 for allegedly denying the Royal Supremacy, and would end his days in exile on the Continent, having discreetly left the realm in 1564 to live under the more congenial catholic dispensation of the Spanish Netherlands. Yet he was also willing to take an Erasmian line on the reform of abuses within the church and his dramatic canon repeatedly calls for reconciliation between contending factions in the best interests of the commonwealth.[2] At times portraying religious controversies directly, at others alluding to them more obliquely through metaphorical disputes about the state of the weather or the nature of happiness in love, Heywood's plays collectively follow the same path as Thynne and Tuke's *Chaucer*, presenting a powerful vision of a realm riven by dissension and ill-will as a spur to the King to begin the pacification and harmonization of the commonweal.

As a royal household servant, musician, and maker of interludes, Heywood enjoyed considerable opportunity to produce and circulate musical and dramatic texts at the political centre as well as to publish work for a wider audience. His name first appears in court records in 1519, as a singer, and it recurs throughout the 1520s, recording receipt of a salary and other grants as a singer, a 'player of the virginals', and a 'Sewer' or waiter in the King's chamber. Thereafter in the 1530s he seems to have gravitated into the service of the King's marginalized daughter, Princess Mary, providing entertainment and perhaps performing other duties within her household. In his earliest extant interlude, *Witty and Witless*, which was probably written or revived for a performance before the King in 1533,[3] Heywood placed a strongly conservative account of Christian virtue in the mouth of a venerable figure of wisdom, a character pointedly named after the compiler of the vulgate Bible, Jerome. He also counselled Henry directly, wryly referring to the newly minted rhetoric of the Royal Supremacy, and calling for indifferent royal patronage for all his subjects, regardless of their position in contemporary controversies.

> Yf the glos of Gods schyne not bright eche way
> In them who having a realme in governall
> Set forthe theyre governans to Gods glory all,
> Charytably aydynge subjects in eche kynde,
> The schynyng of Gods gyfts wheer schall we then fynde?
>
> And of this hye sort the hy hed most excelent
> Ys owr most loved and drade supreme soferayne,
> The schynynge of whose most excellent talent
> Ymployde to Gods glory above all the trayne
> Syns wytt wantyth here recytall to retayne,
> And that all hys faythfull fele the frewte of hys fame.
> Of corse I pray pardon in passyng the same.
>
> (678–89)

This call for impartial treatment and the accommodation of difference ('Charytably aydyng subjects in eche kynde') was voiced in each of his subsequent interludes. In *The Pardoner and The Friar* (printed in 1533) he presented a dramatic analogue of the religious controversies of the early 1530s, as a ranting friar mouthing stock tags of evangelical reform contends with a corrupt pardoner vaunting the authority of his bulls from Rome over which of them should occupy the playing space. The result is the collapse of the parish community as the local priest and Neighbour Pratt, seeking to end the dispute, are routed in a stand-up fight. Against this model of disruptive contention, Heywood set the virtues of tolerance and an acceptance of the status quo. In *The Play of Love* (printed 1534), a four-handed dispute over who is happiest and unhappiest in love, debate is only resolved when each of the disputants accepts the merits of the others' cases and is prepared to compromise to gain a share in the final reconciliation. The same pattern recurs in *The Four P's*, in which a contest between a Pardoner, a Palmer, an Apothecary, and a Pedlar is ended only when each of them withdraws his claim for supremacy over the rest.

Each of these interludes, written and performed in or around the royal court and subsequently printed by William Rastell, sets out to address the problems of a commonwealth divided by dissension and threatening to slide into chaos. At a time in the early 1530s when England, as we have seen, was experiencing an unprecedented assault upon the rights and authority of the Church, and disputes between evangelicals and conservatives were dividing Parliament and court alike, they had an obvious contemporary relevance. The solution which Heywood offered—the need to compromise and tolerate difference—might appear commonplace and anodyne, a retreat into idealism in the face of the pressing problems of real political strife. Indeed, even sympathetic critics have tended to see Heywood as an idealist, a rare voice of moderation and compromise inevitably drowned out by the shrill demands of confessional partisanship. But this is to read the plays out of context. In the circumstances of the early 1530s, at a time when reformers in parliament and council were seemingly in the ascendancy, and those, like Thomas More and bishop Stephen Gardiner who stood out directly against change had been effectively side-lined, the demand for reconciliation was itself a shrewd political tactic, an attempt to continue the defence of orthodoxy by other means.

Throughout this period the King's professed position was that of mediator between the contending parties; the concerned monarch anxious to root out dissension and restore good order to the commonweal. He had posed as an impartial judge between the contending Commons and spiritual peers during the opening session of the Reformation Parliament in 1529.[4] Official pronouncements proclaimed the King's desire for quietness and stability. There was, then, good cause for Heywood to assume that appeals to Henry couched in the language of moderation and accommodation might find a ready ear. But his plays do more than simply echo royal rhetoric concerning the need to impose an end to contentious disputes. Seizing the licence afforded the good counsellor, he offered the King clear advice on how to use his power once he has intervened. Implicit in *The Play of the Weather* and explicit in *The Four P's* is a plea for the church to be left alone to bring about the reforms which all sides in the debates accepted were needed.[5] In each play it is necessary to impose an end to disputation from the outside. But it is also notable that the external authority, having brought about a reconciliation, determines to leave the situation much as it was before the dispute began. In *Weather*, as we shall see, Jupiter takes it upon himself to reward each of his suitors according to their deserts. But as each is now equally determined to conduct him or herself in the best interests of the commonweal, it is clear that no drastic alteration of the *status quo* will be necessary. And in *The Four PP* no sooner has the Palmer gained 'lordship' over the other characters but he hands it back, paving the way for the Pedlar's exhortation that no one should take it upon themselves to reform ecclesiastical abuses. Thus Heywood gives the court a positive analogue for the role of the King in settling religious debate, but he makes it abundantly clear that, having suppressed the disorder, Henry would be best advised to leave things as they stand. For the playwright the Royal Supremacy should lead to reformation from within not without.

The plea for moderation and accommodation voiced in the drama was continued in Heywood's poetry; albeit he was not averse occasionally to adopting a more assertive stance. His most obviously conservative gesture was a poem in praise of Princess Mary, 'Give Place Ye Ladies' written in 1534, which elevated its subject above all the other women of the court.

> Geve place, ye ladyes, all bee gone,
>   Showe not your selves at all.
> For whye?, beholde, there cumeth one
>   Whose face yours all blanke shall.
>
> (lines 1–4)[6]

To produce such a text at the time when Mary was being deprived of her royal title and the Henrician court was re-forming around the new queen, Anne Boleyn, gave the claims for Mary's timeless beauty and virtue a powerful political charge. In such circumstances the claim that 'She doth as farre exceade / These women nowadayes, / As doth the flowre the weede' (lines 65–7) could not help but be read as tacit criticism of Queen Anne and her circle. But the bulk of Heywood's courtly verse adopted a less confrontational tone. The spirit of contentment and recon-ciliation which dominates the interludes also characterizes many of the lyrics. In 'Man, for Thine ill Life Formerly',[7] for example, the speaker commends just such a humble attitude to adversity as was advocated in *The Four P's*.

> And yf thy foes delyghtfully
> Show yll for good most spightfullye,
> Show good for yll most wyllynglye,
> To showe Godes woord fulfyllynglye.
>
> (lines 17–20)

'Be Merry, Friends',[8] provides a protracted defence and justification of the strategy of contentment with one's lot.

> In suche thynges as wee can not flee,
> But neades they must abydden bee,
> Let contentashyn be decree,
> Make vertue of necessytee,
>   Be merye, frendes.
>
> (lines 46–50)

'Gar Call Him Down',[9] condemns slander and detraction and strongly appeals to readers not to judge others in case they be judged themselves; a theme taken up

again in 'Bear no Malice to no Wight [person] Human'.[10] The latter calls for a
genuine reconciliation between enemies on both theological and purely pragmatic grounds,

> Whoever thow hate is good or yll.
>   Yf he be good, hate showth the[e] nowght.
> Yf he be yll, and yll shalbe styll,
>   Wherby at end he hath so wrowght
> That to damnacion he be browght,
>   Then charity showth much more reson
> To pitye hys payne, than malynge hys p[e]rson.
>
> Man, yf thow mynd heven to obtayne,
> Bere no males to no wyght humayne.
>
> If he be nowght to whom thow art fooe,
>   And shall here after so amend
> That he be savid, and thow allso,
>   Then shall he love the[e], tyme without end.
> Then why showldes thow thys tyme pretend
>   In mallys towardes him to persever.
>
> Man, yf thow mynd . . . [etc.]

> (lines 3–18)

The most explicit, and probably the most aesthetically satisfying of his accommodating ballads is, however, the semi-autobiographical 'Long Have I Been a
Singing Man', with its eloquent metaphorical defence of the *via media* in all
aspects of life.[11]

> The base and the treble are extrems,
> The tenor standyth sturdely,
> The Cownter rangyth: then, me sems,
> The mene must make our melodye,
> Wherby the mene declareth well
> Above all partes most to excell.
>
> Mark well the maner of the mene,
> And therby tyme and tune our songe,
> Unto the mene, where all partes lene,
> All partes ar kept from syngyng wrong.
> Thowghe syngyng men take this not well
> Yet doth the mene in thys excell.

> (lines 7–18)

Finally, Heywood returned to the theme in his extended allegory of religious
factionalism, *The Spider and the Fly*, published in 1556 but begun, on the

author's own testimony, *c.* 1536. Here he reverted to the familiar strategy of having order imposed upon a disputatious and divided commonwealth (in this case of insects) by an external authority, this time his own employer, the future Queen Mary, figured as the cleaning maid with the proverbial new broom (which the author assures his readers is 'not sword of rigor, / But the branche of mercie'). 'Mysorder', the Maid tells the chastised spiders and flies:

> . . . bringing you thus confused,
> Let order, by your leaving of mysorder,
> Quietnesse on your sides and all sides forder.
>
> By order (from misorder) you to redeeme,
> (From sorowes of all sorts to solace so sorted)
> Is cause of my cuming. Not by meanes extreeme,
> But by most milde meanes: that maie be imported
> In order to set you, and see you comforted
> To kepe order wherin you obeying mee,
> We may live in love all eche in his degree.[12]

Such was also the spirit that had animated the most explicitly critical of Heywood's dramatic mirrors for Henry VIII, *The Play of the Weather*.

The Play of the Weather in Context

Scholars have long suspected that Heywood's ostensibly playful and inconsequential interlude, based upon a minor dialogue of the second-century Syrian satirist, Lucian, actually reflects some of the most contentious events of the period from the fall of Cardinal Wolsey to Henry VIII's adoption of the title of Supreme Head of the Church in England. The play it is now agreed, was almost certainly performed at court around Eastertide 1533,[13] and so presented its 'mery' account of the court and person of Jupiter, king of the gods, a supreme royal figure who had clear associations with Henry VIII,[14] to the King and his court at the precise moment when Henry's royal ambitions were seemingly at their peak and his assertions of jurisdictional omnicompetence in both secular and ecclesiastical politics at their most vehement and contentious.[15] *Weather* may well thus have been, as Richard Axton and Peter Happé suggest, Heywood's 'most politically audacious' interlude;[16] for, as we shall see, it subjects the King, through his divine classical analogue Jupiter, to deflating irony and wit in an Erasmian, 'Lucianic', attempt to laugh him out of folly and counsel caution in his use of his new-found Supreme authority.[17]

Another courtier-poet, Sir Thomas Wyatt, was, as we shall see in a later chapter, to hit upon an aptly Jovial meteorological metaphor for the extreme perils of life close to the seat of power in Henry's court, borrowing the tag '*circa regna tonat*' ('He thunders around thrones') from Seneca's *Phaedra*.[18] But, in crafting *The Play of the Weather*, Heywood seems to have been oblivious to the threat of thunderbolts from a King notoriously protective of his royal prerogative and honour. How and why this might have been so tells us a good deal about the licence afforded to the dramatic counsellor, about Heywood's own position at court, and about the moment at which he was writing. But, in order to appreciate the full significance of his most daring act of counsel, it is necessary briefly to consider the ways in which the play—in which Jupiter enters the playing space announcing his adoption of new and far-reaching powers over the weather, and then settles down to receive petitions from his earthly subjects concerning how best to exercise them—alludes to the political and religious contexts in which it was written.

Jupiter's account, in his opening speech, of a parliament in heaven 'late assembled by comen assent / For the redres of certayn enormytees' (24–5) strongly suggests an allusion to the Reformation Parliament,[19] which Lord Chancellor Sir Thomas More, standing at the right hand of the king, had opened with an account of the need to reform both the 'very insufficient and imperfect' old laws and the 'diverse new enormities . . . sprung amongst the people, for the which no law was yet made to reform the same . . . ' Rather than settling down to peaceful debate as instructed, however, the assembly had quickly degenerated, as I suggested in Chapter Three, into fractious disputes between the clergy and laity which contributed in no small part to the 'common frenzy' of division that broke out in the realm thereafter.[20]

There may be direct allusions to prominent contemporary individuals in Jupiter's account of the four 'weather gods', Saturn, Phebus, Eolus, and Phoebe and their dispute in the Olympian parliament.[21] But there is also a more general resonance to these lines with their sense of a pervasive turbulence in a trouble-some parliament, and in a wider realm divided between hostile social classes. This fraught social situation is explored further by Heywood through those representative estates figures who voice their self-interested and mutually contra-dictory petitions in the remainder of his interlude.[22] And beyond the possibly specific allusions, the play is rooted more generally in contemporary English culture and events, revealing in particular an abiding interest in the textures and material culture of life in the royal household, an interest reflected most obvi-ously of all in the figure of Mery Report, the play's central comic character and most striking creation. He is the mouthpiece for a variety of perhaps genuine concerns as well as a good deal of in-house humour concerning the staff and protocols of the English royal household with which Heywood was intimately familiar.

In Mery Report, as I have argued elsewhere, Heywood offers a representation of contemporary worries concerning the unruly court 'hanger-on' as a source of both social and sexual misrule.[23] The character, identified on the title-page of the printed text as 'the Vice', oversteps the accepted protocols of courtly behaviour in both the political and moral spheres, treating Jupiter with an informality border-ing on disrespect, and subjecting the suitors to his court with a mixture of social and sexual harassment, bawdy wordplay, and abuse. Such behaviour seems, in part at least, to draw its energy from an ongoing concern among legislators and pedagogues alike with the inappropriate and unruly conduct of certain suspect social groups at court (generally grouped together under the categories of 'rascals', 'vagabonds', or 'boys'); a concern that permeated the courtly conduct books and surfaced from time to time in prohibitive ordinances and legislation.[24]

There is probably also an element of criticism here of those household officers and royal companions—most obviously the Yeomen Ushers of the Chamber, whose job it was to guard the Chamber doors and ensure that no undesirable persons were allowed access, and the Gentlemen of the Privy Chamber, the newest and most intimate of household offices, who gained authority and influence from their proximity to the King, and who were appointed directly by the sovereign according to his whim or personal preference, so by-passing the normal channels of patronage and recommendation.[25]

If, as seems likely, Heywood himself played the part of Mery Report, leading a cast otherwise made up largely, or even exclusively, of boy actors drawn from among the choristers of the Chapel Royal or St Paul's,[26] then the potential ironies and inversions of role and expectation involved in the performance would have been all the more rich and various, and the potential mockery of the King implicit in the play all the more obvious. Jupiter, as he is presented in the text of the interlude, is a magisterial figure, certainly, but in a humorous, ironic vein rather than a straightforwardly portentous one. The printed text is unequivo-cal—if somewhat bathetic—in its description of the character as 'Jupiter, a god', but this is of little help in describing the nature and impact of the role. The question arises, what did contemporary audiences, who did not have the benefit of this explicatory list of *dramatis personae* before them, *see* when they looked at this Jupiter, and (perhaps more importantly in a culture that habitually spoke of going to *hear* a play) what did they hear from him when he spoke?

The visual impact of the figure raises some interesting possibilities. As Axton and Happé suggest, the actor may well have worn a golden mask and crown, as those playing the god-king at John's College, Cambridge did in the 1540s.[27] Such props would have acted as markers of royalty and dignified otherness, and would have associated the character with the iconographic tradition behind representations of God the Father and the risen Christ in the religious drama, where gilded faces and masks were also used. But, if, as has been suggested, Jupiter was played here by a child-actor (of whatever age), then much if not all of the potential dignity and grandeur of the role would have been compromised in performance. What audiences would have seen was not maturity and authority but youth and physical limitation: all the more so given that the majority of the god-king's scenes place him alongside Mery Report, probably played, as we have seen, by Heywood himself, a man who seems to have been tall, even by adult standards.[28] The king who claimed supreme power for himself would thus have seemed comically ill-suited to exercise it in the vast majority of the scenes in which he appears.

Much of the impact of the two central performances, Jupiter and Mery Report, would have relied upon the precise degree of the actors' submergence in their roles, and the extent to which they allowed themselves temporarily to re-emerge from them for comic effect. In a case such as Heywood's, where the identity and 'character' of the actor is as well (or better) known to the audience than the role he portrays; specific lines, even whole scenes, might take on a special resonance precisely because it is Heywood that is playing the role. Because many of the members of a courtly audience would have had some familiarity with him, with his offstage roles as a court body-servant and musician, and perhaps even with his life history and opinions, the potential for extra-textual meanings, unscripted asides, gestures, and 'in-jokes' of all kinds was considerable. Such interactive performative effects are very difficult to reconstruct from the bare record of the written text. Much of the comic dynamic of Mery Report's relationship with Jupiter, would, of course, have depended upon the fact that Heywood, the author of the interlude and 'master' of his troupe of schoolboy players, took the servant's role and one of his pupils the god's. The onstage relationship between the two would thus have been the exact reverse of that suggested by the written dialogue alone (or at least it would when the actors chose to make it so). Rather than an all-powerful god-king and a powerless (if mischievous) servant, the spectators would have seen an adult comedian and his juvenile 'feed' or straight-man. Words, phrases, and actions that seem entirely innocuous on paper might thus acquire significant comic or dramatic potential when accompanied by particular facial expressions or gestures. When, for example, Jupiter referred to his servant as 'son' (which he does five times in the course of the interlude), the incongruity of the child-actor speaking the word to his adult master would give rise to significant comic potential. Indeed there seems to have been a running joke on the theme, probably marked by double-takes and other business. Hence also the conscious harping upon distinctions of height and age in the play (little Dick, the Boy—specifically referred to on two occasions as 'the le[a]st [i.e. shortest] that can play'—refers to Jupiter as his 'godfather', and puns on 'greatness', height, and his 'unmissable' shape (1000–1005) with Mery Report at various points). Such banter would serve further to widen the disjunction between human actor and divine role, character and performance, an aspect of the play that Heywood developed, not simply for comic effect but to make a wholly more serious point about the dangers implicit in Henry's own piece of super-human role-playing, the claim to Supreme authority.[29]

As Axton and Happé suggest, the idea of Mery Report emerging from the audience to take a role in the play seems to borrow from another interlude, Henry Medwall's *Fulgens and Lucres*, in which two characters referred to only as 'A' and 'B' step from among the spectators to volunteer as servants to the protagonists, with somewhat alarming consequences.[30] And, as I have argued elsewhere, the opening exchanges between Mery Report and Jupiter also seem consciously to echo those in another, more recent drama, John Skelton's *Magny-fycence* (probably performed at court in 1519), in which another representation of Henry VIII, the eponymous Prince Magnyfycence, confronts his Vice-like minion Fansy.[31] In accepting Mery Report into his service, Jupiter thus seems to be revealing his own immaturity and folly; committing the cardinal sin of the prince in the Morality tradition by inviting into his confidence a Vice figure with no concern for either justice or protocol, whose sole aim is to follow his own inclinations. Indeed, in his lengthy speech of self-justification, Mery Report tacitly puns on the senses of disinterested and *un*interested, claiming that his fitness for appointment as a royal herald is evident most obviously in his capacity to be 'indyfferent' and 'wythout affecyon' (154–5) towards any of the petitions that are likely to arise.

> Son lyght, mone lyght, ster lyght, twy lyght, torch light,
> Cold, hete, moyst, drye, hayle, rayne, frost, snow, lightnyng, thunder,
> Cloudy, mysty, wyndy, fayre, fowle, above hed or under,
> Temperate or dystemperate—what ever yt be,
> I promyse your lordshyp all is one to me.
>
> (156–60)

Thus the carelessness and irresponsibility of the Vice are misleadingly repre-sented as the impartiality of the good counsellor and the honesty of the loyal servant. But the appointment of a rogue to a position of influence at court, a move that in Skelton's play proved a recipe for political catastrophe and personal ruin, is in Heywood's interlude merely the cue for a series of comic vignettes, suggesting a comedy of manners rather than a political satire. Jupiter's negligence provokes no catastrophe. The state does not totter, even a little, and everything turns out well in the end, with Jupiter being able to please everyone—seemingly all of the time—without ever exercising his new-found powers. This is possible, Heywood suggests, because inaction is the wisest response; nothing is funda-mentally wrong in the world of the play. The petitions of Jupiter's subjects do not identify real injustices, they are merely self-interested pleas for advancement, attempts to unsettle a stable polity in the pursuit of personal comfort or prosperity. Hence the best solution is simply to ignore each of the requests while seeming to listen to them all; a policy that the self-centred and solipsistic Jupiter is ideally suited to perform. Heywood flatters Henry and his courtly audience with a drama that represents a state secure in its fundamentals; the only threat to which comes from the partisan motives of the citizenry beyond its doors; a situation that seems inescapably to allude to the 'common frenzy' of dissension currently troubling English society.

Heywood's interlude is thus 'Lucianic' not only in its comic spirit and inspiration but also in its outcome and political ethos. For, as Robert Bracht Branham puts it, the dialogues of the Roman satirist themselves ultimately 'evoke a static mythical world at once strange and familiar; rather than tell a story...

[e]ach conversation coheres as a unit . . . with a beginning, a middle, and an end, which, far from surprising us with a punch line or unexpected . . . ending, usually serves to return us to the beginning'.[32] In this aspect of the dialogues Heywood found a usefully flexible, serio-comic, approach to parody and satire, imitation of which allowed him to tilt at serious targets playfully—the feature which arguably commended Lucian most obviously to Erasmus and More in the heyday of humanist reform in the first decades of the century.[33] But in Lucian, Heywood also found an ultimately conservative ethos, and a wry but essentially tolerant attitude to the absurdities of the *status quo*, that equally suited his own agenda in the very different circumstances of the period 1529–33.

Under the licence provided by the Lucianic spirit, Heywood is able to make extremely daring jokes about some of the most contentious issues of the moment. The scenes between Mery Report, Jupiter, and the Gentlewoman, for example, seem to contain a series of in-jokes concerning Anne Boleyn, her pregnancy, and Henry's willingness or otherwise to marry her. (He had already discreetly done so in January 1533, a fact that was probably an open secret in inner-court circles by March.)[34] Henry's desire to keep his marriage secret, and the likelihood of Anne's pregnancy, may well be alluded to in the exchanges between the god-king and his squire:

MERY REPORT   And yf yt be your pleasure to mary
              Speke quyckly, for she [the Gentylwoman] may not tary.
              In fayth I thynke ye may wynne her anone,
              For she wolde speke wyth your lordshyp alone.
JUPITER   Sonne, that is not the thynge at this tyme ment.

                                                        (782–6)

The Gentlewoman scenes may also draw upon another source, this time a literary one: Leon Battista Alberti's *Virtus* (1494), one of his *Intercenales* or 'Dinner Pieces'. This dialogue between Mercury and Virtue was itself a conscious imitation of the Lucianic style and mode, and was even printed among Lucian's works in Italy in 1525. In it Virtue waits at Jupiter's door in the hope of an audience in which she can complain about her ill-treatment at the hands of Fortune. She is, however, put off with ever more trivial excuses, being told, for example, that all the gods are busy checking that butterflies have correctly painted wings, or that gourds are flowering in the proper way. Thus she appeals to Mercury to intercede with the father of the gods on her behalf. He, having listened to her suit, chooses not to intervene, however, and advises her instead to lay low until Fortune's hostility subsides: another 'merry' and politically quiescent 'solution' to a problem. The dialogue was the inspiration for two works by the Ferrarese painter Dosso Dossi, both given the modern titles *Jupiter, Mercury, and Virtue*, one, a painting of *c.* 1524 now in the Kunsthistorisches Museum in Vienna, the other a fresco in the Sala del Camin Nero in the Castello del Buonconsiglio, in Trent.[35] Thus, if the Gentlewoman evoked echoes of Alberti's *Virtue* as well as of Henry's

Anne, this may well have helped to mitigate some of the potential controversy that the scene might otherwise have aroused.

Certainly Heywood shows no sign of having caught a tiger by the tail, despite what may be quite bawdy references to the prospect of the King's change of wives, figured as the fashioning of a new moon to replace an old, unattractive one that had worn out its welcome.

> For olde moones be leak[y], they can holde no water.
> But for this new mone, I durst laye my gowne,
> Excepte a few droppes at her goyng downe,
> Ye get no rayne tyll her arysynge . . .
>
> (799–802)

> This new moon shal make a thing spryng more in this while
> Then a[n] old moone shal while a man may go a mile.
> By that tyme the god hath all made an ende
> Ye shall se how the wether wyll amende.
> By saynt Anne, he goth to worke even boldely!
>
> (808–12)

How was it that he felt able to treat such subjects in so open—and so openly comic—a fashion in a courtly play? A number of cultural traditions provided the playwright with the licence to play with royal (and divine) authority in the ways that Mery Report contrives to do. The notion of good counsel that had motivated Thynne and Tuke was obviously central. But Heywood also enjoyed other privileges. The principle that drama in particular could provide a moral mirror in which princes might view both good and bad examples and judge their own behaviour by analogy, was another medieval idea that had gained added impetus from humanist educational theory, offering opportunities for the playwright to couch political advice and personal criticism in improving, moral terms. As Thomas Elyot observed in *The Book Named the Governor*, 'interludes in English' were, like sermons, public works in which 'some vice is declared', albeit only to teach their audiences to reject it and to receive wise counsel. 'By comedies', he concluded, 'good counsel is ministered'.[36] The classical sources from which the play borrowed its plot and much of its ethos; chiefly Lucian's dialogues, with their tradition of treating serious matters *sub specie lusus* ('in the guise of a game'),[37] and the comic dramatic tradition of Plautus and Terence, in which mischievous servants play (over-)familiarly with their less street-wise masters,[38] similarly gave Heywood licence both to portray Jupiter in a comic mode and to touch on some sensitive contemporary cultural nerves. But awareness of these traditions does not quite prepare one for the degree of audacity with which the playwright deploys his material in presenting the character of Jupiter, most obviously in that long speech of self-justification which opens the play, to which I will turn later in this chapter, before returning to the question of Heywood's motivation at the end.

Heywood's Jupiter and the Rhetoric of Supremacy

The crucial aspect of Jupiter as a literary and iconographic figure—the factor that arguably commended him to Lucian as well as to humanists like Erasmus and Heywood—was that he was profoundly, indeed fundamentally, ambivalent. He was a god with many attributes, many roles and embodiments, and a complex and deeply ambivalent personal—not to say sexual—history. For every story that revealed the god-king's wisdom and benevolence there was another that betrayed his self-interest, lust, or manipulative nature. He was, as Frances van Keuren has recently suggested, a symbol of both potent personal authority and of magisterial, even profligate male sexuality, 'the ever-potent father of countless gods and mortals, most of whom were conceived outside the . . . marriage bed'.[39] He was a father and ruler, but also an adulterer, a rapist, and a paedophile (hardly the sort of figure to sit easily with Henry VIII's current assertions of the impeccable moral reasons behind his need to be released from his marriage to Katherine of Aragon). Even his control over the weather, the aspect of his authority that is the focus of attention in Heywood's play, was a site of deep contradiction, for his use of that power was, as readers of Ovid's *Metamorphoses* would have known, all too often capricious, self-interested, and intimately bound up with his own libidinous agenda, as when, in Ovid's first book, he gathered clouds and darkness to inhibit the flight of the nymph Io and to cover his sexual assault upon her.

Hence any representation of Jupiter, and any statement about him, carried a potential for double meaning. He was a text that always already carried its own parodic subtext around with it. Even the brief account of his own adoption of supreme power offered in the opening lines of Heywood's interlude alluded to a contested mythological narrative, a story in which Jupiter was potentially either a conquering hero or a usurping tyrant, depending upon one's viewpoint. While the dominant tradition saw Jupiter's conquest of his father Saturn as instigating the Age of Reason, a period of justice and plenty as noble in its own way as the preceding Golden Age, a rival tradition interpreted it as doing precisely the reverse. In the *Epitomes* of the third century Christian euhemerist Lactantius, the Golden Age of Saturn was interpreted, following the inspiration of Hesiod, as the prelapsarian Age of monotheism, equality, universal peace and morality; a period brought to an end by Jupiter's usurpation and his establishment of a cult in his own honour. What followed was the fallen Age of Jupiter, the time of men, of division, of the seasons, and hence, significantly for our purposes, of variations in the weather. In this model, then, the original sin was the pride of the divine monarch himself rather than that of his mortal subjects.[40] Hence, when Heywood's Jupiter reminds the audience of his relationship to his 'auncyent' father, Saturn, he was drawing their attention to a story with more than one possible moral. And Heywood exploited such ambiguities to the full before an educated audience that was well equipped to appreciate them.

Again, for those schooled in the traditions and history of ancient Rome, the representation of Jupiter was in itself rich with implicit ironies, frequently undercutting claims to omnipotence and pomposity. For, in the central Roman ceremony of the triumph, the honourand enacted just such an impersonation of Jupiter as Heywood's interlude involves, even down to the use of face-paint. On the day of the triumph, the *triumphator* was driven in a two-wheeled chariot—the *currus triumphalis*—to the temple of Jupiter Capitolinis, where he would achieve his apotheosis and make his sacrifice to the *optimus maximus*. He did so clad in the *ornatus Jovis*: the embroidered purple toga and tunic that were—depending upon which source one follows—either those that normally adorned the central statue of the god himself, or replicas of those garments. Carrying in his left hand a laurel branch and in his right a sceptre crowned with an eagle, Jove's bird, the *triumphator* appeared transfigured, his hands and face covered with the pungent red pigment cinnabar (another borrowing from representations of the god, redolent of his adopted otherness and divinity), while above his head (which already bore a laurel coronet) a slave held the heavy golden *corona Etrusca* (again, perhaps, taken from the statue of Jupiter Capitoline itself). But, famously, as he neared his apotheosis, that same slave (a role with more than a passing resemblance to that played by Mery Report in the interlude) would repeat in his ear the deflating words '*Respice post te, hominem te esse memento*': 'Think of what follows; remember that you are [only] a man', as an antidote to over-weaning pride. To play Jupiter was, then, even for the victorious Roman commander in his pomp, also to be reminded of how far short of divinity a human actor really was.[41]

If the visual presentation of Jupiter in Heywood's play suggests implied comic distinctions between role and performance, however, the aural element—the words he speaks—most obviously in his opening speech, create still more potent ironic effects. There is an interesting, and potentially paradoxical tension in that speech between the god's eternal and immutable aspirations and the merely temporal and contingent nature of the events and powers he describes. That he is, as he claims, 'Beyond the compas of all comparyson' (9), and has possessed a matchless glory since his father's fall in 'auncyent' times, sits awkwardly against the stress upon the present moment ('at this season' and 'for tyme present') as the zenith of his powers:

> For syns that heven and erth were fyrste create
> Stode we never in suche tryumphaunt estate
>
> As we now do . . .
>
> (13–15)

Jupiter's 'auncyent estate' seems to have been crafted suspiciously recently. Or perhaps it, like Henry VIII's Royal Supremacy, is an 'ancient' jurisdiction that has only recently been 'rediscovered', having been there all along, unnoticed and un-thought-of, until its (re)assertion by a 'parliament . . . late assembled'.[42]

The speech begins with an extended *occupatio* that effectively casts doubt upon the supposedly self-evident nature of the truth it seeks to establish.

> Ryght farre to[o] long as now were to recyte
> The auncyent estate wherin our selfe hath reyned,
> What honour, what laude, gyven us of very ryght,
> What glory we have had dewly unfayned
> Of eche creature whych dewty hath constrayned ...
>
> (1–5)

> If we so have ben as treuth yt is in dede
> Beyond the compas of all comparyson,
> Who coulde presume to shew for any mede
> So that yt myght appere to humayne reason
> The hye renowme we stande in at this season?
> For syns that heven and erth were fyrste create
> Stode we never in suche triumphaunt estate
>
> As we now do, wherof we woll reporte
> Suche parte as we se mete for tyme present,
> Chyefely concernynge your perpetuall conforte
> As the thynge [it]selfe shall prove in experyment,
> Whyche hyely shall bynde you on knees lowly bent
> Soolly to honour oure hyenes[s] day by day.
> And now to the mater gyve eare and we shall say.
>
> (8–21)

The assertive digressions and qualifications ('If we so have ben ...', 'As the thynge [it]selfe shall prove ...') that qualify rather than assert the points being made; the insistence upon the need to demonstrate and verify those claims ('So that yt might appere to humayne reason' (11), 'As the thynge [it] selfe shall prove in experyment' (18)), coupled with the repeated assertion that such things are beyond merely mortal comprehension, all add up to a speech that ultimately registers self-contradiction and inadequacy rather than omnipotence. While the final determination to return to the point ('And now to the mater gyve eare and we shall say ...' (21)), merely points up the digressive, indirect nature of what has gone before.

The language of consent and consensus dominates Jupiter's account of his supremacy ('They have in conclusyon holly surrendryd / Into our handes ... / The full of theyr powrs for terme everlastynge' (71–4)—a surrender 'as of our parte, no parte requyred / But of all theyr partys ryght humbly desyred' (76–7)). But despite this, and despite his talk of the tranquillity and comfort that his regime will bring to all, this is not one of those long opening speeches that in the mouth of God the Father in the religious Cycle plays or virtues such as Mercy in the Moralities would call for understatement and a calm, measured delivery. Such speeches, helpfully described by Alexandra Johnston as part of a stagecraft of stillness, are central to the essentially Augustinian moral and theological economies of the overtly Christian drama, in which the calm, wholeness, and stasis of virtue are set against a fragmented prosody and the frenetically *active* dramaturgy of evil.[43] But the cadences of Jupiter's speech are not those of scripture or moral treatises, and the vocabulary avoids the heavily Latinate terms of Mercy's invocation of the presiding values of *Mankind*. Jupiter's speech echoes rather (as I shall suggest more fully in a moment) the assertive, repetitive tones and convoluted syntax of Henrician statute and proclamations. And it does so in ways that seem to subvert the authoritative resonances of that language rather than reinforce them. The speech calls, not for the understated, self-effacing delivery of a Mercy, who subordinates 'character' to the dictates of regular meter and syntax, letting the verse itself speak the moral, but a far more proactive, performative delivery, alive to the many potential ironies in the lines. The syntax itself, the enjambment of lines and over-run stanza breaks, the insistent rhymes, and the very distinctively Heywoodian delight in puns (note the neat play on 'high' and 'low' in the god's claim that his justice 'hyely shall bynde you on knees lowly bent' (19)) and repetitions ('Whyche thynge, as of our *parte*, no *parte* requyred / But of all theyr *partys* ryght humbly desyred' (76–7)), turning a single word over and over on the tongue until every possible flavour, sense, and nuance has been explored—all these suggest a self-conscious cleverness and a delight in language for its own sake that distract attention from what is being said to *how* it is being said, by whom, and for what effect. This is a speech of potentially self-entangling persuasiveness rather than of calm authority, a vaunting that has reminded some critics of the ineffectual boasting of the tyrants of the mystery plays: Pilate or the York Herod, who bathetically talks of both felled giants and slaughtered swans in the same breath. Such speeches, of course, serve to problematize the very authority they assert.[44]

But Jupiter does not rant and threaten in the manner of Herod, Pilate, or the other tyrants of the religious drama. As Stephen May pointed out, what distinguishes tyrants from good kings in such plays tends to be, not *whether* they threaten but *whom* they threaten. Tyrants rage against Christians whereas good kings menace pagans and the enemies of Christ.[45] But, beyond that passing reference to his commanding a loyalty from his subjects that 'shall bynde you on knees lowly bent' (19), Jupiter threatens no one. He thus seems neither very tyrannical nor truly very 'good'. What Jupiter does is talk at length, with considerable pomposity and a degree of self-deflating contradiction about his superiority to his fellow gods, his wisdom, and his powers.

> And also that we, evermore beynge,
> Besyde our puysaunt power of deite,
> Of wysedome and nature so noble and fre —
> From all exremytees the meane devydynge,

To pease and plente eche thynge attemperynge —

They have in conclusion holly surrendered . . .
(66–71ff)

The convoluted syntax, the enjambment-ridden lines, the repeated deferral of the completion of the main clause by the accumulation of repeated variations on a given theme, all of these traits are characteristic, not of the blustering tyrants of the Cycle plays, but of Henrician statute and formal declaration. The terms of Jupiter's speech betray Heywood's acute ear for the cadences and tropes of Henrician public utterances, the same sensitivity to the language and tones of formal situations and specific groups and communities that informed his earlier interludes, furnishing the legal pastiches of the *Play of Love* and the confessional polemic in *The Pardoner and The Friar*. Perhaps there is even a direct echo of the Act of Appeals (1533) itself here, the founding document of Henrician 'imperial' authority and independence from Rome, which, beyond its famously sonorous opening declaration, enacts just such a piling-up of syntactically tortuous, sense-deferring clauses in search of a full-stop, and the gathering together of at times near synonymous words and phrases without the drawing of any obvious distinctions between them. Extensive quotation from the first paragraph of the Act (in reality a single extended and seemingly infinitely extendable sentence) will both give a sense of the text as a whole that takes one beyond the apparent succinctness of the endlessly quoted opening clause, and indicate the habitual modes of Henrician statute more generally.

Where by diverse sundry old authentic histories and chronicles it is manifestly declared and expressed that this realm of England is an Empire, and so hath been and accepted in the world, governed by one supreme head and king having the dignity and royal estate of the imperial crown of the same, unto whom a body politic, compact of all sorts and degrees of people, divided in terms and by names of spirituality and temporality, be bounden and owen to bear next to God a natural and humble obedience; he being also institute and furnished by the goodness and sufferance of Almighty God with plenary, whole, and entire power, pre-eminence, authority, prerogative, and jurisdiction to render and yield justice and final determination to all manner of folk residents or subjects within this realm, in all causes, matters, debates, and contentions, happening to occur, insurge, or begin within the limits thereof, without restraint or provocation to any foreign princes or potentates of the world, the body spiritual having power when any cause of the law divine happened to come in question or of spiritual learning, then it was declared, interpreted, and showed by that part of the said body politic, called the spirituality, now being usually called the English Church, which always hath been reputed and also found of that sort that both for knowledge, integrity, and sufficiency of number, it hath always been thought and is also at this hour sufficient and meet of itself, without the intermeddling of any exterior person or persons, to declare and determine all such doubts and to administer all such offices and duties as to their room spiritual doth appertain; for the due administration whereof and to keep them from corruption and sinister affection the king's most noble progenitors, and the antecessors of the nobles of this realm, have sufficiently endowed the said Church both with honours and possessions: and the laws temporal for trial of propriety of lands and goods, and for the conservation of the people of this realm in unity and peace without ravin or spoil, was and yet is administered, adjudged, and executed, by sundry judges and administrators of the other part of the said body politic called the temporality, and both their authorities and jurisdictions, do conjoin together in the due administration of justice, the one to help the other...[46]

More closely analogous still, within a year of the likely date for the perform-ance of *Weather*, the Act of Parliament that formally recognized Henry as Supreme Head of the Church in England was to make a very similar claim to that advanced in Jupiter's speech, announcing, with seemingly unconscious irony, that, although the King's authority over 'his' church was manifest, just, and universally recognized within the realm, it was nonetheless necessary to announce and establish it in the present parliament in statutory form.

Albeit the King's Majesty, justly and rightfully is and oweth to be the supreme head of the Church of England, and so is recognised by the clergy of this realm in their convocations, yet nevertheless for corroboration and confirmation thereof, and for increase of virtue in Christ's religion within this realm of England, and to repress and extirp all errors, heresies, and other enormities and abuses heretofore used in the same, be it enacted...that the king our sovereign lord, his heirs and successors kings of this realm, shall be taken, accepted, and reputed the only supreme head in earth of the Church of England called *Anglicana Ecclesia*, and shall have and enjoy annexed and united to the imperial crown of this realm as well the title and style thereof, as all honours, dignities, pre-eminences, jurisdictions, privileges, authorities, immunities, profits, and commodities, to the said dignity of supreme head of the same church belonging and appertaining.[47]

There may also be, in some of Jupiter's more delightfully self-regarding utterances ('And now, accordynge to your obedyens / Rejoyce ye in us wyth joy most joyfully, / And we our selfe shall joy in our owne glory' (183–5); 'we nede no whyte our selfe any farther to bost, / For our dedes declare us apparauntly / .../ Our prudens hath made peace unyversally. / Whyche thynge, we sey, recordeth us as pryncypall / God and governour of heven, yerth, and all' (1241–2, 1245–7)), conscious echoes of the kind of vaunting descriptions of Henry's qualities to be found in statutes such as the Act Concerning the Pardon of the Clergy of 1531 (which talked of 'his Highness, having always tender eye with mercy and pity and compassion towards his said spiritual subjects, minding of his high goodness and great benignity so always to impart the same unto them as justice being daily administered, all rigour be excluded'), and would later produce, in the Act Concerning Payment of First Fruits and Tenths of 1534, a description of the king as his subjects',

most dread, benign, and gracious Sovereign Lord, upon whom and in whom dependeth all their joy and wealth, in whom also is united and knit so princely a heart and courage, mixed with mercy, wisdom, and justice, and also a natural affection joined to the same, as by the great, inestimable, and benevolent arguments thereof being most bountifully, largely, and many times showed, ministered, and approved towards his loving and obedient subjects hath well appeared, which requireth a like correspondence of gratitude to be considered according to their most bounden duties[48]

Heywood seems, then, to be playing with a range of representations of Henry VIII in this presentation of Jupiter, drawing his inspiration from both earlier classical and courtly entertainments and the King's official self-presentation in proclamations, speeches to parliament, and statutes. And what he creates from this bricolage of ingredients is not a god-king awesome and magisterial in the full panoply of his new-found, 'ancient' powers, but a monarch with feet of clay. He turns an association between the English King and his Olympian counterpart inside out and then back again, transforming what had been a panegyric device in Skelton's *Speke, Parott* into a much more mischievous exploration of Henry VIII's current political and marital ambitions. It is a relatively affectionate portrait, certainly, far from the contemptible tyrants of the religious drama, but it is a deeply ironic and 'merry' portrait nonetheless.[49]

What Heywood's treatment of Jupiter suggests, then, is a clear sense of licence on the part of the playwright to touch upon highly sensitive political and personal issues central to the King's current preoccupations in a comic vein, apparently without fear of recriminations, and seemingly in the expectation of a favourable reception. This speaks volumes for the robust confidence of Heywood himself in both the King's tolerance and his own position at the beginning of Henry's Great Matter and the first years of the break with Rome. Heywood's aim, in part at least, would seem to have been to open an obvious ironic distance between the vaunting language of Jupiter's assertions and the more pragmatic realities of political action—or, as here, of inaction—required to solve the dilemmas raised during the play. Just as the god-king's claims to absolute and immutable power and authority prove largely irrelevant to the situation in which he finds himself in the play, so the drama suggests that the language of those Henrician proclamations and statutes associated with the break with Rome and the Supremacy—the vaunting, discursive language that Sir Geoffrey Elton associated with the ministry of Thomas Cromwell and the notional revolution in government that Elton claimed he inspired—so that language, and the authority it proclaims are equally inappropriate in the context of the disputes provoked around the Reformation Parliament.[50] The moral of the play seems thus to have been the same as that of Heywood's roughly contemporaneous interludes *The Four Ps* and *The Pardoner and the Friar*: the best response to the current wave of confessional strife was not inflammatory rhetoric and radical legislative action, especially not of an anticlerical kind, but sober common sense and tolerant accommodation.[51] Rather than assert new and unsettling powers, the King is best advised to restore the *status quo ante*, allowing all sides to assume that they have got what they wanted, albeit if only for some of the time.

Such an ironic, comedic approach to contemporary politics relies, of course, on a number of assumptions: that the King is willing to listen, and willing to accept such well-intentioned, 'merry' criticism cast in an 'Erasmian vein' on a matter close to his heart. It assumes that the 'private' Henry VIII, the man who would take Thomas More by the arm in his garden and encourage him to argue politics with him, the King who had told his counsellors in 1519 that they should intervene if ever those close to him—and by implication he himself—began to behave inappropriately, was detachable from the sovereign of public policies and formal utterances; that Henry, that is, was able to read his own publicity ironically, see the joke in Jupiter, and take the point. It may well have been that March 1533 was the last moment at which such assumptions held good at court, and at which a writer in Heywood's position was able to attempt such liberties with the King, risking Jove's thunderbolts in order to offer him the good counsel that all princes needed. Within little more than a year such confidence in the capacity of literature and drama, and of well-intentioned good counsel more generally, to speak harsh truths to power in Henry VIII's England would, of course, be in tatters. The experience of the small circle of writers, entertainers, and scholars around Thomas More and the courtly humanists would be engaged with the far more earnest endeavour to find a mode of operating at court, and remaining true to their ideals, that did not run the risk of condign punishment of a very earthly and murderous kind.

PART II

'TO VIRTUE PERSUADED'?
THE PERSISTENT COUNSELS
OF SIR THOMAS ELYOT

7

Sir Thomas Elyot and The King's Great Matter

> There is a tide in the affairs of men
> Which, taken on the flood, leads on to fortune;
> Omitted, all the voyage of their life
> Is bound in shallows and in miseries.
>
> (*Julius Caesar*, iv.ii.270–3)

These sentiments, spoken by the good counsellor Brutus in Shakespeare's *Julius Caesar*, were not penned until 1599, but the notion they express was a commonplace of early Renaissance thinking.[1] Certainly Sir Thomas Elyot, Henry VIII's late ambassador to the court of the emperor Charles V, could have been forgiven for pondering it, and its application to his own situation as he stepped ashore on his return to England on or around 1 June 1532. For Elyot was about to face what was to prove the climacteric of his brief career as a courtier and diplomat when he delivered the final report on his embassy to the King. Apparently convinced that the moment was right to offer Henry rather more than a simple factual account of his mission, Elyot travelled to court determined to remonstrate with his master and tell him some sharp truths about the way the world in general, and the Empire in particular, interpreted his current behaviour and policies. Confronting the King with a mirror of his own actions in this way would, Elyot clearly believed, prove in the long term to be in the best interests of both Henry and his kingdom. In time, no doubt, the King would come to thank and reward the counsellor who had had the courage and integrity to speak up and save him from what appeared in the eyes of the world to be his own folly. As time was to prove, this decision was to cost Elyot dear; for he was never to work as an envoy or ambassador again. But the significance of the moment, and of the attitude towards royal service that it embodies, goes well beyond its material consequences for Elyot's career.

Exactly what Elyot intended to say at this meeting, and what actually transpired, will always be a matter for conjecture, as our only evidence of the event is provided in a brief account in a despatch from that tireless reporter of political intrigue and gossip at the English court, the Spanish ambassador, Eustace Chapuys. Writing to the Emperor on 5 June, he noted that,

The day before yesterday Master Thomas Heliot, on his return from Your Majesty's court, where he has been residing as ambassador, came to visit me, and told me a great deal about his conversation with this king, which he said had been greatly to the benefit of your majesty, of the Queen, your aunt, and principally of the King, his master, who (he said) knowing about it, still showed great desire to hear all the particulars of his mission.[2]

The terms that Elyot is reported to have used, linking the advantages to the Emperor and his aunt Katherine of Aragon to those of King Henry himself, suggest the degree of conflict in the mind of the returning ambassador. For, as we shall see, the terms of his mission left little room for the consideration of anyone's interests but the King's. What had brought Elyot to this state of mind, and what exactly did he hope to achieve by his frank conversation with his king? From Chapuys' letter it seems clear that the matter that so exercised him was the same one that was intriguing much of western Europe at the time, the 'Great Matter' of Henry VIII's campaign to annul his marriage to Queen Katherine of Aragon and so free himself to marry his long-time mistress Anne Boleyn.[3] For, as the ambassador ruefully suggested,

whatever may be Master Heliot's assertions, I have strong doubts of his report having produced as good effect as he says on the King, for whatever remonstrances have been addressed to him by different parties have hitherto been disregarded, and a smile or a tear from the Lady [Anne Boleyn] has been enough to undo any good that might have been done in that quarter.

But, he added, he would nonetheless continue 'to try to sound out the Ambassador [Elyot] and pay him as much court as possible for the better success of the Queen's case'.

Chapuys was not Elyot's only confidante where his fateful interview was concerned. Sir Thomas also wrote up an account, in a specially prepared cipher, of what passed between himself and the King for a Spanish diplomat, Don Fernando de la Puebla, with whom he had become acquainted at the imperial court.[4] This was a remarkably bold, indeed, potentially treasonous thing for an English diplomat to do, suggesting an extreme commitment to the issues at stake.[5] But why was Elyot so exercised by the King's divorce campaign at a time when, some years after the initial furore created by Henry's declaration of his intention to seek an annulment (and the failure of the papal court at Blackfriars to provide one), the whole matter had become rather bogged down in procedural disputes in Rome? On a personal level at least, Elyot clearly had considerable sympathy for Katherine of Aragon and her plight, as can be judged from what he said and did in the following years. On 10 May 1533, for example, Chapuys reported that so great was the affection of the English people for their former queen and her nephew the Emperor that royal ministers were considering provoking civil disorder as an excuse for raising an army to destroy her supporters. His source for this contentious information was, he said, Sir Thomas Elyot. Later, in January 1534, Chapuys reported Katherine's request that 'men of influence' be sent by the Emperor to speak for her in the English parliament, noting that Elyot had already made the same request independently.[6] Given Sir Thomas More's well-known reluctance even to receive an encouraging communication from the Emperor at this time, Elyot's capacity to leak rumours concerning royal policy to Chapuys and advise him on the best tactics to adopt to counter it seems a clear indication of his willingness to take risks for the Queen's cause.[7]

But Elyot's concerns about the King's actions went well beyond a sense that Queen Katherine was being unjustly treated. It was the consequences of the divorce campaign rather than the legal or moral issues that it raised which had roused him to action, and it was those consequences that prompted him to dedicate much of the rest of his life to speaking out, both publicly and privately, about the religious and political turmoil that Henry's actions had provoked. For the face-to-face remonstrance of *c*. 1 June 1532 was only the most direct example of a whole series of warnings and counsels that Elyot had been offering his King since well before he set out on his embassy to the Emperor in the autumn of 1531, and which he would continue to offer throughout the following decade. A consideration of the nature and, more particularly, the form of those counsels reveals a great deal, both about Elyot's own views, and about the nature of political debate in England in these years. And much of the next four chapters will be devoted to exploring the subtle shifts and nuances in Elyot's position and his approach to the theory and practice of counselling Henry VIII through a period of seemingly perpetual crisis. But it is important first to get a clearer sense, both of Thomas Elyot himself, and of the situation in which he found himself at the beginning of the 1530s.

The Public Career of Sir Thomas Elyot

Sir Thomas Elyot (*c*. 1490–1546) was, like the other writers who feature prominently in this book, a servant of the crown, a man who found both his daily employment and his intellectual and cultural foundations in the service of the Henrician state. As Pearl Hogrefe suggested in what is still probably the most readable and consistently astute study of his life and work, Elyot was arguably the most aristocratic as well as the most intellectually rigorous of the humanist scholars associated (however loosely) with the circle of Sir Thomas More.[8] Although not a provincial magnate, he was a solid gentleman landowner with substantial property in Oxfordshire and the west of England. In the course of the 1520s and 1530s he acquired further estates in Oxfordshire and Cambridgeshire through inheritance or purchase sufficient to make him a major figure in his locality.[9] As such he served the crown, as men of substance and influence were obliged to do, across the gamut of local offices and commissions, acting as a Justice of the Peace, Sheriff, and a Member of Parliament in 1539, and as a member of numerous commissions of oyer and terminer, gaol delivery, tax assessment and collection, in addition to more prominent roles at the political centre. Elyot was thus a member of that class of men who saw themselves as the backbone of Tudor England, a stakeholder in the administration as well as a small but important cog in its machinery. This sense of personal investment in the fortunes of the nation was to lead not only to his lifelong patriotic commitment to furthering the well-being of the realm, but also to some perhaps unrealistic expectations about the role he might play in the more substantial political dimensions of national government.

Elyot's earliest paid employment was as clerk to the justices of assize on the western circuit, a post he almost certainly owed to the influence of his father, Sir Richard Elyot, who was one of the justices and a King's Sergeant at Law. It was this post, which he occupied for over a decade, that gained him his knowledge of—and lifelong interest in—the common law, and won him admission to his father's Inn of Court, the Middle Temple, in 1510. At some point in late 1523 Elyot was invited by the Lord Chancellor, Cardinal Thomas Wolsey, to become clerk to the King's Council, a substantial elevation into the heart of national affairs for a man whose life had hitherto been spent primarily in assisting the administration of the law in the provinces.[10] The new appointment was, however, not without its difficulties. Years of legal dispute with the previous incumbent, Richard Eden, over who had the right to the appointment and the fees that it carried with it, were to result in Elyot's dismissal after Wolsey's fall from power in 1529, and the upholding of Eden's appeal for reappointment. So, not only did the 1520s sow the seeds of Elyot's interest in national government and his preoccupation with counselling the King, they also created that longstanding sense of grievance at his own treatment at the hands of the state that would also colour much of his correspondence in the next decade.[11]

The Embassy to the Emperor

Elyot's period of unemployment following the loss of the secretarial position was, however, to be short-lived. There was probably barely time for him to complete the text of his first substantial publication, *The Book Named The Governor* (1531) and see it through the press, before he was called upon to undertake the most politically sensitive task of his career. During the summer of 1530 a rumour was circulating that he was in line for a very significant promotion, to the Mastership of the Rolls, a post that would take him into the administrative heart of the government. But this was not to be.[12] What followed was rather the commission to undertake a diplomatic mission for Henry as ambassador to the court of the Emperor Charles V. Charles had summoned a chapter of the Order of the Golden Fleece (the Burgundian equivalent in status and dignity of the English Order of the Garter), of which Henry VIII was a knight, and Elyot was chosen to represent his king at the meeting.[13] While at the imperial court, however, he was also to take the opportunity to further the Great Matter of the King's divorce. He was to ascertain Charles's intentions regarding the ongoing case in the Roman courts and attempt to draw him out over the extent of his opposition to the King's proceedings.

The degree of Henry's personal involvement in Elyot's mission, and the importance it had in his eyes, can be judged from the instructions that he gave to his fledgling ambassador. Elyot was 'to fish out and know in what opinion the Emperor is of us, and whether despairing of old friendship towards him, or fearing other new communication with France, he seeketh ways and means that might be to our detriment or no'.[14] He was to remind Charles that he had once said that 'he would not meddle otherwise than according to justice' in 'our great cause between us and the queen' and to tell him that the Pope's citation of Henry's case to Rome was a clear case of injustice against him and his princely prerogative. Warming to his theme, Henry began to imagine the Emperor's likely response to such claims, and so to ventriloquize the whole conversation in advance for Elyot's benefit:

and if the Emperor . . . shall ask what the Pope doth wherein we think our self wronged, ye may say, in calling and citing us to Rome, which is contrary to all laws, as all lawyers affirm, and especially them in France, as friends indifferent . . . and if the Emperor shall reply to know what the universities affirm and what the Chancellor and other the Presidents of the court of Parliament of Paris do say, ye may answer how they say that we may not be cited to Rome, there to appear by us or our proctor and that such a citation is not only naught, and all their process there upon following, but also manifest injury and wrong, which [we] trust, ye may say, th'Emperor of his honour will not maintain.

Thus fortified with arguments and a due sense of the importance of the task allotted him, Elyot set out at some point in late October 1531 (having drawn up his will on 29 August in advance of the journey) for Tournai, where the chapter was appointed to meet on 2 November. He was to remain at the peripatetic imperial court until April 1532, after which point Thomas Cranmer, who had been despatched to replace him, took over the duties of resident ambassador in his stead.[15] Travelling slowly back from Germany (the court having by then moved to Regensburg) and stopping in the Low Countries in an unsuccessful attempt to find and apprehend the Lutheran scholar William Tyndale, whom Henry wanted to be brought back to England, Elyot arrived on English soil on or about 1 June 1532. Immediately upon his return he travelled to the court to deliver his final report to the King and the frank remonstrance over his marital and diplomatic policies.

Whether as a direct result of what he said at that meeting, or of other factors beyond his control, the embassy was to be Elyot's last major encounter with international politics.[16] Thereafter, with the exception of one brief session as a Member of the House of Commons in the spring of 1539, he was called to serve his king only in local government and on those occasions when the provincial gentry appeared en masse to swell a crowd or furnish a room.[17] While not, perhaps, the record of 'dismal failure in office' described by one scholar, Elyot's period of regular employment at court had clearly ended disappointingly prematurely from his own point of view.[18] Yet, considered objectively, his career was an entirely respectable one for a substantial gentleman with a sound legal training. Only his own sense of his potential as a counsellor to kings in general and Henry in particular made that record seem unsatisfactory. What is most interesting here, however, is not whether Elyot was underused in government service as a result of his remonstrance, but what he did in response to his lack of promotion, and his evident dissatisfaction with the direction of English policy. For Elyot's response was to write, and write copiously. In the course of the next twelve years he produced at least seven books, all of which addressed, to one degree or another, the political situation of the moment. And these books sought to do vicariously what he could not do in person and *ex officio*: counsel the King on his personal conduct and the public policy of the realm.

Scholarship, Friendships, and Religion

Elyot drew his mandate to counsel his prince from a combination of his own patriotism and concern for the commonwealth and his erudition and learning.[19] Yet his education was far from typical for a man of his class and time. He was, according to his own account, largely self-taught, and never attended a university. In the Latin preface to the first edition of his *Dictionary* (printed in 1538) he described himself as 'educated in his father's house and not instructed by an other teacher from his twelfth year, but led [by] himself into liberal studies and both sorts of philosophy'.[20] But, despite the lack of a lengthy formal education he went on to become probably the most prolific and influential scholar of his generation, producing, not only the hugely popular *Dictionary* (reprinted in a substantially revised second edition as the *Bibliotheca Eliotae* in 1542), but also the definitive English guide to princely education and conduct (*The Book Named the Governor* (1531)), a handbook of popular medicine (*The Castle of Health*, published in 1536 and in five further editions during his lifetime), and a collection of maxims (*The Banquet of Sapience* (1539)), as well as translating or adapting works of political philosophy from the Latin and Greek.[21]

Elyot's intellectual interests and abilities alone would suggest that he was likely to have been drawn into some contact with Sir Thomas More and the group of humanists that gravitated to his household to form the epicentre of most of the scholarly activity in England in the 1520s. A number of accounts have, however, suggested that his links with More were more substantial and closer than this. More's son-in-law and biographer William Roper placed Elyot and his wife Margaret among the group of More's 'friends' at an (at least partially fictional) gathering in his house after his death. A subsequent biographer of More, Thomas Stapleton went further, suggesting not only that Elyot himself was one of More's 'friends and companions in the pursuit of polite literature', but that Margaret Elyot, his wife, 'also gave herself to the study of literature in Sir Thomas More's school'.[22] Scholars have struggled to reconcile these statements with the fact that More nowhere mentions Elyot in his voluminous writings and correspondence, and more troublingly, with the fact that Elyot himself later repudiated any strong association with More in two letters written to Thomas Cromwell after the former Chancellor's fall from grace. The issues are worth considering, if only briefly, before we move on.

On 20 December in either 1534 or 1535 (by which time More was either in prison for his refusal to subscribe to the oath attached to the Act of Succession of March 1534, or already dead),[23] Elyot wrote to Cromwell to assure him of his loyal adherence to the Royal Supremacy, and to refute the suggestion that he was keeping seditious (that is pro-papal, or anti-divorce) books in his houses. 'Sir', he wrote,

As ye know, I have been ever desirous to read many books, especially concerning humanity and moral philosophy, and therefore of such studies I have a competent number. But concerning holy scripture I have very few, for in questionists [scholastics] I never delighted, unsavoury glosses and comments I ever abhorred: the boasters and advauntars [braggers] of the pompous authority of the Bishop of Rome I never esteemed. But after that by much and serious reading, I had apprehended a judgement or estimation of things, I did anon smell out their corrupt affections, and beheld with sorrowful eyes the sundry abusions of their authorities adorned with a licentious and dissolute form of living, of the which, as well in them as in the universal state of the Clergy, I have oftentimes wished a necessary reformation.[24]

He then turned to the more specific question of his personal allegiances, claiming that, as a result of his opinion regarding the necessity of reform,

hath happed no little contention betwixt me and such persons as ye thought that I have specially favoured, even as ye also did, for some laudable qualities which we supposed to be in them. But neither they might persuade me to approve that which both faith and my reason condemned, nor I might dissuade them from the excusing of that which all the world abhorred, which obstinacy of both parties relented the great affection between us and withdrew our familiar repair.

That the adherent to papal authority he had principally in mind was Sir Thomas More (and perhaps also bishop John Fisher, one of whose books he later admitted having purchased, albeit, he assured Cromwell, more for the Latin translation by Richard Pace than for the author or the matter in it) seems highly likely on internal evidence, and is confirmed by a second letter, written to Cromwell at some point after 2 July 1536.[25] Here, having thanked Cromwell for intervening with the King on an unidentified matter on his behalf, he turned to address once more what he perceived to be the minister's doubts concerning his commitment to religious reform.

And where I perceive that ye suspect that I savour not truly holy Scripture, I would God that the king and you might see the most secret thoughts of my heart. Surely ye should then perceive that, the order of charity saved, I have in as much detestation as any man

living all vain, superstitions, superfluous ceremonies, slanderous jonglings [games/tricks],
Counterfeit Miracles, arrogant usurpations of men called Spiritual and masking Reli-
gions, and all other abusions of Christ's holy doctrine and laws. And as much I enjoy at
the king's godly proceeding to the due reformation of the said enormities as any his
Graces poor subject living. I therefore beseech your good lordship now to lay apart the
remembrance of the amity between me and sir Thomas More, which was but *Usque ad
aras*, as is the proverb, considering that I was never so much addict[ed] unto him as I was
unto truth and fidelity toward my sovereign lord, as God is my Judge.

The proverb to which Elyot is alluding here, '*usque ad aram amicus sum*: up to the
altar I am your friend', was attributed to Pericles and taken from Gellius and
Plutarch. It would be succinctly glossed in the 1552 continuation of Elyot's own
Bibliotheca Eliotae as: 'to do all the pleasure that a man can for his friend, saving
his conscience'.[26] Thus the implication would seem to be that, whatever affection
and friendship Elyot had for More, it would not lead him to defy his conscience
or jeopardize his honesty on his behalf. (The metaphor of oath-taking and altar
touching is particularly apt, given that More's treason lay precisely in his refusal
to take the oath attached to the Act of Supremacy, whereas Elyot's compliance
with the Supremacy was indicated by his willingness to do so.)

What seems clear is that Elyot may well have been an associate of More's in the
1520s, although the early biographers' use of the term 'friend' to describe their
relationship may indicate nothing closer than the kind of scholarly 'amity' that
European humanists, often of only the most limited acquaintance, expressed
towards each other in imitation of classical scholarly practice. More and Elyot
clearly shared a number of important intellectual and spiritual affinities at this
time, both being advocates of the kind of moderate, liberal approach to religious
and social issues that is often referred to by the shorthand term 'Erasmian'. But in
the 1530s they seem to have drifted apart, perhaps socially, and certainly
intellectually, as they followed markedly different courses in response to the
break with Rome and the Henrician Reformation. Whereas More took up the
polemical struggle against religious reform directly, refusing to compromise with
the Royal Supremacy, Elyot took a more moderate course, apparently accepting
that some benefits could follow from the King's religious policies, and focusing
his literary endeavours upon counselling Henry to exercise caution and moderation in implementing them.[27] Thus there is no need to see Elyot's comments to
Cromwell as representing a betrayal of More's friendship, or a cowardly attempt
to distance himself from his example and so save his own skin.[28] As will become
clear in the course of this book, writers reacted very differently to the demands
placed upon them by the new conditions created by the royal divorce and the
Supremacy, and Elyot was not stretching the truth in acknowledging the fact that
he and More had finally chosen to follow very different paths.

Despite his consistent sympathy for Katherine of Aragon and his unusually
warm relationship with the Spanish ambassador, then, it is clear that Elyot's
religious views were not those of a simple, diehard reactionary. Rather, he

combined a conservative opposition to many aspects of evangelicalism with a moderate, Erasmian commitment to the reform of abuses in the church, and a degree at least of commitment (however reluctant and pragmatic) to the Royal Supremacy. In 1532, while in Nuremberg, he, in the company of the French ambassador, pointedly walked out of a reformed church service rather than take communion of a Lutheran kind, 'Which caused all the people in the church to wonder at us, as [if] we had been greater heretics than they'.[29] Similarly, he had found the city of Worms even less congenial than Nuremburg, complaining that 'almost the whole is possessed with Lutherans and Jews', while the bishop was either unwilling or unable to act against them. Such statements suggest an attitude towards protestant heresy that would align Elyot with Thomas More's uncompromising oppositional stance. Yet, unlike More, he seems to have remained on good terms with Thomas Cromwell throughout this period, a fact which has, as we have seen, prompted suggestions of time-serving and equivocation on his part. But it seems more accurate to see in Elyot's position a genuine attempt to argue against doctrinal innovation while simultaneously seeking common ground with the future Vicegerent-in-Spirituals on less directly contentious questions of reform. As the letters quoted earlier reveal, he was keen to assure Cromwell on a number of occasions that he had no time for the more obvious abuses of traditional, popular religious practice, and was fully prepared to accept the machinery of the Royal Supremacy as a means of bringing about necessary reform in the Church, albeit only if it would also forestall the more radical innovations that were being advocated at the same time.

It is important to note just how carefully Elyot chose his words in those two letters to Cromwell. While he was willing to acknowledge the legitimacy of the Supremacy, and to reject the 'pompous authority of the Bishop of Rome', both of which were by that time ideas established by statute and enforceable at law, he was not prepared unequivocally to condemn any aspect of orthodox belief or practice. It was the abuses of current practice that he condemned, not the practice itself. Hence he condemned the 'sundry abusions' of supporters of the papacy, and wished for a necessary reformation of the 'licentious and dissolute form of living' practised among the clergy rather than any aspect of ecclesiastical juris-diction or doctrine. Such a position was entirely compatible with the orthodox 'anti-clericalism' of Erasmus, the younger More, or indeed Thynne and Tuke's Chaucer edition. Similarly, in the second letter, written after July 1536, it was again abuses that were singled out for criticism. It was vain superstitions, *superfluous* ceremonies, *slanderous* 'jonglings', *counterfeit* miracles, and 'all other *abusions* of Christ's Holy doctrine and laws' that Elyot said he detested and wished to see reformed. Necessary ceremonies, legitimate miracles, and those aspects of belief and the liturgy that were not abused were, by implication, free from criticism. All of these statements were carefully in line with government policy of the moment, which cited the removal of abuses from current practice to restore the pristine purity of true religion as its primary aim.

Given that this letter was written at a time when, in the wake of the adoption of the Ten Articles on doctrine and belief, the most controversial issue of the moment was the government's reduction of the number of legitimate sacraments from seven to three, it is striking that Elyot made no mention of specifically sacramental issues. Moreover, given that he began his apologia with the observation that he feared Cromwell suspected him of not 'savouring' Holy Scripture in the approved evangelical manner, it is notable that at no point does he affirm his commitment to the primacy of the biblical word or the need to provide a vernacular Bible to bring the gospels to the people.[30] It is thus difficult to avoid the conclusion reached by Pearl Hogrefe that Elyot was walking a fine line in these letters, and treading it with great skill, 'hoping to remain a conservative, but sound like a radical'.[31]

Elyot, as his published works suggest, was not averse to some barbed, Erasmian asides at the lack of learning and dullness of preaching friars, or the luxury and self-indulgence of some priests.[32] But on matters of doctrine, he was far less ready to compromise. His commitment to the catholic interpretation of the mass and the doctrine of transubstantiation runs consistently through his writings, as does a firm belief in the importance of good works in the economy of salvation. He drew up his last Will and Testament, as we have seen, in 1531, at a time when these doctrines had not begun to be questioned in official pronouncements on the faith, but he ratified its terms again on 23 March 1546, by which time more than a decade of reform had cast the value of works in general and the Mass as a propriation and petition and prayers for the dead for remission of sin in particular, into considerable doubt. Thus it is striking that he left provision for prayers to be said for his soul at St Paul's Cross in London once in each legal term, and by three poor men each Friday throughout the year, and for an annual obit at Weston Colville church, in which ten priests would sing a solemn mass and nine low masses for him, his parents, and all Christian souls.[33]

More significantly in the extended exposition of his own faith, *The Preservative Against Death*, which he published in 1545, the doctrine of works provides the cornerstone of the advice he offers to his readers on the best route to salvation. Citing the nineteenth chapter of Mark's Gospel, he states his position plainly at the beginning of the text: 'Christ calleth oftentimes to us: keep (sayeth he) the commandments. Do works of repentance, watch and pray, give in my name and ye shall receive an hundred times as much as ye give, and have life everlasting' (Av(v)).[34] Much of the book is taken up with an anticipation of what the devil, supported by his enticing sisters the World and the Flesh, will say in order to tempt the good Christian away from the road to salvation. What the infernal trio say turns out, in part at least, to be a parodic version of the views of Luther and the more radical evangelicals on faith, works, and predestination. 'Prayer (saith he) is nothing but lip labour or vain occupation.' Fasting and alms-deeds are worthless:

Presumest thou, ignorant fool, to attain to the kingdom of heaven by thy works? Thinkest thou that alms deed, fasting, or prayer, or that foolishness which thou callest virtue, have power to bring thee to any other estate than God hath ordained thee] According as he hath predestined thee, so shalt thou be: he never changeth his purpose; his judgement is constant, like as his knowledge is from the beginning. If he hath ordained thee to be saved, do all thing that thine appetite liketh thee, and thou shalt be clean in his sight. If he hath predestined thee to be damned, take all the pains that thou canst imagine, and all shall not help thee.

(*Preservative Against Death*, Di(v)–Dii)

Against these satanic blandishments, the author asserts his trust in God's word,

Not that I will compel thee to save me; but that I believe that thou hast all ready saved me by thine only son Jesu Christ, according unto his saying: He that believeth (sayeth he) hath life everlasting.

(Dii–Dii(v))

And he asserts that he shall undertake works of charity,

Not presuming to have thereby the kingdom of heaven, but that by doing the works of our father, our father may know us, that we be his own sons, whom he hath predestinate and also called.

(Dii(v))

Thus far the statement might be compatible with an evangelical stress upon works as merely the outward sign of election, albeit they are equally compatible with the thoroughly orthodox Augustinian doctrine of prevenient grace.[35] But Elyot goes on to say,

But yet from the beginning that he ordained mankind, he left him in the power of his own counsel, which is his free will. Albeit of his infinite mercy, where it pleaseth him to show it, if we draw out of the true path, with his whip of grace he some time easily, some time sharply, with trouble, sickness or poverty essayeth to turn us into the right way.

(Diii)

Again, despite his stated abhorrence of vain superstitions and superfluous ceremonies in the letters to Cromwell, the importance of properly ordered ceremonies in the life of the Church was a theme that Elyot was eager to defend, and on which he was anxious not to be misunderstood. In *The Governor*, for example, having praised the servant who honours his master 'with much humble reverence' rather than with lavish and insincere extravagance, he felt it necessary to add an immediate coda,

Yet would I not be noted that I would seem so much to extol reverence by it self that churches and other ornaments dedicate to god should be therefore contemned. For undoubtedly such things be not only commendable, but also expedient for the augmentation and continuing of reverence.

(Yii).

Noting that the Bible records how Christ commended rituals of purification, baptism by water, and ceremonies such as the laying down of palm leaves and garments before him when he entered Jerusalem, at which time 'great routs of people...went before him in form of a triumph': all this while he was still on earth, Elyot asked rhetorically, '[then] how much honour is due to him now that all power is given to him, as well in heaven as in earth[?]' (ʏii(v)–ʏiii).[36]

Criticizing the inconsistency of those like Tyndale who accepted the use of ceremonies in the honouring of mortal kings, yet condemned them in honouring the heavenly king, he lambasted such heretics as the epitome of hypocrisy:

O creatures most unkind and barren of Justice, that will deny that thing to their god and creator, which of very duty and right is given to him by good reason afore all princes... by which opinion they seem to despoil him of reverence, which shall cause all obedience to cease, whereof will ensue utter confusion, if good Christian princes, moved with zeal, do not shortly provide to extinct utterly all such opinions.

(ʏiii(v))

Here and elsewhere Elyot's attitude towards Lutheranism and evengelicalism does seem to echo More's.[37] The kind of apocalyptic streak apparent in this passage, with its warnings of 'utter confusion' and the end of all obedience, shares something with the former Chancellor's views, and does not seem in either case to have been merely a rhetorical device. Both men seem genuinely to have feared that all heresies, however apparently rational or moderate they may initially seem, lead inevitably down a slippery slope to the kind of anarchy exhibited by the German Peasants' War of 1524–5, and later epitomized in the Anabaptist commune in Munster in 1534–5. In *The Governor* (1531) Elyot felt the need to strike out in passing against evangelicals whose emphasis on Scripture, and what he saw as their wilful misreading of the biblical text, threatened to overturn all precedent and order in both religion and society. If order as a concept was in itself commendable, he asked,

Howe far out of reason shall we judge them to be that would exterminate all superiority, extinct all governance and laws, and under colour of holy scripture, which they do violently wrest to their purpose, do endeavour themselves to bring the life of man into a confusion inevitable, and to be in much worse estate than the...beasts.

(*The Governor*, sig. ʏvii(v))[38]

But beyond such brief polemical outbursts it is striking how little time Elyot spends in *The Governor* in outlining the King's relationship with God or his responsibilities as an example of good religious conduct, or a defender of the faith of his people. The spiritual dimension that was fundamental to Erasmus's conception of the Christian prince in *The Education* is markedly downplayed in Elyot's book. And again it seems wise to see this as a strategic response on his part to current religious controversies. By not exploring in detail the religious responsibilities that devolve upon the governor, Elyot was able to avoid contentious questions about ecclesiastical jurisdiction or the spiritual powers of the prince, and so maintain the stance of a peacemaker, offering his ruler impartial advice on how to end the schisms between clergy and laity, king and bishop.

Elyot's sense of foreboding concerning the direction of religious policy and the pressure of events can nonetheless be judged from a letter he wrote to Sir John Hackett, then serving as ambassador to the Low Countries, on 6 April 1533. 'I would that I had some comfortable news to send you out of these parts', he wrote,

But the world is all otherwise. I beseech our lord amend it. We have hanging over us a great cloud which is likely to be a great storm when it falleth.[39]

Given that Anne Boleyn was to appear publicly as Queen for the first time a week after this letter was written, scholars have tended to see the 'great cloud' as an allusion to the King's clandestine marriage, which would have become common knowledge at about this time.[40] But Elyot's sense of a growing storm seems to have encompassed rather more than simply the King's marriage. While he, as we have seen, clearly had sympathy for Katherine of Aragon's plight, what seems to have troubled him most, both here and elsewhere in his writings, was not the specific outcome of Henry's divorce campaign, but what it implied about the King's character and methods of government, for were not his efforts to divorce Queen Katherine and marry Anne a prime example of a king placing private desires above the public good, and was not this a classic symptom of tyranny? Most of all he was exercised by the damage that pursuing the campaign had done to the social and cultural fabric of the nation. Hence Elyot's stress in the remainder of the letter upon the continued need to counsel the King in the interests of truth, and on the plight of the clergy, two issues that he clearly saw as intertwined:

The King's highness, thanked be God, is in good health. I beseech God continue it, and send his comfort of spirit unto him, and that trute may be freely and thankfully heard. For my part I am finally determined to live and die therein. Neither mine importable expenses unrecompensed shall so much fear me, nor the advancement of my successor the bishop of Canterbury so much allure me that I shall ever decline from truth, or abuse my sovereign lord unto whom I am sworn. For I am sure that I and you also shall one day die, and I know that there is a God and that he is all truth, and therefore he will grievously punish all falsehood and that everlastingly. Ye shall hear ere it be long, some strange things of the spirituality. For between themselves is no perfect agreement. Some do say that they digged the ditch that they be now fallen in, which causeth many good men the less to pity them.

Elyot's words do not sound like those of a man who saw the inevitable collapse of all his plans less than a week away, as would have been the case if the Boleyn marriage were the sum total of the great cloud that he feared. Rather they suggest someone steeling himself for a struggle ahead: a struggle in which the fate of the clergy would be a significant issue and the attempt to bring truth to the ears of the King would be the principal weapon. How did this situation come about? To answer this question we will need to backtrack for a moment to see how the question of Henry's divorce, and the consequences to which it gave rise, had developed to the point when Elyot took up his pen.

The King's Great Matter

The precise origins and mixture of motives behind Henry's fateful decision to seek the annulment of his marriage to Katherine of Aragon will almost certainly never be fully known. What can be said with some confidence is that by early 1527 the King had come to the conclusion that his marriage was not valid, and had never been so in the eyes of God. A keen amateur theologian and avid reader of the Bible, Henry had convinced himself that the injunction in the twentieth chapter of Leviticus: 'He that marrieth his brother's wife doth unlawfully, he hath uncovered his brother's nakedness. They shall be without children' had a chilling aptness to his own situation, and his lack of a legitimate male heir seemed to confirm its relevance.

Troubled in his conscience by what he had read, spurred on by his desire for a male heir, and also for his current mistress Anne Boleyn, Henry concluded that his marriage must be declared invalid, freeing him to marry Anne and produce the heir that his kingdom needed. But trying to convert his own convictions into effective action raised profound legal and diplomatic as well as theological questions. Anxious to convince others of his 'discovery', Henry initially consulted those about him whom he could trust to give informed and discrete guidance. Thomas More's son-in-law and biographer William Roper relates how the King consulted More on the issue, 'showing him certain places of Scripture that somewhat seemed to serve his appetite'. When More tried to excuse himself from commenting on so sensitive a matter, Henry 'sore still pressed upon him', telling him to read the relevant texts and to consult bishops Cuthbert Tunstal of Durham and John Clark of Bath and Wells and other counsellors who were privy to the matter.[41]

Although More remained unconvinced,[42] Henry pressed ahead with his secret consultations regarding what would quickly become known in court circles as his 'Great Matter'. Determined to secure a quick and decisive judgement that he could present to Katherine, her Habsburg relatives, and the nation at large as a *fait accompli*, he had Cardinal Wolsey set up a secret court in his house in Westminster on 17 May to reach what he hoped would be a clear and negative judgement on the marriage.[43] But the trial got only as far as the initial statements and rebuttals when, on 31 May, it was suddenly abandoned, and it was decided to seek further theological advice before proceeding further.[44] It was not until 22 June, once the decision had been made to seek an annulment through more orthodox channels from the Pope, that Henry finally told his wife about his 'scruple of conscience' and the matter became public knowledge in political circles.

The failure of the secret Westminster court would prove to be symptomatic of the progress of the Great Matter for the next four years. Henry's impatience to have the marriage dissolved faced a series of increasingly daunting obstacles and delays. International politics and the influence of Catherine's nephew, the Emperor Charles V, thwarted all attempts to gain a positive verdict through swift papal intervention, and, after the failure of a papal hearing held at Black-friars in London and presided over by Wolsey and Cardinal Campeggio, sent from Rome for the purpose, Henry's case quickly became bogged down in a morass of appeals and counter-appeals in the Roman courts. English tactics turned from optimistically pushing for a quick and positive verdict to increasingly vociferous efforts to forestall a judgement in Katherine's favour, and to prevent the King being summoned to Rome (whether in person or by proxy) to face the humiliation of hearing his case thrown out of court.

With a positive verdict from Rome seeming increasingly unlikely, Henry's strategy shifted in the years following the Blackfriars trial towards a domestic solution to his problems. But this added a whole new set of constitutional questions to the wrangles over canon law at the heart of the initial case. For how could an English court settle a problem that had been revoked to Rome, traditionally the highest court of appeal for cases involving spiritual issues such as marital law? The prospect of gaining a verdict in England that was both favourable to the King and secure from papal interference seemed remote. Not only were the principal English clergy unwilling to try the case without papal sanction, but the Great Matter itself was proving an increasingly contentious and unpopular affair in the country at large. The chronicler Edward Hall, who can normally be replied upon to offer the official Henrician line on any subject, offers a telling insight into the unpopularity of the divorce proceedings and of Anne Boleyn at the time of the Blackfriars trial. 'The common people', he wrote, 'being ignorant of the truth, and especially women and other that favoured the Queen, talked largely, and said that the King would for his own pleasure have another wife, and had sent for this Legate to be divorced from his Queen, with many foolish words, insomuch that whosoever spake against the marriage was of the common people abhorred and reproved.'[45]

After Blackfriars, Henry's first and most difficult task remained to convince his counsellors, and his bench of bishops in particular, that a domestic solution to the divorce crisis was just, valid in canon law, and politically plausible. Determined, initially at least, to carry as many of them as he could with him, he summoned a grand Council of his leading subjects to guide him on 12 June 1530. Far from endorsing his view of the legal situation, however, the assembled aristocrats and ministers told him that the divorce could be settled only in Rome. Dissatisfied with that response, he summoned a meeting of lawyers and theologians to Hampton Court in October 1530,[46] asking them 'whether in virtue of the privileges possessed by this kingdom, Parliament could and would enact that, notwithstanding the Pope's prohibition, this case of the divorce [could] be decided by the Archbishop of Canterbury?' But the lawyers too affirmed that the divorce could not be determined by the Archbishop acting independently of Rome. Henry, it was claimed, angrily prorogued Parliament as a result.[47]

Unable to persuade his advisers of the legality of a domestic solution, he appealed to a still wider forum. He consulted opinion in the universities, first in England, then abroad, and individual experts were canvassed on the validity of the papal dispensation and the King's present marriage. If the canon lawyers could not see a practical way to help him, the theologians could determine the questions from first principles. The greatest minds of Europe would pass opinion on his Great Matter. No King, Henry was to claim, had ever taken counsel so widely, nor been so spectacularly vindicated by learned opinion. When the exercise was completed, the scholarly conclusions (or at least those favourable to the royal position) were read out to Parliament by Tuke and More and printed for circulation abroad.[48] Pamphlets in support of the King's case were commissioned and circulated, those in Latin for European audiences, those in English for consumption at home.[49] But, despite having elevated his marital difficulties into an international *cause célèbre*, Henry could still not persuade his subjects to defy the Pope and do as he asked them. The more he pushed, it seemed, the more apparent resistance he encountered. And his public stance that he was simply taking counsel on a matter of conscience became increasingly difficult to maintain with any credibility.

Covert royal pressure, aimed at softening clerical resistance to the divorce and reminding the Pope of the vulnerability of his interests in England, had begun in the first session of the Reformation Parliament in November 1529. Henry had stood back from the heated disputes between members of the Commons and the clergy in the Lords over the bills condemning pluralism (the holding of more than one benefice at the same time), non-residence (the inevitable consequence of pluralism), and excessive exactions such as probate charges and mortuary fees (the property claimed by the priest for officiating at a burial). Posing as an impartial judge between his contending subjects, he met delegations from each side and tried to resolve the arguments by appointing committees of both houses to discuss them. It is clear, however, that he was not at all averse to seeing the bishops discomforted at a time when he needed their agreement to achieve an annulment in England.[50] Significantly it was a member of the royal household, his comptroller, Sir Henry Guildford, who provoked the attack on mortuary fees in the Commons.

Religious and legal reformers took advantage of the divorce debate to encourage Henry to curb ecclesiastical power and privilege and to assert his own authority. Lay lawyers such as Christopher St German argued that the English common law and Parliament were superior to Roman law and the ecclesiastical courts, implying that they offered a surer means than petitions to Rome of achieving the royal divorce. In his influential legal textbook, *Doctor and Student*, St German argued that the English church owed its allegiance primarily to the King in Parliament, and called upon Henry to use his authority to force the clergy to reform. In defending the anticlerical legislation of the 1529 session, St German offered what looks like a tacit acceptance that, where church reform was concerned, Might made Right:

I hold it not best to reason or to make arguments whether they [the Commons] had authority to do what they did or not. For I suppose that no man would think that they would do anything that they had no power to do.[51]

All matters of clerical jurisdiction and authority, he argued, were essentially questions of property ownership, and therefore subject to the common and not the canon law.[52]

More importantly, a team of scholars led by Edward Fox (and later to include Thomas Cranmer), that was working on the justification for Henry's claims to be exempt from citation to the Roman courts over the divorce, had, by early 1530, broadened the scope of their work to the point where they were prepared to assert that the English crown was entirely free of obligation to any foreign authority. It was, in their telling phrase, a 'crown imperial', sufficient to itself in all matters temporal and spiritual. The conclusions of this covert think-tank of inner counsellors were presented in the *Collectanea satis copiosa*, the 'sufficiently large collections' of examples and precedents for 'imperial' kingship assembled from an array of texts from Anglo-Saxon charters and Geoffrey of Monmouth's *Chronicle*, to the work of the Church Fathers and Henry's beloved Old Testament.[53] Henry had a copy of the *Collectanea* in his hands by September 1530, and read it actively, as the abundant annotations in his own hand testify. It contained the most welcome and effective piece of counsel yet, and in it Henry found confirmation of what he had always felt instinctively to be the case. As early as 1515 he had asserted that 'by the ordinance and sufferance of God we are King of England, and the kings of England in time past have never had any superior but God alone'.[54] The *Collectanea* offered the detailed justification for that statement. He was not beholden to the Pope for adjudication on matters of canon law, his own clergy, loyal to him alone, could settle his Great Matter themselves, on his authority. But, if Henry had always been convinced of the theory, the failure of the clergy to agree to his demands over the divorce suggested that putting it into practice would prove difficult, and require rather more force than he had initially expected.

The first obvious sign that Henry was prepared openly to go beyond the appearance of consultation and argument in order to get his own way was the legal action begun in King's Bench against a number of clerics, some of whom had taken Katherine of Aragon's side in the Blackfriars trial.[55] Ambassador Chapuys shrewdly observed that the charges were aimed at getting 'the prelates and clergy so in his [the King's] power that they shall sanction this marriage, which he has always said should have the advice and authority of the Anglican church'.[56]

In January 1531 Henry widened the threat, demanding £100,000 from Convocation in return for a royal pardon for the clergy for having 'illegally' exercised a rival jurisdiction in the church courts. The financial demand was thus linked to a tacit recognition that all ecclesiastical jurisdiction was rightly exercised under the King's authority, not independently of it. Southern Convocation sued for pardon on 24 January, duly offering the £100,000 demanded to the King in return. But, in February, Henry suddenly increased the stakes, telling Archbishop Warham that the clergy must also, if they wanted their pardon, acknowledge the King 'sole protector and supreme head of the English church and clergy'. This was a novel imposition indeed, and the higher clergy, with Katherine's champion John Fisher prominent among them, raised objections in Convocation, striving to limit and circumscribe the King's demands. In the end, anxious to offer something positive, they agreed to acknowledge the royal supremacy, but only 'as far as the law of Christ allows', a qualification which allowed each side a degree of latitude in terms of interpretation.[57]

A number of clerics did object formally to the King's demands. In the northern Convocation Bishop Tunstal of Durham entered a protest into the official register of its proceedings, and in May 1531 he wrote directly to Henry, insisting that the King could not claim authority over the Church in spiritual matters.[58] Some members of the lower house of southern Convocation also signed a letter of protest, which asserted that the King's new title should not be interpreted to involve any diminution of papal authority over the Church, or to indicate any shift in the traditional role of the Crown as its guardian in temporal matters only. Nor should it be thought to sanction any future limitation of ecclesiastical liberties.[59] But as Christopher St German wrote in the *New Additions* to his *Doctor and Student*, published in 1531, and reflecting current government thinking, the King in Parliament was 'the high sovereign over the people, which hath not only charge on the bodies, but also on the souls of his subjects'.[60]

The King's scruple of conscience over his marriage had led, in the course of three years, not only to the dramatic appearance of the schism within the spiritual community discussed in the previous chapters, but to the Church in England itself being subordinated to the supremacy of an 'imperial' royal head: a jurisdictional revolution with as yet unknown and potentially incalculable consequences. And the King, advised by a narrow group of highly partisan counsellors, rather than seeking to heal the divisions and moderate constitutional change, was the driving force behind the entire process. This was the unprecedented situation in which Sir Thomas Elyot, then newly dismissed from the Clerkship of the Council, wrote his first major published work, *The Book Named the Governor* (1531), and presented it to the King. The bulk of the next chapter will be devoted to a close reading of that text. For, although a glance at the conventional criticism on the subject would suggest otherwise, it was actually a remonstrance far more insistent and sustained in its focus than anything that Elyot could have said to his King on his return from embassy in the June of the following year.

8

The Book Named the Governor

Good Kingship and the Royal Supremacy

Scholarly criticism of *The Book Named the Governor* has fallen roughly into two camps: one (the smaller) contending that the text is essentially educational in focus, and so has little of value to say about politics, particularly of the contemporary sort, the second asserting that it *is* a political tract, but should be read as a contribution to government propaganda in favour of the Royal Supremacy and the Henrician Reformation.[1] Neither view, I will suggest, is a fair account of the complex and carefully crafted book that Elyot offered as his suggested remedy for the crisis afflicting England in 1531.

The idea that *The Governor* is really a text for and about the schoolroom has led its advocates not only to miss the book's crucial political dimension but also to undervalue its intellectual and aesthetic qualities. Scholars of this school have asked why a treatise on the education of young aristocrats should begin with a lengthy justification of monarchy as a system of government, the implication being that the two subjects are, if not completely incompatible, then at least highly incongruous bedfellows. Various theories have been offered in an effort to explain why the two might have been brought together, the most notable suggesting a two-stage writing process in which an educational handbook was converted into a text suitable for presentation to the King by the hasty addition of three new chapters dealing with questions of political philosophy.[2] Their conclusion has usually been to dismiss the text from consideration as a political document on grounds either of its alleged incoherence or its primarily educational aims, or both. If the bulk of the book was never intended to be political, and the opening chapters were only a last minute addition, then neither can have very much to tell us about contemporary events or their interpretation, the argument runs. But such readings profoundly underestimate *The Governor*'s value as a political document. For, on closer inspection it is neither incoherent nor apolitical, and it is precisely its political agenda that provides its coherence. A brief examination of the ways in which politics and education had been discussed in other contemporary texts will help to explain why.

Education and The Prince

As the opening chapter suggested, late-medieval and Renaissance notions of good kingship and models of the ideal relationship between princes and their counsellors adapted ideals of political conduct developed for the senators of ancient Rome to fit conditions at the courts of contemporary princes, with the honest and eloquent orators who spoke for the common good in the Senate transformed into honest and eloquent counsellors who spoke in the ears of their king.[3]

The central figure in the early Renaissance reconception of classical political thinking was Desiderius Erasmus, whose writings offered a comprehensive critique of contemporary princely government, its strengths and shortcomings. *The Education of a Christian Prince*, the treatise he wrote for the young Charles V, stressed the crucial importance of education and good counsel to the proper functioning of the state. The principal problem for monarchical states, as he noted with frank clarity, lay in the institution of monarchy itself. 'On board ship', he observed,

We do not give the helm to the one who has the noblest ancestry... the greatest wealth, or the best looks, but to him who is most skilled in steering, most alert, and most reliable. Similarly, a kingdom is best entrusted to someone who is better endowed than the rest with the qualities of a king: namely wisdom, a sense of justice, personal restraint, foresight, and concern for the public well-being.[4]

The choice of a sovereign would thus be a difficult business, even under ideal circumstances. But the subjects of most kingdoms did not, of course, ever face such a choice, as kings were almost universally selected by birth and succession rather than election. So the choices facing the state were few. In 'The Godly Feast', one of his *Colloquies*, Erasmus offered an allegorical account of them. When deciding whether to admit the princely lion within its walls, he claimed, a city could do one of three things:

The first, perhaps, will be not to receive the lion into the city. Next, by authority of Senate, magistrates, and people, to limit his power in such a way that he may not easily break out into tyranny. But the best safeguard of all is to shape his character by sacred teachings while he is still a boy and doesn't realise he's a ruler. Petitions and admonitions help, provided they are polite and temperate.[5]

Outlining this preferred idea of shaping the prince to fit the role of government was the purpose behind *The Education of a Christian Prince*. Within its pages Erasmus set out a prospectus for the grooming of a young prince to meet his royal destiny:

When the prince is born to office, not elected, which was the custom among some barbarian peoples (according to Aristotle) and is also the practice almost everywhere in our own times, then the main hope of getting a good prince hangs on his proper education, which should be managed all the more attentively, so that what has been lost with the right to vote is made up for by the care given to his upbringing. Accordingly, the mind of the future prince will have to be filled straight away, from the very cradle (as they say), with healthy thoughts while it is still open and undeveloped. And from then on the seeds of morality must be sown in the virgin soil of his infant soul, so that, with age and experience, they may gradually germinate and mature, and, once they are set, may be rooted in him throughout his whole life.[6]

The young prince should be brought up to admire the great rulers of the past and fear above all things gaining a reputation as a tyrant in later life. And the lessons in virtue, sobriety, and good conduct taught him in his youth must be constantly reinforced throughout his later life, 'kept fresh in the memory in all sorts of ways: sometimes in a moral maxim, sometimes in a parable . . . they must be carved on rings, painted in pictures, inscribed in prizes . . . so that they are always before his mind, even when he is doing something else'.[7] Above all else, the prince should at all times be surrounded with men (and that it should be almost exclusively men is tacitly assumed throughout) who would discretely but honestly remind him of his responsibilities.

The most important figure in the model of government described by Erasmus was, then, not the prince himself, but the good counsellor, the man who would continue to remind the prince of the highest standards of conduct to which he must adhere, and use the store of wisdom at his disposal to advise him of the right course of action in any situation.[8] Such men needed themselves to be educated to the highest standards in literature, philosophy, politics, and the sciences, in order that they could impart the necessary wisdom to their royal charges, and they needed to deploy the rhetorician's skills of persuasion and logic to convince the prince of the value of the lessons they offered. Thus the seemingly distinct subjects treated in *The Governor*: the education of the governor and the merits of monarchy are actually aspects of the same subject. For elite education, courtier-craft, and good government were intimately related, and together formed the basis of humanist political theory.[9] That *The Governor* was on one level a discussion of an ideal programme of education enhanced rather than invalidated its potential to address contemporary political issues.[10] Indeed, as we shall see, Elyot's 'schoolroom text' offered both an acute diagnosis of the ills of contemporary politics and a clear suggestion for their remedy.

The relationship between prince and counsellor was, then, the lynchpin of the humanist conception of the state, and each party needed to understand and fulfil the role allotted to him. Castiglione's *The Courtier*, a work whose reputation and influence rivalled those of Erasmus's *Education*, stressed, as we have seen, the crucial importance of counselling the prince to the role of the courtier.[11] Elyot would make the same point in *The Governor*, arguing with characteristic literalness and precision for the centrality of the counsellor's role in the life of the state:

The end of all doctrine and study is good counsel, whereunto, as unto the principal point, which Geometricians do call the Centre, all doctrines, (which by some authors be imagined in the form of a circle) do send their effects like unto equal lines.

(*The Governor*, sig. i iv)

The courtier and counsellor thus needed to ensure that their skills and learning were always directed by honesty and an overriding loyalty to the well-being of the whole kingdom, not simply the private interests of the prince. And their analysis of any political situation needed to be dispassionate and rigorous. As Elyot was to put it, borrowing from Cataline, the good counsellor was one who, 'while he consulteth in doubtful matters, is void of all hate, friendship, displeasure, or pity' (*The Governor*, sig. i iv(v)). Good kings in their turn did not have to be perfect, only to be willing to listen to the well-intentioned criticism of those advisers who revealed their faults and weaknesses for them. As Erasmus advised his prince, he must 'accustom his friends to the knowledge that they find favour by giving frank advice'.[12] This quality of open-mindedness in the prince was described by Elyot as affability and it lay, as we shall see, at the heart of his conception of the ideal ruler. The 'uncounselled king' was, almost by definition, a tyrant, the good king's antithesis and dark shadow. The utility of this model of royal affability and conciliar frankness was that it enabled a political dialogue to take place in a system that otherwise prized obedience and unanimity over pluralism and debate. Theoretically at least, it opened up a space for alternative voices at court and in government, allowing critics of current policies the opportunity to raise their concerns and to suggest alternative courses of action, and for princes to receive criticism and alter policies without appearing to be weak or vacillating. Thus, in theory, were the social and intellectual elites bound to the crown by mutually informing concepts of honesty and affability.[13]

Such notions of good kingship and the theory of counsel that underpinned them, were well-known in England, and not least, as I suggested in Chapter 1, to Henry VIII himself. He had learned the lessons of how to embrace the princely virtues and shun the vices that led to tyranny from his tutors, and from the books he had read as a youth.[14] And the King's behaviour in the first two decades of his reign had given every indication that he had taken such examples to heart and intended to live by them. He appeared to be, as Lord Mountjoy declared at his accession, if not quite a philosopher king, then at least a king for philosophers, a royal Maecenas to whose court would flock the best of Europe's scholars and counsellors.[15]

It was precisely this golden promise, and the history of Henry's early reign, that made what followed so troublesome to a man like Elyot who not only understood the tenets of the *Mirror for Princes* tradition, but believed in them passionately. For, as we shall see, Henry's fall into what seemed to be the textbook tyrannical traits of self-indulgence, favouritism, and violent intimidation left the traditional methods of political participation compromised and ineffective, at the same time as few alternative modes of loyal criticism suggested themselves. Men in Elyot's position would thus, as the 1530s progressed, be faced with an unwelcome choice between silent compliance in policies with which they profoundly disagreed, or outright opposition to them that confounded their powerful sense of loyalty to the crown. It is the beginning of such a dilemma that, I would argue, one can detect in the pages of Elyot's first major discussion of contemporary politics, *The Governor*.

The Governor *and Good Counsel*

On one level, *The Governor's* great achievement was to translate into contemporary English terms the principles, originally distilled from classical precedents, that Erasmus had set down for the benefit of Charles V some fifteen years earlier in *The Education of a Christian Prince*.[16] Indeed, on first reading, Elyot's text seems to follow the central tenets of the earlier book like a blueprint. He provides the recommended catalogue of good and bad examples for his readers to consider: the virtuous princes to be admired and copied, the hateful tyrants to be reviled. There are the learned princes: the Emperor Augustus, who read Cicero and Virgil to his children and 'nephews', or the tyrant Dionysus of Sicily who reformed himself by reading Plato while in exile (sig. ciii). There are the princes who acted as patrons to learned men: Augustus (again), 'Nerva, Trajan, Hadrian, the two Antonines [Marcus Antoninus Aurelius and Antoninus Pius], and the wonderful emperor Alexander, for his gravity called Severus', whose palaces were 'always replenished with eloquent orators, delectable poets, wise philosophers, most cunning and expert lawyers, prudent and valiant captains'. One might judge the qualities of such rulers, Elyot claimed, by the company they kept; just as such 'monstrous emperors' as Nero and Caligula, announced their vices by 'nourishing about them ribalds and other voluptuous artificers' (Nvi(v)).

Over and over again the importance of affability and the careful selection of good counsellors is driven home by maxim, example, and analogy. The greatest of emperors were made ready for greatness by the teachings of their tutors: 'What manner a prince Alexander [the Great] was made by the doctrine of Aristotle, it shall appear in diverse places of this book: where his example to princes shall be declared' (Dv); 'what caused Trajan to be so good a prince . . . but that he happed to have Plutarch the noble philosopher to be his instructor[?]' (Dv(v)). Some princes may be naturally inclined to virtue, but good instruction and advice will make even these men much better rulers in time.[17] Thus, even as an infant the future governor should be provided with juvenile good counsellors, morally upright 'companions and playfellows' who would not 'avaunt him with flattery', but 'persuade him to virtue, or to withdraw him from vice in the remembering to him the danger of his evil example' (ci(v)).

The book commends the affability of Artaxerxes, King of Persia, who gratefully received a gift of 'clean water' from the rough hands of a poor husbandman: an emblem of his openness to even the lowliest of his subjects (aii(v)). Marcus Antonius is praised because he sought out the 'most homely and plain men' in Rome and had them secretly brought to his chamber,

Where he diligently enquired of them what people conjectured of his living: commanding
them upon pain of his high indignation to tell him truth, and hide nothing from him.
And upon their report, if he heard anything worthy never so little dispraise, he forthwith
amended it.

(Pi)

Exemplifying the maxim that 'the sufferance of noble men to be spoken unto is
not only to them an incomparable surety, but also a confounder of repentance,
enemy to prudence' (Piii), Elyot cites Plutarch's story of Philip of Macedon who,
after dozing through a trial, would have given a rash and erroneous verdict, had
not the defendant, a soldier, boldly cried out, 'I appeal!' ' "To whom wilt thou
appeal[?]", said the king. "To thee" (said the soldier), "when thou arte thoroughly
awaked" '. With 'which answer the king suspended his sentence; and more
diligently examining the matter, found the soldier had wrong', and judged in
his favour, thus saving his own reputation for probity (Piii–iii(v)).[18]
   There are a number of stories concerning the Emperor Antoninus, who was so
affable that he forbad his guards from barring anyone from his presence (Piv),
and on one occasion, visiting the house of 'a mean gentleman', was rebuked by
his host for being too inquisitive concerning the origin of its furnishings. 'Sir',
advised the gentleman, ' "when ye come into any other man's house than your
own, ever be you both dumb and deaf"; which liberal taunt that most gentle
emperor took in so good part that he oftentimes rehearsed that sentence to
other[s] for a wise and discrete counsel' (Piv). When the emperor Augustus
learned that 'many men in the city [of Rome] had of him unfitting words',
Elyot noted, 'he thought it a sufficient answer that in a free city men must have
their tongues needs at liberty. Nor never was [he] with any person that spoke evil
of him in word or countenance worse discontented' (c ii–ii(v)). While, when
Julius Caesar was the subject of 'contumelious or reproachable verses' written by
the poet Catullus, 'he not only forgave him, but to make him his friend, caused
him oftentimes to sup with him' (c i(v)–ii).
   Likewise Elyot cites the dire consequences that befell those princes who
chose to reject affability or to surround themselves with flatterers and yes-men:
'O, what damage[s] have ensued to princes and their realms where liberty of
speech hath been restrained?' (Pi(v)). Chief among these are the once affable
rulers who fell into vice and self-indulgence later in their reigns. What caused the
premature death of Alexander, Elyot asks, but his neglect of his former openness
to criticism?

Where, if he had retained the same affability that was in him in the beginning of his
conquest and had not put to silence his counsellors which before used to speak to him
frankly, he might have escaped all violent death . . . For, after he waxed to be terrible in
manners and prohibited his friends and discrete servants to use their accustomed liberty
in speech, he fell into a hateful grudge among his own people.

(Pi(v)–Pii. See also Evii(v)).

Similarly, Julius Caesar had 'abandoned his natural disposition' and sought,

New ways how to be advanced above the estate of mortal princes; wherefore little and little he withdrew from men his accustomed gentleness, becoming more sturdy in language and strange in countenance than ever before had been his usage. And to declare more plainly his intent, he made an edict or decree that no man should please to come to him uncalled, and that they should have good await, that they spoke not in such familiar fashion to him as they before had been accustomed: whereby he so did alienate from him the hearts of his most wise and assured adherents, that from that time forward, his life was to them tedious; and abhorring him as a monster or common enemy, they being knit in a confederacy, slew him sitting in the Senate.

(Pii)

'Who beholding the cause of the death of this most noble Caesar', Elyot asked,

will not commend affability, and extol liberty of speech, whereby only love is in the hearts of the people perfectly kindled, all fear excluded, and consequently realms, dominions, and all other authorities consolidate and perpetually established?

(Piii).[19]

But, rather than simply reproduce Erasmus's material uncritically, Elyot's text actively deployed the model of literary counsel that *The Education* offered to address specific contemporary issues. Nowhere is this more obvious than in his extended discussion of consultation, a section of *The Governor* which seems to have no single immediate source in the works Elyot is known to have used elsewhere.[20] The last two chapters of the book are devoted to a sustained discussion of the importance to the well-being of the realm of both counsel and consultation (which is the more formal collective version of counsel in which 'men do devise together and reason what is to be done' (i ii(v)).[21]

When the public weal is stricken with griefs or ailments, 'than cometh the time and opportunity of consultation, whereby . . . is provided the remedies necessary for the healing of the said griefs' (i ii(v)).

It is therefore expedient that consultation (wherein counsel is expressed) be very serious, substantial, and profitable. Which to bring to effect requireth two things principally to be considered. First that in every thing concerning a public weal no good counsellor be omitted or passed over, but that his reason therein be heard to an end . . . [Second] that the general and universal estate of the public weal would be preferred . . . before any particular commodity and the profit or damage which may happen within our own countries would be more considered than that which may happen from other regions.

(sigs. i iv(v) and i vi(v))

It was, then, his counsellors and not the King himself, who had the prime responsibility to consider the problems facing the commonwealth and devise the means to resolve them. They must gather around their sovereign, to investigate or enquire exquisitely the form and reason of the affair, and in that study to be wholly resolved so effectually that they which be counsellors may bear with them out of the council house, as it were on their shoulders, not only what is to be followed and exploited but also by what means or ways it shall be pursued . . . wherefore counsel, being compact of . . . [justice, goodness, and honesty] may be named a perfect Captain, a trusty companion, a plain and unfeigned friend.

(i iii(v))

Thus the reader is continually reminded of the overriding importance of counsel to the smooth running of the state. Elyot characteristically draws his examples widely from both the Bible and classical history. 'My son, without counsel see thou do nothing, and then after thy deed thou shalt never repent thee' (Ecclesiastes) (i iii(v)). Without recourse to open and honest counsel, the realm is destined for chaos and disorder.[22] 'Tulli [Cicero] affirmeth in his book of office [*De officiis*]. Arms without the doors be of little importance if counsel be not at home' (i iii(v)). Thus the ruler is advised to 'consult before thou enterprise any thing', 'and after thou hast taken counsel, it is expedient to do it maturely', that is, 'with such moderation that nothing in the doing may be seen superfluous or indigent' (Liv(v)). He is also to practise providence in the exercise of authority, 'whereby a man not only foreseeth commodity and incommodity, prosperity and adversity, but also consulteth, and therewith endevoureth as well to repel annoyance as to attain and get profit and advantage' (Lv).

Critics have sometimes taken Elyot's advocacy (here and elsewhere) of widespread consultation, and of the need to exclude no one, however humble, from the process ('that in every thing concerning a public weal no good counsellor be omitted or passed over, but that his reason be heard to an end'), as very personalized in their motivation.[23] Such passages, it is suggested, are Elyot's plea for his own return to royal service after his dismissal from the clerkship of the Council, a reflection of the feelings of resentment and frustrated ambition that surface in a number of the letters written to Cromwell in the 1530s. But this is, perhaps, too narrow and uncharitable a reading. It is clear that Elyot did harbour a sense of personal entitlement, based upon his past service, lack of appropriate financial reward for his labours, and his learning and experience, which led him to hope throughout the 1530s for a return to governmental service in due course. And this, coupled with this oft-professed opinion that scholars were a necessary part of the machinery of royal government, may have led him to harbour unrealistically high expectations of his future usefulness to the state.[24] But, given the contemporary circumstances, it is probably wise to give the author the benefit of the doubt where personal ambition is concerned, and read such passages as primarily promoting a more consensual, and hence less radical, approach to the pursuit of the King's Great Matter. If Elyot himself could be called to counsel, then that would be the ideal solution to both his own and his country's ills. But what mattered above all was that some dissenting conservative voices should be heard at the council table, even if his was not one of them.

At another time or in another place it might have been possible to dismiss these sentiments as timeless platitudes. But read in London in 1531 they could not but have been seen as pointed reflections on the crisis provoked by the King's Great Matter: a crisis whose effects every politically active citizen would have experienced, and whose full consequences none could yet foresee. Henry had raised the question of consultation himself, seeking to present his own divorce case as an example of affable kingship in action, portraying himself as a man troubled in his conscience who sought the advice of his counsellors concerning his dilemma. But, as his Great Matter progressed (or rather failed to progress), as his public consultations brought only unwelcome advice and efforts to settle the case in the Roman courts ran into the sand among legal and diplomatic wrangling, Henry had responded more aggressively to critical voices and taken his counsel from an ever tighter circle of government advisers, chief among them evangelicals such as Cromwell and Cranmer and the team of scholars that had produced the *Collectanea satis copiosa*. The motives of such men were hardly disinterested. In such circumstances, for Elyot to stress the importance of consulting as wide a cross-section of informed opinion as possible; of heeding all the voices that could speak on an issue, and taking no offence when those voices offered criticisms of the prince's behaviour, was hardly a politically neutral observation. To critics of the divorce such as Elyot, the King's actions would have seemed the absolute antithesis of good princely practice, involving as they did the rejection of honest counsel in favour of a potentially tyrannical reliance upon a narrow clique of self-interested advisers.

For those privy to events at court, the creation of the *Collectanea* and its delivery to Henry VIII in September 1530 would have provided ample evidence that radical ideas concerning the King's sovereignty were being touted (and, more importantly, given credence) at the heart of government.[25] Was not Henry, like Caesar in the anecdote cited by Elyot, seeking 'new ways how to be advanced above the estate of mortal princes'? But, even without privileged insight into the workings of Foxe's team and of Henry's own mind, there was enough happening in the full glare of public attention to cause Elyot and others like him to worry. The divisive debates in the 1529 session of Parliament were, as we have seen, clearly deeply troubling to many, conservatives and moderates alike. The fall of Wolsey and the *praemunire* charges against leading churchmen, the increasingly rancorous debate over the right to try the King's divorce, in which Henry was seemingly setting his own will against the conclusions of his most experienced counsellors; all of these factors created a volatile political environment in which the idea of good counsel could become a rallying point for those seeking political stability and a return to traditional modes of government.

Read in this context, Elyot's stress upon the virtue of consultation, the importance of receiving critical counsel affably, and the need to banish time-serving or partisan advisers, became a very direct contribution to the debates over the King's affairs. In *The Governor* Elyot effectively reminded the King of the need to make good the claim to affability, and see the consultation process through to its logical and necessary conclusion. Henry needed to heed all the counsels offered to him on the subject rather than merely those whose conclusions he wished to hear, and accept the judgement of the wisest heads without regard for partiality or his private desires. In any gathering, Elyot suggested, 'many will speak warily for fear of displeasure, some more bolder in virtue will not spare to show their minds plainly; diverse will assent to that reasons [sic] wherewith they suppose that he which is chief in authority will be best pleased' (i v). Thus the prince must ensure the widest participation in his consultations, for, 'where there is a great number of counsellors, they all being heard, needs must counsel be the more perfect' (i v). The King who neglects the well-being of the whole of his realm to pursue a single, partial interest is, Elyot asserts, like the gardener who, focusing on 'one knot or bed of herbs', allows the rest of his plot to become overrun with weeds, 'and all the garden [is] made unprofitable and also unpleasant' (i vi(v)).

> Wherefore the consultation is but of a small effect wherein the universal estate of the public weal do[es] not occupy the most part of the time ... For, as Tulli sayeth, they that consult for part of the people and neglect the residue, they bring in to the city or country a thing most pernicious, that is to say sedition and discord.
>
> (i vii)

Far from being simply an educational treatise, then, Elyot's *Governor* was a text directly prompted by and addressed towards contemporary events. It offered its royal dedicatee, not only a programme for the education of the next generation of ministers and counsellors, but a mirror of his own conduct and the state of his realm.

The Governor *and the Powers of the Prince*

The model of kingship advanced in *The Governor* is in fact far from absolutist in its implications, and far from uncritically supportive of the Royal Supremacy.[26] For in chapter after chapter in the latter part of the book, Elyot lays down a whole network of principles and examples of good and bad conduct the effect of which, if put into practice, would be to reduce the powers of the prince dramatically. Regardless of the prerogatives allotted him in theory, the virtues of self-restraint and circumspection bred in him by sedulous tutors and by copious reading in the classics, coupled with the external encouragement to prudence created by the desire to present an example of virtue to the world, would reduce the good prince effectively to the role of chairman of a board whose other members—philosophers and men of virtue all—he was obliged to consult and respect.

To say that Elyot praises monarchy in general and Henry VIII in particular in *The Governor* is, then, only the first step in any attempt to understand his political ambitions for the text. What we need to ask next is *how* he praises them, and in what context, as it is in the precise nuances of detail and timing that the real agenda and impact of *The Governor* can be judged. It is the qualities that Elyot chooses to celebrate in his kings rather than the fact that they are kings that are really telling so far as *The Governor*'s political agenda is concerned. And here again there is little in the text that would have given comfort to advocates of the Supremacy or religious reformation.

Kings should be merciful (as Julius Caesar and Augustus were (oi–iii)), as mercy was the central humane virtue ('not only reason persuadeth, but also experience proveth, that in whom mercy lacketh and is not found, in him all other virtues be drowned and lose their just commendation' (sig. oi)). They should practise patience ('a noble virtue appertaining as well to inward governance as to exterior governance, and is the vanquisher of injuries, the sure defence against all affects and passions of the soul' (b. viii)). In addition to regal majesty, they should, as we have seen, also display affability ('a wonderful efficacy or power in procuring love … where a man is facile or easy to be spoken unto' (ovii(v)), and placability (whereby, when 'by an occasion moved to be angry', he yet 'either by his own reason ingenerate, or by counsel persuaded, he omitteth to be revenged, and oftentimes receiveth the transgressor, once reconciled, into more favour' (piv(v)–pvi)). He must show prudence (Aristotle's 'mother of virtues' (Liii(v)), and circumspection (Mi), twin aspects of the foresight that will anticipate the consequences of actions and lead to the practice of due care and moderation in the pursuit of policy.

All of these virtues have a long pedigree in handbooks and the mirror for princes tradition, and scholars have spent a good deal of time fruitfully pursuing them to the classical or near contemporary texts that Elyot might have used as his sources.[27] But what interests me about these ideas is not so much where Elyot found them as the use to which he put them once he had done so, and here again the context creates the key to their purpose and likely reception. For it is one thing to praise a king for moderation and placability at a time when the realm is at peace with itself and justice is universally recognized to prevail, quite another to do so when there is the kind of widespread sense of social crisis and internal dissension that existed in the period in which Elyot was writing. In the latter case, the rehearsal of certain conventional platitudes and the failure to rehearse certain others can be, not an exercise in antiquarianism, but a direct intervention in contemporary politics. Hence the obvious significance of *The Governor*'s frequent rehearsal of motifs of reconciliation, tolerance, and healing.[28] Elyot praises the role of the prince as a reconciler of divisions and a conciliator between factions, citing the case of Agamemnon, who was chosen to lead the expedition to Troy, *The Governor* suggests, because he was able to contain the rivalries between the various Greek princes, despite the presence of many greater commanders in the host (Bii).

Alertness to the contemporary resonance to Elyot's consistent stress upon affability, patience, tolerance, consultation, and counsel, makes it impossible to agree with those critics who have read *The Governor* as an apologia for the Royal

Supremacy or even a defence of absolutism.[29] Such claims have generally arisen from considerations of the book in the context of other works of political philosophy rather than as a work in continual dialogue with contemporary events. By shifting the focus from the former to the latter very different emphases begin to suggest themselves.

Stanford Lehmberg, noting the absence of any sustained discussion of the evils of tyranny in the book, saw it as indicative of Elyot's outlook. Unlike the majority of the examples of the mirrors for princes genre produced in the past century or more, he argued, Elyot does not dwell upon the drawbacks and dangers inherent in monarchical government, thus downplaying its adverse implications.[30] Similarly, there is no extended account of the role that might be played by the common law or Parliament in limiting the King's freedom of action. Thus, it has been suggested, the version of royal sovereignty presented in *The Governor* was one that Henry VIII, embarking upon the Royal Supremacy, would have found very encouraging. Indeed, critics have gone so far as to describe the book as 'one of the earliest implicit justifications of the English reformation'?[31] But read in the context of the events of 1529–31, it becomes clear that *The Governor* is far from a justification of the policies of Henry VIII's government, still less an apologia for the reformation. Where the book advocates political philosophies compatible with the Supremacy it does so as limited tactical concessions to seemingly irresistible forces for change, or because the Supremacy represents the least damaging of a range of unsavoury options. Elsewhere in the book Elyot offers a vision of the ideal public weal that is very far from that imagined by Henry VIII when he initiated the break with Rome.

When considering the contemporary impact of *The Governor* it is as important to ask what it does not say as to chart what it does say. For the absences are instructive. There may be, as Lehmberg argues, few references to tyranny, but there are none at all to royal authority over the Church or the sacerdotal powers of kings that Henry was claiming for himself at this time. Nor are there any criticisms of foreign influence or the overweening jurisdictional claims of Rome, or of the English ecclesiastical courts of the sort that one might have expected to find if appealing to the King's current agenda had been Elyot's prime ambition. As we shall see, while Lehmberg may be right in claiming that there was 'nothing at which [Henry] might have grumbled' in *The Governor* (although even this might both underestimate the text's covert assertiveness and overestimate the King's patience), there was a good deal in it that would have given him pause, and much that would have suggested to him a very different conception of his royal prerogative and powers to that outlined for him by the team of scholars working to justify the Supremacy. *The Governor*, as a fine example of the humanist virtue of 'copiousness' (the encyclopaedic gathering of disparate materials into an elegant whole), had the potential to be many things to many people, but an extended appendix to the *Collectanea satis copiosa* it clearly was not.

A complex and at times frustratingly diffuse text, *The Governor* nonetheless marshals its arguments carefully, offering encouragement to its royal reader at the same time as preparing him for less welcome truths later in the same argument. Each chapter is thus an exercise in the Erasmian art of panegyric, offering correction and instruction even as it bestows praise. Hence the prospectus for monarchy and the powers of the prince set out in the opening chapters is initially impressive, both in its scope and the terms it employs. But we do not have to read too far into the detail before the qualifications and limitations of what it is offering the King by way of a philosophy of royal government become abundantly clear. Having outlined in detail why the concept of the state defined in Latin as the *res publica* should be translated into English as a 'public' rather than a 'common' weal (sigs. Ai–Aii(v)), and why a hierarchical society is the divinely ordained model for the best ordered collective life (Aii(v)–Av(v)), the text moves on in the second chapter to justify the claim 'That one sovereign governor ought to be in a public weal' (Avi). First the alternatives to a monarchy are rejected. Aristocracy (the rule of an elite, as practiced in classical Thebes) is too riven by personal ambition and factional fighting among the elite to be a stable form of government. Democracy (the Athenian model, called 'in English, the rule of the comminalty') is equally prone to misgovernment and also to chaotic mob rule ('which might well be called a monster with many heads, nor never was certain nor stable, and often times they banished or slew the best citizens').[32] Finally, the only acceptable alternative is described by analogy with the divine and natural orders:

Undoubtedly, the best and most sure governance is by one King or prince, which ruleth only for the weal of his people to him subject: and that manner of governance is best approved . . . and is most ancient. For who can deny but that all thing in heaven and earth is governed by one God, by one perpetual order, by one Providence? One sun ruleth over the day, and one Moon over the night . . .

(Avii(v))

But Elyot's advocacy of rule by a singular, princely ruler falls well short, even here, of a justification of the kind of limitless, unchecked sovereignty usually understood by the term 'absolute', or even the more modest claims of Henrician 'imperial' sovereignty. The analogies Elyot cites are conventional enough, and being, as they are, drawn from the divine order of the cosmos would seem to be non-negotiable as evidence of how the microcosm of human politics should be organized. But, politically speaking at least, they are something of a mixed bag. The analogy with the single God in heaven, uncreated maker of all things, is promising enough in absolutist, caesaropapist terms. But the next example, one sun in the day, one moon at night, already hints at the possibility of a mixed polity, a division of labours and jurisdictions under the aegis of a notionally unified sovereignty which would be ill-suited to encourage a king set upon the absorption of the separate jurisdiction of the church under a single, 'imperial' crown.[33]

Still more obviously, the third analogy that Elyot cites, the example of the beehive, argues overtly for a very distinct and limited form of sovereignty. And it does so in terms that would have resonated very powerfully among the participants in the political disputes of 1529–31, the period during which Elyot was preparing his text for the press. For the 'king' of the bees, as Elyot describes him, is explicitly denied any form of compulsive force with which to enforce his authority. His rule is founded entirely upon the good example of experience and wisdom that he can offer to his subjects and the good of the common weal that it can foster. The hive is, Elyot asserts,

as it seemeth, a perpetual figure of a just governance or rule: who hath among them one principal Bee for their governor, who excelleth all other in greatness, yet hath no prick or sting, but in him is more knowledge than in the residue . . . [hence all look to him for guidance]

(Avii(v) –Aviii)[34]

This idea that the king of the bees could not compel his subjects to follow him had been used to argue for mercy and self-restraint in rulers in a number of influential texts of the previous century and a half. John Trevisa's translation of Bartholomaeus Anglicus', *De Proprietatibus Rerum* (*On the Properties of Things*) had declared that bees 'choseth to [i.e. choose as] her king thilke that [that which] is most clear in mildness, for that is chief virtue in a king, for, though the king have a sting, he useth it not in wreche [anger]'.[35] Thomas Hoccleve had been still more explicit about the lesson to be learnt from the monarchy of the bees in his *Regiment of Princes*. In his section on *Misericordia* he argued:

> Senek [Seneca] seith how the Kyng and the leder
> Of bees is prikkelees; he hath right noon
> Wherwith to styngen or annoye or dere,
> But other bees prikkes han everichoon [each one].
> Nature wolde hee sholde it forgoon,
> And do no crueltee unto the swarm,
> But meekly hem governe and do noon harm.
>
> Of this ensample sholde kynges take,
> And princes that han peple for to gye [govern],
> For to hem longeth it for goddess sake
> To weyve crueltee and tirannye,
> And to pitee hir hertes bow and wrye,
> And reule hir peple esyly and faire.
> It is kingly [to] be meek and debonaire.[36]

Still more anti-absolutist in its use of the material was the anonymous Ricardian poem *Mom and the Sothsegger*, which argued from the example of the 'king' of bees both that human kings should be merciful and that they should rule by consensus among the commonwealth.

The moste merciful among theym and mekkest of his deedes
Ys King of bees comunely, as clergie it telleth,
And sperelees, and in wil to spare that been hym under,
Or yf he have oon [i.e. a 'spere' or sting], he harmeth ne hurteth noon in sothe.
For venym doeth not folowe hym but vertue in alle workes,
To reule thaym by reason and by rightful domes,
Though content of the cumpaignie that closeth alle in oone.[37]

Most recent, and perhaps uppermost in Elyot's mind as he was writing was, however, Erasmus's deployment of the idea in his *Education of a Christian Prince*. He too used it as a lesson in limiting the prince's capacity for violent coercion.

The counterparts of King and Tyrant can be found even among the dumb animals themselves. The king bee has the largest room, but it is in the centre [of the hive], as if in the safest place for the king. And indeed he has no work to do, but is the one who supervises the work of others. If he is lost, the whole swarm disintegrates. Moreover, the king has a distinctive appearance, being different from the rest in both the size and the sheen of his body. But this feature, as Seneca said, most reliably distinguishes him from the rest: although bees are very angry creatures, so much so that they leave their stings in the wound, the king alone has no sting. Nature did not want him to be fierce and seek a revenge which would cost him so dear, and she deprived him of a weapon, leaving his anger ineffective. This is an important example for powerful kings.[38]

That Elyot chose to cite the commonwealth of the bees for his third analogue for princely government was thus, again, no neutral act. He chose a model that had been consistently deployed by writers in the *speculum principis* tradition as an example of a moderate, restrained authority that was unwilling to resort to violence or coercion, whether domestically or in foreign wars.[39] Moreover he used it in such a way as to make its relevance to domestic policy abundantly clear. Unlike the authors cited above, Elyot does not go on to make the political lesson of the analogy explicit. Rather, he coyly observes that, 'I suppose who seriously beholdeth this example, and hath any commendable wit, shall thereof gather much matter to the forming of a public weal' (Aviii), and then, blaming lack of time to say more, points his readers towards Virgil's *Georgics*, Pliny's *Natural History*, and Collumella's *On Agriculture*, where, he says, they 'will find the example more ample and better declared'. Unlike these writers, who use the bee-king's lack of sting to discuss the role of the commonwealth in wartime (whether, like Pliny or Virgil, to vaunt the collective rigour of the swarm in protecting the King in battle, and the King's organizational powers as a military commander, or, like Erasmus, to argue for a pacific foreign policy), Elyot sticks resolutely to the domestic benefits of the King's non-coercive rule, citing his organization of the labour force, forward planning, and his policing of the hive to remove unprofitable drones. Even when the opportunity to discuss warfare and foreign policy suggests itself, as when he discusses the relationship between the King and other rival 'captains' (the part of the story that prompted Virgil, Pliny, and Erasmus to move on to military matters and foreign policy), Elyot turns it into an allegory of the peaceful division of domestic space. When the number of bees in the hive increases to the point at which they follow a new king, he notes, the two cannot be suffered to exist together:

Wherefore this new company gathered in to a swarm, having their captain among them: and environing him to preserve him from harm, they issue forth seeking a new habitation: which they find in some tree, except with some pleasant noise they be allured and conveyed unto an other hive.'

(Aviii)

For Elyot, then, the commonwealth of the bees offered a model of domestic, not international politics, and one that, more conventionally, argues for the limitation of royal powers rather than their extension.

There were a number of writers in Henrician England who *were* willing, in pursuit of their own radical doctrinal agenda, to vaunt the powers of a truly untrammelled royal supremacy. William Tyndale, as Lehmberg points out, had recently done just that in *The Obedience of a Christian Man*, published in 1528. Tyndale offered his readers a paraphrase of chapter thirteen of St Paul's Letter to the Romans that eulogized Henry's royal office in ways that made its affinities to divine authority all too clear.

The powers that be are ordained of God. Whosoever therefore resisteth the power resisteth the ordinance of God...God hath made the king in every realm judge over all, and over him is there no judge. He that judgeth the King judgeth God, and he that layeth hands on the King layeth hand on God, and he that resisteth the King resisteth God...Hereby seest thou that the king is in this world without law and may at his lust do right or wrong and shall give accounts but to God only.[40]

When set against such statements as this, the limited nature of Elyot's suggestion that a king is like God in heaven, the sun and moon in the sky, and the stingless principal bee become rather more obvious. And tellingly, when Elyot does make a similar point in *The Governor*, claiming that 'the hearts of princes be in God's own hands and disposition'(Biv(v)) (one of the few occasions in the text where he discusses the consequences of princely actions in anything beyond a purely human and historical framework), the moral that he draws from it concerns not the freedoms that this unique relationship with the divine bestows, but the increased obligation that it places on the prince 'to be virtuously occupied' and avoid lechery and gluttony (Bv). That princes are ultimately responsible only to God was for Elyot not a liberation but a further onerous burden that they bore, one further reason why they should discipline themselves yet more strictly than their fellow human beings and choose their advisers with ever greater care.[41]

This image of the monarch 'who excelleth all other in greatness, yet hath...no prick or sting' is central to Elyot's conception of monarchy, and it is one to which he returns frequently both in *The Governor* and his later political writings. For nowhere does Elyot offer an encomium of the King that does not carry a further agenda designed to limit the nature of the authority it describes and deprive Henry's imperial kingship of its scope and sting. To exemplify this point we need only to leap ahead of ourselves for a moment and consider those other places in his work in which the nature of kingship in general and Henry's royal authority in particular are explicitly discussed. For each of these references, even where it initially seems to offer precisely the kind of vindications of the royal supremacy that critics have suggested are characteristic of Elyot's work, proves on closer examination to be a far more pointed and subtle description of the limits to the King's authority and the potential uses to which it might be put. Even Elyot's overt 'defences' of the Royal Supremacy, that is, need to be read in the wider context of his concern for moderate reform of the church and his defence of orthodox doctrine.

Perhaps the most extended and extravagant apologia for Henry VIII and the divinity that hedges a king was to come in the Preface to Elyot's *Dictionary* of 1538. Addressed 'To the most excellent prince, and our most redoubted sovereign king, HENRY the VIII, king of England, and France, defender of the faith, lord of Ireland, and supreme head in earth immediately under Christ, of the Church of England' (Aii), the encomium Elyot provides (concluding in the wake of the Pilgrimage of Grace that 'they which rebel against kings be enemies to God, and in will confounders of natural order and providence'), might well suggest, if read in isolation, a fulsome and uncritical assertion of Henry's 'imperial' sovereignty. It is worth quoting at length. 'Truly I am', Elyot wrote,

and ever have been of this opinion, most noble, most puissant, and most virtuous Prince, that the Royal estate of a king here on earth, next unto god, is of men most to be honoured, loved, and feared in an incomparable degree and fashion . . . Unto that office of governance is (as it were by the general consent of all people) one name appropred, in the which, although by diversity of languages, the letters and syllables are oftentimes changed, yet the word spoken hath one signification, which implieth as much as a KING in English, as it may appear to them which do read holy scripture, and well mark how often God is there called king, and also the prophets do so frequently name him. More over the paynims [pagans] being only led with natural affections, called Jupiter, to whom above other their gods they reserved the power universal, king of gods and of men: as who sayeth, there may be no greater name given unto him whom they supposed to be the giver of life unto creatures. To the which example, for the similitude of that divine office men did attribute unto their sovereign governors that excellent denomination, calling them semblably kings, and assigning to them the common distribution of Justice: whereby the people under their governance, should be kept and preserved in quiet life not exercised in bestial appetite, but passed forth in all parts of honesty, they finally should of God be rewarded with immortality. This well considered, it shall be to all men apparent, that they which rebel against kings, be enemies to God, and in will confounders of natural order and providence.

(Aii)

Here at last, one might be forgiven for thinking, is the sort of assertion of the Supremacy and absolute sovereignty that one would expect from an apologist for Henry VIII. And in fusing together divine and royal authority in this way Elyot does indeed seem to be offering an account of the sanctity of the Crown to match that offered by Tyndale in *The Obedience of a Christian Man*. Moreover, one sees here stress on two things that Elyot had been hitherto seemingly very reluctant to discuss, the responsibility of kings to ensure the spiritual well-being of their subjects (so that 'they finally should of god be rewarded with immortality'), and their role as law givers and judges of their people (having 'the common distribution of Justice' in their hands). And Elyot makes the personal applicability of all this to Henry VIII and the Royal Supremacy abundantly clear, extending the discussion to declare that,

Above all things, I have in most admiration, the majesty of you, which be very [i.e. true] kings reigning in Justice, when I consider, that therein seemeth to be a thing supernatural, or (if it may be spoken without derogation unto God's honour) a divine influence or spark of divinity: which late appeared to all them that beheld your grace sitting in the Throne of your royal estate, as Supreme Head of the church of England next under CHRIST . . .

(Aii)

But this is another of those occasions on which context is everything. For Elyot's decision finally to produce, some six years after the declaration of the Supremacy, an open and approving account of its principles, has very little to do with any change of attitude on his part towards the political and religious issues at stake and everything to with the political events of 1538. For, as he goes on to say, it was *how* Henry had chosen to use the Supreme authority at his disposal at that time that had granted Elyot his vision of that spark of royal divinity. Elyot's praise of Henry's office was not an end in itself but a prologue to his account of the King's actions as presiding judge and principal prosecutor at 'the decision [trial] and condemnation of the pernicious errors of the most detestable heretic John Nicholson, called also Lambert' in November 1538:[42]

At the which time your highness, more excellently than my tongue or pen can express, declared to be in your royal person the perfect image of kingly majesty, compact of these excellent qualities: true Religion, Sapience, Justice, and Mercy, all men rejoicing at the manifest and most honourable declaration of your evangelical faith: marvelling at the fulmination of the most vehement arguments proceeding from your highness in the confutation of abominable heresies, extolling the just reprehencions of the perverse opinions and interpretations of the arrogant masters of the said Lambert, in whose writings and his own proper wit he more trusted (as your highness truly alleged against him) than in the plain context of holy scripture, and the determinate sentence of holy and great learned doctors.

It is hardly coincidental that it was at this trial that Elyot had witnessed the spark of divinity in the heart of the King, for it was there that Henry had offered his most conservative statement on the fundamentals of the faith since the advent of the Supremacy, setting himself squarely against Sacramentarianism, one of the most radical and divisive of protestant doctrines, and offering a passionate and highly personalized defence of the Real Presence and the Miracle of the Mass.[43]

Coming after the radically inflected Ten Articles of 1536, Cromwell's accompanying Injunctions, and the publication in 1537 of *The Institution of a Christian Man* (the, so-called, *Bishops' Book* on doctrine) Henry's stance at Lambert's trial represented the first hint to conservatives that there were grounds for optimism concerning the direction of religious policy. The King's judgement and the terms in which he had conducted the trial demonstrated that there were limits to the kinds of radical reforms that he would countenance, and that he was distinctly more conservative on a number of the central issues of faith than his counsellors. To laud Henry's authority as a judge of his people and the guardian of his subjects' spiritual welfare at this moment was, then, a carefully calculated intervention in the religious debate. The *Dictionary* Prologue was no thoughtless piece of royal propaganda but a prime example of the Erasmian panegyric in action, an exercise in praise that actually seeks to fashion the prince in its own image.[44] Elyot praises Henry as a semi-divine ruler at precisely the moment that he was using his powers as Supreme Head to restrain the radical elements in the religious debate raging around him, and he did so in the evident hope that the King would continue on that same course.

Significantly, Elyot's only comparable encomium of royal power couched in terms of divine inspiration came at another time in which religious stability seemed to be a priority on the royal agenda. The revised form of the *Dictionary*, the *Bibliotheca Eliotae*, or *Eliotis Librarie* was printed in 1542, a moment when in the wake of the Act of Six Articles of 1539 and the brutal execution in 1540 of Robert Barnes, Thomas Cromwell and others, policy seemed again to be set on a more conservative course. In the 'Proheme', again addressed personally to Henry as 'defender of the faith, and of the Church of England, and of Ireland, in earth the supreme head' (Aii), Elyot cites Plutarch, 'most worthy master to Trajan the emperor', on 'what is signified by the dignity and name of a king'. Again comparison is made to the examples of God in heaven and the sun in the sky ('that which god is in heaven, and the sun in the firmament, the same in earth is a king to those whom he governeth' (Aii)). But significantly, there is on this occasion no reference either to the complementary jurisdiction of the moon at night, or to the still more troublesome notion of the emasculated, stingless 'principal bee'. Elyot has come here not to rein in the royal authority with examples of regal restraint but to praise the King for his delivery of justice for those who have gone too far in religious innovation. And in his account the administration of royal Justice lies primarily, not in the punitive correction of sinners and heretics, but in the reward offered to deserving scholars and Henry's use of learned men in his councils:

Likewise that king which governeth for the weal of his country, beholding benignly them that be studious or occupied about things that be virtuous . . . rendereth to their wits more sharpness, with a prompt dexterity armed with hardiness. It is therefore no marvel that great kings have in their councils most witty persons, seeing that the making of great wits is in their puissance, although virtue proceedeth immediately from god, and sapience likewise.

(Aii)

The exemplary anecdote that Elyot proceeds to deliver on this occasion is, however, not another case of Henry's harsh treatment of heretics, but his offer of a measure of patronage for the author's own labours in compiling his new dictionary. But, even here the political is not entirely subsumed within the personal. For Elyot takes the opportunity to assert once again the importance of opposing heresy and of kings seeking counsel from a diverse cross-section of the wise.[45]

Seemingly enthusiastic about religious reform only when it suited his own agenda to be so, Elyot praised the King in the preface to *The Castle of Health*, printed in 1539 precisely for his devotion to religious policy: because he 'daily prepareth to establish among us true and uncorrupted doctrine'. The language Elyot uses here is that of evangelical reform, but, as Pearl Hogrefe observed,[46] the sentiments expressed are essentially conservative. For the idea of Henry toiling to define pure and uncorrupted doctrine would have meant something very different to Elyot after the passing of the Act of Six Articles (a statute that he himself would have had a minor role in approving as a member of the Commons in the 1539 Parliament) than it would have done before that date. Similarly, the laudatory sentiments expressed in the Preface to *The Image of Governance* (1541) concerning Henry's religious endeavours need to be read in context if their intended impact is to be fully appreciated. Had not Henry,

Thereby... sifted out detestable heresies, late mingled among the corn of his faithful subjects, and caused much of the chaff to be thrown in the fire? Also hypocrisy and vain superstition to be clean banished? Whereof I doubt not but that there shall be, ere it be long, a more ample remembrance to his most noble and immortal renown.

(Bi)

Here Elyot apparently offers a measured defence of the Henrician *via media*, echoing the balanced terms of statutes and royal proclamations concerning the need to extirpate the errors of both papist superstition and heretical zeal. But his choice of terminology suggests where his sympathies really lie. Evangelical heresy is 'detestable', we note, but superstition merely 'vain', and, moreover, the removal of the latter is described as a matter already settled and dealt with (hypocrisy having been 'clean banished'), while the extermination of heresy is still work in progress, in which 'much', but crucially not all, of the chaff has been consigned to the fire. Thus the implication is that the more ample memorial to Henry's good intentions to follow will involve further purification of heretical opinions rather than further assaults on orthodox ones.

And it is this sense of unfinished business, of the Six Articles and Henry's involvement in heresy trials not having quite purged the new Church of England of its heretical elements, that seems to have prompted Elyot to add a catalogue of 'detestable heretics' to the second edition of the *Dictionary*, published as the *Bibliotheca Eliotae* in 1542. As he explained in the Preface, he had felt the need to expand the coverage of natural and historical phenomena for the new edition of the work, adding accounts of geographical features, flora and fauna, and the major personages of history:

[But] I also thought it necessary to interlace the detestable heretics with their sundry heresies concerning the substance of our catholic faith, justly condemned by the whole consent of all true Christian men, to the intent that those heresies being in this wise divulgate may be the sooner espied and abhorred in such books where they be craftily interlaced with wholesome doctrine.

(Aii(v))

Elyot's approval of the Royal Supremacy, then, went only so far. When Henry's authority was deployed in the interests of moderate reform, or to condemn radical doctrines, then Elyot was willing to praise it, albeit always in ways that made clear his idea of how it should be exercised. When it was deployed in other ways, he was swift to point out the necessary curbs and limitations on princely authority created by self-restraint. His was never an uncritical or open-ended obedience to royal policy.

In a letter to Thomas Howard, Duke of Norfolk, written from Regensburg on 14 March 1532, Elyot had included a telling remark concerning his dedication to his royal master. In assuring his correspondent that he would 'endure all that shall be his [i.e. Henry's] pleasure, employing my poor life gladly in that which may be to his honour or wealth of his realm', he pointedly declared himself to be 'all the king's, *except my soul*' (my italics). In the context of Christopher St German's claim in the previous year that the King-in-Parliament 'hath not only charge on the bodies but also the souls of his subjects', the qualification was a crucial one, and it seems indeed to have marked the limits of this otherwise extremely loyal servant's commitment to the King's causes.[47] As we shall see in the next chapter, this idea of the individual soul as the inviolable inner sanctum of the just man offered Elyot a final refuge to which he might retreat from an unjust world.[48] But it also provided the foundation upon which to construct his engagement with that world. As the seat of his conscience it provided the motivating force for his efforts to counsel the King and address the problems of the realm. Rather than withdraw into stoic self-sufficiency, he continued to enter the public arena through his books, convinced that it was his duty as a just man and honest counsellor so to do.

The Governor *and Parliament*

Another aspect of *The Governor* sometimes cited to support the idea that Elyot was offering an apologia for the Royal Supremacy or absolutism (the ideas are frequently blurred into a single idea of untrammelled Henrician authority) is the book's curious and ambivalent handling of the role of Parliament in the ideal public weal. In his discussion of early Roman history, for example, Elyot took a somewhat unexpected line in lauding the stability of the city under the rule of the Tarquin Kings and condemning the weakness of the Senate and the early Republic. 'The Romans', he claimed,

during the time that they were under kings, which was by the space of [one hundred and forty] years were well governed, nor never was among them discord or sedition.

(Biii)

Only with the expulsion of the Tarquins was disorder introduced, as,

Consequently the comminalty more and more encroached a licence, and at last compelled the Senate to suffer them to choose yearly among them governors of their own estate and condition whom they called Tribunes, under whom they received such audacity and power that they finally obtained the highest authority in the public weal, in so much that oftentimes they did repeal the acts of the Senate, and to those Tribunes might a man appeal from the Senate or any other office or dignity...

(Biii)[49]

Only the onset of war prompted the people to come together in fear to elect a single leader again in the form of a 'Dictator' on whom they bestowed sovereignty for the duration of the crisis.

Taken out of context as an exercise in political history Elyot's portrayal of the Tarquins as the repository of good government and the Republican Senate as a weak and ineffectual institution does seem to invite a reading favourable to the Henrician Supremacy. Was not Elyot here justifying precisely the sort of gathering of legislative authority in the hands of the prince that Henry and his ministers would welcome?[50] But read in the light of the events of 1529–31 the political pressures that might produce such a reading become more obvious. What Elyot seems to be doing here is, not taking every available opportunity to praise the exercise of royal power and downplay every potential rival institution, but treading a very careful line between two undesirable alternatives. He praises the Roman kings, not to laud their governance *per se*, but rather to show what happens when a senatorial assembly takes too great a degree of power and authority upon itself at the King's expense.

In part Elyot's imagined public weal is a version of the state described by the fifteenth-century jurist Sir John Fortescue as a mixed monarchy (the *dominium politicum et regale* or 'political and royal dominion'), in which effective rule by the sovereign is combined with the essential safeguards for the rights of the people.[51] Unlike Fortescue, however, Elyot could not look to the obvious curb and counterweight to royal authority provided by Parliament,[52] for it was precisely from the common lawyers in the House of Commons that the principal agitation against the jurisdiction of the church and opposition to heresy trials had come in 1529. Furthermore, it was the King-in-Parliament that St German claimed had dominion over the souls as well as the bodies of Henry's subjects. To argue for greater powers for Parliament was, then, out of the question for Elyot. And so, unwilling to argue that the constitutional initiative should pass either to Parliament or to the Common Law itself as defined by radical advocates of the supremacy such as St German, he was forced to fall back still more obviously upon the humanist ideal of the sovereign who himself establishes the safeguards against his falling into tyranny through the exercise of reason and virtue and his choice of sober, moderate counsellors.

Elyot was clearly not opposed in principle to the political role and influence of Parliament as an institution. Elsewhere in *The Governor* he was quite prepared to applaud the role of the Roman Senate, and he would take a seat in the House of Commons himself in 1539 as junior knight of the shire for Cambridgeshire.[53] Earlier than that, indeed, he was, as we have seen, one of a number of men whom Chapuys cited as advocates of the view that the Emperor should send representatives to England to appear in Parliament to encourage his fellow conservatives to speak out on behalf of Katherine of Aragon and the Church.[54] As with many of his other analogies and arguments in *The Governor*, Elyot's discussion of parliament was a strategic response to contemporary circumstances, not an unqualified statement of first principles. He clearly saw the two Houses, and the Commons in particular, as too unreliable an instrument, as they were currently constituted, to be the repository of the decisive authority in his conception of the ideal state. He was not alone in this, for a number of other conservatives had also decided at this time to support a Royal Supremacy in which they had little faith, rather than allow the Commons a greater say in the government of the Church. Thus the bishops in convocation had agreed, reluctantly, to acknowledge Henry as their Head, 'so far as the law of Christ allows', rather than be governed through the instrument of parliament.[55] And thus Elyot's fellow author, John Heywood, could, in *The Play of the Weather*, encourage Henry VIII to take on greater royal authority himself, even as he mocked the means by which he did so. Like these men, Elyot seems to have concluded that, in 1530–31, King Henry himself was a more likely source of the kind of policies he wished to see enacted than a parliament dominated by common lawyers and vaunted by St German as the engine of an all-embracing secular and spiritual supremacy. 'Better the devil you know' would seem to have been Elyot's maxim here: not least as in *The Governor* he had argued that a single monarch offered the best form of government precisely because he was a single individual toward whom the concerted counsels of the wise and the persuasions of the virtuous could be directed.

Elyot's Treatment of the Law in The Governor

A similar constraint colours Elyot's discussion of the other conventional curb upon the untrammelled exercise of royal authority, the common law, and for the same reasons. Political theorists from Plato onwards had argued that the best form of government was a monarchy confined within the precepts of the law. This was also the principle that underpinned Fortescue's notion of the 'mixed' monarchy.[56] But, Elyot argues, crucially, not that the common law binds the prince of necessity, but rather that the good prince (unlike the tyrant) chooses to accept the same restrictions on his conduct as the rest of his countrymen, freely and willingly. Thus the thorny question of how far the sovereign may be constrained by law is avoided in a plethora of anecdotal accounts of how good princes accept the restrictions of the law even when they need not, while tyrants never do.[57]

The most striking of these anecdotes occurs in the chapter dealing with the virtue of placability, and its vicious opposite, wrath. Wrath, Elyot argues, turns a noble man into an irrational beast, and a prince into a tyrant.[58] He cites as examples Ovid's Gorgon—the symbol, according to the classical poet, of the man of ire—and the historical rulers Alexander, Sulla, and Claudius, each of whom were made vengeful owing to wrath, only to regret it afterwards. He then turns to placability, and cites the examples of King Pirrhus, who forgave two drunkards who insulted him at a feast, and Julius Caesar, who took no offence when Sergius Galba criticized his handling of Marc Antony's estate. Finally he offers a 'domestical example ... one which in mine opinion is to be compared with any that ever was written of in any region or country'. This is the story of Prince Henry (the future Henry V), who, while still a reckless youth, was 'incensed [by] ... light persons about him' to go to the court of the King's Bench to demand the release of one of his servants who was being tried there for unspecified crimes. The anecdote is worth quoting at length, as it reveals both Elyot's political priorities and his gifts as a storyteller.

The Prince, the very picture of a wrathful man, storms into the court, sword in hand, to demand his servant's freedom. But he finds himself facing a presence of equal weight and gravity, an immovable object every bit as resolute as his own irresistible force, in the person of the Chief Justice of the King's Bench. The latter, looking up at the royal intruder, at first responds diplomatically, and

> Humbly exhorted the prince to be contented, that his servant might be ordered according to the ancient laws of this realm, or if he would have him saved from the rigour of the laws, that he should obtain, if he might, of the king his father his gracious pardon, whereby no law or justice should be derogate.
>
> (pvi(v))

But the Prince is 'nothing appeased, but rather more inflamed' by this, and moves to take away his servant by force. At this the Chief Justice, 'considering the perilous example and inconvenience that might thereby ensue',

> With a valiant spirit and courage commanded the prince upon his allegiance to leave the prisoner and depart his way. With which commandment the prince, being set all in a fury, all chafed and in a terrible manner, came up to the place of judgement, men thinking that he would have slain the judge or have done to him some damage; but the judge, sitting

still without moving, declaring the majesty of the King's place of judgement and with an assured and bold countenance had to the prince these words following: 'Sir, remember yourself. I keep here the place of the King your sovereign lord and father to whom ye owe double obedience, wherefore eftsoons [i.e. again] in his name, I charge you desist of your wilfulness and unlawful enterprise, and from henceforth give good example to those which hereafter shall be your proper subjects. And now, for your contempt and disobedience, go you to the prison of the King's Bench, whereunto I commit you, and remain ye there prisoner until the pleasure of the king your father be further known.' With which words being abashed and also wondering at the marvellous gravity of that worshipful Justice, the noble prince laying his weapon apart, doing reverence departed, and went to the King's Bench as he was commanded.

(Pvii (v)–Pviii)

The episode is, as the author of the late-sixteenth-century drama, *The Famous Victories of Henry The Fifth* was to realize,[59] wonderfully dramatic, evoking a set-piece confrontation between two vividly drawn characters, each speaking for a vital principle of late medieval government. Any writer in search of a memorable demonstration of a prince's subjection before the Common Law of England need look no further. But what is striking about Elyot's deployment of the story is that he uses it to vaunt neither the independence of the law nor the supremacy of the courts over the prerogative of the Crown. In his hands the confrontation is one of personalities rather than institutions or constitutional principles, and each of the participants emerges from it vindicated in one way or another. The Crown indeed ends the episode with its authority strengthened rather than weakened.

The Chief Justice is the hero of the tale, clearly, and his moral courage stands out as its strongest element. But it is not the principle of the law for which he speaks, still less the capacity of the courts to curtail wayward princes. Rather it is for royalty itself that he stands. For, as he himself tells the young prince Hal, 'I keep here the place of the king your sovereign lord and father'. His authority is thus a reflection of the authority of the Crown not of any alternative principle set against it. Similarly, the court itself is 'the king's place of judgement', and the Prince is not commanded to respect the sanctity of the law, but asked to 'be contented' that justice take its course, ordered 'upon his allegiance' to leave the prisoner, and on his 'double obedience' to his king and father to obey the judge's sentence, a sentence itself delivered in the King's name and to last only 'until the pleasure of the king your father be further known'. It is even suggested that, if he returns with a pardon from his father, he can achieve his manifestly unjust desires, and 'no law or justice should be derogate'. Thus the clash as Elyot represents it is not between the rights of the King and the demands of the law, but between two aspects of royal authority: the renegade capacity for tyranny that unchecked royal privilege might indulge, and the sober, mature royal authority that is invested in the paternal sovereign Henry IV and devolved upon the Chief Justice. It is a clash between incipient tyranny and royal justice—between the bad prince and the good king—that is fought out here. And royal justice triumphs, not once but twice, for, not only is the King proved to be just in his judgements and wise in his choice of servants, but the Prince himself proves capable of redemption, as his willing submission to the sentence of the just judge reveals. It is left for the sovereign, Henry IV to give the final verdict on his son's behaviour. 'Ravished with gladness' at the Prince's submission, he offers thanks to God 'for that ye have given me a judge who feareth not to minister justice, and also a son who can suffer semblably and obey justice' (pviii(v)).

'Now here a man may behold three persons worthy excellent memory', Elyot concludes, making the moral of the tale explicit,

first, a judge who, being a subject, feared not to execute justice on the eldest son of his sovereign lord, and by the order of nature his successor. Also a prince and son and heir to the king in the midst of his fury more considered his evil example and the judge's constancy in Justice than his own estate or wilful appetite. Thirdly, a noble king and wise father who, contrary to the custom of parents, rejoiced to see his son and the heir of his crown to be for his disobedience by his subject corrected.

(pviii(v))

Elyot's deployment of this resonant anecdote consequently has much to tell us about his political agenda. He has no interest here in either seeking to establish the constitutional limits of royal power or in describing the effective external checks and balances that might safeguard the public weal from royal tyranny.[60] The crucial checks in his story are psychological and interpersonal, and the lessons he draws from it concern the education of a prince. The story is yet another example of the value of good counsel, and the crucial importance of frank and courageous speakers of truth to the smooth running of royal government. Once again his focus is on the Prince as the recipient of advice, and on the King as the source of the justice that the Chief Justice exercises. Self-restraint— the placability that turns away wrath—is, after all, the virtue to be learned here, not an understanding of the role of the courts in the administration of justice.

The story also suggests a good deal about Elyot's own ambitions and aspirations as a writer and counsellor manqué. For in the figure of the Chief Justice we surely see an idealized representation of the kind of man whom Elyot wished to be. The fearless upholder of truth and justice who, with virtue on his side and eloquence at his disposal, can persuade the prince out of his folly is the humanist hero personified. As a Ciceronian ideal, his authority comes not from his office as a judge, but because he represents justice and reason in his own actions. The full scope of the authority that such a counsellor might exercise is evident in the fact that, far from limiting himself to the strict interpretation of the law (indeed, he is remarkably vague about precisely which statutes the prince has contravened by bursting into the courtroom sword in hand), he moves from offering generalized moral advice ('desist of your wilfulness'), through legal judgement ('and unlawful enterprise'), to fatherly instruction and political counsel ('and from henceforth give good example to those which hereafter shall be your proper subjects') in a single sentence, before finally giving judgement ('And now for your contempt and disobedience, go you to the prison of the King's Bench, whereunto I commit you'). His is the good counsel of a good man skilled in speech,[61] rather than the legal judgement of a personified institution. And, as what follows will suggest, this ideal of the royal servant who, because of his personal virtues, his experience, and his eloquence, can act as both a minister of the Crown and a tutor to his sovereign, was one which would reappear in various guises in Elyot's dialogues over the following decade.

If Elyot was interested in defending or asserting the importance of the law in *The Governor*, it was, then, only in so far as it suited his own specific and contemporary purposes. Just as he was prepared to celebrate the Royal Supremacy only when it enabled him to counsel Henry VIII towards moderation in his pursuit of religious reform, so he was prepared to argue for the role of lawyers and the principles of equity, justice, and the common law, only in the context of counselling the King to moderate his own behaviour. Ironically given his own saturation in legal culture, his experience in the Inns of Court and in working for the Justices of Assize, Elyot was extremely wary of engaging in any discussion of the role of the law that was not subsumed within a discussion of the conduct and responsibilities of the prince. Tellingly, while he was willing to praise the lawyers of classical antiquity, he deferred any explicit and extended discussion of the contemporary legal system and its practitioners to a second volume, which he promised would follow *The Governor*, 'wherein I will render mine office or duty to that honourable study, whereby my father was advanced to a judge and also I myself have attained no little commodity' (Gviii(v)). Yet, when he did produce the work that he said fulfilled that promise, *The Image of Governance* (1542), the book offered no sustained discussion of the role of the law in the ideal public weal. Rather it offered yet another representation (albeit this time, as we shall see, an ironic one) of the good prince, his character and qualities, in the form of an aphoristic 'life' of Alexander Severus. While he clearly revered the English common law, its principles and institutions,[62] Elyot evidently did not feel it necessary to discuss its relationship to the crown at any length, or to offer it as a potential solution to the crisis of 1529–30. Such problems, he clearly believed, must be placed at the door of the King alone.

The Governor *as Mirror for a Prince*

So, having examined some of the more striking elements of *The Governor's* discussion of political issues, it is now possible to say something rather more confidently about both what sort of treatise it is, and, equally importantly, what sort of treatise it is not. To take the latter first: it is clear that it is not simply an educational treatise, not least because the notion that education could or should be divorced from politics or the wider social context in which it took place would not have occurred to a writer like Elyot who was so steeped in humanist notions of the cultural utility of literature and learning. Secondly it is not (or again, not *simply*) an apologia for royal absolutism, the Henrician Royal Supremacy, or religious Reformation. On questions of ecclesiastical jurisdiction and reform, or the extent of papal authority (precisely the areas in which any justification of Henry VIII's Supremacy would have made its boldest claims) it is resolutely silent. On matters of royal authority it is studiedly ambivalent. On the one hand, it asserts the superiority of hereditary monarchy and the royal estate over all alternative forms of government, and downplays the other national institutions that might have set a curb on royal power: the common law and Parliament. Yet on the other, it fashions the education of the prince and the strict regime of self-regulation to which the governor should subscribe so restrictively that the good ruler could never conceive of exercising his somewhat vaguely defined constitutional powers except in a moderate and highly conventional fashion. Elyot's *Governor* is rather a handbook of liberal kingship and a series of carefully modulated lessons in virtue designed for the ruling classes in general and Henry VIII in particular. Its definitions of the princely virtues and examples of good and bad practice are all in one way or another conventional enough, but the way in which they are chosen and organized suggests the contemporary purpose that their author had in mind for them. They present the fashioning of a prince in such a way as to suggest that any good king would have to intervene to halt the more radical and divisive trends in contemporary politics and heal the dangerous schisms developing between conservatives and reformers, clergy and laity. Finally, with due regard for the author's own circumstances and ambitions, *The Governor* makes the case for the employment of experienced, learned, frankly-spoken men such as himself in the counsels of the King.

What is perhaps most striking, indeed, about *The Governor*, is the way in which, despite Elyot's later claims to have spared no class or group from his admonitions,[63] the text never allows its universalizing rhetoric to dilute the specificity of its political focus. Unlike more generalized handbooks or political treatises, Elyot never seriously claims that *everyone* is to blame for the current ills of the realm, nor that everyone has an equal role to play in its recovery. It is the prince and his counsellors who are the target for his accusations, and it is to them that he returns again and again in his discussion. His is thus a very different analysis of politics to that offered by Hythlodaeus in More's *Utopia*, who had blamed 'a certain conspiracy of rich men' for the decay of his commonwealth, or Thomas Starkey's claim in his *Dialogue Between Pole and Lupset* (probably written *c.* 1529–32) that princes, lords and governors all share in the mismanagement of society: 'every one of them looketh chiefly to their own profit, pleasure, and commodity'.[64] Elyot's analysis proves on close inspection to be far more specific and far more specifically political, than More's reputedly more radical and pertinent text, and more determined to focus on the specific remedies that need to be introduced to correct the current imbalances in government policy. Revealingly, where *Utopia* saw the nobility as a class as a principal cause of the social malaise, and so attacked their ostentation, pretensions, and personal indulgence with vigour, Elyot offers a very different account of their significance. He sees their involvement in the political process as counsellors (albeit only those who have been educated to the highest standards according to the curriculum he describes) as the crucial element in its cure. Hence there is little in *The Governor* of the criticism of aristocratic practices that characterizes *Utopia*: no critique of the social consequences of sheep farming or agricultural enclosures, no attacks on bastard feudal retaining, maintenance or bearing; indeed little discussion of any of the issues that one would expect to find in a handbook aimed at improving the conduct of aristocratic families, had the nobility and gentry really been the prime audience for which the book was intended. Rather *The Governor* is focused consistently on the problems of princely government. Its analysis of aristocratic behaviour is presented almost exclusively in the context of their capacity to provide honest and effective advisers to the prince.

The fact that Elyot persists in addressing political issues on the level of personal morality, stressing always the virtuous qualities and the intellectual training necessary in the good governor, should not tempt us to conclude that he was ducking political questions in favour of conventional moral platitudes.[65] If, as he clearly believed, it was the King himself who was at the heart of the problem, provoking schism and encouraging civil dissention through the wilful pursuit of his private desires, then to remind him that the public good should supersede private passion, that affability, placability, generosity, and moderation were the hallmarks of good lordship, and that the duties of the good counsellor were to speak boldly in order to dissuade the King from error and folly, was to address precisely the core of the problem. Elyot's focus on monarchy, and the person of the King, is thus, crucially, double-edged. He identifies the fashioning of a virtuous prince as the solution to the nation's woes, essentially because he saw the prospect of Henry VIII becoming a negligent or tyrannical prince as the central problem.

In this context it is instructive to consider just how resolutely domestic and political Elyot's conception of aristocratic and princely virtue is. Had *The Governor* been either an educational manual designed solely to create an aristocratic class fit for royal service or a Machiavellian treatise on 'imperial' kingship, one would have expected to find within it far more material on the martial and chivalric aspects of aristocratic life, some advice on military tactics, or the upkeep of armour and weapons, horses and their equipment than it actually contains. But beyond a few token references to the military value of horsemanship, martial sports, and draughtsmanship, there is little or nothing in *The Governor*'s more than 250 pages to meet this obvious, practical need. One might be tempted to see this as a reflection of a characteristic Erasmian disdain for chivalric blood sports and warfare. But the silences in the text are more pointed than that and more revealing, for nor is there anything in *The Governor* about the advantages of a peaceful foreign policy, no notes on effective diplomacy or advice on the best ways to stay on good terms with one's European neighbours, no models of

conduct for neophyte ambassadors and envoys. Still less are there any Machiavellian tips on how one might divide one's rival princes among themselves. Even
when the anecdote concerning the stingless principal bee provided him with the
ideal cue to make an Erasmian point about the benefits of a pacific foreign policy,
Elyot turned it down in order to make further points about domestic concord
and prosperity.

Beyond some general assertions concerning the need for a prince to win
honour in the eyes of the world, the international dimension to princely politics
might as well not exist in Elyot's account.[66] In his conception of the state the
threats to political stability, peace, and justice are likely to come from within
rather than without, and from above rather than below. Thus protecting the
prince from himself, through good education, moral exhortation, and continual
counsel, was also the most effective way of protecting the public weal from harm.
So, while the prince is the focus of attention in Elyot's political system, he is not
its *raison d'etre*. Unlike Machaivelli's *Prince*, *The Governor* does not show the
monarch the best way to rule the people for his own advantage; it shows him only
what he ought to know if he is to rule for the benefit of all. Princely government
may have been his ideal form of sovereignty, but only because it was the most
effective means of ensuring the public good. Princes, that is, existed for the public
weal, not vice versa.[67] In such a context to ask whether or not Elyot favours an
absolutist position on monarchy is *un question mal posé*. For in his view, the
notional powers of the prince are irrelevant to the smooth running of the public
weal, for the good prince will never use the more extreme measures at his disposal
and the bad prince will not need constitutional sanction for oppressing his
subjects. What matters is rather the prince's willingness to take counsel from a
wide cross-section of his subjects and heed their advice, a practice that will
inevitably lead to moderate, consensual policies.

Critics have also largely taken Elyot at his word when he claimed to have
aimed his criticisms in *The Governor* and elsewhere at no man in particular, and
have concluded that, for better or worse, he offered no specific criticism of the
King himself in his earliest and most substantial text.[68] But the more closely one
examines *The Governor*, the clearer it becomes that it was written with Henry
VIII in mind. Even when its author is outlining a general educational principle or
exploring a philosophical issue, he always has at least one eye on its particular
application to the case of the King and the problems of the moment. The text is
thus a *speculum principis* in which Henry, if he would but look into it, would see a
highly critical reflection of his current behaviour, attitudes, and policies. The
reflections of royal actions are both generalized and highly specific, adding up to
a comprehensive critique of his royal lifestyle and policies. A minor and, so far as
I am aware, previously unnoticed, glance at contemporary events will illustrate
the degree of specificity that Elyot was prepared to employ in order to catch the
conscience of the King.

In the course of a substantial discussion of the importance of learning in a king (a subject close to the author's heart), Elyot cites the contrast between Henry 'Beauclerk' [Henry I] and his less educated brother William Rufus. The latter,

For his dissolute living and tyranny being hated of all his nobles and people, was suddenly slain by the shot of an arrow as he was hunting in a forest, which to make larger and to give his deer more liberty, he did cause the houses of xii parishes to be pulled down, the people to be expelled, and all being desolate, to be turned in to a desert and made only pasture for beasts savage, which he would never have done if he had as much delighted in good learning as did his brother.

(Fiii–Fiii(v))

The story as Elyot tells it here is nicely constructed. The fact that William's self-indulgence both generates ill-feeling towards him among those whom he has dispossessed to create his park, and provides the engine of his downfall (his artificial 'wilderness' (the New Forest) being so large that he can be isolated from his retainers within it and murdered) brings a nice irony to the lesson that learning brings wisdom, and wisdom teaches self-restraint. But the story has a further critical edge to it, and one more directly pertinent to Henry VIII than the truism that self-indulgence in a ruler is a bad thing. For at precisely the time that Elyot was writing *The Governor*, his sovereign was embarking upon ambitious plans to demolish virtually an entire district of Westminster in order to expand the buildings of York Place, the palace he had acquired from Cardinal Wolsey at his fall in November 1529.[69] The result would be the magnificent new palace of Whitehall, the largest royal complex in Christendom at the time, and a new and spacious park (modern St James's) in which Henry could ride and hunt.

While Henry's ambitions did not run to the destruction of twelve parishes, the devastation caused was to be substantial in the compact urban environment of Westminster. As the Venetian ambassador reported during Christmas 1529–30, 'the plan is on so large a scale that many hundreds of houses will be levelled'. During 1530, while investigations were underway to identify the leaseholders of the various properties involved, royal surveyors were already at work mapping the buildings and boundaries in King Street, and making plans for the massive demolition project that would follow. In early 1531 orders were issued to the civic authorities that the royal works should have priority over all other construction in the city, and workmen, materials, and the wagons to transport them were made subject to a form of compulsory purchase by the crown. Anyone refusing to cooperate was to be imprisoned. On 14 May Chapuys noted that access to the King's new 'great park' would be facilitated by the building of 'a very long gallery... for which purpose a number of houses [have been] pulled down, to the great damage and discomfort of the proprietors'. Two days later the main programme of demolition began, with hundreds of workers moving onto what had become a giant construction site to clear the tons of wood, tiles, brick, and other rubble removed from the existing buildings.[70]

Had Henry needed to be reminded of the applicability of Elyot's strictures concerning wisdom, learning, and the dangers of ignoring the wishes of his subjects to his own case, he had only to look up from the book and glance out of the windows of the palaces of Westminster or York Place. Only a fool would have missed the pointedness of the allusion, and, as Elyot knew, Henry was no fool. Hence he built into his discussion of good governorship and personal development regular reminders of the specific pertinence of their principles to his royal dedicatee. Chapter by chapter, *The Governor* built up into not merely a comprehensive account of personal virtue and princely probity, but a personalized account for Henry VIII of how far he himself was currently falling short of those ideals.

Read as a mirror for Henry himself and a diagnosis of the specific sicknesses afflicting his realm, as well as a treatise on the general principles of good government, new features of the text come into prominence, and familiar ones appear in new and more striking light. Thus we get a sense of what it would have been like to read *The Governor* in 1531 as a living text, responding to real events, rather than merely another example in a long tradition of treatises on political philosophy.

As Pearl Hogrefe suggested, the stress in the text upon sexual morality, personal continence, the virtues of matrimony, and the evils of adultery cannot but have taken on a particular sharpness when read in the heat of Henry's campaign to resolve his Great Matter.[71] Similarly, the criticisms of those who indulge their personal desires and appetites at the expense of the public good would have carried a different emotional and political charge at a time when the King was at pains to assure both his own subjects and the world at large that he was pursuing the annulment of his marriage for the good of his realm and the settlement of his troubled conscience rather than for any private desire for Anne Boleyn. In such circumstances the conclusion to Elyot's chapter on continence would surely have carried a hint of the *ad hominem* about it, not least when the author claimed to have discussed the matter in such detail,

To persuade men of good nature to embrace continence; I mean not to live ever chaste; but to honour matrimony and to have good await that they let not the sparks of concupiscence grow in great flames, wherewith the wits shall be dried up and all noble virtues shall be devoured.

(Ei)

Could Henry have read such a passage without considering his own case and circumstances? Similarly, could he have considered with equanimity the passage describing the exposed position of princes (conventional though it was), mindful of the efforts of his ministers to downplay the stories concerning his love for Anne Boleyn in the public arguments for his divorce? Princes, Elyot observed,

Should consider that by their pre-eminence, they sit as it were on a pillar on the top of a mountain, where all the people do behold them, not only in their open affairs but also in their secret pastimes, privy dalliance, or other unprofitable or wanton conditions, which soon be discovered by the conversation of their most familiar servants.

(Nvi)

These are hardly the sort of sentiments that a writer anxious to flatter or appease his king would write, knowing that he was the text's principal intended reader. And yet Elyot did not hold back from relating stories and principles that addressed directly the questions of marriage, fidelity, and personal sacrifice in the interests of public utility.

Equally, a reader in 1531 might well have seen implications in *The Governor*'s treatment of the virtue of constancy for a king who was in the process of dissolving his marriage of over twenty years and breaking with centuries of political and ecclesiastical tradition. In this section it was Elyot's claim that there was no value in any of his other personal qualities, if the ruler did not ally them to the abiding virtue of constancy:

He that hath all the gifts of nature and fortune, and also in his childhood is adorned with doctrine and virtue, which he hath acquired with much travail, watch, and study, if he add not to [them] constancy when he cometh to the time of experience, which experience is, as it were, the work of the craftsman [i.e. his masterpiece], but moved with any private affection or fear of adversity or exterior damage will omit any part of his learning or virtue: the estimation of his person immediately ceaseth among perfect workmen, that is to say, wise men: and finally nothing being in him certain or stable what thing in him may be commended?

(Eii)

And would not those implications have been made more obvious and personal by the author's further observation (surely informed by thoughts of Queen Katherine) that people have called inconstant men 'womanly'; 'all be it some women nowadays be found more constant than men, and specially in love towards their husbands, or else might there happen to be some wrong inheritors.' (e ii(v))?

Such is the nature of schemes of virtues and vices, of course, and such is the universal scope of their potential applicability, that any discussion of the sort Elyot offers in *The Governor* could be interpreted to touch upon the failings (or indeed the strengths) of any given individual. But this does not mean that such schemes can never be topical and specific as well as universal. Again, one must be aware of context, and the special resonances it creates. To say in 1531 that a prince should be moderate in his habits, sexually continent, and faithful in marriage; dignified, honourable, and constant in his behaviour, and affable, patient, placable and merciful in his administration of justice, was both to offer a series of timeless moral platitudes and to deliver a very pointed and direct rebuke to a king who, in the eyes of many observers, was behaving immoderately and incontinently in his personal affairs, intemperately and unjustly towards his critics, and inconstantly towards his former queen and familiar counsellors, to the point where he was bringing himself and his crown into dishonour both at home and abroad.

There does seem to be further implicit criticism of Henry VIII, as well as matter designed specifically to attract his attention, in the chapter on the virtue of circumspection, defined by Elyot as 'a deliberation, in having regard to that that followeth' (Mi). Here the text offers two principal exemplars of that trait for consideration: the Roman commander Fabius, who defeated Hannibal by patient attrition and the avoidance of pitched battle, and a much more recent figure, Henry's own father, Henry VII. And when one examines the extended portrait of the latter it is hard to avoid the conclusion that it too was intended as an indirect commentary on Henry VIII; the text forming, as it were, one half of a moralized diptych, with the living son providing the other half himself. And in that diptych the father evidently stands for the virtues that Elyot wishes the son to embody:

What more clear mirror or spectacle can we desire of circumspection than King Henry the seventh of most noble memory, father unto our most dread sovereign lord, whose worthy renown, like the sun in the midst of his sphere, shineth and ever shall shine in men's remembrance[?]

(Mi)

Despite his 'long absence out of this realm', Elyot declares, Henry Tudor was able, on his return, to restore order to a realm divided by civil war:

By his most excellent wit, he in few years, not only brought this realm in good order and under due obedience, revived the laws, advanced justice, refurnished his dominions, and repaired his manors, but also with such circumspection treated with other princes and realms of leagues, of alliance, and amities, that during the more part of his reign, he was little or nothing inquieted with outward hostility or martial business. And yet all other princes either feared him or had him in a fatherly reverence.

(Mi–Mi(v))

Representing Henry VII as a pacifier of domestic struggles and a peacemaker and bridge-builder abroad at a time when Henry's Great Matter had opened up a furious schism at home and was threatening to provoke international conflict with both the Pope and England's long-term ally the Emperor, was again no neutral or naïve exercise, but a studied example of the classical panegyric in action. As Elyot went on to assert, Henry VIII had been the beneficiary of his father's legacy of peace, honour, and domestic stability, hence, by implication, he had a duty to maintain and enhance the legacy for his own heir, as all good sons and fathers should:

For, as Tulli sayeth, the best inheritance that the fathers leave to their children, excelling all other patrimony, is the glory or praise of virtue and noble acts, and of such fair inheritance his highness may compare with any prince that ever reigned, which he daily augmenteth, adding there to other sundry virtues which I forbear now to rehearse, to the intent I will exclude all suspicion of flattery, since I myself in this work so specially reprove it. But the which is presently known, and is in experience, needeth no monument. And unto so excellent a prince there shall not lack hereafter condign writers to register his acts with most eloquent style in perpetual remembrance.

(Mi(v))

Thus Elyot paints Henry VII, not as he was, but as he would like his son to be, and praises the son for enhancing his father's peaceable legacy at the very moment when he was in the greatest danger of squandering it, in the hope that this might prompt him to be more moderate in pursuing his Great Matter. Similarly the references to the importance of an honourable legacy raise the issue of what Henry VIII will leave to his own future heirs. If he was indeed, as he claimed, pursuing an annulment in order to provide the realm with a legitimate male heir, Elyot implies here that the achievement would prove a hollow one if he were to squander the best legacy that he could leave such an heir, a stable throne and a peaceful realm, in the very process of engendering him.

Similar contemporary reverberations underscore the text's discussion of justice and equity. At a time when long-neglected precedents and incidents were being resurrected to provide the grounds for *praemunire* cases against leading clerics, Elyot's declaration concerning the decline of justice in England ('what marvel is it, though there be in all places contention infinite and that good laws be turned into sophisms and insolubles, since everywhere fidelity is constrained to come in trial, and credence (as I might say) is become a vagabond?' (zv(v))) would have had a more specific and powerful resonance than normal. As assuredly would statements such as that 'it is faint praise that is gotten with fear, or by flatterers given. And the fame is but fume which is supported with silence provoked by menaces' (Nvi). 'It is to be wished', noted Elyot, citing Cicero, 'that they which in the public weal have any authority may be like to the laws, which in correcting be led only by equity and not by wrath or displeasure' (Ri). Rather than judge on grounds of enmity, grudge or wrath, the ruler is repeatedly advised to exercise mercy and benignity, patience, caution and moderation; conventional virtues that again took on a contemporary specificity in the light of the aggressive prosecutions of 1530–1. Elyot quotes Cicero, Pliny, Seneca and others in support of the idea that benevolence in a prince is a greater safeguard of his throne than terror (Rvi–vi(v)). 'The most noble emperors', he argued, citing Julius and Augustus Caesar, 'which for their merits received of the gentiles divine honours, vanquished the great hearts of their mortal enemies in showing mercy above men's expectation' (Qi(v)).

Likewise the sentiments in verses of Claudian that Elyot recommended should be read by all rulers once each day, and which he freshly translated himself for the purpose, would have had very different implications for a king embarking on a campaign to assert his own 'imperial' authority against the jurisdiction of the Pope, and to bring the church in England under his own 'supreme' personal authority, than they would have had for other readers (even princely ones) with more modest aspirations.

> Though thy powar stretcheth both ferre and large,
> If feare the[e] trouble, and small thinges the[e] offende,
> Corrupte desire, thyne harte hath ones embraced,
> Thou arte in bondage, thyne honour is defaced ...
>
> What thou mayst do, delite nat for to knowe,
> But rather what thinge wyll become the[e] best.
> Enbrace thou vertue, and kepe thy courage lowe,
> And thinke that always measure is a fe[a]ste.
> Love well thy people, care also for the le[a]ste,
> And whan thou studiest for thy commositie,
> Make them all partners of thy felicitie.
>
> Be nat moche meved with singuler appetite,
> Excepte it profite unto thy subjectis all;
> At thyne example the people wyll delite,
> Be it vice or vertue, with the[e] they rise or fall.
> No lawes availe, men tourne as doth a ball,
> For where the ruler in lyvyng is nat stable,
> Bothe lawe and counsaile is tourned in to a fable.
>
>   (sigs. Nvi(v)–Nvii(v))[72]

Once the attempt has been made to read the text, not in the context of other mirrors for princes, but in the light of the events of 1529–31 and the dedication to Henry VIII as its principal intended reader, other additional resonances suggest themselves. Might coded criticism of the Royal Supremacy as a means of pursuing the royal divorce have been read into Elyot's otherwise somewhat opaque citation of Plato's dictum that counsel and consultation should direct themselves at the root causes of problems and their solutions, rather than risk creating further problems by piling secondary questions on top of primary ones?

Plato in his book of fortitude sayeth in the person of Socrates, when so ever a man seeketh a thing for cause of an other thing, the consultation ought to be always of that thing for whose cause the other thing is sought for, and not of that which is sought for because of the other thing; as surely wise men do consider that damage oft-times happeneth by abusing the due form of consultation: men like evil Physicians seeking for medicines ere they perfectly know the sickness.

                                                    (i vii(v))[73]

On a more specific level, might Elyot's discussion of the violent misrule of the Anglo-Saxon period ('who would then have desired to have been rather a man than a dog[?]' (Biv)) have been intended as a critical reflection upon the *Collectanea satis copiosa*'s use of the *Anglo Saxon Chronicle* and the history of the early

Saxon kings as precursors of Henry's own imperial authority? If it was, or if it was read in that light, then Elyot's version of the early history of the realm would have offered little comfort or encouragement to the argument that would lead to the statement in the Act of Appeals that 'by diverse sundry old authentic histories and chronicles it is manifestly declared and expressed that this realm of England is an Empire'.[74] Elyot's view of the legal and political culture of the period was uncompromising in its severity:

> where find ye any good laws that at that time were made and used; or any commendable monument of any science or craft in this realm occupied: such iniquity seemeth to be then that by the multitude of sovereign governors, all things had been brought to confusion.
>
> (Biv–iv(v)).

Again, it is hard to judge the precise contemporary impact of a maxim or aphorism upon the book's royal and elite readers, but when so much of the book seems specifically directed at contemporary issues, it is hard to rule out the possibility that even relatively generalized assertions might have been seen as a commentary on current events.[75]

The Sickness of the Public Weal

In the course of his study of *The Foundations of Modern Political Thought*, Quentin Skinner observed that it was characteristic of European humanists of the fifteenth and sixteenth centuries to lament that they lived in a fallen age in dire need of reformation.[76] And, as his magisterial survey of Italian political philosophy in the period amply demonstrates, they did so not because they were slavishly following tradition or adopting a currently fashionable mode, but rather because the politics of the Italian city states were indeed undergoing a profound and unprecedented crisis in the seventy years from 1480 to 1550. A similar awareness of context is necessary for an understanding of Elyot's declarations concerning the fallen state of his world. For, in the light of the events of 1529–30 and the sense of crisis they evoked, his highly impassioned discussion of the perils facing the English public weal seems equally readily explicable.

Elyot used a number of contractual metaphors and similes to describe the process that led him to produce *The Governor*. It was a duty to his prince, the fulfilment of an oath, a religious and patriotic good work, and an obligation incurred by anyone of his learning and experience to better the state of his fellow men.[77] The common theme is the sense of compulsion, the irresistible obligation to repay his King and country with a dividend for the benefits he has gained from his own learning. This is accompanied by a clear sense of greater than human inspiration, of his being 'inflamed with zeal' and 'violently stirred to divulgate or set forth some part of my study' (aii), as a response to the crisis he saw around him, the sickness of a public weal crying out for a cure. *The Governor* was thus not merely a handbook for princes and their ministers, but a book of remedies for a sick nation, a text that a writer trained in both medicine and law as well as government service was uniquely well placed to provide. In this way Elyot was representing himself, not simply as a counsellor to his prince, but also (again to borrow a term from Castiglione used by Quentin Skinner) a 'physician to the body politic'.[78]

Elyot's political theory was no dry abstraction but a lively engagement with the conditions of his own society and its culture. Everywhere his interest in classical principles is informed and driven by a desire to apply them to contemporary practice, a desire rooted in his experiences as a lawyer, scholar, and landowner in the midlands of England, and an administrator at court. The same energies that motivated his analysis of the failings of Henry VIII's political vision also powered his engagement with wider social concerns both great and small. Hence he could turn from a discussion of aristocratic pastimes to lament the decline in use of the longbow (Nvii), or, at another point, interrupt a passage about hawking and falconry with a protest about the damage to poultry and rural hospitality caused by current English practices in the field (i viii(v)). Similarly, his attacks upon the evils of dicing (Mvi(v)ff), the decline in the quality of schoolmasters and aristocratic schooling (Hiv–v(v) and Fii–Fiv), and the failure of noble parents to allow their children to practise craftsmanship (Gvii), are all informed by the perceived failings in these areas now and in England as well as by discussions in other, earlier, treatises.

Elyot writes at times as if he were living in a society facing a crisis of faith, in which the bonds between ruler and ruled, one person and their neighbour, threaten to break down. 'Without faith', he laments, citing a maxim of Cicero, 'a public weal may not continue' (a vii), for faith is the foundation of justice, and justice the mortar that maintains a civil society. And at the centre of the problem, once again, was the failure of the King:

For thereat not only dependeth all contracts, conventions, commutations, intercourse, mutual intelligence, amity and benevolence, which be contained in the word which of Tulli is called the 'society' or 'fellowship' of mankind . . . Wherefore to a governor of a public weal nothing more appertaineth than for himself to have faith in reverence, and most scrupulously to observe it . . . remembering this sentence: of faith cometh loyalty and where that lacketh, there is no surety.

(a vii(v))

And the failure at the centre had profound consequences in the provinces, where misrule and a failure to enforce the laws led to an increase in social dislocation and the multiplication of masterless men and vagabonds across the kingdom:

Behold, what an infinite number of Englishmen and women at this present time wander in all places throughout this realm as beasts brute and savage, abandoning all occupation, service, and honesty.

'Mark well here', Elyot instructed his readers, 'that disobedient subjects and negligent governors, do frustrate good laws' (Qiv(v)–Qv).

The Governor is thus neither a celebration of Henrician kingship nor an account of an ideal state in the making, but a diagnosis of how a realm might be redeemed if the governor took it upon himself to apply the correct remedies to the ills it identifies. The realm is currently far from healthy, but with time, the political will, and God's blessing, it might yet be brought to order at some point in the (seemingly relatively distant) future:

Albeit it is not to be despaired but that the King our sovereign lord now reigning, and this realm always having one prince like unto his highness, equal to the ancient princes in virtue and courage, it shall be reduced (God so disposing) unto a public weal excelling all other in pre-eminence of virtue and abundance of things necessary.

(ʙiv(v))

Elyot's justification of his endeavour in *The Governor* rested squarely on the public utility of the work: its ability to diagnose and offer remedies for the ills of the realm. And this sense of literary creation as a socially beneficial activity went well beyond his idea of this particular text. The Proheme to *The Governor* set all writing, not merely avowedly didactic texts, in the same utilitarian context. In condemning the unnamed 'malign interpreters' who are likely to 'rend and deface the renown of writers', he asserts, with evident relish of the irony, that they do so while 'they themselves being nothing to the public weal profitable' (aiii). This notion that writers were—and had to be—'to the public weal profitable' was the cornerstone of late medieval and humanist literary theory. On it rested the whole justification of authorship in a world in which learning and rhetorical ability were valued not for private gain but public good. And in a personal monarchy such as Tudor England, writing for the public good inevitably meant writing for those who were in a position to effect social change and determine national policy: the counsellors who advised the King, and, ultimately, the King himself.

But Elyot's fusion of political analysis and educational theory also suggests something more fundamental about his literary and cultural assumptions that will become more obvious when we examine the rest of his literary output. For what is obvious from any reading of his works is that classical and contemporary ideas about monarchy, and the relationship between himself as a writer and the person of the monarch as an implied reader are crucial to Elyot regardless of the genre or context in which he is working. It is striking that *The Governor* is far from unique among his published writings in beginning with a discussion of the nature and purpose of monarchy. He saw the 'Proheme' to a collection of aphorisms and the introduction to a medical handbook as equally appropriate places for discussions of kings and their responsibilities. Even the two versions of his *Dictionary* begin, as we have seen, with Prologues addressed to Henry VIII that seek to describe aspects of ideal kingship and the nature of the royal estate. For Elyot, it seems clear, the act of writing was always a political exercise, an attempt to address the problems facing the public weal by counselling the prince. It is tempting to suggest that every text that he wrote was written, as a result, with the idea of addressing the King in mind, whether that address was direct or through an intermediary who might discuss its contents with the King. Elyot thus represents the supreme example of the humanist ideal of literature as counsel. Everything he wrote was written as an act of counsel, an attempt to influence national policy through eloquence and reason.[79] The problems and dilemmas that such a self-imposed mission to counsel the King against tyranny created will be the subject of the chapters that follow.

9

Tyranny and the Conscience of Man

Elyot's Dialogues of 1533–1534

Elyot's first published work after *The Governor* of 1531 and his subsequent personal remonstrance to the King in June 1532, was a small pamphlet, *Pasquil the Plain*, printed anonymously by Thomas Berthelet in 1533. It, like those earlier interventions into the political arena, reflects Elyot's continued concern with the need for plain speaking in the courts of princes and the ruinous, divisive consequences of the failure of counsel at the centre of government. Indeed in the space of a single year, 1533, during which he clearly believed that the King was becoming increasingly reliant upon a small group of evangelical and reformist advisers, Elyot was to write a total of three new texts, each focusing from different angles upon the nature of princely government and the responsibilities of counsellors. First came *Pasquil The Plain*, printed in two separate and distinct editions in the course of the year, then *Of the Knowledge Which Maketh a Wise Man*, a dialogue inspired by Diogenes Laertus's account of Plato's dealings at the court of Dionysius of Sicily, and finally *The Doctrinal of Princes*, a translation of Isocrates's oration to Nicocles of Salamis on the responsibilities of kingship. I shall examine each of these in turn in the course of this chapter, for each represents a significant development in Elyot's literary and political thinking.

Pasquil the Plain

Pasquil the Plain, the first and most acerbic of these texts, addresses directly a world in which 'things be so far out of frame that stones do grudge at it ... and yet counsellors be speechless' (sig. Dv(v)).[1] It describes, by implication, the paralysis that is created at the centre of government when counsellors practise timeserving and flattery rather than offer the King honest advice. Written and printed at precisely the time that the Act of Appeals was declaring the 'imperial' nature of the English crown and Henry's Royal Supremacy was gaining the full force of law, Elyot's text, like *The Governor* before it, set out a radically different and more subversive account of the nature and impulses of princely government. Far from lauding the sovereign as the fount of wisdom and political authority, as royal propaganda would require, he described in *Pasquil* a situation in which princes in general, and the unnamed royal 'master' of the dialogue in particular, are actually political liabilities. Like Erasmus's young lion, the prince described in the text is a wilful, headstrong creature with little natural wisdom to guide him, who must be steered towards virtue by the assiduous labour of his counsellors. And despite his intention to live and rule well, he is always liable to veer from the path of probity and fall into personal vice and tyrannical government under the influence of flatterers or malign advisers. Once such men have 'rooted in [their] ... master's heart false opinions' (Dii), it will be a monumental task to uproot them.

As with the description of princely virtues in *The Governor*, the account of the fallen court in *Pasquil* offers, in addition to a timeless account of the evils of flattery, a direct, and this time still more obviously personalized commentary on the contemporary failings of the Henrician administration as Elyot saw them. The central conceit of this three-handed Lucianic dialogue was drawn from recent Italian history. When, in 1501, a classical statue was unearthed in Rome, Cardinal Oliviero Carafa had it erected adjacent to his palace in the Piazza Novanna, where it quickly became the centre of an academic festival. On St Mark's Day (25 April) each year thereafter, students and their tutors were permitted to dress the statue, which was nicknamed Pasquino, in the likeness of an historical or mythological figure of their own choosing, and to fix to it satirical verses and lampoons concerning individuals or contentious issues in the city. A rival statue, nicknamed Marfono, standing in the Campus Martius, became the site for satirical replies to the so-called *Pasquinades*. Some of the verses and responses were published, further pastiches and scurrilous oppositional sequences claiming to be genuine *Pasquinades* were written and circulated, and a literary tradition was born.[2]

Elyot's decision to domesticate this Italian form in a pamphlet of his own probably reflects the interest in the St Mark's Day festival of his friend and patron Thomas Cromwell. For, in December 1532, Edmund Bonner, the future Bishop of London, then acting as one of the King's agents in Rome, sent Cromwell a copy of the latest set of Pasquino verses along with a note saying that he knew how much the recipient had enjoyed hearing of the war of the statues when he was in Rome.[3] The arrival of this book in London, and the interest shown in it by Cromwell, may well have suggested to Elyot the usefulness of the figure of Pasquil or Pasquillo (the diminutive form of 'Pasquino') as a vehicle for the further exploration of his ideas about political plain-speaking, and as a mouthpiece for a satirical broadside against his personal and political enemies. If so, then this would explain both the immediacy and the intemperate nature of much of the resulting text. For *Pasquil the Plain* must have been written in a matter of weeks after the receipt of Bonner's gift in early 1533, and contains a number of unguarded remarks on policy and *ad hominem* criticisms of individual royal counsellors that the author seems very quickly to have regretted. As we shall see, before the end of the year a second edition was printed, this time under Elyot's own name, that toned down some of the more severe remarks and removed the more obvious personal references. Perhaps Elyot had overstepped the mark in hitting out at important individuals in sensitive positions and had been censured; or perhaps he merely thought better of his unguarded outburst. Either way, the first edition of *Pasquil* represents the high water mark of Elyot's direct assault upon individuals in his attempt to counsel the King towards moderation.

The dialogue, a 'merry treatise wherein plainness and flattery do come in trial' (Ai), sets out its stall on the high ground of political morality, and, like the first book of More's *Utopia*, discusses the efficacy or otherwise of truth-speaking in the counsel of Kings.[4] But, like the *Utopia* itself, it seems to reveal as much about the doubts and anxieties of its author as it does about the principles at stake. On one level at least, *Pasquil* provides a continuation in a more demotic form of the discussion of counsel begun in *The Governor*; for the three characters involved are fuller, animated versions of types (the plain-speaker and two kinds of flatterer) that he had already sketched out in the earlier text. The flatterers, the open prince-pleaser and the puritanical hypocrite, are presented as two sides of the same coin, differing only in that, where the one is voluble in his hypocrisy, the other is taciturn, allowing the appearance of gravity to conceal his pusillanimity. The former, whom Elyot here names Gnatho after a character in *The Eunuch*, a comedy by the classical playwright Terence, is a character who, as the 'Proheme' informs us, 'was brought in by writers of Comedies for such a servant as always affirmed [what] so ever was spoken of his master', and who, because he was 'Greek born', 'savoureth somewhat of rhetoric' (sig. Aii).[5] In *The Governor* Elyot had described such men as the more obvious kind of flatterers, 'which apparently do flatter, praising and extolling everything that is done by their superior, and bearing him on hand [i.e. deceiving him] that in him is of every man commended [that] which of truth is of all men abhorred and hated' (*The Governor*, xiii–iii(v)). A variant of this type he terms 'Assenters or followers', men who will even ape the habits and dress of their master, or of anyone whom he favours, in the hope of commending themselves to him more readily.

The second of Pasquil's adversaries Elyot names Harpocrates, after 'the prelate of the temple of Isis and Serapis, which were honoured for gods in Egypt, whose image is made holding his finger to his mouth betokening silence' (Aii). He draws some of his inspiration from *The Governor*'s 'subtle flatterer', who covertly lays snares for his master by appearing to be a serious and wise counsellor, and who was identified as a particular danger to virtuous princes:

There be some that by dissimulation can ostent or show a high gravity, mixed with a sturdy entertainment and fashion, exiling themselves from all pleasure and recreation, frowning and grudging at everything wherein is any mirth or solace...taunting and rebuking immoderately them with whom they be not contented. Naming themselves therefore Plain men; although they do the semblable, and oftentimes worse in their own houses. And by a simplicity and rudeness of speaking, with long deliberation used in the same, they pretend the high knowledge of counsel to be in them only; and in this wise, pitching their nets of adulation, they entrap the noble and virtuous heart which only beholdeth their feigned severity and counterfeit wisdom.

(*The Governor*, xv(v)–xvi)

Harpocrates similarly 'seemeth a reverend personage', and is, as Gnatho declares, 'cousin germane removed' (Biii) from his more garrulous counterpart, 'I by the mother['s] side, and he by the father'. Their surface differences indicate merely different means to the same self-interested end; for, as Gnatho goes on to admit,

We both have one master. And when he speaketh or doeth any thing for his pleasure: I study with words to commend it. If my cousin stand by, he speaketh little or nothing, but forming his visage into a gravity with silence, looketh as if he affirmed all thing that is spoken.

(Biv)

This duo of flatterers has long been seen as highly topical in its satirical aim. And each of them does seem to hit at very specific contemporary issues. Gnatho, as Pasquil points out as soon as he sees him, is a walking contradiction, an hypocritical assemblage of outward virtues and inward vices. He is an emblem of the times, in which the more strange things are, the better they are liked, and a man must take considerable pains if he is to tell 'an honest man from a false harlot' (Ai). Pasquil readily identifies him as a 'gallant', that is a fashionable man of the court, and one who is already well known to him. For on closer inspection he names him as 'mine old fellow Gnatho' (Ai). Yet he appears to be 'strangely disguised'. His cap, full of 'aglets and buttons', topped with a long ostrich feather and worn with the front 'turned down afore like a prentice' is courtly enough, but his long gown with its straight sleeves is, as Pasquil rebukes him, 'a *non sequitur*', as is the long fur tippet or collar around his neck. These are more suitable for a scholar or theologian than a courtier, and Pasquil assumes that he has stolen them from 'some worshipful doctor' in a dark alley (Aiii(v)). The jarring distinction between his jaunty courtly hat and grave scholar's coat is exacerbated by the books that he carries with him; for he holds a Latin New Testament in his hand, but carries a copy of Chaucer's *Troilus and Crisseyde* hidden in his bosom. 'Lord, what a discord is between these two books!', cries Pasquil; 'yet a great deal more is there in thine apparel. And yet most of all between the book in thy hand and thy conditions: as, God help me, as much as between truth and leasing [lies]' (Aiv).

The fashionable courtier who has adopted the appearance and manner of a scholar and carries the New Testament in his hands is a pointed parody of the Henrician evangelicals, the kind of men who were driving forward the anticlerical initiatives in the Reformation Parliament and increasingly finding favour in the royal administration. Elyot suggests that, like the Assenters or Followers described in *The Governor*, they adopted an interest in the Scriptures and in biblical scholarship at this time merely because the King favoured those who could interpret divine law and the biblical text in the ways that he desired. (Perhaps

Elyot was thinking specifically of men like Edward Foxe or Thomas Cranmer, who helped to produce the *Collectanea satis copiosa* and scoured the libraries of Europe for precedents and arguments that favoured the King's divorce, or Robert Barnes, the apostate friar turned Lutheran who had returned to England from exile to aid the King's campaign.) The real character and tastes of such men, Elyot implies, are far from Christian in their inspiration, hence he has Gnatho carry Chaucer's courtly and amorous romance within his coat, closer to his heart than the Scriptures that he ostentatiously shows to the world. Elyot's sense of both the newfangledness and the insincerity of the evangelical poseur is suggested by Pasquil's quip that 'some will be in the bowels of divinity ere they know what [be]longeth to good humanity' (Aiv). Whether a specific individual is the intended target of this caricature, or whether Gnatho represents the whole class of such men (including Christopher St German, Thomas Audley, Cranmer, and even Thomas Cromwell himself), who had embraced evangelical religion late in life and at a time when it seemed to promise favour at court, is unclear. It has been suggested that, because it is a work of Chaucer's that he carries, William Thynne or Sir Brian Tuke might be the focus of Elyot's ire.[6] But, given that the text in question is seemingly not the 1532 *Works* but either the Wynkyn de Worde (1517) or Richard Pynson (1526) edition of *Troilus*, the identification seems less convincing, and the point may simply be that this is an ostensibly pagan, courtly romance, a work more in keeping with Gnatho's flamboyant hat than with his professed interest in the biblical text.

If Gnatho's characterization gives rise to a number of possible identifications, however, Harpocrates has suggested only one name to most critics, that of Elyot's one-time fellow ambassador to the imperial court, and the current archbishop elect of Canterbury, Thomas Cranmer.[7] The association does seem convincing. Harpocrates, unlike Gnatho, is a real priest and Gnatho subsequently identifies him as 'my lord's confessor' (Bv and Bviii): a role that Cranmer was to play, informally at least, for many years. His principal characteristic is, as we have seen, his silence, with the spurious air of gravity that it conveys, and quietness, with slow deliberation, were aspects of Cranmer's character that his friends and allies commended in him, as Diarmaid MacCulloch's biography of the archbishop demonstrates. Similarly, as MacCulloch also suggests, the rather odd discussion between Pasquil and Harpocrates over free will and grace may be an allusion to discussions between the two men while they were together in Germany.[8]

Cranmer's rapid rise to favour after their period in Germany together clearly rankled with Elyot, and it is understandable how it came to symbolize in his own mind the way in which insincere flatterers were finding favour with the King, when frank-speakers like himself were being marginalized and neglected. Cranmer had been a relatively conservative thinker, doctrinally, during the 1520s, so his evident interest in the protestant services in the German city states that he and Elyot visited in the train of the Emperor in early 1532, and his growing associations with evangelical figures, may well have struck Elyot as precisely the kind of flirtation with newfangled ideas that he was satirizing in *Pasquil the Plain*. Still more contentiously, if Elyot had gained even a hint of the growing relationship between Cranmer and Margaret, the niece of the Nuremberg reformer Andreas Ossiander, that would lead to their secret marriage and Cranmer's abandonment of his clerical vow of celibacy in the months following Elyot's departure from Germany, then his sense of the latter's hypocrisy would have been all the stronger.[9] More gallingly, while Elyot had drifted into relative obscurity after the climacteric of his June remonstrance, Cranmer had been plucked from his embassy to the centre of ecclesiastical politics. In early October 1532 he was recalled from Germany to succeed archbishop Warham at Canterbury (who had died on 22 August), and had clearly been identified as the man who would finally settle the Great Matter of the King's divorce in England. By early January 1533 Cranmer was back on native soil, and by the end of the month he was sitting on committees discussing the royal marriage, living in new quarters in Canon Row Westminster, and signing himself 'Thomas Elect of Canterbury' on official correspondence.[10]

Elyot's sense of grievance at Cranmer's rise, and at his own marginalization comes through very clearly in the letters that he wrote to Cromwell in late 1532 and to Sir John Hackett in April 1533. On 18 November 1532 he informed Cromwell of his joy that the King had returned safely and honourably from a journey to France, suggesting with more than a hint of desperation that

fear of the great adventure of his most Royal person so attached my heart, that since unto this day it hath bereft me of the more part of my sleep, which I pray God may be redubed with these comfortable tidings of his Grace's safe return.[11]

Even given the element of hyperbole characteristic of such letters, Elyot's tone and his talk of fear and lost sleep suggest an excess of emotional investment here, and the object of that investment becomes clear in what follows. For the burden of the letter is an account of the 'grievous . . . great debt' of 'almost six hundred marks above the King's allowance', plus other losses, that he had incurred during his embassy to the Emperor, and a plea that he might, as a result, be released from the expensive obligation to act as Sheriff for the county of Cambridgeshire, should he be nominated for the coming year. Alongside the details of his financial losses, however, is a powerful sense of anxiety concerning how his performance during the embassy had been received at court, and of the still more painful loss of reputation that Elyot felt that he had suffered as a consequence. Assuring Cromwell that he rejoiced not a little that the secretary was daily augmenting his own good reputation with the King, Elyot quickly turned to his own case (or a very loosely disguised version of it) in the wish that, thanks to Cromwell's influence with the King,

I hope the right opinion of virtue shall once more be revived and false detraction tried out and put to silence by whom some true and painful service have been frustrate and kept from such knowledge as had been expedient.[12]

The awkward syntax and mangled tenses here suggest the intensity of the emotions underlying the letter. And, after a lengthy apologia for his own conduct during the embassy ('how I used me in mine access unto the Emperor, God is my judge, that in my replications I have seen him change countenance, which (as they know that have been with him) is no little thing') he returned again to the issue of reputation, this time more directly and specifically:

I perceive the King's opinion [di]minished toward me by that that I perceive other men advanced openly to the place of counsellors which neither in the importance of service, neither in charges have served the King as I have done, and I being omitted, had in less estimation than I was in when I served the King first in his Council, which I speak not for any ambition, but that only I desire that my true heart should not cause me to live both in poverty and out of estimation, for, God judge my soul, as I desire more to live out of debt and in quiet study than to have as much as a King may give me.[13]

The potent mixture of anxiety, resentment, and envy directed at the unnamed 'other men' would very quickly find a direct point of focus in the person of Elyot's erstwhile fellow ambassador.

A further letter of 8 December reiterated Elyot's assertions of loyalty and obligation to the King, assuring Cromwell of his awareness of,

Howe my duty is to serve my sovereign lord truly and diligently, which God, is my judge, I have done to my power with as good a will and as gladly as any man could imagine to do, neither for mine obedience only, nor for hope of promotion, but for very hearty love that I do bear to the king's highness besides mine allegiance.[14]

It was not long, however, before the note of grievance once again appeared from beneath the assertions of good will and obedience. 'But, when I consider mine infelicity and loss of time in unprofitable study', he continued, 'I am enforced to be cruciate in my poor mind, which I confess to be for lack of wisdom.' Enjoining Cromwell to 'take some patience to hear some part of my grief', he related an account of his long period of unpaid service on the King's Council, his difficulties in securing his father's inheritance against his greedy relatives, the expensive litigation that this had involved, and his unrewarded labours on behalf of the King,

In [which] . . . unthankful travail I no thing got but the colic and the stone, debilitation of nature and almost continual distillations of rheums, ministers to abbreviate my life, which, though it be of no great importance, yet some ways it might be necessary.[15]

These are self-evidently not the letters of a contented or emotionally stable man. 'Cruciate' in mind and racked in body, Elyot had become fixated with a sense of his own ill-use and the contrasting good fortune of those who had been preferred above him. In the letter to Sir John Hackett describing the 'great cloud' hanging over the kingdom, written on 6 April 1533, probably the very time that he was completing *Pasquil the Plain* or seeing it through the press, he again reiterated this sense of injustice, this time giving his fortunate rivals a name. Striking a defiant note, he told Hackett that,

Neither mine importable expenses unrecompensed shall so much fear me, nor the advancement of my successor the bishop of Canterbury so much allure me that I shall decline from truth or abuse my sovereign lord unto whom I am sworn, for I am sure that I and you also shall once die, and I know that there is a God and he is all truth and therefore he will grievously punish all falsehood, and that everlastingly.[16]

That he can refer to Cranmer only as 'my successor' (as ambassador) suggests both the degree of animosity he felt towards him at this time, and the equivalence that he believed to exist between them. Not only does Elyot appear to have felt that he and Cranmer deserved equal reward for their services to the Crown, but given that he himself had been the first to take office and (as he made clear in his letters to Cromwell) sustained the heavier personal losses in the process, he clearly thought that his promotion should have been the earlier and the more impressive. Furthermore, the terms of the letter make it clear that he felt that Cranmer had achieved his success by declining from truth and abusing his sovereign, a path that, however 'alluring' it might appear, he himself would not follow. Such was the background, both political and intensely personal, against which he sketched the figures of Gnatho and Harpocrates in *Pasquil the Plain*.

   In satirizing courtiers and confessors who preach virtue but do not practise it, and keep silent when their masters sin or err for their own personal gain, *Pasquil* does seem, then, to have had Cranmer primarily in mind. To Elyot the advancement of the archbishop elect was both a personal affront and a symbol of the favour enjoyed by a whole coterie of time-serving evangelicals surrounding the King. Cranmer was also himself the prime example of the problem of hypocrisy in the royal council, a man whose own sexual and marital history made him the last candidate worthy of elevation to the see of Canterbury, and the least likely to offer impartial and honest advice to Henry VIII over the best resolution of his Great Matter. Hence, perhaps, the edge of bitterness to Pasquil's assertion that Harpocrates's sins of omission, in not telling his master what he should hear, despite both the obligations inherent upon him as his confessor and the licence that this office afforded him to do so, are far worse than the sins of commission committed by Gnatho and his kind. The priest's silence, he tells Gnatho,

might do more harm than all thy flattery, [and] then what mischief might follow of his damnable silence, if in the secret time of confession, wherein confessors have above all men most largest liberty to blame and reprove, he should either dissemble the vices that he knoweth in his master or else forebear to declare to him the enormity of such capital sins as he hath confessed.

(BV(v)–BVi)

Much of Pasquil's disputation with Harpocrates is taken up with a lengthy debate over when a man is obliged to break his silence in order to save his friend or master from danger—a debate which hinges upon rival interpretations of the word 'imminent' ('a word taken out of Latin and not commonly used'), and the various degrees of knowledge which one might have concerning likely dangers (cvi–cviii).[17] All of which leads to Pasquil's conclusion that, if one would speak out to save one's master from physical harm, then one should all the more readily do so to prevent him from falling into infamy, 'avarice, tyranny, or beastly living' (Di), or to forestall 'perpetual infamy, the subversion of the commonweal, or universal destruction of the whole country' (cviii(v)). For, once such things have been brought into existence, it will prove almost impossible to remove them. As Pasquil tells Harpocrates,

> When Gnatho with his flattery and ye with your silence have once rooted in your master's heart false opinions and vicious affects, which is the poison that we so much spoke of, though ye after repent you, and perceive the danger, yet shall it perchance be impossible with speech to remove those opinions and cure those affects, except ye loved so your master that for his health ye would confess your own errors.
>
> (Dii–ii(v))

In this way the philosophical question, 'what is Knowledge?', becomes an intensely political one. For only in applying his knowledge can the philosopher validate his wisdom and benefit the community. Thus understanding, wisdom, and political action are part of the same fundamental question—a question which, as we shall see, Elyot was to explore far more exhaustively in his next dialogue, *Of the Knowledge Which Maketh a Wise Man*.

In Harpocrates and Gnatho, Elyot exploits the licence created by the St Mark's Day *Pasquinade*, when 'once in the year it is lawful to every man to set in verse or prose any taunt that he will, again[st] whom he list, how[ever] great an estate so ever he be' (Ai(v)), to fashion caricatures of both his own personal enemies and the class of men that were blinding the King to his true responsibilities. Against these two dangerous flatterers, he sets the eponymous hero of the dialogue, Pasquillus or Pasquil himself, whom he introduces as, 'an image of stone, sitting in the city of Rome, openly' (Ai(v)). Unlike Gnatho with his Greek origins or the Alexandrian Harpocrates, Pasquil is 'an old Roman', who 'by sitting in the street and hearing market men chat . . . is become rude and homely' in his speech and manners (Aii). So 'foreign' garrulousness and sophistication are set against 'homely' domestic honesty, and flattery and deceit against blunt, plain speaking. Rather than a simple didactic combat between two vices and a single virtue, however, *Pasquil the Plain* is actually a relatively complex text, combining elements of the political satire and the *ad hominem* lampoon with a serious rumination upon the advantages and disadvantages of free and frank speech in the counselling of princes. And its outcome is some distance from the unequivocal victory for Pasquil himself that the simple terms of the prologue might have suggested.

On one level Pasquil's bluntness reflects the kind of determination to commit oneself to truth, come what may, that Elyot had announced in his letter to Hackett in April 1533: 'I beseech God continue [the King's good health] . . . and send his comfort of spirit unto him, and the truth may be freely and thankfully heard. For my part, I am finally determined to live and die therein.'[18] Yet, as Gnatho points out, Pasquil has hitherto achieved only harm and opprobrium through his plain-speaking and criticisms of others:

Yet hast thou wit enough to perceive what damage and hindrance thou hast thereby sustained, and more art thou likely and with greater peril, if thou have not good await [i.e. care] what and to whom and where thou speakest.

(Aiv)

Thus Gnatho advises him to,

leave now at the last thine indiscrete liberty in speech, wherein thou usest unprofitable taunts and rebukes, I may well call them unprofitable whereby nothing that thou blamest is of one jot amended, and thou losest thereby preferment which thine excellent wit doth require, and that worse is, travailest in study of mind to augment thine own detriment, and therein losest much time that might be better employed.

(Aiv(v))

He suggests to Pasquil, citing Aeschylus as his authority, that he practise 'holding thy tongue where it behoveth thee. And speaking in time that which is convenient' (Av). And when asked to explain this, he interprets the playwright's advice to mean that,

it behoveth a man to hold his tongue when he aforeseeth by an experience that the thing which he would purpose or speak of to his superior shall neither be pleasantly heard nor thankfully taken. And in words, opportunity and time always[s] do depend on the affection and appetite of him that heareth them.

(Av(v)–vi)

Pasquil's own reading of Aeschylus's maxim is rather different, however, resting as it does on the need to avoid speaking inappropriately of irrelevant matters in social situations, rather than avoiding difficult subjects that the hearer may not wish to hear. Just as one should not discourse upon astronomy on a battlefield, or geometry at the card table, or on the moderation of diets in the midst of a feast (Avi(v)), so,

where thou seest thy friend in a great presence honoured of all men, though thou knowest in him notable vices, yet there hold thy tongue, and reproach him not of them. // Where thou seest thy lord or master, in the presence of many, resolved in to fury or wantonness, though thou hast all ready advertisements how he shall refrain it, yet hold thy tongue then, for troubling that presence.

(Avii)

But the moral that he draws from the story is that one should offer the correct counsel at a more appropriate time, preferably prior to the event itself, rather than that one should avoid offering it at all:

If thou knowest a vice in thy friend, which is of a few men suspected, ere it be talked of at the tavern or of his enemy reproached, warn him of the damage that may happen if it be not amended. // When thou perceivest thy Master to be resolved in to wrath or affections dishonest, before the wrath be increased into fury and affection into beastly enormity: as opportunity serveth thee, reverently and with tokens of love toward him, speak such words as shall be convenient.

(Avii(v)–viii)[19]

Thus, while the counsellor must choose carefully the moment at which to offer frank and potentially unwelcome advice, he may not shirk the responsibility to offer it altogether:

Opportunity consisteth in place or time, where and when the said affections or passion of wrath be some deal mitigate and out of extremity. And words be called convenient which have respect to the nature and state of the person unto whom they be spoken, *and also* to the detriment which might ensue by the vice or lack that thou hast espied. It ought not to be as thou hast supposed. For opportunity and time for a counsellor to speak do not depend of the affection and appetite of him that is counselled. Mary, then counsel were but a vain word, and every man would do as him list.

(Aviii–viii(v), my italics)

All of this might appear to be merely the rehearsal of traditional maxims. But the contemporary context of the discussion is suddenly glimpsed once more in Pasquil's further retort to Gnatho's quietist exposition:

If thou understandest no better the New Testament (which thou carriest as solemnly with thee as thou shouldest read a privy lesson, hem, I had almost told where openly!), then thou doest Aeschylus's sentence, which as if thou hadest been learned thou toldest to me for a counsel, thy breath will be so hot shortly, that thou wilt make men afeared to come within twenty foot of thee.

(Avi)

Despite all Pasquil's apparent lightness of tone, these are not laughing matters, and the passage speaks eloquently of the tensions and pressures of the period in which Elyot was writing. This is, indeed, Elyot at his most overtly contemporary, writing in the heat of the moment and responding very immediately to the covert evangelical activity at court and in London, and the official persecution of the more extreme reformers that was underway in 1531–3. Suggesting that Gnatho looks as if he is going to a secret meeting at some undisclosed location ('hem, I had almost told where openly [!]') at which the New Testament would be read and expounded, places his character very precisely in the evangelical underworld of contemporary London, with its private conventicles and secret gatherings of the 'known men' and brethren who followed the old heresies of the Lollards or discussed the newer views of Luther.[20] While the sinister allusion to the 'hot' fate awaiting him if he should be caught expressing such views reflects the current wave of public executions and lesser, corporal punishments handed out to heretics in the City at this time. All of this speaks of both the haste of Elyot's writing, and of the intensity of the feelings that drove him. For, if indeed it was the receipt of Bonner's gift of the Italian dialogue that prompted Elyot to use

Pasquil and his 'licence to rail' as the vehicle for his renewed assault upon the evils of contemporary politics, then the text must have been written and submitted to the press within the first few months of 1533, at a time when heresy trials and the advancement of evangelicals at court and in government were very live issues, both in London and in Elyot's own mind.

The wider religious agenda is also a part of Pasquil's sense of what is wrong with the contemporary world. The same concerns for the plight of conventional piety and the fate of the institutional church that Elyot expressed in his letters to Norfolk and Hackett surface again in Pasquil's lament that ten thousand fewer pilgrims now visit St James's at Compostella and St Peter's in Rome than did so a thousand years before,

And men say that in other countries diverse monasteries be like to break hospitality, because their offerings be not the third part so much as they were accustomed. For indeed nowadays men's devotion waxeth even as cold as the monks be in the choir at midnight.

(Bi)

And religion looms larger still in his claim that, if all good counsellors had taken note of his words ('that they called railing'), then 'many things might have been prevented that were after lamented':

Germany should not have kicked again[st] her mother, emperors and princes should not have been in perpetual discord and oftentimes in peril, prelates have been laughed at as disardes; Saints blasphemed, and miracles reproved for jugglings, laws and statutes condemned, and officers little regarded. What must needs follow, since my breath faileth me, I leave that to thee, Gnatho, to conject.

(Bi(v)–Bii)[21]

Gnatho's counsel, as we have seen, is that Pasquil should abandon his unprofitable railing along with the humanistic learning that underpins it, and instead praise and commend those whom he has previously offended, adopting the same evangelical approach to counselling as he himself has done:

And where thou didst wonder to see me have in my hand the New Testament, if thou wouldst do the same, and now in thine age lay apart the lesson of gentiles, called humanity, since thou mayest have good leisure, being not yet called to council, pick out here and there sentences out of holy scripture to furnish thy reason with authority. I make God avow that thou shalt be within three months able to confound the greatest divine in all Italy.

(Biii)

The passage speaks eloquently of Elyot's sense that true wisdom, and the classical scholarship of the humanists, has been replaced by the superficial commitment and tags of the evangelical 'divine', the kind of learning that can be donned as readily as Gnatho's purloined doctor's coat. But what is the true scholar and the honest would-be counsellor to do in the face of such injustices as he sees around him? Is there still a place at court for free speech and frank advice? The dialogue suggests a pessimistic answer, for at the end of their argument, Pasquil identifies himself to Harpocrates as the voice, not of effective counsel in waiting ('Tush man, my plainness is so well known that I shall never come unto privy chamber or gallery' (Dv(v))), but of protest, a voice, if not exactly in the wilderness, at least in the market-place, forced to speak out on just one day in the calendar in the absence of proper counsel and frankness during the remainder of the year:

Mary, if they that be called [to Council] would always[s] play the parts of good counsellors, and both spiritual and temporal governors would banish thee [Harpocrates] and Gnatho out of their courts, except ye amend your conditions, I would speak never a word, but sit as still as a stone. But forasmuch as it happeneth all contrary, and that things be so far out of frame that stones do grudge at it . . . and yet counsellors be speechless, I that am set in the City of Rome . . . once in the year shall hear of the state of all princes and regions . . . then boldly I put forth my verdict, and that openly.

(Dv–v(v))

His purpose is to shame men into reforming themselves by public exposure rather than to advise them to improve, 'that men shall perceive that their vices, which they think to be wonderful secret, be known to all men. And that I hope alway that by much clamour and open repentance, when they see the thing not succeed to their purpose, they will be ashamed' (Dvi). (Again, was he thinking especially of Cranmer's very dangerous secret marriage, which a number of his reformist friends seem to have known all about at this time?) In the absence of good counsel, the politics of naming and shaming seem to be the only recourse left for the honest man.

Despite the vigour of its execution, then, the result of the debate is inconclusive. Harpocrates and Gnatho return to court, while Pasquil is left in the public streets to ruminate with more than a hint of anxiety about what will happen when they get there:

Now when these two fellows come to the court, they will tell all that they have heard of me; it maketh no mater. For I have said nothing but by the way of advertisement, without reproaching of any one person, wherewith no good man hath cause to take any displeasure. Judge what men list, my thought shall be free. And God, who shall judge all men, knoweth that I desire all things to be in good point, so that I might ever be speechless, as it is my very nature to be.

(Dvi(v))

If, then, as Stanford Lehmberg and others have suggested, Pasquil 'speaks Elyot's own mind' in the dialogue,[22] he does so for only one part of a divided mind, allowing the author to explore one of the options available to a man who, since his remonstrance of June 1532, was 'not called to council'. Pasquil may present himself as the honest man and the plain speaker, but there is also, as his antagonists point out, more than a hint of the railer to him, of a Diogenes figure whose criticisms are ineffective, despite their honesty and acuity, because they are too sharp and wounding to be born with equanimity. Hence, despite the fact that Harpocrates is reduced to confusion by Pasquil's arguments ('I can not shortly tell, I am so abashed at thy forward reason' (Div)) it is he and not the plain-speaking statue that finds a place at court at the end of the dialogue.

Some critics have seen the scenario outlined in the dialogue, and the figure of Pasquil himself, as a direct allusion to the fate of Sir Thomas More.[23] More had, after all, been excluded from the Council following his principled resignation from the chancellorship, and spent his time 'railing' against heresy in a series of polemical tracts. But, if More was the inspiration for the piece, then its conclusion would, for the reasons outlined, have been little comfort to him. It seems more sensible to assume that More's particular situation was just one aspect of the wider social crisis that Elyot was describing. And rather than defending his stance, or, as has also been suggested, declaring Elyot's own resolution to follow his example and 'abandon political discretion for plain-speaking',[24] *Pasquil* seems, as we have seen, to be evidence of work in progress, more an attempt to think through the issues at stake than a declaration of their resolution.

As More had done with Morus and Hythlodaeus in the first book of *Utopia*, Elyot uses the figures of Pasquil and Gnatho to explore both the importance of the role of 'free-speaker' and also the limitations and perils that it involved. When Gnatho informs Pasquil that he has achieved only personal damage through his railing ('nothing that thou blamest is of one jot amended, and thou losest thereby preferment which thine excellent wit doth require' (Aiv(v)) this is no empty argument for Elyot. As his letters to Cromwell and Hackett reveal, he was extremely mindful of the loss of reputation and income that his exclusion from government service entailed, and sought long and hard to redeem them. Thus Pasquil's failure to follow Harpocrates and Gnatho to court, or even to influence their conduct when they got there, must be seen as a defeat in Elyot's own terms. He may, like Pasquil, have won all the arguments (in his own mind at least), but the victory was pyrrhic, as nothing was indeed, 'one jot amended'.[25] Elyot was thus not contentedly committing himself to a life of stoic resignation, or of unrewarded truth-speaking from the margins, rather he was exploring the most effective means of continued political engagement in the circumstances in which he found himself in 1533. And he seems, through *Pasquil*, to have finally rejected not only self-interested flattery, but unrestrained 'railing' too as practical options. For, as he hinted to his readers in the introductory missive, *all* the 'personages that do reason [in the dialogue] be of small reputation' (Ai(v)).

Written in the heat of Elyot's disappointment over not being preferred to more substantial office, and with the promotion of Cranmer to an unimaginably high position at the same time, Elyot had let fly under cover of anonymity against the evangelical cadre of advisers surrounding the King. The mixture of personal grievance and political philosophy that Pasquil represents was not, however, a happy one, and it is perhaps symbolic of a more general return to personal balance and moderation, that he was to rewrite parts of the text almost immediately after they were published, perhaps, as suggested earlier, as a result of direct criticism of the work, perhaps in anticipation of such criticism before it arose. Either way, at much the same time as he was drafting a more substantial and considered exploration of the issues of good counsel and bad government in *Of the Knowledge that Maketh a Wise Man*, he removed the more obviously *ad hominem* references in the second edition of *Pasquil* (again published by Berthelet, but this time under Elyot's own name), and toned down the identification of Harpocrates as his master's confessor, and hence the direct association with Cranmer.[26] Similarly the statement that Gnatho is a 'gallant' is replaced by the observation that he is a 'gentleman' (Aiii), references to 'my lord' are replaced by the less class-specific 'my master' (Aiii, Biv(v)), and the statement that the two flatterers go back 'to the court' (Dvi) is replaced by the less specific suggestion that they go back 'to their master'. Thus the curial element in the satire is effectively downplayed. Yet simultaneously Elyot also added, after the statement that 'no good man hath cause to take any displeasure' at the text (Dvi(v)) the remark 'and he that doeth, by that which is spoken he is soon spied to what part he leaneth', and added two anecdotes that increased the specificity of the advice offered concerning counselling princes.[27] The author might have been reducing the *ad hominem* specificity of his diatribe, but the issues that it raised would clearly not go away. Indeed Elyot was to return to them still more insistently in the longer, more substantial dialogue that he was almost certainly already writing while the first edition of *Pasquil* was at press. At heart that dialogue, published as *Of the Knowledge which Maketh a Wise Man* is a lengthy discussion from first principles of the question that had preoccupied Pasquil's debate with Harpocrates, what is Knowledge? But, characteristically, this philosophical question is prompted by a discussion of a much more directly political one, and this is once again, a question of counsel.

Of The Knowledge which Maketh a Wise Man

'The Proheme of Sir Thomas Elyot, Knight' to *Of the Knowledge* is not addressed to any given individual, although, typically, it refers directly to Henry VIII on a number of occasions. Rather it seems to evoke an intended readership of English subjects, individuals who had already read Elyot's earlier works and needed to be instructed further as to their nature and purpose. At times the text reveals Elyot at his most portentous, writing directly for an imagined posterity concerning the significance of his life and writings, yet at others it shows him at his most contemporary and specific, striking out once more against real or imagined critics, impugning their motives and defending his own endeavours.

The 'Proheme' presents the text that follows as the distillation of a lifetime's reading and scholarship, finally published, as *The Governor* was, as a patriotic duty,[28] the result of a 'constant intent to profit thereby to my natural country, whereunto according to the sentence of Tulli, we be most specially bounden' (Aii). But the prologue also serves as a defence of his earlier works, and *The*

Governor in particular, against two criticisms which Elyot seems to have found equally hurtful: that he used neologisms, 'strange terms' drawn out of Latin and Greek, where simpler English words would do, and that his criticisms of the vices of others were hypocritical and aimed 'to rebuke some particular person'. As a result, he claims, some unnamed, malicious readers have sought 'to bring my works and afterward me into the indignation of some men in authority' (Aii(v)). The resentment and anxieties concerning detraction and his own reputation at court that had characterized his letters to Cromwell thus spill out again in to the more public arena of the printed page:

Such is of some men the nature serpentine that, lapping sweet milk, they convert it forthwith into poison, to destroy him of whose liberality they late had received it.

(Aiii)

To confound such allegations Elyot cites the case of his most significant and illustrious reader, Henry VIII himself, whom he represents as the ideal enlightened scholar, understanding and appreciative of all that the author had sought to do in *The Governor*:

How incomparable be these [malicious] men unlike to the most excellent prince, our most dear sovereign lord? Whose most royal person I heartily beseech God to preserve in long life and honour. His highness benignly receiving my book, which I named the Governor, in the reading thereof soon perceived that I intended to augment our English tongue, whereby men should as well express more abundantly the thing that they conceived in their hearts... as also interpret out of Greek, Latin, or any other tongue into English as sufficiently as out of any one of the said tongues into another. His grace also perceived that throughout the book there was no term new made by me of a Latin or French word but it is there declared so plainly by one mean[s] or other to a diligent reader that no sentence is thereby made dark or hard to be understand [*sic*].

(Aiii–iii(v))

And if Elyot's linguistic strategies were clearly appreciated by his king, so too were his political intentions:

Ne the sharp and quick sentences, [n]or the round and plain examples set out in the verses of Claudian the poet in the second book, [n]or in the chapters of Affability, Benevolence, Beneficence, and of the diversity of flatterers, and in diverse other places, in any part offended his highness: but (as it was by credible persons reported unto me) his grace not only took it in the better part, but also with princely words full of majesty commended my diligence, simplicity, and courage, in that I spared none estate in the rebuking of vice.

(Aiii(v)–Aiv)

This encomium of Henry as the ideal reader is clearly, as Hogrefe suggests,[29] another of those Erasmian panegyrics that presents its subject as he ought to be rather than as he necessarily is. For it recalls to Elyot's mind the example of the Emperor Antoninus ('called for his wisdom Antonine the philosopher') who retained 'a plain and rude person, which always[s] spoke in the rebuke of all men, and never praised any man', in order that he should tell him his faults, and paid him 'double wages' for the privilege. The lesson offered is directed both at the King who had failed to offer the plain-speaking Elyot his due reward for his loyal service, and the detractors who had criticized his works. For Antoninus had provided through his openness to criticism, Elyot declares, an example 'more profitable unto the public weal of the city than any other thing in his person or dignity' (Aiv(v)). And,

> In like wise our most dear sovereign lord perfectly knew that no writer ought to be blamed which writeth neither for hope of temporal reward nor for any private disdain or malice, but only of fervent zeal toward good occupation and virtue. Perdie [By God!], man is not so yet conformed in grace that he cannot do sin. And I suppose no prince thinketh himself to be exempt from mortality. And forasmuch as he shall have more occasions to fall, he ought to have the more friends or the more instruction to warn him.
>
> (Av)

The defensiveness of this Proheme, coupled with Elyot's decision to add those comments to the end of the second edition of *Pasquil the Plain* regarding readers who did 'take displeasure' at its contents, strongly suggest that he had overplayed the specificity of his criticisms in his earlier works—or at least feared that he had. And it seems to have been *Pasquil* rather than *The Governor* that was the prime cause of his anxiety. For he specifically defends that text against the charge of *ad hominem* criticisms here, despite the fact that the first edition of the work had been printed anonymously:

> As for my part, I eftsoons [once again] do protest that in no book of my making I have intended to touch more one man than another. For there be Gnathos in Spain as well as in Greece, Pasquils in England as well as in Rome, Dyonisiuses in Germany as well as in Sicily, Harpocrates in France as well as in Egypt, Aristippuses in Scotland as well as in Cyrene. Platos be few, and them I doubt where to find. And if men will seek for them in England which I set in other places, I cannot let [i.e. prevent] them.
>
> (Av)[30]

By tacitly acknowledging authorship of the earlier dialogue in this way (an acknowledgement that he formalized in the second edition by naming himself as the author at the head of the preface), Elyot was simultaneously both defending the text's integrity and reasserting its political nature. Indeed, his arch assertion that there are 'Pasquils in England', coupled with the suggestion that he cannot help it if readers will seek for his characters at home despite the Italian setting of the dialogue, would seem designed to encourage rather than deter topical readings of the text.

   The dialogue that follows is a lengthy philosophical disquisition on the nature of knowledge. It seeks to demonstrate that true knowledge is an aspect of Wisdom, which is in turn a function of the human soul, true and just in its similitude to God. To know and be true to oneself in honesty, justice, and virtue is thus to be truly wise. But the occasion for this discussion is typically no academic symposium but a very practical debate concerning the responsibilities of the honest man in the court of a tyrant. Just as *Pasquil the Plain* took as its theme the need for the honest counsellor to speak truly at the courts of princes, so *Of the Knowledge* returns to that idea, and seeks to elevate it to the status of a philosophical obligation. Indeed, at first glance, the protagonists of the debate seem to be a reworking on a grander scale of the roles and positions adopted by Pasquil and Gnatho in the earlier dialogue.

Taking as his inspiration an episode in the life of Plato drawn from the *Lives of Eminent Philosophers* by the third-century author Diogenes Laertius,[31] Elyot imagines an encounter between the philosopher and an antagonist, Aristippus of Cyrene, over whether or not Plato was correct to accuse King Dionysius of Sicily of behaving like a tyrant. What should he have done when confronted with evidence that the King was acting tyrannically? It is Plato's contention that, being a wise man and true to himself, he could have done nothing else but confront the King directly, whereas Aristippus argues that there were more pragmatic and circumspect options available to him that would have achieved the same ends without provoking Dionysius angrily to sentence him initially to death and finally, after a change of heart, to slavery among the Aeginites.

Plato declares that he could not know that Dionysius was a tyrant and fail to inform him of the fact, for the knowledge of the wise man must be reflected in his actions. Thus he was compelled to speak as he did, both to cure Dionysius of tyranny and vindicate his own claim to wisdom.[32]

Plato, as Elyot presents him, is thus, like Pasquil before him, characterized by a single-minded and seemingly absolute commitment to truth. 'Neither the cruelty of king Dionise, nor the malicious decree of the Aeginites', he declares,

might remove my courage from virtue and truth, no more than the twice selling of me, nor this vile habit of a slave or bondman may change mine estate or condition.

(Bv–v(v))

He advocates the rule of reason and the soul over the bodily senses, the rejection of worldly values in favour of higher spiritual ones, the conformity of outward life and appearance to inner belief, and the need for knowledge to reveal itself in action in the world if it is to be of value.[33] Against him is set Aristippus whose highest end is 'the voluptuary of the body and senses' (Bviii(v)), and whom Plato mocks as a flatterer and prince-pleaser. Thus far the two do indeed seem to mirror the roles of Pasquil and Gnatho in the earlier dialogue, but, as we shall see, they also display interesting variations upon those characters which further complicate what is possibly Elyot's most complex and conflicted political treatise.

The episode that prompts the dialogue is given only the briefest of treatments in Diogenes Laertius's *Lives*. The relevant passage relates how Plato made three visits to the Sicily of Dionysius, only the first of which (which was undertaken 'to see the island and the craters of Etna'), got him into difficulty:

On this occasion, Dionysius, the son of Hermocrates, being on the throne forced him to become intimate with him. But when Plato held forth on tyranny and maintained that the interest of the ruler alone was not the best end, unless he were also pre-eminent in virtue, he offended Dionyius, who in his anger exclaimed, 'You talk like an old dotard'. 'And you like a tyrant', rejoined Plato. At this the tyrant grew furious and at first was bent on putting him to death; then, when he had been dissuaded from this by Dion and Aristomenes [other philosophers at court], he did not indeed go so far, but handed him over to Pollis the Lacedaemonian, who had just arrived on an embassy, with orders to sell him into slavery.[34]

From these bare details Elyot wove a complex and colourful account of the story, recollected by Plato in relative tranquillity after his escape, and added to it an extended discussion of the significance of the incident focused on the question: what should the wise man have done in that situation?

The dialogue begins when Aristippus, recognizing a figure approaching him in the street as Plato, decides to approach him, even 'though there were some debate between us in Sicily... For in wise men resteth no malice, although diversity in opinions or form of living causeth sometime contention between them' (Bi). When asked why he is on the road in such poor clothes, Plato reveals that he has just escaped from slavery, having earlier survived the sentence of death issued by King Dionysius. This news astonishes Aristippus, for, as he says, 'when I went from king Dionise, he might not suffer that thou mightest be one hour from him' (Bi(v)), and 'for the incomparable favour that the king bore to thee, thou were in the court almost in as much reverence as the king's own person' (Bii). Plato's explanation of how this situation had changed (the details of which are Elyot's own elaboration upon the bare narrative in the *Lives*) has suggested to many scholars a clear, if exaggerated, commentary on Henry VIII's descent from affability to repression in the period from 1529 to 1533:[35]

Soon after that thou hadst obtained licence of the king to go into Athens, he became wonderful sturdy, insomuch as no man might blame any thing wherein he delighted, nor praise any thing which was contrary to that that he used. And that sober and gentle manner in hearing sundry opinions reasoned before him, whereto of a custom he was wont to provoke thee and me, was laid apart, and, supposing that by hearing of sundry philosophers dispute and reason he himself had attained to a more perfect knowledge than any other that spoke unto him, began to have all other men in contempt. And, as it were Jupiter, who (as Homer sayeth) with a wink made all heaven to shake, he would with a terrible countenance so visage them whom he knew would speak of their opinions freely, that they should dread to say anything which they knew should be contrary unto his appetite.

(Bii(v)–Biii)

Only Plato had the courage to speak out in this intimidatory atmosphere:

Notwithstanding, on a time he willed me to declare in his presence the majesty of a king, and how much he excelled and was above the estate of any other person: which request

I gladly heard, thinking to have good opportunity to warn him of his blindness and folly. Therefore I began to commend the perfect image or figure of God, which was manifest in the estate of a king who ruled himself and his people for the universal weal of them all ... Afterward I studiously did set out a Tyrant in his proper colours, who attendeth to his own private commodity. Here at King Dionise frowned and became angry. And interrupting my words said unto me:

'This is a tale of old fools that cannot be otherwise occupied.' And I answered again that those words of his savoured of Tyranny.

(Biii–iii(v))

Those readers who had followed Elyot's discussion of the correct manner and time to offer counsel in *Pasquil the Plain* would not be surprised to read of Aristippus' astonishment at both the boldness and the timing of such a response:

I marvel, Plato that thou spokest so unadvisedly; I do mean, since thou knewest well enough King Dionise's nature and disposition, that thou, perceiving him to be moved, wouldst so suddenly embraid him of his words so despitefully.

(Biii(v)–Biv)

And, indeed, Plato does seem to have been flying in the face of the very wisdom that Pasquil had extolled in the pamphlet produced only months earlier. There the debate between Pasquil and Gnatho had, as we have seen, revolved precisely around the need to chose the moment to offer good counsel with care, not least on those occasions when, as here, the intended recipient was 'resolved into a fury' and so unlikely to take a rebuke with equanimity. In *Pasquil* it was the eponymous plain-speaker himself who had argued that,

Where thou seest thy lord or master in the presence of many resolved into fury or wantonness, though thou hast all ready advertisements how he shall refrain it, yet hold thy tongue then, for troubling that presence.

(*Pasquil*, Avii)

Rather, he added, one should,

before wrath be increased into fury and affection into beastly enormity, as opportunity serveth thee, reverently and with tokens of love toward him, speak such words as shall be convenient.

(*Pasquil*, Aviii)

Hence it is perhaps no surprise that Plato's blunt words to Dionysius prompted an extreme and hostile reply. As he describes it to Aristippus,

The king being inflamed with fury, forthwith would have slain me. But, being entreated importunately by Dion and Aristomenes, he withdrew his sentence, notwithstanding to the intent that he would be avenged, he gave me to Polides, who was then Ambassador sent to him from the Lacedemonians.

(Biv)

But it is worth dwelling upon Pasquil's argument for a moment here, because it highlights a dilemma that *Of the Knowledge* was seemingly designed to resolve. Pasquil's lesson, as we have seen, gives rise to the lengthy disquisition on the nature and purpose of counsel that is the substantive conclusion of his discussion with Gnatho:

Opportunity consisteth in place or time, where and when the said affections or passion of wrath be some deal mitigate and out of extremity. And words be called convenient which have respect to the nature and state of the person unto whom they be spoken, and also to the detriment which might ensue by the vice or lack that thou hast espied, [and] it ought not to be as thou hast supposed. For opportunity and time for a counsellor to speak do not depend of the affection and appetite of him that is counselled; Mary, then counsel were but a vain word, and every man would do as him list. For, if he listed not to hear any counsel, he should never be warned of his own error.

(*Pasquil*, aviii–viii(v))

Rather than set out a clear case for the right use and moment for counsel, however, this passage seems to reflect an ambivalence that Elyot was yet to resolve. There is an equivocation at the heart of the ostensibly plain-speaking Pasquil's declaration between the idea that counsel is entirely independent of political calculation, unconcerned with 'the affection and appetite of him that is counselled', and a sense that it must nonetheless conform itself to opportunity and occasion, choosing its moment carefully in order to be most effective. Should the mood of the prince influence a counsellor, then, or should it not? Would any attempt to compromise the rigour of plain-speaking turn counsel into 'a vain word', and the counsellor into a mere lackey to power, or does good counsel only become truly effective when it conforms itself to the nature and state of the person to whom it is spoken? How *should* the wise man comport himself in the face of tyranny?

Evidently still working through the issues in his mind, Elyot returned to this passage in *Pasquil* later in the year, almost certainly after he had drafted the debate in *Of The Knowledge*, and reworked it. The changes that he made, however, raise more questions than they answer. For in the passage concerning princely fury he changed just two words, replacing the phrase 'beastly enormity' with 'voluptuous appetite' (Aviii). The effect of the change is hard to judge. Did it, for example, make the allusion more or less pertinent to Henry VIII? Was it more potentially insulting and contentious in its new form, or less? Perhaps, while it makes the sexual implications of this particular princely indulgence slightly stronger, and so links it to Henry's desire for Anne Boleyn a little more obviously, it also reduces the severity of the condemnation a degree or two, returning the vice being deplored from the realm of abhorrent beastliness to the field of at least recognizably human desire. Perhaps, then, Elyot was still unsure of the degree of directness that it was appropriate to apply, and so, consciously or otherwise, was still hedging his bets. But he also added to the debate a further example of when to hold one's peace and when, conversely, to speak out, and this too, typically, was a case involving the counselling of the prince:

Where thou art sitting in council about maters of weighty importance, talk not than of pastime or dalliance, but omitting affection or dread, speak then to the purpose.

(*Pasquil*, 2nd edn, Avii)

Against this he offered a further counter-case:

If thou be called to council, after thou hast either heard one reason before thee, or, at the least way, in the balance of thine own reason pondered the question, spare not to show thine advice, and to speak truly, remembering that God is not so far off, but that he can hear thee.

(*Pasquil*, 2nd edn, Aviii)

The need to speak out, the awareness of the presence of God as the nearby, sharp and judicious spectator to all that one does or says, these are Elyot's most obvious current obsessions revisited, as is the scenario itself in which the phrase, 'when', 'where', 'if thou be called to council' acts almost as a refrain. But here they gain an even sharper insistence. This additional passage speaks of an almost childlike compulsion to speak out that will manifest itself regardless of circumstances, and is kept in check only by the most obvious and strenuous effort of will. If one is called to counsel, Pasquil asserts, one should listen to one other person's opinion (but seemingly no more than one is necessary for the sake of protocol) before one speaks up oneself. But if one really cannot wait even that long, then one may speak first, and 'spare not', so long as one has thought about what one will say sufficiently first. Elyot had clearly thought long and hard about what he wanted to say, and his thoughts came tumbling out in *Pasquil* and *Of the Knowledge*. But at times they suggest rather more about the author's concerns and anxieties about the wisdom of such speech, and the nature of true wisdom and its role in the world, than they do about the correct course ahead for the Henrician ship of state.

An interesting insight into Elyot's thinking, and the, as yet unresolved, dilemmas that it involved, can be gained from his choice of the source for his most extensive foray into the dialogue form. The anecdote from Laertius's *Lives* no doubt commended itself to him because, despite its brevity, it addressed directly the clash between philosophical principles (and who better to represent philosophy than Plato?) and tyrannical power. But his use of the story also committed him to a cast of characters that advanced the debate significantly beyond the ground covered in *Pasquil the Plain*, with interesting consequences for his argument. Aristippus, as he is described in the *Lives*, is no flattering Gnatho, a man with no moral or intellectual integrity beyond his commitment to please. He is a more complex and substantial figure, combining a love of pleasure and felicity with an affability and ability to accommodate himself to the conditions of the moment in much the same manner as the ideal counsellor imagined by Pasquil:

He was capable of adapting himself to place, time, and person, and of playing his part appropriately under whatever circumstance. Hence he found more favour than anybody else with Dionysius, because he could always turn the situation to good account. He derived pleasure from what was present and did not toil to procure the enjoyment of something not present. Hence Diogenes called him the king's poodle [or 'royal cynic'].[36]

Hence he is able to extract rewards and concessions from his tyrannical master when others cannot, and can, under cover of a jest, retain Dionysius's good will in the process:

Dionysius met a request of his for money with the words, 'Nay, but you told me that the wise man would never be in want.' To which he [Aristippus] retorted, 'Pay, and then let us discuss the question,' and when he was paid, 'Now, you see, do you not', said he, 'that I was not found wanting'.[37]

His capacity to accommodate himself to the situation in hand does not, however, prevent him for speaking sharp words to his patron when the situation warranted it:

Being once compelled by Dionysius to enunciate some doctrine of philosophy, 'It would be ludicrous,' he said, 'that you should learn from me what to say, and yet instruct me when to say it'. At this, they say, Dionyius was offended and made him recline at the end of the table. And Aristippus said, 'You must have wished to confer distinction on the last place'.[38]

On another occasion,

He made a request to Dionysius on behalf of a friend, and, failing to obtain it, fell down at his feet. And when some one jeered at him, he made reply, 'It is not I who am to blame, but Dionysius, who has his ears in his feet.[39]

Rather than represent a wholly antithetical corpus of values to Plato, as Gnatho and Harpocrates had done to Pasquil, Aristippus, as Laertius presents him, actually shares many of the same ideals and attitudes exemplified by his fellow philosopher, a fact that Elyot himself acknowledges by stressing their shared intellectual heritage as students of Socrates. Both men believe in moral integrity and consistency of belief and conduct, both value the vocation of the philosopher above worldly power or authority,[40] and both revel in exposing the hypocrisy of others. Indeed Aristippus is every bit as honest as Plato, albeit in acknowledging the truth of his own pleasure-seeking nature. The *Lives* record an occasion on which he was given a sum of money by Dionysius at the same time as Plato was given a book:

When he was twitted with this, his reply was, 'Well, I want money, Plato wants books.'[41]

So alike are they at times, indeed, that it is difficult to tell the two men apart, a problem exemplified by the fact that, as Laertius acknowledges, a number of the anecdotes that he relates concerning Aristippus had been attributed by other writers to Plato, and vice-versa:

Dionysius having repeated to him [Aristippus] the lines;
> *Whoso betakes him to a prince's court*
> *Becomes his slave, albeit of free birth.*

He retorted:
> *If a free man he come, no slave is he.*

This is stated by Diocles in his work, *On the Lives of Philosophers*; other writers refer the anecdote to Plato.[42]

What distinguishes the two men is precisely that Plato is inflexible, especially in his relationship to power and authority, where Aristippus is not:

One day Dionysius over the wine commanded everybody to put on purple and dance. Plato declined, quoting the line [from Euripides's *Bacchae*],

> *I could not stoop to put on women's robes.*

Aristippus, however, put on the dress and, as he was about to dance, was ready with the repartee [also taken from the *Bacchae*];

> *Even amid the Bacchic revelry*
> *True modesty will not be put to shame.*[43]

Thus Aristippus both outdoes his rival in the duel of witty quotation, and steals the moral high ground without losing either his own integrity or the King's favour. It is Plato and not Aristippus who emerges from the story looking foolish. The latter is prepared to accept unwelcome events, slights, and minor humiliations as *adiaphora*, things indifferent, to be born with equanimity in pursuit of a higher goal, even if that goal is only personal reward or, his chief desideratum, worldly felicity:

He bore with Diogenes when he spat on him, and to one who took him to task, he replied, 'If the fishermen let themselves be drenched with sea-water in order to catch a gudgeon, ought I not to endure to be wetted with negus in order to take a blenny?'[44]

Hence, while on one level the Aristippus of the *Lives* provides a useful antagonist for Elyot's conception of Plato (and, indeed Laertius explicitly states that the two men were rivals),[45] on another he is a poor choice, if a foil for the latter's arguments was all that was needed, and actually leads to some, perhaps unwitting, complications in their arguments.

The Plato of the *Lives* is in many ways a model of Elyot's plain-speaker, a man of wisdom who does not flinch at speaking harsh truths to those in power. He is also mindful of the need to govern all things by reason, and so, it is said, would not discipline his slaves when he was in a passion, in case he should punish them too severely, a story that Elyot himself used in *The Governor* to exemplify the virtues of moderation and temperance (*The Governor*, c viii). Yet his virtues were also potential weaknesses. He was, as Laertius records, unyielding in matters both great and small, unwilling to concede a principle, however slight the consequences might be:

A story is told that Plato saw one playing at dice and rebuked him. And, upon his protesting that he played for a trifle only, 'But the habit', rejoined Plato, 'is not a trifle'.[46]

An unflinching opposition to dicing, a vice that Elyot found particularly contemptible, was unlikely to strike the latter as problematic.[47] But it is clear that Plato's inflexibility on matters of principle made him at times politically ineffective, and excluded him from a central role in the diplomatic events of his region. The *Lives* record that,

Pamphila, in the twenty-fifth book of her *Memorabilia*, says that the Arcadians and Thebans, when they were founding Megalopolis, invited Plato to be their legislator, but that, when he discovered that they were opposed to equality of possessions, he refused to go.[48]

Similarly, on a more personal level, on the third occasion on which he travelled to Sicily,

He came to reconcile Dion and Dionysius, but, failing to do so, returned to his own country without achieving anything. And there he refrained from meddling with politics, although his writings show that he was a statesman. The reason was that the people had already been accustomed to measures and institutions quite different from his own.[49]

Thus his inability to accommodate himself to the systems and values of others disabled him from the very role for which his virtue and intellectual training commended him. It would not be stretching things too far to see such a figure as an exploration of Elyot's own inability to find favour in the court of Henry VIII.

The relevance of Elyot's treatment of Plato's story to contemporary circumstances is clear. The portrait of a king who has slipped into voluptuous self-indulgence, refuses to listen to anyone who does not confirm his own opinions, and has taken to interrupting and insulting those who offer him critical advice would seem to have drawn its details very obviously from Henry VIII's recent behaviour.[50] He had indeed seemingly turned his back on his former taste for debate and discussion and closed his ears to criticism. He had also, as we have seen, interrupted a preacher in full flow in April 1531, very much in the manner of Dionysius interrupting Plato, and told him that he was spreading lies when he had dared to argue against the Royal Supremacy.[51] The last incident, indeed, may have been the case that brought Plato's story to mind and prompted Elyot to revisit it in the dialogue. But the decision to locate his second formal debate on freedom of speech and counsel in the court of Dionysius, seems to have liberated Elyot to address his own situation still more directly and candidly than he had in *Pasquil the Plain*. For in the philosophers presented in Laertius's *Lives*, he found, not just a protagonist but a whole cast of characters seemingly ready made to comment upon the strengths and weaknesses of his own position. Rather than gaining extra distance and a new perspective on events by moving from the contemporary Rome of *Pasquil* to ancient Sicily and Athens, Elyot seems to have discovered there a world which was almost too like his own for comfort. The result was a far more complicated, and in many ways more candid and self-critical account of his own political position than anything that he had offered to date.

If in Plato we see a representation of Elyot's own idealized self: honest, eloquent, and committed to truth, we also detect an acknowledgement of why such a figure could never prosper in the courtly world to which Elyot so obviously still hoped to gain entry. His inflexibility, his insistence upon speaking at all costs, these are, Elyot seems to acknowledge, weaknesses as well as strengths in the real world of princely politics. So much had been conceded in *Pasquil the Plain*. But there the truth-speaker had been pitted against self-evidently contemptible sycophants who could offer no real intellectual challenge to the integrity of his position. Better to stay in the streets with Pasquil than live in a court populated by simulacra of Harpocrates and Gnatho would be a logical response to that text. In selecting Aristippus as the antagonist for Plato in the subsequent dialogue, however, Elyot opened up a far more nuanced and equivocal contest, and one which seems to carry more obvious and personal contemporary implications. For, whether he did so consciously or not, he seems to have revealed in these two disputants a very close analogue to the very different approaches to counselling Henry VIII adopted by himself and his fellow conservative John Heywood, and the comparison was not always to his own advantage.

In the Aristippus of the *Lives* Elyot found, as we have seen, the figure of a successful court philosopher, accommodating, witty, and socially agile: a man who can make similar points to those made by Plato himself, but, by presenting them in the guise of a merry jest, causes no offence and so retains his place and favour at court. This would seem a strikingly accurate sketch of John Heywood the Lucianic writer of 'merry' interludes, who could mock the Supremacy in the King's presence and seemingly provoke only laughter. Plato, on the other hand, is presented, like Elyot himself, as less culturally agile, less flexible, held back from a full engagement with the court by debilitating doubts about the intellectual and moral validity of compromising with kings, agonizing over every decision, and in the end reduced to repeating the same repertoire of stances and gestures without conspicuous success.

If in *Pasquil*, then, Elyot considered whether to speak plainly, in *Of the Knowledge* he adds a concern with *how* best to do so when the need and opportunity arose. And it is a discussion in which Plato, despite his intellectual superiority, does not win all the arguments. Indeed, even when he is successful, he, like Pasquil before him, cannot persuade his antagonist to join him in his stance. Aristippus admits at one point that Plato 'hast almost made me change mine old opinion' (Mvii). But that 'almost' is telling. And while he finally admits that Plato's logic 'hath made me to change somewhat of mine old opinion' (Piv), he reserves judgement on other matters ('Well, Plato, in such experience of wisdom I will not follow the[e]' (Piii)), and so the final resolution of the debate is deferred until another occasion ('The next time that we meet I will make thee to change all, if thou wilt hear and abide reason' (Piv–iv(v)), vows Plato). Aristippus is left only partially convinced that Plato's stand was the correct one (although he accepts that Dionysius acted tyrannically towards him), and Plato's position is thus only partially vindicated. The result is the more frustrating because the truth-speaker is debating, not as Pasquil was with a personified political vice, who could not be expected to accept the logic of a virtue, but with a philosopher very like himself. Much of Plato's hostility towards Aristippus, evident in his rebukes and asides, stems from the knowledge that they were both pupils of Socrates and schooled in the same values. Yet Aristippus has chosen to apply his wisdom in a very different way. And despite Plato's repeated assertions that his antagonist's philosophy of felicity is a betrayal of Socrates' teachings,[52] there is more than a hint of admiration, even, perhaps, of envy, in the way that Elyot presents Aristippus in the text; such that, while Plato may win most of the arguments, Aristippus appears the more amiable, decent, and ultimately more humane of the disputants.

Where Plato's speeches are punctuated with personal insults, jibes at Aristippus's favour with Dionysius and rebukes concerning his lifestyle,[53] Aristippus retains an evident respect for his adversary, and continues their discussion in an equitable, accommodating tone that suggests, not the studied ingratiation of the flatterer, but the genuine respect of one professional for another. While the best that Plato will say of Aristippus is that he is often wise or honest despite himself,[54] the latter is frequently found conceding a point with good grace or acknowledging the skill with which his opponent argues. When Plato suggests that he might fear that he was being flattered, Aristippus remarks amiably,

No, no, I perceive where about thou goest; thou wouldst with persuasion, wherein I know thou art marvellous, withdraw me if thou might from my professed opinion, but that is now no part of our matter.

(Fvi(v))

Similarly, when forced to concede a point, he does so with evident admiration for, and interest in, the construction of his opponent's argument,

Now on my faith Plato, thou art a wonderful fellow, for by the subtle persuasions brought in by induction, which form of arguing I know is most natural, thou compellest me to assent to thy reason. For now me thinketh that none may be called a wise man except unto that knowledge wherein is wisdom he joineth operation, but for what purpose, I pray thee, hast thou brought in now this last conclusion?

(Niii)

Whereas Plato's response is a terse, 'Art thou so dull-witted, Aristippus, that all this while thou dost not perceive it?' Later Aristippus concedes that in banishing Plato, Dionysius was, 'more liberal than wise. For he had been better to have given to him six the best cities in Sicily than to have departed from such a counsellor' (Iviii).[55] A point to which he returns in his final remarks:

PLATO   What sayest thou, then, by king Dionise? Whom instructing to know himself thus much displeaseth, and instead of thank and preferment hath rewarded me with danger and bondage?

ARISTIPPUS   On my faith, I think that he hath both lost himself, by refusing the said knowledge, whereby he should have been delivered from the said transformation [from man to tyrannical beast], and also that he hath most foolishly lost thee, Plato, in putting thee from him, which by thy counsel shouldst have been to him so royal a treasure, and the same do I think also of Polides the ambassador, and of the Egenites.

(piii(v)–piv)

While there is more than a hint of flattery implicit here, Plato's pleased response ('Gramercy Aristippus, for thy gentle audience, now be we come to the town, and made a good end both of our journey and also of our communication' (piv)) is a tacit validation of its effectiveness. The two one-time rivals part as friends, resolving to meet again and continue their discussions. The search for truth, it is implied, need not be conducted solely in harsh, abrasive language. Soft speech can serve knowledge as readily as it can further ignorance.

There is, conversely, in Plato's handling of the situation at the court of Dionysius a political maladroitness that shows through clearly even in his own self-justificatory account of his actions. He clearly had not expected the King to behave as he did, even though he was well briefed concerning his moods and habits. What he expected was for Dionysius to accept the counsel he offered with good grace, and reward him for it.[56] Hence he presents what followed his accusation as a complete surprise to him:

Now, when he gave not to me condign thanks, as my benefit deserved, but accounted me to have been idle whiles I instructed him, then it seemed that Understanding was absent and fled from the soul...wherefore his ingratitude declared his words to savour of tyranny: which I rehearsed unto him to th'intent that he, perceiving by my words in what peril he was in, might...revoke again understanding, and subduing the effects, be eftsoons restored unto his dignity. Howe sayest thou, considering well all that which is before said, were my words ill as they were spoken?

(oiv–oiv(v))

When Aristippus replies that it was not so much what he said but how he said it that was problematic ('Nay, as thou hast declared them, but yet me seemeth they were very sharp' (o4)), Plato offers a series of curious arguments to prove that his 'shortness' with the King should have been entirely uncontentious. Dionysius, he suggests, being ignorant of the truth, was consequently inferior to Plato, who possessed it. And a man may always speak sharply to his inferior without fear of rebuke. Moreover, he did not actually accuse the King of tyranny, merely of *sounding* tyrannous, a claim which ought not to have offended him. And indeed, he suggests, the observation was actually very politely delivered:

Therefore I spoke as I did to King Dionyse, yet did I it with such a temperance that, if he had not been a Tyrant indeed, he would never have been discontented. For I did not call him a tyrant or reproached him of any tyranny: but only said that his words savoured of tyranny.

(oiv(v)–ov)

Finally, had Plato been giving the King a lesson in rhetoric rather than kingship, he would have accepted criticism of his methods with equanimity,

how much more ought he then to take in good part those words that I spoke in correcting his words whereby he seemest to refuse wisdom, which a little before he so much coveted to hear declared?

(ov(v)–ovi)

Such hair-splitting and psychological naivety hardly deliver a ringing endorsement of Plato's claims to wisdom and the omnicompetence of his philosophy. Aristippus's response, however, is not to rebuke his opponent but to raise an objection that takes us back to the debate in *Pasquil* over the best occasion for offering counsel:

In good faith . . . that is very well spoken. But peradventure thou spakest too soon. And if thou hadst forborne a day, two, or three, until his fume had been passed, and that he had used eftsoons with thee some familiarity, peradventure thy words would have been more easily taken, and thereunto thou shouldst have founden more opportunity.

(ovi(v))

Against this objection (and notably Aristippus is suggesting only that Plato time his admonishments more carefully, not that he refrain from delivering them), Plato's words are uncompromising and go to first principles:

But take one thing with thee, Aristippus, in the office of a wise man that word 'Peradventure' is never heard spoken: No more than in the end of his works these words: 'had I wist [i.e. (only) known]'. For he hath always[s] the three times in remembrance, Time present, time passed, and time to come. And reforming all thing to necessary cause, or (as I said long ago) unto providence, reputeth nothing to Fortune. (Ovi(v))[57]

In the course of this exchange Plato comes closest to confirming a suggestion that has been implicit in much of the dialogue thus far: that plain-speaking of the sort that he advocates is simply incompatible with princely politics in all but the most ideal of circumstances. For, outside that honoured cadre of idealized role models from the past to whom Elyot and others pay homage in their treatises, kings simply would not tolerate for any length of time the kind of indiscriminate, abrupt, and uncompromising didacticism that Plato insists is the only form of advice that the truly wise man can offer.

The problem with Plato as a model for Elyot's own conduct lies not simply in the fact that he was banished from Sicily, and so, like Pasquil before him, was excluded from the place where his wisdom would have been of most use. He was always only a visitor there in the first place. He had, as he claimed in his own defence, never sought 'to serve King Dionyse or to receive by him any commodity' (Nvi). As an itinerant philosopher he could thus pick and choose where and when to make his services available to worldly governors, and need never learn to accommodate himself to the demands and foibles of any one monarch. Hence for him at least, the life of the 'independent scholar', self-aware and resolutely 'true to himself' is sufficient recompense for his dedication to the pursuit of wisdom. As he tells Aristippus, the wise man is 'so armed again adversity that whatsoever the body feeleth, yet the very [true] man, which is the soul, feeleth no disease, or, as I might say, is never inquieted, but is ever entire and in his true proportion and figure, that is to say like unto God.' (Piii-Piii(v)). And, should he fail to dissuade a prince from tyranny, he can always retire to Athens and continue his life there.

For Plato, then, the knowledge of his own integrity is sufficient satisfaction (albeit Elyot, characteristically gives him in addition a strong desire to be acknowledged as wise and honest in the eyes of the world, and a curious need on his own part to live up to 'that good opinion that King Dionyse had of me' (Pii–iii)). He is free to speak against tyranny or folly wherever he finds it as he is indebted to no patron (at least not for long) for his worldly sustenance, and tied to no nation by bonds of patriotism and duty. For Elyot, whose writings were fired by a strong sense of patriotism and personal entitlement in equal measure, such independence would never have been an entirely satisfactory condition for political freedom.[58] Hence his Plato will never quite accept the logic of his own conclusions and circumstances. The need to influence events, to make his wisdom available to the prince and to gain his due recognition and reward for doing so, will never completely go away, however forceful his arguments against them. If Aristippus seems to represent a Heywoodian philosophy of 'merry' accommodation to princely politics, then, Plato does not offer a truly antithetical position from which to attack it. Once again the two antagonists seem to fall short of providing each other with the perfect foil for their views. For Plato's inflexibility does not mark the extreme case of uncompromising rejection of the court and its allurements. This role is played by a third figure who appears frequently in the *Lives*, and seems to haunt Elyot's dialogues in spirit if not in person: Diogenes the cynic.[59]

Diogenes, as Laertius presents him in the *Lives*, *is* a completely uncompromising, acerbic thinker who will have nothing to do with princes or their courts. A number of the stories that Laertius relates concern the obvious contempt with which he treats the archetypal princely patron, Alexander the Great:

When he was sunning himself in the Cranium, Alexander came and stood over him and said, 'Ask of me any boon you like.' To which he replied, 'Stand out of my light.'[60]

Alexander having on one occasion sent a letter to Antipater at Athens by a certain Athlios, Diogenes, who was present, said:

'Graceless son of a graceless sire, to graceless wight by graceless squire.'[61]

And yet, in a quirk of fate that must have galled Elyot intensely when he read of it, Diogenes was admired by the very men whom he so regularly abused. Hence, Alexander famously declared that, 'had I not been Alexander, I should have liked to be Diogenes'.[62]

Diogenes' disengagement from the court and his fellow philosophers, and from civil society as a whole, is symbolized by his decision to live in a tub set up in the market place, from which he can rail and spit at anyone who passes (in the certain knowledge that many will). His scorn for anyone who does not come up to his own standards of poverty or self-denial, who exhibits signs of pretension, or who defies common sense in the pursuit of fame, is everywhere evident in the *Lives*:

The school of Euclides he called bilious, and Plato's lectures [a] waste of time, the performances at the Dionysia great peep-shows for fools, [and] the demagogues the mob's lackies.[63]

He is presented as a self-conscious swimmer against the tide of common human behaviour, whose only consolation for his isolation from the rest of the community is that sense of self-sufficiency and immunity from the blows of Fortune that Plato would claim to be the reward of the wise man at the end of *Of the Knowledge*.[64] Wholly indifferent to public opinion,[65] and able to get the better of anyone in a duel of wits, Diogenes is yet excluded from human society by the aggressive, railing nature of his arguments. Such a man has many admirers, but, as he himself concedes, no followers, and few people are persuaded by his harangues to change their behaviour.[66] Like Elyot's Pasquil, then, he is left in the streets, contented that truth stays with him, while falsehood follows the well-beaten track to court. Indeed, as we have seen, the plain-speaking statue of Elyot's earlier dialogue would seem to have been consciously modelled on Diogenes' type of rough and homely speech rather than on the more sophisticated terms of Plato, an identification made more obvious by Gnatho's description of his 'bourding and *currish* philosophy' (*Pasquil the Plain*, Bii, my italics).

The distinction between the two plain speakers is underlined by the fact that Plato is himself the butt of many of Diogenes' attacks upon hypocrisy, vanity, and self-contradiction in the *Lives*. And, although he is occasionally permitted to get the better of his currish adversary,[67] he is generally discomforted by the directness of his rival:

Diogenes once asked [Plato] . . . for wine, and after that also for some dried figs, and Plato sent him a whole jar full. The other then said, 'If some one asks you how many two and two are, will you answer, Twenty? So it seems you neither give as you are asked, nor answer as you are questioned.' Thus he scoffed at him as one who talked without end.

Plato had defined man as an animal, biped and featherless, and was applauded. Diogenes plucked a fowl and brought it into the lecture-room with the words, 'Here is Plato's man'.[68]

And yet the value systems that the two men proclaim are again, like those of Plato and Aristippus, very similar, revolving around the paramount importance of personal integrity, the rule of reason over passion and the senses, and freedom of speech.[69] Hence Plato is willing to acknowledge kinship of a sort with Diogenes' philosophy, attributing it to a debased form of the teachings of his own master, Socrates.[70] So it again is no surprise to find stories that supposedly exemplify Diogenes' character and opinions being recycled by other writers, and even by Laertius himself, as tales with Plato or Aristippus as the protagonist. The observation that men will try out a jar or dish to see if it rings true before buying it, whereas in choosing men they will select on outward appearance alone, Laertius includes in his lives of both Aristippus and Diogenes. An exchange between Diogenes and Plato over the latter's decision to eat olives at a banquet is ascribed elsewhere to Aristippus and Plato.[71] And another anecdote that presents Plato as the object of Diogenes's sarcasm concerning flattery, reappears in slightly different form as a criticism of Diogenes anti-social conduct delivered by Aristippus. In the first version, Plato sees Diogenes washing lettuces and, approaching him,

> Quietly said to him, 'Had you paid court to Dionysius, you wouldn't now be washing lettuces'; and . . . he with equal calmness made answer, 'If you had washed lettuces, you wouldn't have paid court to Dionysius.'

In the alternative version it is Diogenes who, spotting Aristippus passing by, looks up from his lettuces to say, 'If you had learnt to make these your diet, you would not have paid court to kings.' To which Aristippus replies, 'And if you knew how to associate with men, you would not be washing vegetables.'[72]

No doubt such cases of multiple attribution attest primarily to the confused state of the stories and apocrypha that had built up around the lives and writings of each philosopher by the time that Laertius came to compile his biographies. And his acknowledgement of the inconsistencies reflects an admirable desire to be true to his material, while retaining as many good stories and witticisms as he could for each Life. But, for Elyot, the confusion raised more intractable difficulties. The virtual interchangeability of the philosophers in his source threatened to undermine his attempt to use them as representatives of fixed positions in a moralized topography. If at one moment Plato could stand for simplicity and integrity, yet at another he could advocate prince-pleasing to Diogenes, and at a third be rebuked himself for self-indulgence and pride, or if Aristippus could in one place speak up for luxury and the quiet life and in another expose the self-indulgence of others, then all sense of moral absolutism has been lost. Rather than speak for such enduring certainties, the stories in the *Lives* present a coterie of professional philosophers of roughly similar principles who are engaged in ongoing competition to outmanoeuvre each other and occupy the intellectual high ground: a struggle in which wit and quick thinking are the principal weapons. Where Diogenes, Plato, and Aristippus differ, then, is not so much in their fundamental beliefs, but in the strategies they adopt to realize those beliefs, and there, whether he realized it at the outset or not, lay their principal usefulness to Elyot. For Laertius' text offered him an ideal opportunity to re-examine the possible paths to effective counsel that he had sketched out in *Pasquil the Plain*, and to reconsider his own self-image as a Platonic wise man and counsellor-in-waiting, who could right the wrongs of the Henrician Supremacy.

In this curious trio of philosophers, it is Plato's position that is in many ways the least tenable. Whereas Aristippus chooses to make his way at court, and makes the personal compromises necessary to facilitate that choice, and Diogenes rejects the court altogether, living instead in his tub and scorning princes and their wealth at every opportunity, Plato alone seeks to be in the court but not of it, to engage with politics and hope for thanks and reward, yet at the same time remain unsullied by materialism and worldly calculation. It is little wonder, then, that his path is the least successful of the three. And in this it seems to offer the best analogue for Elyot's sense of the frustrations inherent in his own position.[73] Elyot was himself torn between the attractions of the two modes of possible dissent: the jesting, engaged, playful mode of Aristippus and Heywood, who each found favour by 'adapting himself to place, time, and person', and could 'always turn the situation to good account', and the snarling, spitting, railing withdrawal of the cynic Diogenes. Admiring (perhaps despite himself) the integrity of each stance, and yet simultaneously aware of the limitations of each as a means to satisfy his own conflicting desires, he was ultimately unable to adopt either with any real conviction. His writings thus act as a space in which he could return again and again to the dilemma, rehearsing the options through surrogates and analogues, and always finally leaving the issue unresolved. In the final analysis this irresolution was a product of his own equivocation between principle and the hope of reward, withdrawal and engagement, rather than anything fundamentally intractable about the choice itself. To go to court or stay away: either was a plausible option, but to hope to influence princes without compromising with their demands, to hope to be called to counsel without courting favour, these were never realistic ambitions.

The tensions and anxieties that this internal conflict created for Elyot can be glimpsed, not only in the rather pathetic pleadings and presumptuous demands of his letters to Cromwell, but also in the evasions, internal contradictions, and frequent outbursts of lacerating invective that he directs against his surrogates in the dialogues. His acknowledgement that the railing cynicism of Pasquil has achieved 'not one jot' of reformation, for example, is given a biting edge in the identification of the statue as a homely, churlish cur (in Elyot's hands the term 'homely' carries both a positive and a negative charge, the implications of unaffected honesty vying for supremacy with the author's gentlemanly disdain for any kind of baseness). Pasquil is a lumpen stock, a piece of timber, a stone: the latter being a synonym for ill-educated, uncritical stupidity for both the humanists and their classical forebears.[74] His 'overthwart fashion' aligns him, as Gnatho suggests, not with men of principle, but with the mad in his inability to look to his own profit.[75] But, even here Elyot found himself divided in his attitude, for such 'madness' as Pasquil exhibits required a fixity of will and purpose and an immunity to the lures of a place and influence at court that his creator did not fully possess. Similarly, Elyot's distaste for the compromises that life at court entails emerges not only in the snarling ferocity of Pasquil's attacks upon Gnatho and Harpocrates, but also in Plato's contempt for Aristippus, and his constant reminders that his accommodation to the way of the world was a betrayal of the legacy of Socrates.

Close attention to *Of the Knowledge* and its source provides, then, a valuable insight into the contradictions that Elyot was working through in the spring and summer of 1533, while he came to terms with the consequences of his remonstrance of the previous year and the King's failure to call him to counsel thereafter. Although he was not engaged in active government service in these months, and was seemingly going about his life in London and on his estates in the midlands quietly enough, a great deal was clearly going on in his mind, and issuing forth in torrents from his pen. Thus the man who, to his own deep disquiet, was not called to counsel, sought to influence policy nonetheless, and agonized in his own mind about how best to do so. In an attempt to explain Elyot's failure to take a more obviously active role in national politics, whether by intriguing with like-minded conservatives, or even taking up arms against the Supremacy and all that it entailed, Pearl Hogrefe suggested that he, like many Henrician conservatives, may have followed a policy of 'passive obedience' to the King's demands.[76] But such an idea is misleading if it leads us to underestimate the degree to which Elyot was engaging with the events he witnessed through his writings. Elyot's obedience was in this sense anything but passive. He strove vigorously to counsel the King and his ministers in favour of self-restraint and moderation, protested at the conduct of counsellors whom he saw as corrupt and self-serving, and issued dire warnings of the calamitous consequences of current trends and policies. But he did this while remaining entirely loyal and obedient to the crown under the law and in his work as a local administrator. He defied no statute and refused no oath, yet he nonetheless did all that he believed it was possible for a loyal subject to do to influence policy and effect change. If not exactly 'resistance' in the modern sense of the word, this was at least an active, shaping, form of compliance.

What limited the effectiveness of such political engagement as Elyot could attempt, was, of course, not only his own doubts concerning the best means of effecting good counsel, but the very nature of counsel itself. For counsel by definition lacked compulsion. The counsellor, as Plato's case revealed all too clearly, relied upon the prince's willingness to listen to him and to act upon what he heard. The kinds of elaborate checks and balances on which both the mirror for princes tradition and humanist political theory rested were thus all entirely permissive. The prince's desire to maintain his own honour, to ensure himself a good reputation after his death, to be loved by his subjects and favoured by God, all these things relied upon the sovereign having internalized and committed himself to the same set of values as the counsellor espoused. Only such a prince would recognize the virtues of good counsel and feel the force it exerted. Only an already 'good' prince, that is, was susceptible to good counsel. If the monarch, on the contrary, took a pragmatic decision to follow a Machiavellian route, favouring *realpolitik* over the self-restraint that chivalric honour-culture imposed, or if, conversely, he encountered a personal or political crisis so intense and compelling that it overrode even the desire for honour, then all the theories of good counsel and good lordship were as nothing. Hence the almost obsessive concentration on the virtue of affability in Elyot's early writings, and the strenuous efforts to construct Henry VIII as a good prince, the ideal reader of constructive criticism in his prologues. For once the prince stopped listening, or refused to read further, the whole apparatus that the author had erected to influence him would be useless. Where counsel was concerned, there was no Plan B.

We can, then, detect something of what Alistair Fox has perceptively described as a wider 'humanist dilemma' in Elyot's writings of 1533. Faced with a King whose need to marry Anne Boleyn overrode all other considerations, Elyot was always fighting a losing battle to be heard amid the clamour of voices that offered to promote Henry's Great Matter and advance the Supremacy. In Fox's view the dialogues of 1533–4 represented 'the end of a cul-de-sac' in Elyot's attempt to apply the humanist principle of good counsel as the remedy for England's ills, and marked his realization that the only consolation available to the wise man was the withdrawal into stoic fortitude that Plato seems to offer at the end of *Of the Knowledge*.[77] But there was, perhaps, a political route out of the cul-de-sac, despite the frustrations and equivocations that Elyot was experiencing. For *Of the Knowledge* shows signs of exploring further the alternative model of political engagement that Elyot had already hinted at in *Pasquil the Plain*.

When Dionysius asked Plato to declare 'the state and pre-eminence of a king' (Nvii), his response stressed the qualities of a good man rather than the nature and responsibilities of royal office:

> By the said knowledge of the which we so long have disputed, I set out and expressed such a man, in whom the soul had entire and full authority over the senses, and always kept the affects in due rule and obedience, following only the counsel of Understanding, and by that governance was most like unto God. This man I called a king, although he had no more in his possession than had Crates the Theban. And if that such a one were by the free consent of the people chosen or received to be a principal ruler and governing them in like manner as he doth himself, then is he a great king or Emperor.
>
> (Nvii(v)–viii)

To argue in such terms is to give a new and very different emphasis to the conventional dictum that the good king must be first a good man that Elyot had explored at such length in *The Governor*.

To begin with the good man, and make kingship only a secondary attribute or condition of his goodness, is to reverse the priorities of both *The Governor* and

Pasquil the Plain. And by placing the individual soul or conscience, which is the seat of that knowledge Plato describes, at the centre of the political universe, Elyot was offering himself a very different perspective upon that universe to that defined in those earlier works. Rather than begin with the fundamental reality of monarchy itself, and work outwards from the needs of the king to the responsibilities of the subject, he begins here with the integrity of the subject, and makes that subject's engagement with the king an only secondary and conditional project. It was to prove a liberating manoeuvre, and one that offered its author the foundations of a framework for real political resistance. But it was a manoeuvre that Elyot, schooled as he was in intellectual and cultural traditions that placed the prince at their centre, would take some time to explore and develop, and which he would never fully embrace as his own. The early fruits of this change in thinking can, however, be detected in Plato's attitude in this dialogue. In suggesting that a poor man may be a king, in and of himself, and that kings might be 'by the free consent of the people chosen and received' he had come a long way from the opening chapters of *The Governor* with their careful negotiation of the senses in which monarchy was a reflection of divine order. And there is certainly a new degree of hostility, even a hint of militancy underlying the otherwise conventional criticism of flatterers and the kings who succumb to their wiles, in Plato's affirmation that,

Such a king, stablished in the said knowledge, can never be deceived by his most pernicious and mischievous enemies, which be flatterers and glosers, by whom princes be devoured alive, and their souls utterly consumed with most mortal pestilence, wherewith their countries and people be also in peril to be lost and destroyed.

(Nviii(v))

Elyot may have had to travel to ancient Greece in order to be able to imagine a world in which kings could be chosen rather than simply obeyed, but the relevance of the idea to his own dilemmas was certainly not lost on him, hence, perhaps, the triumphant final flourish in the statement 'then is he a gret king *or Emperour*', with its obvious glance towards Henry VIII and the 'imperial' aspirations behind the Supremacy.

And if Elyot was now able to imagine a world in which kings could be chosen on grounds of personal virtue and wisdom, he was also able to conceive of circumstances in which they might relinquish their right to govern through viciousness or ignorance. Significantly it is the usually accommodating Aristippus, and not Plato, who first draws this bold conclusion from their discussion:

For me seemeth that thy description of a king was wonderful true and necessary, and also therein was the knowledge whereof thou hast treated compendiously, and plainly declared. And me thinketh that the words that king Dionise spoke beseemed not a king, but were much rather the words of one that lacked that knowledge wherein is wisdom.

(oviii)

To which Plato adds the further observation that,

> Since these ungentle words of King Dionise beseemed not a king to speak, it appeareth that they beseemed him that was contrary unto a king, which is a Tyrant. And, being the words of one that lacked knowledge, it accordeth also that they were the words of one that was ignorant, and ignorance is most contrary to wisdom, and, as I have said, transformeth a man into a beast or monster.
>
> (oviii–viii(v))

This radical verdict, that Dionysius has foregone his claim, not only to kingship, but to humanity itself, as he 'knew not himself' (oviii(v)), and self-knowledge was the essential condition of humanity, is confirmed once more by Aristippus. The radical implications of such conclusions would, however, take some time to work themselves through to the surface in Elyot's writing. In the short term, the frustrations implicit in *Of the Knowledge* led him to take a step backwards, in political terms at least, and return to a genre, the handbook of advice to princes, that he had first experimented with in *The Governor*. If the need to find a place for himself at the King's council table raised too many difficulties and complications for him to resolve at present, he could at least offer the King good counsel through the traditional surrogate of a book of advice. And, typically, he did so with a text that was both strikingly experimental and apparently designed with some care to catch the eye of Henry VIII over the yuletide season of 1533–4.

The Doctrinal of Princes

Having set out a blueprint for the personal redemption of the prince and the renewal of the political nation in *The Governor*, railed against those who found the favour which he himself craved in *Pasquil the Plain*, and explored the lot of the good counsellor in the court of a tyrant in *Of the Knowledge Which Maketh a Wise Man*, Elyot returned to the political fray in late 1533 with what was in many ways a still more ambitious project: *The Doctrinal of Princes*. He had argued for the importance of counsel, denounced its antithesis, and offered advice of his own obliquely in all three of his earlier works; now, in his fourth political text in less than three years, he turned to offer counsel directly and unambiguously to the King. He did so by translating into English from a Greek original (very probably the first time that this had been attempted)[78] an oration written by the political and moral philosopher Isocrates for his former pupil Nicocles when the latter became King of Salamis around 372 BC. This earlier treatise, given the title *To Nicocles* by modern editors, was described by its author as an 'oration', but was in reality a combination of a moral handbook and a prototypical *speculum principis*, designed to be read rather than heard. Either way, it provided Elyot with ideal ammunition for his continued campaign to counsel Henry VIII towards political, religious, and personal moderation.

Elyot, like many of his fellow northern humanists, was clearly already captivated by Isocrates and his work before he decided to turn his hand to translating him directly for publication. In *The Governor*, he had offered lavish praise of both the style and the content of the philosopher's writings, singling out *To Nicocles* and its analogue *To Demonicus* for special mention as worthy additions to the young governor's library:

Isocrates concerning the lesson of orators is everywhere wonderful profitable, having almost as many wise sentences as he hath words: and with that is so sweet and delectable to read, that after him almost all other[s] seem unsavoury and tedious; and in persuading as well a prince as a private person to virtue, in two very little and compendious works, whereof he made the one to king Nicocles, the other to his friend Demonicus, would be perfectly conned and had in continual memory.

(*The Governor*, Eiv–iv(v))

In part at least Elyot's admiration for Isocrates probably reflected a sense that the philosopher's career provided an ideal to which he himself, still struggling with the dilemmas associated with winning a place at court, might aspire. As George Norlin describes him, Isocrates offered the disappointed counsellor an ideal model for an alternative, and entirely congenial means to exert political influence from outside the charmed circle of government. Throughout his life, Isocrates,

endeavoured to direct the affairs of Athens and of Greece without ever holding an office, and to mould public opinion without ever addressing a public assembly, by issuing from his study political pamphlets, or essays in oratorical form, in which he set forth the proper conduct of the Greeks in the light of broad ideas.[79]

It is not hard to see why Elyot should have found such a figure congenial. In search of a model of conduct to adopt in response to his own continued failure to win a recall to government office, he would have found Isocrates's glorification of the life of retirement, peace, and tranquillity, free from the cares of a political career, combined with his continued—and apparently successful—engagement with politics through his writings, doubly appealing. Moreover, a number of the philosopher's central preoccupations: his advocacy of the moral basis of rhetorical training, his intense patriotism and sense of duty to his home city of Athens, his defence of true learning (and intemperate assaults upon those teachers and thinkers who seemed to offer superficial and less taxing routes to eloquence), and his insistence that ideals and ideas were only of value if they were put into action for the benefit of the commonwealth, all of these were positions that resonated with Elyot's own thoughts, and could be readily adapted for his own use.[80]

As we shall see, translating *To Nicocles* also allowed Elyot to address directly to the King many of the same points that he had made indirectly in his earlier treatises without appearing to be overtly contemporary or *ad hominem* in his choice of targets: an important consideration if he had indeed, as he claimed, been criticized in high places for the contents of his first two political texts. But, if the suitability of the material explains *why* he chose to translate Isocrates, it remains unclear exactly *when* he chose to do so. The first edition of the text, printed once again by Berthelet, is undated, but scholars have tended to follow the suggestion in the *Short Catalogue of Printed Books* that it probably dates from 1534.[81] This raises an interesting possibility. For, having chosen to offer the book as a contribution to his ongoing political campaign, Elyot needed to find an occasion to present the work, whether to the King himself or to a wider public readership, on which it would be both noticed and welcomed by its intended readers. As he himself had acknowledged in all his previous works, and would reiterate in one of his few additions to Isocrates' own prose in *The Doctrinal* itself, the art of counselling relied to a great degree on finding the opportune moment to speak: 'they that be counsellors ought to have consideration of the occasion, time and opportunity' before offering their advice (*Doctrinal* ci(v)–cii).

Could it be, then, that Elyot initially intended *The Doctrinal* as a New Year's gift to Henry VIII, perhaps taking or sending a manuscript copy to court for 1 January 1534 and then printing it with a new prologue for a wider audience later in the year? The suggestion is prompted by the fact that Isocrates's text presents itself as a gift for a king offered among many other more material offerings. As a gift for Henry VIII on 1 January 1534 the text's opening remarks concerning those presents sent to kings in the hope of reciprocal rewards or favours could be recycled as a witty commentary on the foodstuffs, plate, and jewellery that poured into the royal household during the traditional Tudor gift-giving ceremony. Indeed, a remark of the sort was very likely to catch the jaded eye of the King as he doled out the annual largesse to the courtiers, gentlemen, and other hangers-on who queued to present themselves in the royal presence each New Year's Day.

> They that be wont, Nicocles, to bring to you that be kings, garments, vessel, or plate, or other like jewels, whereof they be needy and ye be rich and have plenty, they plainly seem unto me not to present you but to make open market, selling those things much more craftily than they that confess themselves to retail. For my part, I suppose that to be the best gift and most profitable, also most convenient as well for me to give as for thee to receive, if I might prescribe unto thee by what studies desiring and from what works abstaining thou mayest best order thy realm and city.
>
> (*Doctrinal*, Aiii)

Given that, during the royal New Year ceremony, the King was expected to reciprocate in still more lavish fashion to each of the more important gift-givers (Elyot himself was to receive 13s and 4d on 1 January 1542, the only year in which he is known to have attended the ceremony in person),[82] as a sign that he had their well-being in mind and that even more significant favour might follow in the coming year, Isocrates' observation that such gifts were not given freely but brought to 'open market' would have gained an additional sharpness in this new context.

Whatever the specific occasion and form of its publication, however, the value of the text to Elyot's political campaign was clear. It allowed him, as I have suggested, to revisit the central themes of *The Governor*, *Pasquil*, and *Of the Knowledge*, this time with the added authority of Isocrates' name to endorse the comments on the importance to the good prince of heeding good counsel, banishing flatterers, behaving moderately, and governing benignly. It also allowed Elyot to say what he wanted to say directly, as if to the King himself in *proper persona*, thus bypassing all of the political and moral dilemmas about how to gain the chance to counsel that had so exercised him elsewhere. With this text he could return directly to the counsel table, albeit only imaginatively, as he had done in *The Governor*, the only other of his texts that had (if the unnamed 'credible persons' cited in *Of the Knowledge* were to be believed) found favour with Henry VIII himself. 'Think that the best and most sure guard of thy person', Isocrates observed,

be friends virtuous and honest, loving and benevolent subjects, and thine own will stable and circumspect: for by those things authority is obtained and longest preserved

(Bi).

Think not them to be loyal or faithful that do praise all thing that thou doest, but them that do blame the thing wherein thou errest. // Give to wise men liberty to speak to thee freely, that in things whereof thou doubtest, thou mayest have them with whom thou mayest try out the certainty. // Discern crafty flatterers from them that do serve thee with true heart and benevolence, lest the evil men receive more profit by thee than they that be honest and virtuous.

(Biii)

'Show thyself princely', Isocrates counselled Nicocles, 'not in sturdiness or punishing cruelly, but in surmounting all other in wisdom, that they may suppose that thou canst counsel them better for their weal than they can themselves' (Bi(v)–Bii). Indeed:

Make much of them that be wise and do perceive more than other men, and have good regard toward them, remembering that a good counsellor is of all other treasure the most royal and profitable, and think verily that they which can most aid and profit to thy wit or reason shall make thy kingdom most ample and honourable.

(cii)

All of these sentiments Elyot could reproduce almost verbatim from Isocrates' original text. The philosopher even afforded him the opportunity to make another direct appeal to the King to be more conservative in his religious policies through the maxim,

In the honour due unto God [Isocrates, of course, has 'the gods'] observe diligently that which is left unto thee by thy progenitors and suppose verily that sacrifice to be most acceptable and service most thankful to God, if thou endeavour thyself to excel all other men in virtue and justice. For, undoubtedly thereby shall thou obtain more reasonable petitions than if thou didst give unto him great treasure or offerings.

(Aviii(v))

Again, the applicability of such sentiments to the predicaments of both the fourth century BC and the 1530s alike might suggest merely the timelessness of the injunctions that made up the exhortatory tradition. If Elyot could take each of these maxims almost word for word from Isocrates' original, how, it might be asked, can they be said to be specifically relevant to the circumstances of 1533–4?[83] Isocrates provides part of the answer to such queries himself, offering a detailed exposition of the importance of the conventional nature of his own oration to its specific contemporary impact. For it was the very fact that such orations could claim to be the repository of ancient wisdom that gave them the authority to address contemporary issues, and the leverage to prompt men into action in the present. In Elyot's translation the argument runs as follows:

Marvel thou not that I have now rehearsed many things that thou knewest before, nor that forgot I not, but knew well enough that being such a multitude as well of princes as of private persons, some of them have spoken the same that I did, and many have heard it. Notwithstanding in matter concerning instruction novelty is not to be sought for, for therein ought not to be found either singular opinion or thing impossible or contrary to men's conjecture; but suppose that to be in hearing most gracious or pleasant which being sown in the minds of other, may assemble most matter to the purpose, and the same declare best and most aptly.

(Bvii)

Such sentiments were as relevant to Elyot's strategy of counsel as they were to Isocrates's eighteen hundred years earlier. The trick lay in choosing the most apt and persuasive maxims, examples, and injunctions from the traditional palette, and shading them sufficiently to fit the particular recipient and the specific circumstances they were intended to address.

Thus we can find Elyot making some subtle adjustments to his source text, despite the overall faithfulness of his translation. Some of these, such as changing references to 'the gods' into the singular form, were obviously necessitated by the shift from a pagan to a Christian culture, but others were more artful. Elyot drew one such change to his readers' attention himself in his prologue. Where Isocrates spoke of the gifts to kings being 'articles of dress or of bronze or of wrought gold' (*To Nicocles*, p. 41), Elyot changed this slightly to 'garments, vessel, or plate, or other like jewels' (Aiii). Given the possibility suggested above that the text was intended as a New Year's gift, the change may have been affected to fit more obviously the kind of gifts that the King and his courtiers habitually exchanged. This might also explain the author's rather arch comment in his introductory epistle that 'And where I have put at the beginning th[ese] words: "vessel", "plate", or for that which is in Greek, "brass or gold wrought", it is perceived of every wise man for what intent I did it' (Aii(v)). The reception for a brass vessel as a gift at Henry's court was presumably unlikely to be a warm one.

More significantly, perhaps, that same desire to focus more squarely upon domestic politics that had informed *The Governor* seems to lie behind the toning down of references to foreign advisers and legislation in Elyot's translation. Thus, where the philospher had enjoined Nicocles to 'associate yourself with the wisest of those who are about you and send for the wisest men from abroad whenever this is possible' (*To Nicocles*, 47), Elyot, perhaps thinking of the protestant advisers from the Continent or returning exiles such as Robert Barnes, whom Henry had sought to enlist in his campaign over his Great Matter, amended this to the more neutral instruction to,

Be also most familiar with them which being about thee be wisest, and get other such as thou mayest come by most like unto them.

(Avi)

Again, where Isocrates advocated the adoption of foreign laws when they improved upon domestic practice,[84] Elyot removed the allusion to other countries and replaced it again with a more general instruction to,

Repeal or change such laws and ordinances as be not well constitute, specially be thou the author of those that be good, or at the least the follower of them that were well made by other.

(Avii(v))

A reference (albeit negative) to an expansive foreign policy ('Emulate not those who have most widely extended their dominion, but those who have made best use of the power they already possess' (*To Nicocles*, p. 55)) was also removed, leaving an injunction that concentrated solely on domestic authority: 'Follow not them that do obtain greatest authority, but them that best use things that be present' (Bii(v)), a decision that may have been motivated to address more directly the question of the Royal Supremacy. In a similar vein, Elyot also chose not to translate a remark concerning the tactical advantages of feigning royal wrath for political advantage ('Do nothing in anger, but simulate anger when the occasion demands it' (*To Nicocles*, p. 53)), leaving only the advice to 'Do thou nothing in fury, since other men know what time and occasion is meetest for thee' (Bi(v)). This too may have been politically shrewd at a time when the royal ire, simulated or otherwise, was being exercised by Henry in person against those, like More and Fisher, who would not accept the justice of his actions, and institutionally by the courts against those churchmen who would not subscribe to the Act of Succession. Finally, Elyot took a further opportunity to assert the prime importance of consultation in all political affairs by replacing Isocrates' suggestion that the king should trust to his own deliberation in important matters ('what seems to you upon careful thought to be the best course' (*To Nicocles*, p. 61), with one that advocated the use of counsellors above all else: 'things that *in counselling* seem to be best, those execute thou in proper acts' (Bvi, my italics).

That Elyot chose this text of Isocrates to translate rather than any other of his orations, suggests strongly that it was the desire to speak truth to Henry's power concerning the role of the King rather than a scholarly desire to test his aptitude for translation that recommended the work. Indeed, the royal focus of the printed text was further reinforced by the inclusion, in the three and a half pages that would otherwise have been left blank at the end of the booklet, of an 'Addition to fill up vacant pages' (cii(v)), drawn from Solomon's words on the responsibilities of kings in the Books of Wisdom. Again the significant point about the passages selected was that they stressed the need for a king to behave in ways that commended him to God ('so fram[ing] . . . all his acts, as knowledging and minding that whatsoever he doeth, he doeth it before his eyes who is no less judge over kings than over common people' (ciii)). And once again the virtues of moderation and mercy, justice and affability lie at the heart of the message imparted:

What prescribeth Sapience to Kings? Mercy (sayeth she) and Truth do keep the king, and his throne is made strong with Clemency. He showeth Mercy in succouring the oppressed, Truth in judging truly, Clemency in tempering the severity of the laws with leniency.

(civ–iv(v))

Kings should succour widows and orphans, and 'deliver and defend all that are oppressed from injury' (civ(v)):

Truth hath two companions, Sapience and Constancy. Sapience giveth light unto the eyes, whereby is perceived what is right and what not, what is profitable for the weal public and what is contrary to it. Constancy causeth that the mind, overcoming all covetous desires, neither with ire nor with love, nor with hatred, is moved from honesty. Clemency tempereth with leniency necessary Severity. Clemency is not forthwith to go in hand with war, when cause of war is given, but he leave no reasonable mean unassayed to see whether the matter may be determined without war. And otherwise it is better to dissemble the injury than to revenge it by force of arms.

(civ(v)–cv)

Failing that, war should be conducted as defensively and concluded as swiftly as is humanly possible, so as to avoid as much bloodshed as may be:

For this wisdom that bringeth all good things with it, Solomon prayed for, that she should alway be assistant to his Throne, as a most faithful and trusty counsellor.

(cv)

The basic message was once more the same, but here again we see Elyot experimenting with literary forms and voices, seeking the best means of conveying that message to his intended royal and courtly readers. Having explored the issues of counselling at court and reached no satisfactory resolution in *Pasquil* and *Of the Knowledge*, Elyot tried more overtly literary methods in *The Doctrinal* and its 'Additions'. From writing texts that were in one way or another preliminaries to, or a prospectus for, his own call to counsel *in propre persona*, he turned to writing texts that counselled directly. And if his own voice could not gain a hearing, he tried ventriloquizing the voices of others, co-opting the proven authority of first Isocrates and then Solomon to speak for him in the attempt to persuade Henry VIII to virtue. It was a strategy that he was to explore further, and with more striking effect in his next publications, as the evidence of King Henry's need for moderation and wisdom grew ever greater, as we shall see in the following chapter.

10

From Supremacy to Tyranny, 1533–40

A Sweet and Devout Sermon *and*
The Banquette of Sapience

During the summer and autumn of 1533 opposition to both the King's marriage and his religious policy had continued to be voiced, and had met with an increasingly violent response. On 22 June the evangelical author John Frith and a like-minded apprentice tailor, Andrew Hewet, were burnt at Smithfield for their heretical beliefs. On 23 August two women, one very obviously pregnant, were stripped to the waist, beaten, and nailed by the ears to the Standard in London for claiming that Katherine of Aragon was the true Queen of England. Meanwhile, another outspoken woman, Elizabeth Barton, popularly known as the Nun of Kent, was gathering support among conservative church-men and the laity through a series of miraculous visions which she claimed had revealed to her that King Henry would be deposed and damned if he did not abandon Anne Boleyn and return to his true wife. Barton had even chastised Henry to his face on the matter, a feat which had only increased her reputation for sanctity. Such courage was to lead to her undoing, however, for she and her followers were to be arrested in July 1533, and subjected to the full force of the government's retribution in a series of public humiliations prior to their eventual execution in the following year.[1]

At the same time as Elizabeth Barton was being arrested in England for condemning the Boleyn marriage, events were taking a still more decisive turn in Rome. On 11 July the Pope formally pronounced judgement on Katherine of Aragon's appeal, finding in her favour and ordering Henry to return to her by September on pain of excommunication.[2] The Act of Succession, passed in the Spring of 1534 was Henry's defiant response. It was intended to end such rumbling discontent against the Boleyn marriage as Elizabeth Barton and her followers represented, and to enable the government to punish any further opposition as high treason. Attached to the Act was an oath, to be taken by both the clergy and laity, 'without any scrupulosity of conscience', affirming their loyalty to Anne as Queen, and to the offspring she would produce as heirs to the throne. Those individuals known to be critical of the divorce were called to be sworn first, on 13 April, as examples to the rest. Some, like Rowland Philips, hitherto an outspoken defender of the former queen, took the oath, but others refused. Most dramatically Sir Thomas More would not swear, and was imprisoned in the Tower. His ally Bishop Fisher soon joined him, and others followed. Dr Nicholas Wilson, another of Katherine's supporters, Richard Reynolds, a Bridgettine monk of Syon House, and all the Friars of the austere order of the Franciscan Observants at Greenwich and Richmond met a similar fate when they too refused the oath.[3] On 20 April the citizens of London were sworn *en masse* in their gild halls. As a further encouragement to conform, Henry chose that day for the public execution of Elizabeth Barton and her followers. In all five members of the regular religious died at Tyburn as the capital queued to subscribe to the legality of the King's new marriage.[4]

Further legislation established still more exacting tests of loyalty, and claimed further victims. In November 1534 the Act of Supremacy imposed a second oath, this time upon the clergy alone, formally renouncing all allegiance to the Pope and acknowledging Henry as Supreme Head of the Church in England. In a concerted act of defiance the monks of the London Charterhouse all refused this new oath, and were imprisoned in chains as a result.[5] In November 1534 the Treason Act widened the scope of those actions deemed to be treasonable and so subject to the death penalty beyond merely plotting or 'imagining' the King's death. Once the Act came into force in February 1535 it became a capital offence to speak 'maliciously' (a word the lawyers in the House of Commons fought hard to have included) against either the King's dignities and title or the Supremacy itself, or to 'slanderously and maliciously publish and pronounce by express writing or words that the King our sovereign lord should be heretic, schismatic, tyrant, infidel, or usurper of the crown'.[6] Words alone would now constitute treason in King Henry's commonwealth.

It was not long before Henry's more vocal critics began to die. In May 1535 the first group of Carthusian monks, including the prior of their London house, John Houghton, were convicted of treason and dragged together through the streets from the Tower to Tyburn and there hanged, drawn, and quartered. Henry had almost the whole court turn out to watch them, with a number of the gentlemen of his privy chamber leading the revels disguised in masks and wearing armour for the occasion.[7] Other more prominent victims soon followed. On 19 June three more Carthusians died. On 22 June John Fisher, by that time a Cardinal, having been raised to that dignity while he languished in prison, was next, with his severed head being set on London Bridge (so that it might look in vain for his Cardinal's hat coming from Rome, Henry joked). On 6 July Thomas More was executed, himself finding time to exchange jests with the sheriff's officers and the headsman as he ascended the steps to the block. London was mortified by the deaths, and the whole of Christian Europe was scandalized.[8] Henry, however was evidently enjoying himself. On St John's Eve (23 June) he travelled some thirty miles overnight to watch, incognito, an outdoor play based upon the Book of Revelation. It was evidently staged by evangelicals, for a central feature of the action was the beheading of a number of priests. According to Ambassador Chapuys, the scene so delighted the King that,

in order to laugh more at his ease, [and] also to encourage his people to persevere in such amusements, he [threw off his disguise and] sat bareheaded. Indeed the thing seemed so good to him that the next day he sent his lady [Anne Boleyn] a message that she would do well to come and assist in the representation of the same mystery, which was to be acted on the Eve of St Peter [28 June].[9]

While Henry was contriving to act like Caligula, all references to Rome were being removed from religious life in his kingdom. The parish clergy were ordered to scratch out all mention of the Pope's name, his office, or his pardons from their mass books, and to preach against his usurped authority in their churches.[10]

It was as this assault upon traditional loyalties and beliefs was beginning to take effect that on 1 July 1534 Elyot completed the Preface to the next of his treatises to be published.[11] This was a translation of *A Sweet and Devout Sermon of Holy Saint Ciprian*, printed (like all of his works, by Thomas Berthelet) along with a shorter work, *The Rules of a Christian Life made by Picus, earl of Mirandula*, both translated from the Latin by Elyot himself. At first sight this slim volume would seem to have little to connect it to the pressures and anxieties created by the Act of Succession and the death of Elizabeth Barton and her associates. But, as Pearl Hogrefe pointed out, the text is very much a product of the long, repressive spring of 1534.[12] For it was dedicated 'To my right worshipful sister dame Susan Kingston' and their two 'sisters religious' Dorothy and Elinor Fetti-place, all three of whom were probably sisters of the Bridgettine House of Syon in Isleworth at this time.

Given that the charismatic monk-priest of Syon, Richard Reynolds, was one of those men imprisoned in the Tower for refusing the Succession Oath, and that the more prestigious religious houses, of which Syon was one, were subjected to particular pressure to conform to Henry's new dispensation, the spring and summer of 1534 were doubtless times of considerable tribulation at Syon.[13] Indeed the example provided by the Franciscan Observants, whose houses were all suppressed during the summer in the wake of the friars' refusal of the oath, would raise serious questions about the future of the order itself if the monks and nuns did not handle royal demands with care. Hence there is particular poign-ancy to Elyot's dedication of his text to his spiritual sisters at this time. For the *Sweet and Devout Sermon* is, as Elyot affirms in the preface, an encouragement to Christian witness for those facing oppression, 'excellently declared and taught by the holy doctor and martyr saint Cyprian' in his Carthaginian diocese, 'in the time when there was continual persecution of [i.e. by] paynems, and also mortality by general pestilence' (Aii(v)–Aiii).[14] That Elyot should have turned to such a text, designed to arm the good Christian against 'the most certain sickness and final dissolution of nature called corporal death, as also against all worldly vexations and troubles, called the toys of fortune and the cranks of the world' (ʌii–ii(v)) at this time was thus no coincidence. Contemplating his own dilemma now that the storm carried by the 'great cloud' he had seen approaching in his letter to Hacket of the previous year had finally broken, he set about translating a text that spoke powerfully to the circumstances of his fellow conservatives in their own time of trial. His personal investment in the text can be judged from the dedication to his sister Susan, in which he described the work as,

a token that ye shall perceive that I do not forget you and that I do unfeignedly love you, not only for our alliance, but also much more for your perseverance in virtue and works of true faith, praying you to communicate it with our two sisters religious, Dorothe and Alianour, and to join in your prayers to God for me, that I may be constant in his service, and perform well such other works as been in my hands only to his honour and glory.

(ʌiii(v)–ʌiv)

The sermon itself is aimed, not at those of steadfast heart and soul, who will remain unmoved 'with the hugeness of this present mortality', but rather at those 'which either by weakness of courage, or by the delicateness of their kind, or (that which is a more heavy thing) being deceived in the opinion of truth, do not stand fast ne set forth the divine and invincible might of their stomachs' (ʙi–i(v)). The abuses of the current times are presented as the prelude to imminent dissolution:

The world decaying and in point to fall, and also compassed with tempests of evils continually assaulting it. Also we perceive that great mischief is all ready begun, and we know that much greater is coming: Let us reckon the greatest advantage to depart shortly from hence, which shall be for our special commodity.

(ᴅviii(v))

In this context the sermon aims to reassure waverers that the coming apocalypse will be a test of their faith and resolve (quoting Ecclesiasticus 2:5, he enjoined them to 'suffer both in grief and in fear, and have patience in thine humility, for as well gold as silver be tried with fire' (ʙvii(v)).[15] God had warned his followers 'that toward the end of the world, adversities and troubles should more and more be increased. Now behold, all that which he spake or hath happened, and has come among us.' Yet, just as he warned that the signs of tribulation would arise, so he promised that 'what time ye shall see all these things come to pass, then be you sure that the kingdom of heaven is at hand'(ʙii(v)). Thus, the true believer should welcome persecution, and even death itself, as a means of escaping the snares of the world and the Devil to join Christ and the saints in Heaven.[16] There is, of course, a conventional quality to all such *memento mori*, but Elyot, contemplating his own fate, and those of folk still less willing to conform to the Royal Supremacy and Henry's reforms than he was, could be forgiven for believing that the sentiments had a particular timeliness and urgency.

Significantly, given that both Elyot and his sisters were to take the Succession oath and conform to the government's demands, what the sermon offers is not a rallying cry to resistance or opposition, but words of comfort in the face of adversity. Readers are, consequently, encouraged not only to welcome their own death, but to be reconciled to the deaths of their friends and fellow believers.[17] But it is the patience of Job and Tobias that is commended rather than the defiance of the eager martyr (ci(v)–cii). 'The fear of God and faith should make thee ready to sustain all thing' (ciii(v)):

Truly dear brethren, we ought not to murmur or grudge in adversities, but to suffer strongly and patiently all that shall happen unto us, since it is written: the spirit that is troubled is a sacrifice to God.

(ciii)[18]

Even when Cyprian's text specifically mentions the pressures of the world, by which, as Elyot translates it, 'Thou art compelled to swear, which is unlawful' (BV), he passes up the opportunity to exhort any more than passive resistance.[19] Similar sentiments also inform Mirandola's *Rules of a Christian Life*, which Elyot translates in the remaining pages of the pamphlet. There the reader is assured that 'there is no passion or trouble that shall not make thee in some part conformable or like unto Christ' (EV). But the text is also at pains to exhort the Christian witnessing under oppression to avoid the sin of pride and exultation in his or her own virtue. Thus Elyot would seem to be attempting to reconcile his 'sisters religious', and himself too, to the realization that they would not follow the direct opposition of a More or a Reynolds, but take the quieter, less demonstrative path of passive resistance. As Hogrefe suggests, by translating these works at this time, and dedicating them to Susan Kingston, Elyot 'clearly wished to hearten the Fettiplace sisters at Syon . . . to strengthen himself through their prayers, and to encourage all who wished to remain loyal to the faith'.[20] But beyond that, it seems, he was not prepared to go. While others took the more resolute path to martyrdom, Elyot appears to have retained his faith in the doctrine of good counsel, conforming outwardly to all the government's demands,[21] but seeking once more to deploy his skills as a maker of books to restore order and sanity to the world around him. Hence, within months of the completion of the *Devout Sermon* he was at work on another text, again directed toward the King, and again designed to counsel moderation and self-awareness in its intended royal reader. That text was the *Banquet of Sapience*.

The Banquet of Sapience

Although no copy of an edition earlier than 1542 survives, it seems, from the evidence of the title-page of that edition, which carries the date 1534 in its ornamental frame or cartouche, that *The Banquet of Sapience* was the next of Elyot's texts to be published.[22] Having presented the King with a New Year gift in the form of *Of the Knowledge*, he seems to have hit upon a similarly timely literary conceit when he presented his new work later the same year: this time a collection of maxims presented as a springtime banquet for the King's table following a period of Lenten abstinence. Elyot's Preface presents the work to the King with an engaging vision of convivial feasting, both literal and metaphorical, after the period of self-denial:

> After long fasting and also much travail, it hath been thought ever, most noble prince, not only convenient but also to stand with good reason to have a dinner or supper provided with meats sufficient as well to recreate the vital spirits as to restore eftsoon the strength abated by labours.
>
> (Aii)

Conjuring an evocative image of pastime with good company at court, Elyot observes that, especially in the springtime,

> the nature of them in whom is any spark of gentle courage requireth to solace and banquet with mutual resort, communicating together their fantasies and sundry devices, which was not abhorred of the most wise and noble philosophers, as may appear to them that have vouchedsafe to read the works of Plato, Xenophon, and Plutarch, which they named *Symposia*, called Banquets in English.
>
> (Aii)

The Preface thus suggests that the book might be a domesticated version of those classical *symposia*. But, rather than offer a close and conscious imitation of the 'table talk' of Plato or Putarch's *Moralia*, it is rather a 'feast' of *apophthegma*, a *florilegium* or collection of choice 'flowers' of wisdom, drawn from various sources and presented in an anthology for the reader's instruction and delectation. Prominent examples of the genre were the *Adagia* of Erasmus and Dominico Nani Mirabelli's *Polyanthea*, a text from which Elyot may indeed have borrowed some of the aphorisms he cites.[23] And as he presents it, the feast on offer has as many affinities, as we shall see, with the Banquet of Wisdom described in Proverbs 9: 1–5 as it does with classical sources.

What follows these lines is a passage redolent of Elyot at his most inspired and convivial, exploring the metaphor of Wisdom's banquet as if he were present himself, dining and communing with the ancient philosophers. In his account of the dishes to be served and the pleasures they afford, he evokes a sense of sheer enjoyment and an infectious generosity of spirit on his part that he could rarely summon when contemplating the ills and perils of his own society. But even here it is not long before the good life in ancient Greece is interrupted by the pressing matter of contemporary politics. For, as he goes on to declare, the book was primarily inspired, not by the thought of enjoying the fruits of wisdom for their own sake, but by the more immediate needs of the King and commonwealth:

> I being stirred, most excellent Prince, by a like imitation considering the long abstinence and fasting of the present Lent, with also the continual travail that your highness, your council, and diverse your subjects have sustained in consulting about the weal public of

this your grace's most noble realm, I have provided this little banquet (so is this little treatise entitled) composed of sundry wise counsels gathered by me out of the works of most excellent persons as well faithful as gentiles.

(Aii–ii(v))

This little work with my labours have I dedicate unto your highness, unto whom of bounden duty being your humble servant I owe all my studies, prayer, service, and loyalty, beseeching your grace to receive this little work as a token of my sincere mind and intent, according to your accustomed and incomparable gentleness.

(Aii(v)–Aiii)

Hence Elyot returned once more to the task of counselling his king. Having already addressed Henry in the words of Isocrates, he now did so in the voice of Wisdom herself, quoting from the sapiential books of the Old Testament, most notably Psalms, Proverbs, Ecclesiastes, Wisdom, and Ecclesiasticus, that grant him a new and imperious tone in which to utter his advice and admonitions:

Sapience hath builded a house for herself, she hath prepared her wine, and laid forth her table, she calleth out abroad in the streets, and in the chief assembly of people, and at the gates of the city she speaketh with a loud voice: 'Ye babies, how long will ye delight in your childishness? And how long will fools covet those things which shall hurt thee? . . . Come on and eat ye my bread and drink my wine that I have ordained for you. To me do belong counsel and equity, mine is prudence and mine also fortitude. By me kings do reign and makers of laws do determine those things that be rightwise. By me princes do govern and men in authority do give sentence according to justice.'

(Av(v))[24]

Never before had Elyot spoken with such a bold and compelling voice. By co-opting the words of Scripture to his cause, and delivering them *in propre persona*, he was able both to speak to kings in that voice of authority that he had always believed was the prerogative of the wise man, and also to offer his most comprehensive affirmation to date of the centrality of knowledge and wisdom to the well-being of the public weal:

I love them that love me, and they that wake early shall find me; with me do remain both substance and renown, stately riches and justice; my fruit doth excel gold and stones precious, and my branches are better than fine tried silver; my walks be in the high ways of justice, and in the middle of the paths of judgement, to the intent that I will make them rich that do love me, and fill up their treasures.

(Av(v))[25]

This sustained direct address of Wisdom to Elyot's intended royal reader was not continued beyond the initial pages of the text. Thereafter the maxims of biblical, patristic, and classical wisdom were digested and divided into nuggets arranged alphabetically under general headings from Abstinence and Adversitie to Virginity and Wrath, but the initial experiment with this new voice of command was nonetheless impressive. Perhaps Elyot thought that a brief peroration from

Wisdom was all that was needed. Perhaps now, at last, he could be sure that he had gained his King's full attention.

The maxims that follow are, for the most part, familiar, recycling ideas and quotations that he had already explored in detail in *The Governor*, *Pasquil*, and *Of the Knowledge*. The importance of good counsel is, as one might expect, a central theme. It has a section to itself in which the third-century historian Marius Maximus is quoted to the effect that a 'public weal is in better state and in a manner more sure where the prince is not good than where the king's counsellors and companions be ill' (ciii(v)). But, throughout the text even the most unlikely pretexts are used to reintroduce the theme and assert its importance. Under 'Folly' it is observed that 'A fool's way in his own eye is best, a wise man heareth good counsel' (Dii(v)); under 'Sapience' that 'princes become wise by company of wise men' (Gii).[26] The princely virtues of affability and placability, so crucial to the process of consultation as it was described in *The Governor*, are also continually commended. In the section on Flattery, Elyot quotes the Ciceronian maxim,

[He] whose ears be so stopped from truth that he may not abide to hear truth of his friend, his health and prosperity is to be despaired.

(Diii)

Further examples of royal tolerance of harsh truths are offered in the sections headed 'King' and 'Public Weal:'

Theopompus, King of Lacedemony, unto one that demanded of him how a king might most surely keep his realm and defend it, said: 'If he give to his counsellors liberty to speak always truth and to his power neglecteth not his subjects when they be oppressed'.

(Ev)

Similarly, under 'Correction', Elyot cites Solomon (the putative author of the sapiential books) for the maxims, 'Correct not a scorner, lest that he hate thee; correct a wise man and he will thank thee' and 'The ear which will hear his own life rebuked shall dwell in the middle of them that be wise men. (ciii(v)).[27] Symbolically, the final maxim in the collection, introduced slightly incongruously in the section on Wrath, is Plato's response to the question, what is wise man?

A wise man when he is rebuked is therewith not angry nor anything the prouder when he is praised.

(Gvii(v))

Equally familiar to readers of Elyot's earlier treatises, but still as timely and urgent, were those warnings against socially divisive policies and the perils that they create:

They that sustain one part of the people and neglect the other part they bring into the city a thing very perilous, that is to say sedition and discord.

(cvi(v))

Every realm divided within itself shall be made desolate and every city and house divided by mutual contention shall not long stand.

(cvi)[28]

In citing such old said saws, Elyot returns to the well-trodden paths of political counsel. Rather than directly deploring contemporary divisions or criticizing royal policies, he approaches the matter obliquely, as a question of political principle. Moreover, he is echoing current governmental rhetoric, which frequently cited the King's concern for the well-being of his subjects and his search for a *via media* that would reunite his divided people. Seeking to appeal to this aspect of the King's public persona, Elyot was, predictably, encouraging him to return to more consensual paths.

Equally redolent of the current political climate, in which hitherto loyal men were denounced by informers as traitors for opposing the supremacy or criticizing the Boleyn marriage, is Elyot's inclusion, in the section headed 'Report', of these lines from Ecclesiasticus 10: 20:

Among thy friends detract not the King, nor in the most secret place of thy chamber report none evil of a great man, for the birds of heaven will bear about thy voice and they that have feathers will tell thine opinion.

(Gi)

Indeed, it was a danger the author himself would fall into in 1537, when, as we have seen, one malicious reporter, John Perkins, would denounce him to the Privy Council as a favourer of papists and enemy to the King.[29]

Still more engaged with the detail and direction of current policies is Elyot's repeated emphasis on the need for a prince to show moderation, tolerance, and mercy in judging his subjects. The need to avoid hasty judgements, to allow personal feelings no place in the execution of justice, and to rule through love and not fear, are repeated motifs in this book. Under 'Abstinence' it is noted that 'better is a man patient than strong and he that mastereth will surmounteth a conqueror' (Bi). In the section on Cruelty a number of the maxims concern royal justice specifically, exemplifying the idea that 'Never man might be terrible and also in surety' (civ(v)),[30] leading to the potentially radical conclusion that,

A virtuous man should receive rule or authority as if he were thereto compelled, but he that lacketh virtue, though he be compelled, yet let him not take it.

(Bii(v))[31]

The need for a king to rule in the interests of all his subjects is another theme upon which the *Banquet* plays variations, exemplified by Proverbs 14: 28: 'in the multitude of the people is the state of the King' (Dv). The warnings against those who judge falsely or partially are dire:

Hear, therefore, ye kings, and understand ye. Learn, ye judges of all parts of the world. Give ears, ye that rule over multitudes and delight yourself in the trouble of people, for power is given to you from our lord, which shall examine your acts, and insearch your thoughts, for when ye were ministers of his kingdom, ye judged not straightly, ne kept the laws of true justice, ne went after his pleasure. Horribly and shortly he will appear to you for most sorest judgements shall be to them that have rule over other. To the poor man mercy is granted, but the mighty man shall suffer mightily torments.

(Eii(v))[32]

Although on one level, then, Elyot's decision to present a treatise in the form of a collection of quotations from other writers reduced the mirror for princes to its most obviously conventional form, at the same time this paring down of the genre to its bare axiomatic bones was a liberating manoeuvre for him. By reducing his own authorial role apparently to nothing, and allowing the ideas to be spoken wholly through the voices of others, he seems to have gained a confidence that was lacking in his earlier exercises in good counsel. Freed from the need to construct a voice and a role for himself as a royal counsellor, he found a far more potent voice in the words of generations of the wise. Hence, perhaps, he was able to find the confidence and courage to come as close as he had yet come to criticizing royal policies directly in his statements on the law: statements that seem to have been selected specifically to address the legislative programme of the Reformation Parliament.

Significantly it was in the section labelled 'Public Weal' that he quoted the maxim of Plutarch that,

To change suddenly the customs and disposition of people and with new laws hastily to rule them, it is not only hard, but also unsure as the thing that requireth much time with great power and authority.

(Fvii(v))[33]

Similarly in the section headed simply 'Judge', Elyot presented the dramatic censure of oppressive rulers in Isaiah 10: 1–2:

Everlasting woe shall be to them which make unrightwise laws and do write against justice, to th'intent that they will oppress poor men in judgement and violently subvert the cause of the people.

(Eii–ii(v))

In the light of the current repressive measures enacted to secure the Supremacy and the Boleyn marriage, such comments could not but be read as politically charged. The same is true of a further example offered, that of King Antiochus who specifically instructed his subjects that, should he ever command them 'to do any thing that was contrary unto his laws, then as to him that was ignorant they should repugne and deny it' (Evi(v)). Such principles, like the conclusion to *Of the Knowledge*, offered Elyot the prospect of a theory of resistance to royal policies based upon impeccably legitimate sources; for if the good king should order his subjects to disobey him if he acted against the law, then any king who did not do so could not, by definition, be good.

The power that the anonymity of the compiler of maxims afforded Elyot seems also to have allowed him to return to the kind of *ad hominem* criticisms that had marked the first edition of *Pasquil the Plain*. For it is hard to avoid the conclusion that the two passages that he quotes concerning the role of a bishop—an office not otherwise treated in his works but here afforded a section to itself—were added once more to twist the tail of his erstwhile *bête noir*, Cranmer. First he quotes the relevant section of St Paul's Letter to Titus (Titus 1: 6–9) on the duties of the good bishop:

A bishop must be without fault, as the steward of almighty God, not proud, not wrathful, not drunkenly, no fighter, not covetous of dishonest game, but a good householder, bountiful, wise, sober, just, holy, and continent, having the true manner of speech which is according to learning, wherewith he may exhort by wholesome doctrine, and reprove them which will speak to the contrary.

(Bviii(v))

Did Elyot smile to himself as he wrote of the bishop's continence? Given his comments concerning Harpocrates' culpable silence in *Pasquil*, he clearly expected Cranmer to blush if he read of the need for the true bishop to reprove them who do not follow wholesome doctrine. But it does seem to have been Cranmer's private life that was the principal target of his mischief making here, as he added a second reference to bishops' domestic arrangements to the section on 'Example', this time quoting from Jerome:

The bishop's conversation [lifestyle] and household is set as it were masters of common discipline on the top of a mountain, for whatsoever he doth, all other men think they may lawfully do it.

(ciii(v))[34]

If Cranmer's clandestine marriage and breach of chastity were the targets here, the King's own marital history seems to have been an implicit target in the section on marriage later in the book. Certainly the text's royal dedicatee could not have failed to be provoked if he read as far as the injunction:

Depart not from a wife that is sad and wise which thou hast taken in the fear of God, the grace that is in her honesty surmounteth all riches.[35]

Or indeed the further biblical advice on the politics of divorce and remarriage:

Art thou bounden to a wife? Seek not to be loosed. Art thou loose from a wife? Seek not to be married.

(Fi)[36]

In such passages Elyot seems to be writing with a new boldness and lack of discretion. What prompted this change of heart is unclear, but a hint as to his new mood may be found in one further quotation, taken from Plutarch and placed, appropriately, in the section headed 'Quietness of mind', which would seem to have an obvious bearing on his own circumstances:

Art thou put from thine office? Thou shalt be more at home and the better apply thine own business. Thou labourest to be nigh the king, but thou art disappointed; thou shalt live more surely and in the less business. But thou art turmoiled with much care and business; ye warm water (as Pindar sayeth) doth not so sweetly ease and comfort the delicate members as honour joined with authority maketh labour pleasant and to sweat easily.

To him that would be quiet and live in most surety, the right way is to set nought by exterior things and to be only contented with virtue, for whosoever esteemeth anything to be above virtue, yea, or to be good, but virtue only, he setteth forth his breast naked to all the thing that flyeth from the hand of blind Fortune, and with great study and diligence abideth her shot.

(Fviii–viii(v))

Perhaps Elyot had at last decided to have the courage of his stoic convictions and accept that the summons to council was not going to come—and that, if it did, he should not accept it. Freed from the need to modulate his tones in the hope of that long hoped-for call, he may thus have been able to say rather more boldly what he really thought of the King, his ministers and policies, albeit only in this instance, in the carefully chosen words of others. In his last substantial political dialogue, *The Image of Governance*, written after a further six years of Henrician reform and reformation, he was certainly prepared, as we shall see in what follows, to take that boldness further.

For the next six years, however, he seemingly took his own counsel concerning the satisfactions of quietness of mind and retirement to heart. After 1534 he ceased the torrent of dialogues and treatises with which he had hitherto bombarded the King and concentrated instead upon the less overtly politicized texts that would prove his most popular and successful publications: his *Dictionary*, first published in 1538 and reissued in a revised form as the *Bibliotheca Eliotae* in 1542, and the handbook of popular medicine that he dedicated to Thomas Cromwell, *The Castle Of Health*. During the worst years of the Henrician Reformation, as Henry showed increasing signs of paranoia and tyrannical ruthlessness, Elyot kept his head down and wrote, assuring Cromwell of his loyalty to the Supremacy and Reformation, and gaining the King's permission to use the royal libraries for his lexicographical research. But even in the 'quiet years' of the 1530s, he could not entirely refrain from engaging with political debate. For it was in the unlikely forum of the preface to his *Dictionary* that, as we have seen, he took the liberty of commending Henry for his handling of the trial of the sacramentrian John Lambert or Nicholson and 'marvelling at the fulmination of the most vehement arguments proceeding from your highness in the confutation of abominable heresies'.

Treason, Rebellion, and Repression: Henrician Government in the Later 1530s

In 1536, both opposition to the Supremacy and Reformation and its repression reached new and unprecedented levels, and the victims were both closer to home and more widespread. In May Henry's second wife, Queen Anne was suddenly arrested and convicted of multiple adultery and imagining the King's death. Among her alleged lovers were some of Henry's closest body servants and companions, including a number of those men who had disported themselves in fancy dress at the execution of the Carthusians in the previous May. Most prominent in the list was Anne's own brother, Viscount Rochford. Amid accusations of secret depravity and treason at court, they were all executed on Tower Green.[37] In October, a far more significant threat to Henry's regime arose when the commons of Lincolnshire took up arms in protest against the suppression of the smaller monasteries and other reforming measures. Within a month the whole of the north of England had risen, fired by fears of further suppressions, new taxes, and doctrinal change. Determined to march upon London to present their demands for an end to reform and the punishment of evangelical ministers to the King in person, the movement, calling itself the Pilgrimage of Grace, was reputed to number tens of thousands. There were real fears that the rest of the country would rally to their banner of the Five Wounds of Christ. In London the city authorities were so exercised by fears that the clergy would support the pilgrims, that all priests and friars between the ages of sixteen and sixty were ordered to surrender anything that might be used as a weapon, keeping only a single meat knife for their own use. The sanctuaries in the London churches were also locked up to prevent the criminals inside from adding to any potential disorder.[38] The direst predictions of domestic strife that had been voiced in 1529–30 seemed to have been realized.

By a mixture of prevarication and outright deception Henry contrived to stall the Pilgrims while royal armies marched north to meet them. Assurances of the King's good will, and the promise of a parliament in the north to redress their grievances persuaded the protestors to disperse. Once the military threat was over, however, repression quickly followed. At the most conservative estimate one hundred and thirty two of the pilgrims were executed under a variety of pretexts,[39] and many more deaths probably went unrecorded during a brutal period of martial law imposed by the Duke of Norfolk and inspired by a series of ferocious letters of encouragement from the King in London. No major town in the north was without its grizzly reminder of the fate of traitors in the form of a dismembered pilgrim leader.

Meanwhile religious reform continued, with Henry defending his chosen *via media* against radicals and conservatives alike. In 1535 he took the first steps against the Anabaptist and Sacramentarian heresies, ordering all foreign sectaries to quit the country on pain of death. Many fled, but over twenty Dutch Anabaptists remained and were condemned in a mass trial at St Paul's.[40] At the same time the attack upon traditional 'superstitions' gathered pace. The Ten Articles and the Injunctions of 1536 outlawed the 'abuse' of religious images and those sacraments of the church not strictly commended in Scripture, prompting the despoliation of numerous shrines and centres of pilgrimage. St Thomas Becket's tomb in Canterbury cathedral was smashed and its fabulous treasures appropriated by the crown. In May 1538 a macabre pantomime devised by Cromwell and the evangelical chaplain William Latimer was played out in London. One of the suppressed devotional images was that of the Welsh saint Darvel Gaderen, who was the subject of a supposedly ancient prophecy to the effect that one day he would set a whole forest ablaze. In a carnivalesque mockery of such beliefs Cranmer had the image brought to London where it was used as kindling at the burning of the Observant Friar and long-time supporter of Katherine of Aragon, John Forest.[41]

In July 1539 Parliament debated the Six Articles, a new definition of belief and practice that delighted conservatives by reining in some of the more radical implications of the Ten Articles and Injunctions, and reasserting the catholic doctrine of transubstantiation and the value of private masses, vows of celibacy, and the need for communion in or under one kind only (*communio sub una panis specie*) for the laity.[42] In the Lords one temporal peer praised the 'marvellous goodness' of the King in this session, concluding that 'never prince showed himself so wise a man, so well learned, and so catholic as the King hath done in the Parliament'. Evangelicals were dismayed. Thomas Broke, a Calais burgess, spoke against the Bill, singling out its stress upon the doctrine of Transubstantiation. In response, Sir William Kingston, the comptroller of the royal household, declared that if Broke were to repeat his opinions once the bill was made law, he would prove himself a heretic, and 'I will bring a faggot to help to burn you withal'.[43] When the bill was duly passed two of the more evangelical bishops, Hugh Latimer of Worcester and Nicholas Shaxton of Salisbury resigned their sees in protest.[44]

Significantly, perhaps, it was in this Parliamentary session, running from 28 April to 28 June, and characterized by its leading historian as 'poorly organized, inadequately prepared for, divisive, [and] full of opposition to government measures', that Thomas Elyot was to have his one taste of government service, acting (perhaps through Cromwell's patronage), as a Knight of the Shire for Cambridgeshire.[45] What he saw during this brief but intense experience of national government in action seems to have prompted him to return to his political writings. For early in the next year he published a short pamphlet in commendation of womanhood, *The Defence of Good Women*, dedicated in an ill-judged gesture to Henry's fourth wife Anne of Cleves, but in reality a coded reassertion of the virtues of the late Katherine of Aragon (who had died in 1536) and the conservative values she represented, presented as another paean to moderation in political life.[46] But any thought of further attempts to influence the King by appealing to his better nature with books of straightforward counsel seem to have been banished by the savage events of the first half of that year.

Henry VIII was nothing if not even-handed in his repression. Following the formalization of official doctrine in the Act of Six Articles, he provided a powerful demonstration of the boundaries of acceptable belief. On 7 July 1540 a reformer, one William Collins, was burnt in London, and during the following summer over five hundred suspected evangelicals were arrested and questioned concerning alleged transgressions of the Six Articles in the City.[47] All those caught in this sweep were eventually released without trial, but not everyone had been so fortunate. On 30 July three further evangelicals, one of them the apostate friar and author Robert Barnes, were executed, condemned as heretics by act of attainder. From the scaffold, Barnes made it clear who and what he thought were responsible for his own death and the ills of the nation, praying to the King, who had two days earlier married his fifth wife, Catherine Howard, 'that matrimony be had in more reverence than it is and that men for every light cause invented cast not off their wives'.[48] On the same day three long-term prisoners, all of them conservative opponents of the Supremacy, were brought from prison and hanged, drawn, and quartered as traitors. Such defiance on Barnes's part, and such deliberate and bloody parallelism on Henry's, would have created more of a stir had it not been for the fact that, some two days earlier, Henry had claimed a still more influential and unexpected victim in the form of his vicegerent-in-spirituals and the alleged architect of his reformation, Thomas Cromwell himself. On 10 July Cromwell was arrested on charges of treason. On 28 July he was dead. It was this act, and the manner in which it was performed that prompted Elyot to write the last and I would argue the most daringly oppositional of all his political treatises, *The Image of Governance*.

11

The Apotheosis of Sir Thomas Elyot

The Image of Governance

In the Preface to *The Image of Governance*, dedicated 'To All the Nobility of this Flourishing Realm of England' (aii), Elyot relates an engaging story about the origins and gestation of the book. It was, he claims, while he was searching through his papers for some reading matter,

whereof I might recreate my spirits, being almost fatigate with the long study about the correcting and amplicating of my Dictionary... [that] I happened to find certain quires of paper which I had written about ix years passed.

(aii)

These quires proved to be his own translation of a Greek life of the Emperor Alexander Severus (AD 222–35) written by his secretary 'Eucolpius', a work that had so 'marvellously ravished' Elyot when he first read it that he had immediately attempted to translate it into English for the benefit of his countrymen. The copy of the original text that he was using had, however, only been loaned to him by a Neapolitan gentleman named Pudericus, who had unexpectedly asked for it back, forcing Elyot to leave the project unfinished.[1] On returning to the material later, he was again struck by its eloquence and utility, and, recalling his promise in *The Governor* 'to write a book of good governance' as a companion volume to that text, saw that this translation might redeem that pledge, since 'in this book was expressed of governance so perfect an image' (aii(v)). So, having made good the untranslated portion of Eucolpius's text, 'as well I could with some other Authors, as well Latins as Greeks', he now offered the completed text for publication.

The story is, on first reading, a plausible one. The bulk of *The Image* seems to have been prepared for the press in late 1540, and the Preface (traditionally the last section to be written and printed) was completed in early 1541.[2] So the original translation would have been undertaken, on Elyot's estimate, in around 1532 or 1533, the time at which he was working on *Of the Knowledge* and his other translations and adaptations from classical sources. Notes produced at that time might plausibly have been put aside to lie unconsidered until they were fortuitously rediscovered in 1540. Yet, as Uwe Baumann and others have suggested, there is an artfulness to Elyot's presentation of the details that casts doubt upon the supposedly simple story he relates.[3] Indeed, the seemingly idiosyncratic details prove on closer inspection to be very carefully chosen. That nine-year gap which Elyot cites between starting the translation and publishing it, for example, actually conforms to Horace's dictum that any book should be allowed to lie fallow for nine years to allow time for reflection and amplification before publication.[4] More fundamentally, the original Greek text written by 'Eucolpius' which Elyot cites as his source seems to have been itself an invention. Certainly no such text has survived or is known to have been extant in Elyot's lifetime. Elyot's citation seems actually to be part of a complex game of literary allusion. For what he was really translating was not a lost Greek text but an extant Latin one, the *Lives* of Alexander Severus and Heliogabalus attributed to Aurelius Lampridius and contained in the so-called *Historia Augustae*, a text in which he would have found one '*En*colpius' named as the Emperor's secretary and biographer.[5] Furthermore, modern scholarship suggests that this text was itself a clever literary hoax, purporting to be a compilation of *Lives* written between the late third and early fourth centuries AD by six different hands, but probably the work of a single author, writing a century later.[6]

That Elyot was translating from the *Historia* and not the spurious Greek text is evident from the printed marginalia in *The Image*, which actually cite 'Lampridius' as the relevant authority at various points. So Elyot was not only failing to do what he claimed to be doing in his Preface, but revealing as much to his readers as he did so. Not that his more scholarly readers would have needed such obvious clues to the spuriousness of his claims, however, for the decision to cite the mysterious 'Eucolpius' as his source would almost certainly have already aroused suspicions. For the original 'Encolpius' (seemingly itself an onomastic pun—literally 'windy one' or perhaps, 'windbreaker') was a wonderfully apt name for the author of a fraudulent biography, especially so inflated a text as Elyot was finally to produce. Rather than giving the spurious nature of his source away completely at the outset, however, he chose to amend the name slightly to '*Eu*colpius' a less obviously comic name (although he might have intended it to suggest 'good wind', 'blown up' or, even, 'very windy'),[7] leaving the full extent of the joke to be discovered by those willing to trace his sources back to the *Historia* itself. Such name games were the lifeblood of humanist humour, as Thomas More's account of *Utopia* ('Nowhere'), supposedly related by Hythlodeus ('Skilled in Nonsense') to Morus ('A Fool' / Thomas More) demonstrates.

A further hint that *The Image* should not be read simply at face value is offered in the final section, where the story of the fateful interruption by the Neapolitan bibliophile Pudericus is itself cast into doubt. For there the text offers a rather different reason for its own abbreviation, based on the state of the manuscript rather than the needs of its owner:

HITHERTO is the report of Eucolpius: much more he wrote, as it seemed, for diverse quires lacked in the book. Wherefore, to make some perfect conclusion, I took the residue out of other which wrote also the life of the Emperor.

(cc iii)[8]

Hence not only the manuscript but the owner too, the otherwise unknown Pudericus and his need to recover his book, may have been Elyot's own invention.[9] But why this elaborate but deliberately self-defeating subterfuge? In Baumann's view, Elyot was following a vogue for games of 'literary hide-and-seek' instigated by the publication of Antonio de Guevara's *Libro Aureo*, which first appeared in 1528 and was published in an English translation by Lord Berners *c.* 1535. This book claimed to be a biography of the emperor Marcus Aurelius copied from an original manuscript found in the Medici Library ('in Florence, among the books left there by Cosme de Medicis, a man of good memory'),[10] but was in fact Guevara's own creation. Was Elyot simply indulging in a humanist *jeu d'esprit* in response to Guevara's work, offering a *Life* of Alexander Severus that revealed itself to the initiated to be an amalgam of authentic history and pure invention? As I suggested a moment ago, there were other, earlier, examples of such puzzling amalgamations of fact and fiction still closer to Elyot's own experience. The most notable was More's *Utopia* itself, which claimed to be the account of a meeting between More and the imaginary traveller Hythlodeus in the garden of the real scholar and citizen of Antwerp, Peter Gilles. But the existence of such precedents does not explain why Elyot chose to produce his most deliberately puzzling and comically allusive text at the point that he did, and why he wrote *The Image*, the successor to *The Governor* and the last of his *specula principium* (a genre he had hitherto treated entirely seriously) in this curiously ironic manner.[11]

As we shall see, *The Image of Governance* proves, despite its reputation among scholars as an anodyne and politically irrelevant work,[12] to be a very powerful and original political text, in many ways Elyot's equivalent of More's *Utopia*.[13] It, like More's text, uses a range of ironic and satirical effects to explore contemporary social and political issues. And Elyot had still more obvious reasons to fictionalize the contemporary origins of his work than the former Lord Chancellor. He employed his text to touch upon some extraordinarily sensitive and urgent issues in the spring and summer of 1540; issues that, if he had discussed them directly, would have brought him into grave danger of prosecution under the Treason Act. For Elyot, while on one level commending his royal subject, would nevertheless also bring the authority and dignity of the King into question, and in ways that would be hard to defend against allegations of malice. His version of the life of Alexander Severus is not a faithful translation of the account in the *Historia*, but a carefully chosen selection of the material presented there, expanded and arranged in such a way as to point up its relevance to contemporary issues and events. Hence Elyot's stress upon the alleged age of the text. For placing its origins 'about ix years passed' would locate it safely beyond the events and issues of the moment and so deflect allegations of specific and malicious political intent. It may have been that Elyot did indeed write some portion of the text in 1532–3, although it is also possible that he did not. Either way, he almost certainly fashioned the most significant portions into their published form during the summer of 1540, intending them as a coded commentary upon what was probably for him the most personally traumatic event of the Henrician Reformation, the fall and execution of his friend and patron Thomas Cromwell, and the culmination of his own long campaign to counsel Henry VIII towards virtue and cure the ills of the public weal.

The Preface offers the text to its noble readers as a *speculum principis* in its classic form, 'both pleasant and marvellous, and no less profitable to governors that do prefer their public weal before wilful appetite and particular pleasures' (aii(v)). Predictably it draws together Elyot's major preoccupations: education, good counsel, and tyrannical government, presenting the exemplary stories of two emperors, the one, Heliogabalus (Marcus Aurelius Antoninus, or Antoninus Elagabalus, ruled AD 218–22) an archetypal tyrant, the other, his successor, Alexander Severus, described, as he is in the *Historia*, as an ideal prince. With this in mind he exhorted his intended audience,

That reading it distinctly and studiously, first ye mark diligently how by the lascivious and remiss education of Varius Heliogabalus he grew to be a person most monstrous in living . . . Then shall ye note diligently how much it profited to Alexander, who next did succeed him, that he had so wise and virtuous a mother and that he was brought up among so wise counsellors.

(bi(v))

The contemporary relevance of the text is, however, also hinted at early in the Preface, for it is not long before Elyot refers directly to King Henry, citing him as a prime case of the 'exactly well learned' monarch whose example refutes the assertion that scholars make bad governors. Once again the aspect of Henry's alleged sagacity that he commends is carefully chosen, though, and the terms employed well measured. For, picking up on the repeated stress upon the *via media* and the elimination of extreme opinions in recent royal proclamations and statutes, Elyot asks of those who might conceivably be unaware of the fruits of the King's learning,

Hath not he thereby only sifted out detestable heresies late mingled among the corn of his faithful subjects and caused much of the chaff to be thrown in the fire? Also, hypocrisy and vain superstition to be clean banished? Whereof I doubt not but that there shall be, ere it be long, a more ample remembrance to his most noble and immortal renown.

(bi)

In the light of the recent repression of Sacramentarians and Anabaptists, and the simultaneous deaths of catholic traitors and evangelical heretics, Elyot's balancing of the sifting out of heresies and the banishment of superstition would seem designed to court royal approval. Yet, as I suggested earlier, there is in that claim that 'a more ample remembrance' of Henry's credentials as a wise ruler will follow, more than a hint that any such remembrance should involve the casting into the fire of the remaining heretical chaff rather than any more evangelical reform, all of the hypocrisy and superstition having been already 'clean banished'.

Was Elyot using the life of Alexander Severus, then, as a means of applauding legislation such as the Act of Six Articles and the purges of evangelicals that followed? Certainly there is a good deal of material in the *Historia Augusta* that would further an attempt to fashion the emperor as a moderate conservative in matters of religion. And Elyot developed that material further. The Alexander of the *Historia* was tolerant of Christianity when most of those around him were not. This was the result of his encounter with Origen, the Christian bishop of Alexandria, whose piety and wisdom had impressed him. (Elyot went so far as to suggest, following patristic tradition, that the Emperor was 'persuaded...to embrace the profession of Christ's faith and doctrine' (oiii) by Origen's words, and so became, like his mother, a closet Christian – quite literally in his case, as we shall see.)[14] He favoured the early Christians in a dispute between them and the innkeepers (Elyot says the cooks) of Rome over the use of a plot of land in the city, declaring that it should be set aside for worship rather than worldly ends (oiii(v)),[15] and spoke favourably about Christian belief and virtue when judging a dispute between two members of the church (oiii(v)–oiv). And, although he 'durst not attempt to publish the Christian faith by his authority, the persecution of Christian men being but late ceased, and they being yet odious to the Senate and people', he nonetheless tolerated the exercise of the faith tacitly, and showed signs of following it himself in the privacy of his own palace. For he set up the images of Christ, Abraham, and Moses, among the statues in his privy closet,[16] and cited versions of the, so-called, Golden Rule of Luke 6:31 ('that which to thyself thou wouldst not have done, do not in wise unto an other' (oiv(v))) in his execution of justice.[17] 'And being by himself he honoured one god': an observation that Elyot attributes to his imaginary source, Eucolpius himself, 'as I myself, being oftentimes secret with him, did well perceive' (oiii).

With still greater relevance to Henry's policies, the *Historia* cites an attempt by the Emperor to dedicate a temple in the city to the Christian God, which failed when the Senate united in opposition to his proposal,

Wherewith they all were sore grieved and did obstinately deny it, saying that they had counselled with the goddess, of whom they had answer that if that were suffered all men should be Christians, and all other temples should be made desolate. Wherefore he ceased his enterprise, but alway[s] he was studious in the books of Christian men and oftentimes used their sentence.

(oiii)[18]

An emperor who tolerates the practices of Christians (as opposed to heretics), keeps religious images in his privy closet, and seeks to build temples (rather than suppressing monasteries) would certainly offer a pointed contrast to Henry's policies of the later 1530s. And was there also, perhaps, in the statement that Alexander was a Christian at home but dare not be so in public, an implied tweak to the conscience of a King who, while practising 'creeping to the Cross' and other conventional observances in his own chapel at Easter 1540, was prepared to countenance government sponsored preachers criticizing such practices at Paul's Cross and elsewhere? Once again Elyot seems to be encouraging the King to have the courage of his more conservative convictions. Not least as he added the detail that it was the Senate and not the priests who opposed the creation of a Christian temple. Elyot's Alexander would fail to advance true religion through lack of nerve to confront his critics in the legislative assembly, not religious belief alone.

That Elyot should use every opportunity offered by the *Historia* to applaud his King's more reactionary measures in religious policy and call explicitly for the suppression of heresy, should, of course, come as no surprise. But the call for further repressive measures is rather more problematic here than it had been in his earlier works. For the most recent and contentious act of repression had, of course, been the execution of Elyot's own friend, Thomas Cromwell.

The Degradation of Thomas Cromwell

Cromwell's fall had been as swift as it was spectacular.[19] On 10 April 1540 the French ambassador, Charles de Marillac, reported that Henry was planning 'a great change' involving his ministers, and was beginning to recall to favour those whom he had earlier rejected and was 'degrading those he had raised'. Cromwell was said to be a prime target for degradation, and his office as vicegerent-in-spirituals was reportedly already ear-marked for the conservative bishop Cuthbert Tunstal.[20] But Henry had confounded such rumours only days later—whether through genuine indecision over what he wanted, or as part of a sadistic game of cat and mouse is hard to say—when he elevated his chief minister to the ranks of the higher nobility as the Earl of Essex. This dramatic social promotion for a man whose father had been a humble blacksmith was, however, to prove only the prelude to a more emphatic and brutal degradation. For at 3 o'clock on the afternoon of Saturday 10 June, as he sat at the Council table among his fellow peers, the Captain of the Guard interrupted the meeting and arrested Cromwell in the King's name on charges of high treason. The minister was momentarily nonplussed. But he had seen too many such arrests to be ignorant of his likely fate. Getting to his feet he angrily threw his bonnet to the ground and defied his fellow councillors by asking them directly on their consciences whether he was a traitor or not. When no answer was returned he said simply that he hoped the King would allow him a swift and early death.

What followed was, however, a grotesque pantomime of social humiliation. The Duke of Norfolk stepped forward and reproached Cromwell with his 'villainies' (the word was carefully chosen, redolent of aristocratic contempt for the churlish behaviour of a 'villein' or social inferior), and then tore the insignia of the Order of the Garter from around his neck. Then William Fitzwilliam, the

Earl of Southampton untied the garter itself and pulled that off. Cromwell was literally stripped of his honour and dignity before men, many of whom he had assisted to their present positions. He was then led through a postern gate to a boat waiting to convey him to the Tower.

The symbolic degradation meted out by Norfolk and Southampton was given more concrete form within hours of his arrest. Royal agents descended upon Cromwell's properties in London and seized them and their contents for the Crown: a sure sign that the accused was already guilty in the eyes of the King. He was formally deprived of all his titles, honours, and prerogatives, and even his household servants were ordered no longer to wear his livery. The recently created Earl was being systematically erased from the annals of the peerage. It was soon being reported that he would even be denied the swifter and cleaner death by beheading that was the entitlement of every nobleman and would instead be forced to endure the agony of being 'dragged up as an ignoble person and afterwards hanged and quartered'. Indeed, on 6 July Norfolk was gloating to ambassador Marillac that the former minister's death would be 'the most ignominious in use in the courts'. His death warrant, it was said, would read simply 'Thomas Cromwell, shearman'.[21] The minister's aristocratic enemies were enjoying extracting the last ounce of humiliation from his plight, and King Henry was seemingly happy to indulge them.

The crimes of which Cromwell was accused were an eclectic mix, combining accusations of Sacramentarianism, the protection of known heretics from justice, and the frustration of Henry's attempts to establish a moderate religious settlement with wilder claims that he had offered to fight in person against the King for his beliefs and coveted the Crown for himself. Whether Henry was simply punishing Cromwell for failing to extricate him quickly enough from his recent disastrous marriage to Anne of Cleves, as he had done to Cardinal Wolsey in similar circumstances a decade earlier, or whether he genuinely believed that he harboured Sacramentarian beliefs is unclear, as is whether Norfolk, Southampton, and other noblemen, and conservative bishops such as Stephen Gardiner of Winchester had instigated these allegations themselves or were simply taking the chance to rub salt into the wounds of the fallen 'upstart'. Henry's self-pitying remark later in the year that he had been tricked into discarding the best servant he ever had by faithless counsellors hardly counts as evidence either way.[22] Neither the veracity nor the origins of the charges was ever tested, however, for Cromwell was convicted, not by the courts but by parliamentary Act of Attainder, and he was not given the opportunity to speak in his own defence. The Act was passed first in the Lords and then in the Commons without apparent opposition. It condemned Cromwell as both a heretic and a traitor, allowing the King to decide whether to burn him as the former or behead (or hang and quarter) him as the latter at pleasure. On 28 July he was taken to the scaffold and, after an eleventh hour act of clemency by his sovereign, spared the full horror of quartering by the headsman's axe (albeit the executioner made so poor a job of it that several blows were needed before his head was finally off). Henry was, after all, in giving mood, for he had chosen the day of Cromwell's death for his own wedding to his fifth wife, the young and vivacious Catherine Howard, and holiday spirits prevailed. Again, a grotesque air of carnival presided over one of Henry's direst acts of brutality.

The issue of Cromwell's social origins continued to dominate his fall to the last. In making the expected dignified confession of his sins (but not his guilt), and commending both the King and the system of justice that had condemned him, the fallen minister himself drew attention to his humble background for one last time. 'It is not unknown to many of you', he told the assembled spectators,

That I have been a great traveller in this world, and being but of a base degree, was called to high estate, and since the time I came thereunto, I have offended my Prince, for the which I ask him heartily forgiveness, and beseech you all to pray to God with me that he will forgive me.[23]

Cromwell's Fall and Elyot's Image

Given the immediacy of these events, and the obvious humiliation and injustice that they visited upon a man whom Elyot had been used to referring to as his most special and assured friend, even 'the Prince of friends',[24] how is it that he could cite Henry's burning away the residue of the heretical chaff with such apparent approval in *The Image of Governance*? It is a question that takes us to the heart of the ironic strategy behind the text, and our attempt to answer it will make clear just how audacious were the literary games that Elyot was playing in this, the last political treatise that he was to publish. For, far from avoiding the awkward question of Cromwell's punishment and the difficult associations that it carried, he seems to have written them in one form or another into almost every major anecdote *The Image*, returning again and again to the motifs of the fall of favourites, the punishment of erring ministers, and the merits or otherwise of judicial severity towards those servants closest to the royal person.

Already in the Preface Elyot was preparing his readers for the text's focus on the offences and punishments of royal servants, and stressing the value of such stories as exemplary tales for contemporary governors. The 'marvellous proceedings' of the Emperor Alexander, he observed, were evident in his handling of malefactors against his state and person, and,

In his acts and decrees, what Justice and prudence were in them contained, what severity he used, sparing neither himself nor his friends and ministers. Finally, all his life is a wonderful mirror if it be truly read and justly considered, which if ye do often look on, ye may thereby attire yourself in such fashion as men shall therefore have you in more favour and honour than if ye had on you as rich a garment as the great Turk hath any.

(bi(v)–bii)

It was, of course, a major shift in emphasis for Elyot to praise the severity and lack of mercy of a ruler, when the burden of all his previous publications had been to commend moderation and benevolence in princes. But, if the general sentiments of the Preface may have given his regular readers pause for thought, the specificity of the allusion to Alexander's sparing 'neither himself nor his friends and ministers' could not but have prompted thoughts of Cromwell and his death. Could it really be that Elyot was seeking to justify the execution of his patron and assured friend on the grounds of necessary severity, even at the expense of his own intellectual credibility? If so, then this was *a volte face* against which his criticisms of Thomas More would pale into insignificance.[25]

Such hints are, however, only part of the author's longer, ironic game plan. For, rather than endorse Henry's destruction of Cromwell, Elyot, it soon becomes clear, uses *The Image* to criticize it, indeed to present Cromwell's death as an emblem of the reign as a whole, in which royal good intentions had given way to anger and cruelty, the hallmarks of tyranny. Very much in the spirit of *Utopia* and *The Praise of Folly*, he comes ostensibly to praise Alexander Severus, and through him Henry VIII, but contrives instead to chastise him through a mixture of ironic affirmations of his virtue and accounts of deeds and policies so severe and repressive that they are, cumulatively, incompatible with any notion of a just and tolerant regime. Yet *The Image* is, characteristically, no clinical exercise in satirical character assassination. Like *Of the Knowledge*, Elyot's other extended exercise in augmented translation, the end result is a complex and at times disorienting text that seems to strike out in a number of directions at once, discharging an excess of critical and emotional energy upon diverse and sometimes mutually contradictory targets.

Given that the most obvious and disturbing aspect of Cromwell's fall was, as we have seen, the evident glee with which the established nobility, in some cases only very recently established at that,[26] fell upon the new earl, deriding his humble origins, it is perhaps not surprising to find that the issue of low birth is a prominent theme in *The Image*. What Elyot offers is, however, not the sort of defence of the virtuous man of low birth that he had provided in *The Governor* and elsewhere, following the humanist commonplace that gentility was based upon personal virtue not family history, but a series of angry sketches of the viciousness of the low-born, and the folly of raising them to high office at the expense of the established elite. One of the most deplorable aspects of the reign of Heliogabalus, the text asserts, was his elevation of vicious churls to high office:

He...promoted to the greatest dignities of the public weal common bawds, notable ribalds, solicitors and furtherers of dishonest appetites, oftentimes cooks and devisers of lecherous confections and sauces. Semblably, by such persons he sold dignities, authorities, and offices in the public weal. He also elected into the Senate and to the rooms of great captains, dukes, and governors of countries, most vile personages not having regard to any age, gentleness of blood, merit, possessions, or substance. He had of his privy counsel in all his acts, two carters, the one named Protogenes and the other Cordius.

(Aiv–iv(v))[27]

Dismissing noble councillors such as Sabinus and Ulpian, and having 'Silvinus the noble orator' put to death, 'the greatest rooms and affairs of the empire he committed to minstrels, players of interludes, and disards':

Also of his rabble of brothels, to some he gave the rule and governance of the youth of the city, some he made rulers of the Senate, to other he gave pre-eminence and sovereignty over all them that were gentlemen.

(ʙi(v))[28]

Elyot reserves particular hostility for a low-born servant for whom Heliogabalus had special favour:

one named Zoticus, who for familiarity used between them was taken of all the chief officers for the emperor's husband. This Zoticus, under the colour of the said familiarity, sold all the sayings and doings of the emperor, intending to accumulate abundance of riches by promising fair to many men but finally deceiving all men. For, coming out of the emperor's privy chamber after that he had heard every man speak that sued unto him, to some he would say, 'This said I to th'emperor of you', unto an other, 'Of you I heard the emperor say this today'. To diverse he would say, 'Your matter or request shall come thus to pass'. As is the fashion of such manner of persons, which, being from a base condition admitted of princes into overmuch familiarity, they sell the fame and renown of their masters.

(ʙi–i(v))[29]

Eventually the Emperor's support for such folk became intolerable to his more virtuous and high-born subjects, and his soldiers and household servants allied together to murder him, to everyone's evident relief.

What are we to make of these passages? Here indeed is all the lofty contempt for one of low birth raised to high office that had spilled out from Henry's councillors when they were let loose on Cromwell. And in the figure of Zoticus there is not a little of Cromwell himself, in his manifestation as patronage broker and principal conduit for contact between many an importunate suitor and the King.[30] Indeed, might we not detect here more than a hint of Elyot's own frustration at the years that he spent petitioning Cromwell with little success for redress of his financial losses in royal service? Certainly a good deal of hostility seems to have gone into the portrait of the minister who emerges from the King's chamber to assure suitors that all is well, when nothing has actually been said to improve their fortunes. Perhaps again it is wise to conclude that Elyot never writes from a dispassionate, objective position, and that his own emotions and personal obsessions colour and animate the fictions he creates, even at times giving them a life of their own, and taking them into areas of himself that he might in other circumstances have wished to leave unexplored.[31] But if, in associating such low-born counsellors as Zoticus with the tyranny of Helioga-balus (who 'with voluptuous and monstrous living in such wise corrupted the city of Rome that therein unneth [hardly] remained any step of virtue or honesty'

(Aii)) Elyot was able both to imply his support for the destruction of Cromwell and exorcize some of his own demons with regard to his lack of promotion and favour, what followed would offer considerably less comfort to Henry VIII and his counsellors.

Alexander Severus's first act on being elevated to imperial office on the death of Heliogabalus was, Elyot notes, to purge his own palace of all the low-born sycophants and hypocrites whom his predecessor had brought there, and to reduce the royal household to a reasonable size (BV):

> First he discharged all ministers which the monstrous beast Heliogabalus had indiscreetly promoted of most vile and dishonest personages, banishing also out of his palace all such as he might by any means know to be persons infamed. Semblably flatterers as well those which therefore were favoured of his predecessor as them whom he apprehended abusing him with semblable falsehood.
>
> (Dv(v)–Ei) [32]

Likewise, 'the whole Senate and judges' were purged of such men and the civil administration and military garrisons staffed with more virtuous and reliable men.

That the new Emperor shared the contempt for low-born upstarts voiced by the narrator is made abundantly clear, for readers are told that another of his early decrees stated that henceforward no descendant of a bondsman (slave) could become a Senator, but rather, 'the order of Knighthood was the place from whence were fetched the plants of the Senate, that is to say, from whence the senators were elected' (Fi). And yet, despite the conspicuous talk of reform and renewal, the first sustained example of life at the Alexandrian court that Elyot relates takes us back to precisely the same situation that he had described in his account of Zoticus and his crimes. There was in Alexander's service, Elyot observes, 'an ambitious and vainglorious counsellor', whose corrupt practices the Emperor eventually discovered and punished condignly. Indeed, it is his punishment that is the point of the story, for as the text goes on to explain, this counsellor, one Vetronius Turinus, was subjected to a torment that might initially strike readers as 'over vehement and grievous', but it would prove upon fuller explanation that the Emperor's 'said rigour in judgement was necessarily used, and with equality in justice, deserving in no part to be reprieved' (Fv). The crime that warrants such rigorous punishment has its own interest for us, however, as it again concerns the proximity of a counsellor to his imperial master, the trust that is placed in him, and the way that he abuses it to frustrate suitors to his own advantage.

Turinus, Elyot declares, so delighted in the company of his prince, and in the favour afforded him, that he sought by every means to increase Alexander's reliance upon him:

> And therefore he had continual suit made unto him, as well by them that had suits to the emperor in their particular causes as others that looked for offices or great promotions. To every man apart he would promise his favour, and therefore received great rewards and presents... And oftentimes in a day he would come from the emperor into the chamber

of presence or place where suitors awaited, and of whom he had received money to them would he say that he had remembered them and in their request or matter received good comfort, when indeed he spoke not thereof one word.

$$(\text{fv}(\text{v}))^{33}$$

The similarities between the stories of Turinus and Zoticus are too obvious to be accidental, and Elyot's choice to narrate both cannot have been made without careful thought. It is possible that he intended them to emphasize the contrast between the treatments of the two offenders, setting Alexander's righteous indignation against Turinus against Heliogabalus's apparent toleration of Zoticus and his abuses. Certainly it was possible to use the Turinus story to reflect well upon Alexander, as Erasmus had done in his *Adage* 'Fumos vendere' ('To Sell Smoke').[34] But if a contrast between the emperors was what was intended, the stories also illustrate the similarities between Alexander and his monstrous cousin. For both men fall victim to the same abuses, and both allow them to continue, apparently oblivious to their effects for some considerable time. It is notably only when Turinus had 'gathered much treasure' and was grudged at by many of those whom he had deceived, that word of his behaviour 'came to the emperor's ear, by what means I know not' (fv(v)–gi). And, given that the *Historia* has Alexander in control of Turinus's exposure from the outset, 'deputing' a suitor to set a trap for him which he will later spring, rather than simply waiting to hear of his crimes by unknown means, Elyot actually increases the sense of his Emperor's culpability in retelling the story. There is consequently a nice irony to his comment that 'such abuses cannot be long hid from princes' (gi) that serves to undercut the apparent praise of his actions. Indeed, if anything, the story of Turinus is more destructive to Alexander's reputation in Elyot's account than that of Zoticus was to his predecessor. For it follows a passage in which Alexander delivers a lengthy lecture on his intention to be affable and accessible to all his subjects ('[That is] not only mine opinion herein, but also my determined sentence' he had announced), rejecting the suggestion of one of his older counsellors that he should appear only rarely in public and give audience to few (di–div(v)).[35] That he should soon after fall victim to an abuse that centres on him not seeing his suitors in person but relying on an intermediary to conduct his business, doubly undermines his position.

Having finally been made aware of Turinus's deceit, Alexander subjects him to a very public arrest with distinct echoes of Cromwell's own fall.[36] And the swift conviction and exemplary execution that followed were indeed savage, as Elyot had warned that they would be:

He was judged by the emperor to be led into the open market place where most resort was of the people, and there being bounden to a stake, with smoke made of green sticks and wet stubble to be smouldered to death. And during the time of his execution the emperor commanded a beadle to cry, 'With fume shall he die, that fumes hath sold'. But to the intent that men should not think that for one offence the judgement was too cruel and rigorous, or ever Turinus was condemned to die the emperor made diligent search and by evident process it was found that Turinus had often and in many causes received money of both parties, promising to advance their cause to the emperor.

$$(\text{Gi}(v))^{37}$$

Even in a London growing used to the gruesome spectacle of public burnings and the disembowelling of convicted traitors, the notion of deliberately choking a victim to death prior to burning would probably have seemed a little too ingenious in its cruelty to accord with justice; not least because of the detail of the grotesque pun intoned as a parodic litany as Turinus died: 'with fume [smoke] shall he die, that fumes [lies] hath sold'.[38] Did Elyot, when reading the relevant passage in the *Historia* (or his notes from that text), hear a dim echo of the punning death of Friar Forest that increased the contemporary resonance of the scene?

Whereas the account of Turinus in the *Historia* ends with his execution, Elyot adds critical emphasis to his story by appending a further passage of his own devising, in which Alexander and his counsellors discuss the merits of the fallen servant's punishment. Notionally the scene should precede the execution itself, but in Elyot's text it follows it. And, interestingly, given the fact that Cromwell's fate was judged by Parliament and not in the courts, it is in the Senate that Elyot chooses to place the debate. (Gi(v)–Gii). Unlike the supine Lords and Commons of 1540, however, the Roman Senate proves a less tractable body, suggesting a range of punishments for Turinus' offence from a public rebuke and restitution to the injured party to beheading, all of which fall short of the grizzly death determined by Alexander (Gii–ii(v)). Thus the Emperor is forced, in a speech several times longer than the account of Turinus's crimes and punishment, to justify the severity of his verdict to a sceptical audience. It is a theme that will become his signature contribution to political debate in the course of *The Image*, repeated in numerous scenes and passages. Here his argument rests upon the personal nature of Turinus's treasons and the potential damage that he has done to the Emperor's good name through his betrayal of trust:

The treason done to me aggrieveth the trespass. Is it not treason to conspire the destruction of thy sovereign lord most of all, of whom thou art entirely favoured and put in great trust[?] Is there any diversity between the sticking of him with a dagger or killing him with poison and by some circumstance to cause his people to rebel against him and in their fury to slay him?

(Giii)

All of this might appear as something of an overreaction to Turinus's offence, but Alexander persists, and it quickly becomes clear that it is the sense of personal betrayal that drives his determination to punish his former servant with the utmost severity:

[A]fter I was elect emperor, he, craftily smelling out my disposition, by little and little acquainted himself with some of those of whom for their virtues I had best opinion, and counterfeiting their manners, he at the last so aptly set forth such gravity, which he adorned also with a wonderful sharpness and promptitude of wit, that he obtained to be highly recommended unto me by the wisest men of my counsel, by whose advice first I made him one of my treasurers.[39] Finally I called him near me and made him of my privy council, wherein we found him so necessary that in our opinion his sentences were equivalent and sometime surmounted them that had been in most estimation.

(Giii(v))

As a consequence, Alexander declares, 'I did advance him, as ye know, to the highest dignities within the city, except the consul[ship]' (Giii(v)–Giv). Yet, since his promotion, Turinus has repaid his master's generosity with treachery:

[H]e hath deceived and mocked us with his hypocrisy, abusing our simplicity and winning our favour, and not our favour only, but also our credence and trust, whereby he might finally work to his private commodity and to our confusion...But principally and above all other am I most indamaged. For I, unawares and innocent, being brought into the hatred of men, should be destroyed before that I might know that I were in peril...

(Giv–iv(v))

Thus both the severity of the punishment and its novelty are justified by analogy with the personal nature and 'singularity' of the crime:

And as he was with us in singular favour and trust, and therein like to none other, so ought his death to be singular and strange, that by the novelty thereof it may be more terrible, whereby other may fear from henceforth to abuse such manner our affability.

(Hi)

But Alexander has not finished. There are still more extravagant analogies to work through before his argument can be completed:

Finally, if any common person, never receiving of me any benefit, would report in the ears of the people that I went about to change the estate of the weal public of this noble city, to slay all the senators, to withdraw the people from their ancient liberties, and finally to bring the majesty of the empire into a tyranny, and by false information exciteth and stirreth the Senate and people to hate me and covet my destruction, [and] such one proved at the last to have said falsely, I believe ye would not think [him] only worthy to die, but ye would with your own hands dismember him and pluck him in pieces.

(Gv)

Consequently, if they thought such a person worthy of death,

Why should you not think that Turinus, whom I most favoured and was about me most secret, not by reporting evil of me (which perchance would not be believed), but by actual deeds and openly...and by these means quenching the good opinion and love that all men had toward me, and changing it to a grudge and hatred, they thinking that Turinus did all thing by our appointment...why should ye not, I say, think that such a one deserved to die[?].

(Gv(v)–Hi)

At the conclusion of this curious amalgam of arguments and assertions, the assembled Senators appear stupefied, abashed by the vehemence and volume of Alexander's speech rather than convinced by its logic:

There was no man offered to reply thereto, perceiving him rather moved with zeal than with any particular displeasure, and to say the truth, when they had pondered his considerations, not finding sufficient argument to confound his opinion, finally, they all being in number fifty wise and honourable counsellors, rejoiced that they had so wise and virtuous an emperor, which preferred Justice and the weal of his people before any private affection of singular appetite.

(Hi)

The silence which greets the conclusion of the speech, while the Senators seek to explain to themselves the nature of the Emperor's very apparent distress—settling in the end for the diplomatic conclusion that it is 'zeal' rather than real displeasure—is only one manifestation of their awkwardness.[40] They then, rather than being immediately convinced, consider possible ripostes to his claims, eventually failing to respond through lack of 'sufficient' material rather than the will to oppose, before 'finally' (and Elyot's positioning of that word just where it can exert the maximum comic leverage on the scene shows that he can write with great wit and subtlety when he chooses) they break out into their far from spontaneous bout of 'rejoicing' at their ruler's wisdom. It is a scene of masterful dry irony. *Finally* the Senators realize that a complete affirmation of Alexander's angry tirade is the only response that will be acceptable to him, and set about the task of providing it; but the penny takes an awfully long time to drop.

That irony is the presiding genius of this scene is evident from the nature of Alexander's assertions as well as the manner of their reception. For the Senators' celebration of his putting 'justice and the weal of his people before any private affection of singular appetite' sits extraordinarily awkwardly following a speech that is one long testimony to the private motives and sense of personal betrayal that have prompted the Emperor's judgement. His speech proceeds from the claim that 'the treason done to me aggrieveth the trespass', through a series of allegations of personal injury ('he hath deceived and mocked us', 'abusing our simplicity and winning our favour', 'principally and above all other men am I most indamaged') to the conclusion that it is the close and personal nature of Turinus's relationship with the Emperor that justifies the extraordinary severity of his death ('as he was with us in singular favour and trust...so ought his death to be singular and strange'). The whole speech, carefully crafted by Elyot himself, is a monument to self-regard and wounded pride (precisely the kinds of 'private affection' that the Senators commend it for *not* displaying) in which variations of the personal pronoun appear no fewer than fifty-three times and its possessive variants a further twenty-three times. Hence it would not take too great an effort on the part of Elyot's readers to realize that he is taking them deep into ironic territory in this particular depiction of Alexandrian justice. Indeed, what is true of this scene is equally so of *The Image* as a whole. For the book offers in its portrayal of its imperial hero a decidedly *Utopian* exercise in ironic wit, in which both a knowledge of classical literature and a sharp eye for internal inconsistencies provide the keys to its hidden satirical meanings.

If Elyot really did begin his translation in the early 1530s, he may not have initially intended it as an ironic exercise. Indeed he may have translated those passages from the *Historia* which he eventually reproduced in *The Image*, as he suggests in the Preface, with the intention of their forming the basis of a companion volume to *The Governor*, dealing with governmental authority and the 'rigour and equality in punishment' characteristic of the Roman state at its best. For he had promised in the earlier text to 'treat more amply' that theme 'in a place more propitious for that purpose'.[41] In this context the material in Lampridius's *Life* of Alexander might of itself form the basis of a quite straightforward exposition of the benefits of a severe but just governor. But, by the summer of 1540 the notions of severity and 'rigour and equality in punishment' in the state had taken on other, more powerful and rebarbative associations in Elyot's mind, and his enthusiasm for eulogizing them in a *speculum principis* had waned. At that point he may well have looked at his notes (if notes they were) about an Emperor who was 'given the name of Severus by the soldiers because of his strictness, and his punishments were in some cases too harsh',[42] in a new light, seeing in them the potential foundations of an ironic commentary on contemporary events. Perhaps, as Baumann suggests, taking his cue from the ironic pastiche of an imperial biography in Guevara's *Libro Aureo*, he then spent the second half of the year working the material up with that daring, savagely critical new agenda in mind.[43] He used roughly half of the material in Lampridius's *Life* in his own text, adding to it anecdotes, speeches, and a copious amount of new exposition of his own devising,[44] turning the original encomiastic narrative into a far darker, more grimly comic portrait of a tyrant. And he hinted at the liberties that he had taken with his source text by attributing the new work, not to Lampridius but to the archetypally insubstantial figure of 'Eucolpius'. The elaborate fiction of the disappearing Eucolpian text, the equally unlikely sounding Neapolitan bibliophile Pudericus, and the chance recovery of his notes when searching for other things, served to cover Elyot's tracks sufficiently to escape accusations of political malice, but equally well signalled his real intentions to his more astute readers. Once alerted to his contemporary purpose, those readers are led by the narrator into a looking-glass world of reversal and inversion in which cruelty is commended and tyranny presented as good kingship. For *The Image* proves to be a mirror for princes in the literal sense, as the neat image of the reader using its reflection to dress himself before stepping out to meet his public suggests. And mirrors, of course, show the world its image in reverse. If any reader had not taken the hint from the games with lost books and imaginary authors in the Preface, and turned to the text still expecting to find a straightforward translation of the work of the mysterious Eucolpius, then Elyot's marginal citation of his real sources in the pseudo-history of Lampridius were there to offer a further clue to his real strategy.

Satire and Irony in the England of Henry VIII

The value of irony as a satirical device had, of course, been displayed to spectacular effect in Chaucer's *General Prologue* to *The Canterbury Tales*, a text that, as we have seen, had gained a new currency for Henrician readers through Thynne and Tuke's 1532 edition of the poet's *Works*. And irony had taken on a new life in scholarly circles as a result of the humanists' recovery of classical satire, both through translations, such as Erasmus and More's edition of the Dialogues of Lucian, and original compositions such as *Utopia* and *The Praise of Folly*. Such works, written in happier times before Luther's challenge to Rome and Henry's Great Matter, were so resistant to simplistic readings that they still challenge scholars to account for the full range of their effects and intended meanings. But in subsequent, more troubled times, others were willing to explore the uses of irony in more direct ways to challenge the internal contradictions and injustices of Henry VIII's Reformation.

On Passion Sunday (2 April) 1536, John Skyp, one of Anne Boleyn's more independent-minded chaplains, had preached a sermon before the King in the Chapel Royal that had used irony and analogy to savage effect in mocking the motives and morality of those who advanced the case for religious reform in Council and Parliament. Skyp was later called in for interrogation by the Privy Council, and the surviving list of the questions put to him on that occasion leaves no doubt about either the nature of his sermon or the sensitivity with which it was received by the King and his court. A number of those questions are worth quoting in full, as they also have an obvious bearing on Elyot's dialogues in general and *The Image of Governance* in particular. Skyp's interlocutors asked him,

Whether a preacher speaking generally of any notable crime or vice in such wise as all his audience doth as plainly perceive what person he meaneth as though he specified him by his name, doth slander that person?

Where he sayeth that nowadays councillors will not move a King otherwise to anything but as they see him disposed and inclined to the same . . . whether by these words he do not accuse the King's council as flatterers and deceivers of the King's grace[?] . . . If he will say that he meant not of the King's council, then was his sermon not mete for the audience for there were none other councillors of any other king present.

To what end tendeth th'example of Solomon, which he sayeth in the beginning of his reign was much beloved of his people because he governed them very gently and wisely, ever having respect to their common wealth, but after was un-noble and defamed, himself taking many wives and concubines and laying sore burdens and yokes on his subjects, but that he intended in his mind to touch the King's grace with the said similitude, albeit he showed not his mind in plain and express words[?]

What goodness or honesty is in the said preacher to use such ironies or mocks against the Parliament as he spoke under this manner in his sermon: 'It is not to be thought that there is anything done but for the commonwealth in his high council or court of Parliament'... Item, let the preacher be examined upon his oath whether he spoke not all this sentence ironice or mockishly in displeasure and rebuke of the Parliament... for in all ironies the meaning is contrary to the words.[45]

Such questions suggest a good deal about Elyot's own ironic and allusive literary strategies; for he used many of the same devices himself. The claim to be speaking generally on moral issues, and defaming no man in particular, although 'all his audience doth as plainly perceive what person he meaneth as though he specified him by name', was one which he had deployed himself more than once, and would seem a particularly apt summary of his treatment of Cranmer in *Pasquil the Plain*, as well as his allusions to Henry VIII throughout *The Governor* and in *The Image*. Similarly, the fact that Skyp's interrogators were ready to apply any general comments about counsellors 'now a days' to specific contemporary circumstances, for otherwise 'was his sermon not mete for the audience for there were none other councillors of any other king present', suggests the acute receptiveness of Tudor audiences, and especially courtly ones, to the possibility of contemporary allusions in what they were hearing or reading. Hence men like Skyp and Elyot could make their political points through analogy, 'ironice or mockishly', confident that their intentions would be detected and understood by their intended audiences.

Still more pointedly, the questions posed to Skyp reveal how sensitive—and how habituated—courtly and elite audiences could be to the possibility that any allusion to vice or virtue in kings could be a comment upon Henry VIII himself, even (or perhaps especially) if such allusions touched upon the acutely sensitive subjects of the taking or rejecting of wives, the placing of undue burdens on subjects, or the sudden loss of royal popularity. Thus we gain a sense of how resonant the numerous comments on the sanctity of marriage and the virtues of wives that litter Elyot's works may have been for their original readers. One thinks not only of *The Defence of Good Women* but also to the passage in *The Image*, published less than a year after Henry had contracted his fifth marriage and Robert Barnes had harangued him from the block on the importance of marital fidelity, in which Elyot imagines Alexander Severus outlining some extremely negative views on the possibility of an emperor ever contracting a wholly satisfactory marriage:

I find in my fantasy that the taking of a wife should be to the public weal and to myself more dangerous than fruitful... if she shall be much younger than I am, perchance she shall not be so apt for generation of children... If she shall be as old, or older, then shall I bring myself to much unquietness and trouble of mind, for... it is not... four years ago that the abominable monster, my kinsman Heliogabalus left not only the city of Rome, but also all . . . Italy . . . polluted with detestable lechery . . . Wherefore, if I should marry one of the said city or territory, although I found her by fame and experience a maiden, yet should not that discharge my mind of suspicion, thinking always that she was rather so kept by restraint of liberty than by her own chastity, considering that she did hear or see daily such wanton allectives and provocations to lechery . . .

(oiv–iv(v))

The potency and specificity of the passage would, of course, only increase during the following year, when Catherine Howard herself proved to be no maiden on her marriage and was executed for adultery.

As in *Utopia* or *The Praise of Folly*, the irony in *The Image* is not consistently or universally applied. Each text offers its readers what appears (to modern eyes at least) a bewildering mixture of the admirable and the seemingly grotesque presented as if it were all of equal merit and virtue. At times each author seems to provide a genuinely idealistic account of how the world might be if all men and women acted with good will and for the good of the commonwealth. At others the practices described seem to be the most savage or absurd exaggeration of contemporary vices or social ills. Thus in *The Image* Alexander is at times presented, as we have seen, as a religious conservative of a kind that would have appealed to Elyot's sensibilities. And elsewhere he is described as an ideal blend of affability and self-denial,[46] dedicated to physical and mental self-improvement ('he of his own courage never suffered any day to pass without exercising himself in letters or in feats martial' (Aii)) and with an attitude towards scholars and writers that was everything that the Elyotian good counsellor could desire ('he loved all men that were learned and feared them also, lest they should write if him anything sharply or to his rebuke' (Aii(v)),[47] yet elsewhere he seems the epitome of cruelty and self-regard.

There is, at first glance, much to commend in a good deal of what the text says of Alexander and his governance. His first action on gaining his imperial powers is, as we have seen, to purge his own household of sycophants and libertines. And in many ways the polity that he establishes from the ruins of his predecessor's regime does appear to be a humanist ideal.[48] His reforms, all enacted 'by the consent of the Senate and people' (Iii(v)), provided for the education of all children and youths in letters, physical sports, and the basics of a trade (for boys) and housekeeping and morality (for girls). Sixty 'Conservators of the weal public' were appointed to oversee the well-being of all children, to ensure that householders kept a moderate diet (Mi(v)–Mii), and observed the sumptuary laws that regulated the dress appropriate to each social class. Markets were carefully regulated and the prices and quality of the goods sold were monitored. Idleness, the root of vice and disorder, was banished from the state by the establishment of programmes of exercises for each class, and in a measure close to Elyot's heart, all those found guilty of dicing were treated by the law as if they were madmen or natural fools, their goods and money being put into trust on their behalf until they could prove that they had abandoned their pernicious pastime (Lii(v)–Liii). Public bathhouses were renovated or built afresh, with pleasant gardens for recreation and the practice of athletic sports placed conveniently adjacent to them (Iiv(v)–Kiii).[49] The result was a state in which public conduct and private morality were brought into harmony through a combination of good example and judicial severity (Hiv(v)–Ii). Public works throughout Italy extended the benefits of Roman renewal across the peninsula. Elyot even allows himself a momentary reverie in contemplating the creation of a grand new municipal library, a subject wholly of his own devising. Built in circular fashion with separate galleries for each of the Arts and Sciences, each decorated with appropriate tables and figures, this library is designed around a central garden in which readers,

might walk or sit at their pleasure, and communicate each with other that which they had read or perceived. And to these place there failed not to come daily a great number of gentlemen.

(Li(v))

Ever mindful of the practicalities, even in such a haven of scholarly endeavour, Elyot is also careful to lay down a series of strict by-laws against the theft or defacing of books, each of which would be secured in its own 'hutch' or receptacle, as in a late-medieval chained library, and brought to readers one at a time.[50]

While some of the Alexandrian reforms seem to be exercises in wish-fulfilment on Elyot's part, however, others seem to fly in the face of common sense, and to promise quite the reverse of prosperity and tranquillity for the commonwealth. As a good humanist, Elyot probably sympathized with the Emperor's insistence that strangers and visitors to Rome should be welcomed and well treated, yet restricted to a strict quota so as not to arouse resentments at their numbers or prosperity. He might also have seen merit in having all 'vile' manual labour performed by bondsmen and strangers, leaving Roman citizens free to ply trades that would not leave their natures corrupted or their bodily strength decayed (Iiv(v)). Similar proposals appear in *Utopia*, and have impeccable classical origins. But could he, with his experience of both the law courts and the turbulent politics of London's mercantile culture, have really thought that banning all citizens from acting as 'merchant adventurers' and placing the wholesale importation trade in the hands of strangers would lead to fairer treatment for native craftsmen and lower prices at market? (Iiv(v))[51]

But if some of the policies that Elyot seems to commend appear merely a little foolhardy, others seem to offer a more pointed commentary on the failings of the Henrician regime. In the wake of the dissolution of the smaller monasteries, considerable controversy had arisen over how the revenues of the suppressed estates should best be used for the benefits of the nation. It was a central theme of 'Erasmian' arguments for the reform of 'unproductive' religious houses that the wealth invested in them was essentially lost to the commonwealth; wasted on keeping the supposedly poor brethren in an indolent and self-indulgent lifestyle. Hence evangelicals and reforming catholics alike could find common ground in the idea that some at least of the dissolutions were beneficial to society if the wealth created was to be used in founding schools, the relief of the poor, and the repair of the decaying fabric of towns and villages. This was a case that Anne Boleyn and a number of heads of religious houses had tried to put to Henry VIII just before her fall. But the revenues of the Henrician suppression had not been diverted to such good causes, and by 1540 a good deal of the former monastic land had been sold to the existing landed elite (indeed Elyot had himself bought up lands in Cambridgeshire once owned by Eynsham Abbey in 1539)[52] as a means of securing their compliance in the reforms and bringing ready cash into the royal coffers. In the light of the inevitable sense of disillusionment that followed, Elyot's description of the expensive programme of public works funded by Alexander's reform of the Roman state would have had a particular edge to it. Nowhere would this have been more obvious than in the statement, added by Elyot himself, that the revenues raised by the suppression of traditional Roman festivals and religious practices ('the plays called *Florales* and *Lupercales* and the abominable ceremonies of Isis' (Miii))[53] were spent immediately on the creation of four new hospitals for the poor and needy in the city itself and just outside its walls; so here at least Alexander's actions offer an implied rebuke to Henry's own self-interested behaviour.

But, over and above the potential for irony and subversive comment in the detail of Alexander's reforms, there is a wider and more direct criticism of his governance, and hence of the Henrician regime, in the very presentation of the Emperor's character itself, and in the characteristic severity with which he imposed and was prepared to enforce his reforms. The Alexandrian state is, as has been implied, a regime founded on fear. Ministers and courtiers are savagely punished if they fall short of the Emperor's requirements, and the populace as a whole is held in check by the prospect of Alexander's vengeance should they transgress his laws. Indeed, hardly a page passes without the reader finding some reminder of aptness of the Emperor's adopted epithet 'Severus' and the effect of his severity upon his subjects. It is a point that Elyot goes out of his way to emphasize, extending and reinforcing those references to severity that appear in his source text, and excluding or ironizing those statements and speeches of the Emperor's in the *Historia* that tend to soften his image, suggest a modest side to his character, or demonstrate his milder character traits.[54] Despite the frequent reassurances that he is in fact affable and slow to anger, it is clear that his subjects thought otherwise and acted accordingly. Even the examples cited of his benevolence and willingness to be corrected by his people tend to create the opposite impression.

When, for example, he tours the city in disguise to check up on his officers and hear what the people say of him and his regime, his subjects, we are told, occasionally recognize him, but rather than approach him, they 'durst not salute him or make any sign of knowledge unto him', 'dreading his severity' (Miv(v)): a point not made in the *Historia*. When a retired soldier abused an old woman, the Emperor, hearing of it, degraded him to the status of a slave and gave him to the woman to work for her upkeep. When 'the residue of the soldiers were therewith grieved, he persuaded them to be therewith contented, and did put them in fear to grudge at it (Rii(v)).[55] And Elyot leaves little room for doubt about how compelling Alexander's persuasions could be. 'Oftentimes', he notes, 'he discharged whole legions, never fearing his army', and proceeds to relate a story of how, on one occasion, because his garrison in Antioch had frequented the 'brothels, taverns, and bains [bathhouses] in the Greek fashion' (Rii(v)–Riii(v)), he had imprisoned the offenders, and threatened to deprive the remainder of the legion of their citizenship if they protested further about their fate. Having put down the threatened mutiny he magnanimously restored the imprisoned soldiers to the ranks, but had all of their officers beheaded 'because that through their negligence the soldiers passed their time riotously' (Riii(v)).[56]

Elyot even contrives to make Alexander's offers of patronage sound like veiled threats:

If he found any man to whom he had either given nothing or that which in value was not equal unto his merits, he called him and said: 'What is the cause that thou asketh nothing of me? Desirest thou to have me thy debtor? Ask somewhat that, lacking promotion thou complain not of me'.

(Hiii)[57]

And always it is the merciless severity, the seemingly excessive and often grotesquely apt or 'witty' nature of the punishment meted out to offenders, that is stressed, and which provokes horrified responses from the Emperor's subjects:

To one of his secretaries which forged an untrue bill in his council, he commanded the sinews of his fingers wherewith he did write to be cut, and so to be utterly banished, wherefore he was called Severus, which is as much to say as sharp or rigorous, for severity is rigour in punishment according to the quality of the offence, having respect to a good purpose without any desire of vengeance.

(Fiv(v))[58]

But, as the example of the 'smouldering' of Turinus that Elyot goes on to narrate at this point amply demonstrates, when the definitions of the quality of the offence and the goodness of the purpose are the prerogative of the Emperor himself, the line between punishment and vengeance is easily crossed and the desire to produce a fitting punishment can often be hard to distinguish from a sadistic delight in devising ever more novel and horrific punishments.

The text is, like the *Historia*, swift to assert that anger was an emotion unknown to Alexander. Despite working late into the night and rising before dawn to resume his labours when the needs of the state required it,

Notwithstanding he never showed countenance of weariness, ne to be in any part froward or angry, but had always one manner of visage and in all things seemed merry and pleasant.

(Nii–ii(v))[59]

But, read in the context of *The Image* as a whole, such assertions can only appear ironic, the kind of *faux naïve* statements that Chaucer put into the mouth of the narrator of his *General Prologue* when exposing the vices and failings of his more culpable pilgrims. For it was not many pages earlier that the narrator had described the quite extraordinary anger and very un-'merry' visage with which the Emperor always greeted cases of bribery and extortion, when 'he immediately would vomit up choler and his face being as it were on fire, of a long time [he] might not speak one word' (Fiii).[60]

Indeed, anger is a regular feature of Alexander's response to situations of all kinds as *The Image* describes them, most notably when justice and punishment are the issues under discussion. When he observed a group of commoners provoking and insulting some gentlemen who were wrestling in the grounds of the imperial palace (again it is interesting that it is the 'upstart' rudeness of the low-born to their social superiors that provokes Alexander's wrath), he took 'a vehement displeasure' at their presumption, and 'being therefore so angry as erst he was never', he summoned all the commons of the city to the amphitheatre, where he 'abashed' them 'with a displeasant countenance' and berated them as traitors to Rome unworthy of the title 'good Romans' (Piii(v)–Qiv(v)). Only after securing the submission of the whole class to his will did he return to the palace to order the particular unruly individuals (each a substantial property owner in his own right) to be degraded and bound as a slave to one of the gentlemen he had insulted until he had made him richer than he was (Ri(v)). When, on another occasion (again, seemingly of Elyot's own invention), the son of a senator disdainfully refused to acknowledge Alexander as they passed each other in the street, the Emperor 'incontinent discharged the father of the said young man out of the Senate, saying that he was not worthy nor mete to be of that reverend company... since he had so ill brought up his son' (Pii(v)–Piii).

The obvious disparity between the narrator's frequent praise of Alexander's lack of anger or desire for vengeance and his accounts of his actual behaviour undermines much more than our since of the Emperor's personal equilibrium, however. For the good ruler, as Elyot had repeatedly asserted in *The Governor* and his dialogues, was characterized above all else by his capacity to judge transgressors of his laws free from all ire and rancour. Hence, to draw attention by such ironic means to Alexander's frequent anger at offenders against his person or regime—to the extent that he would become speechless and vomit up choler at the thought of bribery and extortion—was tacitly to demonstrate that he was no good governor. Similarly the ineffectiveness of his justification of the extravagant cruelty meted out to Turinus and other malefactors, serves to undercut the claims that such punishments are just. Rather than present a straightforward portrait of an ideal emperor as it claims to do, then, the text actually presents the mirror image of such a king, a tyrant who dresses himself in the rhetoric and trappings of virtuous rule.

Elyot is neither coy nor overly subtle about the suggestion that tyranny is an issue where Alexander is concerned. For, far from the word being unspoken in the text, the Emperor repeatedly has to defend himself before his subjects against allegations, whether real or imagined, of tyranny. On the occasion that he rebuked the entire common estate in the amphitheatre, for example, he had begun by acknowledging that, perhaps his subjects thought he was 'moved with some private displeasure for something touching our person, or that we were altered from our late temperance unto a tyranny' (Piv(v)–Qi). He was quick to assure them that this was not the case. 'Tyranny, as we have ever had it in extreme detestation, so do we now most abhor it' (Qi). Unlike his predecessor and 'cousin germane' Heliogabalus, he had not, he claimed, been roused to anger by any damage to his private person, but by the slight to the entire aristocracy and so to the City itself (Qi–Qii). Yet, however hard he tries, Alexander can never quite shake off the association with the tyrannous methods deployed by his predecessor. Like those other 'cousins germane', Gnatho and Harpocrates in *Pasquil the Plain*, Heliogabalus and Alexander seem to share as many similarities as they have differences. Indeed, even as the latter rebukes the Senate and people that they had chosen and elected the tyrants Caligula and Heliogabalus, and so shared in the responsibility for their crimes, one cannot help recalling that they had also chosen him for government, and by the same process.[61]

To be accused of tyranny once would seem unfortunate, to be accused on numerous occasions begins to look more ominous. And Alexander is accused repeatedly in the text, often in the most unlikely places. Having, he claims, described 'the virtuous severity of sharpness' of his subject, Elyot then proposes, three-quarters of the way through *The Image*, to turn to a description of his 'gentilesse, patience and affability' (Siv(v)). But, even here the discussion returns almost immediately to the themes of punished servants and tyrannous rule. For the only example cited of imperial benignity is, again, apparently one of Elyot's own devising. It concerns an agreement brokered by Alexander between the city's usurers and their debtors,[62] a settlement that was so harsh for some of the more culpable debtors that it left them enslaved 'in most vile servitude' to their creditors for a period of years, and prompted accusations of tyranny against its architect:

This ordinance being put in due execution, it was thought at the first of some men to be very cruel, but after it was once perceived what a marvellous frugality or temperance of living was suddenly found . . . then extolled they the excellent wit and virtue of the most noble emperor. And, where afor they called him cruel and tyrannous, they ceased not to name him equal to the gods, most benign and most gracious, confessing that, had not been his severity, they all, with the city and empire had utterly perished.

(Tiii)

Elyot's characteristic method is to show Alexander behaving in an apparently arbitrary and tyrannical manner, and then to have him convince his subjects (with varying degrees of success) that he was acting in the best interests of everyone. But where one such example might be taken at face value, a whole series of them has a quite different effect. If Alexander looks and acts like a tyrant, is frequently seen by his subjects as a tyrant, and even his eulogizer's examples of his benign character end in accusations of tyranny, readers are entitled to conclude that there may be truth in the accusation after all.

An insight into Elyot's likely intentions here can be gained from another anecdote he cites concerning Alexander's punishment of 'one of his most privy servants' who had been discovered promising to advance a suitor to an office in the judiciary in return for a bribe of 100 pieces of gold. The man (another of those individuals who had been appointed by the Emperor as part of his anti-corruption drive, but who had proved to be not such a good choice after all) was hanged in the public highway where all the other court servants might see him as they passed in and out of the city. Having handed down the sentence and seen it carried out, Alexander once more found himself defending his actions against an accusation of tyranny, and this time from a very interesting source:

When Ulpian, one of the sage men of his council, blamed his sentence as cruel and representing a tyranny, he [Alexander] patiently heard him and answered immediately, saying, 'The residue of my manners declareth me not to be furious or to take pleasure in cruelty, specially in them whom I favour and have next about me.

(Hiii(v)– Hiv)[63]

Even ignoring the fact that the claim itself is a highly unconvincing one, given that his treatment of Turinus and others reveals that he was especially cruel in punishing those whom he favoured and were next about him, the argument is a specious and circular one. The fact that his other actions are not tyrannous does not, of course, affect the question of whether this one is. The passage ripples with a still greater irony, however, for those of Elyot's readers who were familiar with his classical source and the other early accounts of Alexander's reign, as we shall see in a moment. But it is worth pursuing the Emperor's argument a little further first, because he goes on to justify his severity by citing two analogous cases. If, he argues, all the year were perpetual springtime, then worms and flies would so multiply that they would quickly consume all the fruits of the earth. Hence it was necessary to let a 'sharp and terrible winter' alternate with the milder weather of spring and summer to purge these parasites and so preserve nature's store. Similarly,

If the ancient laws of this city judgeth him to die that spitefully pulleth down or defileth th'emperor's image, or counterfeiteth his coin, seal, or sign manual, of how much congruence and more with justice is it that he should suffer death which with selling of the administration of justice plucketh down and defileth among the people the good renown of the Emperor, which is his very image immortal, whereby both the prince and the people suffereth incomparably more damage than by forging of money... Wherefore, if ye consider everything well, ye shall find no cause to blame me of cruelty or resemble me to a tyrant.

(Hiv–iv(v))

Rather than judging each case on its own merits, then, Alexander here comes close to arguing, after Machiavelli, that a degree of cruelty is a necessary instrument of state, as important to good government as the moderation with which it alternates.[64] Hence, in the interests of a stable regime, someone must suffer exemplary punishment from time to time regardless of the nature or extent of their crimes. His interlocutor, Ulpian, seems, however, to be entirely convinced by his master's reasoning:

With these words Ulpian found himself satisfied and, wondering at the Emperor's wisdom, ceased to speak any more against him in any semblable judgement.

(Hiv(v))

But, as Elyot's better informed readers would have realized, there is a further irony to this image of the lawyer Ulpian absorbing from his master the wisdom of a little judicious severity to purge the caterpillars of the commonwealth, just as there was to his initial objection to the Emperor's cruelty. For in Christian apologetics, drawing on patristic sources such as Lactantius, with which Elyot was certainly familiar,[65] Ulpian was presented as the great codifier of imperial laws against Christians and himself a cruel persecutor of the early church throughout the Empire.[66] That it was Ulpian who was the one to quail at the Emperor's severity here, and who was the recipient of his lecture on the need for severity, thus gives an added emphasis to the suggestion that Elyot's Alexander was far from the affable and benign figure that the narrator seems to believe.

As Alexander himself is frequently at pains to point out, the principal difference between a true ruler and a tyrant is that the former governs in the best interests of the public weal as a whole, while the latter is motivated by purely personal interests (a distinction that Elyot's readers would also have found at numerous points elsewhere in his works). And, as Emperor and narrator alike claim, Alexander was never moved by purely private motives.[67] Yet, as the text also makes clear at a number of crucial points, it is extremely difficult to disentangle purely private motives from concern for the public good when the private individual in question is the Emperor, in whose person political and judicial authority and the state as a whole are embodied. In his case it is hard to imagine a private interest that does not also have public and political implications, or at least can be made to appear to have them after a little judicious persuasion. Hence Alexander's habitual recourse when arguing his way out of a charge of tyranny is to move immediately from the private to the political aspects of his person, arguing that a crime or slight against him as an individual is also a crime or slight against the Empire and the Senate and people of Rome, and deserves to be punished accordingly. If a man who seeks to destroy the City by fire warrants death, so does the man who seeks to destroy the reputation of the Emperor, in whom the well-being of the City is embodied. If the man who seeks to kill the Emperor with knife or poison is a traitor, so is the man who seeks to destroy his reputation, the lively image of his public person and the cornerstone of his Empire's happiness. Hence what might be seen as his 'private displeasure' provoked by an insult or a betrayal of his trust is argued to be a public matter, evidence or a just concern for the public good rather than the private grudge of a tyrant.

What Elyot seems to be doing in *The Image of Governance* is, then, to present, in the wake of Cromwell's death, a mirror of contemporary policy that suggests the tyrannical motives and methods behind the claims to reform and sound government. Like its humanist forbears *The Praise of Folly* and the second book of *Utopia*, and like the courageous sermon of John Skyp, it offers a criticism of contemporary ills dressed up as a eulogy of an ideal state, mingling idealistic aspirations for the future with bitter reflections upon present practice. And he did so with the intention, if not of accusing Henry VIII directly of tyranny (for that would have been high treason, however carefully he sought to conceal his intentions behind ironies and mocks), at least of rebuking his aristocratic ministers for conniving in and encouraging his increasingly tyrannical methods and behaviour. *The Image* is, after all, pointedly dedicated to 'All the Nobility of this Flourishing Realm of England', with the wish that it will bring them 'increase of virtue and honour' (aii). And it is hard to escape the conclusion that on one level at least it is Elyot's bitter offering to those noble councillors who helped to bring Cromwell down and revelled in his subsequent humiliation. Thus his wish that Alexander's life,

> may worthily be a pattern to knights, an example to judges, a mirror to princes, [and] a beautiful image to all them that are like to be governors, whereby they may have in continual remembrance to embrace and follow his most excellent qualities
>
> (cc iv(v))

must be read as a final ironic parting shot. For his intended noble readers had already demonstrated their capacity to embrace Alexander's methods and act with equal severity towards the man they helped to destroy.[68] And just in case the intended rebuke is missed, it is emphasized one more time in Elyot's marvellously arch comment in the Preface that, if his readers follow the example set out in the text correctly, they will win more honour and favour among men than if 'ye had on you as rich a garment as the great Turk hath any' (bii). For in English culture the Great Turk was synonymous with rapacity and cruelty.[69]

If *The Image* is read as an ironic condemnation of its intended readers, of the nobles who had degraded Cromwell, and the King who had ordered them to do it, a number of the apparent inconsistencies in the text seem less problematic. Not least among them is the fact that its subject, Alexander Severus, was actually remarkably short-lived for an apparently ideal monarch, having only reigned for some thirteen years before being murdered by his own soldiers who could no longer stomach his severity. At least one critic has seen this historical detail as a serious flaw in Elyot's argument, suggesting that the author must have been unaware that he was actually presenting his readers with a cautionary tale of political failure.[70] But the irony was clearly intentional, and Elyot was well aware of the significance of the Emperor's early end in determining the lessons that readers were likely to draw from his text. As he himself emphasized, it was when his soldiers 'would not suffer any longer his rigorous gravity' (cc iv(v)) that they killed him, just as they had done with his predecessor, the monster Heliogabalus. Such was, indeed, the usual fate of tyrants, however carefully they tried to dress their tyranny in the robes of virtuous kingship.

But, if in some parts *The Image* is a destructive work, a savagely witty outburst against the cruelty and rapacity of Henry's noble councillors and the King whose values they reflect, we should not be blinded by the angry glare of its irony to its other more positive aspects. For there is also a good deal of evidence within its pages of further serious consideration of those problems of government and counsel that had exercised Elyot throughout his writing career and had proved so troublesome in *Of the Knowledge Which Maketh a Wise Man* in particular. Indeed in this respect *The Image* probably presents Elyot at his most constructive and radical in his thinking about the systems and mechanisms of government as well as his most bitter and pessimistic about the realities of contemporary governors. And the combination is probably not coincidental.

As with his previous extended foray into classical politics in *Of the Knowledge*, writing *The Image* allowed Elyot to explore a world that was both very similar and very different to his own in both its values and its institutions. And, as with that earlier exercise, the experience was liberating. As the lengthy letter of self-justification that he sends to his counsellor Gordian demonstrates (Di–Div), Alexander's world was considerably more brutal and precarious than that described in either *Pasquil the Plain* or *Of the Knowledge*. It was a world in which emperors were not born to office but raised by the legions or chosen by the Senate and people, and needed to maintain the confidence of a number of powerful interest groups, including the Senate itself, the army, the mass of common citizens, and their own household servants, if they were to govern effectively or even survive into old age. For, as Alexander recognizes, Roman history was littered with examples of rulers who were murdered by their own subjects when they failed to retain their love and support. He himself cites Julius Caesar and Germanicus as well as his own predecessor Heliogabalus, and astute readers would have mentally added his own name to that list as they read it.[71] Hence, there is an inherent irony in his stated determination to fulfil the humanist dictum that it is more important for a ruler to be loved than feared:

He much erreth (in mine opinion) that prefereth fear before love, without which (witnesseth Socrates) nothing either with God or with men may endure or abide . . . Suppose not ye that he was a wise man that said, 'Men, whom they fear they hate, and whom they hate they would were destroyed'?

$$(\text{DIV}-\text{DIV(V)})^{72}$$

To be the emperor was thus a risky business, especially if one were pathologically inclined to severity.

Thinking about political life, and the means of realizing the humanist ideal of a good governor in such an environment seems to have freed Elyot to consider more fundamental and radical changes to systems of government than he had done in any of his previous treatises. Perhaps paradoxically, considering a world in which emperors were worshipped as gods but also slaughtered as cattle seems to have removed some of the divinity that hedges kingship in Elyot's mind, allowing him to propose, albeit still only hesitantly, some far-reaching solutions to the perennial problems of bad government.

In the descriptions of Alexander's council in the *Historia*, Elyot found material that answered directly the questions pondered in *Pasquil* and *Of the Knowledge* concerning the limitations of advice and the powers of the counsellor. As Elyot translated it, the Emperor's first constitutional act after gaining power was to elect 'out of all parts of the empire a convenient and honourable company of wise and honourable counsellors' (EI), which would attend him at all times. This council, made up of 'the most excellent lawyers of whose sentences is made the text of the law civil gathered in the books named the Digests', offered a ready analogue to the early Tudor Privy Council of which Elyot had personal experience, which similarly combined judicial, administrative, and advisory functions.

That Elyot, who had in *The Governor* shied away from any direct discussion of the idea that the law should limit the freedom and prerogatives of the crown, should now portray with evident approval a system in which lawyers are the principal councillors of state, suggests the degree to which his thinking had changed in the course of the 1530s concerning the freedom which it was safe to allow to the King. For, as his phrasing suggests, Elyot was here describing a body of councillors that did not merely advise their sovereign, but had a key role in the making of both law and policy.[73] His account of the workings of the Alexandrian council is indeed his most substantial and concrete exposition of the case for the council as an instrument of government as well as a forum for advice and discussion. It is worth quoting at some length:

First all matters and causes civil of great importance he [Alexander] caused to be examined and brought in order by the great lawyers before rehearsed, of whom Ulpian was chief, and they made true report thereof unto him. Moreover, he would never make decree or ordinance without [twenty] lawyers substantially learned, and fifty other expert men and eloquent. Every man's opinion and sentence was thoroughly and quietly heard, without interruption or altercation. Thereto were assigned viii secretaries or clerks, men of quick and substantial memory, who in brief notes or ciphers made for that purpose, wrote every word that by those councillors was spoken. Moreover, a competent time was given to every councillor to study and seek for such reason as he would purpose, to the intent they should not speak unadvisedly in things of importance. // It was also this Emperor's custom that when he treated of laws and matters politic, he called thereto learned men and such as were eloquent and well reasoned...And after that all their opinions and sentences were written by the secretaries...and that they, conferring together, had made thereof one perfect minute of every man's saying and delivered it to the Emperor with as much haste as was possible. Then he in a place secret, perusing the minute and assembling and pondering the sentences thoroughly, after a competent time therein bestowed either gathering of them one perfect conclusion or else adding to [them] some thing of his invention, he finally opened his conceit among all his councillors whom he had before heard, notwithstanding he gave to them liberty either to allow his sentence, or if any man had anything newly devised, eftsoons to declare it. And that sentence which was of most wise men approved, that always prevailed, and he thereto consented. For he was of such moderation of mind that nothing more pleased him than to hear any man with a substantial and true reason to confute his opinion, which caused him to bring to pass things to be marvelled at.

(Ei(v)–Eii)

This extended and in many ways remarkable description of the Alexandrian council at work shows both the pragmatic and the radical sides to Elyot's character. The basic framework he took from the *Historia*, but much of the detail is his own invention. And everywhere his own experience of Henrician politics illuminates the text. If George Cavendish's *Life* of Cardinal Wolsey could famously be caricatured as 'history as it appears to a gentleman usher', then this chapter of Elyot's is clearly politics as designed by a clerk of the Privy Council. The provision of eight learned secretaries trained in an early form of shorthand to take minutes of the proceedings (Elyot had managed single-handedly), the assurance that everyone spoke without interruption or altercation, in proper sentences and paragraphs (ideal for transcription) and all of it to the point, the speakers having been given ample time to prepare their thoughts beforehand, and the generous provision for the secretaries to gather together, compare notes, and produce a perfect record of every man's saying before submitting their minutes to the Emperor: all of this was surely a vision of paradise for a man who had struggled to record the, no doubt frequently confused and acrimonious, deliberations of the Henrician Council in the 1520s.

But the importance of this passage goes beyond its reflection of Elyot's personal administrative experiences. Here was a council that was not only efficient and well informed, but which formulated policy by democratic vote. Alexander's stated willingness to accept the views of the majority of his advisers, even when they directly contradicted his own—indeed nothing more pleased him than when they did—seems to place him in the categories of the ideal and the fantastic, until we realize that this is Alexander Severus who is being described, and we have already been given sufficient examples of his behaviour when subject to criticism to see the irony implicit in this account. Indeed, despite the assertion to the contrary here, the text provides in all its length not a single anecdote in which the Emperor changes his mind on the strength of criticism or advice from a councillor. We are thus once more in the looking glass world of *Utopia*, examining a council not as it was or is, but as it ought to be: a standing rebuke to the imperfect councils of the fallen, real world of the here and now. Yet in imagining perfection, even if only as an ironic exercise, Elyot was able to explore a possible solution to the problems of his own situation. And interestingly he found that solution, as had Thomas Starkey in his *Dialogue between Pole and Lupset*, in the creation of a powerful council that might overrule the sovereign by a bare majority in a free vote. Typically Elyot had come to this radical proposal through a characteristically conventional humanist route, the fashioning of an ideal prince. Unlike Starkey, who had envisaged a constitutional revolution in order to protect the commonwealth from a tyrannical ruler, Elyot first imagined the perfect sovereign, and let the ideal form of constitutional government flow from aspects of his benevolent character, reflecting his desire for expert counsel and his willingness to heed good advice.[74]

But having pursued the institutions described in the *Historia*, and imagined their utility in his own world, he was prepared to explore their implications to the full. Not only did Alexander bind himself to accept the judgement of the civil lawyers on his council, he also provided for the appointment of four 'censors or correctors of manners', elected 'according to the ancient and laudable custom of this noble city' (Eii(v)–Eiii).[75] These men would be of good life and reputation,

furnished with wisdom and gravity, void also of all private affection, fear, avarice, and flattery, who like good surgeons should not forbear with corrosive and sharp medicines to draw out the festered and stinking cores of old marmols [ulcers] and inveterate sores of the weal public, engendered by the long custom of vice.

(Eiii(v))

They were, according to Elyot (and again the relevant passage is almost all his own addition)[76] given extraordinarily wide-ranging powers, and were clearly imagined by him as a cadre of senate-appointed moral watchdogs, whose brief to reform the commonwealth involved policing the social elite rather than the commons, and ran even to the removal of imperial ministers and courtiers should the need arise:

The office of Censors was to note the manners of every person which was in any degree of honour, that is to say, above the estate of the common people, wherein was showed such rigour that no man was spared, so that if a knight, a judge, or a senator had used any unseemly thing, appairing or staining the estimation of the degree which he represented, it was in the authority of the Censors to degrade him or discharge him of his office or dignity.

(Ev)

In practice, Elyot's Censors not only furthered Alexander's purge of Heliogabalus's corrupt appointees ('degrading all knights which were shameless lechers, maintainers of thieves, or themselves robbers', and removing all those officers and judges appointed by the previous regime (EV(v))), but also, when that was done, turned their attention to Alexander's own officials to exemplary effect:

Ne [i.e. not even] the emperor's palace was exempt from their jurisdiction: In so much as Aurelius Philippus, who was sometime a bondman, not withstanding that he was manumitted [freed], and had been the emperor's schoolmaster, and after wrote his life, forasmuch as he did ride in a chariot and would be saluted as a senator, the censors caused him to be led to prison and prohibited him from coming to the emperor's palace but only on foot and [with] his copped cap on his head, which fashion only was used of them that were enfranchised. And although for his good learning and honesty some noble men advised the emperor that he should require the censors that they should withdraw their rigour in correcting Philippe, he nothing would do to let or restrain the sharp correction of the Censors, but much extolling their constancy, he answered: 'If the common weal may have ever such officers, in short space there shall be found in Rome more men worthy to be Emperors than I at my coming found good senators.

(EV(v)–FI)

Again, the passage is Elyot's own invention. That he feared he might be tacking too close to the wind in imagining so powerful and intrusive a role for the Censors here, is suggested by the fact that he cites a seemingly irrelevant source, 'Marius Maximus' as a cover in the margin at the start of the discussion.[77]

Such caution even when he was being at his boldest in imagining an alternative political system to Henry VIII's imperial rule, suggests the limits of Elyot's political journey in the course of his literary career. His was no long march from absolutism to republicanism, but a more measured response to the realities of oppressive government. When Erasmus set out the options for good princely rule in *The Godly Feast*, he had described shaping the character of the prince by 'sacred teachings' as the best safeguard against tyranny. The next best, he claimed, was 'by the authorities of the senate, magistrates, and people, to limit his power in such a way that he may not easily break out into tyranny'.[78] What Elyot had done in the long decade of Henry's brutal reformation was, slowly, agonizingly, learn to accept second best from his prince. He seems finally to have concluded, resignedly, that Henry was not capable of redemption by eloquence (although he never quite gave up trying to persuade him to virtue, and would add one final encouragement to religious orthodoxy in the Preface to his *Bibliotheca Eliotae* in 1542). So, in *The Image of Governance*, he returned to the model of the omnicompetent council of all talents that he had first imagined in *The Governor*,[79] and gave it coercive force. Rather than simply trusting the King to listen to good advice as he had in his earlier work, he now imagined forcing him to do so by designing a council in which majority votes carried the day. And, rather than allowing his prince to reform his own morals and conduct, he surrounded him with powerful, independent-minded officers, whose role it was to correct those abuses that he would not address himself.

Virtue Rewarded: The Apotheosis of Sir Thomas Elyot

If Elyot was able to use *The Image* to suggest some radical constitutional solutions to the problems of governance with which he had been struggling throughout the 1530s, it also afforded him the opportunity to resolve (if only vicariously) a long-standing and more personal grievance. In the Preface the familiar sense of Elyot's personal grievance concerning his lack of reward and recognition for his admin-istrative and literary labours surfaced once more, displaced this time onto unnamed critics, who had dismissed his previous writings as thankless and worthless acts. Against them he offered a defiant retort. 'Yet am I not ignorant', he wrote,

> that diverse there be which do not thankfully esteem my labours, dispraising my studies as vain and unprofitable, saying in derision that I have nothing won thereby but the name only of a maker of books, and that I set the trees but the printer eateth the fruits. Indeed, and though disdain and envy do cause them to speak it, yet will I not deny but that they say truly, for if I would have employed my study about the increase of my private commodity which I have spent in writing of books for others necessary, few men doubt (I suppose) that do know me but that I should have attained ere this time to have been much more wealthy and, in respect of the world, in a more estimation.
>
> (aii(v))

He has laboured, he argues, with 'more regard to my last reckoning than to any riches or worldly promotion' (aiii), bestowing that poor talent that he has been allotted, after the parable in Matthew 18, in the service of God and his fellow Englishmen. Although there is a note of resignation behind the bold defiance here, an apparent acceptance that a life of unrewarded and unrecognized obscurity may have to be his lot for following his conscience and speaking uncomfortable truths to those in power; there is nonetheless also in the text that follows a sense that Elyot was preparing for himself a triumphant last laugh, aimed both at his unnamed critics and the King who had been so slow to reward his labours. And it was, fittingly, to be a laugh fashioned out of his unique position as a maker of books, a man who could fashion a fictional world more to his liking than the real one if he chose to do so.

The Image of Governance is, as we have seen, a work even more obviously and generously populated with surrogates and analogues of Henrician figures than Elyot's earlier treatises. In Zoticus and Turinus and the various other victims of imperial severity one sees variations on Thomas Cromwell's brutal fate, just as in Alexander and Heliogabalus, Ulpian and Gordian we see variously idealized, inverted, ironized and refracted images of Henry VIII and his counsellors. But beyond the narrator figure (whether he is assumed to be Eucolpius, Lampridius, 'Thomas Elyot, knight', or a combination of all three) there does not seem at first glance to be an immediate analogue for the author: a figure to which he could attach his own fears and aspirations and his ongoing preoccupation with the plight of the good counsellor. That is until we reach the point, almost three-quarters of the way through the book, when he introduces us to 'a gentleman called Sextilius Rufus', the subject of another of those exemplary case studies that displays aspects of Alexander's relationship with the people he governs. This Sextilius (who appears nowhere in Elyot's sources) was, we are told, 'right well learned in all parts of philosophy, and also in the sciences liberal'. (ui(v)–uii).[80] Having noted the vagaries and injustices of political life in the capital, he has withdrawn to his country estates, and there,

he desired nothing so much as quietness of mind and to solace himself in the most pleasant harbour of science, and visiting the most delectable works of ancient writers.

(uii)

This scholarly paragon nonetheless has his critics at court, chiefly among the lawyers as a result of his criticisms of the ambiguities and deliberate obfuscations of the law (one thinks, perhaps, of Elyot's swipes at the barbarisms of legal training in England and the obfuscatory glosses in legal textbooks in *The Governor*).[81] Hence, when it is proposed that Sextilius be appointed to the Senate, the suggestion is opposed by one 'Alphenus, a great lawyer', who dismisses him as an amateur with no real legal knowledge and a man 'of no great policy': the 'aptitude' of whose nature 'was only in studious meditation of sundry science, and in writing more than in doing'

(uii).

The 'maker of books' has, however, his champions in Rome, chief of whom is the Emperor himself. The latter thus rebukes Alphenus, saying that he knows that he bears a grudge against Sextilius since he,

in one of his books hath sharply noted the detriment done unto justice by covetous lawyers, which by their subtle wits have involved the laws civil into such obscure and ambiguous sentences that no man without their [i.e. the professional lawyers] declarations may know how to do or minister justice in cases, for the which the said laws have provided . . . these and like annotations of Rufus do not a little offend you that be lawyers.

(uiii)

As a result of this intervention Sextilius is indeed appointed senator, with only a handful of lawyers opposing him, as he 'as his learning and honest manners required, was beloved and commended of all men, except very few, whom envy and private displeasure continually fretted'

(xiv(v)).

Sextilius's rise to national prominence was not, however, to be unproblematic: given Elyot's doubts over the wisdom and morality of going to court, how could it be? For Alexander next resolves to nominate him as Praetor, an office equivalent to the Tudor Lord Chancellor, combining the roles of chief minister and principal judge. Rather than accept a post for which he feels himself unsuitable, however, Sextilius flees to Athens to resume the life of quiet study which he had so recently and so reluctantly abandoned. Yet his apparent act of disloyalty leads, against all of the expectations of his enemies, only to a second and still greater affirmation of his worth, for rather than being scandalized by his disobedience, Alexander interprets his actions as further confirmation of the wisdom of his appointment. 'We now deem him more able for the refusing', the Emperor announces, 'For, truly, authority ought to be given to such as careth least for it and kept from them which press fastest toward it'

(ɣi(v)).

Thus Sextilius is afforded a second summons to Rome that amounts to a virtual apotheosis, his Emperor's words still ringing in his ears as he ascends to the Capitol:

Return, therefore, with honour, gentle Sextilius, satisfy the desire of me that am both your emperor and lover, rejoice the Senate and people, shame your enemies, and recomfort your friends.

(ɣii)

It is the summons to counsel that Elyot himself had always wanted. And there is the unmistakable sense of the author having fun here, fashioning for his surrogate the glorious vindication for his life and labours that he himself had been denied in life. Liberated, perhaps, from his ongoing craving for recognition, by his advancing age and disillusionment with the prospect of ever redeeming Henry VIII by counsel alone, and by a final resolution to put conscience and 'regard to my last reckoning' before political engagement, he could now relish the long-looked-for summons vicariously from the comfort and safety of his study. Having toiled at the literary forge for so long, hoping to change the world by his labours, he was now at last able and willing to settle down and enjoy the pleasures of the text on their own terms, 'in writing more than in doing'.

So he prolonged the enjoyable sensations just a little longer with further quotation from the letter of summons that Alexander sent to Sextilius in Athens. Its terms were a veritable epitome of Elyot's own philosophy of counsel:

In vain were your long travail in study and learning if actual experience did not show forth their fruits... [To serve the public weal in person not merely through writing] is your chief office and duty. For so God hath ordained you, nature commandeth you, your country compelleth you, and philosophy biddeth you. Return, therefore, hardily, and accept with good courage and thankfully the reward of your virtue.

(ɣii)

Before finally consummating the apotheosis which was also to be his farewell to his efforts to influence policy and to gain a place in the perilous and contingent world of real politics (a world glimpsed for the last time in Sextilius's vision of the perverse arena 'wherein diligence shall be cause of displeasure... friendship dangerous, every man's countenance pleasant, [but] many men's minds offended' (yiii)), he affords his readers a glimpse of his triumph in a literary world. Here at least ideals are achievable, philosophers really can be governors, and the problems of the commonwealth can actually be solved:[82]

And so he departed and in short space arrived at Rome, where with many noble senators and the chief of the people he was gladly received. Many other wise and well learned men did this noble prince elect and most gently invite unto the ministration of the weal public, by occasion whereof, oppression, extortion, bribery, and other corruption of justice were out of the city of Rome during this emperor's life utterly exterminate.

(yiii)[83]

PART III

THE DEATH OF COUNSEL: SIR THOMAS WYATT AND HENRY HOWARD, EARL OF SURREY

12

Sir Thomas Wyatt

Poetry and Politics

Elyot's *Image of Governance* was not the only text in which the fall of Thomas
Cromwell found a powerful literary echo. Thomas Wyatt, the poet and diplomat,
whose relationship with the fallen secretary has been closer even than Elyot's,
adapted a sonnet of Petrarch's to mark the passing of his friend and patron:

> The piller pearisht is whearto I lent,
> The strongest staye of myne unquiet mynde;
> The lyke of it no man agayne can fynde
> From east to west still seking though he went,
> To myne unhappe, for happe away hath rent
> Of all my joye the vearye barke and rynde;
> And I (alas) by chaunce am thus assynde
> Dearlye to moorne till death do it relent.
> But syns that thus it is by destenye
> What can I more but have a wofull hart,
> My penne in playnt, my voice in wofull crye,
> My mynde in woe, my bodye full of smart,
> And I my self my self always to hate
> Till dreadfull death do ease my dolefull state?[1]

When Tottel came to print this poem in his *Songs and Sonnets* (1557) he entitled
it 'The Lover laments the death of his love', but generations of scholars have seen
it as a political rather than an amorous lament. In Petrarch's original, '*Rotta è
l'alta colonna e 'l verde lauro*' ('smashed is the tall column, smashed the green
laurel'),[2] the imagery makes clear the dual object of the poet's loss, punning on
the names of his patron, Cardinal Giovanni Colonna, and his beloved muse,
Laura. Wyatt dispenses with the latter allusion and focuses upon a single loss,
a single cause for mourning, echoing, as Petrarch's first allusion had, the image of
the column that Horace had coined with reference to his own patron, Maecenas:

> *Maecenas, mearum / grande decus columenque rerum.*
> ('Maecenas, the great glory and prop of my own existence.')[3]

But Wyatt is not merely borrowing Petrarch's sentiments to mark his own loss. His
translation characteristically recreates his source to do new work in a new context.

Whereas Petrarch had spoken merely of the loss of joy and the horror prompted by a realization that even the most precious things are mutable and transient, Wyatt adds a sense of the devastating psychological impact of the loss he is describing. So, where Petrarch referred to the dead patron having provided 'cooling shade to my weary thought' ('*Che facean ombra al mio stanco penseri*'),[4] Wyatt talks of a more fundamental support, of a mind not merely weary but 'unquiet', in need of external buttressing if it is to remain stable. He describes 'the veary barke and rynde' of his joy having been ripped away, and of a subject left both desperate and divided ('My mynde in woe, my bodye full of smart, / And I my self my self always to hate / Till dreadfull death do ease my dolefull state.').[5] These terms, wholly characteristic of Wyatt's later poetry as they are, inevitably suggest to modern readers an immediacy and psychological verisimilitude that transcend the conventions and commonplaces of the lyric tradition.[6] Scholars have, however, frequently been puzzled by the apparent intensity of emotion displayed here. Why should Cromwell's death have proved so devastating to Wyatt, and why should it have prompted the feelings of self-loathing so evident in the final lines? Did the poet feel in some way responsible for his patron's fall? Did he feel that he might have prevented it had his diplomatic missions been more successful?[7] Wyatt and Cromwell were certainly close, both professionally and personally, as the following chapters will demonstrate.[8] On more than one occasion Cromwell would act or speak on his behalf, shielding him from the full consequences of a judicial investigation. And, while he was abroad on his many diplomatic missions, it was Cromwell who kept an eye on Wyatt's financial fortunes, offering him gentle warnings when those relatives and friends whom he had left in charge of his affairs seemed not to be exerting themselves sufficiently on his behalf, assuring him that 'in the mean season, as I have been, so shall I be, both your friend and your solicitor'.[9] There was more to these protestations than simply the rhetorical flourishes that covered formal business dealings. Cromwell was a friend as well as a patron and ally to Wyatt, and his unexpected and violent death must have come as a severe shock to the poet.

The evidence suggests that Wyatt was present on Tower Hill when Cromwell met his death on 27 July 1540, and that the two men exchanged words. But what precisely was said remains something of a mystery. The version of Cromwell's speech from the scaffold recorded by the chronicler Edward Hall (which he implies was drawn from official documents, although he seems also to have been an eyewitness) notes merely that, having enjoined the crowd to pray for him, for the King, and 'after him that his son, Prince Edward, that goodly imp, may long reign over you', he knelt to pray further:

> And then made he his prayer, which was long, but not so long as both godly and learned, and after committed his soul into the hands of God, and so paciently suffred the stroke of the axe, by a ragged and Butcherly miser, which very ungodly performed the office.

As H. A. Mason discovered, however, two other semi-formal documents survive in which a further sentence is added to this account. What appears to be a handwritten draft or copy of an official printed account of the minister's death reads, after the material quoted from Hall:

and after this prayer, he stood up again and said, 'pray for our prince and for all the Lords of the Council, and after for all the communality, and now I pray you once again that ye will pray for me', and he turned him about and said, 'farewell Wyatt, and gentle Wyatt pray for me'.[10]

The same additional passage was included in the version (perhaps copied from the printed text) written into the commonplace book of Richard Cox, Bishop of Ely, a man who was obviously interested in Wyatt and his work, as the same manuscript also contains copies of two of the poet's more politicised poems, 'Myne owne John Poyntz' and 'Like as the bird'.[11]

Either a version of this fuller printed account or the personal testimony of Cromwell's son Richard informs the more florid and embellished story related in the *Cronica del Rey Enrico Otavo de Ingaletera*, a Spanish account of events in England in the period, that goes on to observe that, 'there had always been great love between him [Cromwell] and this Master Wyatt', adding that 'Wyatt could not answer him, for his tears came too fast'. This outpouring of emotion on the poet's part, the chronicler alleged, prompted Cromwell to attempt to allay suspicions that Wyatt was implicated in the crimes for which he was being punished by declaring. 'Wyatt, do not weep for me; if I were no more guilty than you were when you were arrested, I should not now be standing where I am.'[12] These last words may well be the chronicler's own addition, or family recollections of what Cromwell ought to have said. But that he did say *something* to Wyatt, asking him in particular among all those standing around the scaffold to pray for him, seems clear. Why the official account should have initially recorded those words but then omitted them from a second draft (if that is indeed what happened) is less easy to determine. Most plausibly such a detail would have humanized Cromwell to a degree unhelpful to a government anxious to justify his execution. Yet, as Cox's commonplace book suggests, those who knew Wyatt and valued his work, recalled the minister's words to him and recorded them as part of their own memorialization of the event.

Wyatt's friendship with Cromwell ended in the most violent and horrific of circumstances, and the poet's copious tears and inarticulacy in response to the minister's words would seem entirely consistent with the degree of grief and devastated self-examination evident in his elegiac sonnet. Such emotions as Wyatt's sonnet expresses do not need an immediate and direct source in a specific sense of guilt or responsibility. They seem more plausibly to embody that general sense of culpability and self-reproach that is also suggested at times in Elyot's letters and dialogues: a sense that Cromwell's death was merely the most palpable and shocking example of how far the moral standards of Henrician political culture had declined since the establishment of the Supremacy, and how far men like Elyot and Wyatt had compromised themselves and their ideals by collaborating—and continuing to collaborate despite their self-reproach—in its operation.

The Unquiet Life of Sir Thomas Wyatt

Thomas Wyatt was born in 1503, son to Sir Henry Wyatt of Allington Castle in Kent.[13] Like all the writers discussed in this book, he was a life-long servant of the Henrician regime, an administrator and courtier; both nominally and literally one of the King's men. At the age of twelve he had entered St John's College, Cambridge where he gained his grounding in literature and languages, and probably forged the friendships with such scholars as the future antiquary John Leland that were to last throughout his life. By 1516, however, he was already embarked upon the career as a crown servant that was to dominate his professional and intellectual life. At court he became first a sewer extraordinary to the Crown, then an esquire for the King's body. By 1524 he had moved up to the more substantial role of clerk of the King's jewels, a post that would probably have required his full-time attendance at court, so ending his formal studies. And alongside his household duties he began to play a role in the recreational and ceremonial culture of the court. At Christmas in the same year he appeared as one of the performers in an allegorical entertainment, the Siege of the Castle of Loyalty, presented in the tiltyard at Greenwich alongside his brother-in-law Sir George Cobham, and three of the King's 'minions', Henry Norris, Sir Francis Bryan, and John Poyntz or Poins. This appearance was another foretaste of later connections. Bryan and Poins were to be lifelong associates and the dedicatees of some of his more substantial poems; Norris, like Cromwell, was to die a traitor's death as Wyatt watched, prompting one of the poet's most moving and powerful verses.[14]

Wyatt quickly gravitated from domestic to diplomatic service. In May 1526 he accompanied Sir Thomas Cheney on embassy to the French court. In January the following year he travelled with Sir John Russell to Rome, a mission that saw him unexpectedly take on more significant responsibilities when Russell broke his leg. Wyatt travelled on alone to Venice, during which time he was briefly imprisoned by Spanish troops before making his escape. The two envoys finally returned home together just before the Sack of Rome by imperial forces in May 1527.[15] Other more substantial diplomatic roles would follow in the course of the 1530s. But this first embassy provides a useful insight into aspects of Wyatt's character that would resurface later in his life to both good and ill effect: specifically his frustration with what he saw as hypocrisy and his tendency to speak his mind freely, seemingly regardless of the consequences. The poet's grandson Sir George Wyatt is our source for the story that, on the return journey through Italy, while waiting for a change of horses and musing on 'the want of success of the King's affairs' in the papal curia, Wyatt sketched a political cartoon or *impressa* on the wall of his chamber. It depicted 'a maze, and in it a minotaur with a triple crown on his head, both as it were falling, and a bottom [ball] of thread with certain gives [shackles] and broken chains there lying by'. Above the sketch he wrote a line quoted from the one hundred and twenty third psalm:

> *Laques contritus est et nos liberati sumus*
> ('the snare is broken, and we are delivered').

The quotation was aptly chosen to register a sense of release and liberation. The relevant psalm, entitled '*Nisi quia Domini*: The Church giveth glory to God for her deliverance from the hands of her enemies', speaks of the relief of the chosen nation of Israel at its liberation from the snares of its heathen enemies, and the full text of the relevant verse (Psalms 123:7) reads '*anima nostra sicut passer erepta est de laqueo venantium laqueus contritus est et nos liberati sumus*': 'Our soul hath been delivered as a sparrow out of the snare of the fowlers: The snare is broken, and we are delivered'.

Hindsight suggests an evangelical edge to the *impressa*, linking it to Henry VIII's Great Matter and the Break with Rome. As a consequence, critics have tended to see it as evidence of reformist doctrinal sympathies on Wyatt's part. Certainly that is the context in which Sir George Wyatt, probably following a family tradition, chose to repeat it.[16] And there is undoubtedly a strong anti-papal sentiment implicit in the image of the fall of the triple-crowned Minotaur. But, it is not clear that Wyatt intended the sketch and legend to imply the escape of the English church from papal authority. The spring of 1527 is almost certainly too early for such long term implications to have been in the poet's mind as he sketched. In London the King's Great Matter was still a closely guarded secret at that time, and England would remain resolutely loyal to Rome in matters of ecclesiastical authority for another year and more before the possibility of defiance became part of official statements on the divorce. So the Roman maze from which Wyatt saw himself escaping was probably a diplomatic rather than a spiritual one, having more to do with the difficulties of securing a clear commitment from the papal curia to English plans for a European peace settlement that would contain Imperial ambitions in Italy (the substance of Wyatt and Russell's brief) than with questions of ecclesiastical jurisdiction or Henry's scruple over his marriage.[17] The warning implied by the toppling of the papal tiara probably concerned the danger posed by the Emperor's German troops, from whose clutches Wyatt himself had only recently escaped and who were currently descending upon Rome. Indeed, within days of Wyatt's departure they would send Clement VII scurrying for sanctuary in the Castel Sant'Angelo. Moreover, given that the best-known use of the biblical quotation had been anti-Imperial rather than anti-papal, Wyatt may well have intended a double significance to the Minotaur and the fowler's snare.[18] Perhaps the *impressa* symbolized his escape from both the labyrinth of curial politics *and* the clutches of the Emperor's soldiers, and the poet was wishing confusion on both their houses.

If Sir George Wyatt's account is to be believed, however, it was the anti-papal implications of the image and text that had the greater impact at the time. When the *impressa* was discovered, and a copy was sent to the Roman court, the Pope and Cardinals, it was said, were 'troubled' by it, especially when they knew of its origins. But, when Henry VIII heard the story he took 'pleasure to hear the discourse of it . . . and it was thought an occasion to the King of his employing Sir Thomas the more in his services of importance and trust ever after'.[19] Again, hindsight may colour the Wyatt family tradition here, but, by the time of Wyatt's return, Henry was certainly intent upon securing a settlement to his Great Matter by hard bargaining in Rome, and would have seen the value of an envoy with an independent, even disrespectful attitude towards Papal dignity. If the *impressa* was read at court as an anti-papal statement, it would not have harmed Wyatt's prospects of further employment.

By this time Wyatt must already have established something of a reputation for scholarship, especially in the sphere of humanist translation, and may well already have written and circulated a number of the courtly lyrics (many translated or adapted from French and Italian models) that would characterize his early poetic output. For soon after his return to England in 1527 Queen Katherine asked him to translate for her a text of Petrarch's *De remediis utriusque fortunae* ('The Remedy for Ill Fortune'). Having begun the task, however, Wyatt subsequently gave up the attempt, citing the 'tediously' repetitive nature of the exercise by way of excuse, and on New Year's Day 1528 presented the Queen instead with a text of Plutarch's *Quiet of Mind*, translated into English from a Latin translation by Budé.[20] Critics have conventionally taken Wyatt's explanation of the change of texts at face value; but there may have been more to it than he suggested. In formally requesting that one of the court's best known poets translate for her a text that discussed the responsibilities of the virtuous soul in an unjust world, the Queen was offering an implicit comment on her own situation. For Wyatt to present her with a translation of Petrarch's text might have been seen as a tacit acknowledgement that she was indeed facing undeserved adversity in a hostile environment, pressed by the King's supporters to agree to a one-sided 'investigation' of the validity of their marriage. By courteously refusing that particular commission, and offering instead a text that focused on the need for the virtuous soul to reconcile him or herself to fortune and adversity, Wyatt was deftly signalling his willingness to meet the Queen's wishes, while simultaneously refusing to compromise his loyalty to the King on the most important issue of the moment. The following passage gives a flavour of the text that Wyatt presented:

So may we mend and turn another way fortune, when she chanceth otherwise than we would. Diogenes, because of his exile, left his country, it was not so greatly ill, for it gave him occasion of learning philosophy. Zenon of Citius, that had but one ship, when he heard that it was perished, the mariners, the merchandise, and (as they say) every crumb; 'Fortune', quoth he, 'thou dost very well with me, that drives me to mine old cloak, and to the porch of philosophy'. What, therefore, shall let us, that we may not follow them? Thou art fallen from some rule or authority?: thou shalt live in the country, applying thy private business with great compass; assaying to advance thyself in the prince's favour.

Thou art refused?: thou shalt live surely everywhere with no business laid unto thee. Warm water doth not cherish so much tender members (as sayeth Pindarus) as honours and glory joined with power doth make labour sweet and sufferable. But some offence doth trouble thee, of backbiting, of envy, or naughty slander, the best remedy is with the muses, or in some place of learning to suffer over... Therefore it is of no little effect for the quietness of mind diligently to mark noble and famous men if they have suffered any like thing by those same causes, as by example, want of children maketh thee sad?: Look on the Roman Kings, of whom never a one dying left his reign to his child.[21]

The stress upon reconciling oneself to loss, to making the best of diminished favour and fortune, and the specific (if rather brusque) comfort offered to those afflicted by 'want of children'; all make the text particularly apt for Queen Katherine's predicament.

Alongside such delicate diplomatic and intellectual manoeuvres came more martial duties: the foundations of the poet's reputation as the model exponent of the 'mixed life', who would wield both pen and sword in the service of King and country.[22] Between 1529 and 1530 he acted as Marshall of Calais, and in 1532 was made Justice of the Peace for Essex. In June 1534 he was commissioned to raise troops in Kent for the defence of the county, and granted a licence to retain twenty men in his personal livery.[23] Yet Wyatt, for all his civic responsibilities, was evidently not suited to be a staid pillar of the establishment. The same rebellious streak that prompted him to taunt papal and imperial authority with his satirical *impressa* surfaced again in 1534 with more serious consequences. In May of that year a terse record notes that a sergeant at law, one of the senior members of the metropolitan legal community, had been slain 'in a great affray between Master Wyatt and the sergeants of London'.[24] What prompted the affray, or just how culpable Wyatt was in the sergeant's death is not recorded. He was imprisoned briefly in the Fleet, but within a month was released and was raising troops in Kent in the King's name. Indeed, only a year later he was knighted.[25] Evidently Henry at least took as indulgent a view of the poet's actions in this respect as he had towards his anti-papal graffiti.

Wyatt's private life was as turbulent as his public career. In 1520, at the age of seventeen, he married Elizabeth Brooke, the daughter of Thomas Brooke, Lord Cobham: a political alliance that established the young Esquire for the Body firmly in the ranks of the aristocracy. The couple had a son, Thomas the younger, and perhaps also a daughter named Elizabeth; but theirs was not a happy match.[26] By the later 1520s Wyatt had rejected his wife, reputedly as a result of adultery on her part, and would refuse for some years to maintain either her or her servants, despite the entreaties of her Brooke relatives. Something of both the regret and the anger that he felt over the failure of the relationship can be seen in a letter to his son written soon after the latter's own marriage in 1537. 'Love well and agree with your wife', he admonished the younger Thomas,

for where is noise and debate in the house, there is unquiet dwelling. And much more where it is in one bed ... And the blessing of God for good agreement between the wife and the husband is fruit of many children, which I for the like thing do lack, and the fault is both in your mother and me, but chiefly in her.[27]

In its balance of introspection and self-justification, and the pointed apportioning of blame ('chiefly in her'), the letter reflects the attitudes evident in some of the poet's more aggressively misogynistic lyrics. In the absence of a stable and fulfilling marital relationship Wyatt evidently pursued a number of affairs with women in and around the court in the later 1520s and 1530s. Some of these may well have been alluded to in his amatory verse, with its repeated motifs of the cruel courtly mistress and the pains of unrequited desire. The most notorious of these affairs involved Anne Boleyn, and brought the poet into the heart of some of the most contentious events of the reign.

Trying to untangle the precise truth about the relationship between the poet and Henry VIII's second and most controversial queen is an almost impossible task, given nearly five centuries of anecdote, romanticized biography, and polemical assertion and counter-assertion. What it is probably safe to conclude is that, at some time in the mid-1520s, prior to Anne's attracting the eye of the King, Wyatt was her suitor. She was then a young woman newly returned from France and attracting considerable attention at court owing to her sophisticated French manners and fashionable interests in francophone poetry and religious writings. The two may briefly have been lovers (although this is far from certain), and their 'courtship' was at least partly played out in the verses that Wyatt wrote and circulated at court at this time.[28] But once the King had made his interest known, the poet seems—despite the existence of some rather implausible stories of the two men competing for her favour—to have beaten a careful retreat.[29]

What is also evident, however, is that Wyatt's desire for Anne, and the subsequent experience of her being taken beyond his grasp by the attentions of the King, furnished material for a number of his most powerful amatory lyrics. The story of the young suitor who pursues a lofty, disdainful lady of superior status is, of course, the archetypal scenario of the courtly love lyric. But the particular circumstances of Wyatt's relationship with Anne give his own poetic explorations of furtive desire and a painful unrequited love that could not speak its name except in riddles a special poignancy and power.

That Henry knew about Anne's past seems clear from the surviving evidence, although it is unlikely that the poet ever formally confessed his desire for her to the King in the way that some catholic sources suggest.[30] But the possibility that the poet retained feelings for the future queen, which he could no longer voice with any safety, adds a special charge to such cryptically allusive verses as:

> What wourde is that that chaungeth not,
> Though it be tourned and made in twain?
> It is myn aunswer, God it wot,
> And eke the causer of my payn.
>
> (Muir and Thompson 50, 1–4)

The unspoken answer to the poet's question is almost certainly 'Anna', as would have been obvious in oral performance, where the third line could have been heard to declare: 'It is mine Anne, sir, God it wot.'[31]

Other verses seem more obviously and straightforwardly autobiographical. Hence the *strambotto*, 'Some tyme I fled the fyre that me brent' seems to allude directly to Wyatt's feelings during a journey to France in the entourage of Henry and Anne in 1532:

> Some tyme I fled the fyre that me brent
> By see, by land by water and by wynd;
> And now I folow the coles that be quent [quenched]
> From Dover to Calais against my mynde.
> Lo! how desire is boeth sprong and spent!
> And he may se that whilome[i.e. once] was so blynde;
> And all his labor now he laugh[s] to scorne.
> Mashed in the breers that erst was all to torne.
>
> (Muir and Thompson 59)[32]

Similarly the 'question and answer' sonnet 'If waker care, if sodayne pale coulour' (Muir and Thompson 97) seems to bury its autobiographical content very near to the surface. There the speaker responds to a playful demand to tell his audience who it is he loves with the declaration that 'Th'unfayned chere of Phyllis' has now taken the place in his heart once filled by 'Brunet', 'Her that did set our country in a rore' (8). Indeed the particularity of the allusion to the most controversial woman in England may have been too obvious here, for Wyatt later changed the relevant line to 'Brunet that set my welth in such a rore.'[33]

Most obviously and most powerfully, Wyatt gave a new specificity and resonance to Petrarch's enigmatic *Rime* 190, translating it from a delicate religious allegorization of secular love and its loss through death into an openly autobiographical reminiscence of his complex feelings for a living woman, Anne.

> Who so list to hounte, I know where is an hynde;
> But as for me, helas, I may no more:
> The vayne travaill hath weried me so sore,
> I ame of theim that farthest cometh behinde;
> Yet may I by no meanes my weried mynde
> Drawe from the Diere: but as she fleeth afore
> Faynting I folowe; I leve of[f] therefore,
> Sithens in a nett I seke to hold the wynde.
> Who list her hount I put him owte of dowbte,
> As well as I may spend his tyme in vain:
> And graven with Diamondes in letters plain
> There is written her faier neck rounde abowte:
> '*Noli me tangere* for Cesars I ame,
> And wylde for to holde though I seme tame.'
>
> (Muir and Thompson 7).[34]

Where Petrarch's sonnet spoke of the release of the deer ('dear') through death, Wyatt's talks of its capture and possession, despite its fleetness of foot. Petrarch's Caesar was God, whose claim upon Laura freed her from the snares of her earthly life; Wyatt's was Henry VIII, whose interests were more mundane and personal. So Wyatt's overt association of the deer with Christ through citation of the Latin motto *'noli me tangere'* (Petrarch had used the vernacular: *'nessun mi tocchi'*), a repetition of Christ's words to Mary Magdalene in John 20: 17 ('Do not touch me (for I am not yet ascended to my Father)') seems to place the poem in the curious liminal period of Henry's extended courtship of Anne. Not yet married and so not yet 'ascended' to her destined position on the throne, Anne is yet marked out as 'Caesar's' and so inaccessible to other men. Prior to the sexual consummation of their long relationship (which probably did not occur until late 1532) Anne remained overtly, indeed ostentatiously, chaste, yet was also clearly the sexual property of the King, hence, perhaps, the enigmatic play in the text with the idea that she is both wild (sexually available, even enticing) and tame (chaste), free (to run fleetly from the chasing pack of courtiers) and constrained (by the collar of diamonds and its emphatic, spondaic declaration of ownership).

These poems do not suggest that Wyatt was conducting an illicit affair with the Queen, nor even that he maintained a secret, unrequited desire for her throughout the years of her marriage to the King. The implication of 'Some tyme I fled the fyre' is, after all, that the fires which once burnt him are now 'quent', or extinguished. But they do imply that the relationship with Anne, whatever form it took, had once been of vital importance to the poet, and that it still had implications for his current feelings and conduct. To have once been in love with the woman who was now the Queen clearly had powerful personal implications for his relationships both with her and with the court over which she presided.

The dangers implicit in continuing even to reflect upon past desire once Anne was Queen, if only within the circumscribed conventions of courtly verse, became suddenly and terrifyingly apparent in May 1536. Anne's arrest on charges of multiple adultery led to the imprisonment and interrogation of a whole swathe of courtiers who had at least paid lip service to the idea of courting her during the period of her ascendancy. Henry Norris, the King's Groom of the Stool, Francis Weston, William Brereton, and Mark Smeaton of the privy chamber; another courtier, Sir Richard Page, and Anne's own brother, George, Viscount Rochford, were all arrested between 30 April and 8 May on charges of having committed sexual acts with the Queen and imagining the King's death. And with them to the Tower, as the net widened and other possible suspects were drawn in, went Wyatt. He would later admit that he suspected that the influence of Charles Brandon, Duke of Suffolk lay behind his arrest, although he did not say why. Brandon and his wife, Mary, sister to Henry VIII, had resented the precedence granted to Anne at public events while she remained merely the King's consort. As the King's sister and dowager Queen of France, Mary considered herself and not the King's mistress to be the premier noblewoman of the realm, and evidently smarted under the indignity of having to take second place. Hence, when the opportunity arose, the Suffolks may well have taken a measure of revenge on the fallen Queen by suggesting more crimes against her, forwarding the names of further potential lovers to blacken her name, among which may have been Wyatt's.[35] Or so he may have thought. The charges against him certainly struck Anne Boleyn as far-fetched. When she heard of Wyatt's arrest and learned that he was lodging in the Tower with her brother, himself an amateur poet, she joked that 'they might make ballads well now'.[36] The investigations were no joke, however. For a time it seemed likely that all those arrested would die. That at least was one rumour. On 12 May John Hussee wrote to Lord Lisle from London, reporting that Wyatt and Page were imprisoned 'without danger of life'. But on the following day he corrected himself, suggesting that some observers at least were convinced that 'Wyatt and Master Page are as like to suffer as the others … If any escape it will be young Weston, for whom importunate suit is made.' A week later, with Anne and the inner group of her co-accused, Weston among them, already convicted and executed, Hussee was still casting around for definite news of the remaining prisoners, suggesting that 'Master Page and young Wyatt are in the Tower. What shall become of them God best knoweth.'[37]

Wyatt's fate had, however, been decided much earlier. Evidently the lack of evidence against him was decisive,[38] as it had been for Sir Francis Bryan, another courtier-poet with a reputation for promiscuity who had been questioned by Cromwell but then quickly set free. By 11 May Cromwell had sent word to Wyatt's father that his son would be released unharmed in due course. Sir Henry wrote back immediately, thanking the Secretary for the news, and assuring him that:

When so ever it shall be the king's pleasure with your help to deliver him, that ye will show him that this punishment that he hath for this matter is more for the displeasure that he hath done to God [than] otherwise—Wherein I beseech you to advertise him to fly vice and serve God better than he hath done.[39]

Quite when Wyatt's own anxieties over his fate were relieved is less clear. Certainly his period in the Tower would have more horrors in store for him than interrogation alone before he was eventually released. From a grated window in the bell tower he was able to look down upon Tower Hill where the execution of all Anne's alleged lovers took place on a single day, 17 May. This at least was the claim he made in a poem written at this time, probably while he was still imprisoned. 'Who lyst his welthe and eas retayne' (Muir and Thompson 176) is an extraordinarily vivid account of the events of 'these blodye dayes' and the terrors they inspired in him. The refrain *circa regna tonat* ('around thrones he thunders'), taken from Seneca's tragedy *Phaedra*, sums up the dangers of existence at what he would elsewhere call 'the slipper top' of palace life, in a poem that intersperses general maxims with flashes of intense personal experience.[40]

Who lyst his welth and eas Retayne,
Hym selffe let hym unknowne contayne;
Presse not to[o] ffast in at that gatte
Wher the Retorne standes by desdayne:
For sure, *circa Regna tonat.*

The hye montaynis ar blastyd oft,
When the lowwe vaylye ys myld and soft;
Ffortune with helthe stondis at debate;
The ffall ys grevous ffrome Aloffte:
And sure, *circa Regna tonat.*

These blodye dayes have brokyn my hart;
My lust, my youth dyd than departe
And blynd desyre of astate;
Who hastis to clyme sekes to revert:
Of truthe, *circa Regna tonat.*

The bell towre showed me suche [a] syght
That in my hed stekys day and nyght;
Ther dyd I lerne out of a grate,
Ffor all vavore, glory or myght
And yet *circa Regna tonat.*

By proffe, I say, ther dyd I lerne:
Wyt helpythe not deffence to yerne,
Of innocence to pled or prate;
Ber low therfor, geve God the sterne,
Ffor sure *circa Regna tonat.*

Critics have often categorized works such as this as Wyatt's 'occasional verse',[41] as if the fact that it was prompted by a particular event might in some way lessen a work's claim to poetic merit. In this case nothing could be further from the truth. In these stanzas Wyatt forges poetry from the raw emotions of personal experience, or rather uses verse as a means of reflecting upon and containing emotion that might otherwise prove uncontrollable. It is the specificity with which he relates the events of 1536 and his own response to them that gives the poem its capacity to shock, even after almost half a millennium. Thus, while the text clearly attempts to set those events into the wider context of a general truth (emblematized by the Senecan tag), any attempt to see it as simply a didactic exploration of a universal theme that employs the executions for rhetorical effect seriously undervalues its impact.

The refrain itself suggests the dangerous specificity of the poem. It should be translated, not as some critics have suggested, as 'around the throne it thunders', or 'around the throne the thunder roles', but 'around thrones *he* thunders'. The source in Seneca's tragic drama reveals that it is no abstract or impersonal agency that produces the thunder but Jupiter, King of the gods.

Juppiter alto vicina petit
non capit umquam magnos motus
humilis tect plebia domus.
circa regna tonat.

['Jupiter is attacking places from on high. The modest dwelling and the humble roof are never troubled by the great tumult, around thrones he thunders.'][42]

Was Wyatt suggesting, then, that the god was picking out those who chose to live around the King for his victims? Or were the wrath and the violence the King's own? For Jupiter, as we have seen, as well as symbolizing the Christian Creator, had more than once been used by his courtiers as a figure for Henry VIII himself. Either way the implication is clear, to live close to the King was, as many another courtier would discover, to court disaster: *ira Regis mors est.*

Similarly striking in its specificity, although less impressive, perhaps, as verse, is a second, longer reflection on the fates of Anne's alleged lovers: 'In mo[u]r-nynge wyse syns daylye I increas'(Muir and Thompson 146). Apparently composed somewhat later, following the executions, this poem is written in the manner of a moralized reflection on the characters of each of the men addressed. Yet, once more it focuses, initially at least, on the poet's own emotions rather than the universal significance of the events discussed. Hence it begins, not allegorically or from first principles, but with the poet himself, hamstrung and disoriented by grief, buttonholing the reader like Coleridge's ancient mariner to unburden himself of his story:

> In mo[u]rnyng wyse syns daylye I Increas,
> Thus shuld I cloke the cause of all my greffe;
> So pensyve mynd with tong to hold his pease,
> My reasone sayethe there can be no relyeffe:
> Wherffor geve ere, I umble you requyre,
> The affectes to know that thus dothe mak me mone.
> The cause ys great of all my dolffull chere,
> Ffor those that were, and now be dead and gonne.

> (1–8)

The poem that follows is a curiously partial text (in every sense of the word) that confounds conventional expectations of either the encomium or the moralized epitaph.

With disabling frankness the narrator declares that he will not describe his grief for all of those who were executed, and will not grieve equally for those he will discuss ('As ffor them all I do not thus lament, / But as of Ryght my Reason dothe me bynd' (17–18)). Anne herself he ignores entirely. Perhaps he thought that she was justly condemned, and so has no place in the lament. He does offer a rather elliptical acknowledgement of the justness of the guilty verdicts for those he does address:

> What thoughe to Dethe Desert be now ther call,
> As by ther ffautis yt dothe apere ryght playne,
> Of fforce I must lament that suche a ffal
> Shuld lyght on those so welthy dyd Raygne.
>
> (9–12)

Indeed, his response to their sentence seems, here as elsewhere, curiously displaced: more concerned with the impact of fortune on the mighty than with the alleged crimes that brought their downfall. More plausibly, he may have thought that any discussion of the fallen Queen's behaviour, however circumspect, would have been too contentious, or too painful, to risk. Either way, he confined himself to bemoaning the deaths of each of her supposed lovers, one at least of whom gets relatively brusque treatment:

> Brewton [Brereton], ffarwell, as one that le[a]st I knewe.
> Great was thy love with dyvers as I here;
> But common voyce dothe not so sore the[e] Rewe
> As other twayne that dothe before appere [i.e. Norris and Weston]
>
> (41–4)

Of those for whose death he does express seemingly genuine regret, Rochford is the first to be addressed, an honour in keeping with his superior social rank. And here the implication would seem to be that the Viscount's haughty and provocative demeanour during his trial (he had, for example, insisted on reading out a note concerning the King's sexual impotency in open court rather than silently acknowledging its contents as his judges had requested) was what brought about his condemnation rather than the validity or otherwise of the charges against him:

> Some saye, Rochefford, hadyst thou benne not so prowde,
> Ffor thy gryt wytte eche man wold the[e] bemone;
> Syns as yt ys so, many crye alowde:
> Yt ys great losse that thou art dead and gonne.
>
> (21–4)

The stanza addressed to Sir Henry Norris, Henry's Groom of the Stool and closest personal companion, is similarly noncommittal concerning the nature of his guilt. He had been the first of those accused to be arrested, and it may well have been that Wyatt and the others who were arrested later suspected (wrongly) that it was his testimony that had implicated them. This may be the sense behind Wyatt's declaration,

> A! Norrys, Norres, my tearys begyne to Rune
> To thynk what hap dyd the[e] so le[a]d or gyd,
> Wherby thou hast bothe the[e] and thyn undone.
>
> (25–7)

Regarding Weston, Wyatt comments only that the stories that are circulating about his offences prevent a universal lamentation at his death.

> And we that now in court dothe le[a]d our lyffe
> Most part in mynd doth the[e] lament and mone;
> But that thy ffaultis we daylye here so Ryffe
> All we shuld weppe that thou art dead and gone.

(37–40)

Finally, after passing over Brereton with the comments mentioned earlier, Wyatt devotes a stanza to the court musician Mark Smeaton, the lowest born of the victims, whom he presents as a classic over-reacher brought down by his excessive ambition.

> A! Mark, what mone shuld I ffor the[e] mak more?
> Syns that thy dethe thou hast deservyd best,
> Save only that myn eye ys fforsyd sore
> With petus playnt to mone the[e] with the Rest.
> A tym thou haddyst above thy poore degree,
> The ffal wherof thy frendis may well bemone.
> A Rottyne twygge apon so hyghe a tree
> Hathe slepyd thy hold and thou art dead and goonn.

(49–56)

The final stanza seeks to end the narrative of these foreshortened lives with a communal act of piety, a conventional prayer for the souls of the departed:

> And thus ffarwell eche one in hartye wyse!
> The Axe ys home, your hedys be in the stret;
> The trykklyngge tearys dothe ffall so from my [e]yes,
> I skarse may wryt, my paper ys so wet.
> But what can he[l]pe when dethe hath playd his part,
> Though naturs cours wyll thus lament and mone?
> Leve sobes therffor, and every crestyn hart
> Pray ffor the sowlis of thos be dead and gonne.

(57–64)

Yet, despite this gesture towards closure, which sets the individual stories of the dead into the wider frames of nature and eternity, there is nonetheless a sense of unfinished business to the text. The curious brusqueness of the sentiments ('The Axe is home, your hedys be in the street'), and the trite, lacklustre acknowledgement of grief ('The trykklynge tearys dothe ffall so from my [e]yes'), seem to belong to a different realm of experience to that which prompted 'Who lyst his welthe and eas Retayne'. Indeed, so hard is it to imagine the same sensibility that conceived of the lines 'The bell towre showed me suche a syght / That in my hed stekys day and nyght' (16–17) finding 'And thus ffarwell eche one in hartye wyse!' a suitable response to the same events, that a number of critics have argued that the later poem cannot be Wyatt's work at all.[43] The evidence, however, suggests that it was, leaving readers to ponder why there should be such a disparity in both style and content between the two texts.

Here what the poem does not say is as significant as what it says merely inadequately. There is, as we have seen, no open or unequivocal statement of the guilt of the accused. Nor is there any overt discussion of the crimes alleged against them. In the light of so scandalous a series of sexual allegations against the Queen: multiple adultery, public indecency, incest, it is remarkable that Wyatt never once mentions lust or sexual immorality as the presiding vice of any of those accused. Rather he dwells upon ambition, pride, misfortune ('hap' or 'a rotten twig') the conventional engines of ruin in the narratives of the 'fall of princes' tradition. Consequently, the poem has something of that air of abstract didacticism about it that is so obviously absent from 'Who lyst his welth and eas Retayne.' It suggests a public poem written to record a formal statement of regret rather than a private text created to exorcize a personal reaction. Could Wyatt have been obliged to write it as part of the conditions of his release? Or might he have felt so obliged? Or is the very conventionality of the poem a clue to a deeper need on the poet's part to distance himself from the immediacy of the events? Was he perhaps trying to fit those events into a recognizable and reductive literary framework in order to render them manageable; and does the poetic failure of that attempt suggest that he was as yet unable to do so? The opening stanza implies an intention to examine closely the impact of the courtiers' deaths on the narrator himself, but thereafter the poem shies away from such introspection towards formality and a concern with the public reaction to each man's death. In this context the absence of Anne from the poem is surely significant. It is hard to conclude that Wyatt thought her unequivocally guilty, given that he was so carefully equivocal regarding the guilt of her alleged accomplices. But the thought that the King might have destroyed his wife without cause, whether wittingly or otherwise, is a thought that no courtier could voice in so public a text, however elliptically he sought to do so.

As Muir and other critics have suggested, the Wyatt who emerged from the Tower, and (following royal instructions) absented himself from courtly felicity for a period of internal exile at Allington, seems to have taken to heart the lessons of his own stoic verse.[44] Both the change in his outlook and the terms of his release into his father's charge are suggested in the latter's letter to Cromwell written in mid-June 1536:

After I had considered to my great comfort with myself the king's great goodness toward my son with his so favourable warnings to address him better than his wit can consider, I straight called unto me my said son, and, as I have done oft, not only commanded him his obedience in all points to the king's pleasure, but also the leaving of such slanderous fashion as hath engendered unto him both the displeasure of God and of his master, and as I suppose, I found it not now to do in him but already done. And further, on my blessing I have charged him not only to follow your commandments from time to time, but also in every point to take and repute you as me, and if whilst he liveth he have not this for sure printed in his heart, that I refuse him to be my son.[45]

Wyatt, that is, was sent 'homeward' to Allington not merely as a punishment, but as an exercise in self-improvement. He was to learn 'to address him better', to abandon his immoral lifestyle (his 'slanderous fashion of living') and learn sobriety and circumspection. And, if his father's letter is to be believed, Wyatt had already taken such injunctions to heart.[46] The resulting period of self-discipline and reflection was to bring about a profound alteration in the nature of his poetic output in the period between his release from prison in June 1536 and his return to royal service in the following October or November, when he joined the royal army that was sent north to quell the popular rising known as The Pilgrimage of Grace, leading 350 men raised in Kent for the campaign.[47]

13

Tyranny Condemned

Wyatt's Epistolary Satires

It would be unwise to underestimate the psychological impact of Wyatt's imprisonment and the executions of May 1536 upon the nature of his literary output. Indeed, as we shall see, he himself attests to the effects of those 'bloody days' a number of times in his verse.[1] But there may well have been other more pragmatic factors behind his decision to turn to longer, satirical works during his period of enforced rustication at Allington. Deprived of regular access to the courtly circles that had provided both the subject matter and the audience for his amatory lyrics, the poet almost of necessity had to adapt his mode of writing if he was to maintain a relationship with a community of courtly readers. Short poems that adopted the fiction at least of oral performance had to give way to more obviously textual forms,[2] since they would have to be despatched to geographically distant readers if they were to be read. Hence the epistolary poem was an attractive and obvious choice. And, given his location on his father's rural estates, satirical reflection upon the differences between the courtly life of his readers and his own rustic existence was an equally obvious mode for Wyatt to employ. The poet's inward state and outward circumstances may well thus have contributed in equal measures to the powerful outpouring of wit and anxiety that constituted his three epistolary satires, at least the first two of which were written at Allington in the second half of 1536.

'Myne Owne John Poyntz'

Wyatt's period at Allington was not the first time that he had turned his pen to political issues. He had never been averse to offering advice to his sovereign in the manner of the conventional poetic good counsellor. Indeed he had drawn upon the language and sentiments of the classic *speculum principis* in a number of the shorter poems written during his time at court in the earlier 1530s. In 'If thou wilt mighty be' (Mew and Thompson 261), for example, he shaped material from Book 3 of Boethius's *Consolation of Philosophy* into a textbook lesson on the theme that the monarch must cure himself of all sensual distractions, subduing his own vices and passions before he might legitimately claim the right to rule others:[3]

If thou wilt mighty be, flee from the rage
Of cruell wyll, and see thou kepe thee free
From the foule yoke of sensuall bondage,
For though thy empyre stretche to Indian sea,
And for thy feare trembleth the fardest Thylee [Thule],
If thy desire have over thee the power,
Subject then art thou and no governour.

If to be noble and high thy minde be meved,
Consider well thy grounde and thy beginnyng,
For he that hath eche starre in heaven fixed,
And geves the Moone her hornes and her eclipsyng:
Alike hath made the[e] noble in his workyng,
So that wretched no way may thou bee
Except foule lust and vice do conquere thee.

All were it so thou had a flood of golde,
Unto thy thirst yet should it not suffice.
And though with Indian stones a thousande folde
More precious then can thy selfe devise
Ycharged were thy backe, thy covetise
And busye bytyng yet should never let
Thy wretchid life, ne do thy death profet.[4]

And, as we shall see, he would return to these ideas, and the Boethian text that inspired them, in the second of his epistolary satires. But what the period at Allington seems to have engendered is a very different attitude to the nature and purpose of political verse. Having tried his hand at the poetry of princely counsel, he seems to have lost confidence in the capacity of such verse to move his prince towards virtue, and instead redirected his gaze towards other members of the courtly community, fellow courtiers and diplomats, men very like himself, aiming thereby to fashion a small community of like-minded readers united by their shared interests in the commonweal and its renovation. In such verse the prince would become the implied subject rather than the intended reader of the political discourse.

As John Scattergood suggests, all three of Wyatt's satires are 'bookish poems', texts that 'recognise and draw attention to their bookishness'.[5] Like many of the stronger of his lyrics, they are in one form or another translations of earlier texts, newly adapted for contemporary purposes. The first, 'Myne own John Poyntz' (Muir and Thompson 105), openly gestures towards other texts, as Wyatt reminds its recipient, a fellow courtier and royal servant, of their shared memories of writers from Juvenal, Horace, and Seneca, through Chaucer and Alain Chartier, to Skelton and contemporary Continental poets, pointing up the relevant wisdom they each offer to Henrician readers. The form and scenario of the poem, written by a poet in rural retreat to a friend at court, recalls the

Satires of Horace (especially the second) and Juvenal (especially the tenth),
Seneca's *Moral Letters,* and medieval English examples of anti-curial writing
such as Chartier's *Curial.*[6] In each of these poems the virtues of the country are
extolled and the vices of the court condemned.

Indeed, Wyatt had earlier sketched out the lineaments of the conventional
neo-stoic position on the superiority of the quiet rural life over the precarious,
violent world of the court in a lyric based upon a passage from Seneca's *Thyestes*:

> Stond who so list upon the slipper toppe
> Of courtes estates, and lett me heare [here] rejoyce;
> And use me quyet without lett or stoppe,
> Unknowen in courte, that hath suche brackish joyes.
> In hidden place so lett my dayes forthe passe,
> That when my yeares be done, withouten noyse,
> I may dye aged after the common trace.
> For hym death greep'the [i.e. grips] right hard by the croppe
> That is moche knowen of other, and of him self alas,
> Doth dye unknowen, dazed with dreadfull face.

(Muir and Thompson 240)[7]

Here, as in the satires, Wyatt energizes a seemingly conventional sentiment by
the addition of a striking detail. In this text it is the sudden intrusion of violence
in the allusion to the courtier whom death has gripped 'hard by the croppe', an
image redolent of the violence pervading his own life, in which many courtiers
had died 'dazed with dreadfull face' before his own eyes.

In his first satire he returned to discuss the 'brackish joyes' of the court in
greater detail and with still more urgent political intentions. The reference in the
opening lines to 'the presse of courtes wher soo they goo' (3) recalls the first lines
of Chaucer's most overtly politicized ballad: *Truth: Ballade de Bon Conseyl,* with
its Boethian emphasis on the value of simple sufficiency and honesty:

> Flee fro the prees and dwelle with sothfastness;
> Suffyce unto thy thing, though it be smal,
> For hord [possessions] hath hate, and climbing tickelnesse,
> Prees hath envye, and wele blent overal,
> Savour [desire] no more than thee bihove shal,
> Reule wel thyself that other folk canst rede,
> And trouthe thee shal delivere, it is no drede.

(1–7)[8]

But Wyatt's principal source was not an authoritative text from the past, but a
highly contemporary political satire taken from the *Opera Toscani* of Luigi
Alamanni, printed in Lyons on 1532–3. Alamanni, a Florentine stoic, wrote
the *Opera* while in exile in France, having fled from his native city as a result of
his republican opposition to its Medici overlords. And his tenth satire, addressed
to his friend Thommaso Sertini, reflected both his immediate experiences of

political oppression and exile and his anti-monarchical views. So, in the very choice of this particular text to translate, and in adapting it to his own circumstances, Wyatt was already tacitly making a daring political statement,[9] implying the relevance of ideas forged in the notoriously corrupt and despotic world of the Italian city-states to recent English experience.

Typically, however, Wyatt does not draw immediate attention to his borrowings. Rather he takes over the sentiments of Alamanni's satire and makes them his own so that the text appears, not an exotic importation, but something that has grown organically from roots deep in the English landscape and vernacular culture. Where the Florentine poet grounded his text in the classics, differentiating between good and bad Greek and Roman poets, for example, when he wished to exemplify courtly sycophancy, Wyatt refers to Chaucer's *Canterbury Tales* and distinguishes between two romances, the neo-classical *Knight's Tale* and the parodic *Sir Thopas* (50–1). Where Alamanni condemned hypocrisy by saying he cannot praise a Thersites as if he were refined, or call a coward a Hercules, Wyatt declares that he cannot commend a crow for singing like a swan, or condemn a lion if it 'cannot take a mows as a cat can' (44–6). Such homely, domestic examples ensure that the sentiments expressed in Wyatt's verse have both a local habitation and a name. Similarly, where Alamanni is comprehensive in his contempt for human weakness, bemoaning not only the life of the court but life everywhere else too, ending with a denunciation of the Provencal backwater in which he was writing,[10] Wyatt exempts the Kentish countryside from criticism, presenting his father's estates as an arcadian space for physical recreation and intellectual labour.

> . . . here I ame in Kent and Christendome
> Emong the muses where I rede and ryme;
> Where if thou list, my Poynz, for to come,
> Thou shalt be judge how I do spend my time.
>
>   (100–3)

It is this apparently autobiographical dimension to the satire that gives 'Myne Owen John Poyntz' its special novelty and power. In this poem, as in a number of the lyrics cited earlier, Wyatt achieves an apparent particularity, a rootedness of the narratorial 'I' in the quotidian detail of the poet's own life and experience, coupled with a technical mastery of form and metre (here the novel Italian importation, *terza rima*), that had rarely if ever been achieved in English verse since the days of Chaucer. The satire, with its very particular locus 'in Kent and Christendom', leaves readers in little doubt about either who wrote it or why. There is, indeed, a seemingly robust honesty to the poet's opening acknowledgement of the real reason for his residence in the country:

> Myne owne John Poyntz, sins ye delight to know
> The cawse why that homeward I me draw,
> And fle the presse of courtes wher soo they goo

> Rather then to lyve thrall under the awe
> Of lordly lookes, wrapped within my cloke,
> To will and lust lerning to set a lawe,
> It is not for becawsse I skorne or moke
> The power of them to whome fortune hath lent
> Charge over us . . .
>
>   (1–9)

This recognition that the narrator (unlike the poets of his immediate sources who chose retirement for themselves) is in Kent for a period of enforced corrective discipline, 'learning to set a law' to 'will and lust', sets the poem squarely in the context of Wyatt's dismissal to Allington to learn 'to addres him better'.[11] And that note of compulsion and punishment returns later in an acknowledgement that his pleasure and liberty are limited by a metaphorical 'clog'—a wooden block tied to the feet of prisoners and domestic animals to restrict their movements:

> This maketh me at home to hounte and hawke
> And in fowle weder at my booke to sitt.
> In frost and snowe then with my bow to stawke,
> No man doeth marke where so I ride or goo;
> In lusty lees at libertie I walke,
> And of these newes I fele nor wele nor woo,
> Sauf that a clogg docth hang yet at my hele:
> No force for that, for it is ordered so
> That I may lepe boeth hedge and dike full well.
>
>   (80–8)

Albeit he insists that the restraint does not prevent him from ranging widely within his father's estates, the acknowledgement of the 'clog' must nonetheless have been a painful one for a poet who had previously celebrated his escape from Italian 'gives' and 'chains' with such obvious exultation in his *impressa*. Once again, it seems, as in the 'bell tower' poems, Wyatt knew what it was to be fettered, and was writing about the experience in verse.

The specific pretext for the poet's exile and his recent experiences in the Tower seem also to have been written into the early lines of the text, if we follow Scattergood in taking the references to those who have the power 'to strike the stroke' (9) to refer both to his own punishment, and to the specific strokes of the headsman that killed Queen Anne and her fellow victims.[12] Either way, the poet's statement that he does not 'skorne or moke / The power of them to whome fortune hath lent / Charge over us, of Right' (7–8) offers the first hint of the poem's highly critical attitude towards royal authority. Even the hasty qualification, 'of Right', which has no equivalent in Alamanni's text, cannot efface the scepticism explicit in the claim that the power 'to strike' is merely lent to those in authority by Fortune, rather than by God or justice (Alamanni's text has spoken, more directly still, of 'those to whom Fortune has given the power to govern us,

whether on account of their birth or for their great possessions').[13] The idea that
Fortune presides over the life of the courtier, making or breaking careers as she
chooses, is a commonplace of anti-curial satire. But specific contexts suggest
specific meanings. And here the republican sympathies of the Italian text seem to
chime with the particularities of Wyatt's recent experience to produce an especially pointed observation on contemporary politics. This, the poem implies, is a
poet speaking freely and from the heart about the conditions that have driven
him from court into the Home Counties of an idealized rural England.

   Again, there is an engaging honesty to the speaker's acceptance that he is not
immune to those attractions of court service that motivate men, like Poyntz, who
remain in the King's household:

> I grawnt sumtime that of glorye the fyar
> Dothe touche my hart: me lyst not to report
> Blame by honowr and honour to desyar;
> But how may I this honour now atayne
> That cannot dy the coloure blake a lyer?
>
> (14–18)[14]

But, for Wyatt as for Alamanni, that honesty is an integral part of the poem's
rhetorical strategy: an initial concession that allows him to launch an assault
upon the dishonesty of the court with greater force and conviction. It is not the
idea of a life at court that repels the speaker, he claims, but his specific experience
of *this* court *now*. With its inverted value system and capacity to destroy all those
who resist its pressures, the English court offers a particular model of rapacity and
corruption that his viewpoint from the untainted Kentish landscape allows him
to see clearly for the first time. To demonstrate the truth of this observation the
poet characteristically intersperses conventional criticisms, translated faithfully
from his Italian source, of the drunkenness, greed, and hypocrisy of courtiers,
with flashes of specific and dangerous contemporary resonance. And here it is
clearly implied that the problem with the English court is not simply the general
immorality of its residents, but the particular cruelty and despotism of its ruler:

> I cannot crowche nor knelle, nor do so great a wrong
> To worship them like God on erthe alone
> That are as wollfes thes sely lambes among.
>
> (25–7)

Again, such sentiments are on one level only an intensification of ideas familiar
from other anti-curial satires, but in the contexts of Henry's Supremacy and the
deaths of Anne and her fellow defendants, it is hard not to see in them a more
immediate implication. Significantly Alamanni's text declared only that its
speaker could not kneel to worship treacherous and wicked people more than
he did the immortal gods.[15] The notions of worshipping a figure who is himself
godlike, 'on earth alone' (with its clear echo of Henry's claim to be sole and

supreme Head of the Church on earth) and who is like the ravenous wolf among
the innocent lambs, are Wyatt's own additions and appear to speak to personal
concerns. Similarly the lines that follow:

> I cannot with my wordes complayne and mone
> And suffer nought; nor smart without complaynt,
> Nor torne the worde that from my mouthe is gyven...
>
> (28–30)

have a very different implication when spoken by someone who was known to be
'smarting' under enforced rustication after unjust imprisonment than when read
in a text written by a foreign author whose exact circumstances are less well
known. (It was later alleged against Wyatt that he 'doth often call to his
remembrance his imprisonment in the Tower, which seemeth so to stick in his
stomach that he cannot forget it', to which he replied: 'If they take grudging for
being sorry or grieving...I grant it'.)[16] And such immediate implications could
only have been heightened by the poet's decision to substitute at key moments a
singular oppressive ruler for the many 'masters' alluded to in Alamnni's text.
Thus where the latter has,

> *Non saprei dentro all'alte soglie infide*
> *Per piu mostrar amor, contr'à mia voglia*
> *Imitar sempre altrui se piange, oride.*

[In the treacherous high halls of the mighty I could not try to show devotion by going against
my inclinations and crying when my masters cried or laughing when they laughed.][17]

Wyatt writes that he cannot,

> Grynne when *he* laugheth that bereth all the swaye,
> Frowne when he frowneth and grone when he is pale,
> On others lust to hang boeth nyght and daye.
>
> (53–5, my italics)

As the poem progresses, this focus upon a single oppressive ruler and the
particular pressures of a cruel, despotic regime become more apparent and
specific.

> I cannot wrest the law to fill the coffer,
> With innocent blode to fede my sellff ffat,
> And doo most hurt where most hellp I offer.
> I am not he that can alow [praise] the state
> Off highe Cesar and dam Cato to dye,
> That with his dethe dyd skape owt off the gate
> From Cesares handes, if Lyvye do not lye,
> And wolld not lyve whar lyberty was lost:
> So did his hart the commonn wele aplye.
>
> (34–42)

At the same point in his satire, Alamanni had cited not Cato but Brutus:

> *Non di loda honorari chiara immortale*
> *Cesare, & Sylla, condannando a torto*
> *Bruto, & la schiera che pui d'altra vale.*

[I could not honour with bright immortal praise... Caesar and Silla, while wrongfully condemning... Brutus and the company which has no peer in worth.][18]

Why the poet should have omitted reference to Brutus and substituted Cato Uticensis here has provoked considerable debate among critics.[19] Cato fought against Caesar at the battle of Thapsus (46 BCE) and lost, subsequently taking his own life rather than allowing himself to be taken prisoner and paraded in triumph. He was thus an open opponent of the Emperor rather than a conspirator and regicide. Was the poet, then, merely censoring an overtly anti-monarchical reference in favour of something marginally less offensive? The question goes to the heart of the problem facing opponents of princely government—or the government of particular princes—in this period. For, given that religious, political, and legal theory alike forbad the killing of one's anointed sovereign, however tyrannical he might be, the options facing someone who found intolerable the regime under which they were living were few indeed. If Wyatt could not openly applaud a regicide without following Alamanni into opposition to the princely subject of his verse: a position which a lifetime in royal service would militate against, he could at least celebrate a more passive, stoical act of resistance. And Cato's taking of his own life in order to thwart the designs of a proto-tyrant offered an example that other sixteenth-century writers had already singled out for praise. As Mason notes, Erasmus had celebrated Cato's 'honourable' death in his *Apophthegms*.

Cato maluit honestam mortem quam oppressa publica libertate cuiquam servire.
   [Cato rather chose death with honour than after the oppressing of the public liberty and freedom to be as a bondservant to any person.][20]

Closer to home, Elyot's *Governor* had made very clear the respective worth of Sylla and Caesar on the one hand and Cato on the other. In his chapter on 'Ambition', Elyot cited both Sylla and Caesar among those cruel emperors 'by whose ambition more Romans were slain than in acquiring the empire of all the world'.[21] Conversely Cato appeared as an example of the virtue 'Constancy or Stability':

The constancy of Cato Uticensis was all way immoveable, in so much as at sundry times, when he in the Senate eagerly defended the public weal with vehement and long orations against the attempts of ambitious persons; he was by them rebuked and committed to prison; but, he therefore not ceasing but going toward prison, detected [revealed] to the people as he went the unlawful purposes and enterprises of them by whom he was punished, with the pile [spoliation] that was imminent to the public weal: which he did with such courage and eloquence that as well the Senate as the people drew so about him, that his adversaries were fain for fear to discharge him. Who can sufficiently commend this noble man Cato, when he readeth in the works of Plutarch of his excellent courage and virtue? How much worthier had he been to have had Homer the trumpe[t] of his fame immortal than Achilles, who for a little wench contended with Agamemnon only, where Cato for the conservation of the weal public contended and also resisted against Julius Caesar and the great Pompey, and not only against their menaces, but also against their desires and offers of alliance.[22]

Hence by siding, not with Brutus but with Cato, the champion of the commonwealth against proto-tyrants, Wyatt aligns himself with an ideal of stoic constancy and dedication to the public weal. Significantly too, as Elyot declares, Cato represented resistance to the allure of compromising with cruelty as well as the fear of succumbing to its threats. By rejecting both the 'menaces' and the 'offers of alliance' presented by Caesar and Pompey, he offered an example for the courtier who, like Wyatt, must choose between remaining in the honest backwater of Allington and returning to court when and if the offer of further employment came.

What this small but significant variation from his source suggests is that Wyatt was already thinking carefully as he wrote this first satire about the responsibilities of the subject under an oppressive regime, and beginning to differentiate a distinctly English response to the problem. Rather than adopting wholesale Alamanni's classically based republican admiration for Brutus, he chooses a figure more amenable to his own situation, a stoic defender of liberty who was free of the ambiguous legacy of regicide. In alluding to Cato's case, Wyatt considered a man whose experience encompassed both absolute engagement with public life through advocacy and argument in the Senate and absolute withdrawal from that life through suicide. And his stated response suggests that, at this stage, the choice between them represented a real and unsolved dilemma for the poet. The text thus suggests a kind of paralysis, with the narratorial 'I' torn between two competing impulses neither of which he was prepared completely to embrace. Hence he defines himself, here as elsewhere, not by active choice of what he wishes to be, but by a statement of what he cannot be, what he is not able or prepared to do. He cannot praise the state of high Caesar, if that will consequently damn Cato to die.[23] But he cannot explicitly damn high Caesar either. His resistance is thus passive and implicit rather than active and open.

There is a clear sense in these lines, nonetheless, of the attractiveness to Wyatt of Cato's chosen destiny, to 'skape owt off the gate' and so deprive Caesar of his triumph. If he cannot approve of the kind of regime that forces lovers of liberty and the commonweal to die, Wyatt can nonetheless admire the courage of such men who choose death rather than live where liberty is lost. There is a hint here, then, that the poet is skirting around the deeper issue beneath the surface of his anti-curial satire. He might present his own withdrawal to Kent as a superior alternative to life at court, but the citation of Cato and his fate signals an awareness that rustic retreat was not the real answer to the dilemma of whether or not to engage with the demands of a despotic regime. To live a life of ease, hunting when the weather permits and reading when it does not, is not the real answer. What rustication offers Wyatt is simply a vacation from the pressures of the court, a period of liberty in which to consider what he really intends to do. And 'Myne owne John Poyntz' suggests that he was not yet ready to answer that question with any certainty.

Hence in the catalogue of simple pleasures that he offers as a prospectus for the self-sufficient completeness of the rural life he nonetheless always keeps one eye (and often both) on the court that he ostensibly vilifies. Such was often the way in anti-curial satire. Writers from Juvenal onwards had derided the corruption of city and court and extolled by contrast the honest virtues of the country. And the humanists of the sixteenth century took up and rehearsed those positions almost verbatim, making them their own in so doing. And yet such authors nonetheless flocked to court at every opportunity and sought employment there with tireless commitment. How can such obvious self-contradiction be accounted for? The easiest recourse would be to dismiss such behaviour as hypocritical, the mouthing of conventional virtues to gloss the pursuit of simple self-interest or to make a virtue of necessity.[24] But it was more than that. These contrary impulses speak to a deep-seated contradiction at the heart of humanism itself. The Senecan and Ciceronian values that underpinned the humanist position were active, civic values. They found their fullest expression only in the pursuit of the public good and service of the state.[25] Hence men like Wyatt, Elyot, and Sir Thomas More were drawn to court and to royal service by principle as well as personal ambition. They sought to improve and redeem the state, even—indeed especially—when they saw it to be fallen and corrupted; a task that could only be performed at the heart of the political machine: at court and in counsel.

Repulsion and attraction were thus in endless unresolved conflict when such men considered the question of whether or not to 'go to court'. This was the dilemma that animated the first book of More's *Utopia* and gave it its cutting edge. Every courtly reader—every reader who was touched by or recognized the humanist impulse—would appreciate its relevance to their own lives. And yet every reader would also recognize that the outcome of the debate was inevitable. Regardless of the contradictions implicit in the decision, the humanist *had* to go to court, to take up a place on the royal council if he could. In order to remain true to his civic ideals every gentleman must devote his life to the service and betterment of the state. The kind of neo-stoicism that praised the comforts of the rural life *and stayed there to enjoy them* was simply not an option for the humanists. And yet, as Wyatt's verse reveals, the virtuous path of returning to court and bringing the values of the country and neo-stoic self-sufficiency to the task of governing the realm better was problematic too, especially if the conventional avenue of engagement with public life—counselling the prince—was itself closed off, whether through exclusion from court or the failure of the prince to listen to counsel. For Wyatt, then, the problem was especially intractable. As a man in exile he did not have the option to return to court, however strong the desire to do so may have been. And yet he also had good reason to doubt whether going to court would allow him to put his humanist principles into practice anyway. What could he do, then, but lament his fate as eloquently as possible? The evidence of 'Myne own John Poyntz' implies, as I suggested earlier, that Wyatt's solution was to seek out a form of political engagement, and a form of writing about politics, that circumvented the impulse to counsel the King, and created instead a new community of readers with a very different set of political concerns and priorities.

In the discussion of Cato, as in the poem as a whole, Wyatt was beginning to find a voice for himself under the new conditions created by the events of May 1536 and his exclusion from London. The writer who had hitherto presented himself in his verse as a creature fundamentally in and of the court, entertaining it with his lyrics and recycling its amorous intrigues, petty jealousies, and gossip in his verse, now sought instead to define himself by his separation from that environment. As Stephen Greenblatt put it, the satires as a whole, and 'Myne Owne John Poyntz' in particular, mark Wyatt's 'struggle to clear himself from the entanglements that had nearly brought him to the scaffold and to achieve a new mode of address', to write into being a new public identity and 'discover... his true voice', a process of defining himself as a writer that would also redefine him as a person. 'The goal [was]... to take control of one's life by finding within oneself a sustaining center.'[26] And Wyatt found that centre in the 'new stoic identity' suggested by Alamanni's text and the traditions which it shared with the writings of Erasmus, More, and Elyot.[27] The value of this stoic identity, as Colin Burrow suggests, lay precisely in its capacity to identify and locate that stable, 'sustaining centre' of identity within the subject himself rather than in his relationship to his sovereign or the court: 'it enabled writers excluded from court to present themselves as possessed of inner power and autonomy'. For Wyatt it turned 'the experience of exclusion' (to borrow Burrow's apt formulation) into an experience of going 'homeward' to a firmer, truer centre.[28]

So Wyatt was able to speak in this satire in ways that he could not have risked in the medium of courtly lyric, voicing his independence repeatedly in terms of what his new self was unable to do. In so doing he could turn the initially disabling lack of affirmation into a decisive negative energy. Increasingly the poem makes clear that what Wyatt 'could not do' was compromise with the specific policies and personality of his prince. He could not, he claimed, name 'crueltie' 'Zele of justice and chaunge in tyme and place' (68–9), tacitly associating the unprecedented political and religious changes of the 1530s with the viciousness that he identified at court. Finally he came as close as he could under the terms of the 1534 Treason Act (which made it a specific offence to call the King a tyrant) to protesting that Henry VIII was sliding into despotism, and liberty really was in danger of being lost here and now in England, when he declared that he could not call:

> The letcher a lover, and tirannye
> To be the right of a prynces reigne.
>
> (74–5)

The collation of lechery and tyranny, the one masquerading as courtly love, the other as good kingship, is Wyatt's own addition to his source. And it demonstrates that Wyatt had but one prince and one state in mind as he wrote, the prince who had married Jane Seymour mere days after he had executed Anne Boleyn, and had spent most of May 1536 seeking to refute those rumours of his impotence that had surfaced during the treason trials by provocatively revelling with a succession of ladies to the consternation of foreign observers.[29]

That these lines mark the emotional climax of the text for Wyatt is made clear by the remarkable irruption of personal emotion that punctuates the verse at this point, stopping the narrative in its tracks with a series of staccato denials with no precedent in the poet's source:

> I cannot, I; no, no, it will not be!
>
> (76)

In that decisive 'no, it will not be!' Wyatt acknowledges both the identity of the problem that the poem could not name, and his chosen solution to it. Thereafter, he turns away from describing the horrors of the court to discuss the pleasures of the country, and both syntax and vocabulary proclaim that the psychological climacteric of the text has passed. Although he still cannot state openly the obvious fact that it is the king's despotism that keeps him from the court, the narrator nonetheless writes hereafter as if he has explained the matter to Poyntz's full satisfaction. '*This* is the cause that I could never yet / Hang on their slevis' (77–8, my italics), he concludes, as if 'this' was now fully understood. '*This* maketh me at home to hounte and hawke' (80), and *this* is why he has chosen to reject the life of the courtier in favour of study and writing 'in Kent and Christendome / Emong the muses where I rede and ryme' (100–101). Wyatt had found his voice and deployed it as effectively as the law allowed him to protest against the events that he had witnessed in May 1536.

'My Mother's Maids'

The question of how to address the literally unspeakable thought that the king had fallen into tyranny also haunts the second of Wyatt's satires, 'My Mother's Maids', which was similarly addressed to John Poyntz, and almost certainly written at Allington in the late summer or early autumn of 1536. Like its predecessor, it too circles around the naming of the dread truth, proceeding from a conventional model to the particular case, and investing borrowed material with lines that speak directly to Wyatt's own thoughts and experience.

While precisely rooted in the details of Wyatt's life (claiming as it does to be a recollection of a song of his mother's serving women), the poem begins nonetheless with a series of effects which problematize its connection to his own inventive mind. Given the distance that it will travel in the course of its 112 lines of *terza rima* towards denouncing the Henrician state as tyrannical, it is perhaps no surprise that the poet should seek to disguise the originality of the work, and downplay its claims to literary authority. Hence he presents it as a work song, a *chanson de toile*, recalled from his childhood; a song which itself drew upon an ancient fable, by implication already well known to both the poet and his intended audience:

> My mothers maydes when they did sowe and spynne,
> They sang sometyme a song of the feld mowse,
> That forbicause her lyvelood was but thynne,
> Would nedes goo seke her townyssh systers howse.

> (Muir and Thompson 106, 1–4)

The formulation '*a* song of *the* feld mowse' implies the precise balance of familiarity and distance between reader and narrative that Wyatt desires to convey. The root story of the mouse, it suggests, is well known (indeed it had first appeared among the fables attributed to Aesop in the fifth century BC, and was subsequently reworked many times, most recently in Caxton's translation of Aesop of 1484, and by the Scottish Chaucerian Robert Henryson among his *Moral Fables*, written at the end of the fifteenth century).[30] The version that Wyatt intends to repeat is, he suggests, just another version of that old story, hence his variations upon its traditional theme would be obvious and noticed. And by identifying it as a worksong, sung by women simply to pass the time and ease their labours, he reduces the apparent contemporary relevance of the text still further. How could a women's song based upon an ancient fable, recalled from a distant Kentish childhood, have any bearing upon current events? And yet, of course, to base the poem in fable and the proverbial wisdom of working women (however genteel their actual 'labour') was also, paradoxically, to claim for it another form of authority, rooting it in the timeless folk-wisdom of the countryside and the rhythms of the labouring year. As he read those opening lines Wyatt almost certainly intended John Poyntz to feel the pressure of both claims: to the safety of universality and to the authority of timeless wisdom.

A similar artfulness, a light-fingered dexterity at play with the competing claims of rustic simplicity and wisdom, is evident in one of the poet's principal sources for this part of the text, Horace's *Satire* II, vi. There Horace had presented his own life, retired from Rome on his Sabine farm, as the perfect existence, free from the snares of the city: 'a piece of land, not so very large, where there would be a garden, and near the house a spring of ever-flowing water, and above these a bit of woodland...I am content. Nothing more do I ask, O son of Maia [Mercury], save that thou make these blessings last my life long.'[31] And as an apparently independent endorsement of that message he had introduced Aesop's story of the town mouse and the country mouse, ostensibly as an anecdote told by his country neighbour Cervius, among a series of 'old wives' tales'.[32] Wyatt takes up Cervius's story and retells it as a product of his own childhood memories. But, as with his treatment of Alamanni's satire, he adapts his source, turning it in the act of translation into a tool suitable for his own particular ends. The Aesopian fable, like Cervius's retelling of it, involved parallel exchange visits, first of the town mouse to her sister's country home, and then of the rustic mouse to the former's house in the city. The disadvantages of country life as seen through the eyes of the town mouse evidently did not interest Wyatt, however, nor did they serve his satirical ends. For he dispensed with the first half of the conventional diptych entirely, concentrating instead almost exclusively on the perils of the court as they manifested themselves to the country mouse. The hardships of rural living are briefly sketched out in the opening lines as a means of establishing the country mouse's motive for moving to court ('The stormy blastes her cave so sore did sowse / That when the forowse swymmed with the rain / She must lyve cold and whete in sorry plight' (6–8)), but the remainder of the fable is devoted to an acute and chilling anatomization of the paranoia induced by life at court.

In order to give still greater sharpness to the theme, the poet altered the ending of the traditional tale too. Rather than having the country mouse return reconciled to her humble home, relieved to have escaped the urban hell that is her sister's lot, he leaves her in the court, trapped as the narrative section of the poem closes, in the instant of the cat's terrifying assault. We leave her, presumably on the point of death, but forever frozen by the poet's failure to complete the story, in an endless moment of dying:

> At the threshold her sely fote did tripp,
> And ere she myght recover it again,
> The traytour Catt had caught her by the hipp,
> And made her there against her will remain
> That had forgotten her poure suretie and rest
> For semyng welth wherin she thought to rayne.
>
> (64–9)

By turning away from the story at precisely this point to address his intended reader directly ('Alas, my Poyntz, how men do seke the best . . . '), Wyatt, with his own variety of feline mischief, plays cruelly with his reader's expectations of narrative closure, prolonging the mouse's death-throes to an infinity of irresolution. But then, it is the moral that he seeks to draw from the tale rather than the tale itself that is crucial, so for him the narrative can be put aside as soon as it has done its work. Hence he turns briskly from his tale to consider its implications for himself and his readership.

Quite what moral should be drawn from that tale is no simple question to answer. The fable operates on a number of interconnected levels. Ostensibly its targets are the misconceptions that prompt individuals to search for happiness in situations that can only bring greater danger and misery. In this respect it follows its sources all the way back to their Aesopian progenitor, and the moral it conveys is politically quiescent: be content with one's lot, since the lives of one's betters, however superficially alluring, are likely to prove much worse. This was the moral that Caxton drew from his translation of the tale, which he closed with the words: 'therefore it is good to live poorly and surely, for the poor liveth more surely than the rich'.[33] But beneath that conformist narrative, and underpinning it, Wyatt develops a far more politically engaged and radical agenda concerning *why* it is that life at court should be so dangerous to the unwary. Here the poet goes much further than most previous exponents of anti-curial satire in suggesting, not simply that all courts are endemically corrupt and dangerous, but that the English court is particularly so at present, and for very specific reasons. To develop the point the poet moves from one set of source texts to another, turning his attention from Horace and the Aesopian tradition to the works of Persius, Boethius, and Chaucer.

To Cervius's picture of a physically dangerous townhouse, overrun with 'Molossian hounds', Wyatt adds an element of psychological danger, of a fear not simply of death or discovery, but of words themselves, and the dangers they bear. The theme is introduced in the marvellously well-observed vignette of the country mouse's arrival at her sister's home:

> And to the dore now is she come by stelth
> And with her foote anon she scrapeth full fast.
> Th'othre for fere durst not well scarse appere,
> Of every noyse so was the wretche agast.
> At last she asked softly who was there;
> And in her langage as well as she cowd,
> 'Pepe', quod the other, 'Syster I ame here.'
> 'Peace', quod the towne mowse, 'Why spekest thou so lowde?'
>
> (36–43)

As Colin Burrow suggests, there is a political edge to this scene, created by the context of the 1534 Treason Act, which made words alone sufficient proof of treason.[34] This is a poem marked by silences and whispers, into which the country mouse is drawn before she is even aware of the precise nature of the danger to which she has exposed herself. That danger is represented by the courtly cat, a neat variation on the dogs that inhabit both Horace and Caxton's texts.[35] It is no mere hunter of flesh and bone, but a psychologically unsettling presence, in Burrow's phrase, 'a terrifying projection of ill-defined, almost extra-linguistic... fears'.[36] An apt embodiment, perhaps, of the particular terrors generated by life under the 1534 Act, a threat that can be seen only by the 'ascaunce' (sideways) glance, lurking dangerously beyond the threshold of full visibility. To describe it, as the text suggests in its anxious flitting between the source of the threat and the emotions of the witness, is to describe fear itself:

> . . . as she loked ascaunce
> Under a stole she spied two stemyng ise [i.e. eyes]
> In a rownde hed with sherp erys; in Fraunce
> Was never mowse so ferd, for tho th'unwise
> Had not i-sene suche a beest before,
> Yet had nature taught her after her gyse
> To know her ffoo and dred hym evermore.
>
> (53–8)

Wyatt probably found his model for this allusive, cruelly comic passage in his reading of Chaucer.[37] For in the latter's best-known beast fable, *The Nun's Priest's Tale*, the narrator had introduced the 'col fox', ostensible assassin of the cockerel Chanticleer, with a similar vagueness regarding his appearance, in a dream vision of a doglike beast characterized by details of bright eyes and pointed ears:

> Me mette [dreamt] how that I romed up and doun
> Within our yeerd, wheer as I saugh a beest
> Was lyk an hound, and wolde han maad areest
> Upon my body, and wolde han had me deed.
> His colour was bitwixe yelow and reed,
> And tipped was his tayl and bothe his eeris
> With blak, unlyke the remenant of his heeris;
> His snowte smal, with glowynge eyen tweye;
> Yet of his look for feere almoost I deye.
>
> (CT VII, 2897–906)

There too Wyatt could have found a similar point about a vulnerable creature's instinctive capacity to 'know her ffoo' regardless of previous experience:

> For natureelly a beest desireth flee
> Fro his contrarie, if he may it see,
> Though he never erst hadde seyn it with his ye.
>
> (4076–8)

But, if the allusion to Chaucer was intended to be recognized, it was with mischievous intent, for Chanticleer would escape the clutches of his putative nemesis, outfoxing him at his own smooth-talking game and ascending triumphantly to safety in a nearby tree. No such salvation awaited the country mouse, as we have seen. The moral of her story is not the possibility of redemption for all who err, nor even that one might learn a lesson and return home a sadder and a wiser mouse, but the inescapability of the dangers of the court, and an awareness that those dangers were linked bafflingly but inextricably with violence and death. If Wyatt and Poyntz had read *Piers Plowman*, they would have given a particular name to the source of those dangers, for in the Prologue to that text the 'cat of the court', that 'cam whan hym lyked', and overleapt the lowly cats and mice, 'laught [seized] hem of his wille / And pleide with hem perillousli and possed [dashed (them)] aboute' (149–51), was the King, and the mice and rats the Commons and Lords of Parliament, 'Comen to counseil for the commune profit' (148).[38]

Wyatt had explored the dangers of courtly life before in a remarkable, 'suicidal' poem perhaps written during the dark days of May 1536. It still more explicitly imagined the pressures and paranoia of life in the Henrician court as a ravenous animal presence lurking on the margins of experience:

> Like as a byrde in the cage enclosed,
> The dore unsparred and the hawke without,
> Twixte deth and prison piteously oppressed
> Whether for to chose standith in dowt.
> Certes so do I, wyche syeke to bring about
> Wyche shuld be best by determination,
> By losse off liefe libertye or liefe by preson . . .
>
> But deathe were deliveraunce and liefe lengthe off payne:
> Off two ylles, let see nowe chuse the lest:
> This birde to deliver youe that here her playne,
> Your advise, yowe lovers, wyche shalbe best
> In cage thraldome, or by the hauke to be opprest;
> And which for to chuse? Make playne conclusyon,
> By losse off lieffe libertye or liefe by prison.
>
> (Muir and Thompson 246, 1–7, 22–8)

Whether they were figured as a hovering hawk or a stalking cat, the implied message was the same: to be at court was always to be subject to predatory forces, and the freedoms that such a life offered were merely illusory.

The final lines of 'My Mother's Maids' identify both the true target of the satire as a whole and the nature of its political agenda. Having turned directly to the moral of the tale ('Alas, my Poyntz, how men do seke the best / And fynde the wourst by errour as they stray!' (70–1)), Wyatt makes clear that he has a very particular sort of 'men' in mind as the subjects of his anger:

> Hens fourth, my Poynz, this shalbe all and some:
> These wretched fools shall have nought els of me
> But to the great god and to his high dome
> None othre pain pray I for theim to be
> But when the rage doeth led from the right
> That lowking backward vertue they may se,
> Even as she is so goodly fayre and bright,
> And whilst they claspe their lustes in armes across [ie embrace them]
> Graunt theim, goode lorde, as thou maist of thy myght,
> To fret inward for losing such a losse.
>
> (103–12)

A number of critics have seen this passage as an anomalous conclusion to the satire, finding the sudden outburst of emotion concerning these unnamed 'fools' an incongruous intrusion into the text, unmotivated and unheralded by what had gone before.[39] But the outburst is actually the heart of the poem, the point to which it has always been leading and the moment in which Wyatt makes clear its purpose. For these are no generalized lines of moral opprobrium. They are translated directly from Persius's Third *Satire*, and their targets are tyrannical governors:

> *Magne pater divum, saevos punire tyrannos*
> *Haut alia ratione velis, cum dira libido*
> *Moverit ingenium ferventi tincta veneno:*
> *Virtutem videant intabescantque relicta.*

> (*Satire* iii, 35–8)

[O mighty Father of the gods! Be it thy will to punish cruel tyrants whose souls have been stirred by the deadly poison of evil lust in no other way but this—that they may look on virtue, and pine away because they have lost her.][40]

Even though Wyatt substitutes an inoffensive, generalized 'they' for the 'inhuman tyrants' who were Persius's explicit target, the implications of these lines would have been clear to anyone who knew the text from which he was translating. And the implication of both of these 'bookish' satires addressed to John Poyntz was that he and other educated readers would indeed have known all of the texts from which the poet was drawing his material. He would know that Persius's third *Satire* spoke directly to Wyatt's current condition, and was probably in his thoughts as he wrote each of the texts that the poet had addressed to him, for it too deals explicitly with the difficulties of writing and with the life of the gentleman in country retreat. More pointedly it also discusses the case of Cato Uticensis, recalling an oration devised to be delivered by the stoic hero prior to his suicide that the youthful narrator hated to recite (*Satire*, iii, 45–50). Hence it may well have been his reading of Persius that inspired the poet to use Cato in the place of Brutus in 'Myne owne John Poyntz'.

By concluding his text with this passage, Wyatt makes clear the specifically political target of the satire: the despotic sway of tyrants. But the nature of his moral is implicit throughout the second section of the text, from the moment that the narrator abruptly turns from the unfinished beast fable to address his reader so directly. The tale of the mice—or rather of the one mouse who was tempted to enter the court in search of a better life—has become in Wyatt's hands an allegorical demonstration of the foolishness of wilfully seeking fulfilment in places where it manifestly cannot be found. And, as he goes on to illustrate for Poyntz's benefit the various forms in which such foolishness might manifest itself, as men erroneously seek for the best, but find the worst, it quickly becomes clear that the particular case of foolish kings is what he has foremost in his mind. That focus governs both the kinds of folly that he describes and the sources to which he turns for his illustrations.

The idea of the 'sight oppressed' man led into the ditch by a blind guide he found, of course, in Matthew 15:14: 'And if the blind lead the blind, both fall into the pit.' But, despite the suggestion that 'Eche kynd of lyff hath with him his disease' (80), he soon turns away from biblical material and homely questions of poor travellers and ditches to focus upon the follies of those who have the power to rule kingdoms and make policy:

> O wretched myndes, ther is no gold that may
> Graunt that ye seke, no warre, no peace, no stryff,
> No, no, all tho thy hed were howpt [hooped] with gold,
> Sergeant with mace, hawbert, sword, nor knyff
> Cannot repulse the care that folowe should.
>
> (75–9)

As Mason suggests, the poet was probably adapting these lines from a passage in the sixteenth poem in the second book of Horace's *Odes*:

> *non enim gazae neque consularis*
> *summovet lictor miseros tumultus*
> *mentis et curas laqueata circum*
> *tecta volantes.*

[For 'tis not treasure nor even the consul's lictor that can banish the wretched tumults of the soul and cares that flit about the panelled ceilings [of the great].][41]

Significantly, where the Horatian text places the subject in the role of lictor, suggesting merely that the achievement of high office cannot dispel a citizen's cares, Wyatt makes his domestic equivalent, the sergeant, attendant upon the troubled king. It is thus not the delusions of Everyman that concern him, but those of one man in particular, the prince. Not all the prerogatives of the crown, he suggests, not the power to make war or peace, nor the servants and powers at his disposal, can protect the king from his own folly:

> Lyve in delight evyn as thy lust would
> And thou shalt fynde whan lust doeth moost the[e] please
> It irketh strait and by it self doth fade.
>
> (81–3)

'Lust' here might mean no more than a generalized desire, but, given the context, it might also have carried an additional sexual resonance for courtly readers. Certainly in a year in which the King had executed one queen and married another there was a political edge implicit in any discussion of the soon-cloyed tastes of a pleasure-seeking mind—and such implications could only have been sharpened by any hint that the pleasures sought were sexual.

The curious excursion into the rhetorical trope of 'impossibilities' that follows might suggest a widening of focus, a dilution of the political material by a more generalized discussion of folly. But close attention to Wyatt's sources suggests a more specific intention. It would not take much to correct such foolishness as his targets reveal, he suggests, 'A small thing it is, that may thy mynde apese' (84).

> None of ye all there is that is so madde
> To seke grapes upon brambles or breers,
> Nor none I trow that hath wit so badd
> To set hay for conys [rabbits] over Ryvers,
> Ne ye set not a dragg net for an hare,
> And yet the thing that moost is your desire
> Ye do mysseke with more travaill and care.
>
> (85–91)

The most immediate source for such ideas was the *Adagia* of Erasmus, and a passage that Wyatt had already borrowed to flesh out his translation of *The Quiet of Mind* at the point where it describes the folly of an unstable mind. Such minds, Wyatt's earlier text suggested, blamed fortune when they could not achieve their impossible ambitions:

as it were to be angry with fortune that thou canst not shoot an arrow with a plough, or hunt an hare with an axe, and that some cruel god should be against them that with vain endeavour hunt an hart with a drag net and not thy attempt to do those impossibilities by their own madness and foolishness. Surely the cause of this error is the naughty love of our self.[42]

Such self-love he associates once again with those who sought authority with princes and with the excessive ambitions of tyrants:

Denys the elder [Dionysus of Sicily] thought it not enough to be the greatest tyrant in his time, but evil content also that he was not so good as the poet Phylarenus in poetry, and as Plato in the craft of reasoning, moved with ire, him he put into a dungeon, and th'other he sold and banished in to Aeginas.[43]

A second likely source for such ideas also linked them to the theme of tyranny. For, as Scattergood observes, a similar interest in the wilful pursuit of the impossible characterizes the discussion of despotism in Boethius's *Consolation of Philosophy*, a text itself written from a prison cell by another victim of an oppressive regime.[44] Wyatt would have found the relevant passage translated by Chaucer in Thynne and Tuke's edition of the poet's *Works*:

Alas! Which folly and which ignorance misleadeth wandering wretches from the path of very good. Certes ye ne seek no gold in green trees, ne ye ne gather not precious stones in vines; ne ye ne hide not your gins [traps] in high mountains to catch fish, of which ye may make rich feasts.

And if you like to hunt to Roes [roe deer], ye ne go not to the fords of the water that hight [i.e. are called] Thyrene.[45]

Wyatt clearly had Boethius in his mind as he was writing this part of the satire, for he had taken the comment cited earlier about the 'small thing' that would appease the troubled mind from *The Consolation of Philosophy*.[46] And he turns to the same text again in the subsequent lines in which he describes to Poyntz the alternative philosophy that would bring peace to the unquiet mind:

> Make playn thyn hert that it be not knotted
> With hope or dred and se thy will be bare
> From all affectes [mental attributes] whome vice hath ever spotted;
> Thy self content with that is the[e] assigned,
> And use it well that is to the[e] allotted.
> Then seke no more owte of thy self to fynde
> The thyng that thou haist sought so long before,
> For thou shall fele it sitting in thy mynde.
>
> (92–9)

Boethius had made the same point in a passage that Chaucer had translated as:

O ye mortal folk, what [why] seek ye then blissfulness out of your own self, which is put in yourself? [Error and folly confoundeth you].

(*Works*, fol. 243(v))[47]

This moral had arisen out of what is probably the definitive exposition of the Boethian neo-stoic position:

This same place that thou clepest [call] exile is country [home] to them that inhabit here, and forthy [therefore] nothing wretched but when thou weenest [think] it; as who sayeth: thou thyself ne no wight else nis [is not] a wretch but when he weneth himself he is a wretch by reputation of his courage. And, agenward [contrarily], all fortune is blissful to a man by the agreeability or by the egality of him that suffereth it. What man is that that is so wealful [fortunate] that nolde [would not] change his estate when he hath lost his patience? The sweetness of man's wealfulness is spraint [mingled] with many bitternesses. The which wealfulness, although it seem[s] sweet and joyful to him that useth it, yet may it not be withhold that it ne goeth away when it will.

Then it is well seen how wretched is the blissfulness of mortal things that neither it endureth perpetual[ly] with them that every fortune receive agreeably or egally, ne it desisteth not in all to them that be anguished.

(*Works*, fol. 243(v))

That the secret of survival in an unjust world was contentment with one's lot and the disciplining of an infected will; that 'hope and dread', the products of that will, were alike the enemies of quietness: these were ideas central to the neo-stoic position.[48] Wyatt had drawn heavily upon them in his translation of *The Quiet of Mind*, and, as Mason suggests, the poet was probably recalling that text when he warned Poyntz that if he 'Let present passe and gape on tyme to come', he would only 'diepe' himself in 'travaill more and more' (101–2).[49] He deployed them again in the brief mirror for the prince he had earlier translated from Boethius, which enjoined its readers to 'flee from the rage / Of cruell wyll' and from 'the foule yolke of sensuall bondage' (Muir and Thompson 261, 2–3). But crucially, for Wyatt, such a philosophy was not primarily a transcendent guide to self-preservation and the virtuous life as it was for Boethius. For him it was always primarily associated with questions of government and kingship. That is, the problems of the wilful man were always most obviously and particularly the problems of the wilful King, as the 'moral' that he drew from the Boethian lyric suggests:

> If thy desire have over thee the power
> Subject then art thou and no governour.
>
> (6–7)

If all men must discipline their lusts and rule themselves correctly, Wyatt suggests, that need was all the more obvious and pressing for governors.

Wyatt is thus saying allusively here what he had suggested tacitly before in 'Myne owne John Poyntz'. Only here he says it with greater detail and clarity. The reason why the court was so dangerous and so inimical to him, and to all those who thought like him, was because the King had made it so. The prince who had begun his reign so ambitious for virtue, aiming to 'seek the best', had indeed found the worst in its stead, straying through error into the very vice of tyranny that he had so strenuously condemned at his accession. By striving for powers, lusts, and delights above even the exalted status allotted to him, he had ended with the spotted mind and corrupted will of a despot. The return in these lines to that ready collocation of lechery and despotism that he had added to Alamanni's text in 'Myne owne John Poyntz' again signals the particularity of the poet's vision concerning Henry's crimes. Men like Wyatt had sought to counsel him back to the path of virtuous self-sufficiency:

> Thy self content with that is the[e] assigned
> And use it well that is to the[e] allotted.
> Then seke no more owte of thy selfe to fynde
> The thing that thou haist sought so long before,
> For thou shalt fele it sitting in thy mynde.
>
> (95–9)

But such words had fallen on deaf ears. And now the poet was reduced simply to condemning his king with the curse that Persius had passed upon all those rulers who fell into tyranny: may he eat himself away from within with thinking on what he once had been, what he once had possessed, and had now lost for ever. This was a particularly telling invocation given the flamboyant declarations of Henry's accession. It is a devastating moment, born no doubt of the particular circumstances of Wyatt's exile, of the frustrations created by imprisonment and exclusion, and the freedom that exclusion granted him to read widely and write from first principles, unchecked by the habitual caution that was the lot of town mouse and resident courtier alike.

And that moment would pass. Wyatt would, like the good humanist, return to court, and serve once more, loyally and to the best of his abilities, the King whom he had here condemned. Hence he answered the call to arms in October 1536, and joined the royal army mustering under the Duke of Norfolk to oppose the rebels in Lincolnshire and the northern counties, and he would later depart on diplomatic service to the Imperial court in March 1537. But, having once spoken the unspeakable thought, confiding in a friend through the semi-public medium of epistolary verse the treasonable idea that the King was a tyrant, Wyatt had nonetheless crossed the Rubicon in his mind. Thereafter his verse would no longer conform to conventional limits. He had indeed found his voice, and he would use it in future years to considerable effect, not merely in the third and most powerful of his epistolary satires, to which we shall turn next, but in the remarkable prose 'Defence' that he was to write from his cell on the third and final occasion that he was imprisoned by his king. He would use it again, as we shall see, in the last and most substantial of his poetic works, his adaptation of the seven Penitential Psalms. Our task now, however, is to consider the third satire, 'A Spending Hand', which Wyatt addressed to another courtier-poet, a man who like him had been arrested and questioned during the 'bloody days' of May 1536, and had survived to serve the crown again thereafter: Sir Francis Bryan.

'A Spending Hand'

The third of Wyatt's satires may have been written at the same time as the other two, as the poet languished during his five months of rustication in 1536. But, more plausibly it was produced later, in the period from May 1539 to February 1540, once Wyatt had returned from the ill-fated embassy to the imperial court that will be the subject of the next chapter.[50] Wyatt and Bryan had met in Nice during June and July 1537, where the latter convinced the poet to lend him the princely sum of £200 to help meet the costs of his own sojourn as ambassador to the French court.[51] This fact alone would provide ample justification for the poem's proverbial opening:

> A spending hand that alway powreth owte
> Had nede to have a bringer in as fast,
> And on the stone that still [continually] doeth tourne abowte
> There groweth no mosse: these proverbes yet do last.
>
> (Muir and Thompson 107, 1–4)

There is thus a definite edge to these ostensibly conventional sentiments, an evident 'bitchiness' (as Burrow suggests) that becomes more apparent the more one knows about the relationship between the two men.[52] But it is far from clear which of the two was supposed to feel the more embarrassed by these lines. Thomas Cromwell had gently rebuked Wyatt in January 1539 for having lent money that he needed himself to Bryan and to others:

I think your gentle frank heart doth much impoverish you. When you have money ye are content to part with it and lend it, as ye did lately...to Master Hobby [Philip Hoby, a royal Groom of the Chamber], the which I think had no need of then for he had large furnishment of money at his departure hence . . . Take heed, therefore, how ye part of such portion as ye need. And foresee rather to be provided yourself than for the provision of other to leave yourself naked: politic charity proceedeth not that way.[53]

Reflecting on the same theme, Wyatt, in thanking Cromwell 'for giving order for my money that I lent Master Bryan', had observed somewhat ruefully, 'If the King's honour more than his [Bryan's] credit had not been before mine eyes, he should have piped in an ivy leaf [i.e. whistled fruitlesly] for ought of me.'[54] So the poet may well have resented the fact that he had been obliged to be Bryan's 'bringer in'. Yet he also knew about the costs of maintaining an embassy, and was seeking money from Cromwell every bit as importunately as Bryan had sought it from him. Indeed, Cromwell, when agreeing to repay the money owed to Wyatt by Bryan, had pointedly told the poet, 'whosoever ought them, I have disbursed them . . . Other men make in manner of their debts mine own, for very oft where they have borrowed I am fained to pay'.[55] Any resentment towards Bryan on Wyatt's part must thus have been tempered by a sense of his own equal culpability, his own decidedly compromised position when it came to upbraiding those who spend more than they bring in.

Indeed, attempts to see the poem as aimed at humiliating Bryan, or as evidence of an ongoing antipathy between the two men, are overstated. There were more things to draw Wyatt and Bryan together than to thrust them apart. Both were advocates of the neo-stoic positions exemplified by Horace and Boethius. Both had a public reputation for plain speaking, especially in counselling the King: 'Sir Francis doth boldly speak to the King's grace the plainness of his mind', the Abbot of Woburn observed, 'and . . . his grace doth well accept the same'.[56] Both men were also collectors of maxims and nuggets of proverbial wisdom, and each used them in their verses. In the second of the letters written to his son in 1537, Wyatt had advised the younger Thomas of the value of gathering a stock of aphorisms to inform his conversation and actions:

Then too had ye need to gather an heap of good opinions and to get them perfectly as it were on your fingers' ends. Reason not greatly upon the approving of them, take them as already approved because they were of honest men's leavings, of them of God [i.e. biblical aphorisms] there is no question. And it is no small help to them the good opinion of moral philosophers, among whom I would Senek were your study and Epictetus, because it is little to be ever in your bosom [i.e. small enough to carry in your pocket].[57]

Bryan thought similarly. Indeed, he had written a 184-line poem, 'The Proverbes of Salmon [Solomon] do Playnly Declare', constructed almost entirely from aphorisms drawn from Sir Thomas Elyot's *Banquet of Sapience*, a poem to which Wyatt seems to allude at a number of points in the satire.[58] Bryan was also, as Wyatt dubs him, one 'who knows how great a grace / In writing is to cownsell man the right' (9–10). In 'The Proverbes of Salmon' he placed considerable stress upon the classic humanist ideal that good counsel was the mainstay of the commonweal. 'Wyse councell well ordered', he wrote, 'ys a Realmes preservacion' (8):

> They [who] do all thinges by counsel comes bytyde [i.e. are well prepared],
> Call not to counsel that [i.e. those who] lackes dyscrescion,
> For they love nothinge but ther owen apytyde,
> Trust not that man that loves his own affeccions:
> Better ys a just kyng than a counsel full of pryde.

$$(81-5)^{59}$$

The scholar Robert Whittington, in dedicating his own *Mirror or Glass of Manners and Wisdom* (1547) to Bryan, referred to him as one 'that hath delight in moral wisdom'. 'Beside manifold virtues', he claimed,

you have a singular zeal and delight in works that be pithy and politic touching moral wisdom, ever glad (as the noble man of immortal laud and fame Maecenas) to set forward such antique monuments of virtue and good learning... whereof ensueth the advancement of commonwealths.[60]

In the role of Maecenas or patron to works of good counsel he had encouraged his uncle, John Bourchier, Lord Berners, to translate Antonio de Guevara's *Libró áureo de Marco Aurelio* into English as the *Golden Book of Marcus Aurelius* (1532). And Bryan would later publish an English translation of the same author's *Dispraise of the Life of a Courtier* (translated via a French intermediary, Antoigne Allègre's *Le Mesprise de la Courte*), printed in 1548. *The Dispraise*, a moral treatise in the Boethian and Horatian tradition, was very much in the spirit of Wyatt's 'Myne Owne John Poyntz'. Bryan subsequently explained the appeal for him of this text (full of 'grave sentences and persuasion to virtuous life') in the Preface, addressed to William Parr, Earl of Essex:

For as much as the matter was not only pleasant and fruitful but also full in every where of old ancient stories and wise sayings of the noble and notable philosophers and clerks.[61]

The two men were also evidently friends; and Wyatt's decision to address his third and final satire to Bryan was no aberration. At least one other of the poet's works was also written with Bryan as its intended recipient. And that other text was, if anything, more intensely felt and heavily politicized than 'A Spending Hand'. Once more writing from prison—or claiming to do so—the poet wrote a taught *strambotto* whose tortuous syntax spoke powerfully of the anxieties and anguish of the prisoner.

> Syghes are my foode, drynke are my teares,
> Clynkinge of fetters suche musycke wolde crave;
> Stynke and close ayer away my lyf wears;
> Innocencie is all the hope I have.
> Rayne, wynde, or wether I judge by myne eares.
> Mallice assauted that rightiousnes should have.

> Sure I am, Brian, this wounde shall heale agayne,
> But yet, alas, the scarre shall styll remayne.

(Muir and Thompson 244)

The text could have been written either in 1536 or 1541. On each occasion Wyatt was in prison accused of crimes that he was certain he had not committed, and on each occasion he blamed the malice of given individuals (first Suffolk, then, as we shall see, Edmund Bonner and Simon Heynes) for his plight. Critics have tended to favour the later date, however, and this would seem to be the more likely of the two.[62] The poem has attracted a good deal of biographical speculation. It has recently been suggested, for example, that the allusion to the scar that will remain was a covert 'warning' to Bryan not to betray secrets that he and the poet shared, secrets concerning their dealings while abroad that would undo Wyatt should they become public knowledge. In this reading the reference to the scar is taken to be an allusion to Ecclesiasticus 27:21 (Vulgate 22:27), translated in the Matthew Bible of 1537 as,

As for wounds, they may be bound up again, and an evil word may be reconciled, but whoso betrayeth the secrets of a friend, there is no more hope to be had unto him.[63]

But this suggestion seems to miss the point of Wyatt's lines. He speaks of the difficulty of healing a wound, and of the marks that remain even once it has healed,[64] whereas Ecclesiasticus refers to the relative ease with which a wound heals compared to the damage caused by a treacherous friend (and does not mention scars at all). Beyond the fact that they each mentions wounds, there is little to link the two passages. And closer examination confirms that there is no need to link them. For Wyatt is quoting Bryan here, not the Bible.[65] In 'The Proverbes of Salmon' Bryan had written,

> Yt ys a scab[b]e of this world a good man to defame,
> Those men speake evill that be nother juste nor trewe.

(99–100)[66]

Bryan was in turn quoting the chapter on 'Envy' in Elyot's *Banquet of Sapience*, where the line (drawn ultimately from Cicero's letter to Lucio Cornello) read 'It is a scab of this world to have envy at virtue.'[67] Wyatt was thus referring to the malicious allegations that had brought him to prison, allegations that, he claimed, were the product of envy of his virtue, not to any supposed secrets whose revelation might ruin him now that he was there. Such allegations, however groundless, would nonetheless tarnish his honour, leaving a scar that would outlive his formal vindication. His intention was to enlist Bryan's sympathy and support, not to warn him against contemplating treachery.

Support for this reading can be found both in Wyatt's own Defence against allegations of treason, written in 1541, and in another later poem, written by Wyatt's friend Henry Howard, earl of Surrey, when he was himself in prison.

In the Defence, Wyatt turned angrily upon his accusers, 'These men thinketh it enough to accuse, and as all these slanderers use for a general rule, whom thou lovest not, accuse. For, though he heal the wound, yet the scar shall remain.'[68] Surrey quoted Wyatt's words in a lyric addressed to Thomas Radcliffe, lord Fitzwalter, and pointedly associated them in his own verse with Solomon, the putative 'author' of the maxims in Bryan's poem 'The proverbs of Salmon'.

> Yet Saloman sayd, the wronged shall recure [recover]
> But Wiat said true, the skarre doth aye endure.

These lines demonstrate that Surrey recognized both that Wyatt's words had concerned those 'wronged' by slander and malicious allegations and the enduring taint that such charges left behind, and that they alluded in turn to Bryan's Solomonic poem. Bryan, he suggests, may have got it right that slander damages the reputation of its speaker, but Wyatt was the wiser in seeing the long-term damage that it does to the target too. And in his own work he was evoking both the sentiments of Wyatt's text (for he too felt himself to be unfairly accused as he wrote) and the network of humanist friendships and affiliations upon which the earlier poem had drawn (Wyatt quoting Bryan quoting Elyot quoting Cicero). For Surrey's verse was written in the hope of evoking a similarly 'friendly' response from Radcliffe, who might speak up for the writer with his father-in-law, Lord Chancellor Wriothesley.[69] Again a love of justice and a sense of writerly community were being evoked by a poet *in extremis*, casting about for aid through his writing.

In choosing Bryan as the named recipient of his third and most explicitly political anti-curial satire, then, Wyatt was, on one level at least, following an obvious course. What better dedicatee for a poem about the perils of courtiership than a man who shared all of the poet's experiences of courtly life and revered the same precepts of political and moral philosophy? But nothing in 'A Spending Hand' is either obvious or quite what it first appears. The text confounds expectations of straightforward didactic satire, and offers instead a frustratingly ambivalent, enigmatic and open-ended analysis of the perils of court life and the wisest response to them. As such it may offer a valuable insight into Wyatt's own unquiet mind in the difficult period during which it was created.

In 'A Spending Hand' Wyatt presents a dialogue between a cynical courtly narrator and a more idealistic courtier, giving the recipient, Bryan, the latter role and taking the former for himself. Again the text draws upon and translates earlier texts, and an alertness to Wyatt's sources and the intertextual meanings they create is necessary if we are to appreciate the full range of nuances that the poem evokes. Horace and Chaucer again figure prominently (indeed this is probably Wyatt's most openly Chaucerian poem), and the immediate inspiration for the scenario was probably the fifth satire of Horace in which Odysseus asks the blind seer Tiresias for advice about how best to enrich himself when he returns to Ithaca in poverty. That text purports to be a continuation of a scene in

Book XI of Homer's *Odyssey*, but is in fact an ironic dissection of the avarice and corruption of contemporary Rome. For what the old seer offers Odysseus in lieu of sound guidance is a prospectus of the quick profits to be had from legacy-hunting, political marriages, and sycophancy.[70]

Wyatt's poem takes up Horace's satirical spirit and adapts his sketch of the prevailing Roman vices into an anatomy of the ills of the Henrician court. Professing a solicitous concern for Bryan's well-being, the worldly wise narrator offers to reveal to him the wisdom he has gathered from his own scholarly reading: 'When I remember this [the value of proverbs] and eke the case / Where in thou stondes, I thowght forthwith to write, / Bryan, to the[e]' (7–9). He bases his cynical advice on the principle that a wise man should ingratiate himself only with those who can further his own interests. The resulting counsel is thus a mirror image of neo-stoic philosophy and conventional moral counsel. Abandon honest speech, the narrator declares, as 'trowght shall but offend', whereas sycophancy can 'pourchase frendes' (34). Follow fashion rather than integrity, and be sure to divorce your public persona from the real you:

> Use vertu as it goeth now a dayes:
> In word alone to make thy langage swete,
> And of the dede yet do not as thou sayse.
>
> (37–9)

At court every action should be directed towards profit. Never lend money except at interest (an ironic touch, given Wyatt's loan to Bryan), and be like the upstart 'Kitson' who,

> From under the stall withoute landes or feise
> Hath lept into the shopp.
>
> (48–9)

Here the reference is probably to Sir Thomas Kitson (1485–1540), a London mercer's apprentice who rose to wealth, buying a country estate at Hengrave Hall, Suffolk, and becoming Sheriff of London in 1533.[71]

Borrowings from Chaucer and echoes of his work are scattered through the poem, especially where the poet delves into the seamier sides of human behaviour, and they are clustered particularly tightly in this passage. The poet refers to Pandarus, the go-between who facilitates the affair between Troilus and Crisseyde in Chaucer's greatest romance, thus coining the word 'pandar' as a term of abuse. Even he, the text declares, was naive in arranging matters for nothing more tangible than friendship. 'Pandering' should always aim to yield a profit. Similarly, a reference to the 'diligent knave that pikes his maisters purse' (56), yet pleases him so well that he becomes executor to his will, might, as Muir and Thomson suggest, be an allusion to the portrait of the Reeve in *The General Prologue* to *The Canterbury Tales*, of whom it was said,

His lord wel koude he plesen subtilly,
To yeve [give] and lene [lend] of his [i.e. the lord's] owene good,
And have a thank, and yet a cote and hood.

(A610–12)[72]

But, given what follows, it is more likely to have been *The Merchant's Tale* that
Wyatt had in mind as he wrote. For his thoughts were clearly already dwelling
upon merchants and their values, given the allusion to Kitson and his spectacular
'leap' from under the counter. In Chaucer's tale the young squire Damien
performs a similar sleight of hand to that which Wyatt's poem commends, with
his aged employer, January. He offers himself as an obsequious attendant, carves
before his lord each day, yet seeks all the time to bed the latter's young wife, May:

He kembeth hym, he preyneth hym and pyketh,
He dooth al that his lady lust and lyketh,
And eek to Januarie he gooth as lowe
As ever dide a dogge for the bowe.
He is so plesant unto every man
(For craft is al, whoso that do it kan)
That every wight is fayn to speke hym good,
And fully in his lady grace he stood.

(IV(E) 2011–8).

Consequently it is perhaps to *The Merchant's Tale* as well as to Horace that we
should look for the inspiration behind the passage in which Bryan is encouraged
to ingratiate himself with old men and, if that does not win him a legacy, then to
woo a wealthy widow instead. No action, however repellent, should be shunned
in the quest for gain, the narrator assures him. Hang on to the sleeves of wealthy
ancients in the hope of a legacy, or of being made the executor of their wills:

Stay him by the arme where so he walke or goo;
Be nere alway: and if he koggh [cough] to[o] sore,
When he hath spit, tred owte and plesse him so.

(53–5)

And do not baulk at the thought of marrying a rich old woman if the opportunity
arises:

... if so chaunce you get nought of the man,
The wedow may for all thy charge deburse.
A ryveld skyn, a stynking breth, what than?
A tothles mowth shall do thy lips no harm:
The gold is good, and tho she curse or ban,
Yet where the[e] list thou maist ly good and warme;
Let the old mule byte upon the bridill,
Whilst there do ly a swe[e]tter in thyn arme'

(59–66)

The source of the strikingly repulsive image of the widow's wrinkled skin and stinking breath, and especially the contemptuous dismissal of potential qualms about kissing such a woman ('A tothles mowth shall do thy lips no harme!' (62)), may well have been the scene in Chaucer's story in which the young and lusty gold-digger, May, is brought to January's bed. There a similar attention to the grotesque details of the aged lover's flesh is evident, and, ultimately, a similar contempt displayed for the capacity of such old flesh to move the recipient, whether to pleasure or to pain:

> He lulleth hire; he kisseth hire ful ofte;
> With thikke brustles of his berd unsofte,
> Lyke to the skyn of houndfyssh, sharpe as brere -
> For he was shave al newe in his mannere -
> He rubbeth hire aboute hir tendre face,
> And seyde thus, 'Allas! I moote trespace
> To yow, my spouse, and yow greetly offende
> Er tyme come that I wil doun descende.
>
> (IV(E) 1823–30)

> The slakke skyn aboute his nekke shaketh
> While that he sang, so chaunteth he and craketh.
> But God woot what that May thoughte in hir herte,
> When she hym saugh up sittynge in his sherte,
> In his nyght-cappe, and with his nekke lene;
> She preyseth nat his pleyyng worth a bene.
>
> (IV(E) 1849–54)

Given that Wyatt had just translated the passage from Horace that advised the aspirant heir to tread out an old man's spit if he coughed onto the floor ('*si quis forte coheredum senior male tussiet*'), perhaps it was the allusion to senile coughing that prompted him to recall *The Merchant's Tale* again. For one of the more grotesque accounts of the sexual encounters between January and May commences memorably when the old man is jolted awake by his own phlegmy cough, at which point he turns to May and 'Anon he preyde hire strepen hire al naked; / He wolde of hire, he seyde, han som pleasaunce' (IV(E)1957–9).

Finally, Wyatt declares, do not hesitate to prostitute your female relatives if any potential patrons show an interest in them. But, be sure to take a reward for brokering the deal:

> Thy nece, thy cosyn, thy sister or thy doghter,
> If she be faire, if handsom be her myddell,
> Yf thy better hath her love besought her,
> Avaunce his course and he shall help thy nede.
>
> (68–72)

The idea is again taken from Horace's fifth *Satire*, in which Tiresias advises Ulysses,

> *Scortator erit: cave te roget; ultro*
> *Penelopam facilis potiori trade.*

[Is he [the ' "idiot" you wish to cultivate] a libertine? See that he has not to ask you; yourself obligingly hand over Penelope to your better.][73]

The ostensible message of the text is thus straightforwardly satirical: only by taking corruption to its extreme and outdoing its residents at their own self-interested game could Bryan hope to survive and prosper at court. Such advice is, of course, clearly immoral, and, like all good satirists, Wyatt occasionally drops the mask of cynicism sufficiently for his readers to see that this is not the 'real' him speaking but a parodic persona. Indeed, the depth of Wyatt's own contempt for the counsel that his narrator proffers is betrayed by the very language in which it is couched. The imagery of shop(s) (49), profit (42), and gain (52 and 77), of spending hands (1), picking purses (56), and purchasing friends (33), of old mules (65), dogs and cheese (44), places such advice firmly among the sort of mercenary values and bourgeois aspirations for which Wyatt and Bryan alike had nothing but contempt. Such advice is indeed a language sweet 'in words alone', and is effectively undercut by the countervailing current of humanist terms of value that also runs through the poem. The latter draws the reader inescapably away from the goals of financial gain and self-interest back towards neo-stoic integrity. 'Reason' (5), 'grace' (9), 'cownsell' (10), 'serv[ice]' (23 and 25), 'trowght' (33), 'trueth' (34), 'trouth' (35), 'trouth' (36), 'vertu' (37): these words are a litany of Boethian virtues. (Bryan's 'Proverbes of Salmon' declared 'Whoes eares be stopped from trowth, hys helthe ys in dyspare' (169), citing Cicero's *De Amicitiis* via Elyot's chapter on 'Flatterers'). And the cluster of variations on the seminal principle of truth—embodying honesty, integrity, and self-sufficiency—in those lines where the narrator begins to outline his strategy for survival at court, indicates with deliberate self-defeating intent precisely what it is that the reader must sacrifice if he wishes to follow such immoral advice.[74]

There is thus a self-evident air of conviction and 'rightness' to the fictional Bryan's outraged response:

> Wouldest thou I should for any losse or gayne
> Chaunge that for gold that I have tan for best,
> Next godly thinges, to have an honest name?
> Should I leve that? Then take me for a be[a]st!
>
> (81–4)

This is clearly the 'correct' response to any attempt to seduce the upright man from the path of virtue. Indeed Bryan's own poem had quoted approvingly the maxim 'Aboundaunce of ryches ys not lyke a good name' (101), while Wyatt had instructed his son in the second of the letters he wrote to him from Spain in 1537, 'seek not, I pray thee...that honesty which appeareth and is not in deed...If you will seem honest, be honest, or else seem as you are'.[75] Hence the seemingly inevitable conclusion to be drawn is that a successful life at court is not something to which such men should aspire. The poem's Boethian agenda is continued in the narrator's parting shot to the uncorrupted Bryan, delivered as a curse, but actually offered by the poet as a remarkably clear prospectus for the stoic courtier's chosen self-image as set out in the two previous satires:

> Nay, then, farewell, and if you care for shame
> Content the[e] then with honest povertie,
> With fre[e] tong what the[e] myslikes to blame,
> And for thy trouth sumtyme adversitie:
> And therewithall this thing I shall the[e] gyve:
> In this worould now litle prosperite,
> And coyne to kepe as water in a syve.
>
> (85–9)

Bryan would no doubt have concurred that this 'curse' actually represents the preferable course of action; for 'The Proverbes of Salmon' noted that 'Yt perteyneth to vertue to suffer adversyte' (41), sentiments drawn from St Bernard's eighty-sixth Sermon on the Song of Songs (*sermone* 86).

And yet the rhetorical grain of Wyatt's satire does not run truly all in one direction. Merely assuming the opposite of everything the narrator says to be true will not reveal Wyatt's real intentions here. Both structurally and intellectually the text is more complex and more problematic than that, and seemingly more uncertain of its own ironic procedures. Against the ceaseless motion of Bryan, 'that trottes still up and downe, / And never restes; but running day and nyght' (11–12), Wyatt sets a rhetoric of stillness and certainty. The poem lauds not only the stability of rural seclusion ('at home...in thy bed of downe'), but also the fixed certainty of spoken and written truth. Thus the maxims with which it begins and ends are figured as deeply rooted wisdom, unmoved and undiminished by time:

> ...these proverbs yet do last.
> Reason hath set theim in so sure a place
> That length of yeres their force can never wast.
>
> (4–6)

And the appreciation of 'that grace / [That] In writing is to cownsell man the right' is posited as secure knowledge, shared by writer and reader alike.

Wyatt's lines here both allude to and echo the opening of Bryan's own didactic poem:

> The Proverbes of Salmon do plainly declare
> That Wysdome ys the vessel that longest will endure.
>
> (1–2)

Bryan had made grand claims for the capacity of such proverbial wisdom to regulate the governance of individuals and states alike:

> Who cares not for wysdome falles ofte into care;
> The braunches of that frute ys tried hole and sure,
> For powere without wysdome ys a feble foundaccion:
> Wyse councell well ordered ys a Realmes preservacion.
>
> (5–8)[76]

So Wyatt's poem seems to endorse Bryan's sentiments in setting the certainty of wisdom, of words and writing, against the perennial uncertainties and compromises of the active life in royal service. Yet it soon becomes apparent that his text lacks the courage of these borrowed convictions. Indeed, its method is to unsettle all fixity in a flux of ironic implication. The wisdom of counsel may have grace, but not when it is the kind of counsel that the narrator offers Bryan here, advice that instructs him to abandon neo-stoic, Boethian principles and embrace financial gain as the only good. Such advice is, of course, far from 'the right' in both Wyatt and Bryan's own philosophy: 'He that maketh hast to be ryche, of all ys despysed', stated 'The Proverbes of Salmon'; 'To a covetous [man] no sweter bate then ryches to lewre, / Poverte lackith many thinges, the covetuus lackith all' (61–3),[77] and the text declares as much even as it offers it.

Even as it heaps righteous scorn upon the corruption of the court in the guise of pragmatic advice for the courtier, the text nonetheless tacitly demonstrates the power and intractability of the humanist dilemma. For the poet cannot finally envisage the alternative to the public life of the court and princely service as anything other than itself a moral abdication of responsibility, a retreat into self-indulgence. As David Starkey observes, 'Bryan's rejection of the contemplative life in the country—'so sackes of durt be filled up in the cloyster' (22)—is as contemptuous as it is peremptory, and gains the ready approval of the narrator: 'By god, well sayde!' (28).[78] Thus, as the narrator offers Bryan the prospect of that life of rustic withdrawal that Wyatt had so lauded in 'Myne Own John Poyntz', he lets his voice slip perceptibly into the tones of the Vice of the Morality Plays, offering sloth and luxury rather than moral integrity as the real alternatives to public service:

> Why dost thou wear thy body to the bones
> And mightest at home sleep in thy bed of down,
> And drink good ale so nappy for the nonce,
> Feed thyself fat and heap up pound by pound?
> Likest thou not this?
>
> (14–18)

When the antithesis between court and country is put in such terms, the reader cannot but sympathize with Bryan's indignant retort:

No ... For swynne so groyns
In stye and chaw the tordes molded on the grownd,
And dryvell on pearles, the hed still in the manger,
Then of the harpe the Asse to here the sownd.
So sackes of durt be filled up in the cloyster,
That servis for lesse then do thes fatted swyne.

Tho I seme lene and dry withoute moyster,
Yet woll I serve my prynce, my lord and thyn,
And let theim lyve to fede the pa[u]nche that list
So I may fede to lyve both me and myn.

(18–27)

The life of the courtier is thus presented as both more and less virtuous than that of the country landowner, and the latter is, again, revealed not to be the real answer to the courtier's dilemma. The court is finally presented as both a swamp of mercenary values and the only arena in which the upright man of honour can be true to his principles. What is the virtuous man to do, then, if he is to serve the commonweal and avoid corruption? Such 'writing' as Wyatt offers can thus hardly 'cownsell man the right' in any clear or effective sense.

It is tempting to see such ambivalence as a direct response to the kind of naïve sententiousness that Bryan had advanced in 'The Proverbes of Salmon'. Bryan, it seems, was happy to settle for the simple comforts of Horatian neo-stoicism. In his *Dispraise of the Life of the Courtier* he would write, seemingly without irony, that,

Mine advice is that the sage person chose to live in a quiet state and to dwell in such a place, that he may lead a life without reproach and Christianly to die.

(cii(v))

It is possible also that he may actually have upbraided Wyatt about the contradictions in the poet's own position regarding the court during their meetings in France or elsewhere. For other passages in the *Dispraise* seem to have a direct bearing on the stance that Wyatt had adopted in his first two satires. Both men agreed that the court was a place of venality and danger. Bryan would translate Guevara's sentiments approvingly:

Favour and covetousness guideth the Courtier, so the one groweth with the other and at the end [all are] converted from the manner of Christians to Courtiers. For all men knoweth that the court is a place where men may get wealth and likewise ye place of men's undoing.

(cvii(v))

But Bryan's text would also offer a caustic commentary on the motives of those who leave the court and berate it from outside.

We have already rehearsed the occasions why men do withdraw them from the court, some for lack of money, some for poverty, or not being in favour, or for age, all these things be of necessity and nothing of free will, nor yet praise to them that so withdraweth them for the causes aforesaid. But the true leaving of the Court, and of the world, is, when ye courtier is young, strong, in favour, rich and in health, then with good heart to leave the court, to find in other places honest rest after his degree.

                                                                    (cvii(v)–cviii)

Still more pointedly, he wrote,

To leave the court and after return to it is so open a fault that it cannot be hid, except ye will say he goeth to sell virtue and to buy riches.

                                                                    (Di)

Did Bryan have Wyatt's case in mind as he penned these lines? For Wyatt, as we have seen, had left the court of necessity and condemned it from exile, only to return again as soon as the opportunity arose. The chronology allows no certainty, although we do know that Bryan was rehearsing Horatian sentiments as early as May 1538, talking of his wish that the King would recall him from ambassadorial duty and allow him 'to repair to his country and to make merry among his loving friends'.[79] But the possibility that Bryan had already voiced such opinions to Wyatt, conventional as they were, would lend considerable weight to Wyatt's stance in 'A Spending Hand' which otherwise seems merely self-defeating and irresolute in its political implications. For, as a number of critics have pointed out, there is yet another level of irony to the poem that Bryan, and anyone who was aware of his public reputation, could appreciate.

Sir Francis, unlike the 'Bryan' of Wyatt's poem, was no naive innocent at court. Rather he was a cynical, worldly backwoodsman with a reputation not only for plain speaking but also for philandering and self-interest.[80] Affectionately dubbed 'the vicar of hell' by his sovereign,[81] he had indeed seemingly put into practice a number of the ruses that Wyatt's narrator recommends to his fictional counterpart. As both Greenblatt and Starkey note, Bryan had already married one wealthy widow, Philippa, Lady Fortescue, in 1517, and would subsequently marry another, the Countess of Ormonde, in 1548. His two sisters had each married influential members of the King's privy chamber, thus adding an additional 'bitchiness' to the reference to pandering 'Thy nece, thy cosyn, thy sister or thy doghter' (68). And, to Wyatt's painful knowledge, not only did Bryan not lend money freely, but also borrowed without offer of interest or apparent intention to repay the loan.[82]

The poem is thus triply ironic. Not only is the narrator peddling a philosophy that the poet does not believe in as a means of covertly asserting a position in which he seems ultimately to have little faith, but he is doing so for the benefit of a reader, Bryan, who was himself a figure of irresolvable contradictions. Bryan was a plain-speaking deceiver who embodied both of the positions that the poem evokes at the same time: being both a successful exponent of the arts of courtly acquisition outlined in 'A Spending Hand' and a prime example of the principle of frank speech in action that was posited by Wyatt as its antithesis.[83]

Such mischievous play with inversions of character was probably initially suggested to the poet by his classical source. In his fourth Satire Horace had made similar ironic play with the reputations of his speakers. The immoral counsel for survival in a corrupt city he placed in the mouth of the archetypal truth-speaker Tiresias, who, as Odysseus noted, 'never spoke falsely to any man' ('*nulli quicquam mentite*'), while he cast Odysseus himself, the wiliest and most self-interested of the Greeks, in the role of the naive neophyte in worldly affairs.[84] What Wyatt seems to have done in rewriting such material in an English context was to add still further levels of irony to Horace's already deeply ironic text, creating a vessel for satire that consciously sinks itself with its own cleverness. This was a text so riddled with ironic effects and self-contradictions that it could carry its precious contents: wisdom, truth, and even meaning itself,[85] only, as Wyatt's final maxim suggests, like water in a sieve. And yet this allusion too was probably one last ironic barb at Bryan's expense; for the one person who had been able to carry water in a sieve was the vestal virgin Tuccia, whose story was related in Petrarch's *Triumph of Chastity*.[86] To be able to perform that miracle, one had to be pure of heart and body, and Bryan, as both poet and reader well knew, could not claim to be either.

Wyatt seems, then, consciously to revel in the contradictions thrown up by the poem, and by the 'Bryan' persona whom he crafted as both its subject and intended reader. Indeed, it is tempting to see the poem as deliberately attempting to perform too many tasks simultaneously, of drawing attention to too many aspects of Wyatt's relationship with Bryan to work successfully as satire. On one level it seems to make a point about Bryan's profligacy, satirizing his monetary debt to Wyatt and to his problems in royal service. For, as we shall see, he had been singularly unsuccessful in his most recent embassy, and at least one contemporary commentator attributed his failure to money problems. Hence in suggesting to the fictional Bryan that, if he should pursue the cynical practices recommended in the poem, he would become a prosperous and successful courtier, Wyatt was drawing attention to the addressee's failings in a doubly insulting way. For Bryan *had* done these things, and was still short of money and favour. The poem also seems intent on undermining Bryan's stated faith in the power of literature—of maxims and aphorisms—to bring about a just commonweal. By offering itself as a programme of good counsel, but actually recommending vicious behaviour, and doing so in such a way as to leave the reader uncertain of the moral it conveys, the satire effectively demonstrates the maleability of the supposedly durable and fixed wisdom of words.[87] Words, it implies, can be used to further any cause, or to frustrate it, or to do both things at once, depending upon who it is that crafts them into counsel. In this way the poem's very irresolution and apparent slipperiness as a vehicle for counsel conveys its intended agenda perfectly. Even a poem seemingly stocked full of maxims, the text suggests (with pointed reference to Bryan's 'The Proverbes of Salmon') need not be capable of persuading its readers to follow its advice or of doing any practical good in the real world.

This playful attention to the contradictions inherent in the position and persona adopted by Francis Bryan was more than simply a clever game between friends. And there was more to Wyatt's presentation of 'Bryan' than a series of witty inversions of character. The two men seem also to have taken different approaches to the rather more serious problems of Henrician government and despotism, and Wyatt was seemingly addressing that fact too. Bryan, like Wyatt, had witnessed from the inside those dramatic changes undergone by both King and court in the course of the 1530s. He, like Wyatt, had evidently felt their weight and pressure, yet he, unlike Wyatt, had still insisted upon absolute and unflinching loyalty to the crown as the only appropriate response. In 'The Proverbes of Salmon' he had warned of the dangers of despotism: 'Where affeccion [favouritism] blyndeth ther ys small equyte.../ A ravening reler [ruler] ys a fowle devowrer' (37 and 40); 'He that ys in auctoryte let hym loke wisely / Howe to governe the thinges that he hathe to gyde.../ Yt ys harde to denye that will have no naye; / High auctoryte ys always in perell to decaye' (43–4; 47–8). Yet, where Wyatt had responded with satire and complaint, Bryan had ultimately counselled passive obedience, and offered an explicit warning against attempts by the Commons to resist the demands of the King:

> A realme not obedient, there growes no good thing:
> Better ys obedience then londes or possessions;
> He that resysteth auctoryte resysteth hys kinge;
> Ye servauntes, obey your soverayn, for that ys to be don,
> Yt ys not lawfull for subjectes newe lawes in to bringe,
> W[h]ere commons will governe, there raignes oppressioun;
> The lawes of God we shulde at no tyme forsake,
> Nor agaynste our Kinge newe lawes for to make.
>
> (145–52)[88]

And yet, despite evident material prosperity and despite his conspicuous loyalty, Bryan had patently not, as I have suggested, been successful at court. It had been his capacity for frank speech (often enhanced by the effect of alcohol) that had been his undoing. Bryan had returned from his embassy to France to find his king furious at his failure to prevent a Franco-Imperial rapprochement and incensed by his apparent inability to guard his tongue. Frustrated by his own inability to prevent Francis I from meeting the Emperor, Bryan had used 'proud' language to the French king and delivered a demand for the repayment of money owed to Henry as part of his French 'pension' '*simpliciter*', without due regard for diplomatic niceties. When the suggestion of a meeting between Henry and Francis had been politely declined, he had asked abruptly, 'and should the King my master ride post to see you, would you shut the gates of your kingdom in his face?'[89]

Such bluff directness had its place, but it was disastrously inappropriate for the kind of delicate, poker-faced negotiations that were called for during July 1538.

Both protocol and royal *amore propre* were offended, and Henry himself had been made to look foolish (and, worse still, desperately importunate) in the process. Bryan reported finding the French king colder than usual in their dealings, and his letters became increasingly cynical and assertive about French motives. The French ambassador, Castillon, sensing the tone of the despatches from France, suggested they were written 'after dinner', that is while Bryan was drunk. The ambassador was manifestly becoming a liability, and Henry was not one to conceal his irritation. He complained about being misled by his ambassadors, Wyatt and Bryan being singled out for particular blame, and called the latter 'a drunkard whom he would never trust again'. Castillon predicted 'evil cheer' for Bryan on his return. Indeed he was recalled so suddenly that there was not time for the French to present him with the traditional farewell gifts on his depart-ure.[90] Terrified at what this suddenness portended, Bryan fell into 'a burning ague' during his return journey and got such a bad reception from the King that he retired to his sickbed for over a month. He was said to be in danger of death for much of that time, and joked about being sent into internal exile in Calais to keep his friend Lord Lisle company there. In the end, his disgrace was not quite so disastrous. He lost his principal office as Chief Gentleman of the Privy Chamber and was '*chassé hors de la Chambre*' for a time, as a result, Castillon said, of '*les folles*' that he had written in his despatches, after he had lost all his money when he was in Provence. He had to content himself with a couple of months touring the Home Counties buying up deer to restock the King's parks, but no worse fate ensued. He returned to court, yet he never regained Henry's full confidence, and had to endure being described as a 'wretch' by the King as late as New Year's Eve.[91]

The real Bryan had thus experienced 'adversity' as a result of both his free and frank speech and his financial mismanagement, precisely as the poem had predicted he would:

> Content the[e] then with honest povertie,
> With fre tong what the[e] myslike to blame,
> And for thy trouth sumtyme adversitye:
> And therewithall this thing I shall the[e] gyve -
> In this worould now litle prosperitie,
> And coyne to kepe as water in a syve.

> (86–91)

And neither his faith in wisdom and good counsel, nor his conspicuous loyalty had saved him. In fact, his attempts to speak freely to the King about what he saw as French duplicity had precipitated his disgrace.

There is thus a kind of savage irony prevailing over what Wyatt presents as the neo-stoic idealism of his Bryan figure. On one level these lines seem to return us to the fable of the town and country mice of 1536, belatedly providing the moral conclusion to that tale which Wyatt had earlier denied his readers. In the role of country mouse, Bryan is allowed to walk into a neo-stoic future resolved to the 'honest povertie' and adversity that are the fate of those who choose the 'country' virtues of simplicity, plainness, and honesty over the corruption of the court. But events had moved on since 1536. The aspiration to be an independent private citizen, poor but free to speak or write what was on one's mind, like the aspiration to be a bold, honest counsellor, free to tell his king the harsh truths that would save him from wilfulness and tyranny, was by the end of the 1530s self-evidently deluded. While it might have been possible in 1536 for Wyatt to believe what he had told Poyntz in his first satire, that in Kent 'No man doth marke whereso I ride or go' (83), three or more years later such sentiments would have been naive in the extreme. In a world of surveillance and investigation, complaint and denunciation, the rural landowner speaking over-boldly at the dinner table, or arguing contended points of doctrine with his parish priest in his closet was as likely to find himself reported to Cromwell and under investigation for sedition as the courtier or preacher who spoke out in London.[92] Freedoms were everywhere receding in England, as Wyatt and Bryan had each found to their cost, and writers were having to come to terms with the fact. 'Thought is free' was therefore no longer a consoling maxim, but a potentially seditious remark. The events of Wyatt's embassy to Spain would, if nothing else, have taught him the wisdom of that conclusion.

14

Wyatt's Embassy, Treason, and 'The Defence'

Wyatt's brief as Henry's resident ambassador at the Imperial court of Charles V was complex and delicate. At its broadest his mandate was to keep Henry appraised of the Emperor's attitudes and policies, to 'fish out the bottom of his stomach and advertise his majesty [Henry] how he [Charles] standeth disposed towards him' and 'to the continuance of the amity between them'.[1] But, beyond that there were more specific and pragmatic issues to be attended to, of which preventing Charles from reaching any accommodation with France, keeping a track on the activities of English catholic exiles such as Cardinal Reginald Pole, protecting English mercantile interests in Imperial territories, and trying to woo the Emperor with the prospect of a dynastic marriage involving Princess Mary (still legally illegitimate but Henry's *de facto* heir until the birth of Prince Edward in October 1537) were only the most pressing.

The moment was not unpropitious for such a mission. The death of Charles's aunt, Katherine of Aragon in January 1536 and the execution of Anne Boleyn less than six months later had removed the most obvious impediments to closer Anglo-Imperial ties. But the ever shifting nature of royal demands and the rapid pace at which European diplomacy was moving meant that Wyatt was continually at risk of either overstepping the mark or missing an opportunity in his negotiations with Charles and his ministers. Not that he was to help himself in such matters. For in an environment in which the only safe option was absolute compliance with each new royal demand (and even that was not always safe) he was dangerously willing to act on his own initiative and instincts when he saw fit, even when it involved ignoring direct instructions. When, for example, soon after his arrival, he was told to pass on a letter written (under government pressure) by Princess Mary to the Emperor, in which she acknowledged the invalidity of her mother's marriage to Henry and accepted her own consequent illegitimacy, Wyatt simply failed to do so. This prompted an angry rebuke from Cromwell, who had, he said, been forced to cover for his failure with the King:

It is much marvelled that you have not yet delivered my Lady Mary's grace['s] letters. It was a part of your Instruction, and therefore very negligently pretermitted.[2]

Perhaps, as Muir suggests, Wyatt thought that passing on a document so obviously created under coercion would damage rather than improve Anglo-Imperial relations.[3] Perhaps his inactivity was simply the result of an oversight. Either way it was a startling omission, and it would take further orders from both Cromwell and Wriothesley before he finally passed on the letter. A similar sense of independence, indeed what looks very like a belief that he as the man on the spot knew better how to handle matters than anyone in London, coloured many of the letters he wrote from Spain and the allegations made against him by his fellow ambassadors in the course of the summer of 1538.

Given his obvious personal hostility to Wyatt, one has to handle the evidence of Edmund Bonner with care, but there is a degree of plausibility to his account of a number of incidents during his time with Wyatt that transcends his obvious malice. Bonner had been sent to Spain along with Simon Heynes, the dean of Exeter, at the end of April 1538, on a special mission to deliver new arguments developed by Henry VIII concerning the powers of the Papacy regarding general councils of the Church (a particular concern at that time as the prospect of a general council was being mooted by several parties, including Henry himself). On arrival, Bonner seems to have taken an almost instant dislike to Wyatt, and Wyatt in turn seems to have resented the disruption that these new envoys, and the more aggressive arguments they brought with them, caused to his carefully developed charm offensive on the Emperor. The result was a fractious summer of petty arguments and squabbles over precedence among the English diplomats, culminating in a formal letter of complaint sent by Bonner to Cromwell on 2 September, 'briefly touch[ing] diverse things wherein I cannot commend but mislike the doing of Master Wyatt'.[4]

One of the allegations that Bonner would level at Wyatt was that he deliberately underplayed and frustrated any attempts to put the case concerning the Pope's powers regarding councils in discussions with the Emperor and his ministers, in order to favour his own arguments and ongoing negotiations. Wyatt had, Bonner claimed, been characteristically blunt about his feelings, telling him that:

Ye shall do no good with th'emperor, I know it, and I have told the King myself in my letters that he lanceth the sore before it be ripe.

Hence, when they appeared together before the Emperor, he had neglected the case *'de potestate pontificis et de concilio'* that Bonner wanted to press, instead 'setting forth old things begun by himself and passing over ours'. As they left the audience, he had turned to Bonner and said:

'Ye have spun a fair thread. I knew well enough how you should speed.' And he spoke the words so, as though he rejoiced that we had not sped, lest our speeding should have been a dispraise to him, who, speaking afore therein could not prevail.[5]

Part of the difficulty was created, paradoxically, by the very success of Wyatt's personal relationship with the Emperor. The two men obviously enjoyed each other's company, and Wyatt, it was claimed, 'rejoiced' in the chance to dine at the Imperial board and be well thought of by Charles. Back in London, indeed, Henry was heard to say that he thought of Wyatt as more Charles's ambassador than his own.[6] The remark was no doubt intended as a joke, a means of preventing the real Imperial envoys inquiring too closely into the latest dispatches from Spain. But it nonetheless identified a real dilemma at the heart of Wyatt's role. Like Elyot before him, Wyatt no doubt *did* feel a potential conflict of interest, however slight, between his functions as Henry's representative and his status as a gentleman and a scholar at the court of Charles V. As a gentleman—a man of honour—his sense of his own chivalric identity would have transcended national boundaries, not least those between England and her traditional allies Spain and the Imperial territories. Such men had much in common with their imperial counterparts, especially if they added an enthusiasm for humanist learning to their aristocratic preferences. For them the Emperor was not simply a foreign monarch but Europe's premier prince, *ex officio* the descendant of the Caesars, beneficiary of the *translatio studii et emperii*, and the repository of the values of the Roman cultural imperium.

But did such concerns, coupled with his evident personal empathy with Charles V, prevent Wyatt from performing his role as Henry's representative to the best of his abilities? Bonner alleged that they did. In his view, the 'great mark' at which Wyatt shot was not the service of his King but 'to please th'emperor and Grandevelle [Charles V's Chancellor, Antoine Perrenot de Granvelle], and to be noted to be in th'emperor['s] favour, whom he magnifieth above all measure'.[7] Accordingly, Bonner claimed, Wyatt was loathe to 'expostulate' with the Emperor on the King's behalf, seeking rather to mollify him whenever possible. How much truth there was in such suspicions it is hard to judge, but it may well be that political principle rather than social ambition motivated Wyatt's behaviour. Perhaps, like Elyot, he hoped to use his office to bring about a reconciliation between his King and the Emperor that would be in the long-term interests of both parties. It may well have been that this was why he pressed every occasion to promote the dynastic marriages proposed at various points by Charles V, even when Henry himself seemed reluctant to advance them, thereby, as Bonner would allege, 'putting th'emperor in great expectation and hope thereof', and becoming frustrated when the King and his Council in London were slow to follow his promptings.

Certainly during his first embassy Wyatt was noticeably more enthusiastic when ensuring the King of Imperial goodwill than when relating news of setbacks in his negotiations.[8] Indeed at times he seems almost to have convinced himself that only matters of definition and a willingness to agree to differ over key points stood between the two sovereigns and a lasting peace. Hence in June 1538 he informed Henry that Charles was only too eager to reach an agreement over their religious differences:

if in these things your Majesty will hearken to the reconciling with the Bishop of Rome, he [Charles] would be glad to travail in it; but if not, yet would he go through with you and will continue ever in that mind the same notwithstanding, and like as he is not lettered, so would he not charge your majesty for th'argument of the Bishop's state, but leave it alone to them that toucheth, knowing well your wisdom and learning to be such as ye are [able] to justify yourself, both to God and to the world.[9]

Henry's refusal to accept such offers of goodwill at face value evidently left Wyatt deeply frustrated.

Such frustration, indeed, was the source of the most contentious of those remarks spoken by Wyatt that would lead to allegations of treason from Bonner and Heynes and his interrogation before the Privy Council in 1541. As Bonner reported it, the poet had announced, when discussing the apparent lack of dispatch with which Henry was responding to Imperial overtures:

By god's blood, ye shall see the king our master cast out at the cart's tail, and if he so be served, by god's body, he is well served.[10]

The occasion, Bonner claimed, was a dinner at which Wyatt, his friend Sir George Blage, and his secretary John Mason, Heynes, and Bonner were present, during which the poet was:

so hot herein and so oft spoke at the table hereof... that, by the charge of my soul, my stomach biled and I could not keep in, but said, 'No, sir', quoth I, 'it were not mete that his grace should be so served.'

When Wyatt asked why, Bonner, by his own account, loyally replied,

'Because the king, our master, hath heretofore showed so much kindness, both to th'emperor and the French king that they cannot with their honour cast him out at the cart's tail.' Mr Wyatt, perceiving that I spoke very earnestly... he began to call himself home and to speak of another sort, but angry surely he is that his travail bringeth forth no better issue.

The precise words spoken on this occasion became the subject of considerable debate when the poet came to defend himself in 1541. Was Wyatt treasonably implying that Henry would be *thrown* out of a cart by his fellow monarchs like a criminal strung up for hanging: a remark that, as well as being deeply insulting, would fall dangerously close to 'imagining the King's death' under the terms of the 1534 Treason Act?[11] Or was he, as he later claimed, arguing that he would be merely '*left* out of the cart's arse' (as he more colourfully put it), like an over-looked piece of luggage as France and the Empire moved on without him? 'But ye know, masters', he would later tell his judges,

it is a common proverb, 'I am left out of the cart's arse', and it is taken upon packing gear together for carriage. That that is evil taken heed to, or negligently slips out of the cart and is lost.[12]

The difference between the two phrases was the difference between treason and mere discontent. What Wyatt did not deny was that a conversation along the broad lines that Bonner described had indeed taken place, and that he himself, frustrated that the King would not follow his advice, had grumbled publicly that royal reticence was endangering his entire strategy, and, moreover, had suggested that Henry was reaping the inevitable reward for his prevarication. Even if one takes Wyatt's version of the exchange at face value, this was a remarkably bold attitude for a subject to take about his king.

Yet Wyatt was proved right. While he was despatched back to London to consult King and Council over a proposed marriage between Princess Mary and Don Lodovic of Portugal, Francis I and Charles V concluded a truce in his absence, and England faced the prospect of a Continental catholic alliance ranged against them. That Wyatt felt he had been tricked, having been assured by the Emperor that no arrangement would be made without his cognizance, hardly made the situation easier to swallow. Nor did it make it easier to face a rebuke from the King, when in his view it was Henry's own fault that England had not been included in the agreement.

These were perilous times in England. The Pilgrimage of Grace, the great popular rising against the dissolution of the monasteries and Henry's religious reforms that convulsed Lincolnshire and the northern counties between October 1536 and Spring 1537, had seemingly confirmed royal fears about the secret disloyalty of sections of the population—especially monks and other regular religious persons, and rendered the realm acutely vulnerable to outside intervention and attack. Wyatt, who had served for a time in the royal army sent north under Norfolk to suppress the rebellion, would have seen the scale of the discontent at first hand. Norfolk, outnumbered and outmanoeuvred, was forced to temporize with the rebels, offering them in Henry's name a general pardon and the promise of a free parliament held in the north to redress their grievances. But, once the Pilgrims had dispersed to their several counties, the full force of martial law was unleashed upon the ringleaders and other convenient victims, with the regular religious suffering most. 'All these troubles', Henry told Norfolk in a letter of 22 February 1537, 'have ensued by the solicitation and traitorous conspiracy of the monks and canons of those parts.' And he confided to Sir William Fitzwilliam and Sir John Russell that he would never consent to the restoration of the suppressed abbeys, as the Pilgrims had requested. The Earl of Derby, commander of one wing of the royal army, was ordered that, should he find that the monks of Sawley Abbey had been restored to their house by the rebels, he should take the Abbot and his principal brethren and hang them 'upon long pieces of timber or otherwise out of the steeple; and the rest to be put to execution in such sundry places as you shall think meet for the example of others'.[13]

Once order was restored in the north, Henry moved decisively to remove the remaining larger abbeys across the country as a whole. Having seen the dangers inherent in a mass, enforced, dissolution, he moved more circumspectly this time. Over the next two years the abbots of the greater monasteries were

individually bribed or pressed—sometimes to the point of blackmail—to surrender their houses to the King, signing fulsome confessions (prepared for them
by the government) admitting to the sinfulness of their lives and the worthless-
ness of their contemplative vocation. Even such 'voluntary' submissions could be
brutally peremptory. A note in a Bible used at Evesham Abbey records how the
royal commissioners burst into the chapel during evensong on 30 January 1539
and ordered the monks to surrender the house there and then, 'not even suffering
them to make an end of the service'. Those heads of houses who refused to
surrender were subjected to still more brutal persecution. The Abbots of Reading, Glastonbury, and Colchester were all executed for upholding the Pope's
authority and denying the Supremacy by opposing the royal will.[14]

During the Pilgrimage and its immediate aftermath, fears of a Continental
invasion inspired by Cardinal Pole's diplomacy, and enabled by a rapprochement
between France and the Empire were justifiably intense; and anxieties about
potential sedition at home, especially in the south of England which had been
relatively untouched by popular unrest thus far, were equally high. Henry saw
traitors everywhere, and moved swiftly to nip in the bud any suggestion of
potential discontent or treachery. Of particular concern was the possibility that
relatives and associates of Cardinal Pole were feeding him information about the
state of domestic politics and helping him to foment unrest in preparation for an
invasion.

As recent research has shown, Henry had no long-term Machiavellian policy to
destroy either his dynastic rivals or the old catholic nobility. He was simply
reacting on an ad hoc basis to perceived threats.[15] But the problem was that the
policies of the 1530s in and of themselves created so much discontent, so many
potential enemies and threats, that the net effect was almost indistinguishable
from a predetermined cull. Henry would not cease to dip his hand in blood, the
French ambassador, Marillac, reported in August 1540, as long as he doubted his
people.[16] And his own policies, and the level of obedience that he demanded
from his subjects, ensured that he would never be rid of such doubts.

On the strength of confessions obtained from Geoffrey Pole, the mentally
unstable younger brother of Cardinal Pole, key members of the last remaining
noble house with a serious claim to the throne, the Courtneys, were arrested on
charges of treasonable conspiracy with the exiled Cardinal. Henry Courtney,
Marquis of Exeter, Henry Pole, and Sir Edward Neville were tried and executed
in December 1538. Further rumours of conspiracy led to the arrest of Lady
Margaret Pole, Countess of Salisbury in 1539, and her eventual execution in
April 1541. Among all of Henry's brutalities, it was probably the death of the
septuagenarian Countess, so infirm and weakened by interrogation that she
had to be carried to the scaffold in a chair, that marked the nadir of royal
vindictiveness. Undoubtedly it was her death that Sir Walter Raleigh had
principally in mind when he penned his powerful condemnation of Henrician
brutality in the preface to his *History of the World*: 'how many princes of the

blood (whereof some of them for age could hardly crawl towards the block) with a world of others of all degrees (of whom our chronicles have kept account) did he execute?'[17]

It was at the time of the Exeter conspiracy, and the fears that it prompted in the Council regarding Pole's connections among the English aristocracy, that Bonner sent his complaint about Wyatt to Cromwell. Wyatt had, Bonner claimed, sent John Mason to speak with Cardinal Pole, implying that unspecified treasonable intentions lay behind the mission. Wyatt was clearly discontented, Bonner claimed, for he repeatedly complained about his own treatment at the King's hands, grumbled about royal policy, and about his own imprisonment in the Tower in May 1536 in particular. Might he not, the letter insidiously implied, have sought a measure of revenge against the King who had so singularly humiliated him, through his dealings with Pole? When Cromwell received Bonner's letter, he took steps to investigate the allegations. Mason was interrogated by Cromwell, Bishop Tunstal, and the Duke of Suffolk, in September 1538. Observers assumed that, although Mason was the one being questioned, it was Wyatt's activities that were the real target of the questions. 'They meant at Mason, but they shot at thee, Wyatt', Cromwell allegedly said of the accusers.[18] But the minister seems quickly to have concluded (correctly) that there was little substance to the claims. He quietly dropped the inquiries, and assured Wyatt that there was nothing for him to worry about. 'After I came home', the poet recalled, 'I was in hand with th'earl of Essex for it. He desired me to let it pass. I was cleared well enough.'[19] Ever the dutiful bureaucrat, however, Cromwell filed away Bonner's letter among his correspondence, and it was there, among his papers, that it was rediscovered at some time after his own fall in June 1540. And at that point a new enquiry was begun, this time with a less sympathetic set of investigators.

From Wyatt's written responses to his judges, it seems clear that what particularly concerned the Privy Council was, not only the more obviously treasonable potential of Wyatt's alleged use of Mason as a go-between between himself and Cardinal Pole, but also what the poet may have said about the King during his sojourn in France. As Wyatt himself was later to summarize it,

these be the ii marks whereunto mine accusers direct all their shot of eloquence—a deed and a saying. After this sort in effect is the deed alleged with so long words: 'Wyatt, in so great trust with the king's majesty that he made him his ambassador...hath had intelligence with the king's rebel and traitor Pole.' Touching the saying, [it] amounteth to this much: 'the same Wyatt, being also ambassador, maliciously, falsely and traitorously said that he feared that the king should be caste out of a cart's arse and that by God's blood, if he were so, he were well served, and he would he were so.'[20]

As a result of the unearthing of Bonner's letter, Haynes, Mason, and Bonner himself were questioned, and Mason was subsequently arrested again and interrogated further.[21] On 17 January 1541 Wyatt was seized from his lodgings at the

Crutched Friars in London, and marched, his hands bound before him, to the
Tower, accompanied by twenty-four royal archers. So dramatic and public an
arrest made a considerable impact upon those who saw or heard of it. Marillac,
the French ambassador, reported that everyone 'supposed ill' of Wyatt's chances,
given that he was seen with his hands tied at the time of his arrest:

For it is the custom of this country to take them to prison unbound, being well assured
that they could not escape. It is the third time that this Wyatt has been taken there; (and
doubtless it will be the last), for it is bound to be a grave charge, since he has earned the
malevolence of all those who leagued against Cromwell, whose favourite he was. Although he is more regretted than any man arrested in England these three years, both by
Englishmen and foreigners, no man is bold enough to say a word for him, and by those
fine laws he must be judged, without knowing why.[22]

Equally suggestive of Wyatt's likely fate was the fact that, on 20 January the Privy
Council ordered the seizure of all his property at Allington, and the conveyance
'with all convenient diligence' of his plate and such household stuff 'mete for the
king's majesty's use together with all the stuff of the armoury, guns, jennets, and
great horses'. Wyatt's servants were to be dismissed with half a year's wages, and
the house sealed awaiting the King's pleasure. Evidently Wyatt was not expected
to return. His mistress, Elizabeth Darrell, who was pregnant with their child, was
to be encouraged to leave, unless to do so would endanger her unborn infant (if
that is what is meant by the cryptic allusion in the instructions to Sir Richard
Southwell, that he might allow her to stay if 'he might conjecture that might
perish which she had conceived'), in which case she might remain there until
alternative provision might be made or nature take its course.[23]

Meanwhile, Wyatt himself, in the Tower, was directed in the King's name to
draw up a statement of:

such things as have passed me whilst I was in th'emperor's court by word, writing,
communing, or receiving with or from any man whereby I know myself to have offended
or where I might run in suspect of offence, namely in the time of that court being at Nice
and Villa Franca.[24]

At this stage the poet had evidently already been questioned at least once by
members of the Privy Council,[25] but clearly knew little of the precise allegations
made against him, save that they emanated principally from Bonner (he entitled
the 'Declaration', written in response to the Council's demand, 'A declaration...
of his Innocence... upon the false accusation of Doctor Bonarde'). He was thus
reduced to trawling his memory for anything potentially incriminating that
might have occurred during his lengthy embassy.

Wyatt's tone in this first formal response to the Council is understandably
anxious and tentatively apologetic. He sought his judges' tolerance if he erred in
recalling 'those things that be not fresh in my memory', asking that 'no captious
advantage...be taken of me' as a result of any oversights. He declared that he
had done nothing 'wherein my thought could accuse my conscience' 'in crime

toward the Majesty of the King my master or any his issue in deed, word, writing or wish'. Having been informed, or having guessed, that his dealings with Pole and other traitors formed the substance of the allegations against him, he declared that:

As touching word with any the king's enemy or traitor, in my life I remember not that ever I spoke with any, knowing him at that time to be a traitor or enemy, but to Braunceter [an Englishman in imperial service whom Wyatt had been instructed to apprehend during his second embassy to Charles V in 1539–40] at his apprehension in Paris, and to Frogminton [Throckmorton, a servant of Cardinal Pole] at S. Davis [St Denis] that would have brought me a present of wine from Pole, which processes I doubt not but it is well in your lordship's remembrance.[26]

Then he added, seemingly as an afterthought, that he had also spoken with 'a light fellow, a gunner, that was an Englishman and came out of Ireland with an Irish traitor called James (I have forgot his other name)' and an Irish fool called Rosarossa ('because he wore a red rose on his breast'). And, as he asserted, 'there was no substance of these things'.

There is a sense of genuine anguish to the Declaration, the sense of a man fighting in the dark against accusations that he does not fully understand, in a political landscape that he does not fully recognize:

God knoweth what restless torment it hath been to me since my hither coming to examine myself, perusing all my deeds to my remembrance, whereby a malicious enemy might take advantage by evil interpretation.

There is also a sense of that instability—that slippery 'tickleness'—of the political environment that was a regular theme of his verse. As he implied himself, the difficulty with listing all of his dealings with traitors, was that a number of individuals with whom he had worked on crown service (of whom Cromwell was only the most obvious) had subsequently been accused of treason, so the list was likely to have been a long one.[27]

Having no specific charges against which to defend himself, Wyatt was driven back on a general defence of his probity and diligence in royal service, and of his dealings with Bonner and Haynes in particular. And it was here that he gave the frequently quoted account of his ambassadorial labours that echoed so obviously the language of 'A Spending Hand', with its cynical conclusions about the value of exerting oneself in royal service:

So rested I not day nor night to hunt out for knowledge of those things [i.e. the negotiations between France, the Empire and the Papacy], I trotted continually up and down that hell, through heat and stink from Counsellor to Ambassador, from one friend to another, but the things then were either so secretly handled or yet not in coverture that I with all mine acquaintance ... could get [no] ... knowledge.[28]

But there was one further matter that Wyatt knew had to be mentioned, the occasion that linked him, Bonner, and Haynes with Mason, the man who had preceded him to the Tower, and whose testimony he knew had been damaging to him.[29] There had been, he recalled, a dinner with no one present 'but we three and Mason, and the servants being from the board', when he had asked for advice from his fellows about a possible stratagem for circumventing the wall of silence surrounding the negotiations in Nice. He had then, he admitted, made a daring proposal:

What if Mason should insinuate himself [into Pole's household], dissembling with Pole to suck something worthy of knowledge in these great matters?[30]

Both Bonner and Haynes had agreed to the plan, he claimed ('both thought it good'), and Mason 'was content to essay it when he should see time and occasion'.

The plan was, however, a failure. Mason was able to infiltrate Pole's household, but could get nothing from him, 'for that he seemed to suspect him'.[31] He had, therefore, to content himself with forwarding a report of his actions to Cromwell, who, despite Bonner's subsequent complaint, had been satisfied that nothing untoward had been intended. As Wyatt claimed, both men were only doing what they could in difficult circumstances to further the cause of their king. Indeed, if Wyatt had acted without first seeking royal approval, and had been involved in some surreptitious matters, then this was no more than an ambassador was appointed to do. For the exercise of initiative and subtlety were the very essence of his role:

If these be the matters that may bring me in to suspect, me seemeth, if I be not blinded by mine [own] cause, that the credit that an Ambassador hath or ought to have might well discharge as great stretches as these. If in these matters I have presumed to be trusty more than I was trusted, surely the zeal of the King's service drew me to it. And I have been always of opinion that the King's majesty either should send for Ambassadors such as he trusteth or trust such as he sendeth.

And, he asked his judges:

Weigh in this mine innocence as you would be deemed in your first days when you have charge [responsibility] without experience; for if it be not by practise and means that an ambassador should have and come to secrets, a prince were as good send naked [i.e. unencrypted] letters and to receive naked letters as to be at charge for Residencers [resident ambassadors]. And, if a man should be driven to be so scrupulous to do nothing without warrant, many occasions of good service should scape him.[32]

The Declaration is in many ways a disturbing document, the statement of a man who feared he might never have the chance to prove his innocence in a fair trial. Yet it is not without its rhetorical flourishes, and moments of bold self-assertion. The suggestion that, when choosing his ambassadors, Henry ought either to send those whom he trusts or trust those he sends was a telling thrust against royal paranoia and interference, and reflects something of the author's own confidence in his own record and abilities, even *in extremis*. And amid the frustration there is also a quiet rage against those men whose complaints had brought him to this pass:

Touching the Bishop of London and Haynes' calumny in this matter, when it shall please your lordships to examine me I shall sincerely declare unto you the malice that hath moved them. And if I might be examiner in my own cause I know they cannot avoid their untruth in denial of their consent in this cause of Mason.[33]

What would eventually secure Wyatt's pardon and release was neither the eloquence of his Declaration and the subsequent, longer Defence, nor the likelihood of his innocence, but that more familiar engine of Tudor justice, patronage. It was a well-judged intervention on his behalf by Henry's new queen, Catherine Howard (perhaps prompted by her cousin, Wyatt's friend and fellow poet Henry Howard, Earl of Surrey) that persuaded the King to order his release. According to the Spanish ambassador, it was during a journey by barge from Whitehall to Greenwich on 19 March 1541 that Catherine:

took occasion and courage to entreat the King for the release of Master Wyatt . . . which petition the king granted, though on rather hard conditions, the first of them being that the said Wyatt should confess the guilt for which he had been arrested; and, secondly, that he was to resume conjugal relations with his wife, from whom he had been separated for upwards of fifteen years. Wyatt had cast her away on account of adultery, and had not seen her for many years; he will now be obliged to receive her and should he not do so, and not lead a conjugal life with her, or should he be found to keep up adulterous relations with one or two other ladies that he has since loved, he is to suffer pain of death and confiscation of property.[34]

These were indeed hard conditions. But Wyatt seems to have accepted them. For on 26 March the Privy Council wrote to Lord William Howard reporting, amongst other matters, that the poet had:

confessed upon his examination all the things objected unto him, in a like lamentable and pitiful sort . . . which surely were grievous; delivering his submission in writing, declaring the whole history of his offences, but with a like protestation, that the same proceeded from him in his rage and foolish vainglorious fantasy, without spot of malice; yielding himself only to His Majesty's mercy, without the which he saw he might and must needs be justly condemned. At the contemplation of which submission, and at the great and continual suit of the Queen's Majesty, His Highness, being of his own most godly nature inclined to pity and mercy, hath given him his pardon in as large and ample sort as His Grace gave the other to Sir John Wallop, which pardons be delivered and they be sent to come hither to His Highness at Dover.[35]

By the end of the month Wyatt had knelt before the King at Dover, no doubt biting back the obvious rejoinder when his sovereign lectured him on the subject of marital fidelity, and received his absolution. By 10 April he was on his way to Calais on royal service, leading a troop of 300 horsemen to protect the city while the fortifications were being repaired.[36] He was restored to the courtly fold; but at what cost?

Critics have made a good deal of Wyatt's submission, suggesting that it marks a shift in his poetic outlook, even the end of his personal happiness, and inaugurated a period of profound self-doubt. Alistair Fox has perhaps gone furthest down this psychoanalytical path, suggesting that 'Wyatt capitulated and saved his neck, but in doing so he lost the last vestiges of his self-respect.'[37] Fox's reading of both the situation and its effects on Wyatt's subsequent verse is a powerful one and in many ways persuasive, but it may go too far. It is not necessary to assume that Wyatt was 'broken' by his experience in prison and by the pressures placed upon him by his King upon his release. Nor is it necessary to assume that he was forced to 'suppress his original defence and submit'. The evidence allows for some latitude in interpreting precisely what Wyatt had to do to satisfy the Privy Council of his contrition. They declared that he had 'confessed his guilt'. But did this mean that he must therefore have repudiated his Declaration and the Defence, which also asserted his innocence? The two texts are not incompatible with the idea of a confession. As Muir suggests, 'passages in both . . . could be twisted into a confession to save the faces of his accusers'.[38] Indeed, the Council, upon discovering that the King was minded to pardon Wyatt, would have had to do very little in the way of twisting to turn the Defence into a confession of guilt. For Wyatt's case in that text was not that he had not said the things accused against him, but simply that they did not carry the implications that Bonner had inferred, and did not, under the terms of the 1534 Act, constitute treason.

As he argued at length in the Defence, the crucial question was whether he had spoken the contentious words about the King and the 'cart's arse' maliciously, and this he emphatically denied. His judges seem to have accepted the claim. For they noted in their letter to Lord William Howard that he had offered a frank history of all his offences, but with the protestation that 'the same proceeded from him in his rage and foolish vainglorious fantasy, without spot of malice'. That he had spoken incautiously and, as Bonner alleged, in heat, Wyatt acknowledged in the Defence. And he was willing, for the sake of argument, to allow that he might be thought a 'naughty . . . knave and not all of the wisest', all of which might be taken by his judges as an admission of a degree of culpability. Yet he was not, he insisted, 'so very a fool' that he would talk of the King in the 'abominable' terms that were implied, and confide in Bonner of all people in so doing. His words should be interpreted in the context of the daily frustrations of his ambassadorial role.

A case in point was the accusation that he harboured resentment against the King as a result of his imprisonment in 1536. Wyatt was scathing in his rejection of the claim:

Wyatt grudged at his first putting in the Tower. Ergo (say they) he bear malice in his heart and it is like that [he] sought intelligence with Pole and also he wished the king's affairs to miscarry because he would t'on way or t'other to be revenged . . . But let us examine every point thereof: 'Wyatt grudged at his first putting into the Tower'. If they take grudging for being sorry or grieving, I will not stick with them. I grant it; and so I think it would do to any here. But if they [use] that word 'grudging' including a desire to revenge, I say they lie. I never so grudged. Nor they nor any other man can either prove that or maybe a likelihood of a proof thereof. Mason sayeth he hath heard me complain thereof. What then? Doth Mason say that thereby he reckoned I meant revenging, bearing malice in my heart? I know him so well that he will not so interpret complaining or moaning to revenging.[39]

To admit even to complaining and moaning about one's treatment by the King was a dangerous thing in the paranoid climate of January 1541. But Wyatt was sufficiently confident in his own understanding of the law, and sufficiently angry at the insufficiency of the charges against him, to speak plainly on the matter, and to record his complaints in writing. Still more remarkably, he was also willing to admit that he had doubts and misgivings about the whole drift of royal policy, even about specific Acts of Parliament including the Supremacy itself, albeit with the crucial reservation that such misgivings did not compromise either his loyalty to the King or his ability to serve his country.

Discussing the questions concerning Wyatt's behaviour that were put to Mason, the poet turned to the query 'whether he thought I could be a good subject that misliketh or repugneth his prince's proceeding'. Given the context, his response was perhaps the most remarkable of the entire Defence:

I say here as I said unto it, as far as misliking or repugning includeth violent disobedience or seditious persuasion, I think he is no good subject. But to mislike a building, a choice of an Ambassador, or the making of a law, obeying it nevertheless, or such things proceeding, although, peradventure, it may be done out of time and place, yet I think it may be without hurt of allegiance, unless there be a law made to the contrary which I know not.[40]

Even so general a statement of the freedom of a subject to think that his king was in error is striking among the increasingly sycophantic utterances of these years. But Wyatt went on to make more specific and detailed admissions:[41]

What say I then to the law of words [the 1534 Treason Act], which Mason should say that me thought very hard and that the first devisers were well served in falling into it, which he thinketh I meant by the lord Rochford or the lord of Essex? This, and it were offence it is uncertain by his own saying. And yet I never remember I said so unto him. But what is it to treason? Do I maintain against the law? Do I persuade any violence against the law? It rather includeth allowance of the law if they were well served that they suffered for offending in that.[42]

In admitting to finding the Treason Act 'very hard', and seeing a grim irony in Cromwell and Rochford's falling foul of the law that they themselves drafted, Wyatt was sailing close to the wind, if not in legal terms, certainly politically. Others had drawn the royal wrath upon themselves for less open statements of criticism. But there was more to follow, as he turned to consider the Supremacy itself.

Again, sayeth Mason, that I should say unto him that it was a godly act, the act of Supreme Head, speciously [especially?] the king's majesty being so virtuous, so wise, so learned and so good a prince; but if it should fall into an evil prince that it were a sore rod. I suppose I have not miss-said in that, for all powers namely absolute are so rods when they fall into evil men's hands, and yet I say they are to be obeyed by express law of God, for that there is no evil prince but for the dessert of the people, and no hand over an evil prince but the hand of God. This upon examining of as many men as have been familiar with me, among whom some words might have escaped me and sucked out both of them and of me with such interrogations. Yet is nothing found of me of treason. Yea, and when there is any toward my master, within this heart a sharp sword go thither withall.[43]

Here is the classic defence of the conventional liberties of the subject under the law. While the King might command their obedience and the loyalty of heart and body, 'thought is free': a proverbial idea about which, as we have seen, Wyatt had already suggested some cynicism in 'A Spending Hand'. For in Henry's Reformation, as Wyatt's own satires had implied, thought was increasingly not free. The Acts of Succession and Supremacy had looked beyond word and deed to the thoughts that lay behind them, declaring his subjects guilty of treason even if they swore the oaths attached to these acts while secretly harbouring reservations in their hearts. Even absolute obedience to the letter of the law was no longer sufficient unless the subject believed equally absolutely in what they were doing. Such at least was the theory. Yet Wyatt here staked his claim to innocence on precisely the grounds that he had obeyed the letter of the law despite having misgivings about the spirit.

A number of critics have seen the sort of characteristic plain-speaking evident here as a pose, part of a bluff persona that Wyatt adopted for rhetorical advantage in his verse and other writings.[44] And it would be rash to deny any element of conscious self-fashioning in what he said, either here or elsewhere. But the fact that the poet could be so open about his doubts concerning recent legislation, and so willing to concede an element of culpability here—albeit only to deny the substance of the accusations against him—surely goes beyond image-making. Wyatt was arguing for his life in the Declaration and Defence, and it is tempting to conclude that here, at bay, we see the true Wyatt emerge. The writer of the Defence reveals himself as a paradoxical figure: a man confident in himself and in his own ability to understand both the demands of the law and the dictates of human nature, yet frustrated at the malice and hypocrisy of his accusers and the timidity and potential complicity of his judges. Rhetorical skill and truth need not be mutually exclusive, of course. Indeed, the Ciceronian tradition so fundamental to humanist thinking insisted that the first could find its true value only in the defence of the second.[45] And here we see a vindication of that principle in action. Here was Wyatt, a man at the height of his rhetorical powers, using them to assert what he saw as the truth, and to fight back in true Ciceronian fashion against the prospect of deep and personal injustice. Having at some point following the composition of the Declaration evidently seen the full extent of

Bonner's complaints against him, he used the Defence both to rebut them one by one and to school his judges in the provisions and limitations of the legislation under which they were investigating him:

Rehearse here the law of words. Declare, my lords, I beseech you, the meaning thereof. This includeth that words maliciously spoken or traitorously against the King's person should be taken for treason. It is not meant, masters, of words which dispraise the King lightly, or which are not all the most reverently spoken of him, as a man should judge a chase against him at the tennis, wherewith he were not all the best contented. But such words as bear an open malice or such words as persuade commotions or seditions or such things.[46]

As the Defence makes clear, Wyatt feared the 1534 Act. It was a severe law indeed that made mere words treason, but the safeguard provided by the stipulation that such words had to be spoken maliciously in order to be treasonable was crucial, and Wyatt's hopes of freedom rested upon it. Such indeed was the safeguard at the heart of humanist notions of good counsel too. For the frankness of the good counsellor was always well intentioned, however harshly or bluntly he spoke truth to power, whereas the honeyed words of the flatterer were always filled with secret malice.

The Defence is a devastating refutation of the charges against him, and all the more devastating as it is so honest in its admissions. But, despite its evident self-confidence, there is nonetheless an unanswered question implicit in each of its statements. What if this is not enough? What if Innocence, Truth, and Faith, the three virtues inscribed as a protective cordon around the poet's name in the Blage Manuscript, were not sufficient to protect him from his enemies? What if the 'innocence' which he declared to Bryan 'is all the hope I have' in his prison sonnet 'Syghes are my food' (that may well have been written at this time) proved a false hope? What if his fate was already sealed by something over which he had no control or immediate influence: the whim of the King? Such questions lurk just below the surface of the conclusion of the Defence, when, in perhaps the boldest passage in the text, Wyatt turned to his judges directly and instructed them how they, as fellow men of honour, should—must—proceed in reaching their verdict:

The confidence put in my affairs is for you to acquit me. And it is an naughty fear if any man have any such, to think a quest [jury] dare not acquit a man of treason when they think him clear, for it were a foul slander to the King's majesty. God be thanked, he is no tyrant. He will no such things against men's conscience. He will but his laws and his laws with mercy. What displeasure bear he to the lords for the acquitting the Lord D'acres?: never none, nor will not unto you if you do as your conscience leads you. And for the great cause the law ministereth betwixt the King and his subject an oath to the quest in favour of the Subject; for it supposeth more favour to be born to the prince than to the party, if the oath bound not Christian men's conscience... and afore God and all these men I charge you with my innocent truth that in case, God defend, ye be guilty of mine innocent blood, that ye before his tribunal shall be inexcusable.[47]

In the collocation of those two sentiments, 'God be thanked, he is no tyrant... he will but his laws and his laws with mercy' and 'in case... ye be guilty of mine innocent blood' lies the whole story of the Henrician Reformation; the story of the gradual loss of confidence in the King experienced by men such as Wyatt. While the poet might comfort himself with the thought that Henry, whom he had known and served loyally for over two decades, still adhered to the classical virtues of the good king: justice, affability, and mercy, he nonetheless acknowledged the reality: that the likelihood was that mercy would not be the royal response. For a good deal of innocent blood had already been shed by those who had crossed the King's wishes in matters of high policy and low pragmatism since the establishment of the Supremacy.[48] And the King whom the poet had cursed as a tyrant with the words of Persius in 'My Mother's Maids' was no longer a man prone to spontaneous acts of mercy.

Yet, as we have seen, it was to be royal mercy that would, against the odds, bring about Wyatt's release, albeit the mercy of a king so besotted with his new queen that he was only too happy to grant her anything she asked. Rather than praising his sovereign for his liberality, and affirming the royal virtues celebrated in the conventional *speculum principis*, however, the Wyatt who emerged from prison for the third and last time in March 1541 immersed himself in the longest and most seemingly introspective of his poetic projects. This work, a translation and adaptation of the seven Penitential Psalms, was traditionally an act of repentance and a preparation for death. For Wyatt, however, it would bring a measure of conclusion to a decade of rumination on the nature of princely power and the responsibility of the virtuous subject under tyranny.

15

Pleading with Power

Wyatt's Penitential Psalms

It was almost certainly during this second period at Allington Castle in 1541, as Wyatt came to terms with both his freedom and the conditions on which it had been granted, that he turned to the last and arguably the greatest of his poetic achievements, his *Paraphrase of the Seven Penitential Psalms*.[1] Like the Satires of 1536, the *Paraphrase* was a work born out of a real and pressing sense of personal adversity, and like those earlier texts it was a direct response to that adversity and to the national crisis that had provoked it. Alistair Fox has read the *Paraphrase* as a direct reaction to the terms of Wyatt's second 'internal exile', and in particular Henry's injunction that he should send away his mistress Elizabeth Darrell, and return to his estranged wife Elizabeth Wyatt née Brooke.

The only way he could bring himself to give up his mistress was to persuade himself that God, morality, and his own conscience required him to do it as much as the king, but this he found hard to accept with total conviction. Part of the purpose of the Penitential Psalms was to help make him believe it . . . An equally powerful function of the work, one suspects, was to purge Wyatt of the guilt he felt over his surrender of integrity.[2]

And characteristically, Wyatt's *Paraphrase*, for all its conventionality, *does* suggest a very autobiographical aspect to its narrative of suffering and redemption.[3] The need to banish Elizabeth Darrell from his life, and with her the earthly affections and desire she represented does seem to resonate in the lines in which the psalmist describes the snares of an explicitly sexualized sin and temptation.

> By nightlye playntes in stede of pleasures old
> I wasshe my bed with teares contynuall,
> To dull my sight that it be never bolde
> To stirre mye hart agayne to suche a fall.
> Thus drye I upp amonge my foes in woe,
> That withe my fall do rise and grow with all,
> And me bysett evin now where I am so
> With secret trapps to troble my penance.

> Sum do present to my weping [e]yes, lo,
> The chere, the manere, the beaute and countenance
> Off her whose loke alas did mak me blynde;
> Sum other offer to my remembrans
> Those plesant wordes, now bitter to my mynd . . .
>
> (148–60)[4]

The experience of condemnation and imprisonment, and the desertion of such friends and colleagues as Thomas Wriothesley (and perhaps also John Mason himself, whose testimony provided evidence against the poet) seems to be reflected in Wyatt's particularly bitter expression of the psalmist's sense of his own isolation and desertion by his friends.

> And when myn enmys did me most assayle,
> My frendes most sure, wherein I sett most trust,
> Myn own vertus sonest then did ffaile,
> And stoud apart, reson and witt unjust,
> As kyn unkynd were fardest gone at nede
> So had thei place theire venim owt to thrust
> That sowght my deth by nowghty word and dede:
> Theire tonges reproche, their wittes did fraude aplye.
>
> (364–71)

On one level Wyatt is clearly referring to the failure of his own senses, the 'virtues' of the rational, mortal subject that undermine his search for spiritual cleansing, the 'heart', strength, 'sight', 'Eyes' and 'look' that 'decays and faints' in the face of temptation and fear.[5] But the more worldly, political implications of these lines remain present and, given Wyatt's recent experiences, offer a more obvious subtext to the poem.[6] Those who 'sowght my deth by nowghty word and de[e]d' are not merely the senses that draw him towards Elizabeth Darrell and the sins of the flesh, but the more mundane figures of the venomous former associates who have prospered during his own time of trouble: Bonner (now promoted to the bishopric of London), Heynes, and Wriothesley (Cromwell's one-time secretary, now swiftly ascending the steps that would lead him to the Chancellorship in 1544). Hence the pointed reference in the following lines to the success of his persecutors:

> In the mene while myn Enmys saffe encresse
> And my provokars herby do augement,
> That withowt cawse to hurt me do not cesse
> In evill for good against me they be bent
> And hinder shall my good pursuyte off grace.
>
> (385–9)

Elsewhere, as we have seen, the same point was made with greater economy,

> Thus drye I upp among my foes in woe,
> That with my fall do rise and grow with all . . .
>
> (152–3)

And everywhere in the *Paraphrase* the psalmist's discussion of the foes surrounding him is given a particular and contemporary twist, reflecting Wyatt's sense that those who had tried to bring him down in 1536 and 1538 still pursued him after his release from prison in 1541. Thus in Wyatt's version of the psalmist's text, spiritual aestheticism and political stoicism combine to identify and characterize the speaker as the archetypal virtuous man surrounded by foes both literal and metaphorical.

The solution to such adversities posited by the psalmist is the same as that outlined in 'Myne Owne John Pyntz': virtuous retreat. Here the voluble courtly poet, tracing the biblical David's flight from his palace, withdraws into that ultimate rustic sanctuary of the dark cave, from where he claims the absolute self-sufficiency of silence as his safeguard, and places his trust in the only true friend and patron, God himself.

> And I like deffh and domme forth my way yede,
> Lyk one that heris not, nor hath to replye
> One word agayne, knowyng that from thi hand
> Thes thinges procede and thow, o lord, shalt supplye
> My trust in the[e] wherein I stikk and stand.
>
> (372–6)

But this 'solution' is no more satisfactory to the poet here than it had been in the earlier satire. In Wyatt, the active humanist subject and the wily courtier and diplomat alike rebel against such quietist behaviour: the former because he knows that virtue consists in action and purposeful, truthful speech, the latter because he understands only too well that, at court, silence is no defence; one has constantly to defend oneself against slander, while the patronage of a lord, even a divine one, can never be assumed and must always be worked for. Hence the narrator candidly undermines his declaration of blind, deaf, and dumb faith in the very next line:

> Yet have I had gret cawse to dred and fere
> [Tha]t thou woldst gyve my foos the overhand;
> Ffor in my ffall they shewd suche plesant chere,
> And therewithall I alway in the lashe
> Abyd the strok; and with me every where
> I bere my fawte, that gretly doth abashe
> My dowlfull chere, ffor I my fawt confesse,
> And my desert doth all my conffort dashe.
>
> (377–84)

And the passage ends not with resolution but with a further urgent supplication:

> My lord, I ame, thow knowst well, in what case.
> Fforsak me not, be not farre from me gone:
> Hast to my help; hast, lord, and hast apace,
> O lord, the lord off all my helth alone.
>
> (391–4)

Wyatt's God, like his earthly master Henry VIII, cannot, it seems, be relied upon absolutely, but needs to be reminded, prompted, and cajoled to deliver on his promises. Even that trust that claims to stick and stand, remains precarious, in Wyatt's favoured word: 'tickle', and must be sured up and endlessly pursued with a stream of words. Hence in the midst of prayer Wyatt ends, characteristically, not with abject submission but with the peremptory tone familiar from his petitionary letters to Henry and Cromwell written in Spain. Desperation and abject reliance are coupled with an injunction not merely to help him but to do so quickly, now! 'Hast to my help, hast Lord, and haste apace' (393). This blurring of the psalmist's tones with those of Wyatt the courtly diplomat and rhetorician is, as we shall see, a characteristic of the *Paraphrase*; a sign of the worldly, political dimension to the text. Even here, in a work devoted to withdrawal from the world, Wyatt was still engaged with the problems of negotiating with power.

Wyatt's Paraphrase: Translation and Adaptation

Translating the psalms, especially those seven that were grouped together as The Penitential Psalms (Psalms 6, 13, 37, 50, 101, 129, and 142 in the Vulgate),[7] was a spiritual exercise that gained significantly in popularity during the early sixteenth century. Conventionally the repetition of these psalms was imposed as an act of penance, and so their translation might be seen as a kind of higher penitential exercise for scholars, a more substantial and taxing act of self-mortification and cleansing of the soul.[8] In the testing time of the early Reformation, catholics and reformers alike would turn to these texts both for spiritual consolation and as a preparation for ordeals to come. Sir Thomas More, during his incarceration in the Tower in 1534–5, compiled psalmic meditations in Latin and English, in order, as Rivkah Zim suggests, 'to remake his spiritual identity in preparation for a martyr's death' and become 'a new David: a man according to the will of God'.[9] Similarly, in 1543, the reformer Thomas Sternhold, imprisoned in the Fleet under suspicion of supporting the sacramentary Anthony Parsons, composed thirty-seven metrical psalms in English, while three years later in December 1546, Henry Howard, Earl of Surrey, was, as we shall see, to write verse paraphrases of a number of psalms, and of the first five books of Ecclesiastes, almost certainly while he was in the Tower awaiting his execution for treason. For each of these writers, as Zim suggests:

> The choice of the Psalms, with [their] themes of despair and acute misery, a trial of faith and the denunciation of treachery by former friends, seems peculiarly appropriate to these last weeks.[10]

'In such circumstances', Zim observes,

> prisoners approached the Psalms in expectation of finding vehicles for their own supplications to God, sources for comfort in the affliction, guides to their spiritual self-scrutiny, and patterns for remaking their spiritual identity.[11]

It was almost certainly with precisely such motives that Thomas Wyatt turned to the psalms as he reflected upon his recent imprisonment and faced his uncertain future in 1541. Yet, if he did set out to translate them purely as an exercise in penitential self-abnegation, that anti-egotistical ambition did not survive much beyond the opening lines. Surrounded by the texts and commentaries that he had to hand (the Vulgate, perhaps the Matthew Bible's English translation, Pietro Aretino's fashionable Italian prose translation of the Penitential Psalms (*I Sette Salmi*), the Latin translation of the Hebrew text in the *Enchiridion Psalmorum* of Joannes Campensis, published in 1532,[12] the Latin psalter of Tomas de Vio, Cardinal Cajetan, and the paraphrase of Ulrich Zwingli) and drawing from memory recollections of other texts, translations and commentaries by Erasmus, John Fisher, and perhaps others too,[13] he began to shape a paraphrase that would attempt, not to efface the personal and political aspects of his own recent experience, but rather to engage with and resolve them.

King David is, at first glance, an unlikely object of spiritual veneration. His life and character (in so much as it was hinted at in the biblical texts) were profoundly ambivalent. He was the leader of the Chosen People, the archetypal *beatus vir*, the man beloved of God, a priest, king, and poet, the precursor and prophet of Christ; but he was also an adulterer and murderer, a traitor twice over (once to his master Saul, once to the Philistines), a betrayer of loyalties and a deserter of causes, whose enemies had good reason to mistrust and despise him. Yet it was his combination of these 'ideal traits and his remarkably human failings' that, as Michael P. Kuczynski suggests, made him so useful an emblem of Christian penitence and for Wyatt in particular, as he sought a means both to explore his own culpability and to further the critique of contemporary politics and the King's condition that he had begun in the satires.[14]

While on one level Wyatt's translation is self-evidently a meditative exercise (or series of exercises), an exploration of his own sinfulness and a quest for personal redemption through prayer, it is clearly also a text with profound and potentially unsettling public implications. It is, paradoxically, an intensely private text that achieves its full potential only in its engagement with a wider public readership.[15] It is, in addition to everything else, a demonstration of Wyatt's own vatic powers, a public exhibition of his capacity to mediate biblical and political truth through his verse, an attempt to wrestle with and domesticate the Davidic text (to 'draw [it] into English metre' as the title-page of the printed text would put it) on behalf of his fellow Englishmen.[16] Hence, although he wrote the text into a manuscript in his own keeping and it was not printed during his lifetime, he almost certainly intended it to be circulated among those friends and companions who made up his social and intellectual circle.[17]

In addition to their meditative function, Wyatt's psalms are also a uniquely powerful anatomization of the royal condition, a work that has Henry VIII as well as Wyatt himself at the centre of its excoriating gaze.[18] The biblical David is pre-eminently a sinful and repentant *king*, and a priest-king at that (the 'chief pastor of the Hebrews assembly' as Wyatt would insist (204)); the supreme ruler of Church and state brought to abject humility as a consequence of his misuse of power and his lustful desire for Bathsheba. The collocation of sexual sin and murder in a king who had lost sight of wisdom and the demands of his own royal office was the hallmark of Wyatt's presentation of Henry's tyranny in his satires, and he was to make the most of the obvious and close connections between the biblical sovereign and his Tudor equivalent in the *Paraphrase*.[19]

Wyatt followed Aretino's prologues to each of the psalms in setting David's sin and subsequent repentance firmly in the context of his own life, specifically his adultery with Bathsheba and the murder of her husband Uriah:

> Love to gyve law unto his subject hertes
> Stode in the Iyes off Barsabe the bright;
> And in a look anone hymsellff convertes,
> Cruelly plesant byfore kyng David syght;
> First dasd his Iyes and forder forth he stertes
> With venemd breth as softly as he might
> Towcht his sensis and over ronnis his bonis
> With creping fyre, sparplid for the nonis.
>
> (1–8)

> So that forgot the wisdome and fore-cast
> (Wych wo to Remes when that thes kynges doth lakk)
> Forgettyng eke goddes majestie as fast,
> Ye[a] and his own, forthwith he doth to mak
> Urye to go in to the feld in hast,
> Urye I say, that was his Idolles mak,
> Under pretence off certen victorye
> For enmys swords a redy pray to dye.
>
> (18–24)[20]

This narrative of a besotted king drawn to murder and repression by his desire for an otherwise unobtainable woman gave the story an obvious and immediate relevance to Henry VIII's own recent marital and political history. And Wyatt would use it to his advantage, taking on, through the narratorial voice of the prologues, the role of Nathan, the prophet whose rebuke set the King on the path to repentance:

> But Nathan hath spyd out this trecherye
> With rufull chere, and settes afore his face
> The gret offence, outrage and Injurye,
> That he hath done to god as in this Case,
> By murder for to clo[a]k Adultery;
> He sheweth hym ek from hevyn the thretes, alas,
> So sternly sore, this prophet, this Nathan,
> That all amasid this agid woofull man.
>
> (33–40)[21]

But Wyatt did not need Aretino's example to read the psalms as a direct consequence of David's historical sins, for commentators from Augustine onwards had written about them in relation to the events narrated in the Second Book of Kings. Indeed many early printed psalters contained woodcut illustrations depicting the King overlooking Bathsheba bathing, while the *tituli* attached to the individual psalms in the Vulgate text made explicit the connection between the poems and this and other events of David's life.[22]

So, just as the 'enemies' besetting the narrator vacillate between aspects of his own sinful flesh and will and the external, human enemies who condemned Wyatt for treason and continued to seek his destruction, so the figure of David himself, the speaker of the psalms and the subject of the narrative links, *is* both Wyatt's mouthpiece and a figure of Henry VIII. The prayers of the psalmist are thus translations, autobiographical utterance, and acts of ventriloquism at one and the same time. The consoling fantasy of imagining the King repenting of his lusts and despotism, and adopting instead a life of repentance and atonement merges in the text with an exploration of Wyatt's own sense of himself as a sinful, fallen human being, giving the *Paraphrase* its unique potency as both politically and psychologically radical writing.

David is both a humbled king, 'this agid woofull man' (40), possessor of 'palais, pompe, and ryches' (164), and, as the 'dowble diadem' of line 163 suggests, head of the Church ('chief pastor of th'ebrews assemble' (204)). Yet he is simultaneously a vulnerable, mortal man, subject to pain and torment like any other. Thus he is utterly prostrated when confronted by Nathan's rebuke:

> Lyke hym that metes with horrour and with fere,
> The hete doth strayte forsake the lyms cold,
> The colour eke drowpith down from his chere,
> So doth he fele his fyer maynifold.
> His hete, his lust and plesure all in fere
> Consume and wast, and strayt his crown of gold,
> His purpirll pall, his sceptre he lettes fall,
> And to the ground he throwth hym sellff withal.
>
> (41–8)

Wyatt's exploration of the psalmist's corporeal vulnerability gives rise to some of his most powerful images of human suffering and subjection to external forces:

> ...thi arrows off fere, off terror,
> Of sword, of sekenes, off famine and fyre,
> Stikkes diepe in me. I, lo, from myne errour
> Ame plongid up, as horse owt of the myre
> With strok off spur: such is thi hand on me,
> That in my fleshe for terrour of thy yre
> Is not on[e] poynt of ferme stabilite,
> Nor in my bonis there is no stedfastnes;

> Such is my drede of mutabilite,
> Ffor that I know my frailefull wykednes.
> For whyy? My sins above my hed ar bownd,
> Like hevi weight that doth my force oppresse
> Under the wych I stopp and bowe to grownd,
> As whilow plant haled by violence;
> And off my fleshe ech not well curyd wound
> That festred is by foly and neclegens,
> By secrete lust hath ranklyd under skyn,
> Not duly Curyd by my penitens,
> Perceyving thus the tyranny off sin,
> That with his wheit hath humbled and deprest
> My pryd, by gruging off the worme within
> That never dyth, I lyve withowten rest.
> So ar myn entrayles infect with fervent sore,
> Fedyng the harme that hath my welth oprest,
> That in my fleshe is lefft no helthe therefore.
> So wondrous gret hath bee my vexation
> That it hath forst my hart to crye and rore.

> (331–57)

As Stephen Greenblatt has observed, 'the desire for chastisement is central to the process' of salvation described in the *Paraphrase*,[23] and Wyatt seems to embrace that masochistic desire, suggesting that the stability that he seeks and the stoic-identity he is crafting for himself are ultimately to be found only through violent physical discipline. Hence, as Greenblatt notes, he adds the element of self-knowledge expressed in the second line here to the image of punishment found in his sources:

> For thou didst lift me up to throw me down
> To teach me how to know myself again.

> (575–6)

But even here the self-lacerating overtones are mingled with a sense of political triumph, of achieving through verse what could not be done in the real world. For King Henry himself was fond of thinking and speaking of himself as a new David, and so speaking of David allowed Wyatt to speak, *sotto voce* and by implication, about Henry. The *Paraphrase* gave him the freedom to imagine and to inflict vicariously upon the King each of the torments suffered by the psalmist. Each act of cringing self-abnegation, each word of contrite regret that he speaks as of himself he also speaks on behalf of his sovereign, imaginatively crafting the King's own humiliation and repentance for a decade of lustful tyranny. Hence pain and pleasure were both probably present in his mind as he penned these lines, and the many others like them that form the backbone of the psalms.

One can, perhaps, sense the degree of satisfaction which Wyatt might feel, along with the self-mortification, in imagining the prince who claimed for himself sole prerogative to determine the divine will on behalf of his subjects voicing such seemingly pointed sentiments as,

> Lorde here my prayer and let my crye passe
> Unto the[e] lorde, withowt impediment.
> Do not from me torne thy mercyfull fase,
> Unto my selff leving my government.

(541–4)

Redeeming the King?

As Rivkah Zim observes, on one level the seven Penitential Psalms offer a potentially satisfying narrative of sin and redemption—a narrative that, when read against the biographical details provided in Aretino's prologues, offers a plausible account of the fall and rise of the repentant King. The David of the first psalm (Psalm 6: *Domine ne in furore*) is proud and overweening, naively confident in his own misreading of the demands of penitence and grace, locked as he is in a very material sense of God's need for 'recompense' (91). In the following psalm (Psalm 31: *Beati quorum remisse sunt*) he flounders in his own terror and self-pity, wavering between despair and false confidence in God's redemptive intentions, until he reaches a nadir of anguish and contrition. In the third psalm (Psalm 37: *Domine ne in furore tuo arguas me*) he has the first inklings of divine grace, unprovoked and freely bestowed upon him, a grace symbolized by the first arrival of light in the dark cave ('a beme that bryght sonne forth sendes' (309) that 'percyth the cave and on the harpe discendes' (311)). This grace allows him spontaneously to voice his repentance in prayer, 'surprisd with joye by penance off the herte' (316). And thereafter he begins the process of renewal that will culminate in a notionally secure sense of redemption.[24] But, as Zim and Halasz point out, this narrative stream runs neither smooth nor clear. Wyatt's David remains unstable and fragmented throughout the sequence, and appears conflicted in his sense of his own worth even at the end ('Hast to my help, o lord, afore I fall, / Ffor sure I fele my spryte doth faynt a pace.' (753–4)), prompting Halasz to conclude that the poet intended him to be perceived as an ultimately 'unregenerate' figure, representing a tacit rebuke to the poet's royal master.[25] Wyatt was thus, she suggests, demonstrating that 'David's example can be enacted in bad faith, his voice assumed for interested purposes' as well as self-abnegating ones, just as Henry VIII himself, perhaps, was adopting a Davidic persona when promoting his claims to wisdom and spiritual overlordship.[26]

Wyatt's *Paraphrase* thus continues where the third of his satires left off. Like 'A Spending Hand' it is a text so rich in implication, so ambitious in its attempt to encompass multiple meanings, to perform multiple tasks, that it becomes almost indecipherable in its complexities. Just as 'A Spending Hand' produced a Bryan figure who was both the object and the subject of the poem's address, who was mocked, cajoled, satirized, teased, and applauded by turns, so the *Paraphrase* creates a David who is both a mouthpiece for the poet's own spiritual quest and a vehicle for the satirical criticism, counsel, and imagined redemption of the King. Again Wyatt complicates any notion of simple, monologic didacticism through the addition of a second voice within the text, here the narrator who comments on David's words and state of mind, distancing the reader from his prayers and conditioning their response to him.[27] And, as with the earlier satire, much of the richness of implication, the complexity of agenda, is created by the poet's own insistent presence in the text, a presence inevitably burdened with a sense of its own culpability. Just as in the satire Wyatt's position as narrator was both compromised and enabled by an awareness that he too was guilty of many of the failings that he ascribed to 'Bryan'—financial mismanagement, overly frank speech, political ambition, a residual faith in 'Counsel' and the principles of neo-stoicism—so in the *Paraphrase* the narrator's own sinfulness, lusts and anger constantly inform and complicate his criticism of the King. As Halasz argues in her powerful reading of the text, Wyatt 'addresses the King with a consciousness of loss. He can call the King to account, but he cannot do so from a position of innocence.'[28] Hence as well as being Wyatt's most ambitious literary endeav-our—an attempt simultaneously to domesticate the divine word, to imagine the thought processes of the biblical David, and to arraign his own sovereign at the bar of divine justice, the *Paraphrase* is also his most fractured and difficult text to read politically. And the multiple focus of that ambition in great part creates its difficulty and fascination as a political text.

Wyatt's Religious Position

One aspect of the difficulty of the *Paraphrase* arises inevitably from its religious context, from its status as a biblical translation. Given the intense contemporary controversy over biblical translation, and the wider confessional battles in which that controversy played a crucial part, it is almost irresistibly tempting to see Wyatt's decision to translate the psalms as a contribution to doctrinal debate. To engage in a translation of the Penitential Psalms in the spring and summer of 1541 was necessarily a controversial act, and critics have traditionally interpreted it as a statement of radical confessional intent on Wyatt's part—an attempt to set his own doctrinal position on record as part both of his private reckoning with God and his public reckoning with his king. Such an assumption, understand-able though it is, has had a distorting effect upon our sense of both Wyatt's own beliefs and the nature of the *Paraphrase* itself. For the latter is a politically and poetically radical text, but it is not its doctrinal content that gives it its radicalism. In confessional terms the poem is carefully conformist, taking a distinctly 'Henrician' line on the principal matters of faith that it discusses. But this conformity in matters of doctrine only makes its personal and institutional critique of the King the more surprising and powerful.

It is common for critics to stress the evangelical qualities of Wyatt's translation, citing both those passages with an evident doctrinal agenda and the pervading 'inwardness' of the psalms' language of self-examination and recrimination as evidence of its 'protestant' sensibility.[29] The first observer to claim Wyatt for protestantism, indeed, was his friend and fellow poet, Surrey, who, as we shall see, sought to weld the poet's reputation for political and intellectual integrity onto a distinctly evangelical position. But this attempt had more to do with Surrey's own religious agenda than with Wyatt's beliefs, as the next chapter will demonstrate. Surrey was followed by Sir John Harrington who, in collaboration with the evangelical printer Thomas Reynold, produced the first printed edition of the *Paraphrase*. He dedicated it to William Parr, Marquis of Northampton in explicitly reformist terms, describing its dedicatee as 'a worthy patron for such a man's work...whom I have always known to be of so godly a zeal to the furtherance of God's holy and secret gospel'.[30] Subsequent critics have generally taken this claim at face value.

It is important to pause here, however, before moving on to the psalms themselves, to consider Wyatt's religious position. How convincing is the suggestion that he was an evangelical? The evidence of his poetry as it has been considered so far here has been inconclusive concerning his religious views, but in so far as it has suggested a position at all it has been a conservative one. The poet claimed in his Defence that he was no papist, declaring indignantly that 'I think I should have more ado with a great sort in England to purge myself of suspect of a Lutheran than of a papist', and asking his judges to recall 'what hazard I was in in Spain with the Inquisition only by speaking against the bishop of Rome'.[31] But these sentiments should not be taken to imply that Wyatt thought himself to *be* a Lutheran. The concession was purely rhetorical, and designed to refute suggestions that he had confessional affinities with Cardinal Pole. And the evidence he cited of his 'Lutheranism' here amounted to no more than speaking loyally in defence of the Supremacy. Elsewhere in the Defence he expressed (again, not without polemical intent) far more conservative views. He had, he claimed, in partnership with John Mason, pressed his fellow envoys and future accusers Bonner and Heynes to attend Mass while they were in Spain, 'because of the name that Englishmen then had to be all Lutherans...that we might sometimes show ourselves in the church together, that men conceived not an evil opinion of us'.[32] The claim was, of course, aimed at tarring Bonner with a Lutheran brush, but it suggests at very least that Wyatt had no passionate objection to hearing mass in the traditional Roman form, and indeed that he thought that to be suspected of Lutheranism was to invite 'an evil opinion'. Elsewhere in his writings the poet speaks, apparently approvingly, of conventional catholic practices such as prayers for the dead, pilgrimages, and good works. Such things were part of the orthodoxy of the Henrician church at the time, so to approve of them does not make him a dissenting conservative, but neither does it suggest any radical tendencies. It is, of course, possible, that Wyatt changed his position in the course of the 1530s (or, as Mason suggests, in the course of writing the psalms themselves). But other evidence implies a longer-term commitment to conservative beliefs, or at least to toleration of them in someone very close to him.

At some point following the death of Anne Boleyn, possibly as early as the summer of 1536 and certainly by the middle of 1538, Wyatt had met Elizabeth Darrell, the woman who would become his long-term mistress. If the lyric, 'If waker Care' is indeed assumed to be a posthumous farewell to Wyatt's desire for Anne, then Darrell may well be the 'Phyllis' whose 'Unfeigned cheer' replaced the wild 'Brunet' in his heart.[33] Certainly, as the poem implies of Brunet and Phyllis, Anne and Elizabeth were very different figures, both emotionally and politically. Where Anne was associated at court with religious reform, Darrell seems to have been firmly in the conservative camp.[34] Her father, Sir Edward Darrell of Littlecote in Wiltshire, was vice-chamberlain to Queen Katherine of Aragon, and it was no doubt through his influence that she became a maid of honour to the Queen, probably at some point in 1529 or 1530. This was a troubled time in which to join Katherine's household, in the midst of Henry's Great Matter, and to do so argues for a conscious choice of loyalties. In March 1529 Sir Edward died, but Elizabeth remained in service (or perhaps this was the occasion of her joining the retinue of the embattled queen) and followed Katherine as her household was cut back under royal pressure, moved around the country to ever more meagre accommodation, and subjected to intense pressure to conform to Henry's demands. Katherine, however, resisted all attempts to coerce her into submission, and Elizabeth Darrell, it seems, remained loyal throughout. When the Queen, demoted to Princess Dowager—a title she never recognized—refused to subscribe to the Oath of Supremacy, Elizabeth, along with many of her ladies, did the same. When, in January 1536, her mistress died, she rewarded that loyalty, leaving Elizabeth £200 as a dowry against any future marriage.

Further evidence of Darrell's religious leanings can be gleaned from the fact that, on the dissolution of Katherine's household, she thought first of joining that of Princess Mary, finally rejecting the idea on the grounds that the post would be too precarious, given the Princess's reputation for defying her father. After exploring the possibility of serving her kinswoman Jane Seymour, she eventually became a maid to the Marchioness of Exeter, dowager head of the premier catholic family in England. It was there that she became embroiled on the fringes of the Exeter conspiracy, and there that she and Wyatt probably became lovers, when, in the summer of 1539, during a brief respite from diplomatic duties, the poet visited the Marchioness's household, and spent time with Darrell, as several witnesses attested.[35] By 1540 Darrell was living with Wyatt at Allington, and, as we have seen, she was carrying their child when the house was seized by the Crown following his arrest in January 1541. On 12 June 1541, following his release and the King's insistence that he sever all links with Darrell and return to his estranged wife, Wyatt drew up his will. He left lands in Dorset and Somerset to his former mistress and to their infant son Francis Darrell.[36]

Wyatt's lengthy and very close relationship with Darrell casts an interesting light on his own religious affiliations during this time. Clearly friendship, love, and sexual desire could cross confessional divides, not least during the dramatic shifts of official belief and practice of the 1530s, when doctrinal positions were neither clear nor stable. But, had Wyatt been the kind of 'hot' evangelical that some critics have suggested, it is unlikely that he could have remained attached to, and evidently lived so happily and tranquilly with, someone whose conservative beliefs he had come to despise.

Wyatt's Religion and the Psalms

But, if the details of Wyatt's personal life cast doubt upon claims that he was an earnest evangelical, what about the *Paraphrase* itself? That Wyatt should have used phrases from the works of Luther and Zwingli in translating the biblical text is often cited as evidence of evangelical intentions. But neither case is particularly convincing. The borrowings from Luther are few and, as we shall see, at best ambivalent. Those from Zwingli are slightly more numerous, but no less problematic. As Helen Baron has demonstrated in her detailed examination of Wyatt's sources, the text of Zwingli's Latin *Paraphrases* which Wyatt used was that printed with the Commentary of Campensis by Gryphius in 1533. There the reformer's text is printed anonymously alongside the orthodox commentary, so Wyatt may well have thought that he was drawing upon the work of the conservative Campensis rather than that of the radical Zwingli.[37] Moreover the borrowings from the reformers were far less copious than those from thoroughly orthodox, indeed by 1541 dangerously conservative, sources such as John Fisher's *Meditations*, which inform both Wyatt's translations of particular phrases and his treatment of wider themes, suggesting that the poet had a considerable familiarity with Fisher's text at least.

Wyatt's 'protestant' sympathies are, it is often asserted, revealed especially in his discussions of the nature of Justification: the way in which the soul achieves salvation. The first of these comes at the start of his translation of Psalm 31 (*Beati quorum remisse sunt*), a text that one critic has described as 'virtually the battle-hymn of the Lutheran republic of the spirit': a text whose 'verses had become a code for justification by faith and for the imputation of God's righteousness'.[38] The Vulgate text reads simply:

Beati quorum remissae sunt iniquitates et quorum tecta sunt peccata.
[Blessed are they whose iniquities are forgiven and whose sins are covered.]

The question of whether 'covered' implied that sin was merely struck from the record and not taken into account, as Luther argued, or that it was completely eradicated, as orthodox commentaries asserted, was a crux of Reformation disputation. And Wyatt's expansion of the passage accordingly has a distinct doctrinal and expository edge, suggestive of a poet anxious to clarify his position on a deeply contentious issue:

Oh happy ar they that have forgiffnes gott
Off their offence (not by their penitence
As by meryt wych recompensyth not,
Altho that yet pardone hath non offence [i.e. no effectiveness]
Withowte the same), but by goodnes
Off hym that hath perfect intelligens
Off hert contrite, and coverth the grettnes
Off syn within a marcifull discharge.

(217–24)[39]

Critics have quite correctly pointed out the close correspondence between Wyatt's text here and his principal source for this portion of the translation, Aretino's *I Sette Salmi*, which entangles itself in a similar string of self-qualifying clauses.[40]

Aretino's Italian text, cited in John Hawkins' translation, reads:

O blessed they whose iniquities God pardoneth, leaving them unpunished, not through the works of contrition, nor other acts hence arising, as austerities, and denying themselves, although without them our sins acquire not remission, but through the benefit of his grace, whose goodness taketh merciful notice of a tender mollified heart, and by means of his compunction inclineth to hide his sins under the skirts of his mercy.[41]

And such critics have identified both of these expositions with a Lutheran insistence in the irrelevance of good works and the all-important status of faith in the process of salvation.[42] But, more significantly on a doctrinal level, Wyatt's pained exposition of the relationship between penitence and salvation, with its convoluted and awkward 'not as a result of . . . yet also not without' formula, is a close paraphrase of the official pronouncements on the matter promulgated by the Henrician regime.[43] *The Institution of a Christian Man* (the, so called, *Bishops' Book*) of 1537 set out the official position (drawn verbatim from the Royal Articles of 1536) in its discussion of Penance and Justification.[44] In the crucial passage explaining 'The Article of Justification', the *Bishops' Book* offered a painstakingly balanced exposition of the Henrician 'middle way' between justification-by-faith-alone and an unqualified belief in justification by works. 'As Touching the order and cause of our justification', the bishops declared:

We think it convenient that all bishops and preachers shall instruct and teach the people committed unto their spiritual charge that this word Justification signifieth remission of our sin and our acceptation or reconciliation into the grace and favour of God, that is to say, our perfect renovation in Christ.[45]

They went on to clarify the process.

Item, that sinners attain this justification by contrition and faith joined with charity, after such sort and manner as is mentioned and declared in the sacrament of penance. Not as though our contrition or faith or any works proceeding thereof can worthily merit or deserve to attain the said Justification. For the only mercy and grace of the Father promised freely unto us for His Son's sake, Jesu Christ, and the merits of His blood and passion be the only sufficient and worthy causes thereof. And yet that, notwithstanding, to the attaining of the same Justification, God requireth to be in us not only inward contrition, perfect faith, and charity, certain hope and confidence, with all other spiritual graces and motions, which, as was said before, must necessarily concur in remission of our sins, that is to say, our Justification, but also He requireth and commandeth us that after we be justified we must also have good works of charity and obedience towards God in the observing and fulfilling outwardly of His laws and commandments. For, although acceptation to everlasting life be conjoined with Justification, yet our good works be necessarily required to the attaining of everlasting life. And, we being justified, be bound, and it is our necessary duty to do good works.[46]

So, if Wyatt was indeed following Aretino's Italian text as he began to translate his version of the second Penitential Psalm, he did so, in part at least, because it allowed him simultaneously to follow precisely the twists and turns of the clearest and most recent official pronouncements on doctrine and the subject of justification issued by the Crown and the Henrician bishops. Far from boldly asserting a reformist line at odds with official policy, the poet was carefully following that policy to the letter, even where its own internal inconsistencies and tensions made the precise tenor of the policy hard to ascertain. Where the Ten Articles and the *Bishops' Book* insisted that sinful humanity was saved neither through contrition, works, nor faith alone, but only through the grace of a merciful God and the sacrifice of Christ, *and yet, notwithstanding*, God also required sinners to perform outward good works if justification was to have effect, so Wyatt declared that the forgiven sinner is redeemed 'not by their penitence / As by meryt wych recompensyth not'—although 'pardone hath non offence / Withowte the same'—'but by goodness / Off hym that hath perfect intelligens / Off hert contrite, and coverth the grettnes / Off syn within a marcifull discharge'.

Wyatt, unlike the Henrician bishops, was not writing a systematic exposition of religious faith. To do so in the wake of the proclamations and statutes of the later 1530s banning biblical translations in English would have been reckless indeed for one so closely associated with government service, and so frequently under official scrutiny for his political and religious beliefs. But where the text does offer what amounts to a clear gloss on a question of doctrine or belief, he was careful to ensure that, as here, it conformed closely to the official Henrician view. Here, as the text's similarity to Aretino's prose account suggests, both Wyatt and the bishops were not straying far from the conventional catholic position that works, like faith, were not sufficient contributory factors in the process of Justification, but they were both—and faith pre-eminently so—necessary conditions for and consequences of the justificatory process.

Once the similarity between Wyatt's account and the *Bishops' Book* has been noted, other apparently radical passages in the psalms also appear in a new and more moderate light. The bishops' exposition of the two-part process of contrition, in which the sinner must first conceive 'great sorrow and inward shame' that he or she has offended God, along with 'great fear of God's displeasure', but then conjoin and replace that fear with 'a certain faith, trust, and confidence' in God's mercy, ('whereby the penitent must conceive hope and faith that God will forgive him his sin and repute him justified and of the number of his elect children'),[47] seems to be what Wyatt is describing in another passage, taken from the Fifty-First Psalm (*Misere me Domini*), conventionally cited as evidence of his Lutheran sympathies.[48]

> To the[e] alone, to the[e] have I trespast,
> Ffor none can mesure my fawte but thou alone;
> For in thy syght I have not bene agast
> For to offend, juging thi syght as none,
> So that my fawt were hid from syght of man,
> Thy majestye so from my mynd was gone:
> This know I and repent; pardon thow than,
> Wherby thow shalt kepe still thi word stable,
> Thy justice pure and clene; by cawse that whan
> I pardon'd ame, then forthwith justly able,
> Just I am, jugd by justice off thy grace.
> Ffor I my sellff, lo thing most unstable,
> Fformyd in offence, conceyvid in like case,
> Ame nowght but synn from my natyvite;[49]
> Be not this sayd for my excuse, alase,
> But off thy help to shew necessite;
> Ffor lo thou loves the trowgh off inward hert,
> Wich yet doth lyve in my fidelite;
> Tho I have fallen by fraylte overthwart,
> Ffor wilful malice led me not the way,
> So much as hath the flesh drawn me apart.
>
> (445–65)

The 'certayne faith and hope' in God's mercy that follows shame and fear seem evident in the sentiments that Wyatt has David express in a later passage:

> But off thi sellff, O God, this operation
> It must proced, by purging me from blood,
> Among the just that I may have relation,
> And off thy lawdes for to let owt the flood;
> Thow must, O lord, my lyppes furst unlo[o]se:
> Ffor if thou hadst estemid plesant good,
> The Owtward dedes that owtward men disclose,
> I wold have offerd unto the[e] sacrifice.
> But thou delyghtes not in no such glose
> Off owtward dede, as men dreme and devyse.
> The sacrifice that the[e], lord, lykyth most
> Is sprite contrite: low hert in humble wyse
> Thow dost accept, O God, for plesant host.
> Make Syon, Lord, according to thy will,

Inward Syon, the Syon of the ghost:
Off hertes Hierusalem strength the walles still.
Then shalt thou take for good these uttward dedes,
As sacrifice thy plesure to fullfyll.
Off the[e] alone thus all our good procedes.

(490–508)

Indeed the psalms as a whole clearly chart that same process from despair and fear of retribution to hope and exultation, ending in David's discovery of true faith in divine mercy:

Wherby he frames this reason in his hert
That goodness wych doth not forbere his Sonne
From deth for me and can therby convert
From deth to lyff, my synn to salvation,
Both can and woll a smaller grace depert
To hym that suyth by humble supplication:
And sins I have this larger grace assayd
To aske this thing whi ame I then affrayed?

(711–18)

Again the passages cited above have been read as expressing Wyatt's indebtedness to and sympathy for a Lutheran position on Justification. And certainly, as Stephen Greenblatt observes, there is a marked difference of approach in line 496 and following between Wyatt's spiritual Jerusalem and the stress upon Jerusalem as the Heavenly City in works such as Fisher's *Commentary*.[50] But the two interpretations are not mutually exclusive. The venerable medieval practice which ascribed four levels of exegesis to every biblical image, left room for the Jerusalem of the Psalmist to refer both to the celestial city and the soul of the faithful believer. Again, these lines cannot be taken as evidence that Wyatt was advancing a radical theological agenda in advance of the official position outlined in the Articles of 1536 and the *Bishops' Book*.

More specifically, some of Wyatt's phrasing here has been read as a direct and deliberate echo of Luther's. The play on the word 'just' at lines 454–5 in the penultimate passage quoted has, for example, been seen as drawing upon Luther's '*sum Justus et justificatus per justum et justificantem Christum*' ('I am just and justified by a just and justifying Jesus').[51] But, as Mason also pointed out, Wyatt comes closest to Luther's text precisely in those places where Luther relies most obviously upon those commentaries and translations that Wyatt himself was using.[52] Indeed, Wyatt's source for perhaps the most strikingly combative passage in the psalms, the rejection of outward deeds in favour of the 'sacrifice' of a 'sprite contrite' and a 'low hert in humble wyse' (500–1)—a phrase that Mason interprets as 'a "fighting remark" of a Protestant' that 'must have been dictated by anti-catholic feeling'—was probably the psalms themselves.[53] For the Vulgate text itself advances those sentiments in very similar terms:

For if thou hadst desired sacrifice, I would indeed have given it: with burnt offerings thou wilt not be delighted.

A sacrifice to God is an afflicted spirit: a contrite and humbled heart, O God, thou wilt not despise.

(Psalms 50: 18–19)

Far from being a definitively protestant position, the rejection of merely outward contrition in favour of genuine spiritual humility was a central part of conventional catholic doctrine, as the translations of both Campensis ('*Externis sacrificiis non placaberis*': 'Thou wilt not be pacified with outward sacrifices'), and Fisher suggest.[54]

For the striking image of the inward Zion, the Zion of the ghost or spirit, Wyatt probably looked, as Mason suggests, to two catholic sources, Aretino (who observed in the commentary on Psalm 101, that '*il Signore ha edificato Sion nelle sincere menti de gli huomini eletti dallo Spirito santo*' ('the Lord has built Sion in the pure minds of the men elected by the Holy Spirit'), and the *Sancta admodum ac religiosa pietate refertissima expositio in quinquagesimum psalmum*, printed in Paris in 1523. In the latter, the poet would have found reference to 'that inward Jerusalem which is my soul', and the assertion, drawing upon a lengthy tradition of fourfold exegesis of the figure of Zion:

Sion here means the higher part of the soul. Just as in the citadel placed on the high ground of the physical Jerusalem the watchman lying awake used to shout when he caught sight of corporeal enemies, so that higher part of reason, called so because it is built in the highest ground of my soul, looks out and sees spiritual wickedness attacking my inward Jerusalem and constantly roars and cries out against them . . .[55]

Mason also draws attention to Wyatt's use of the word 'penitence' rather than the more conventional 'penance' at line 444 ('Theroff to have more perfitt penitence'), and more explicitly at lines 651–5, where in the prologue to Psalm 129: *De profundis*, the narrator relates how David would measure the extent of his fault against his hope of reward:

> Wherby he takes all outward dede in vayne
> To bere the name of ryghtfull penitence:
> Wich is alone the hert retornd agayne
> And sore contryt that doth his fawt bymone,
> And outward dede the sygne or fruyt alone.
>
> With this he doth deffend the slye assault
> Off vayne alowance off his voyde desert,
> To good [God?] alone he doth it hole convertt.
> His own merytt he fyndeth in default . . .

(651–60)

This use of 'penitence', Mason suggests, was another overtly evangelical gesture, 'very much in the spirit of Luther',[56] citing Tyndale's polemical assault on the whole concept of penance in his *Answer Unto Sir Thomas More's Dialoge* as evidence.[57] But in essence the process that Wyatt describes as 'perfect' and 'ryghtfull penitence' is the same as that 'perfect *penance*' in the *Bishops' Book*, in which Contrition, Confession, and Amendment of former life lead to 'the newe obedient reconciliation unto the lawes and wyl of God'. In each account 'the hert retornd agayne / And sore contryt' is the primary act of Justification, and 'outward dedes' merely 'the sygne or fruyt' of contrition. For the *Bishops' Book* had also described 'exterior acts and works of charity according as they be commanded of God' as those things 'which be called in Scripture, *fructus digni penitencia*: the worthy fruits of penance'.[58] Again similarities of wording between Wyatt's translation and the works of a leading reformer should not distract us from the fact that Wyatt's principal sources for matters of doctrine were the official statements of the faith issued by the Crown and the bishops, not the works of exiled evangelicals.[59] He might use the modish vocabulary of the latest translations, but he used them to describe essentially orthodox doctrinal positions.

Similarly, while there are clear similarities of phrasing and emphasis between Wyatt's text and Luther's *Enchiridion*,[60] sufficient to suggest (but not to prove) that he had read the reformer's work—although whether he knew it to be Luther's when he did so is less clear, as this text too was printed anonymously in the version that was most readily available to him[61]—their theological positions are sufficiently distinct to refute the suggestion that he had been 'converted' to a 'Lutheran' position by his encounter with the reformer's work. Nowhere does Wyatt advance the central and defining Lutheran doctrine of justification-by-faith-alone,[62] and, indeed, closer inspection of some of the similar passages actually suggests that Wyatt's sensibilities may have been markedly at odds with Luther's. Both writers, for example, insert at the end of Psalm 51 a summary of the issues that David has spoken of in that text. Luther informs his readers that:

> We have completed the chief part of this Psalm in which the chief topics of our religion are handled, that is to say, what is Penance, what Grace, what Justification, what are the causes of Justification.[63]

Wyatt, reducing a page of Aretino's prose to a terse summary, has his narrator observe,

> Off diepe secretes that David here did sing,
> Off mercy, off fayth, off frailte, off grace,
> Off Goddes goodnes and off Justyfying,
> The grettnes dyd so astonne hymselff a space,
> As who myght say who hath exprest this thing?
>
> (509–13)

The terminology employed by the two writers may be similar, but how they deploy it is very different. Where Luther's summary reduces David's song to a technical handbook for salvation, an account of a process to be understood and followed, Wyatt offers his readers a more organic assemblage of human and divine attributes. Luther seeks to define the questions: 'what is Justification, and what are the causes of Justification?' in terms of a division of responsibilities between God and humanity: 'what is [human] penitence?'; 'what is [God's] grace?' Wyatt's account describes what seems, by contrast an overtly unequal, non-contractual relationship in which human virtues (faith) and failings (frailty) are merely the precursors to God's forgiveness and his unwarranted benevolence (mercy and grace). Ironically, then, if Wyatt was indeed reading—or recalling— Luther's phrasing as he wrote these lines, he seems to have rejected it, favouring instead a less formulaic and more emotionally resonant account of an utterly unequal confrontation between fallen humanity and the divine. And here we come, I think, to the aspect of the *Paraphrase* that is truly interesting and distinctive about them, although not in terms of doctrine or confessional bias.

The stress upon the intensity and exclusivity of the relationship between David and his God ('To the[a] alone, to the[e] have I trespast, / Ffor none can mesure my fawte but thou alone . . . ' (445–6)) has also often been interpreted as reflecting a markedly Protestant inflection to Wyatt's text. Such inwardness and individualism have suggested to many that the poet was writing out of existence the mediatory apparatus of the institutional church in a way that is indicative of an evangelical and reformist spirit.[64] But Wyatt did not invent the introspectiveness of the psalms. Their intense focus on self-examination and self-awareness was always a part of their theological and aesthetic appeal, an appeal that extended to generations of orthodox writers as well as to reformers.[65] Hence Fisher's paraphrase offered an almost identical translation of the same lines: 'Only to Thee I have trespassed and offended before Thy sight.'[66] Indeed it was almost certainly the inherently introspective cast of the psalms themselves that attracted Wyatt to them, albeit in political rather than doctrinal terms.

What is more striking about the *Paraphrase* in the context of the later 1530s and early 1540s is not its avoidance of the mediating role of the priesthood in the relationship between the sinner and the divine so much as its steadfast silence on the role of the King and the apparatus of the Royal Supremacy in the economy of salvation. In the psalms King David, priest-king of the Jews, is reduced to humble supplication before his God in precisely the same way as his subjects: a point that Wyatt stresses in the course of his translation. Hence what the psalms allow Wyatt to do is to discuss issues of sin and redemption, personal failings and salvation without reference to the single most pressing and contentious issue of the moment: the Supremacy. Indeed he is able, tacitly, to describe obedience to such earthly authorities as one of the distractions on the path to salvation:

> For in thy syght I have not bene agast
> Ffor to offend, juging thi syght as none,
> So that my fawte were hid from syght of man,
> Thy majestye so from my mynd was gone.

> (446–9)

In rejecting the judgement of worldly, political authorities and declaring so clearly that God was the only witness to his sin and transgression, and the only capable judge of his case, Wyatt's David speaks into being a position that effectively circumvented the Oaths of Supremacy and Succession, the Treason Act of 1534, and the steadily accumulating body of Articles, Injunctions, Acts and Proclamations that were defining true and false belief, and distinguishing good and laudable practices from superstitious abuses in Henry's Reformation. Like Thomas More before him, who, when faced with the King's demands for conformity, cited his own conscience and the consensus of fifteen centuries of Christian belief as the higher courts on matters of faith, Wyatt thereby found a way around the apparently universal claims to authority at the heart of the Royal Supremacy. The very act of abjection before the all-seeing, all-weighing divine judge was thus also an implicit act of quiet defiance, a tacit rejection (or perhaps more correctly an avoidance) of the King's claims to spiritual dominion.

The inwardness of the psalmist was thus an effective intellectual solution to the problems faced by a poet hemmed in by injunctions and pressed to breaking point by what he saw as culpable earthly tribunals. By imagining himself as his own advocate in the highest court of appeal, presided over by an infallible, universally competent and merciful sovereign, Wyatt was able to write into being a new identity for himself, an identity in which he was no longer the powerless victim of others' demands and machinations but an autonomous political agent. Moreover, imagining himself as an advocate in this higher court allowed Wyatt to deploy all his own skills and experience as both a poet and diplomat in ways that gave him a distinct advantage. Having been thwarted in his attempts to counsel Henry VIII towards virtue, and so effectively hamstrung in his attempt to bring his Ciceronian skills to bear on the redemption of the state, Wyatt was able to craft in this text a vicarious opportunity to use them in a far higher court. Thus, paradoxically, in following David and withdrawing from the palace into the dark and solitary seclusion of the cave, Wyatt was moving from a world in which he was beset with dangers, both real and imagined, to a situation in which he felt very much at home, a private audience with his divine King and Maker; an audience in which he had an opportunity to negotiate a special deal with the highest of royal authorities.[67]

Translating the psalms, then, gave Wyatt the opportunity, in his imagination at least, to negotiate with those otherwise inscrutable powers whose decisions determined his fate. By imaginatively inhabiting the persona of David, he could bring his rhetorical and political skills to bear upon the task of literally talking his way out of the desperate situation that he was in. As James Simpson notes, Wyatt's David is acutely aware of the importance of words, just as the poet, following the passing of the Treason Act of 1534, was aware of the dangers that an incautious choice of one term over another could bring. His own trial, after all, hinged upon precisely the importance of his having spoken one word rather than another during his conversations in Spain. As he conceded to his judges in his Defence,

It is a small thing in altering of one syllable either with pen or word that may make in the conceiving of the truth much matter or error. For in this thing 'I fear' or 'I trust' seemeth but one small syllable changed, and yet it maketh a great difference.[68]

Hence Wyatt's David tests each word that he will speak, weighing it in his mind before he utters it, planning his approach to God with the meticulous care of the professional orator:[69]

> ... in his hert he tornith and payseth [poiseth]
> Ech word that erst his lypps might forth aford.
> He poyntes, he pawsith, he wonders, he praysyth
> The marcy that hydes off justice the swourd ...
>
>   (518–21)

Wyatt's rhetorical strategy is perfectly replicated in the rhythm of these lines, as the careful hesitancy of 'torneth and payseth', 'poyntes', 'pawsith', and 'wonders' stores up an energy that finally pours forth, once the correct formulation is determined, in the syllabic flood of 'he praysyth / The marcy that hides off justice the swourd'.

By ventriloquizing David's appeals to his God from the depths of his cave, Wyatt is able to turn the psalmist's humble attempts to reach a compact with the divine into an entirely more proactive process. Alexandra Halasz has drawn attention to the way in which Wyatt transforms the humble petition of *Domine ne in furore* into a full-blown attempt to plea-bargain.[70] The Vulgate reads,

Turn to me, O Lord, and deliver my soul: O save me for Thy mercy's sake.
    For there is no one in death that is mindful of Thee: and who shall confess to Thee in hell?

                    (Psalms 6: 5–6)

This becomes in Wyatt's hands an extended demonstration of the courtly counsellor's persuasive art.

> Returne, O Lorde, O Lorde, I the[e] beseche,
> Unto thie olde wonted benignitie ...
>
>   (116–17)

> Ffor if thie rightwise hand that is so juste
> Suffer no Synne or stryke with dampnacion,
> Thie infinyte marcye want nedes it must
> Subjecte matter for his operacion:
> For that in deth there is no memorie
> Amonge the Dampnyd, nor yet no mencion
> Of thie great name, grownd of all glorye.
> Then if I dye and goe wheare as I feare
> To thinck thearon, how shal thie great mercye
> Sownde in my mowth unto the worldes eare?

Ffor theare is none than can thee lawde and love,
Ffor that thow wilt no love among them theare.
Suffer my Cryes thie marcye for to move,
That wonted is a hundred yeares offence
In momente of repentaunce to remove.

(127–41)

The vocabulary deployed here is certainly that of desperate, humble, supplication. But, as Halasz observes, the argument that Wyatt's David advances carries more than a hint of special pleading. Rather than a condemned man facing his judge from the dock, this sounds much more like a barrister trying to do a deal with the judge in his chambers before the case even comes to court. David's 'presumption', she suggests, lies in his daring to suggest to God that it is in His best interests to forgive him for his sins.[71] And, more than this, Wyatt invests David with all the advantages of the courtly counsellor, allowing him to play upon a personal familiarity with his divine judge not available to most petitioners. He refers to God's 'old wonted benignitie' (117), hinting at a history of personal acquaintance that can be appealed to as grounds for special favour.[72] And he even has the temerity to suggest, albeit with the utmost discretion, that God has got Himself into something of a crisis of His own making as a result of His own (by implication injudicious) decisions. It is because He 'wilt no love among them theare' (in Hell) that there will soon be no one left to praise Him if David too is condemned to join the damned. Thus, when David, having outlined what he sees as the dilemma facing God, turns again to supplication with the appeal 'suffer my cryes Thie marcye for to move', it is the solution to an otherwise insoluble dilemma that he seems to be offering rather than the abject plea of a powerless penitent. This is pleading, but of a very special kind indeed.

Wyatt's David returns to this persuasive mode of speech again, and with still greater apparent confidence in the fifty-first Psalm. And the sense of his trying to 'cut a deal with God' is still more obvious here. Finding the bare bones of a plea and a promise in the Vulgate text, Wyatt brings the full range of his skills as a courtier and diplomat to bear upon presenting David's case in the most persuasive of terms. The Vulgate text reads:

Restore unto me the joy of thy salvation, and strengthen me with a perfect spirit.
I will teach the unjust thy ways, and the wicked shall be converted to thee.
Deliver me from blood, O God, Thou God of my salvation, and strengthen me with a perfect spirit.

(Psalms 51: 14–16)

Wyatt expands this to read:

Rendre to me joye off thy help and rest;
My will conferme with spryte off stedfastnesse:
And by this shall thes[e] goodly thinges ensue.

> Sinners I shall in to thy ways addresse;
> They shall retorne to the[e] and thy grace sue.
> My tong shall prayse thy Justification,
> My mowgh shall spred thy gloryous praysis true.

(483–9)

Here indeed is Wyatt in full negotiative flow, engaging in what looks remarkably like an attempt to convince God that he is offering Him a good return on His investment. Wyatt's David, unlike the king of the Vulgate, is careful to spell out the advantages to God in his own redemption, and his own usefulness to his creator as a poet or rhetorician of divine praise. At moments like these the text forcefully reminds us that one of the principal titles of an ambassador in this period was 'King's Orator', a spokesman for his royal master in the courts of his rivals. It is precisely such a role in God's service that Wyatt's David proposes for himself. Redeem me of my offences, he offers, and I shall go out into the world and sing your praises as an orator for God in the lands of the unjust. What is notable in Wyatt's David is the complete absence of any self-doubt about his ability to fulfil this promise. He seems sublimely confident in his own ability to sway audiences to his desired ends: 'Sinners I *shall* into thy waye addresse; / They *shall* retorne to the[e] and thy graces sue'. (my italics). We could, of course, assume that the poet-king's confidence here stems, as it does in the Vulgate text, solely from his trust in God to inspire him to eloquence, but in Wyatt's version of the story David's eloquence seems not a divine gift that will follow from God's mercy, but one of the bargaining chips that he brings to the table in advance of the negotiations. Wyatt's David, that is, seems sure of his own capacity to work out independently and execute whatever was really in his master's best interests, precisely as Wyatt himself had been in Spain.

After such a discussion, the lines that follow sound less like a Lutheran affirmation of the absence of any human agency in the process of salvation and more like a firm reminder that God must fulfil His part of the contract before David will be able to act on His behalf and put right the problems that He has created for Himself:

> But off thi self, O God, this operation
> It must proced, by purging me from blood,
> Among the just that I may have relation;
> And off thy lawdes for to let owt the flood;
> Thow must, o Lord, my lypps furst unlo[o]se . . .

(490–4)

Here again is Wyatt the diplomat, the advocate and orator, seeking to take command of a negotiation and, through the careful deployment of language, conclude it in his own favour. Far from his bringing an evangelical sense of human impotence and abjection to the scenario, we can sense Wyatt here almost pushing the David of the Vulgate aside in his enthusiasm to show just how the negotiation with God should be handled. Hence we find his David suggesting to his silent interlocutor that, if He is to govern His Universe successfully, indeed if He is to remain true to His own promises and intentions, if, that is, He is to remain true to Himself as God, He must accept the logic of His suitor's argument and redeem him on the spot.

We misunderstand Wyatt's position, then, if we see his Penitential Psalms as motivated by a Lutheran doctrinal impulse at odds with the official position of the Henrician church. In doctrine his text was carefully conformist, following the contours of the official statements of faith even where they were implicitly contradictory. Where he was profoundly at odds with Henry and his regime was not over the articles of faith, but over politics and morality. Wyatt had sought, like More, Elyot, Heywood, Thynne, and Tuke before him, to counsel the King on these matters, but partly as a result of his own maladroitness and over-confidence, and primarily because Henry was simply not listening any longer to such unwelcome advice, these conventional methods had failed. Consequently he had sought other literary forms in which to voice his frustrations and disillusionment, and to pursue his ambitions. The first results of this resolution were the satires with their readiness to declare, albeit in subtle, allusive ways, that the King had become a tyrant, and their fraught discussion of the dilemmas facing the humanist man of virtue in a despotic realm. The second was the move to biblical paraphrase in the search for a voice to express the poet's own inability to redeem the King and to overcome it. And in 1541 the psalms offered a ready vehicle for the potent mixture of anger and anxiety provoked by the failure of his mission to the Emperor, the death of his patron Thomas Cromwell, and his own subsequent investigation for treason. The psalmist's fraught attempts to subjugate pride to humility,[73] to discipline sexual desire in the interests of spiritual fulfilment, and most of all his complex attitudes to royal power and authority, all allowed Wyatt to give voice to the issues central to his own situation. His evident and acute difficulty in resolving these issues, and his signal failure to fulfil the injunctions that he voices either simply or irrevocably reveal the depths and severity of his own personal struggle at this time.

What the psalms also allowed the poet to do was much more openly to confront the King with a vision of his own personal and political misdeeds. As Halasz suggests, Wyatt was able, by adopting the persona of David, to do what Elyot had done in *The Banquet of Sapience*, that is co-opt a voice of biblical authority to perform contemporary work:

In using the psalmic voice as his ground, Wyatt claims the position as sacred singer, as one who can call kings to account, counsel kingdoms away from their errors, and articulate the temporal and spiritual desires of a people as well as his own.[74]

Whereas in 'My Mother's Maids' Wyatt had merely voiced the curse levelled by Persius at all tyrants, letting his intended reader make the connection between text and context, in the *Paraphrase* he would arraign the King vicariously, and, more than that, imagine Henry's own response, ventriloquizing his abject admission of guilt, and offering him, albeit after a suitably satisfying degree of contrite humiliation, the prospect of his own redemption, alongside that of the poet himself.

As Elyot had done in his last substantial work, *The Image of Governance*, Wyatt turned to literature and the comforts that its imaginary realm offered as a partial solution to his own dilemma. Just as Elyot both fashioned for himself the perfect satirical weapon with which to attack his sovereign and engineered his own apotheosis in the course of that last and most satirical prose work, so Wyatt in the *Paraphrase* both confronted and acknowledged his own guilt as a fallen sinner and, in the manner of Nathan the Prophet, condemned the lustful self-indulgence and murderous despotism of his king, deploying his rhetorical skills as chief advocate for his own redemption and the King's confession. In doing so, however, he was tacitly admitting defeat. Such things could only be achieved, if at all, within the confines of the literary text. And like Elyot before him, he remained trapped within the paradigm of literature as counsel—a paradigm in which he could have had little faith by this stage in his relatively short but unquiet life. His text, the product of his lifetime of scholarship and diligent service, could only achieve political good in the world if the King chose to read it and to act on its powerful injunctions and imperatives. Such, of course, was the great limitation of good counsel. Wyatt thus left the King, and the world, with one final excoriating piece of literary counsel, a text that would, if it were understood and acted upon, reveal to Henry the harsh truth of his own condition, and offer him the only way to seek his own redemption: the path of contrition, confession, and eventual absolution. Perhaps, finally, no loyal counsellor could do more in the reign of a tyrant.

16

'Wyatt Resteth Here'

Henry Howard and the Invention of Resistance

In November 1541, a final sexual scandal rocked the royal court. Catherine Howard, the young queen upon whom Henry doted and who had secured Wyatt's release from prison earlier that year, was arrested. She was accused, like her cousin Anne Boleyn before her, of multiple adultery: of continuing with two previous, carefully concealed, sexual liaisons after her marriage to the King, and of beginning a new one, with a courtier, Thomas Culpepper, once she had become Queen. Unlike Anne, however, Catherine does seem to have been guilty as charged. On 15 February 1542 she was executed. Henry was said to be devastated by the behaviour of his inconstant wife. What Wyatt thought is unknown, but by the beginning of 1542 he was back in royal service, and gained materially from the division of those court offices that had previously been held by Culpepper.[1] He did not live to enjoy them for long, however. On 3 October he was sent in haste to the West Country to welcome the new Spanish envoy, Montmorency de Courrièrez, who had landed at Falmouth at the end of September.[2] The exertion of the journey after so many years of frantically 'trotting up and down' on his king's behalf, seems to have been too much for him. He did not get beyond Sherborne in Dorset, where he fell ill and had to rest in the house of Sir John Horsey. He died there three days later, on 11 October at the age of thirty-nine.

Within months of his death the printers John Herforde and Robert Toye published a slim volume of poems in English, headed by an anonymous text, 'An Excellent Epitaph of Sir Thomas Wyatt'.[3] Printed beneath a medallion containing an engraved bust of Wyatt in his maturity, the *Epitaph* offered a sustained and powerful tribute to the dead poet's character and reputation:

> Wyat resteth here that quike coulde never rest;
> Whose hevenly gyftes encreased by dysdayne,
> And vertue sanke the deper in his brest,
> Such profyte he of envy could optayne.
>
> A Head, where wisdom mysteries dyd frame,
> Whose hammers beat styll in that lyvely brayne

As on a styth, where some worke of fame
Was dayly wrought to turn to Brytayns gaine.

A Vysage sterne and mylde, where [b]oth dyd groo,
Vyce to contempne, in virtues to rejoice;
Amyd great stormes whome grace assured soo
To lyve upright and smyle at fortunes choyse.

A Hand that taught what might be said in rime,
That reste Chaucer the glorye of his wytte,
A marke, the whi[c]he (unperfited for tyme)
Some may approche, but never none shall hyt.

A Tong that served in foraine realms his king,
Whose curtoise talke to vertu dyd enflame
Eche noble harte, a worthy guyde to brynge
Our Englysshe youth by travayle unto fame.

An Eye whose judgement no affect coulde blind,
Frendes to allure and foes to reconcyle,
Whose pearcynge looke dyd represent a mynde
With vertue fraught, reposed, voyde of gyle.

A Harte where dred yet never so imprest
To hide the thought that might the trouth avaunce,
In neyther fortune lyste nor so represt
To swell in welth not yelde unto mischaunce.

A valiaunt Corps, where force and beautye met;
Happy, alas to[o] happy, but for foos,
Lyved and ran the race that nature set,
Of manhodes shape, where she the mold did loos.

But to the heavens that simple soule is fleed,
Which lefte with such as covet Christe to knowe,
Witnes of faith that never shalbe dredde,
Sent for our welth, but not received so;
Thus for our gylt this jewell have we lost,
The earth his bones, the heven possesse his goost.

AMEN

This tribute to a simple, stoic soul who served his nation and his prince, yet at the same time was able to set the limits for poetic achievement in the English tongue and 'reste Chaucer the glorye of his wytte', was no piece of anonymous hackwork. The author was a nobleman and himself a poet of distinction, Wyatt's friend Henry Howard, Earl of Surrey, the eldest son of Thomas Howard, Duke of

Norfolk. For so distinguished an aristocrat, the heir to the most powerful noble house in England, voluntarily to enter, even anonymously, the still rather vulgar medium of print to eulogize someone who was, after all, merely a knight was, as W. A. Sessions has observed, a remarkable act.[4] To circulate private verses in manuscript would better suit both the tenets of aristocratic taste and the sentiments of private friendship that Surrey expressed here and in other verses concerning Wyatt. Yet Surrey chose to print these lines, and must, as Sessions suggests, have gone to considerable trouble to do so, as he was campaigning in the north of England against the Scots at the time of Wyatt's death, and would have found it difficult both to write the verses and to get them south to London in time for publication. In addition he almost certainly also financed a second printed book published at the same time and also dedicated to venerating Wyatt's poetic and personal reputation: the *Naeniae* composed by the former Howard family tutor, John Leland.[5] Why he did so tells us as a good deal about Wyatt's poetic legacy, but rather more about Surrey's own political agenda and ambitions.

'Reckless Youth in an Unquiet Breast': The Life of Henry Howard, Earl of Surrey

Henry Howard, 'the poet earl of Surrey', was in many ways a prototype for that model of reckless, youthful aristocratic ambition that would later produce Sir Philip Sidney and the Elizabethan Earl of Essex, Robert Devereux.[6] Like Sidney, Surrey was a writer who was adopted after his death as an icon of an idealized, English, reformed Christian manhood by a cadre of protestant writers. Like Essex, Surrey was a political firebrand, fiercely proud of his noble lineage, and intensely politically ambitious for both himself and his family. Those ambitions, and the flamboyant, incautious ways in which he expressed them brought him five separate periods of imprisonment in his brief life—more even than Wyatt himself— before he succumbed, again like Essex, to charges of treason and a traitor's death.

Impatient, rebellious, and highly strung, Surrey was rarely able to brook frustration or sustain a slight, whether intended or imagined, and he frequently clashed with authority in the numerous forms in which it was manifested in Tudor England. His father, the burgers of the City of London, privy councillors, friends and rivals, the conservative clergy, and the King himself: all were the subject of Surrey's resentments at one time or another during his short, turbulent life, and each of these resentments was to find its way into his poetry.

Howard was born in the early months of 1517, the first son of Thomas Howard the younger, third Duke of Norfolk, and grandson to Thomas Howard the elder, the 'Flodden Duke' of Norfolk. On the latter's death in 1534, his father became Duke of Norfolk, and Howard in turn inherited the courtesy title of Earl of Surrey, the prerogative of the Howard heir. His family connections and history inevitably gave him a prominent place in the political nation, and his youth gave him an additional advantage. When, in 1530, Henry VIII sought a suitable aristocratic playfellow for his bastard son, Henry Fitzroy, Duke of Richmond, it was to the thirteen-year-old Surrey, first cousin to his future queen, Anne Boleyn, that he looked, and the boy moved to Windsor to take up residence as the closest companion to the King's only male child. The two young men quickly developed an intense friendship. In the following year the bonds between the Howards and the crown were further strengthened, when Richmond married Surrey's sister, Lady Mary Howard. Meanwhile Surrey himself had forged other bonds within the tightly knit circle of noble families that dominated national politics, having taking for his own wife Lady Frances de Vere, daughter to the Earl of Oxford.

Surrey's family was, then, at the heart of the political nation, its ducal lineage stretching back some three generations: not far by the standards of some noble families, perhaps, but certainly longer than the Tudors' claim to the Crown. And their sense of their own worth—and the entitlement it brought with it—evident in the family motto '*sola virtus invicta*' ('only unconquered virtue'), had both positive and negative aspects. Family pride and class prejudice are often bedfellows, of course, but the Howards in general, and Surrey in particular, seem to have turned them into something of a religion. The Earl's grandfather, Thomas Howard the older, had allegedly, as the Ricardian army collapsed all around him on the field of Bosworth, begged his ally Sir Gilbert Talbot to finish him with his sword, not through shame at having backed the losing side, but to prevent an enemy of non-gentle blood from striking the mortal blow and so tainting his honour.[7] Surrey evidently held similar views. Following Cromwell's death in 1540, he was said by his cousin Sir Edmund Knyvet to have expressed, not the remorse shown by Wyatt, but satisfaction: 'Now is that foul churl dead so ambitious of other['s] blood; now is he stricken with his own staff... These new-erected men would by their wills leave no noble men on life [i.e. alive].'[8] It was precisely the kind of savage, noble hostility that had prompted Elyot to write the *Image of Governance* and dedicate it signally to the noblemen of England. But the corollary of this noble arrogance was a confidence in his self-worth and political destiny that would allow him in his verse to express his disquiet at Henry's tyrannical tendencies, and his personal distaste for the King, in the boldest and most direct terms.

In the space of two months in 1536, however, both of the blood ties between the Howards and their sovereign were severed. In June, Surrey's cousin Anne Boleyn died a traitor's death. On 22 July a death still closer to home followed. Henry Fitzroy suddenly succumbed to a fever and died, probably as the result of a form of tuberculosis.[9] The loss of his royal brother-in-law and closest friend evidently left Surrey emotionally and physically devastated. As late as 12 July 1537, his father reported that the young earl was still 'very weak, his nature running from him abundantly', and that he had been in 'that case' for a great part of the previous year 'for thought of my lord of Richmond'.[10] We should not, perhaps, over-sentimentalize Surrey's emotional reaction here. In Tudor aristocratic society friendship, like marriage, was a political and cultural commodity as well as a personal relationship. His closeness to Richmond, genuine though it seems to have been, was also an indication of his political status, of his family's fortunes, and, in the years before Henry sired a legitimate male heir, a promise of a potentially still more elevated political future. Hence there is more than a hint of self-assertion to his poetic recollection, written some years later when he was himself imprisoned in the same castle at Windsor, of the days when:

> ...I in luste and joye
> With a kinges soon [son] my childishe yeres did passe,
> In greater feast than Priams sonnes of Troye...
>
> ('So Crewell Prison', 1–4)[11]

Richmond's death was not the only blow to the Howards in 1537, however. In the same year, on All Hallows Eve, Surrey's uncle, another Lord Thomas Howard, died in the Tower, having been imprisoned in the previous July for contracting without royal permission a marriage to the King's niece, Lady Margaret Douglas. This was a match that again seemed to link the Howards to the succession in ways which the King, still lacking a legitimate heir (his daughters having each been declared illegitimate by separate Acts of Succession) found dangerous.

After these deaths Surrey's behaviour became more overtly politicized and more wayward. No longer a part of the inner circle of the royal family, he seems both to have sought desperately to win back a role at the political centre and paradoxically to have signalled his resentment at that exclusion with ever more self-marginal-izing acts of bravado. His career thus progressed by fits and starts, as periods of advancement were punctuated and reversed by moments of self-destructive assertiveness. In 1537 he was imprisoned for a time in Windsor, reputedly for striking the young man who was to become his great rival for political favour, Sir Edward Seymour, Viscount Beauchamp. Seymour had allegedly accused both Surrey and his father of favouring the rebels' course during the Pilgrimage of Grace, despite the fact that the young Howard had served loyally in the royal army led by his father that had punished the rebels so brutally earlier that year.

In 1539 and 1540 Surrey's star was once more ascending. In the first of those years he served the crown loyally, organizing the coastal defences in his home county of Norfolk during a period of acute fears concerning an imperial invasion. In 1540 he won plaudits and honour at court by jousting with conspicuous success in the tournament in honour of the King's ill-fated marriage to Anne of Cleves. In the following year, benefiting from Henry's new marriage to his first cousin, Catherine Howard, he attained what was to prove the pinnacle of his courtly career, being elected as a knight of the Order of the Garter, and taking his stall five places from that of the King himself in St George's chapel Windsor.[12] But this, the highest of chivalric honours, did not for long curb Surrey's wayward temper, nor did it improve the fortunes of his family. In 1542, indeed, he was to witness the lowest moment in the Howards' fortunes, when Queen Catherine was executed, just eight years after Anne Boleyn had met the same fate. The Howards may, then, have enjoyed a special, indeed uniquely intimate relationship with their sovereign, but it was an intimacy that bred resentment and periods of intense distrust as well as familiarity. And on the part of the young Howard heir, resentment and bitterness born of thwarted ambition were increasingly becoming the stronger emotions, finding outlets in ever more extreme activities.

In the same year that Queen Catherine died, Surrey took on another military commission, this time campaigning against the Scots, but not before he had spent another period in prison, again for challenging a courtier on a point of honour. And less than a year later, newly returned from campaigning, he was again arrested and brought before the Privy Council, this time for openly defying the prohibition on eating meat during Lent and then leading a group of young followers on a riotous spree through London, breaking the windows of prominent burgesses' houses and shooting stone-bolts at the prostitutes and other nightwalkers of Bankside. A further period of imprisonment followed, during which he wrote a lengthy poem in the style of the Roman satirist Juvenal, arraigning the citizens of London for their religious and moral corruption and presenting his own riotous cavalcade through the streets as the imposition of the scourge of God for their sins:

> London, hast thow accused me
> Of breche of lawes, the roote of stryfe?
> Within whose brest did boyle to see,
> So fervent hotte thy dissolute life,
> That even the hate of synnes, that groo
> Within thy wicked walles so rife,
> For to breake forthe did convert soo
> That terrour colde it not represse . . .
>
> (j33: 1–8)

> This made me, with a reckless brest,
> To wake thy sluggardes with my bowe:
> A figure of the Lordes behest,
> Whose scourge for synn the Scriptures shew.
>
> (19–22)

> Oh membre of false Babylon!
> The shop of craft, the denne of ire!
> Thy dredfull dome drawes fast upon.
> Thy martyres blood by sword and fyre,
> In Heaven and earth for justice call.
> The Lord shall here their just desyre;
> The flame of wrath shall on the[e] fall.
>
> (53–9)

In the following two years Surrey served on two further successful military campaigns, fighting alongside the Emperor Charles V, now Henry's ally, at the siege of Londres in 1543, and then leading the siege of Montreuil as Marshall of the Field. In 1545 Surrey again led the army, this time alongside his sovereign during the capture of Boulogne. But, when he was left in sole charge during the following year, he badly overreached himself, allowing his forces to be outnumbered and routed by a French force around Mont St Etienne, near Montreuil, a reverse that was to lead to his ignominious replacement by his rival Edward Seymour and his recall to England in March 1546. As his troops broke around him on the field of battle, Surrey was said to have begged Sir John Bridges and his other lieutenants to run him through so that he might forget the day, seemingly in conscious emulation of his grandfather at Bosworth. They did not comply, however, and on his return to England he was, reportedly, 'but coldly received' at court and denied an immediate audience with the King.[13]

That Surrey's ambitions were beginning to look beyond merely winning royal favour by acts of conspicuous bravery is suggested by the lavish building project that he embarked upon in his native Norfolk in these years. As W. A. Sessions has described, Mount Surrey, near Norwich, was planned on a lavish scale, advertising not only its owner's status as the principal regional magnate, but his ambitions as a national leader. In both the design and the scale of the project Surrey declared his intentions, not least in the conspicuous use of heraldic devices in the stained glass of the windows, which made much of the Howards' Plantagenet descent from Edward III. These devices—in which Surrey pointedly moved the arms of Edward the Confessor ('azure, a cross fleury between five martlets gold' as his indictment for treason was to describe them) from the second to the first quarter of his shield, decorating them with the 'three labels silver' which were the privilege of the Prince of Wales—were to prove his undoing. For in a culture acutely sensitive to heraldic symbolism they seemed to be an implicit assertion of quasi-regal ambitions. At the same time Surrey commissioned a series of grand, self-glorifying portraits of himself from Hans Holbein, William Scrots, and another unknown artist, presenting him in a variety of heroic guises from the flamboyant Renaissance man of action, leaning ostentatiously upon a broken pillar of gold, symbolizing fortitude in adversity, to the philosophical classical statesman, wrapped in a sober black cloak in the high Roman manner.[14]

Such ostentatious displays of personal and familial ambition would have been dangerous at any time, but in the last years of an obviously dying King they were particularly ill-judged. And Surrey compounded them with dangerously loose talk within his own circle and, more incautiously still, with fellow noblemen. With Henry's health failing week by week, and the question of who would be appointed Protector to the infant Prince Edward becoming ever more pressing, Surrey began to make his play for a Howard protectorate with increasing insistence, and in ways that his father, one of Tudor England's great political survivors, would find suicidally reckless.[15] At a court reception in August 1546 he was reported to have had a public argument with Wyatt's old friend Sir George Blage over the question of the protectorate. Of all those noblemen potentially eligible for the role, he said, 'his father was meetest, both for good services done and for estate'. To this, Blage, by this point probably a convert to sacramentarian views and consequently deeply suspicious of Norfolk's overtly reactionary brand of catholicism, is said to have replied that if this was the case, then 'the prince should be but evil taught . . . Rather than it should come to pass that the prince should be under the government of your father or you, I would bide the adventure to thrust this dagger [in you].'[16] And at his trial other deponents would testify to his having asked other gentlemen in other places the dangerously provocative question 'if God should call the King to His mercy who was so mete to govern the prince as my lord my father?' Still more improvidently, his household servants were overheard suggesting that 'if ought came at the king and my lord prince, he would be king after his father'.[17]

Such talk, encompassing as it did the explicit imagining of the death of the King contrary to both the Treason Act and successive Acts of Succession, was positively suicidal in the fraught atmosphere of 1546. Henry was already preparing for the succession with an almost paranoid concern to exclude from the regency council those who might seek to usurp the authority of the Crown for their own ends. Hence when, for reasons that remain unclear, a former friend and client of Surrey's, his cousin Sir Richard Southwell, reported that Surrey was plotting concerning the succession, and during the searches of Howard residences that followed, witnesses reported what they had seen in the heraldic devices at the Howard's principal residence of Kenninghall, Norfolk, the Earl's fate was virtually sealed. Evidence of Surrey's ill-advised conversations with Blage and others was secured from more or less willing witnesses, and questions concerning the contents of his new coat of arms, and what he might intend it to signify were asked of expert witnesses from the royal college of heralds and former intimates of the Earl himself.

Although the trial covered all aspects of the Earl's conduct, the indictment for treason itself relied upon the heraldic evidence alone to indicate the Earl's treasonable intentions. It alleged that, contrary to the various Succession Acts of the 1530s and 1540s, he had attempted to deprive both the King and his heir of their proper titles, in as much as he had,

falsely, maliciously, and treasonably, and indeed openly and publicly held, displayed, and bore and used . . . [the Arms of St Edward the Confessor, thereby] willing, wishing and desiring and with all his nefarious art and talent imagining, inventing, practicing and attempting to deprive the . . . most illustrious and serene [lord] our King of the rights, dignity, titles and names of his royal estate . . . [intending] . . . the undermining, destroying, annihilating, and scandalizing the true and indisputable title of the said Lord King, [and] . . . no less treasonably . . . disinheriting and cutting off the . . . most excellent Lord Prince Edward from his true and indubitable title from the throne of his kingdom [of] England.[18]

The familiar piling up of adverbs and adjectives that was the hallmark of Henrician statute here indicates an additional and very real animus against the Earl on the part of the King, whose crabbed, failing hand can be seen annotating and amending the interrogatories given to Surrey to sharpen a question or strengthen a rebuke.[19] When he was finally confronted with these charges and informed that it was Southwell who had initiated the investigation, Surrey's first instincts were characteristically aristocratic and flamboyant. He offered to fight his accuser in his shirt, that is to endure trial by combat, allowing his opponent to wear full armour but wearing none himself, trusting in God, his own honour and innocence to protect him. The offer was declined, or rather ignored, but it was of a piece with the spectacle that Surrey would present when cornered by his accusers.

The trial itself was a series of calculated slights to Surrey's heightened sense of aristocratic honour. After his arrest, he had been interrogated at the London residence of Lord Chancellor Wriothesley in Ely Place. Following ten days of close questioning he was taken on 12 December under guard to the Tower to await trial, not in a closed carriage but, like Wyatt before him, openly and on foot through the streets of the City, 'making great lamentation' for all the citizens, whom he had so brazenly rebuked for their vices only three years earlier, to witness. If the *Spanish Chronicle*, a somewhat romanticized account of the events of these years, is to be believed, the trial itself was also a symbolic humiliation, being held, not as was normal for noble defendants, at Westminster, but at the London Guildhall, 'this being the first time that ever such a thing was seen of a gentleman being tried there'. Again the Earl who had set himself up as the judge and jury of the sinful city was pointedly subjected to its gaze and authority.[20]

Surrey's evident contempt for the men of lower rank on Henry's privy council, and his malice towards Edward Seymour in particular, newly elevated to the earldom of Hertford, formed a substantial element in the evidence presented against him during the trial. Sir Gawain Carew, for example, testified that the Earl had remarked to him that 'those men which are made by the King's majesty of vile birth hath been the distraction of all the nobility of the realm'. And Surrey did little to dispel such accusations during the eight hours in which he defended himself before his judges. When evidence was offered concerning an argument between Surrey and a commoner (possibly the exchange with Blage cited above), the Earl asked his judges dismissively 'whether it were probable that this man should speak thus to the Earl of Surrey and he not strike him again?'[21] And when William Paget, the son of the former Mace-bearer of the City of London, interrupted him in mid-flow to accuse him of treasonable intentions, he was subjected to the full glare of the Earl's aristocratic hauteur: 'And thou, Catchpole, what hast thou to do with it?' Surrey retorted. 'Thou hadst better hold thy tongue, for the kingdom has never been well since the King put creatures such as thou into the government.'

Surrey's conduct before his arrest, and his refusal to compromise with his interrogators subsequently, left little room for manoeuvre. Even his closest allies, sensing that matters could end only one way, moved to secure their own safety. His sister, Mary, Duchess of Richmond, provided some of the most damning evidence against him at his trial. Even his father abandoned him. On 12 January, the day before his son's trial was to begin, the Duke confessed to the lesser charge of misprision of treason, thereby condemning his son to death by default. 'I have concealed high treason', he declared, 'in keeping secret the false and traitorous act . . . committed by my son . . . in using the arms of St Edward the Confessor.'[22] Surrey was duly condemned, and was finally beheaded on Tower Green on 19 January 1547. He may have been one of the few victims of Henry's despotic final years who actually invited a violent end by challenging royal authority directly.

Surrey's Life in his Verse

It is interesting to note that in all the testimonies and all the evidence brought against Surrey at his trial in 1546, at no point did anyone allude to his poetry. Details of his conversations, his actions, his use of heraldic devices and his commissioning of portraits were all cited against him and subjected to detailed scrutiny in order to provide evidence of his attitudes and intentions. But the most explicit and extended statements of his attitudes, his resentments, his hopes and aspirations were never exposed to examination. Had his accusers had access to his poetic manuscripts, or even to the printed text of his elegy for Wyatt, they would have found ample material from which to fashion charges against him. For Surrey's verse, perhaps more so even than Wyatt's, is deeply coloured by the extremity of his own personal and political experiences.[23] The exultation of military victory, the pain of personal loss, his intense sense of his own honour and of the honour due to others, the terror of arrest and accusation, the misery of imprisonment, and his fierce opposition to tyranny in all its forms, all have left an indelible mark upon his writing.

Numerous verses speak of the plight of the beleaguered man of honour, beset by foes, or the solitary prisoner brought down by his enemies. One elegiac work was written while he was imprisoned in Windsor Castle, and contrasts his current misery to his former life with the young Duke of Richmond in that same palace:

> So crewel prison howe could betide, alas . . .
> When eche swete place retounes a tast full sowre . . .
>
> Eache stone, alas, that dothe my sorrow rewe,
> Retournes therto a hollowe sound of playnt.
> Thus I alone, where all my fredome grew,
> In pryson pyne with bondage and restraint.

(J27: 1, 5, 49–52)

A sense of Surrey's pride in his own military exploits can be gained from the elegy he wrote for his squire, Thomas Clere, who died in April 1545 from wounds or an infection picked up during the siege of Montreuil the previous September. As

Sessions suggests, the poem reveals Surrey 'claiming' Clere and his heroic example for the Howards' family history—the literary equivalent of their physical interring of Clere's corpse in the Howard chapel at Lambeth. But, even more obviously it shows the poet using Clere's death as an occasion to rehearse and affirm his own chivalric honour. It is principally as a witness to Surrey's campaigns (as he literally follows in his master's footsteps) that the squire is recalled and cherished. His birthplace, his Irish ancestry, his relationship to Anne Boleyn, his love for Mary Shelton: all make brief appearances in the poem, but it is the roll-call of Surrey's battles and sieges (Kelsall (1542); Landrecy (October 1543); Boulogne and Montreuil (both September 1544)) that takes centre stage.[24] It is Clere's service to his lord rather than his lady that is pre-eminently celebrated:

> Norfolk sprang thee, Lambeth holds thee dead.
> Clere of the county of Cleremont thou hight,
> Within the wombe of Ormondes race thou bread,
> And sawest thy cosine [Queen Anne] crowned in thy sight.
> Shelton for love, Surrey for Lord thou chase:
> Ay me, while life did last that league was tender;
> Tracing whose steps thou sawest Kelsall blaze,
> Laundersey burnt, and battered Bullen render.
> At Muttrell gates, hopeless of all recure,
> Thine Earle half dead gave in thy hand his Will;
> Which cause did thee this pining death procure,
> Ere Sommers four times seaven thou couldest fulfil.
>   Ah Clere, if love had booted, care, or cost,
>   Heaven had not wonn, nor Earth so timely lost.
>
>   (J35)

Considerable insight into Surrey's sense of personal and familial honour, and the kind of violent energies to which it could give rise, can be found in a remarkable, semi-allegorical poem that he wrote in the early 1540s: 'Each beast can choose his fere according to his mind.'[25] Seemingly written in response to what might appear at first sight a minor social embarrassment (an aristocratic woman's refusal of his offer to dance with her), this seventy-six line poem of self-justification and threat narrates how a lion 'of noble blood', as 'whyte as any snow' (a transparent allusion to the Howards' emblem of the white lion) while prancing and 'seeking for a make' approaches a she-wolf, 'as white as whale his bone' (line 9). Rather than responding favourably, however, the wolf rebukes his presumption with 'a scornfull cheer', the like of which 'was never seene, I trow. . . to suche as well deservid' (16). Her refusal is superficially courteous, but devastating:

> 'Lyon', she said, 'yf thow hadest knowen my mynde beforne,
> Thow hadst not spentt thie travaile thus, and all thie payne forlorne.
> Do waye! I let the[e] weete, thow shalt not play with me;
> But raunge aboute: thow maiste seeke oute some meeter feere for the[e].'
>
>   (19–22)

The Lion, 'his noble hart moche moved by the same' (24), allows his 'rage [to] asswage' before responding. What he eventually offers is, however, no measured counter designed to brush off the rejection, but a ferocious assertion of his own and his family's purity of blood and honourable history:

> ... farewell, unkynd, to whome I bent so low...
> Syns that a lyons hart is for a wolfe no pray,
> With blooddye mowth of simple sheepe go slake your wrath, I say,
> With more dispight and ire than I can now expresse,
> Whiche to my payne though I refrayne, the cause you may well gesse.

(69, 71–4)

The Lion's response seems hugely out of proportion to its occasion until one notes the political context of the ostensibly minor incident at the heart of the story. For the woman in question, who had so pointedly refused Surrey's invitation to dance, was probably Anne Seymour, Countess of Hertford, the wife of Surrey's *bête noir*, Edward Seymour. Her family, the Stanhopes, had the wolf as their badge, and Seymour himself had a residence at Wulfhall in Savernake forest, so the choice of animal surrogate was an apt one.[26] It was Seymour whom Surrey had allegedly struck within the confines of the court in 1537, an exchange that led to his imprisonment at Windsor and had reportedly 'incensed' Surrey against him.[27] And it was now Seymour (the future Edwardian Protector Somerset) who stood as the Howards' principal (and ultimately successful) rival for the role of guardian to young prince Edward on Henry's death. Both Surrey's invitation and Lady Anne's response were thus highly politicized actions, played out in the full glare of courtly attention. The motive behind the poet's initial proposal is impossible to determine at this distance. It was potentially either a very public attempt to reconcile the differences between the two earls, or a calculated provocation to Seymour—an open flirtation with his wife in the most public arena. As Susan Brigden has shown, the relations between the Howards and the Seymours were not unremittingly hostile during these years of rivalry. Surrey himself dined with the Seymours at least fifteen times between the October and December of 1539, on one occasion with Lady Anne alone. In April 1544 Surrey had formally proposed Thomas Seymour, Edward's brother, for admission to the Order of the Garter. And, during 1546, Norfolk, ever mindful of the Seymours' increasing favour with the King, was proposing to Henry a series of dynastic marriages between his own grandchildren and Seymour's children. But these were attempts to heal a rift, not signs of genuine conviviality, and behind such formalities, Surrey's resentments were clearly undiminished.[28]

Lady Anne evidently responded to the Earl's invitation as if it were hostile, and, if Surrey's account is to be believed, reproved him with a taunt that turned his own chivalric modesty ('with a beck full low, he bowed at her feete / In humble wyse, as who wold say, "I am to[o] farr unmeete" ' (13–14)) against itself. Her words suggest not only that he was indeed both an unsuitable suitor, unworthy of her attention, but also that his suit itself was too frivolous to be taken seriously. Her dismissive 'Thow shalt not *play* with me' (my italics) adds a pointed personal barb to the general social rebuke implied in 'seeke some meeter fere for the[e]', for the young Surrey was to be dogged throughout his short life with taunts that he was a mere 'boy' (indeed, as John Barlow, Dean of Westbury, called him, 'the most foolish proud boy that is in England'),[29] insufficiently mature or experienced to be taken seriously on the political stage.

Surrey depicts this tense pavane of approach and repulsion with the keen eye of one attuned to the niceties of courtly protocol. First the Lion 'gan hym advaunce apace', offering himself up with the vulnerability of the suitor for the lady's grace, then she, rather than step forward to greet him halfway, abruptly starts 'asyde well neare a foote or twaye' (17), making concrete the cultural gap she seeks to preserve between them, before finally dismissing him with an imperious gesture of hand and tongue: 'Do waye!...raunge aboute...seeke oute some meeter feere for the[e]'. And the care with which the narrator records each gesture indicates the weight of political significance they carry. Whatever Surrey's motive was when he stepped across the dance floor to seek out his rival's wife (and a spontaneous attempt to heal divisions or a reckless gesture of derision would each have been in character) it is clear that, in his own eyes at least, he had come out of the encounter distinctly second best, his family's position belittled and his own honour slighted. Thus it was as a direct response to a perceived humiliation that he seems to have produced the poem, intended as a retaliation in kind, a grand social gesture that would claim the cultural and intellectual high ground from his opponent. If Anne Seymour could humiliate him on the dance floor he would do the same to her and her kin in verse, the newly fashionable aristocratic medium that he had mastered but to which she and her husband had no access. But in Surrey's hands what could have been an elegant, Chaucerian satire, a beast fable that wittily mocked the pretensions of his adversary, is turned in the heat of his rage into a blunt instrument for unremittingly violent assault and self-assertion. The poet presents the Lion, and by implication the Howard family for whom it emblematically stands, as living out a history and a destiny worlds removed from the experience of the Seymours, enduring suffering and experiencing triumphs on a level that Lady Anne could not begin to understand. His father's victory at Flodden, the death of his uncle Thomas in the Tower after his illicit marriage to the King's niece, his own military experience against French and Scots enemies and English northern rebels, all formed a part of Surrey's extraordinary torrent of self-justification:

> Crewell, you do me wronge to sett me thus so light;
> Without desert, for my good will to shew me such dispight.
> How can you thus entreat a lyon of the race,
> That with his pawes a crowned kinge [James IV of Scotland] devoured in place,
> Whose nature is, to prea uppon no simple foode
> As longe as he may suck the flesshe, and drincke of noble bloode.

Yf you be faire and fresshe, am I not of your hew?
And, for my vaunte, I dare well say my blood is not untrew;
Ffor you your self dothe know, it is not long agoe
Sins that, for love, one of the race [Thomas Howard] did end his life in woe
In towre both strong and highe, for his assured truthe.
Wheare as in teares he spent his breath, alas, the more the ruthe,
This gentle beast lykewise, who nothinge could remove,
But willinglye to seeke his death for losse of his true love.
Other ther be whose lyfe, to lynger still in payne,
Against their will preservid is, that wold have dyed right fayne.

(27–42)

Surrey, writing as if his approach to Anne had been an unequivocal attempt to reconcile their family differences, to submit himself to her 'mercy', offers a searing contrast between their two natures:

But well I may perceave that nought it movid you
My good entent, my gentle hart, nor yet my kind so true;
But that your will is suche to lure me to the trade,
As others some full many yeares to trace by crafte you made.
And thus beholde my kynd, how that we differ farr:
I seke my foes, and you your frends do threaten still with warr;
I fawne wheare I am fedd, you flee that seekes to you;
I can devoure no yelding pray, you kill wheare you subdue.
My kind is to desyre the honour of the field,
And you, with blood to slake your thurst of suche as to you yelde.

(43–52)

He furiously rejects the role that Lady Anne has allotted him ('I am no man that will be traynd, nor tanglyd bye such hookes' (54)), asserting the untrammelled 'wildnes', so alien to modern notions of gentility, that was fundamental to his own aristocratic self-perception. The conclusion is a naked threat of violence, barely contained let alone displaced by its allegorical context:

...as a ffaulcon free, that soreth in the ayre,
Whiche never fedd on hand or lure, that for no stale doth care,
While that I live and breathe, such shall my custome bee,
In wildnesse of the woods to seeke my prea, wheare pleasith me;
Where many one shall rew that never mad offence:
Thus your refuse agaynst my powre shall bode them no defence.
In the revendge wherof, I vowe and sweare therto,
A thowsand spoyles I shall commytt I never thought to do;
And yf to light on you my happ so good shall be,
I shall be glad to feede on that that wold have fed on me.
And thus, farewell, unkynd, to whome I bent to[o] low,
I would you wist the shipp is safe that bare his saile so low.
Syns that a lyons hart is for a woolfe no pray,

With blooddye mowth, of simple sheepe go slake your wrath, I say,
With more dispight and ire than I can now expresse,
Whiche to my payne though I refrayne the cause you may well gesse,
As for becawse my self was awthour of this game,
It bootes me not that, by my wrath, I should disturbb the same.

(59–76)

Had Surrey's judges sought any further evidence of the young Earl's attitudes and aspirations, of the kind of volatile political energies that made him, in the reported words of one of his prosecutors, 'an unmete man to live in a common-wealth',[30] they needed to look no further than this text. The same ferocious, reckless assertion of family destiny that prompted him to move the arms of St Edward from the minor to the major quarter of his shield, and to display it so openly at Kenninghall, lay behind the defence of the white lion's 'race' here. There is a remarkable confidence in his family status as well as a terrifying familiarity with violence inherent in the rehearsal of recent history that the lion offers. The Howards in this view are the makers and breakers of kings as well as the most reliable guardians of the realm. The pointed recollection that the Flodden Duke had 'with his pawes a crowned kinge devoured in place' is as much a warning to his rivals—and implicitly to the King himself—as it is a reminder of the Howards' greatest service to the nation.

The Howards, of course, like other noble families in this period, carried their heritage around with them, quite literally, on their coats of arms. The Flodden Duke's victory over James IV to which Surrey alludes so proudly here, allowed them to add the Scottish royal arms as a decoration to their own shield, just as their Plantagenet descent allowed them to include those of St Edward the Confessor—albeit only in the second quarter and without the silver labels that were the prerogative of the Prince of Wales. Howard history, the deeds of his forebears and the cultural inheritance of Surrey himself, were thus always on display: a matter of public witness and repeated self-assertion. What Surrey is doing in this poem is in effect offering the Seymours a lesson in that history, a glossed reading of the family shield, in which their royal links and aspirations, their military service, and the terrible price at which their enmity would be bought are all spelled out with chilling clarity.

Surrey's heraldry and his poetry were thus equally functional in displaying Howard claims, and equally reckless in the manner in which they did so. If, as G.W. Bernard has argued, the Tudor nobility were by nature a 'service nobility' who as a class saw their role as to serve and support the crown loyally and generally without quibble,[31] then Surrey is the spectacular exception to that rule. Unlike his father and grandfather, who set loyalty to the Crown above all else and as a result survived into old age, the young Earl was, as his leonine surrogate declares, defiantly proud of his own unwillingness to succumb to such domesti-cation, having 'never fedd on hand or lure'. His stated intention, 'In wildnesse of the woods to seeke my prea, wheare it pleasithe me', is a stark assertion of independence in a culture in which conformity (in politics, in religion, in obedience to protocol) was becoming the *sine qua non* of personal survival. It is hard to see how such energies as this text reveals could have been contained for long within the increasingly restrictive Henrician state without the kind of catastrophic self-combustion that was to be Surrey's fate. And the poem itself seems to acknowledge the fact, mythologizing the martyrdom of previous Howard heroes whom the commonwealth had found unmete (uncle Thomas 'willingly' seeking his death for love and 'his assured truthe' stands in for them here, as do the unnamed 'others' of the Howard race, 'whose lyfe, to lynger still in payne, / Against their will preserved is, that wold have dyed right fayne' (41–2)) as well as those more conventional figures who won glory on the battlefield. It is above all this reckless will to self-determination, even if that self-determination leads to his own destruction, that characterizes the poem. The repetition of 'I shall', 'I would', 'I should', places the lion's destiny in his own hands, just as surely as the realization of that destiny beckons him beyond the bounds of civil society and conventional morality: 'A thowsand spoyles I shall commit I never thoght to do'. In this respect the writing of the text, like the alteration of his heraldic device, is Howard's own grand gesture of suicidal self-determination. Like another 'martyred' uncle, Lord Edward Howard, Henry VIII's Lord Admiral, who, in 1512, had thrown himself into the sea and drowned during a naval skirmish in the waters around Brest rather than be captured by the French, Surrey was here symbolically stepping out onto the parapet and defying his pursuers to follow him.[32]

But, for all the recklessness of its expression, Surrey's literary and political stance was in essence a continuation—albeit with considerable variation—of that adopted more modestly by Wyatt in his own verse. Like Wyatt, Surrey deplored the increasing despotism of Henry's regime and the moral and physical decline of the King himself. And both men wrote about those feelings, and the principles that underpinned them, in their poetry. Unlike Wyatt, however, Surrey was in a position to do something more substantial about them. As the scion of the Howards he was able to envisage a plausible alternative to Henrician rule, to step outside the humanist dilemma of 'to serve or not to serve', and to fashion himself as a plausible redeemer of national honour: a lord protector for the infant Edward VI who would put into practice the ideals that both poets had shared.[33]

Surrey's Wyatt

It is in the light of such attitudes as are displayed in 'Each beast can choose his fere' (written in roughly the same period) that we should read Surrey's poetic responses to the death of Thomas Wyatt, the most substantial example of which, the Epitaph, acted as a prologue to this chapter. For the Earl's recuperation and affirmation of Wyatt's reputation as England's great national poet was equally a part of his own reckless self-assertion in the face of criticism and his pursuit of what he saw as his destiny.

John Leland's dedicatory 'Song', addressed to Surrey in the other text dedicated to Wyatt's memory and probably financed by the Earl, his collection of *Naeniae* ('songs in praise of honourable men'),[34] provides a striking example of this principle at work. As the terms of the dedication suggest, Surrey's swift and dramatic presentation of himself as Wyatt's principal mourner and truest friend was simultaneously an expression of genuine loss and a bold assertion of his own claim to be the poet's literary and political heir. It is the personal relationship between the two poets—the dead diplomat and the living Earl, in life fifteen years his junior—that is stressed in many of the *Naeniae*, most obviously and extremely in '*Unicus phoenix*' ('The Sole Phoenix'):

> *Una dies geminos phoenices non dedit orbi.*
> *Mors erit unius vita sed alterius*
> *Rara avis in terries confectus morte Viatus*
> *Houardum heredem scripserat ante suum.*

> [The World a single Phoenix can contain,
> And when one dies another one is born.
> When Wyatt, that rare bird, was taken away
> By death, he gave us Howard as his heir.][35]

It is this personal relationship that Leland praises in his dedicatory 'Song', claiming again that the intensity of their friendship was such that the younger man was the only fitting heir to the elder's legacy:

> *Accipe Regnorum comes illustrissime Carmen,*
> *Quo mea musa tuum laudavit moesta viatum*
> *Non expectato sublatum funere terris.*
> *Nominis ille yui dum vixit magnus amator.*
> *Tu modo non vivum coluisti candidus illum,*
> *Verum etiam vita defunctum carmine tali*
> *Collaudasti, quale suum Chaucerus avitae*
> *Dulce decus linguae vel juste agnosceres esse.*
> *Perge Hovarde precor virtute referre Viatum,*
> *Dicerisque tude clarissima Gloria stirpis.*[36]

> [Accept, illustrious Earl, this mournful song,
> Wherein I praised your Wyatt, whom in brief space
> Death brought beneath the earth. He greatly loved
> Your name. You revered him while he was alive,
> And since his death have given him due praise
> In such a song as Chaucer had approved,
> As sweet and worthy of his mother tongue.
> Continue, Howard, his virtues to revive,
> And you will confirm it by your honoured race.][37]

Thus Surrey, following Wyatt, takes up the Chaucerian baton as a—or perhaps better *the*—national poet, speaking of and for the nation in new and aureate tones. But this sonnet, like the collection that it introduces, does more than simply claim Wyatt's poetic reputation as Surrey's inheritance. To praise the Earl's 'name', and to vaunt the future glory of the 'honoured race' of the Howards was, in 1542, in the wake of the fall and execution of Surrey's first cousin Catherine Howard, and of his own troubles at this time, both a very public and a highly audacious gesture of personal and dynastic self-assertion.

The song of praise 'as Chaucer had approved' was probably the printed Epitaph. But Leland might also have been thinking of another elegiac poem, less public in form but no less political, that Surrey had written in manuscript. In this text the poet explicitly imagined himself as a mourner at Wyatt's grave, offering the only sincere grief for his loss amid a crowd of hypocritically weeping courtiers:

> Dyvers thy death doo dyverslye bemone;
> Some that in presence of that livelye hedd
> Lurked, whose brestes envye with hate had sowne,
> Yeld Cesares teres upon Pompeius hedd.
> Some that watched with murders knyfe
> With egre thurst to drynke thy guyltless blood,
> Whose practyse brake by happye end of lyfe,
> Weape envyous teares to here thy fame so good.
> But I that knowe what harbourd in that hedd,
> What vertues rare were tempred in that brest,
> Honour the place that such a jewell bredd,
> And kysse the ground where as thy coorse doth rest,
>   With vaporde eyes from whence such streames avayle
>   As Pyramus did on Thisbes brest bewayll.[38]

There is little here of the overt eulogizing of Wyatt that had characterized the earlier Epitaph. Indeed, this elegy is not 'about' Wyatt at all but about Surrey himself, his feelings, and his character. And here, as in 'Each beast', Surrey presents himself as a solitary figure, a lone man of virtue and integrity in a corrupt and dissembling world. As Colin Burrow shrewdly observes, the narratorial 'I' of Surrey's poetry is characteristically set apart, both socially and linguistically from the world around him. The 'But I' of the ninth line here fulfils the same function as the 'save I' and 'yet I' that appear in a number of his lyrics, the 'Thus I alone' of 'So Cruell Prison', or the 'I' of 'Each beast' who defines his own virtue in counterpoint to the vices of the unnamed 'You', the white wolf.[39] Set against the 'Dyvers' and 'some' who adopt conventional postures of grief for the departed poet, having been his enemies and detractors while he lived, this 'I' is no stoic hero, able to suffer in silence the corruption around him, but an alienated outsider. He is literally a malcontent prone to voice his unhappiness in near hysterical outbursts such as the extraordinarily emotive image of the final couplet here: in which again the imagery of heroism and that of suicide forcefully cohere.

As I suggested earlier, such claims to intense friendship may be more than simple statements of personal loss. The two men may have first met while Surrey was still a child.[40] Certainly the families were close enough for the Duke of Norfolk to agree to act as a godfather for Wyatt's son in 1521. But Surrey had probably been close to Wyatt for little more than two years when he died. This would have been long enough to cement a strong personal relationship, certainly, but not perhaps sufficient time to underpin the claims that the younger poet was to advance in this remarkably orchestrated outpouring of structured poetic grief. Again, as with his grief at Richmond's death half a decade earlier, personal loss and personal projection went hand-in-hand. Surrey was acting swiftly and decisively to ensure that Wyatt would be remembered and his poetic and personal achievements appreciated. But it was a particular image of Wyatt and his verse that the young Earl was anxious to foster in the minds of the political nation.

As he is presented in the Epitaph, Surrey's Wyatt was the consummate diplomat and orator:

> A Tong that served in forein realmes his king
> Whose courteous talke to vertue did enflame
> Eche noble hart . . .

He was a hero in the classical, humanist model: a moral authority and example of good conduct to his fellow citizens.

> . . . a worthy guide to bring
> Our English youth by travail unto fame.

And, as that allusion to 'travail' implies, he was also a man who realized his learning and wisdom in action rather than in the quiet, contemplative life of the monastery or schoolroom ('Wyat resteth here that quike coulde never rest'), whose brain hammered out its thoughts 'As on a styth, where some worke of fame / Was dayly wrought to turn to Brytayns gaine'. He was a Ciceronian stoic whose persuasive eloquence was combined with an indifference to worldly fortune ('to lyve upright and smyle at fortunes choyse') and the machinations of his foes:[41]

> Whose hevenly gyftes encreased by dysdayne,
> And vertue sanke the deper in his brest,
> Such profyte he of envy could optayne.

He was, in short, the model humanist statesman. And yet this Wyatt, for all his conventional virtues, was dead. His dedication to royal service and honest counsel had brought him only an early grave. His foes had triumphed, if only by default, and his example was already in danger of being forgotten. Hence it is that Surrey, espousing a very different type of heroic manhood, less stoical, more confrontational, less willing to rely on counsel or to lead by tacit example alone, has to step forward to reclaim the dead poet's legacy from those hypocritical mourners, and to put it to new political work. It is the reckless, youthful Surrey who offers himself as the mature Wyatt's champion. And in his hands the older poet becomes a talisman for those hoping for a thoroughgoing moral reformation of the Henrician regime. Rather than dwell upon the Wyatt of the lyrics, the amorous Petrarchan poet who brought Italianate sophistication to the English courtly love song, Surrey highlights the stern moral teacher, the Wyatt of the psalms. This Wyatt was, the poet suggests, the archetypal good counsellor, a man who was unafraid to confront the King with his own failings ('A Hart where drede was never so imprest / To hyde the thought that might the trouth avaunce' (Epitaph, lines 25–6).[42] Yet his voice was not heeded, and his legacy of poetic counsel now lies unread.

In another complex and anxious poem (made more complex by its problematic syntax) Surrey contrasts the responses to the poet's legacy of his friends—the small group of courtiers whom Surrey himself sought to inspire and lead—with those of his enemies, the rivals who had mourned hypocritically at his graveside, but begrudged him the honourable name that he left behind. Citing the precedent of ancient men, teachers of virtue in a pagan world, whose reputations were now forgotten, to the great impoverishment of later generations, he ponders how best those who treasure Wyatt's legacy should respond to his loss:

> In the rude age when science was not so rife,
> If Jove in Crete and other where they taught,
> Artes to reverte to profyte of our lyfe,
> Wan after deathe to have their temples sought;
> If vertue yet in no unthankfull tyme
> Fayled of some to blast her endles fame:
> A goodlie meane both to deter from cryme
> And to her steppes our sequel to enflame:
> In dayes of treuthe if Wyatt's friends then waile
> (The only debte that ded of quyke may clayme)
> That rare wit spent, employed to our avayle,
> Where Christe is taught, deserve they mannes blame?
> His livelie face thy brest how did it freate,
> Whose cinders yet with envye doo thee eate![43]

What is to be done with Wyatt now that he is dead? It is a question that troubles Surrey both here and elsewhere in his verse. Should contemporary Christian society merely repeat the errors of the past and risk confining his reputation to oblivion? Or was there a greater obligation upon 'Wyatt's friends', in an age when 'science' (knowledge) was more widespread, to preserve his name and legacy? The implied answer to this latter question is, of course, yes. And so, how England dealt with Wyatt's memory became a critical test, not only of the loyalty of his friends, but of the nation's moral health. It was a test, Surrey suggests, that the Henrician regime was signally failing.

In a poem of his own which he added to the manuscript into which Wyatt had written the *Paraphrase of the Penitential Psalms*, the Earl openly invited the English political nation to consider how best it should treasure Wyatt's greatest poetic legacy: a text that he identified as both avowedly protestant in doctrine and anti-tyrannical in intent:

> The great Macedon, that out of Perse chasyd
> Darius, of whose huge power all Asy rang,
> In the riche arke if Homers rymes he placyd,
> Who fayned gestes of hethen prynces sang,
> What holy grave, what worthy sepultre
> To Wyates Psalmes shulde Christians purchase,
> Where he dothe paynte the lyvely faythe and pure,
> The stedfast hoope, the swete returne to grace
> Of juste Davyd by parfite penitence,
> Where Rewlars may se[e] in a myrrour clere
> The bitter frewte of False concupysence,
> How jewry brought Uryas deth full dere?
> In prynces hartes Goddes scourge yprynted depe
> Myght them awake out of their synfull slepe.[44]

That Wyatt's final legacy to his readers should thus be, in this account, a mirror for princes—albeit one that, like the prophet Nathan, offered no concessions to royal sensitivities in the severity of its judgements—indicates precisely the image of the poet that Surrey intended his readers to retain in their memories. He offers the Wyatt of the satires, who cursed Henry in the words of Persius, and the Wyatt of the psalms, who sought to bring home to Henry the depth of his own depravity, as the image of the poet that history should commend and the English nation revere.

Here as elsewhere the community of readers that will receive and cherish Wyatt's legacy is imagined as exclusively protestant. In the Epitaph, his circle of grieving friends had been represented as 'such as covet Christe to know', recipients of his 'witnes of faith that never shalbe dredde'. Here the 'Christians' receiving 'the lyvely faythe and pure' are also by implication reformed. In 'In the rude age', another text written at around this time, Surrey, as we have seen, explicitly denied the community of Wyatt's grieving friends the catholic consolation of praying for his soul, declaring how, 'In days of treuthe', wailing at his loss was 'The only debte that ded of quycke may clayme.' Thus Surrey was recreating Wyatt as a radical author whose texts would energize a future generation of reformist readers—an image of the poet that elides the care with which, as we have seen, he stayed within officially prescribed limits in matters of doctrine.[45]

Such sentiments have prompted a number of scholars to claim Surrey, like Wyatt before him, as an evangelical, one of the 'brethren' or 'new Christians' on the radical wing of those arguing for further doctrinal reform in Henrician England.[46] But a little more caution is necessary here before we assume that

Surrey was necessarily consistently Lutheran in his beliefs. Certainly he frequently portrays himself as a devout Christian, at odds with what he presents as pharisaical cabals in the City of London, or among his persecutors in general, and he was evidently capable of some very radical utterances.[47] And he clearly saw himself as in some sense in sympathy with the evangelical position on a number of issues. Yet it is nonetheless hard to pin him down on any other points of doctrine on which he was markedly in advance of the official position of the Henrician church. He adopted the coterie vocabulary of the evangelicals, talking of his 'secret zeal to God' and stressing the crucial role of grace in his discussions of salvation.[48] But, as we have seen in previous chapters, such emphases were not antithetical to official doctrine in England, or indeed in Rome. And, when he was serving in Boulogne in 1544, the Earl specifically antagonized his more evangelical followers by setting up an altar in a church there in the catholic manner.[49]

His verse, indeed, provides a further useful corrective to simplistic definitions of religious affiliations at this time. In the early stages of the Reformation in England religious differences were far more a matter of different emphases and tendencies than of clear-cut divisions between groups of 'catholics' and 'protestants' with wholly dissimilar sensibilities. For even here, as Surrey seeks to claim Wyatt for a protestant (and protesting) tradition, he simultaneously betrays a powerfully catholic sensibility regarding how best to memorialize his lost friend. Despite Leland's description of Surrey as the 'sole phoenix' who will in and of himself resurrect all that was immortal in Wyatt, the Earl nonetheless seeks other external mementos, and in so doing establishes a whole landscape of sanctified monuments and sites of pilgrimage dedicated to the dead poet. It is, after all, a holy grave, a worthy sepulchre that he attempts to conceive into being in 'The great Macedon', into which the psalms can be literally translated, a shrine at which he and the reformed community of 'Wyatt's friends' may gather to remember and revere their lost mentor. Similarly, Wyatt's physical tomb is memorialized in 'The Epitaph', as Surrey imaginatively undertakes a pilgrimage to his graveside to drop pious tears on his corpse. There he metaphorically dismembers the poet into an assortment of separate body parts ('A Head', 'A Visage', 'A Tong', 'An Eye', 'A Harte', 'A Valiant Corps'), each of which is individually meditated upon as one might piously reflect upon the Five Wounds of Christ. Although the 'symple soul' is fled to heaven, the body itself remains for his friends as a timeless, sacred relic of the newly beatified saint of reform, 'witnes of faith that never shalbe deade':

> Sent for our welth, but not received so,
> That for our gylt this jewell have we lost,
> The earth his bones, the heven possesse his goost.
>
> (36–8)

The vocabulary here of 'corpse', 'jewel', and 'bones' is again redolent of the reliquary. And in the most intensely personal of the elegiac poems on Wyatt,

'Dyvers thye deth doo dyverslye bemone', Surrey, as we have already seen, makes literal the idea of Wyatt's tomb as a shrine to be venerated. He promises, in the kind of emotional, highly eroticized manner redolent of the more flamboyant forms of ecstatic mysticism and late medieval affective piety, to:

> Honour the place that such a jewell bredd,
> And kysse the ground where as thy coorse doth rest
> With vaporde eyes, from whence such streames avayle
> As Pyramus did on Thisbes brest bewayll.
>
> (11–14)

The idea of Wyatt as a protestant saint, and his tomb at Sherborne Abbey, along with his birthplace at Allington, as centres of a topography of veneration, sits awkwardly, at least from a modern perspective, with Surrey's proclaimed self-image as an evangelical reformer. But such odd disjunctions were a common feature of the hybrid religious sensibilities developing during this period of transition. Just as catholic orthodoxy in the century before the Reformation was, in Mishtooni Bose's elegant formulation, 'dappled and variegated'; capable of tolerating marked differences of opinion and belief,[50] so too evangelical reform was a piebald phenomenon, divided not simply between distinct varieties of dissent—Lutheran, Zwinglian, Anabaptist—but variegated within itself. Groups such as the ill-defined coterie of Wyatt's friends alluded to by Surrey might contain various shades of opinion,[51] and so might individuals contain within themselves loyalties and leanings towards aspects of the old faith just as they enthusiastically embraced new ideas that were incompatible with its tenets. Surrey clearly had no qualms about presenting Wyatt as a saint of English reform, a secular, poetic Beckett, whose bones might furnish the centre of a new cult dedicated to aristocratic resistance to Henrician tyranny, a cult with himself as its founder and high priest.

What Surrey was doing in his elegiac verses on Wyatt, then, was fashioning a Wyatt whose example offered two powerful lessons. First it showed that men of honour were not swayed by the lure of personal gain nor daunted by the threat of repression, but necessarily spoke out against tyranny wherever and whenever they saw it. For Surrey, Wyatt was thus symbolic of the good counsellor who repeatedly spoke out against royal injustice, lust, and vindictiveness. As such he was a model of stoic rectitude. But he had failed. Good counsel had not been enough to move the King from his despotic course. The baton of English heroism must therefore pass into more active, determined hands. Thus in his writings Surrey fused this figure of Wyatt the Ciceronian humanist with the new energies of religious reform, energies already finding favour with those evangelical tutors and advisers in the household of the infant Edward VI, to suggest a new political force in waiting, a progressive alternative to tyranny that would take its destined place at the head of the nation once the old King was dead. Surrey's Wyatt was, then, a poet who would have chosen Brutus over Cato every time, and would have had few qualms about doing so.

Surrey's Biblical Paraphrases

In the last year of his life, almost certainly during his final imprisonment itself, either as he awaited trial, or following the trial as he waited for the death sentence to be put into effect, torn between an attempt to reconcile himself to death and the stubborn hope of a pardon, Surrey himself turned to biblical paraphrase and translation.[52] Like Wyatt before him, and using one at least of the same sources as his forebear (Joannes Campensis's *Paraphrase*) Surrey turned to translating a number of psalms, and the apocalyptic first five chapters of Ecclesiastes, another text intimately concerned with issues of justice and injustice, suffering, and the protests of the oppressed.

As Wyatt had done, Surrey used these paraphrases to personal and political ends, in part at least to cement the links between his own experience and that of the earlier poet, and beyond him with the psalmist himself. As Thynne and Tuke had used Chaucer as a model and an authority through which to counsel Henry VIII towards moderation, so Surrey used Wyatt's conception of the psalmist, and the voice of Ecclesiastes to express and enact a more overtly oppositional political position, one that sought to resist and transcend royal authority and power. For Surrey, as for all the writers featured in this book, poetry—and particularly the poetry of biblical paraphrase—was not an end in itself. As Brian Cummings has observed, translating the psalms provided contemporaries with a coded yet powerful means of reflecting on their own experiences, and a useful way of exposing and opposing the excesses of the Henrician regime. In such hands 'the laments of the Psalms became a covert means of expressing the laments of these later days'. Paraphrasing biblical texts also provided Surrey, as it had Wyatt, with a voice through which he could speak truth to princely power, a poetic identity for a man of honour and truth outside of the circle that remained in thraldom to royal authority. In the words of Ecclesiastes, as James Simpson suggests, Surrey could speak 'in the voice of King Solomon to rebuke his own king', and could venture, as Brigden suggests, 'where it was wild folly, or bravery, to stray'.[53]

Surrey's other verse is itself shot through with barbed allusions to the falsity and cruelty of kings. The mourners shedding crocodile tears on Wyatt's grave in 'Dyvers thy death', we recall, 'Yeld Cesares teres upon Pompeius hedd': a pointed reminder that hypocrisy can be found at the very pinnacle of the political nation. And Surrey's biblical paraphrases similarly offer frequent examples of corrupt and decaying royal figures. Indeed, his paraphrase of Ecclesiastes is dominated by a powerful sense that the speaker, Solomon, is a culpable king, and that the story he tells of his journey from folly to wisdom is particularly applicable to those who rule. Even where the speaker's kingship is not explicit in the biblical text, Surrey makes it so through pointed additions and variations of his own. Hence the Vulgate's 'Vanity of vanities, said Ecclesiastes, vanity of vanities, all is vanity' (Ecclesiastes 1:1–2) becomes in Surrey's text:

> I Salaman, Davids sonne, King of Jerusalem,
> Chosen by God to teach the Jewes and in his lawes to leade them,
> Confesse under the sonne that every thing is vayne.

> (J43: 1–3)

And the Vulgate's 'I Ecclesiastes, was King over Israel in Jerusalem, and I proposed in my mind to seek and search out wisely concerning all things that are under the sun' (Ecclesiastes 1: 12–13) becomes:

> I that in Davides seate sit crowned and rejoyce,
> That with my septer rewle the Jewes and teache them with my voyce,
> Have serched long to know all things under the sonne.

> (25–7)

Even where the royal status of the speaker is not explicitly germane, Surrey stresses it, suggesting strongly that it was the sense of a king fallen into vice and corruption and then recalled to wisdom by God that gave the text its resonance and attraction for him. So, whereas the first two verses of the second chapter in the Vulgate read simply:

I said in my heart: I will go and abound with delights, and enjoy good things. And I saw that this was also vanity. / Laughter I counted error, and to mirth I said: Why art thou vainly deceived?

> (Ecclesiastes 2:1–2)

Surrey's protagonist declares:

> From pensif fanzies then I gan my hart revoke,
> And gave me to suche sporting plaies as laughter myght provoke.
> But even such vain delights, when they moste blinded me,
> Allwayes me thought with smiling grace a king did yll agre.

> (J44: 1–4)

Surrey's Solomon, like his David, was then, first and foremost a royal sinner, and it was his royal office that gave his sins their political importance. And it is hard to avoid the conclusion that it was Henry VIII's example that the poet had in the forefront of his mind as he wrote: that he was indeed recklessly taunting the King—among the small circle who read his poems in manuscript at least—with his own failings, and defying him to redeem himself. The same kind of angry self-confidence that recalled the Flodden Duke's 'devouring' of a crowned king seems to underpin the poet's self-projection here as both a tutor and a judge of his sovereign. For his account of princely vanities contains a number of details that seem designed to touch Henry's recent extravagances.

The Vulgate presents a speaker who 'withdrew [his] flesh from wine that [he] might turn [his] mind to wisdom', and began instead to build houses, plant vineyards and gardens, and to make ponds to succour his young trees. The building, for Solomon, is thus part of a redemptive process, a step away from folly toward wisdom. In refiguring that section, Surrey blurs the distinction between fleshly imbibing and constructive labour, offering instead a single process of excessive indulgence in which the building of palaces seems a natural extension of the drunkenness (and, the poet adds, gluttony) of the fallen prince. It is prompted by a pride and restless worldly ambition every bit as culpable as the former fleshly appetite:

> Then sought I how to please my belly with muche wine,
> To feede me fatte with costely feasts of rare delights and fine,
> And other plesures eke, too purchace me with rest,
> In so great choise to finde the thing that might content me best.
> But, Lord, what care of mynde, what soddaine stormes of ire,
> With broken slepes enduryd I, to compasse my desier!
> To buylde my howses faier then sett I all my cure:
> By princely acts thus strave I still to make my fame indure.
> Delicius gardens eke I made to please my sight,
> And grafte therin all kindes of fruts that might my mouthe delight.
> Condits, by lively springs, from their owld course I drewe
> For to refreshe the frutfull trees that in my gardynes grewe...
> Great heapes of shining gold by sparing gan I save,
> With things of price so furnyshed as fitts a prince to have.

(5–16, 19–20)

The references to princely acts, the building of conduits and water-courses, and to delicious gardens and royal sports, may well deliberately echo Henry VIII's current building plans.[54] By the late 1530s he had established a reputation as England's most ostentatious and prolific royal builder. Indeed, his latest and most ambitious project, a hunting lodge at Nonsuch, was indeed established by Act of Parliament, and involved the building of a lengthy conduit to pipe fresh water from a spring in the village of Coddington to a vast tank within the spectacularly decorated lodge. Indeed the whole enterprise of Nonsuch was something of a monument to the kind of royal self-indulgence discussed in Surrey's verse. The lodge had been established precisely so that the corpulent and immobile monarch could continue to indulge his passion for hunting without having to travel too far from Hampton Court. As the Act Book of the Edwardian Privy Council none too tactfully recorded, Nonsuch was built 'in the latter days of the King of famous memory, when his Highness waxed heavy with sickness, age, and corpulences of body and might not travail so readily abroad, but was constrained to seek to have his game and pleasure ready at hand'. Hence, special blocks were built at strategic points around the park, 'that the king's grace may not only get upon his horse easily, but alight down upon the same'. But things did not go entirely to plan. The water pressure could not be sustained along the length of the conduit, and the house probably never enjoyed the quantity or quality of fresh water that the King had demanded.[55] Surrey's allusions to fat kings seeking pleasure from 'lively springs' and delicious gardens, and to the saving of 'shining gold' by frugal planning looks very like an unsubtle reference to a very recent and rather embarrassing enterprise.

All of these royal works cited in Surrey's paraphrase, which were in the biblical text examples of a better kind of human endeavour, investing worldly prosperity in lasting monuments and the betterment of others, are for Surrey part of the same grotesque royal will to self-indulgence. Hence, rejecting the logic of the Vulgate's trajectory from bad (drunkenness) through better (building) to best (true wisdom and contempt for the world), he turns from the lavish princely building schemes not 'upwards' to wisdom, but back 'down' to equally flamboyant sexual self-indulgence:

> Lemans [lovers] I had, so faier, and of so lively hewe
> That who so gased in their face myght well their bewtey rewe.
> Never erste sat theyr king so riche in Davyds seate:
> Yet still me thought for so smale gaine the travaile was to[o] great.
> From my desirous eyes I hyd no pleasaunt sight,
> Nor from my hart no kind of myrth that might geve them delyght;
> Which was the only freute I rept of all my payne:
> To feade my eyes and to rejoyce my hart with all my gaine.
>
> (23–30)

In Surrey's narrative it is not the King's own wisdom that prompts him to see the shallow vanity of such a life, but the sudden irruption of divine grace, bestowed upon the deserving sinner by a merciful God:

> But freshe before myne eyes grace did my fawlts renewe:
> What gentill callings I hadd fledd, my ruyne to purswe,
> What raging plesurs past, perill and hard eskape,
> What fancies in my hed had wrought the licor of the grape.
> The erroure then I sawe that their fraile harts dothe move,
> Which strive in vaine for to compare with him that sitts above;
> In whose most perfect works suche craft apperyth playne
> That to the least of them their may no mortall hand attayne.
> And like as lightsome day dothe shine above the night,
> So darke to me did folly seme, and wysdomes beames as bright.
>
> (35–44)

Surrey's paraphrase is thus very like Wyatt's in both the scope and the direction of its political ambition, albeit it takes that ambition far further, pushing beyond the limits of loyal counsel into a different sort of political engagement with its royal subject. The play that the poet makes with his text is equally complex and multivalent. At times the text thus looks inward to the poet's own soul and his fears of death and humiliation; at others it faces outward to the sins of the King and the failings of the wider political community that has allowed Henry to become what he has become. As with the voice of Wyatt's David, that of Surrey's Solomon sometimes mingles with that of the poet himself, confessing his own sins and protesting at the corruption that he sees around him. At other moments it blurs into the ventriloquized voice of King Henry, speaking the words of self-reproach and abasement that Surrey wished he would speak in proper person, but knew he never would.[56] So it combines complaint, invective, protest, exhortation, and confession into a single potent genre of poetic revelation. Surrey's ostensible aim is to imagine his own and his sovereign's redemption, but in the heat of writing he seems at times to lose sight of the self-mortifying function of the exercise and to immerse himself in the pleasures of figuratively wielding the scourge upon his royal master.

In its most politically engaged passages, the Ecclesiastes paraphrase arraigns the King in the person of Solomon before the court of his own conscience. Like Wyatt before him he uses the potent voices of Old Testament kingship for contemporary work. He deploys them to gain the moral advantage over his sovereign, rehearsing his sins and vanities and projecting, with a mixture of pious hope and vindictive pleasure, the scene of his humble submission to divine authority, when,

> ... eache agrevid mynde,
> Lyke the brute beasts that swell in rage and fury by ther kynde,
> His erroure may confesse, when he hath wreasteled longe;
> And then with pacience may him arme, the sure defence of wronge.

> (Ecclesiastes 3: 49–52)

In the third chapter in particular the criticism of royal degeneracy and corruption, and the implicit allegations of tyranny against the King, were made from the vantage point of personal history, and with a savagery born of experience. Thus the speaker talks, not abstractly of universal truths as the Vulgate text does ('All things have their season, and in their lives all things pass under heaven'), but from the bitter fruit of his own history ('Like to the stereles boote that swerves with every wynde, / The slipper topp of worldley welthe by crewell pro[o]f I fynde.' (J45: 1–2)), before launching into an anatomization of a fallen political world in which injustice reigns and God's judgement is imminent. The Vulgate at this point speaks merely of a world dominated by constant mutability and perpetual inversion in which there is literally nothing new under the sun:

That which hath been made, the same continueth; the things that shall be have already been: and God restoreth that which is past. / I saw under the sun in the place of judgement wickedness and in the place of justice iniquity.

> (Ecclesiastes 3: 15–16)

By contrast Surrey's lines are of a wholly different order of particularity and venom. His theme is not the constant revolution of history but the reappearance in his own time of all the worst excesses of injustice witnessed in the ancient past. It is not that there is nothing new under the sun; rather, things have never been so terrible:

The gresly wonders past, which tyme wearse owt of mynde,
To be renewed in our dayes the Lord hath so assynde.
Lo, thus his carfull skourge doth stele on us unware,
Which, when the fleshe hath clene forgott, he dothe againe repaire.
When I in this vaine serche had wonderyd sore my witt,
I saw a roiall throne wheras that Justice should have sitt;
In stede of whom I saw, with fyerce and crwell mode,
Wher Wrong was set, that blody beast, that drounke the giltes blode:
Then thought I thus: One day the Lord shall sitt in dome,
To vewe his flock and cho[o]se the pure: the spotted have no rome.

(39–48)

Combining personal experience with the prophetic power of Revelation in the repeated use of 'I saw', and adding an element of politic discretion in the claim to have received this vision of tyranny enthroned only when he had 'wondered sore his wit', the poet forges a potent weapon of protest from the already powerful scriptural text.

A similar level of painful contemporary particularity seems to colour the poet's realization of the Vulgate's phrase 'A time to embrace and a time to be far from embraces' (Ecclesiastes 3:5):

Suche as in folded armes we did embrace, we haate;
Whom strayte we reconsill againe and banishe all debate.

(19–20)

This image of love turned to hate and hate as quick returned to love again would have had a real contemporary resonance in a decade that began with Henry's destruction of his closest servant Thomas Cromwell (an act which he later blamed on others whom, he claimed, had convinced him to reject 'the best servant he ever had'),[57] and ended with the king seemingly playing mind games with those closest to him. He set counsellors to arrest first Thomas Cranmer and then Queen Catherine Parr on charges of heresy, then called off the pack and rebuked the would-be inquisitors for their presumption, before restoring the erstwhile victims to his favour.[58]

In translating and transforming the opening chapters of Ecclesiastes, Surrey thus brought to the task a strong sense of his own position as a witness to and victim of tyranny. And what he found in the scriptural text itself was a visionary narrative that ideally met his need to voice his own sense of injustice and to imagine the means of its redress. The heartfelt protest on behalf of the oppressed in the fourth chapter thus spoke directly to his own sense of misuse, and of the plight of the victims of Henrician oppression, whether he thought of those victims primarily in terms of his cousins, Queens Anne Boleyn and Catherine Howard, executed on charges of adultery, the ranks of the godly, condemned for their zeal for religious reformation, or aristocratic figures such as himself, victims of Henry's jealousy and paranoia:

I turned myself to other things, and I saw the oppressions that are done under the sun, and the tears of the innocent, and they had no comforter, and they were not able to resist their violence, being destitute of help from any. / And I praised the dead rather than the living. / And I judged him happier than both of them that is not yet born, nor hath seen the evils that are done under the sun.

(Ecclesiastes 4: 1–3)

Again Surrey brings to these bold declarations a sense of the particular experience of suffering, and the anxious response of the witness:

> When I be thought me well, under the restles soon [sun]
> By foolke of power what crewell wourkes unchastyced were doon,
> I saw wher stoode a heard by power of suche opprest,
> Oute of whose eyes ran floods of teares that bayned all ther brest;
> Devoyde of comfort clene, in terroure and distresse,
> In whose defence none wolde aryse, suche rigor to represse.

(ʃ46: 1–6)

At times the perpetrators of this cruelty seem multiple, suggesting the catholic clergy and defenders of orthodox belief, protecting their wealth and traditions against the simple zeal of the godly. At others King Henry seems the only active agent in the persecution. But, even when he is not directly blaming the King for the crimes he claims to have witnessed, Surrey leaves little doubt that the ultimate responsibility for them lies with the monarch, and offers dire warnings that the redress of such powerful grievances may well involve the violent overthrow of the King. On several occasions he allows himself, with only a little prompting from the Vulgate text, to imagine the sudden death of uncounselled princes and the end of their corrupt regimes:

> In better far estate stande children, poore and wyse,
> Then aged kyngs wedded to will that worke with out advice.[59]
> In prison have I sene or this a wofull wyght
> That never knewe what fredom ment, nor tasted of delyght;
> With such, unhoped happ in most dispaier hath mete,
> With in the hands that erst ware gives to have a septre sett.
> And by conjures the seade of kyngs is thrust from staate,
> Wheron agrevyd people worke ofte[t]ymes their hidden haat.

(35–42)

Again the weight of painful personal experience is wedded to a visionary 'I saw' ('In prison have I sene or this . . . ') to give the passage additional moral and political leverage, turning a general reflection on worldly mutability into a potent instrument of political protest.[60] As Sessions suggests, the prisoner 'That never knewe what fredom ment', may well be an allusion to the young Edward Courtenay, who was in the Tower when Surrey was there, having been imprisoned at the age of twelve in 1538. Courtenay was a member of the de la Pole family, a scion of the line with the strongest claim to the crown after the Tudors themselves. His imprisonment was thus another example of royal insecurity concerning those who—like Surrey—posed a threat to the succession. And the prospect that such a man might one day wield a sceptre in his own hands was a clear political warning to the King who had imprisoned him.[61]

Given the restrictions imposed upon writers imagining the death or deposition of the King, it is vital to note the freedom that translating such passages offered to Surrey, enabling him to voice what would otherwise have been unspeakable in Henry's England: the thought that kings might be deposed and tyrants violently brought to book—even if he did finally place such radical ideas within a conservative moral framework.

> Other with out respect I saw, a frend or foo,
> With feat worne bare in tracing such wheras the honours groo.
> And at change of a prynce great rowtes revived strange
> Which, faine theare owlde yoke to discharg, rejoyced in the change.
> But when I thought, to theise as hevy even or more
> Shalbe the burden of his raigne as his that wente before,
> And that a trayne like great upon the deade depend,
> I gan conclude eache gredy gayne hath his uncertayne end.
>
> (43–50)

Even to broach such ideas within his own circle of intended readers, and so to begin a discussion of when and how the King might meet his end, was a remarkably audacious step, a sign of how far beyond Wyatt's cautious experiments he was prepared to go in using verse to lay the foundation for political action.

Surrey's Psalms

Surrey's paraphrases of the psalms fulfil a similar range of functions to his version of Ecclesiastes. If they were, as most scholars have concluded, written during his final imprisonment, then their self-examinatory aspects, and the pleas that they offer for divine grace and mercy have a special power and poignancy.[62] But again it is the tyrannous behaviour of those in power, and of princes in particular, that provides the focus for the poet's attention, calling forth his greatest vitriol, and engaging his strongest emotional energies. Following hints in Campensis, he turns the Vulgate's criticism of those sinners who prosper in the world,[63] into a bitter condemnation of royal degeneracy, at the heart of which is another obese king with more than a passing similarity to the Henry of the mid-1540s:

> Yet whiles the faith did faynt that shold have ben my guyde,
> Lyke them that walk in slipper pathes my feet began to slyde,
> Whiles I did grudge at those that glorey in ther golde,
> Whose lothsom pryde rejoyseth welth, in quiet as they wolde.
> To se by course of yeres what nature doth appere,
> The pallayces of princely fourme succede from heire to heire;

> From all such travailes free as longe to Adams sede;
> Neither withdrawne from wicked works by daunger nor by dread,
> Wherof their skornfull pryde; and gloried with their eyes,
> As garments clothe the naked man, thus ar they clad in vyce.
> Thus as they wishe succeds the mischief that they meane,
> Whose glutten che[e]ks slouth feads so fatt as scant their eyes be sene.
> Unto whose crewell power most men for dred ar fayne
> To bend and bow with loftye looks, whiles they vawnt in their rayne
> And in their bloody hands, whose crueltye doth frame
> The wailfull works that skourge the poore with out regard of blame.
> To tempt the living God they thinke it no offence . . .

>   (3–19)

Even as he admits his own error in giving himself over to such wrathful thoughts, the verse conveys precisely why he has done so. Such injustice, like the psalmist, cries out for redress, and does so by provoking revulsion in all those who witness it.

Why then do the just tolerate such manifest abuses to persist?

> Suche proofes bifore the just, to cawse the harts to waver,
> Be sett lyke cups myngled with gall, of bitter tast and saver.
> Then saye thy foes in skorne, that tast no other foode,
> But sucke the fleshe of thy elect and bath them in their bloode:
> 'Shold we beleve the lorde doth know and suffer this?
> Foled be he with fables vayne that so abused is!'
> In terrour of [i.e. to] the just thus raignes iniquitye,
> Armed with power, laden with gold, and dred for crueltye.

>   (21–8)

But the text nonetheless allows the poet to imagine his own redemption and the final overthrow of even such powerful entrenched oppressors in the face of divine retribution:

> And they shall fall, their power shall faile that did their pryde mayntayne.
> As charged harts with care, that dreme some pleasaunt tourne,
> After their sleape fynd their abuse, and to their plaint retourne,
> So shall their glorye faade; Thy sword of vengeaunce shall
> Unto their dronken eyes, in blood disclose their errours all.

>   (42–6)

> And suche for drede or gayne, as shall thy name refuse,
> Shall perishe with their golden godds that did their harts seduce.
> Where I, that in thy worde have set my trust and joye,
> The highe reward that longs therto shall quietlye enjoye.
> And my unworthye lypps, inspired with thy grace,
> Shall thus forespeke thy secret works in sight of Adams race.

>   (61–6)[64]

At moments such as these, Surrey's 'foes' coalesce into discrete forms. Frequently, as we have seen, they take the bloated form of Henry VIII. Indeed, it is evident that Surrey could not for long imagine iniquity of any sort without seeing before him the image of his King, the antithesis of all his own ideas of true nobility and masculinity. Hence his sonnet on the suicide of Sardanapulus, that most conventional of tyrants, seems motivated by a particular loathing for a king far closer to home, not least in its stress on the subject's inaptness for military exploits. As Surrey witnessed at first hand, Henry VIII had been so infirm from osteomyelitis and other ailments at the siege of Boulogne that his colossal body had been carried around in a litter:[65]

> Th'Assyryans king, in peas with fowle desyre
> And filthye luste that staynd his regall harte,
> In warr that should sett pryncelye hertes afyre
> Vanquyshd dyd yeld for want of martyall arte...
>
> (J32: 1–4)

> Who sca[r]ce the name of manhode dyd retayne,
> Drenched in slouthe and womanishe delight,
> Feble of sprete, unpacyent of payne,
> When he hadd lost his honor and hys right,
> Prowde tyme of welthe, in stormes appawld with drede,
> Murdred hym selfe to shew some manfull dede.
>
> (9–14)[66]

At other times these foes take on the form of individual acquaintances who have seemingly betrayed his trust or turned against him in some vital matter. Hence Jones suggests that it was the thought of Richard Southwell, who testified against him at his treason trial in 1546 that motivated the sentiments in Surrey's translation of the fifty-fourth psalm:

> Ne my declared foo wrought me all this reproche;
> By harme so loked for, yt wayeth halfe the lesse.
> For though myne ennemyes happ had byn for to prevaile,
> I cold have hidd my face from venym of his eye.
> It was a frendly foo, by shadow of good will,
> Myn old fere and dere frende, my guyde, that trapped me;
> Where I was wont to fetche the cure of all my care,
> And in his bosome hyde my secreat zeale to God.
>
> (J50: 18–25)[67]

But there was also a more pragmatic purpose to Surrey's psalmic paraphrases—or at least to the use that he made of them once they had been written during the terrible weeks of his final incarceration. For the verses became a means of creating or in some cases recreating connections within that small group of significant individuals associated with himself, with the memory of Thomas Wyatt, and with service to the King. On one level these paraphrases, and the verses which he appended to them, addressed to friends and associates of the dead poet, continued the work of linking himself with Wyatt's legacy, and cementing his own role as the central figure in the transmission of that legacy to future generations of readers, the destined redeemer of Wyatt's dream of a just commonwealth. Such work was evidently needed in the wake of his own arrest and social humiliation. But in addition to this general, culturally self-promoting role, the short lyric texts that Surrey dedicated to named individuals also performed a more urgent function. In them he spoke of his own experiences in the Tower and of his use of the biblical texts as part of a personal penitential process. In these texts he set about recreating old allegiances and attempted to forge new ones with individuals who were in positions where they might intervene with the King or his judges to seek a pardon, or at least to ameliorate the terms of his punishment. Whether written before his trial in an attempt to influence the verdict or afterwards to forestall its effects, these poems were evidence of Surrey's writing at its most personal and most instrumental. Quite literally, he was writing for his life.

Hence he dedicated his paraphrase of Psalm 87 to Sir Anthony Denny, Henry VIII's Groom of the Stool, the man who was closest to the ailing King, and so in the best position to make a direct appeal for royal clemency. As one of the keepers of the dry stamp, the wooden press by which the King's signature was affixed to official documents, he was also in a position to defy or delay the execution of justice, if he thought fit.[68] In the dedicatory verse, Surrey announced his own contrition in the clearest possible terms:

> When recheless youthe in an unquiet brest,
> Set on by wrath, revenge and crueltye,
> After long warr pacyens hath opprest,
> And justice wrought by pryncelye equitie;
> My Deny, then myne errour, depe imprest,
> Began to worke dispaire of libertye,
> Had not David, the perfyt warriour, taught
> That of my fault this pardon shold be sought.

> (j36)

His paraphrase of Psalm 72 was despatched to Sir George Blage, Wyatt's friend and Surrey's former ally, with whom he had quarrelled over the protectorship in the conversation that would provide unhelpful evidence at his trial.[69] In the dedication Surrey again announced his contrition, admitting his earlier errors, and even hinting at the kind of religious wavering and final reaffirmation of evangelical commitment of which the radical Blage might have approved:[70]

> The soudden stormes that heave me to and froo
> Had welneare perced faith, my guyding saile,
> For I, that on the noble voyage goo,
> To succhor treuthe and falshed to assaile,

Constrayned am to beare my sayles ful loo
And never could attayne some pleasant gale,
For unto such the prosperus winds doo bloo
As ronne from porte to porte to seke availe.
This bred dispayre, whereof such doubts did groo
That I gan faint and all my courage faile.
But now, my Blage, myne erour well I see;
Such goodlye light King David giveth me.

(j37)

Given that, earlier in the same year, Blage himself had been saved from burning by royal intervention, the prospect of a reprieve was not wholly implausible. Significantly, Blage had himself composed two psalmic verses while he was languishing in prison, a fact that offered both a model of poetic self-fashioning and a potential point of contact between the two men that Surrey's dedicatory poem could exploit. Moreover, the addition of the dedicatory verse to the Earl's paraphrase would, as Elizabeth Heale has suggested, invest the psalmic text itself with new implications that would speak still more pointedly to the poet's condition. Thus in the references in the final lines to the speaker's salvation being achieved by 'thy grace' and 'thy secret works' (lines 65–6) Surrey might appear to be 'perhaps addressing himself as much to a merciful Blage as to God himself'.[71]

To another young noblemen, almost certainly Thomas Radcliffe, Lord Fitz-walter, who as Lord Chancellor Wriothesley's son-in-law was equally well placed to intercede for the poet,[72] Surrey wrote another penitent poem, this time offering counsel of humility to the recipient, and here overtly linking his own case with Wyatt's, and investing Wyatt's words with a kind of Solomonic wisdom:

My Ratclif, when thy rechlesse youth offendes,
Receve thy scourge by others chastisement;
For such callyng, when it workes none amendes,
Then plages are sent without advertisement.
Yet Salomon sayd, the wronged shall recure,
But Wiat said true, the skarre doth aye endure.[73]

That Surrey should be thinking of Wyatt while he himself was in prison is hardly surprising. But it is interesting to wonder precisely which text of the earlier poet he was recalling here. The assumption has always been that it was the short lyric 'Sighs are my food', dedicated to Sir Francis Bryan. Thus Surrey, probably writing from his own prison cell to Radcliffe, cites a poem written by Wyatt when he was himself imprisoned (equally unjustly dishonoured, as he claimed) to another courtier, Sir Francis Bryan, thereby suggesting the existence of what Heale terms 'a virtuous, intellectual community of wise but unfortunate men of affairs, each drawing on the experiences of themselves and others, and grounding their wisdom on the authority of biblical and time-honoured aphorisms'.[74] And, as we have seen, Surrey is clearly recalling Wyatt's poem, and its own allusion to Bryan's 'The Proverbes of Salmon' here. But Wyatt had also, of course, used the same phrase, talking of the scar that never heals, in his prose *Defence*, drawn up during his own imprisonment in the Tower in 1540/1. It is at least conceivable, then, that it was also the Wyatt of the *Defence*, the writer at bay, drawing up his own life-saving apologia that Surrey had in mind when he drafted the poems. He may well have hoped that these texts would secure his own release; or at least persuade those men, many of them evangelicals of humanist sympathies, who held the reins of power while Henry languished on his deathbed, to delay the sentence of execution long enough for the poet to survive the reign. Hence he might emerge during the minority of his successor to fulfil that destiny as royal friend and protector that had been cruelly denied him once before by the death of Henry Fitzroy.

It was not to be, of course. As we have seen, Surrey was beheaded on Tower Green on 19 January 1547, and quickly interred in the church of All Hallows, Barking. Within eight days of his death, Henry VIII was himself dead. The scourge of God had fallen just a week too late. The young poet Earl who had known no other king but Henry and his royal nemesis were each to meet their maker in the same month.

Coda

The last poem that Surrey was to write, if the testimony of his son is to be believed, was a brief, fractured work, 'The stormes are past' (j38), a seventeen-line pseudo-sonnet drawing on a rhyme scheme employed nowhere else in his canon.[75] Printed in Tottel's *Miscellany* with a title drawn from the 118th Psalm that may have authorial authority, it ostentatiously signalled its own status as a work of penitent humility.

Bonum est mihi quod humiliasti me.
[It is good for me that you have humiliated me (so that I may learn your justification).]

The opening lines present an image of stoic resignation achieved by 'patience graft in a determined brest' (line 4), and of new-found freedom won by an acceptance of fate and the surrender of the self into God's gracious hands:

> Thraldom at large hath made this prison fre;
> Danger well past remembred workes delight.
>
> (8–9)

But, as Heale notes in an incisive reading of the poem, this mood suddenly gives way to a 'startling' irruption of anger following lines 10–11.

> Of lingring doubtes such hope is sprong, pardie,
> That nought I finde displeasaunt in my sight
> But when my glasse presented unto me

The curelesse wound that bledeth day and night.
To think, alas, such hap should granted be
Unto a wretch that hath no hart to fight,
To spill that blood that hath so oft bene shed
For Britannes sake, alas, and now is ded.

(10–17)

Surrey's return here to the image of the shameful wound, suggests, as Heale observes, 'the power its Christ-like image of betrayal and martyrdom had for him'.[76] That the wound was intimately associated with slighted personal and class honour is confirmed by the thoughts that are prompted by its contemplation: thoughts of shame and furious resentment against the 'wretch that hath no hart to fight' (surely Southwell, who ignored the poet's offer to fight him in his shirt), yet had contrived to bring about his fall. In the face of this infuriating thought, the poised poetic edifice so carefully constructed in the opening nine lines comes crashing down, and with it crumbles Surrey's stoic self-image and quiet resolve. Thus, in Heale's reading, Surrey's poetic persona reveals itself as 'a shattered man, riven by contradictions'.[77] But there is also a characteristic reckless hauteur at work here. Even while he is penning what is effectively his own epitaph, the Earl cannot restrain his furious sense of noble self-worth, and his resentment at the injustices that have been contrived against him. It is, indeed, somehow fitting that he should not, finally go gentle into the dark night to which he has been consigned by royal justice—despite the promptings of his humanistic training and his own best intentions—but went down raging and snarling to the last, breaking all the codes of social and literary decorum as he did so.

17

Writing Under Tyranny

Wyatt, Surrey, and the Reinvention of English Poetry

In the course of this book we have moved from a case of literary collaboration, the story of two men at the heart of Henry VIII's court labouring together to produce a collected volume for royal consumption, to the tale of a single author, solitary, imprisoned, and excluded from the political centre, reflecting on the possibilities of literary production in a time of tribulation. The shift from courtly collaboration to alienated isolation provides an effective emblem of the impact of Henry's Reformation on the literary community—indeed, on the very *sense* of a literary community—in England in these years.

These were extraordinary times in England. The doyen of Tudor historians, Sir Geoffrey Elton famously claimed that the 1530s saw a Tudor Revolution in Government brought about by the administrative reforms of Thomas Cromwell.[1] His argument, that English government was transformed in this period from a medieval system centred on the person of the monarch to an essentially modern, bureaucratic administration, has been substantially revised and dismantled in the last half century, and even to mention it now is distinctly unfashionable in historical circles. Yet the extraordinary qualities of these years should not be dismissed. Indeed, I would suggest that 'the long 1530s' from the summoning of the Reformation Parliament in 1529 to the King's death in 1547, did witness something revolutionary, albeit not perhaps in the machinery of central government. It is legitimate to call this a revolution in English literary culture, a radical rethinking of the forms and ends of vernacular poetry and prose in response to the unprecedented demands placed upon writers by the King's divorce, the Royal Supremacy and their aftermath. In the course of the Henrician Reformation a confident, seemingly well-established, literate, cultural elite was forced to reassess fundamental assumptions about its own position. Writers had to learn to write very differently in a rapidly changing political situation, and they had to do so quickly as the accepted conventions of political life and cultural exchange collapsed around them. The result was the birth of many of the forms and features of literary writing—and of poetry in particular—that are now perceived as central to the English literary tradition. These writers had to invent—or rediscover—new ways of writing about politics and public life, and in so doing they reinvented themselves and the role of the author in English culture. Paradoxically, they both inscribed a new sense of alienated interiority into English verse and simultaneously began to write into being a new literary polity, a public sphere that could sustain and justify public writing outside the conventions of courtly counsel, and beyond the direct gaze of the monarch who had hitherto been the ultimate patron and arbiter of literary activity.[2]

These are large claims, but the previous chapters have, I hope, demonstrated their validity. It has been my argument that during the 1530s and 1540s a long-standing consensus about the nature of literature (and especially serious, public literature) in England broke down in the face of acute political crisis, leaving a generation of writers profoundly uncertain about the nature and effectiveness of their chosen vocation. Prior to Henry VIII's divorce proceedings and the break with Rome, poets, prose-writers, and dramatists wrote within the guiding and sustaining context of a number of cultural conventions. As they announced to their readers in their prefaces and colophons, they wrote, not to please themselves or to seek personal fame and riches, but for the good of others. They wrote to eschew idleness and to employ their learning and experience in the service of the commonweal by translating or paraphrasing the wisdom of the ancients or the eloquent testimony of other scholars. They wrote because writing was a rhetorical exercise, and rhetoric was a social, persuasive endeavour that found its fullest expression in the public domain. But, above all else, they wrote to advise, inform, instruct, and persuade their prince and his counsellors; because such men needed constantly to be reminded of the importance of virtue, self-restraint, and wisdom in the exercise of government. Underlying this writerly endeavour were the assumptions that the prince and those around him sincerely wished to be virtuous and to be loved by those whom they governed, and that they desired to conform to the principles enshrined in the conventional guidebooks of virtuous princely conduct. Hence they would listen and take notice of what scholars and men of eloquence were saying to them about their responsibilities.

In the 1530s these assumptions broke down under the pressure of political events. As Henry VIII increasingly set his government on a course of confrontation with Rome, with the leaders of the English Church, and with conservative forces in the kingdom as a whole, antagonistic social energies previously kept in check were given newfound freedom. And the King, rather than listening to the criticisms of those who were horrified by these developments, intimidated, imprisoned, or executed his critics in steadily increasing numbers. Writers were consequently faced with a stark choice. They could either turn their pens to promoting the King's Reformation (or, if that was too repugnant to them, cease writing altogether), or they could find new ways to write, new forms in which to address the situation in which they found themselves. Some undoubtedly chose the former course. But others tried to turn literary creativity to new uses, or to new forms that made the old uses effective again. From a culture in which the natural assumption was that all writing was in one way or another writing for the King, whether for his own consumption or to improve his kingdom by educating his subjects in his name, England moved in the space of two decades to a point where the most urgent public literature was no longer 'royalist' in any obvious sense. By the early 1540s the natural supposition of a Wyatt, a Surrey, or an evangelical like the prose writer and dramatist John Bale, was that the sort of directly political literature they were creating was not—and indeed should not be—for the King. Theirs was writing *about* the King, *despite* him, and in many ways *against* him. England had learned the art of writing under tyranny.

In recent years a number of scholars have observed fundamental links between literary production and the political and religious changes of the mid-sixteenth century.[3] Most recently and powerfully, James Simpson has argued for a definitive shift from a 'reformist' medieval literary culture in which 'self-regulating energies' dominated production, to a centralizing, 'revolutionary', authority in the course of the Reformation. The 'central perception' of his groundbreaking volume in the *Oxford English Literary History* is, he suggests, that,

Concentrations of power that simplify institutional structures also simplify and centralize cultural practice, by stressing central control, historical novelty, and unity produced from the top down.[4]

One might argue over whether the Henrician period really saw a simplification of institutional structures, or whether the regime really stressed its own novelty in quite the ways that this model suggests, but the essential insight is illuminating. Simpson's argument is that the Henrician Reformation centralized and simplified power structures and in so doing produced a literature similarly reduced in its outlook and possibilities. It favoured, he suggests, a small core of authorized modes of writing and literary postures, each in its own way 'threatened and mesmerised by... absolute power' and 'unable to escape the historical dislocation and emotional circularities that such a position necessarily entails'.[5] I would qualify those conclusions, at least in so far as they suggest that all courtly writing in the Henrician period was of necessity enthralled to centralizing royal authority. My objections would be as much chronological as hermeneutic. The high point of 'centralization' in literary terms was, I would argue, not coterminous with the period of dramatic political change, but preceded and only partially overlapped with it. It was in the 1510s, 1520s, and early 1530s that the late medieval literary culture of the *speculum principis* combined with the new assertive impulses of the Henrician Supremacy to produce a literature that was almost exclusively aimed (in one way or another) at the King. The early manoeuvres of the break with Rome and the active patronage of polemical literature by the Crown accentuated and intensified those tendencies already apparent in English literary culture which placed the monarch at the centre of textual reception. What followed in the later 1530s and 1540s was not, however, the consolidation of that centralizing tendency as the Supremacy took hold, but its rapid erosion and eventual collapse. Rather than acquiesce entirely in the royal agenda, writers began to record, and in various ways to resist, the tyrannical tendencies that were an increasingly obvious aspect of the Supremacy. The result was a profound loss of confidence in what had traditionally been a centralized literary culture, as successive attempts to redress those tyrannical tendencies through conventional, 'approved' forms of writing: didactic 'mirrors' and critical panegyrics, proved ever more obviously ineffective.

As a consequence, the experience of living and writing under tyranny prompted men such as More, Elyot, Wyatt, and Surrey to explore alternative forms and modes of writing. The *speculum principis*, the panegyric, and the exemplary narrative gave way to the satire, the lyric, and the biblical paraphrase as the most vital emerging literary forms, and the public, petitionary stance characteristic of the late medieval poet and 'maker of books' was replaced by the more inward-looking, self-generating poses now seen as characteristic of 'Renaissance individualism'. Like Simpson, I see these Renaissance innovations as the product of political pressure rather than of any 'liberating' possibilities created by the new learning and the new religion: unlike him I see them as consciously resisting rather than complying with that pressure.

A Revolution in Literary Culture?

The public literature of the fifteenth century; the work of John Lydgate, Thomas Hoccleve, Thomas Malory and the numerous anonymous poets and prose writers who contributed to English political discourse, was a literature born of uncertainty, created amid the dynastic, political, and doctrinal ferment of years of foreign wars and a disputed succession. These writers produced texts that in one way or another voiced their aspirations that civil war would end, that good government would return, that Henry VI would prove a strong king like his father, or that a saviour would be found to end the cycle of war and usurpation that would culminate in the brief reign of Richard III. The political literature of the long period from the death of Richard II to that of Richard III was thus a literature of prolonged, enervating, crisis. But it was also, fundamentally and paradoxically, a literature of hope, born of an incipient confidence that all would be well again in England once a strong king appeared to restore order and renew national confidence. By contrast, what one sees in the verse and prose of the later 1530s is increasingly a literature of despair, provoked by a sense that the strong king was already enthroned, and was settled upon a political course entirely antithetical to the nation's needs; and, moreover, that the only realistic alternative was an inevitably weak and divisive minority.

When William Thynne and Sir Brian Tuke began the grand project of gathering together all the works of Chaucer as a monument to English literary history and national identity, they did so, despite the obviously progressive aspects of their edition, within an essentially conservative and optimistic framework. They assembled a collection of authoritative texts associated with a prestigious national author and conceived of that project as something to be presented to the King for his entertainment and edification. They gave the King a mirror and trusted him (with a little tutorly guidance from their preface and glosses) to consult it and to benefit from its counsel. Their work as literary editors was thus another aspect of their role as servants of the crown. When Wyatt and Surrey began their separate projects to translate the psalms, they did so in a quite different and markedly more antagonistic spirit. Under the strains of the Henrician Reformation the poetry of counsel had become an increasingly shrill call for a return to consensus and accommodation, and as the life was slowly drained from it by the indifference of the King, it had begun to make way for the first signs of a new literature of resistance. Although Surrey would retrospectively describe Wyatt's psalms as a *speculum principis* (in which 'Rewlers may se in a myrrour clere / The bitter frewte of false concupiscence' (J 31: 10–11)), it was a polemical point at Henry's expense that he was seeking to score. He did not seriously expect the King to benefit from Wyatt's mirror in the conventional sense approved by Erasmus. Indeed, the whole purpose of the remark was to condemn Henry for *not* having benefited from Wyatt's counsel. In so doing, Surrey revealed his despair at the failure of the conciliar tradition, and his desire to move beyond it.

The ceaseless, importunate quest for royal approval and patronage that had motivated poets and scholars from Hoccleve and Lydgate to Hawes, Skelton, and even Elyot, thus had neither the same urgency nor the same meaning for Wyatt; and it meant still less to Surrey. Indeed, it would not regain its hold upon the generality of writers until well into the reign of Elizabeth I. The literary community, under the pressure of political events, was beginning to reconfigure itself as an alternative forum for the discussion of moral and political values, a court in the legal rather than the regal sense. The crucial cultural concepts of tradition, continuity, morality, wisdom, and the accommodation of diversity would have to be articulated *despite* the King rather than to and through him. Voicing the idea that the King was no longer the dependable guardian of national virtue, and might actually be its greatest enemy, was a matter of pressing importance, and it became necessary to use the hitherto taboo word 'tyrant' in a domestic context. What had previously been a term for something that happened far away or long ago had become a political reality here, now, in England.

This clear shift in the focus of public poetry in the course of the long decade of Henry's Supremacy was perhaps the most profound change in literary consciousness in a century and a half, amounting to a revolution in sensibility. When all the stable points of the political landscape: church, court, crown, parliament, the law, become unfixed, as they were by Henry's Reformation and the Supremacy through which it was imposed; when the very landscape and cultural geography of the realm themselves shifted, as monastic houses were wound up and pulled down, shrines uprooted, liberties, sanctuaries, and private jurisdictions dissolved, with new diocese and secular estates created, then those who wrote about England and Englishness and what it meant to write in English were forced back upon their own intellectual resources in wholly new and more urgent ways. Wyatt, Surrey, and those who, like them, wrote through the Supremacy and Reformation, were forced to reassess the literary tools bequeathed to them by previous generations of English poets, and to rethink the uses of literature and the role of the writer from first principles.

If the Henrician Reformation did not ultimately bring about the revolution in government described by Sir Geoffrey Elton, it nonetheless shook English culture to its foundations and had a profoundly unsettling effect upon the generations of English men and women who lived through it. A revolution need not be permanent to have permanent consequences. An earthquake may shake houses, break windows, even bring walls and bridges crashing to the ground, but the buildings can be rebuilt and all the damage is eventually made good. Similarly, the Henrician Reformation did not introduce any fundamental changes that were not subsequently reversed, revised, ameliorated, or adapted in later reigns. But those who experienced that Reformation, like those who have lived through an earthquake, were never quite the same thereafter. They never trod the ground with quite the same degree of confidence, never trusted with the same degree of blithe assurance to the solidity of bricks and mortar, and never again took their cultural heritage for granted in the ways they once had.

What is perhaps initially most striking to modern eyes is how quickly a sense that Henry was falling into potentially tyrannical behaviour becomes evident in the literature of the period. It is not the case that the authors we have been following were wrong-footed by Henry's actions, or were lulled into a false sense of security by a gradual and piecemeal slide into unacceptable methods of government. As early as 1530 the signs of potential hazards ahead were evidently sufficiently clear for a number of writers to mobilize the conventional literary methods for seeking political redress. Sir Thomas Elyot's most substantial critical analysis of the ills of society and his most sustained discussion of their remedy, *The Book Named the Governor*, was begun in 1530 at the latest, and was printed for the King's benefit in 1531. Thynne and Tuke's Chaucer edition offered its collective prospectus for moderate kingship and social reconciliation less than a year later. And John Heywood's interludes began to be played at court over much the same period, and were issued in print *en masse* in 1533–4. This is not evidence of a literary community taken by surprise by the events of the royal divorce and the Supremacy, nor of a community cowed into quiet submission by what they experienced. These men saw the dangerous implications of Henry's apparent rejection of consensus in pursuit of seemingly 'wilful' private ends, and they reacted to it in the ways that their reading and education suggested they should. Their problem was that Henry did not respond to the clear and consistent mass of advice literature with which they presented him in the ways that convention and recent experience suggested that he should. Hence the challenge was tacitly thrown down to find ways of writing that would effectively address the new political imperatives.

In Sir Thomas Elyot we see perhaps the strongest advocate and most consistent exponent of the old humanist model of literary counsel. For him, as we have seen, the idea of the *speculum principis* never completely lost its attraction. He continued to write works of advice and instruction throughout his career, hoping through the tried and trusted combination of counsel, criticism, and carefully modulated praise to persuade, cajole, and shame the King into addressing the personal and political crises that he had provoked. Hence even Elyot's last and most savage text, *The Image of Governance*, contained a broad seam of counsel aimed at Henry VIII, offering a vision of good government that he could emulate, even as it satirized the reality of contemporary tyranny in the parodic *Life* of Alexander Severus. Yet, even in Elyot's persistent counsels one can sense an increasing frustration with the conciliar function, and notice attempts to adapt and develop it to meet the new circumstances of Henry's Supremacy. *The Governor*, his first essay in the genre, was both a vehicle for advice and an exploration of the issues involved in counselling princes: it suggests an author thinking aloud on paper for the benefit of his intended royal reader. In *The Image* there is a new and emphatic sense of the text in and of itself creating a space for the realization of the author's desires, a means of resolving problems imaginatively rather than simply publicizing them for solution elsewhere. Hence the sense of writerly pleasure evident in the final anecdote of the call to court of Sextilius Rufus. In this sense, *The Image* offers just a hint of the kind of interiority to be found in the lyrical poetry of Wyatt and Surrey. It reveals, not a retreat from politics into literature, but the re-imagination of literary creativity as a means of realizing a different kind of politics: an alternative means of political engagement through writing that does not rely solely upon the receptiveness of a royal reader.

For others the idea of crafting ever more sophisticated mirrors in which to show Henry VIII both what he had become and what he might be again if only he would return to old ways was evidently no longer sufficient. Such men sought new forms and new audiences through which literary endeavour could be turned to the public good. Sir Thomas More was probably the first mainstream writer to abandon the campaign to counsel the King out of his folly. Having always written for a wider, more diverse, European readership than most of his courtly contemporaries, More probably found the shift in audiences rather easier to make than most. Either way, in his polemical English tracts, beginning with *The Dialogue Concerning Heresies* of 1528, he wrote for a wider 'public' readership, not in the hope of altering royal policy, but with the intention of fortifying the faith of his fellow Englishmen *tout court*. He took up the evangelical challenge of the reformers directly, and sought to refute their claims point by point. His English dialogues mark a sustained turn to the new literature of polemic instigated by Continental protestantism, as he sought to discredit and so disarm the evangelicals as a popular force in England, and to cajole his fellow scholars into taking up their pens to oppose the new learning of the heretics.

Other writers responded to the failure of the literature of counsel in other ways. By the time that he began to write *The Dialogue Between Pole and Lupset*,

Thomas Starkey, for example, had clearly concluded that he could not reform the King's mind or morals through persuasion alone. Consequently, he aimed to win Henry from tyranny not by offering good advice, but by outlining a constitutional solution to the problem of a potentially despotic regime. He described a system of governance in which the King was hedged in with external checks and balances, a standing Council and a dramatically more powerful Constable of England, who would become a kind of Lord Protector for an adult sovereign, and 'see to the liberty of the whole body of the realm', summoning a parliament on his own initiative if he felt there was 'any peril of the loss of liberty of the people'.[6] Perhaps only someone who, like Starkey, was writing in exile could have envisaged so radical a rethinking of the boundaries of English government and of conciliar literature alike. Unsurprisingly his *Dialogue* found little favour at court, and neither Elyot nor his contemporaries were initially prepared to follow its constitutionalist lead.

Elyot rejected such oppositional forms and continued to praise and counsel Henry VIII through the 1530s because, like many of his contemporaries, writers and non-writers alike, he saw little else that he could do to influence events. So he wrote treatises, tracts, and prefaces, 'Prohemes' and epistles either addressed to the King or written with him as their primary intended reader, that restated the conventional tenets of good government and personal morality. He praised extravagantly Henry's more orthodox theological moves (most obviously his condemnation of the Sacramentarian John Lambert) and commended his labours to bring sound doctrine to his subjects in ways that stressed the moderate, Erasmian principles at the heart of royal policies, passing over the more radical edges to Reformation legislation in silence. The fact that he continued to write in this way tells us a good deal. It was not that he simply misjudged Henry's capacity to be persuaded.[7] Elyot's stubborn refusal to abandon the role of the literary counsellor spoke to a much deeper faith in conventional methods of political engagement and in the responsibility of writers to contribute to the discussion of policy and national life. His stress in the *Governor* on the distinctive qualities of English society, like Thynne and Tuke's stress upon the nature and dignity of the English language, was part of a wider claim concerning the nature of English public culture and the role of literature in public life.

For Elyot, as for Thynne, Tuke, Heywood, and those others who wrote critically about Henry's policies, the decision to write a text, to perform an interlude, or to publish the texts or interludes of others, was the consequence of an earlier decision to counsel and influence readers or spectators in their chosen arena. And in the early 1530s at least that arena was almost always the court, and the principal intended reader the King. The idea of literary interiority, of private uses for literary creativity, while it was clearly known to them, does not seem to have suggested itself to these writers, nor to have appealed to their sense of what they were doing at the time. Literary creation, for them, was intimately linked with public politics, and with the lives and responsibilities of governors.

This fact alone meant that writing was already intensely politicized, even before the Acts of Succession and the 1534 Treason Act made specific forms of writing, speaking, and imagining potentially criminal acts in which the state acquired a close interest. And in the later 1530s writing itself came under political scrutiny of a kind and intensity rarely experienced in England before, and acts of censorship, both external and (perhaps more effectively) internal, became a crucial feature of literary creation.

It was in this environment of intense scrutiny—what Seth Lerer has perceptively described as a culture of surveillance and surreption[8]—that the literature of counsel was slowly asphyxiated in Henrician England. And, while Elyot strove vainly to resuscitate it, others, primarily Wyatt and Surrey, turned with a new urgency to other modes and other implicit audiences. Most obviously and powerfully they turned to lyric poetry and the possibilities that it offered of less public, but no less political, forms of address and self-presentation. In the lyrics, the metrical psalms, and the Horatian epistolary satires of the later 1530s, Wyatt and Surrey developed a new poetic voice and a new social energy: the engaged, yet seemingly self-sufficient voice of the poet in exile, alienated and isolated, yet empowered by that isolation, in dialogue with himself, with his God, and with a small group of like-minded fellow courtiers linked by the 'private' medium of manuscript circulation.

Having been smothered in the 1530s, the literature of counsel would not be fully resuscitated until the 1560s, when the government of Elizabeth I restored a degree of confidence in a stable royal polity. By that time, however, the new forms and modes of writing devised by Wyatt and Surrey specifically to address the Henrician crisis had themselves been absorbed into the mainstream of courtly literary practice. The central figure in this process of transformation, as William Sessions has shown, was Surrey. It was he who fashioned the way in which Wyatt's work was received by his contemporaries and by subsequent generations. And he himself was the one poet among his contemporaries equipped with the character, the lineage, and the social position to wield literature in a wholly more combative manner than had previously been attempted. The price he paid for his presumption was death; not for the words he wrote, but for the more immediate and obvious statements of dissent and aspiration that he crafted in the plaster panels and stained glass of Kenninghall and Mount Surrey. Those statements implied that the time for counsel was past and that events called for a wholly more assertive embodiment of the humanist *vita activa* who could redeem and renew both the Crown and the wider realm.[9] These same sentiments also animated his verse, however, and it was their written expression that would have the longer and more significant impact.

Wyatt, Surrey and the Reinvention of English Verse

The literary historian George Puttenham, writing in the second half of the reign of Henry's daughter Elizabeth I, singled out the innovations of Wyatt and Surrey as the moment when the spirit and the techniques of the Continental Renaissance were imported into England, and English poetry was reborn. 'In the latter end of [King Henry's] . . . reign', he claimed, there,

> sprang up a new company of courtly makers, of whom *Sir Thomas Wyatt* th'elder and *Henry*, Earl of Surrey were the two chieftains, who, having travailed into Italy and there tasted the sweet and stately measures and style of the Italian Poesy as novices . . . greatly polished our rude and homely manner of vulgar Poesy.[10]

It was the formal and stylistic innovations of these two 'chieftains', learnt in Italy and brought home to England, that, in Puttenham's view, set the agenda for all future poetic creativity in English:

> I repute them . . . for the two chief lanterns of light to all others that have since employed their pens upon English Poesy, their conceits were lofty, their styles stately, their conveyance cleanly, their terms proper, their metre sweet and well proportioned, in all imitating very naturally and studiously their master Francis Petrarch.[11]

Modern critics have accepted the substance of Puttenham's claims, differing only over the details. But what was it that made Wyatt and Surrey's work so appealing to their successors and so important for what followed? Opinion has generally favoured variations on the idea that it was simply so much better than anything that had gone before. Stephen Greenblatt, for example, has suggested that Wyatt's verse is 'at its best distinctly more convincing, more deeply moving, than anything written not only in his generation but in the preceding century'.[12] This may be too dismissive of the best work of the fifteenth century, not least of the verse of Dunbar, Henryson, and Skelton; but Greenblatt identifies a feature of Wyatt's writing that has often commended itself to critics: its apparent authenticity.[13] The 'moving' quality to his writing lies, in part at least, in the impression it creates of (what seems to modern ears at least) a real speaking voice; of genuine emotion struggling for expression through, against, and at times, seemingly, in despite of the demands of form and metre. Wyatt's poetry, it is often said, is 'rough',[14] both metrically and verbally, and it stakes its claim to verisimilitude through that roughness, and through the expression of idiosyncratic details of thought and observation it deploys, seemingly striving for the unadorned emotion, the thing itself. It is an art that, as Hamlet would later immortalize it, could hold a mirror up to nature, representing a heightened, intensified form of experience that nonetheless appeared to those who witnessed it to be unmediatedly 'real'.

As Sessions has observed, the poetry of both Wyatt and Surrey appealed to successors such as Samuel Daniel and Shakespeare precisely because such writers 'found powerful the realism associated with prose in Surrey's varied rhyme scheme . . . and . . . in the more realistic enjambment, one line overflowing into another to render natural speech'.[15] This prose-like realism, with its impression of a 'plain-speaking' poetic voice was the product of a verse form that elided its own formality even as it announced its technical excellence. The 'dense speech' (as Sessions terms it) of Surrey's verse offered a rhythmically complex yet seemingly spontaneous diction underpinned by satisfyingly complex syntactical patterns, structured around rhetorical figures such as chiasmus (counterpoint), hyperbaton (inversion), and oxymoron.[16] Like the portraits sketched and painted by their contemporary Hans Holbein the Younger, the poets' lyrics—and still more obviously Surrey's blank verse—were the art that concealed art; the exact poetic realization of Castiglione's supreme courtly quality: *sprezzatura*.[17]

It was this capacity to offer a new and more immediate access to emotional authenticity, coupled with its evident and stylish courtliness and the social distinction of its authors, that ensured the survival of Wyatt and Surrey's innovations, and their adoption as the principal lyrical modes for subsequent generations of English poets. Central to the process of transmission was the publication of the anthology of *Songs and Sonnets* (better known as *Tottel's Miscellany*), published by the printer Richard Tottel in 1557. Tottel gathered together a substantial portion of Wyatt and Surrey's work, packaged it with other texts as a compendium of love poems and examples of modish courtly forms of self-expression, and bequeathed it to future generations of aspirant poets as the definitive guide to refined aristocratic and poetic sensibilities.[18] It was no doubt Tottel's collection that Puttenham had in mind when he praised the poets' capacity to inspire a literary Renaissance with their borrowings from Petrarch. Yet Wyatt and Surrey rediscovered the inwardness of Petrarchan lyricism and gave it a new spirit and new functions in England, not because they had travelled to Italy and imbibed the Petrarchan spirit *ad fontes*, but because they stayed at home. Surrey never visited Italy, and Wyatt did so only once. Both absorbed their Petrarchanism at second hand, largely through French intermediaries and the earlier English experiments of Chaucer. The impetus for their innovations came from the fact that they were Englishmen, subjects of Henry VIII, and subjected to the events of the 1530s. They developed the characteristic 'Renaissance' lyrical voice that would prove so amenable to later generations in reaction to the social and cultural pressures of the Supremacy and Reformation.

It is thus only slightly excessive to suggest that Renaissance English poetry, in the forms that now seem definitive of the mode and the age, was created out of the intense political pressure of Henrician tyranny. The sonnet, the *strambotto* and *frottola*, the metrical psalm and the verse satire, blank verse, *terza* and *ottava rima*, and Poulter's Measure, were all invented, rediscovered, or imported into English, developed and popularized in the short intense period of Henry's Reformation, as Wyatt and Surrey sought ways of writing of and for 'this realm of England' that did not necessitate and presuppose a sympathetic royal reader.[19] So too, as Colin Burrow has suggested, was that 'inwardness' or interiority that is traditionally seen as so axiomatic a part of the Renaissance sensibility forged from the pressures of living through Henry's Supremacy.[20] Far from being the product of a joyful embracing of Renaissance optimism; a spontaneous celebration of the infinite potential of humankind newly revealed to them in the writings of the Italian and French humanists, Wyatt and Surrey's adoption of this characteristic subjectivity was an anxious political expedient. It was an expression of what Burrow has called their sense of 'being at odds with the rest of the world' (and, we might add, of not knowing quite how to express and respond to that experience).[21] Political necessity was the mother of their prolific literary invention.

Wyatt was already experimenting with form and genre in the early 1530s. Following humanist impulses he had adopted classical genres as well as classical styles with the intention of enriching and refining his native language and literature. But the onset of the Royal Supremacy and the Reformation that it enabled gave added impetus and urgency to this experimentation. The Italianate forms so useful as vehicles for the new amorous courtly verse were doubly effective for voicing the growing sense of political unease that the events of the 1530s provoked. Both their vernacular inwardness and their ostensibly playful indirection gave them their particular potency in courtly discourse. Similarly, the plain-speaking voice and the tight self-discipline required by the formal strictures of the sonnet and *strambotto*, coupled with their immediate Italianate sources and their classical origins, made them the perfect literary expression of the humanists' favoured stoic philosophy in a courtly context.[22]

Petrarch, the poet whom Puttenham identified as Wyatt and Surrey's greatest inspiration, was, of course, himself adept at both political and amatory verse, and his innovations in each mode provided models for their own work. His elegiac sonnets for his patron, Cardinal Colonna (Rime 269) and his fellow poet Cino da Pistoia (Rime 92) directly inspired Wyatt's 'The Pillar Perisht' and stand behind Surrey's elegies for Thomas Clere and Wyatt himself. Similarly, as Elizabeth Heale suggests, Petrarch's satirical assaults upon the Avignon papacy (*Rimes* 114 and 130–8) provided models for Surrey's most overtly political verse, notably his satires, 'Th'Assyryan King' and 'London hast thou accused me'.[23]

The interiority of the Tudor poets' lyric voices similarly carried a self-evident political charge. In many of his later poems, as Heale has perceptively argued, Wyatt presents himself as a tortured soul, torn and fragmented by cultural tensions and paradoxes which he is unable to contain or reconcile. In Surrey's songs the speaker is similarly an isolated individual, but more often one whose 'private feelings are invested with coherence and nobility in opposition to an outer world marked by change and loss'.[24] In each case, whether they represent themselves as baffled (in the strong, early-modern senses of the word, both 'bewildered' and 'publicly disgraced')[25] by the world around them, or resolute in defiance of it, the poets depict their own condition as one of profound alienation from a courtly environment rendered hostile, unstable, and 'unnatural' by inexplicable and rebarbative change.

Wyatt's courtly verse is characterized by a horror at the endemic fickleness around him. And the ambiguity in many of his texts over whether the capricious object of his address is a woman who has betrayed him sexually or a patron who has deserted him politically is conscious, suggesting a wider instability in the very categories of knowledge prompted by the unfixing of the realm:

> I se the[e] change ffrom that that was
> And how thy ffayth hath tayn his fflyt,
> But I with pacyense let yt pase
> And with my pene thys do I wryt
> To show the[e] playn by prowff off syght,
> I se the[e] change . . .
>
> I se the[e] change, as in thys case,
> Has mayd me ffre ffrom myn avoo [avow],
> Ffor now another has my plase,
> And or I wist, I wot ner how,
> Yt hapnet thys as ye here now:
> I se the[e] change.
>
> I se the[e] change, seche ys my chance.
> To sarve in dowt and hope in vayn;
> But sens my surty so doth glanse,
> Repentens now shall quyt thy payn,
> Never to trust the lyke agayn;
> I se the[e] change.
>
> (Muir and Thompson, 115, 1–6, 19–30)

At times the fluidity of sexual relationships seems to be a function of a wider cultural crisis, a moral and political amnesia at the heart of the realm.

> They fle from me that sometyme did me seke
> With naked fote stalking in my chambre.
> I have sene theim gentill, tame, and meke
> That nowe are wyld and do not remember
> That sometyme they put theimself in daunger
> To take bred at my hand; and nowe they raunge
> Besely seking with a continuell chaunge.
>
> (Muir and Thompson, 37, 1–7)

Elsewhere political failure itself offers an emblem of cultural and moral decay.

> Luckes, my faire falcon, and your fellowes all,
> How well pleasaunt yt were your libertie!
> Ye not forsake me that faire might ye befall.
> But they that somtyme lykt my companye
> Like lyse awaye from ded bodies thei crall . . .
>
> (Muir and Thompson, 241, 1–5)

Such fundamental disorientation and the savage anger that it provokes go well beyond the conventional criticisms of Fortune's fickleness to be found in most late-medieval anti-curial satires. In such an environment, Wyatt suggests, the very principles of virtue and integrity become unfixed and mutable. Hence, as Thomas Hannen has suggested, what in other hands, or in an earlier period, might have been presented as a decorous *demande d'amour*, a rhetorical question set for a courtly audience in order to prompt a series of didactic *sententiae*, becomes an urgent appeal for guidance:

> What vaileth trouth? Or, by it, to take payn?
> To stryve by stedfastnes for to attayne
> To be juste and true, and fle from dowblenes,
> Sythens all alike where rueleth craftines
> Rewarded is boeth fals and plain.
> Sonest he spedeth that moost can fain;
> True meanyng hert is had in disdayn.
> Against deceipte and dowblenes
> What vaileth trouth?
>
> Decyved is he by crafty trayn
> That meaneth no gile and doeth remayn
> Within the trapp, withoute redresse;
> But, for to love, lo, suche a maisteres,
> Whose crueltie nothing can refrayn,
> What vaileth trouth?
>
> (Muir and Thompson, 2)

Again, to say that truth is the first casualty of life at court is nothing new. But Wyatt brings a new sense of urgency and self-criticism to his exploration of the theme. There is no trace here of a dispassionate observer, judging from a moral distance a world whose values he despises. Wyatt's speaker is implicated fully in the confusion of values that he describes, and, as Hannen observes, seems genuinely to want to know the worth of honesty in this new courtly dispensation.[26] Here the roughness of the syntax and apparent irregularity of rhythm serve to accentuate the sense of disorientation, in which even stoicism is built upon shifting sands. What price integrity ('to stryve by stedfastnes for to attayne / To be juste and true . . . ') when there is nothing to which one might remain true, and even the stoics no longer know what truth is?

The precariousness of the courtier's existence is a recurring theme, both in the more overtly political poems ('Stand whose list on the slipper top', etc.) and in less obviously 'public' poems, in which the fickleness and uncertainties of the political world often seem to have been internalized by the speaker, absorbed into his sense of all social relationships and his own identity itself:

> It may be good, like it who list,
> But I do dowbt: who can me blame?
> For oft assured yet have I myst,
> And now again I fere the same:

The wyndy wordes, the Ies [eyes] quaynt game,
Of sodon chaunge maketh me agast:
For dred to fall I stond not fast.

Alas! I tred the endles maze
That seketh to accorde two contraries;
And hope still, and nothing hase,
Imprisoned in libertes,
As oon unhard and still that cries;
Alwaies thursty and yet nothing I tast:
For dred to fall I stond not fast.

Assured, I dowbt I be not sure;
And should I trust to suche suretie
That oft hath put the prouff in ure
And never hath founde it trusty?
Nay, sir, in faith it were great foly.
And yet my liff thus do I wast:
For dred to fall I stond not fast.

(Muir and Thompson, 21)

The difference between such anxieties and the allegorical trepidations of the figures in a previous generation's anti-curial satires, such as Skelton's Drede in *The Bowge of Courte* lies precisely in the sense of alienated inwardness that they convey—the sense that these words were written to explore a felt condition rather than to exemplify a universal truth.

Both Wyatt and Surrey stretch the conventions of anti-curial satire to breaking point, depicting the Henrician polity as a world without the fixed landmarks by which a man of honour might navigate his way. Sometimes that world is explored from the inside, as in Surrey's powerful sonnet 'The soote season' (j2), in which the stable continuities and spontaneous renovative energies of the natural world are contrasted to the anxious sterility of the courtly subject:

The fishes flote with newe repaired scale;
The adder all her sloughe awaye she slinges,
The swift swallow pursueth the flyes smale;
The busy bee her honye now she minges [recalls];
Winter is worne that was the flowers bale.
  And thus I see among these pleasant thinges
  Eche care decayes, and yet my sorrow springes.

(8–14)

But more frequently it is looked at from the sidelines, from the perspective of an observer who seeks to free himself from the toils of a world that fills him with horror. For each poet, as Heale observes, the lyric form 'creates a tiny "private" space in which, by bewailing its own powerlessness, the speaking voice can assert its superiority of judgement and feeling, its integrity, or at least its ironic self-knowledge in a faithless and unsympathetic world'.[27]

Paradoxically, given that the bulk of Wyatt's poetry conveys a sense of helplessness and despair in the face of the all-pervading flux of courtly life, it was his fortitude, the quality stressed in Surrey's elegies and epitaphs, that seems to have appealed most obviously to his successors. It was Wyatt and Surrey's confident attempts to reassert their own integrity amid the chaos that future generations of writers would seize upon and claim for their own. The kind of defiance of fortune evident in Wyatt's 'In faith I wot not well what to say' inspired sonneteers and playwrights from Kid and Daniel to Shakespeare to espouse a renewed faith in the heroism of the stoic subject:

> In faith I wot not well what to say,
> Thy chaunces ben so wonderous,
> Thou, fortune, with thy dyvers play
> That causeth Joy full dolourous,
> And eke the same right Joyus:
> Yet though thy chayne hath me enwrapt,
> Spite of thy hap, hap hath well hapt.
>
> Though thou me set for a wounder
> And sekest thy chaunge to do me payn,
> Mens myndes yet may thou not order,
> And honeste, and it remayn,
> Shall shyne for all thy clowdy rayn;
> In vayn thou sekest to have trapped:
> Spite of thy hap, hap hath well happed.
>
> (Muir and Thompson, 23, 1–14)

That bold declaration: 'Mens myndes yet may thou not order!', born out of the specific circumstances created by the intrusive legislation of Henry's Supremacy, would suggest to future generations a more general statement of stoic integrity, an assertion of the inviolable interiority of the self as a writing subject and generator of meaning. And in the same way, many of Wyatt and Surrey's other formal innovations of the period, designed to meet particular political pressures and perform specific political tasks, would be adapted and popularized as the basis of a new public poetry.

Wyatt's domestication of the Horatian verse satire, and the English 'Horatian' style which he developed in 'Mine own John Poins' and 'My Mother's Maids' (what Stephen Foley has called 'the independent moral voice of the gentlemen in repose'), laid the foundations of a poetry that would 'speak the aspirations (and mask the anxieties) of the English establishment for centuries to come'.[28] Created as a means of negotiating the specific problems of one man's internal exile into a source of moral integrity, it came to epitomize the self-image of a whole class of classically trained English gentlemen with country estates to extol as 'home'.

Similarly, in his elegy for Richmond, and the savage portrait of the effeminate tyrant in 'Th'Assyryans King', Surrey invented the form of sonnet that would carry his name as a means of containing the powerful emotions generated by specific events, the loss of a friend and the apparent failure of his political aspirations. Yet it too proved amenable to far wider use. His innovation, with its capacity to deliver a sententious or ironic 'punchline' in its distinctive final couplet, was taken up by Samuel Daniel for his own sonnet sequence, *Delia*, published in the 1590s, and would spawn the 'sonnet craze' of the next decade, leading ultimately to Shakespeare's definitive foray into the field. As Sessions observed, 'the form changed history, or at least what makes history, its sense and sensibilities'.[29] The elegiac mode itself, learnt ultimately from Ovid, was, as Simpson suggests, ideally suited for Wyatt and Surrey's needs in the 1530s, providing a distinctive forum for the poet who wished to 'turn aside from, yet comment on, the public world'. It presented a self 'fragmented by its thraldom to power',[30] yet capable nonetheless of defying that power, and signifying its tyranny. The example offered by texts such as Wyatt's 'The Pillar perisht' and Surrey's elegies on Thomas Clere, Richmond, and Wyatt would consequently be imitated and endlessly reproduced by successive generations, establishing, as Sessions has suggested, a tradition of English verse commemorating the lives of great men in troubled times that would last well into the twentieth century.[31]

In a similar way the heroic quatrain (a stanza rhyming abab) that Surrey devised for his most sustained exercise in elegy, 'Wyatt resteth here' and his Windsor elegy for Richmond, 'So crewel prison', would provide an example for future poets in search of a suitable form to convey epic sentiments in the English language. And, most obviously and significantly of all, blank verse, that 'strange metre', coined by Surrey for his translation of Book IV of the *Aeneid* to emulate the unrhymed hexameters of Virgil's Latin text, and first presented to a wider reading public in John Day's printed edition of 1554, would spawn a literary tradition of incomparable consequence. It was taken up in Norton and Sackville's groundbreaking verse drama *Gorboduc* (1561–2), would inspire Marlowe's 'mighty line', and become the definitive form of the Elizabethan Renaissance as the basis of Shakespeare's dramatic verse.[32]

The stylistic and formal innovations of the long 1530s thus laid the foundations of the characteristic verse-forms of the Elizabethan Renaissance. But they did not do so as part of a seamless evolutionary development. The inventions and importations of Wyatt and Surrey were forced upon them by the unprecedented political circumstances of the period, a fact which marks a clear disjunction between their work and that of previous generations of writers. The kinds of public oratorical stances adopted by earlier poetic innovators such as Hawes and Skelton had been intimately associated with their quests for patronage, with attempts to claim a public role as the 'King's orator' or poet laureate, and with efforts to be recognized and acknowledged as worthy of a place at court. They consciously fostered the notion of a direct, almost casual, relationship between literary creativity and royal patronage, and the intimacy with royalty associated with the work of the celebrated authors of a previous age. The stories of how Richard II invited John Gower on to his barge on the Thames and asked him to write 'some new thing' for him (a 'commission' that was to lead to the *Confessio Amantis*), or how Chaucer was commanded by Alceste to write a book about virtuous women, 'And whan this book is maad, give it the quene, \ On my behalf at Eltham or at Shene',[33] offered both an attractive model of the poet's role and a heady prospectus of the potential social mobility of their vocation to men such as Skelton and Hawes. The poetic selves they created were thus effectively conditioned by this sense of their own role as a public representative of (and mediator between) the King and the polity they served.

Their attempts to write into being so overtly public and communal a form of individuality led these poets into some very curious convolutions. In *The Pastime of Pleasure* (1509), for example, Hawes's pseudo-autobiographical persona, Graunde Amoure, is so much a function of his public role, so obviously part of a communal allegory, that 'he' is able to write about his own death in the first person, allegorizing it as a moral lesson for a public audience even as he experiences it at first hand ('But whan I thoughte longest to endure, / Dethe with his darte a rest me sodaynly'. 'Out of my body my soule thus it went').[34] Similarly, in Skelton's *Bowge of Courte*, the poet personifies himself as 'Drede', an 'I' who is simultaneously the site of the poem's subjectivity and part of a wider allegorical scheme—his eponymous anxiety seemingly being both a psychological drive and a psychomachian function of his role. And again, the curious conflation of self and role that this persona embodies allows the poet imaginatively to experience his own death, as Drede jumps over the rail of the ship at the end of the poem in a desperate attempt to escape the plotting of his enemies.[35]

That each of these early Tudor public autobiographical experiments should end with the poet writing about (and through) his own death, is suggestive of the problems implicit in this kind of courtly self-fashioning. The subjectivity of Hawes and Skelton did not involve looking inward from world to self, but was rather a profoundly outward looking vision, a writing of the self upon the poetic and cultural landscape. Such a movement could reach its ultimate end only in the loss of self, whether through a formal apotheosis, or the ultimate consummation of death. (In Skelton's *Garlande of Laurel*, the narrator is inducted into the pantheon of immortal poets by Fame at the request of Gower, Lydgate, and Chaucer; in Hawes' *Pastime* Fame eulogizes the fallen narrator alongside the Nine Worthies before Time enters to dismiss the significance of his story in the wider context of eternity.) Either way, the self ends as both more and less than itself, no longer a single subject but part of a wider universal order.

If imagining their own death within their fictions was the solution to the poetic dilemmas of this first generation of Tudor courtly makers, it was the prospect of a far more literal death that created the principal problems for Wyatt and Surrey. In the unprecedented political situation created by the Supremacy, their challenge was to find a way of writing the self that could address political issues but would not provoke an abrupt and violent brush with authority. Rather than seeking out royal attention and approval, as Skelton, Hawes, and Barclay had done (with varying degrees of success), and as Elyot was doing with a new and urgent frankness, Wyatt and Surrey sought to elide the King's functions as the principal validator of literary endeavour. Their energies were engaged in avoiding and circumventing the royal gaze and royal approval in a public arena in which they were almost ubiquitous. It is thus little surprise that translation of the psalms and of anti-curial satire became their ultimate recourse, both as a direct expression of the experience of imprisonment and desolation and as an emblematic reworking of the poet's role. The voice crying in the wilderness was one of the few obvious models of authorized utterance in the approved canon of biblical and classical literature that did not offer its testimony in direct address to political authority. The private space, the dark cave or the rural estate, the distance of isolation, these became the places of the poet, and, paradoxically, offered the readiest means for him to recreate a politically alert audience.

The circle of aristocratic, courtly readers that Wyatt and Surrey addressed in their lyrics, satires, and psalms, was thus a very different audience to the courtly readership sought by Skelton and Hawes. When Richard Tottel came to print those poems in his *Miscellany*, he portrayed it as a privileged clique that had jealously guarded precious texts whose 'stateliness of style' was 'removed from the rude skill [understanding] of common ears'. 'It resteth now (gentle reader)', his Preface declared:

that thou think it not evil done to publish to the honour of the English tongue, and for the profit of the studious of English eloquence, those works which the ungentle hoarders up of such treasure have heretofore envied thee.[36]

But Wyatt and Surry's original readers were no secretive coterie; they were, as we have seen, a cross section of the aristocrats, gentlemen, and civil servants at the heart of the court. What the poets had done was to address them, not as an audience of royal subjects, but as a readership of Englishmen, victims of the same despotic regime, and potential agents of its redemption. That they had thought it necessary, and found it possible to do so is a striking index of the impact of Henry VIII's government on English culture. If, as Maurice Latey suggests, tyranny is a kind of nervous breakdown in the body politic, then the work of Thynne, Tuke, and Heywood, Elyot, Wyatt and Surrey, shows just how aware Henry's subjects were of the nature of the illness, and how ready they were to prescribe its cure. In so doing they not only brought into being a new forum for serious political writing, they changed the face of English literature for ever.

Notes

INTRODUCTION

1. See, for example, Maurice Latey, *Tyranny: A Study in the Abuse of Power* (London, Macmillan, 1969), p. 195, where it is claimed that Henry VIII was 'the greatest of the English home-grown tyrants...He demonstrated many of the classic features of tyranny, above all the progressive corruption of power, aggravated by disease, which converted the brilliant and popular monarch of his younger days into the bloated, morose, and suspicious despot executing his adversaries...and potential rivals... burning for heresy and religious treason those, whether catholic or protestant, who disputed [the Royal Supremacy]'.
2. G. R. Elton, *Policy and Police: The Enforcement of the Reformation in the Age of Thomas Cromwell* (Cambridge, Cambridge University Press, 1973). For more recent explorations of reactions to the Reformation, see J. J. Scarisbrick, *The Reformation and The English People* (Oxford, Oxford University Press, 1984); C. Haigh, *English Reformations: Religion, Politics and Society under the Tudors* (Oxford, Oxford University Press, 1993); Eamon Duffy, *The Stripping of the Altars: Traditional Religion in England, 1400–1580* (New Haven, Yale University Press, 1992); and Ethan H. Shagan, *Popular Politics and The English Reformation* (Cambridge, Cambridge University Press, 2003). The most recent and substantial treatment is G.W. Bernard, *The King's Reformation* (Yale University Press, forthcoming). I am very grateful to Professor Bernard for the chance to read and cite his forthcoming study in the course of this book.
3. The founding text of this faith in the omnicompetence of rhetoric was Cicero's *De Oratore*, in which the author has Crassus observe, 'I think nothing is more admirable than being able, through speech, to have a hold on human minds, to win over their inclinations, to drive them at will in one direction, and to draw them at will from another...what could be...so powerful and so splendid as when a single man's speech reverses popular upheavals, the scruples of jurors, or the authority of the Senate?...I assert that the leadership and wisdom of the perfect orator provide the chief basis, not only for his own dignity, but also for the safety of countless individuals and of the state at large.' Cicero, *On the Ideal Orator*, ed. and trans. James M. May and Jakob Wisse (Oxford, Oxford University Press, 2001), pp. 64–5.

1. THE LONG DIVORCE OF STEEL

1. William Thomas*, The Pilgrim: A Dialogue on the Life and Actions of King Henry the Eighth*, ed., J. A Froude (London, Parker, Son, and Bourn, 1861), pp. 3–9.
2. Thomas, *The Pilgrim*, p. 9.
3. Ibid., p. 12.
4. *LP* IX 594; XII (ii) 908; Elton, *Policy and Police*, pp. 362–3.
5. E. W. Ives, *Anne Boleyn* (Oxford, 1986), p. 191.

6. Thomas Stapleton, *The Life of Sir Thomas More*, ed. E. E. Reynolds and trans. P. E. Hallet (London, 1966), p. 201; *LP* x 975.

7. *LP* xiv (ii) 454; see G.W. Bernard, *The King's Reformation* (New Haven, Yale University Press, forthcoming).

8. William Camden, *History of the Most Renowned and Victorious Princess Elizabeth* (London, 1675), p. 4.

9. *The History of the World*, quoted from Sir Walter Raleigh, *Selected Writings*, ed., G. Hammond (Harmondsworth, 1984), pp. 133–4.

10. The Act sought to give royal proclamations the same status and enforceability as Acts of Parliament. For Joel Hurstfield and others, it was an unsuccessful attempt by the Crown to secure greater 'arbitrary' powers to act independently of Parliament. For Professor Elton it was an attempt by Cromwell to demonstrate that only parliament could grant such powers, and so was an anti-despotic measure. So far advocates of the first position have had the better of the argument. See G.R. Elton, *England Under the Tudors* (London, 1955), p. 269ff; Elton, 'Henry VIII's Act of Proclamations', *EHR* 75 (1960), reprinted in Elton, *Studies in Tudor and Stuart Politics and Government* (4 vols., Cambridge, Cambridge University Press, 1974–92), i, pp. 339–54; and Elton, 'The Rule of Law in Sixteenth-Century England', in A. J. Slavin, ed., *Tudor Men and Institutions* (Baton Rouge, 1972), reprinted in *Studies*, i, pp. 260–84; Joel Hurstfield, 'Was There A Tudor Despotism After All?' *TRHS*, 5th Series (1966), pp. 83–108. On definitions of tyranny more generally, see Latey, *Tyranny*, p. 18: 'a tyrant is a ruler who exercises arbitrary power beyond the scope permitted by the laws, customs, and standards of his time and society and who does so with a view to maintaining or increasing that power.'

11. Thomas, *The Pilgrim*, p. 10. The argument stems ultimately from Plato's *Republic*, where the tyrant is described as a man dominated by desire and passion, lacking all self-restraint. Plato, *The Republic*, ed. I. A. Richards (Cambridge, Cambridge University Press, 1966), 573Bff.

12. Aquinas, *De Regimine Principum*, quoted in J. M. Blythe, ' "Civic Humanism" and Medieval Political Thought' in J. Hankins, ed., *Renaissance Civic Humanism: Reappraisals and Reflections* (Cambridge, Cambridge University Press, 2000), pp. 30–74, p. 37.

13. Again, the idea can be traced back to Plato's *Republic* (see 573cff); see also Rebecca W. Bushnell, *Tragedies of Tyrants: Political Thought and Theater in the English Renaissance* (Ithaca, Cornell University Press, 1990), pp. 10–11.

14. Clarence H. Miller, Leicester Bradner, Charles A. Lynch, and Revilo P. Oliver, eds., *Thomas More's Latin Poems*, The Complete Works of Thomas More volume 3, (New Haven, Yale University Press, 1984), p. 163.

15. Desiderus Erasmus, *The Education of a Christian Prince*, ed., Lisa Jardine (Cambridge, Cambridge University Press, 1997), pp. xii, 34, and 25. The ultimate source here was probably the eighth book of Aristotle's *Ethics*, where it is argued that the tyrant's intention is to pursue whatever brings him profit, while a king's is to do whatever is useful to his subjects.

16. *Complete Works of Thomas More*, iii, p. 165. See also Erasmus, *Education*, pp., 25–35.

17. The *locus classicus* of this model of courtiership is Baldasar Castiglione's *Book of the Courtier* (printed in 1528), especially Books ii and iv. Baldesar Castiglione, *The*

Courtier (Harmondsworth, Penguin, 1976). See also Lauro Martines, 'The Gentleman in Renaissance Italy: Strains of Isolation in the Body Politic', in Robert S. Kinsman, ed., *The Darker Vision of the Renaissance: Beyond the Fields of Reason* (Berkeley, University of California Press, 1974), pp. 77–93.

18. *LP* V 533; G. R. Elton, *Reform and Renewal: Thomas Cromwell and the Common Weal* (Cambridge, Cambridge University Press, 1973), pp. 41–2. Similarly, the first injunction addressed to the prince in Stephen Baron's *De Regimine Principum*, dedicated to Henry VIII in the year of his coronation, was to beware flatterers: 'the flatterer's tongue harms more than the persecutor's sword. Flatterers are scorpions, coaxing with their faces and striking with their tails'. Stephen Baron, *De Regimine Principum*, ed. and trans. P. J. Mroczkowski (New York, Peter Lang, 1990), p. 33.

19. J. A. Guy, 'Tudor Monarchy and Its Critiques', in J. A. Guy, ed., *The Tudor Monarchy* (London, Arnold, 1997), pp. 78–109; Hannah H. Gray, 'Renaissance Humanism: The Pursuit of Eloquence', *Journal of the History of Ideas* 24 (1963), pp. 497–514, p. 504.

20. Castiglione, *The Courtier*, p. 284.

21. Eramus, *Education*, p. 64.

22. Thomas Elyot, *Pasquil the Plain* (London, 1532), sig. A10 (v).

23. Roper, *Life of More*, pp. 56–7.

24. Erasmus, *Education*, p. 26.

25. D. R. Carlson, *The Latin Writings of John Skelton, Studies in Philology*, Texts and Studies, 4 (1991), p. 39.

26. Dermot Fenlon, 'Thomas More and Tyranny', *JEH* 32 (1981), pp. 453–76, pp. 455–6; J. A. Guy, *Reputations: Thomas More* (London, Edward Arnold, 2000), p. 49.

27. Erasmus, *Education*, p. 54.

28. F. M. Nichols, ed., *The Epistles of Erasmus* (3 vols., London, 1901–19) I, 457. Pollard, *Henry VIII*, p. 37; Marie Louise Bruce, *The Making of Henry VIII* (London, William Collins, 1977), p. 11.

29. Skelton, 'A Laud and Praise', lines 40–1, in John Scattergood, ed., *John Skelton: The Complete English Poems* (Harmondsworth, Penguin, 1983).

30. 'On the Coronation Day of Henry VIII, Most Glorious and Blessed King of the British Isles and of Catherine His Most Happy Queen, A Poetical Expression of Good Wishes by Thomas More of London', in Miller, et al., eds., *More's Latin Poems*, pp. 101 and 113.

31. Stanley Wells and Gary Taylor, eds., *The Oxford Shakespeare: The Complete Works* (Oxford, Clarendon Press, 1994). All quotations from Shakespeare's work are from this edition.

32. Skelton, 'A Laud and Praise', lines 23–5.

33. Miller, *et al.*, eds., *More's Latin Poems*, p. 107.

34. Pliny, *Letters and Panegyricus*, ed. B. Radice, Loeb Classical Library (Cambridge, Mass., Harvard University Press, 1969). See also David Rundle, ' "Not so much Praise as Precept": Erasmus, Panegyric, and the Renaissance Art of Teaching Princes', in Yun Lee Too and Niall Livingstone, eds., *Pedagogy and Power: Rhetorics of Classical Learning* (Cambridge, Cambridge University Press, 1998), pp. 148–69; James D. Garrison, *Dryden and the Tradition of Panegyric* (Berkeley, University of California Press, 1975), *passim*.

35. Miller, *et al.*, eds., *More's Latin Poems*, pp. 102 and 107.
36. *Venetian Calendar, 1527–83*, p. 293.
37. For the emulation of his forebears, see Stephen Gunn, 'The French Wars of Henry VIII', in J. Black, ed., *The Origins of War in Early Modern Europe* (Edinburgh, Edinburgh University Press, 1987), pp. 28–51; C. S. L. Davies, 'Henry VIII and Henry V: The Wars in France', in J. L. Watts, ed. *The End of the Middle Ages?* (Stroud, Sutton, 1988), pp. 235–62; and David Starkey, 'King Henry and King Arthur', *Arthurian Literature*, 16 (1998), pp. 171–96. For the Treaty of London of 1518, renamed by Wolsey with characteristic flamboyance as the Treaty of Universal Peace, see P. J. Gwyn, *The King's Cardinal* (London, Barrie and Jenkin, 1990), pp. 96–102, and Scarisbrick, *Henry VIII*, pp. 71–4.
38. Hall, *Chronicle*, p. 598. For a fuller account of this incident, see Greg Walker, 'The Expulsion of the Minions of 1519 Reconsidered', *Historical Journal* 32 (1988) pp. 1–16, reprinted in Walker, *Persuasive Fictions: Faction, Faith, and Political Culture in the Reign of Henry VIII* (Aldershot, Scolar Press, 1996), pp. 35–53.
39. Hall, *Chronicle*, p. 598.
40. W. Shakespeare, *Henry VIII*, i.iii.24–5, 32.
41. Hall, *Chronicle*, pp. 598–9.
42. C. L. Kingsford, *The First English Life of King Henry the Fifth* (Oxford, Oxford University Press, 1911), p. 19.
43. For the Grant and opposition to it, see G.W. Bernard, *War, Taxation, and Rebellion in Early Tudor England: Henry VIII, Wolsey, and the Amicable Grant of 1525* (Brighton, Harvester, 1986), *passim*.
44. Hall, *Chronicle*, pp. 694–703.
45. After a show of justice, the 'rebels' were pardoned, ostensibly at Queen Katherine's request. Thus Henry maintained his reputation for strong kingship, but the rebels got what they wanted. For a detailed analysis of this episode, see G. W. Bernard, *War, Taxation, and Rebellion*. In reality Henry had, of course, been involved in every stage of the demand, as the documents recently discovered by G.W. Bernard and R. Hoyle conclusively demonstrate. G. W. Bernard and R. Hoyle, 'The Instrument for the Levying of the Amicable Grant, March 1525', *Balletin of the Institute of Historical Research* 68 (1994), pp. 190–202.
46. See Sir John Fortescue, *On the Laws and Governance of England*, ed. Shelley Lockwood (Cambridge, Cambridge University Press, 1997), Introduction and *passim*.
47. P. L. Hughes and J. F. Larkin, eds., *Tudor Royal Proclamations* (3 vols., New Haven, Yale University Press, 1964), i, pp. 193–7, p. 194.
48. *LP* viii 921; Bernard, *The King's Reformation*.
49. *LP* xi 956.
50. *Spanish Calendar* iv (ii) 739, p. 175.
51. See, for example, *LP* v 466 and 1109.
52. *LP* v 819 and 820.
53. *LP* v 8181 and 1247.
54. *LP* v 1019; J. A. Muller, ed., *The Letters of Stephen Gardiner* (Westport, Conn., Greenwood Publishers, 1970), pp. 48–9.
55. For More, see *State Papers Henry VIII* vii 370 (*LP* v 1025); *LP* 1046, 1069, 1094. For Pole, *Spanish Calendar* iv (ii) 888 (*LP* v 737). Chapuys is the source of the claim that

Pole had refused the offer of the archbishopric of York because he could not agree with the King over the divorce. Henry had, the ambassador claimed, given Pole a licence to leave for Italy when he said that, if he was still in England when Parliament resumed in January/February 1532, he would have to attend and speak as his conscience prompted.

56. *Spanish Calendar* IV (ii) 646 (*LP* v 120). See also ibid. 962 (*LP* v 1109)

57. *LP* v 614 and 696; 238; *Spanish Calendar* IV (ii) 619 (*LP* v 70) and 739, p. 177.

58. *Spanish Calendar* IV (ii) 739, p. 177.

59. Joel T. Altman, *The Tudor Play of Mind: Rhetorical Enquiry and the Development of Elizabethan Drama* (Berkeley, University of California Press, 1978). Sir Thomas Elyot described the rhetorical exercises of the legal 'moots' of the Inns of Court in his *Book Named the Governor* (London, 1531), sig. Gviii(v) ff. A moot was, he said, a conscious harking back to the rhetorical practices of the classical period: 'a shadow or figure of the ancient rhetoric'.

60. T. W. Baldwin, *William Shakspere's Small Latine and Lesse Greeke* (2 vols, Urbana, Ill., University of Illinois Press, 1944), I, pp. 86–7, 88; Nicholas Orme, *Education and Society in Medieval and Renaissance England* (London, The Hambledon Press, 1989), pp. 130ff.

61. Erasmus, *The Right Way of Speaking Latin and Greek*, ed. and trans. Maurice Pope, in J. K. Sowards, ed., *The Collected Works of Erasmus: 26: Literary and Educational Writings 4* (Toronto, University of Toronto Press, 1985), p. 402. For the example of an informal disputation between two pupils noted in an early-Tudor schoolbook, see Orme, *Education and Society*, p. 141.

62. Cicero, *Orator*, p. 61. Richard Morison's translation of Vives's *Introduction to Wisdom* (1540) similarly advocated the keeping of a commonplace book as a store of terms, analogies, and *sententiae* gleaned from reading or the conversation of wise men to be drawn on in oration or argument. 'And if thou perceive anything taken of the wise sort, or to be spoken quickly [in a lively way], gravely, learnedly, wittily, comely, bear in mind that thou mayest, when thou shalt have occasion, use the same. Thou shalt have always at hand a proper book, wherein thou shalt write such notable things as thou readest thyself, or hearest of other men worthy to be noted, be it either feat sentence, or word, mete for familiar speech, that thou mayest have in a readiness when time requireth.' Richard Morison, *An Introduction to Wysedome, made by Ludovicus Vives* (London, 1540), sig. Cviii(v). See Willaim G. Crane, *Wit and Rhetoric in the Renaissance: The Formal Basis of Elizabethan Prose Style* (Edinburgh, Edinburgh University Press, 1937), p. 32.

63. Vives cited in Baldwin, *William Shakspere's Small Latine*, I, pp. 185–9, p. 194.

64. Baldwin, *William Shakspere's Small Latine*, II, p. 17; Nicholas Orme, *From Childhood to Chivalry: The Education of the English Kings and Aristocracy, 1066–1530* (London, Methuen, 1984), especially pp. 76, 129ff, and 185; Orme, *Education and Society*, p. 132.

65. Elyot, *Governor*, sigs. Eiv(v)–Ev.

66. J. M. Fletcher, 'The Faculty of Arts', in James McConica, ed., *The History of the University of Oxford: III: The Collegiate University* (Oxford, Clarendon Press, 1986), pp. 157–99, pp 168–70; John Barton, 'The Faculty of Law', in ibid., pp. 257–83, p. 270; and S. L. Greenslade, 'The Faculty of Theology', in ibid, pp. 295–334. For

the Inns, see Wilfrid R. Prest, *The Inns of Court Under Elizabeth I and the Early Stuarts* (London, Longman, 1972), especially pp. 116ff.

67. Altman, *The Tudor Play of Mind, passim*. For *Fulgens and Lucres*, see Greg Walker, ed., *Medieval Drama: An Anthology* (Oxford, Blackwell, 2000), pp. 305–47, lines 2210–2. Lucres's response is equally 'academic': 'I wyll not afferme the contrary for my hede, / For in that case there may be no comparison. But, never the lesse, I said this before…' (2216–18). For more general discussions of the importance of this rhetorical training, see Hanna H. Gray, 'Renaissance Humanism', pp. 497–514; Brian Vickers, *In Defence of Rhetoric* (Oxford, Clarendon Press, 1988), Dorothy H. Brown, *Christian Humanism in the late English Morality Plays* (Gainesville, Fl, University of Florida Press, 1999).

68. Thomas More, *Utopia and the Dialogue of Comfort Against Tribulation*, ed., Richard Marius (London, Dent Everyman, 1994), pp. 40 and 42.

69. Thomas M. C. Lawler, Germain Marc'Hadour, and Richard C. Marius, eds., *The Complete Works of St Thomas More: 6: A Dialogue Concerning Heresies* (2 vols., New Haven, Yale University Press, 1981), i, pp. 83, 159, 65, 154, 219, 274. For the stories cited and others, see ibid, pp. 69, 156–7, 297, 134 and 300ff respectively ('if there were a man of Inde [who] never cam out of his country, nor never had seen any white man or woman in his life…'; 'I put case that God would tell you two things; which of them would ye believe best?'; 'I put case now that ye had an inkling or else a plain warning, that some of them [the King's retinue] were his enemies that seemed his best friends…what would you now do…?').

70. More, *Dialogue*, pp. 156–7.

71. *LP* iv (ii) 4027.

72. *LP* xiii (i) 1141 and 1229.

73. *LP* x 346. For a discussion of the case, see Elton, *Policy and Police*, pp. 27–9.

74. There is a relatively full summary of the relevant document in *LP* v 1209. I am grateful to G. W. Bernard for providing a transcript of the original manuscript in the PRO.

75. Another good example of the dangers of giving free reign to this kind of scholarly criticism is provided by the case of Edward Harcocke, prior of the Blackfriars in Norwich. In a sermon delivered in April 1535 he seems to have let his taste for intellectual inquiry get the better of him. He is said to have told his audience that, 'ye shall pray for our sovereign lord, King Henry, of the Church Chief Head, so called. Here riseth a question: may the King be the head of the Church? To this grow two answers. Some say yea and some say nay. They that say nay have Scripture that teaches us Christ to be our Head of the Church…An earthly man, namely a temporal man, may not be Head of the Church. Notwithstanding, seeing that spiritual men have bodies that must be clothed and have bodily substance, the King is their head in temporalities and protector and defender of the same. But that the King should be head in ministering sacraments, or in incensing, or such other, I deny, and will in any place in this world.' (*LP* vii 595, quoted and re-dated to April 1535 in G. R. Elton, *Policy and Police: The Enforcement of the Reformation in the Age of Thomas Cromwell* (Cambridge, Cambridge University Press, 1972), pp. 16–17).

76. *LP* xiii (i) 981 (2).

77. Another advantage of such stories was that they were a common currency that crossed national boundaries. When Eustace Chapuys sought to persuade Henry to allow the Pope's mandates regarding the divorce to be intimated privately to an inner core of the King's ministers rather than forcing him to issue them publicly by refusing outright to receive them in England, he reached for a classical analogy, citing the example of Philip of Macedon, the father of Alexander the Great, who would not dismiss from his service a man who was continually criticizing his own acts and speaking ill of him, because, he said, he preferred the slanderer to remain where he was, and spread his calumnies within the precincts of the palace, to sending him away to spread them through the world. (*Spanish Calendar* IV (ii) 598 (*LP* v 45), 13 January 1531.)

78. *LP* XI 1244, p. 504; John Guy, 'The King's Council and Political Participation', in Alistair Fox and John Guy, *Reassessing the Henrician Age: Humanism, Politics, and Reform, 1500–1550* (Oxford, Basil Blackwell, 1986), pp. 121–47, p. 121.

79. Francis Bacon's aphorism is cited in J.A. Guy, *Tudor England* (Oxford, Oxford University Press, 1988), p. 296.

80. *Statutes of the Realm*, III, pp. 471ff; Elton, *Policy and Police*, pp. 222 and 227.

81. *LP* XIII (ii) 829 (ii).

82. Kenneth Muir, ed., *Life and Letters of Sir Thomas Wyatt* (Liverpool, Liverpool University Press, 1963), p. 126.

83. *LP* XIV (i), p. 126.

84. *Complete Works of Thomas More*, II, p. 93; see Fenlon, 'Thomas More and Tyranny', p. 473.

85. Erasmus, *Education*, p. 28.

2. A GIFT FOR KING HENRY VIII

1. *The Workes of Geffray Chaucer newly printed / with dyvers workes whilche were never in print before* (London, Thomas Godfray, 1532) *STC* 5068. The precise month of publication is unclear. The volume must have been in print before the publication of Thomas Berthelet's edition of Gower's *Confessio Amantis* (*Jo. Gower, de Confessione Amantis*, (London, 1532) *STC* 12143), because Berthelet referred to it in his preface. But, given that Berthelet's text cannot be dated precisely either, the best that can be said on this score is that the *Chaucer* almost certainly appeared before December 1532. The latter must have taken several months to run off in Godfray's print-shop. H. S. Bennett, *English Books and Readers* 2nd edition (2 vols., Cambridge, Cambridge University Press, 1969), I, pp. 228–9, estimates a production rate of one folio sheet per day. As Brian Donaghey notes, the Chaucer ran to almost 200 sheets, and so may well have taken up to seven months to produce. Brian Donaghey, 'William Thynne's Collected Edition of Chaucer: Some Bibliographical Considerations', in John Scattergood and Julia Boffey, eds., *Texts and Their Contexts: Papers from the Early Book Society* (Dublin, Four Courts, 1997), pp. 150–64, pp. 156–7. In what follows I will argue on internal evidence that at least the final quires and the preliminary material of the Chaucer volume were produced in June/July 1532 or soon thereafter.

2. F. J. Furnivall, ed., *Animadversions upon the Corrections of some Imperfectiones of Chaucers Workes . . . sett down by Francis Thynne*, EETS 9 (London, Kegan Paul,

Trench and Trubner, 1865), pp. 12 and 6 (Thynne had 'commission to search all the libraries of England for Chaucer's Works'). Some support for these claims is provided by the marginal note in Longleat House MS 258, a Chaucerian text ('Master Thynne, clerk of the kitchen to our Sovereign Lord, King Henry the Viiith [...] Thomas Godfray'), which suggests that it was in Thynne's possession at the time that the *Works* were in production. There is also evidence that he consulted the Longleat House copy of Caxton's edition of the *Boece*, and another manuscript, Glasgow University Library MS Hunterian v 3.7. See James Blodgett, 'William Thynne (d. 1546)' in Paul G. Ruggiers, ed., *Editing Chaucer: The Great Tradition* (Norman, Oklahoma, Pilgrim Books, 1984), pp. 35–52, p. 39, and James E. Blodgett, 'Some Printer's Copy for William Thynne's 1532 Edition of Chaucer', *The Library* 6th series, I (1979), pp. 97–113, *passim*. One of the stated reasons for the younger Thynne's praise of his father's antiquarian efforts must, however, be qualified in the light of subsequent research. Francis claimed that William's diligence in searching out exemplars could be judged from the note following the text of the *Squire's Tale*, that 'There can be found no more of this foresaid tale, which hath been sought in diverse places' (Thynne, *Animadversions*, p. 6, citing *Works*, fol. xxxii(v)). But, as Stephen Partridge has demonstrated, the annotation seems to have been copied directly from Wynkyn de Worde's earlier edition of *The Canterbury Tales*, where the *Squire's Tale* ends with a similar remark. See Stephen Partridge, 'Minding the Gaps: Interpreting the Manuscript Evidence of the *Cook's Tale* and the *Squire's Tale*', in A. S. G. Edwards, Vincent Gillespie, and Ralph Hanna, eds., *The English Medieval Book: Studies in Memory of Jeremy Griffiths* (London, The British Library, 2000), pp. 51–85. The most detailed account of Thynne's editorial practice is offered in James E. Blodgett's original doctoral thesis, 'William Thynne and his 1532 Edition of Chaucer', Indiana University Ph.D. thesis, 1975. I was fortunate enough to be able to read Dr Blodgett's invaluable analysis at a late stage in the revision of this chapter for publication.

3. Leland, cited in Caroline F. E. Spurgeon, ed., *Five Hundred Years of Chaucer Criticism and Allusion, 1357–1900* (3 vols., New York, Russell and Russell, 1960: first published, London, 1908–1912), I, p. cxvi, and Derek Brewer, ed., *Chaucer: The Critical Heritage*, (2 vols., London, Routledge and Kegan Paul, 1978) I, p. 94. For the full text, and the new translation of it here, see p. 62, below. I am grateful to Dr Anne Marie D'Arcy, Dr Helen Conrad-O'Brian, and Mr Joseph Pheifer for their generous work on the translation.

4. Spurgeon, *Five Hundred Years*, I, p. cxvi; Blodgett, 'William Thynne', pp. 35–52; Alice S. Miskimmin, *The Renaissance Chaucer* (New Haven, Yale University Press, 1975), pp. 244–5; A.S.G. Edwards, 'Chaucer from Manuscript to Print: The Social Text and the Critical Text', *Mosaic* 28 (1995), pp. 1–12, especially p. 12.

5. John Watkins has noted the cultural significance of the *Complete Works* idea ('modelled on European editions of Virgil's *Opera*, Thynne's massive folio volume endowed Chaucer with a canonical identity as a native, gothic laureate'). John Watkins, ' "Wrastling for this World": Wyatt and the Tudor Canonization of Chaucer', in Theresa M. Krier, ed., *Refiguring Chaucer in the Renaissance* (Gainesville, Florida, University of Florida Press, 1998), pp. 21–39, p. 23. As we shall see (pp. 62–3, below), Tuke's close friend and fellow antiquarian, Leland made explicit connection between Chaucer and Virgil in his commendatory verses on English poets, a collection that also

paid tribute to the 1532 edition. For the notion of Chaucer as the 'father' of English poetry, see A. C. Spearing, *Medieval to Renaissance in English Poetry* (Cambridge, Cambridge University Press, 1985), especially pp. 59–110 and 224ff; and Seth Lerer, *Chaucer and His Readers* (Princeton, Princeton University Press, 1993), *passim*.

6. Given Tuke's involvement in the Preface, which I shall explore in greater detail in Chapter Four, it is somewhat awkward to talk of its author as 'Thynne'. Rather than deploy potentially irritating prophylactic quotation marks around his name whenever I am referring to the author of the Preface and the editor of Chaucer, rather than the historical William Thynne, clerk of the royal kitchens, I shall leave the name unsullied by special punctuation, but on the understanding that (somewhat fittingly for the editor of a poet whom we have learned to bifurcate into a 'Chaucer the poet' who wrote *The Canterbury Tales*, and a 'Chaucer the Pilgrim' who narrates them) I am referring to a pseudo-fictional 'Thynne the Editor' who was, as I shall argue, a literary construct created by the combined authorship of Tuke and Thynne.

7. *Works*, fol. Aii. All quotations are from the facsimile edition edited by J.S. Brewer (J. S. Brewer, ed., *Geoffrey Chaucer: The Works, 1532* (Ilkley, Scolar Press, 1974)). I am grateful to the librarians of the Huntington Library, San Marino, California, The Harry Ransom Humanities Centre Library, the University of Texas, Austin, and Clare College Cambridge for the opportunity to consult the copies of the original text in their keeping.

8. For the concepts of the *translatio studii* and *translatio imperii*, see R. R. Bolger, *Classical Influences on European Culture, 500–1500* (Cambridge, Cambridge University Press, 1975); M. A. Freeman, *The Poetics of 'Translatio studii' and 'Conjointure'* (Lexington, 1979); E. R. Curtius, *European Literature and the Latin Middle Ages*, trans. W. R. Trask (London, 1953), esp. pp. 28ff; and E. Jeauneau, *Translatio Studii: The Transmission of Learning: A Gilsonian Theme* (Toronto, 1995).

9. *Works*, fols. Aii and (v). The allusion to the 'Englishman' who produced a French grammar is almost certainly to John Palsgrave, whose *Lesclarcissement de la langue Francoyse* (*STC* 19166) was printed by Richard Pynson and John Hawkyns in 1524 and 1530, respectively.

10. See, for example, T. J. Heffernan, 'Aspects of the Chaucerian Apocrypha: Animadversions on William Thynne's Edition of *The Plowman's Tale*', in R. Morse and B. Windeatt, eds., *Chaucer Traditions: Studies in Honour of Derek Brewer* (Cambridge, Cambridge University Press, 1990), pp. 155–67, p. 157 (which talks of 'William Thynne, acting in concert with the Henrician reforms'); Theresa M. Krier, 'Receiving Chaucer in Renaissance England', in Krier, ed., *Refiguring Chaucer*, pp. 1–18, pp. 9–10 (which claims the 1532 edition 'was one of the many autocratic, centralizing gestures of Henry's regime, and was intended to augment Henry's own glory and strength'); John Watkins, ' "Wrastling" ', pp. 22–3 ('Thynne's project . . . contributed directly to the centralization of the Tudor state by casting Chaucer as a champion of the King against the conflicting claims of church and nobility') and p. 24; Andrew N. Wawn, 'Chaucer, *The Plowman's Tale*, and Reformation Propaganda: The Testimonies of Thomas Godfray and *I Playne Piers*', *Bulletin of the John Rylands University Library of Manchester* 56 (1973–4), pp. 174–92; Robert Costomiris, 'The Influence of Printed Editions and Manuscripts on the Canon of William Thynne's *Canterbury Tales*', in Thomas A. Prendergast and Barbara Kline, eds.,

Rewriting Chaucer: Authority and the Idea of the Authentic Text, 1400–1602 (Colum-
bus, Ohio, Ohio State University Press, 1999), pp. 237–57, especially 246–8; R. F.
Yeager, 'Literary Theory at the Close of the Middle Ages: William Caxton and
William Thynne', *Studies in the Age of Chaucer* 6 (1984), pp. 135–64, especially
150–1; Brian Cummings, 'Reformed Literature and Literature Reformed', in David
Wallace, ed., *The Cambridge History of Medieval English Literature* (Cambridge,
Cambridge University Press, 1999), pp. 821–51; Seth Lerer, *Courtly Letters in the
Age of Henry VIII: Literary Culture and the Arts of Deceit* (Cambridge, Cambridge
University Press, 1997), especially p. 187; A. S. G. Edwards, 'Dunbar, Skelton, and
the Nature of Court Culture in the Early Sixteenth Century', in Jennifer Britnell and
Richard Britnell, eds., *Vernacular Literature and Current Affairs in the Early Sixteenth
Century: France, England, and Scotland* (Aldershot, Ashgate, 2000), pp. 120–34,
especially 129–31. For the most recent restatements of this claim, see David Starkey,
'The English Historian's Role and the Place of History in English National Life', *The
Historian*, Autumn, 2001, pp. 6–15, p. 9; and James Simpson, *Reform and Cultural
Revolution: The Oxford English Literary History: 2: 1350–1547* (Oxford, Oxford
University Press, 2002), p. 41. For the contrary view, see Blodgett, 'William Thynne
and his 1532 Edition', pp. 258 ('the bulk of Thynne's edition does not reflect
political motives, largely, of course, since Chaucer's works reflect no such motives')
and 261 ('the English Reformation, barely getting under way in 1532, seems to have
little affected Thynne's edition').

11. See Spearing, *Medieval to Renaissance in English Poetry*, and Lerer, *Chaucer and His
Readers, passim.*

12. *Spanish Calendar* IV (ii) 429, 433, and 598 (*LP* V 45).

13. The *Collectanea* also cited Constantine as the imperial ruler who had ordered church
councils to be held in all provinces of the western Church. For the *Collectanea*, see
Graham Nicholson, 'The Act of Appeals and the English Reformation', in Claire
Cross, David Loades, and J. J. Scarisbrick, eds., *Law and Government Under the
Tudors: Essays Presented to Sir Geoffrey Elton on his Retirement* (Cambridge, Cambridge University Press, 1988), pp. 19–30. Valla's treatise was to be published in
English by Thomas Godfray in 1534: L. Valla, *A Treatise of the donation or gyfte and
endowme[n]t of possessions gyven unto Sylvester Pope of Rhome by Constantine, emperor
of Rome* (London, Thomas Godfray for William Marshall, 1534), STC 5641.

14. *LP* V 216. The allusion was probably to Constantine's handling of the dispute begun
in AD 313 between the Donatists and Caecilian, bishop of Carthage. When the
former petitioned the Emperor with charges against Caecilian, Constantine refused
to judge it himself, but empowered a series of ecclesiastical panels to settle the case,
culminating in a trial in Arles on 1 August 314. There he, appearing in person,
declared, 'that the judgement of the priests should be regarded as if God himself were
in the judge's seat'. (M. Edwards, ed. and trans., *Optatus: Against the Donatists*
(Liverpool, 1997), Appendix 5.) The Henrician preacher consequently had a
point. But against this Henry might have cited the fact that, as the result of a further
appeal against the Arles judgement, Constantine did intervene and interrogated
Caecilian and his followers personally. Moreover, Bishop Eusabius of Caesarea
spoke of how the Emperor, 'like some general bishop constituted by God, convened
synods of his ministers'. (Eusebius of Caesarea, *De vita Constantinii*, line 44: E. C.

Richardson, trans, *The Life of Constantine*, in P. Schaff and H. Wave, eds, *A Select Library of Post-Nicene Fathers of the Christian Church*, series 2:1, (New York, 1890), pp. 471–559). For an excellent discussion of Constantine's ecclesiastical policies, see H. A. Drake, *Constantine and the Bishops: The Politics of Intolerance* (Baltimore, Johns Hopkins University Press, 2000).

3. THE SIGNS OF THE WORLD

1. C. St German, *A Treatise Concernynge the Division Between the Spiritualitie and Temporality* (London, Thomas Berthelet, 1532), *STC* 21587.5.
2. Hall, *Chronicle*, p. 764.
3. Hall, *Chronicle*, pp. 767–8. The additional complaints against Wolsey's jurisdiction voiced in both the Lords and Commons in 1529 could only have added to the anticlerical climate.
4. *LP* IV (iii) 6011; C. Haigh, *English Reformations: Religion, Politics, and Society Under the Tudors* (Oxford, Oxford University Press, 1993), pp. 96–7; *Spanish Calendar* IV (I) 228; Simon Fish, *The Supplication for the Beggars*, printed in *EHD* v, p. 676.
5. See, for example, the petition discovered by Richard Hoyle, described in R. Hoyle, 'The Origin of the Dissolution of the Monasteries', *Historical Journal* 38 (1995), pp. 275–305, especially pp. 284–5. For Darcy's memorandum, see the transcript in J. A. Guy, *The Public Career of Sir Thomas More* (New Haven, Yale University Press, 1980), pp. 206–7. For the murder of Dr Miles, see Susan Brigden, *London and The Reformation* 2nd edition (Oxford, Clarendon Press, 1991), p. 172, which provides a good sense of the religious ferment in the capital at this time.
6. Hall, *Chronicle*, p. 771; Paul L. Hughes and James F. Larkin, eds., *Tudor Royal Proclamations* (3 vols., New Haven, Yale University Press, 1964), I, pp. 193–7; *Venetian Calendar* III, p. 642; *Spanish Calendar* IV (i) 820–1, 847–8; Susan Brigden, 'Thomas Cromwell and the "Brethren" ', in Cross, Loades, and Scarisbrick, *Law and Government under the Tudors*, pp. 31–49; *LP* v 522, 583, 589, 929.
7. *LP* v 618 and 607.
8. *LP* v 533, 574, 618.
9. Thomas M. C. Lawler, Germain Marc'Hadour, and Richard Marius, eds., *The Complete Works of St Thomas More: 6: A Dialogue Concerning Heresies* (2 vols., New Haven, Yale University Press, 1981), I, p. 374.
10. *Spanish Calendar* IV (ii) 865 (*LP* v 593); 664 (*LP* v 148); IV (i) 547.
11. Thomas Starkey, *A Dialogue Between Pole and Lupset*, ed., T. F. Mayer, Camden Society 4th series, 37 (London, Royal Historical Society, 1989), pp. 56 and 58.
12. *Spanish Calendar* IV (ii) 646; *LP* IV (iii) 6047 (3); Hall, *Chronicle*, pp. 780–1 and 784; *Venetian Calendar* IV, 668, 773, and 701.
13. Brigden, *London and The Reformation*, p. 208.
14. More, *Complete Works*, 6, p. 296.
15. St German, *A Treatise*, printed in J. B. Trapp, ed., *The Complete Works of Thomas More*, 9 (New Haven, Yale University Press, 1979), pp. 176–212, sig. Aii.
16. *LP* v, 50; S. E. Lehmberg, *The Reformation Parliament, 1529–1536* (Cambridge, Cambridge University Press, 1976), pp. 120–1; J. A. Guy, 'The Public Context of *The Debellation*', in J. A. Guy, C. H. Miller, and R. McGugan, eds., *The Complete*

Works of Thomas More, x (New Haven, Yale University Press, 1987), p. xxiiiff. Note also *A Dyalogue between one Clemente, clerke of Convocacyon and one Bernarde, a burges[s] of Parlyment, disputyng betweene them what auctoryte the clergye have to make lawes, and howe farre and where theyr power doth extende*, STC 6800.3, the work of a common lawyer anxious to limit the scope of the ecclesiastical courts' jurisdiction. Brigden, *London and the Reformation*, p. 176.

17. *E.H.D.* v, pp. 732–3.
18. *E.H.D.* v, pp. 734–6. A series of specific measures to limit the jurisdiction and prerogatives of the church courts is set out on pp. 734–5.
19. *E.H.D.* v, p. 733.
20. *Spanish Calendar* IV (ii) 926 (*LP* v 898) and 907 (*LP* v 886).
21. *LP* v 1017.
22. Hall, *Chronicle*, p. 788.
23. Hall, *Chronicle*, pp. 788–9.
24. *Spanish Calendar* IV (ii) 951 (*LP* v 1013); *LP* 1023, 1025, and 1029. Edward Carpenter, *A House of Kings: The History of Westminster Abbey* (London, John Baker, 1966), pp. 92 and 106. Islip had been formally elected abbot in October 1500, although he had been acting informally in that capacity for much of the previous year. The procession of clergy and London layfolk that accompanied his corpse from his house at Neyte to the abbey for burial is said to have filled the entire thoroughfare from Chelsea to Westminster.
25. *LP* v 50.
26. BL MS Cleopatra F II, 223 (*LP* v 49)
27. *State Papers* VII 349 (*LP* v 831); *LP* v 276, VI 433, and VII 411; G.R. Elton, *Policy and Police: The Enforcement of the Reformation in the Age of Thomas Cromwell* (Cambridge, Cambridge University Press, 1972), p. 114; *LP* IX 1059.
28. *Spanish Calendar* IV (ii) 898 (*LP* V 723). As G. W. Bernard and Richard Rex have each argued, Henry's religious policy was from this point increasingly characterized by the desperate search for obedience and order, and the finding of a 'middle way' between radicalism and Rome to which all of his subjects could subscribe and which would still the waters that his divorce campaign and the Break with Rome had enraged. G. W. Bernard, 'The Making of Religious Policy, 1533–1546: Henry VIII and the Search for the Middle Way', *HJ* 41 (1998), pp. 321–49; Bernard, 'The Piety of Henry VIII', in N. Scott Amos, Andrew Pettegree, and Henk van Nierop, eds., *The Education of a Christian Society: Humanism and the Reformation in Britain and the Netherlands* (Aldershot, Ashgate, 1999), pp. 62–88; Bernard, 'The Church of England, c. 1529–c. 1649', *History* 75 (1990), pp. 183–206, reprinted in Bernard, *Power and Politics in Tudor England* (Aldershot, Ashgate, 2002), pp. 191–216; and Richard Rex, *Henry VIII and the English Reformation* (Basingstoke, Macmillan, 1993). For the call for reconciliation, see, for example, Richard Sampson's *Oratio* (1534) (*STC* 21681) which called for obedience to the prince based on the words of John 13:34: 'A new commandment I give unto you: that you love one another as I have loved you . . .' (cited in Elton *Policy and Police*, p. 181). On 7 January 1536 a royal circular letter to all bishops instructed them to suppress contentious sermonizing from both sides of the doctrinal divide, and especially those preachers who 'treat and dispute such matters as do . . . engender a contrariety' (*LP* VII 750, re-dated to 1536 in Elton, *Policy and Police*, p. 244).

29. *LP* v 216.

30. *Spanish Calendar* IV (ii) 739, p. 177 (*LP* v 286).

31. Hall, *Chronicle*, p. 788; *Spanish Calendar* IV (ii) 948 (*LP* v 989).

32. *Spanish Calendar* IV (ii) 648 (*LP* v 124); *LP* v 387 and p. xvi; Hall, *Chronicle*, pp. 783–4.

33. *Spanish Calendar* IV (ii) 888 (*LP* v 737).

34. *Spanish Calendar* IV (ii) 808 (*LP* v 478).

35. Hall, *Chronicle*, pp. 783–4.

36. *LP* v 525.

37. *The Determinations of the moste famous and mooste excellent Universities of Italy and Fraunce that it is so unlefull for a man to marie his brother's wyfe, that the Pope hath no power to dispence therwith* (London, Berthelet, 7 November, 1531), *STC* 14287, and *A Glasse of the Truth* (London, Berthelet, 1532), *STC* 11918.

38. A. W. Pollard and G. R. Redgrave, eds., *The Short Title Catalogue of Books Printed in England, Scotland, and Ireland, 1475–1640*, 2nd edition, revised and enlarged by W. A. Jackson, F. S. Ferguson, and K. F. Pantzer (London, 1976).

39. Frith's *Revelation* is *STC* 11394. Fish's *Supplication* (printed by J. Grapheus), is *STC* 10883, and his *Summe of the Holye Scripture* is *STC* 3036.

40. William Tyndale, *The Pentateuch*, *STC* 2350; *The Practyse of Preleates*, *STC* 244; *A Proper Dyalogue... [with] An ABC*, *STC* 1462.3 and 1462.5; Richard Ullerston (d. 1423), *A Compendious Olde Treatyse shewynge howe that we ought to have ye scrypture in Englysshe*, *STC* 3021; George Joye, *The Psalter of David in Englisshe* (Antwerp, Martin de Keyser), *STC* 2370; Colet, *The Sermon of Doctor Colete made to the Convocacion at Pauls* (London, Thomas Berthelet), *STC* 5550.

41. W. Tyndale, *Exposition of the First Epistle of St John* (Antwerp, Martin de Keyser, 1531), *STC* 2443; Tyndale, *The Prophete Jonas* (Antwerp, de Keyser, 1531), *STC* 2788; Tyndale, *An Answere Unto Sir Thomas More's Dialogue* (Antwerp, S. Cock, 1531); George Joye, *The Prophete Isaye, translated into Englisshe* (Antwerp, de Keyser, 1531), *STC* 2777; Joye, *The Letters which Johan Ashwell, Priour of Newnham Abbey, besid[e]s Bedforde, sent secretly to the Bishope of Lyncolne... Where in the said Priour accuseth George Joye... of Fower Opinio[n]s: with the answer of the said george un to the same...* (Antwerp, de Keyser, 1531), *STC* 845; John Frith, *A Disputacio[n] of Purgatorye* (Antwerp, S. Cock, 1531), *STC* 113861.5; Robert Barnes, *Supplication* (Antwerp, S. Cock, 1531), *STC* 1470.

42. *A Compendious olde Treatyse*, sigs A6–A6v; Anne Hudson, ' "No Newe Thyng": The Printing of Medieval Texts in the Early Reformation Period', in Douglas Gray and E. G. Stanley, eds., *Middle English Studies Presented to Norman Davis in Honour of his Seventieth Birthday* (Oxford, Clarendon Press, 1983), pp. 153–74, p. 157.

43. *The Examinacion of Master William Thorpe, preste, accused of heresye before Thomas Arundel, Archebishop of Ca[n]terbury, the yere of ower Lorde MCCCC and seven, [with] the Examinacion of the honourable knight, Syr Jhon Oldcastell, Lorde Cobham, burnt bi the said Archebishop, in the fyrste yere of Kynge Henry the Fyfth* (Antwerp, J. Hoochstraten), *STC* 24045, and *The Lantern of Light* (London, Robert Redman) (dated *c.* 1535 by *STC*, but probably somewhat earlier) *STC* 15225, respectively. See L. M. Swindurburn, ed., *The Lantern of Light*, EETS os 151 (London, Kegan Paul, Trench, and Trubner, 1917); *The Praier and Compleynte of the Ploweman unto Christe*

(Antwerp, ?von Hoochstraten, 1531), *STC* 20036 and (London, Thomas Godfray, 1532), *STC* 20036.5; *The Plowman's Tale* (London, Thomas Godfray, 1532–3) *STC* 5099.5; Steven Justice, 'Lollardy' in Wallace, *Cambridge History*, pp. 662–89, especially, pp. 687–71, Hudson, 'No Newe Thyng', p. 162.

44. *A Proper Dyaloge*, sig. c6v, quoted in Hudson, 'No Newe Thyng', p. 160.

45. Hudson, 'No Newe Thyng', p. 157.

46. See Hudson, 'No Newe Thyng', *passim*; John N. King, *English Reformation Literature: The Tudor Origins of the Protestant Tradition* (Princeton, Princeton University Press, 1982), pp. 51–2; and, for an account of one *Piers Plowman* manuscript produced in 1531–32, Thorlac Turville-Petre, 'Sir Adrian Fortescue and His Copy of *Piers Plowman*', *Yearbook of Langland Studies* 14 (2000), pp. 29–48.

47. *LP* V, Appendix, 18; Hughes and Larkin, *Proclamations*, I, pp. 193–7.

48. St German's *Treatise* and Skot's *Abuses* are *STC* 10421.5 and 21587.5, respectively. For Tunstal's register, see Anne Hudson, *The Premature Reformation: Wycliffite Texts and Lollard History* (Oxford, Clarendon Press, 1988), p. 490.

49. Fisher, *Two Fruitful Sermons* (W. Rastell, 1532), *STC* 10909; More's *Confutation*, *STC* 18079 was printed in London by William Rastell, Abell's *Invicta Veritas*, *STC* 61, was produced in Antwerp or Luneburg.

50. John Lydgate, *The Serpent of Division* (London, Robert Redman, *c.* 1535) *STC* 17027.5

51. See, for example, C. Haigh, 'Anticlericalism and the English Reformation', published most accessibly in C. Haigh, ed., *The English Reformation Revised* (Cambridge, Cambridge University Press, 1987), pp. 56–74.

52. More, *Complete Works* 6, I, pp. 31–2.

53. *LP* VII 953; Elton, *Policy and Police*, p. 280.

54. *LP* V, Appendix, 14 and 10. The latter is a letter of 13 June 1531 from Thomas Cranmer to the Earl of Wiltshire, describing Pole's project. At the other confessional extreme, Simon Fish's *Supplication for the Beggars* was condemned by More as offering 'sedition under colour of counsel' (More, *The Supplication of Souls* (1529), printed in Frank Manley *et al*, eds., *The Complete Works of St Thomas More volume 7: Letter to Bugenahgen; Supplication of Souls* (New Haven, Yale University Press, 1991).

55. E. V. Hitchcock, ed., *The Lyfe of Sir Thomas Moore, Knight, written by William Roper, Esquire*, EETS os 197 (Oxford, Oxford University Press, 1935), p. 21.

56. For a detailed account of Elyot and Heywood's writing in this context, see Greg Walker, 'Dialogue, Resistance, and Accommodation: Conservative Literary Responses to the Henrician Reformation', in Amos, Pettegree, and van Nierop, *The Education of a Christian Society*, pp. 89–111; and Walker, *The Politics of Performance in Early Renaissance Drama* (Cambridge, Cambridge University Press, 1998), pp. 76–116.

57. This and all the following quotations from Heywood's plays are taken from Richard Axton and Peter Happé, eds., *The Plays of John Heywood* (Cambridge, D. S. Brewer, 1991).

58. More, *Complete Works*, 6, p. 98. The importance of the claim to More, and its association in his mind with Chaucer, is suggested by the fact that it is restated, and in precisely the same terms, at p. 217.

59. Thomas Elyot, *Pasquil the Plain* (London, Thomas Berthelet, 1533), *STC* 7672.5, sigs A3v–A4 ('Lord, what a discord is between these two books: yet a great deal more

is there in thine apparel. And yet most of all between the book in thy hand ['*Novum Testamentum*'] and thy conditions. As God help me, as much as between truth and leesing [lies].').

4. READING CHAUCER IN 1532

1. See, for example, John N. King, *English Reformation Literature: The Tudor Origins of the Protestant Tradition* (Princeton, Princeton University Press, 1982), pp. 306 and 400.
2. Larry D. Benson, *et al.*, eds., *The Riverside Chaucer* 3rd edition (Boston, Houghton Mifflin, 1987), p. 328.
3. Foxe, *Acts and Monuments*, IV, p. 250.
4. A. S. G. Edwards, 'Chaucer from Manuscript to Print: The Social Text and the Critical Text', *Mosaic* 28 (1995), p. 1–12.
5. John Leland, *Commentarii de Scriptoribus Britannicus* [*c*. 1545], see p. 62, below.
6. Thynne, *Animadversions*, p. 6.
7. *Works*, fol. Aii. The syntax is uncertain, but the note seems to mean, following the original punctuation, that Tuke provided the preface for the person who was at the time of its composition ('then being') Master (or Chief) Clerk of the Kitchen (i.e. Thynne, who was to be promoted to Clerk Controller of the Household in 1536 and Master of the Household in 1540), while he, Tuke, was tarrying for the tide at Greenwich. The implication being that Tuke wrote the note at some point after Thynne had been promoted in 1536 and before he himself died in October 1545. The alternative reading: that 'then being' should apply to 'tarrying' (i.e. that Tuke had 'then been tarrying for the tide', or that Thynne had been tarrying and so Tuke had written the request in his absence) seems less attractive. For the latter suggestion, see Yeager, 'Literary Theory', p. 158, where it is suggested that Tuke's writing of the Preface was an unplanned and pragmatic response to a need to produce a text for the printer at a time when Thynne was stuck in Greenwich by the tide. David Starkey's recent assertion that Tuke's note is dated, and so 'we can tell the exact minute at which it was written' is, unfortunately, mistaken. (D. Starkey, 'The English Historian's Role and the Place of History in English National Life', *The Historian* (2001), pp. 6–15). Starkey's further claim that 'The author's copy of the book survives in the library of Emmanuel College, Cambridge, where it is inscribed "written by me waiting for the turning of the tide at Greenwich" ' (ibid) should be treated with similar caution.
8. Tuke was born *c*. 1475. In September 1538 he talked of his father, Richard Tuke (d. 1498?) being 'a gentleman born of the county of Kent' with claims to lands near Hythe and Sandwich (*State Papers*, I, p. 585). He was a Commissioner of the Peace for the counties of Essex and/or Kent from the early 1510s onwards, also acting in that capacity for Middlesex and Surrey at various points in the 1520s (*LP* III (ii) 3586; IV (i) 1136; IV (iii), p. 3076; V 1694). In November 1533 he became Sheriff of Essex and Hertfordshire. He seems to have been knighted in 1518 (but see *LP* IV (ii) 6513 and p. 3076 which suggest 1528–9). In the subsidy returns of 1524 he was valued at the very respectable sum of £1,000 (*LP* IV (i) 969). In November 1527, he was considered influential enough to be granted a pension from the French Crown (*LP* IV (ii) 3619). He was among those giving a personal gift to the King as part of the New Year's Day

ceremony of 1532, presenting six sovereigns in a red satin glove (*LP* v, 666). He was to die at his house at Layer Marney on 26 October 1545. For the above and the information in the following paragraph, see DNB and New Oxford DNB, Tuke, Brian; and *LP* III (ii) 2894, 2965, 3558.

9. In May and June 1528 he was appointed co-commissioner with Bishop Cuthbert Tunstal to negotiate a treaty with the Low Countries and France. See *LP* IV (ii) 4280, 4332, 4376, 4385. The degree of Henry's trust in (and reliance upon) Tuke can also be judged from the fact that, when in June 1528 the King decided to revise his will, it was Tuke whom he summoned to draft it, despite the fact that the secretary was currently bedridden with a bladder infection ('a disease *in vesica*') and unable to travel. (*LP* IV (ii) 4332, 4358). Declining Henry's offer of a litter to convey him, Tuke travelled to the court, which was then at Hunsdon, by mule, moving 'at a foot pace, with marvellous pain' and voiding blood '*per virgam*'. On arrival, on 20 June, he was placed in a chamber directly below Henry's privy lodgings so that he might be at hand night and day, and was put to work at once, with dishes being sent down to him from the King's table at every meal. There he worked, sleeping on a camp bed, until he fell ill of the sweat *c.* 26 June, at which point the King hurriedly decamped for first Hertford, then Hatfield, to escape the contagion, leaving Tuke to make his way painfully back home. (*State Papers*, i, 293 (*LP* IV (ii) 4404); *LP* IV (ii) 4405, 4429, 4510). On 15 July Tuke was still reporting discomfort from his ailments, complaining to his fellow secretary and former employee Thomas Derby that he had tried two days previously to sit upon his mule, 'but it would not be; I am yet so tender underneath, where was like to have been a fistula'. (*LP* IV (ii) 4518).

10. See *State Papers* i cxlvii, p. 300 (Muriel St Clare Byrne, *Letters of Henry VIII* (London, 1968), pp. 73–4). Tuke wrote to Wolsey in July 1528 describing how the King 'cometh by my chamber door, and doth for the most part, going and coming, turn in for the devising with me upon his book and other things occurent'.

11. *LP* v, 488; *Spanish Calendar* IV (ii), 814.

12. *LP* v, 171; Hall, *Chronicle*, pp. 775–82.

13. Anthony Wood was to claim that Thynne 'was, as it seems . . . educated among the Oxonians for a time, afterwards retiring to the Court', suggesting that a formal scholarly training underpinned his 'amateur' endeavours in literary collecting and editing. Wood, *Athenae Oxonienses* (2 vols., Oxford, 1692), i, p. 1368. Blodgett has argued convincingly that the edition shows evidence of scholarly knowledge in its use of Livy's *History* in its revisions to *The Physician's Tale*, where the staunchly medieval-sounding 'churl' was systematically replaced by the more satisfyingly classical 'client', and 'Zanis' is amended to 'Zeusis' ('a learned form closer . . . to the classical Latin form of the Greek name') (Blodgett, 'William Thynne and his 1532 Edition', p. 204). The French text of *The Romance of the Rose* may also have been consulted to supplement doubtful readings in Chaucer's translation (ibid., p. 209).

14. Why Leland should have named Bertholet rather than Godfray as the printer is unclear. Perhaps it was simply a slip of either the pen or the memory. T. R. Lounsbury suggested a confusion of the Chaucer *Works* with Berthelet's edition of Gower's *Confessio Amantis* published in the same year. (Lounsbury, *Studies in Chaucer, His Life and Writings* (3 vols., New York, Russell and Russell, 1892), p. 147.) But it may be that, as Andrew Wawn has suggested (Andrew Wawn, 'Chaucer, *The Plowman's Tale*

and Reformation Propaganda: The Testament of Thomas Godfray and *I Playne Piers*', *Bulletin of the John Rylands Library* 56 (1973), pp. 174–92, pp. 177–83), Bertholet was also involved in the publication in some way. He may have taken a share in the financial risks of so large a project in return for a percentage of the profits. He seems also to have loaned some of the woodcuts used in the volume to Godfray at around this time. Thynne, *Animadversions*, p. xxvi.

15. '*Vicit tamen Caxodunicam editionem Bertholetus noster opera Gulielmi Thynni; qui, multo labore, sedulitate ac cura usus in perquirendis vetustis exemplaribus, multa primae adjecit editioni. Sed nec in hac parte caruit Brianus Tucca, mihi familiaritate conjunctissimus, et Anglicae linguae eloquentia mirificus, sua Gloria, edita in postremam impressionem praefatione elimata, luculenta, eleganti.*' Leland, *Commentarie de Scriptoris Britannicis* [*c*. 1545]. The passage is translated somewhat differently in Brewer, ed., *Chaucer: The Critical Heritage*, I, p. 94. I am grateful to my colleague Dr Anne Marie D'Arcy, and, via her good offices, to Dr Helen Conrad-O'Briain and Mr Joseph Donovan Pheifer of Trinity College Dublin for their advice and guidance in teasing out Leland's Latin syntax.

16. Thynne, *Animadversions*, p. 6.

17. Leland would, indeed, go on to praise Tuke's learning and scholarship in a number of the nine Latin poems addressed to him in the 1530s. See below, n. 20. That Tuke was a scholar of some renown is clear from a variety of sources. In addition to his linguistic skills (he could speak (and perhaps write) Spanish as well as Latin and French) he was also an antiquarian and collector of manuscripts. Leland states that Tuke obtained a copy of Adam Murimuth for him, and, in his *Chronicles*, Raphael Holinshed credited the secretary as the source of a manuscript copy of one of the three, now lost, histories of Babylon by Berosus, the Greek historian of the third century BC. See May McKisack, *Medieval History in the Tudor Period* (Oxford, Clarendon Press, 1971), p. 10, and the valuable information made available by M. Gascoigne at http://www.write-on.co.uk/history/berosus.html. The DNB asserts that Tuke was the author of an antiquarian work critical of Polydor Vergil's *Anglica Historia*, but offers no source for the claim.

18. '*Virgilii Carmen quod non violaverit ignis, / Tucca dedit: tu das Bacchica serta mihi. / Quilibet è doctis versus servaret ab igne, / Principis est hederam sed tribuisse viri. / Quanto privatus minor extat principe tanto / Maior Romano, Tucca Britannus erit.*' John Leland, *Principum, Ac Illustrium aliquot et eruditorum in Anglia virorum, encomia, Trophaea, Genethliaca, et Epithalamia, A Joanne Lelando, Antiquario conscripta nunc primum in lucem edita,* (London, Thomam Orwinum, 1589). Thanks once again to Dr Helen Conrad-O'Briain and to Professor David Wilson-Okamura for their help with the translation of this verse, and to Dr D'Arcy for suggesting the significance of the allusion to Tucca to me.

19. Suetonius, *The Life of Virgil*, in J. C. Rolfe, ed. and trans., *Suetonius*, Loeb Classical Library revised edition (3 vols., Cambridge, Mass, Harvard University Press, 1997), III, pp. 455–6.

20. Leland, *Principium, Ac Illustrium Aliquot et Eroditorum in Anglia*, p. 79. '*In Laudem Gallifrodi* Chauceri, *Isiaci*': '*Dum iuga montis aper frondes dum laeta volucris, / Squamiger et liguidas piscis amabit aquas . . . , / . . . Latinae / Gloria Virgilius maxima semper erit. / Nec minus et noster Galfridus summa Britannae / Chaucerus Musae gratia*

semper erit.... ' ('While the boar will love mountain ridges, / While the joyous bird will love leafy branches, / [Or] scaly fish will love running water, / Virgil will always be the greatest glory of the Latin [language]. / And no less will our Geoffrey Chaucer, by grace of the Muses, be the greatest [glory] of the British [tongue].'). Thanks again to Helen Conrad-O'Briain and Professor Wilson-Okamura for help with this translation.

21. Suetonius, *Life of Virgil*, p. 455.

22. Of those scholars who have allowed Tuke a role in the project, Donaghey, following Francis Thynne's account in the *Animadversions*, was prepared to suggest in passing that Tuke 'helped' Thynne in unspecified ways (Donaghey, 'William Thynne's Collected Edition', p. 151), and Blodgett speculated that Tuke might have been employed by Thynne as a 'learned corrector' of his Latin rubrics—which are heavily corrected in the surviving manuscript exemplars—although he went on to suggest that Thynne himself, or an unknown third party might equally well have performed that role. Blodgett, 'Some Printer's Copy', p. 112. The possibility that Tuke was the corrector of rubrics was advanced more tentatively in Blodgett, 'William Thynne and his 1532 Edition', pp. 76–7.

23. Donaghey, 'William Thynne's Collected Edition', pp. 150–64.

24. It may well, for example, have been Tuke who obtained the manuscript of religious and moral texts, including Chaucer's *Melibee* and *Monk's Tale* (now Huntington Library HM 144), which seems to have been used in the preparation of the *Works*. Tuke was a fellow Commissioner of the Peace for Kent in 1531 with its former owner, John Skinner of Reigate (Blodgett, 'William Thynne and his 1532 Edition', p. 226).

25. *LP* v 311 and 322.

26. Baldasar Castiglione, *The Courtier*, trans. Charles S. Singleton (New York, Doubleday and Co., 1959), p. 43.

27. In February 1524 he was granted the reversion of the office of Cofferer of Rye in Essex, then held by Richard Shirley. On 18 October 1526 he was granted an annuity of £10 from the revenues of the manor of Cleobury Barnes in Shropshire, and on 28 October he gained the offices of bailiff of the town and keeper of the park at Beaudly, Shropshire, vacant on the death of another royal favourite, Henry's Chief Gentleman of the Privy Chamber, Sir William Compton. For this and the information in the rest of this paragraph, see *LP* IV (iii), 2598 and 6038; The Society of Antiquaries, *A Collection of Ordinances and Regulations for the Government of the Royal Household Made in Divers Reigns* (London, John Nichols, 1790), especially p. 217; DNB, New ODNB, and Furnivall's biographical notes in Thynne, *Animadversions*, especially pp. vii–xxvii.

28. See, for example, Spurgeon, *Five Hundred Years*, I, p. cxvi ('Thynne must have been a good hater of Romanism and the priests'); Edwards, 'Dunbar, Skelton, and the Nature of Court Culture', p. 131 ('There is something quite consistent about Thynne's encouragement of radical political literary statements'); Heffernan, 'Aspects', p. 160 ('[John] Foxe could claim that Chaucer's Wycliffite sympathies were utterly transparent...We can imagine that Bale, Godfray, Thynne, and other Henrician propagandists of the mid-1530s would have shared that sentiment'); Wawn, 'The Plowman's Tale', p. 109; and F. J. Furnivall, in Thynne, *Animadversions*,

p. xli ('[Thynne] must have been a hater of Romanism and priestcraft'). See also my own suggestions that 'Thynne may well have been an evangelical' and 'a radical' (Walker, 'John Skelton and the Royal Court', in Britnell and Britnell, eds., *Vernacular Literature*, pp. 1–15, pp. 11–12; and see also Walker, *John Skelton and the Politics of the 1520s* (Cambridge, Cambridge University Press, 1988), pp. 116–17). Needless to say I would now like to qualify those statements in the light of the present chapter.

29. Thynne, *Animadversions*, pp. 9–10.

30. See Thynne, *Animadversions*, p. 5. There is also, as Furnivall noted in his introduction to the text, more than a hint that Thynne felt Speght had, in compiling his edition, used without acknowledgement manuscripts that had originally been discovered by his father, and which had found their way into Speght's possession through third parties to whom Francis Thynne had given them, or (more troublingly) as a result of theft from Thynne's house at Poplar. As Thynne observed, his father had 'added many things which were not before printed, as you now have done, some of which I am persuaded (and that not without reason) the original came from me'. He subsequently spoke of his father's manuscript collection, 'which books being by me . . . partly dispersed about xxvi years ago and partly stolen out of my house at Poplar . . . which being copies unperfected . . . it may happen some of them to come to some of your friends hands; which I know if I see again: and if by any such written copies you have corrected Chaucer, you may as well offend as seem to do good.' (Thynne, *Animadversions*, p. 12).

31. Ibid., pp. 7–9.

32. Ibid., pp. 9–10.

33. See, for example, Blodgett, 'William Thynne and his 1532 Edition', pp. 10–11.

34. See, for example, Mary Rhinelander McCarl, *The Plowman's Tale: The c. 1532 and 1606 Editions of a Spurious Canterbury Tale* (New York, Garland, 1997), p. 16, where it is observed, without qualification, that 'according to Francis Thynne . . . the poem [i.e. *The Plowman's Tale*] was intended to be included in the 1532 edition of Chaucer's *Works*, but was blocked by Cardinal Wolsey'; and Blodgett, 'William Thynne and his 1532 Edition', p. 11, where the suggestion is advanced more cautiously, along with speculation that Francis Thynne may have mistaken Wolsey for Warham in the retelling. The possibility that the two tales were confused in Thynne's mind was raised in the *DNB* article on Thynne written by Sidney Lee and repeated in the revised New Oxford DNB article by A. S. G. Edwards. For a more sceptical reading of Thynne's testimony, see Wawn, 'The Plowman's Tale', pp. 15–22.

35. Thynne, *Animadversions*, pp. 7–9.

36. Ibid., p. 10.

37. Walker, 'The Archaeology of *The Plowman's Tale*', in Anne Marie D'Arcy and Alan Fletcher, eds, *The Key to All Remembrance* (Dublin, Four Courts, 2005).

38. The Bonham and Reynes editions are, respectively, *STC* 5069 and 5070; see Costomiris, 'Influence', p. 247. Francis Thynne's testimony would seem to argue against this suggestion, as he talks of 'my father' placing *The Plowman's Tale* where it stands in the 1542 edition (see the following footnote for quotation of the relevant passage).

39. Francis Thynne assumed a more pragmatic reason for the location of the *Tale*. 'And because my father could not see by any prologues of the other tales (which for the most part show the dependency of one tale upon one other) where to place the

Plowman's tale, he put it after the Parson's tale, which, by Chaucer's own words, was the last tale...' (Thynne, *Animadversions*, p. 69).

40. The will is printed in Thynne, *Animadversions*, p. xl. Notably, however, Thynne's epitaph in the All Hallows' church, Barking, asks worshippers to 'pray for the soul' of the deceased, suggesting belief in the orthodox doctrine of purgatory (ibid., pp. 132–3).

41. That is, the sort of man who might well have favoured the kind of orthodox reforming sentiments voiced in Skelton's Wolsey satires.

42. *Jacke Up Lande, compiled by the famous Geoffrey Chaucer* (London, J. Nicolson for John Gough), *STC* 5098. *STC* dates this text *c.* 1536.

43. For the names of Tuke's children, and his wife, Gissell née Boughton, see *DNB*: Tuke, Brian and *LP* III (ii) 1431. In June 1538 his daughters were still young enough to travel in a 'wagon' rather than on horseback (*LP* IV (ii) 4333). For Tuke's diplomatic stance, see *Spanish Calendar* IV (ii) (*LP* V 1531). I am grateful to G. W. Bernard for the chance to discuss these points with him.

44. Oskar Bätschmann and Pascal Griener, *Hans Holbein* (London, Reaktion Books, 1997), pp. 177–80. Certainly Tuke suffered considerable ill-health in the five years prior to the painting of the portrait. In addition to the problems noted in fn 9, above, there were further bouts of illness in May 1528, July 1529, and early 1533 (see, for example, *LP* IV (ii) 4332 and 4520). The quotation from the Book of Job 10:20 visible on the papers at Tuke's left hand in the portrait ('*Nunquid non paucitas dierum meorum finietur brevi*'—'Shall not the fewness of my days be ended shortly') would suggest a highly fatalistic frame of mind on Tuke's part at the time of the sitting. Confirmation of the date of the portrait is to be found in John Oliver Hand's detailed discussion of it, in Hand, 'The Portrait of Sir Brian Tuke by Hans Holbein the Younger', *Studies in the History of Art* IX (1980), pp. 33–49, p. 49 ('Author's Note').

45. See, for example, *LP* IV (i) 410, 1212, and 1964, although it is difficult to separate Tuke's own views from the warp and weft of government policy at any given moment. There seems rather more than mere diplomatic formality, for example, in his declaration to Wolsey, written at Hunsdon on 23 June 1528, that the King had commended Francis I's harsh dealing with French heretics and the 'damnable and scelerate demeanour of those, worse than Jews, that would do such despite to the Blessed Images'. *State Papers*, I, p. 585. Tuke was also on good terms with that intemperate critic of Lutheranism, Sir John Hackett, who left him a gold chain on his death in October 1534. See *LP* IV (ii) 2903, 4431, 5292. For the bequest, see *LP* VII 1309.

46. See, for example, *LP* III (ii) 1624; V 1047.

47. *LP* VII 171.

48. *LP* V 1531. Given that Chapuys' source for this story is likely to have been Tuke himself, it provides further evidence of his willingness to discuss government business and sensitive information with the Imperial diplomats.

5. THYNNE AND TUKE'S APOCRYPHA

1. Of the two anonymous texts, 'The Eight Goodly Questions' also appears in Trinity College Cambridge MS R.3.15 and in the Ballantyne Manuscript. As Skeat noted, it is a translation and expansion in a style reminiscent of Lydgate, of '*Eorundem septem sapientum sententiae*' by the fourth-century poet Ausonius (W. W. Skeat, ed., *The*

Complete Works of Geoffrey Chaucer: Supplementary Volume: Chaucerian and Other Pieces (Oxford, Clarendon Press, 1897), p. xv. 'When Faith Faileth' survives in the Capesthorne Manuscript (Oxford University Bodleian Library MS Latin Misc. *c.*66), a fifteenth-century verse collection compiled by Humphrey Newton, and in a number of later sixteenth-century collections. It is ascribed to Chaucer only in those manuscripts produced after Thynne and Tuke's edition. See William A. Ringler, Jr, ed., *Bibliography and Index of English Verse in Manuscript, 1501–1558*, prepared and completed by Michael Rudick and Susan J. Ringler (London, Mansell, 1992), pp. 44 and 244. It was printed as three separate poems of six, four, and four lines respectively, in Caxton's edition of *Anelida and Arcite* (*c.* 1477–8), a volume that also contained Chaucer's ballad 'To His Purse' (Beverley Boyd, ed., *Chaucer According to William Caxton: Minor Poems and Boece*, 1478 (Lawrence, Kansas, Allen Press, 1978), pp. xiii–ix.). It may well have been, as Lounsbury suggested (*Studies in Chaucer*, I, pp. 434–5), that the verses' appearance there prompted Thynne (and Tuke) to include them in their edition (see also Yeager, 'Literary theory, pp. 144–5). Certainly Blodgett's textual analysis would seem to confirm that Thynne was aware of that edition, having used it in the collation of the 1532 text of *Anelida and Arcite* (Blodgett, 'William Thynne and his 1532 Edition', p. 110). But, as Skeat and Boyd have pointed out, Caxton himself did not attribute the text(s) to Chaucer, so Thynne need not have believed it/them to be canonical (Skeat, *Chaucerian and Other Pieces*, p. lxxxi; Boyd, *Chaucer According to William Caxton*, p. xiv). The decision to combine them into a single 'Prophecy' with an apocalyptic warning followed by a prescription of the virtuous action required to prevent its realization seems to have been Thynne and Tuke's own innovation.

2. Yeager notes, without further elaboration, that 'historical circumstances, for example, surely lie behind the presence of "To the King's Most Noble Grace", "To the Lordes and Knightes of the Garter", "Eight Goodly Questions", and "Go Forth King". The first three of these poems are concerned with the right behaviour of the King and nobility in a time of religious controversy' (Yeager, 'Literary Theory', pp. 150–1).

3. Lounsbury suggests the poems are there simply to fill an empty space (*Studies in Chaucer*, p. 434). Donaghey argues they were placed there by Thomas Godfray as there was insufficient room for them among the Ballades in the final gathering (Donaghey, 'William Thynne's Collected Edition', p. 163). Had the need been simply to fit in 'extra' pieces, however, it seems more plausible that Godfray would have 'moved' only two of the poems from the rear to the front of the book. This would have allowed him to fit everything in and let the text spread over onto the top half of the final page, leaving the bottom half free for the colophon. This would also have avoided the slightly awkward appearance of the third piece, the Prophecy, printed without a title or incipit, presumably as there was not room at the front of the volume if the three poems were to fit into the space before *The Canterbury Tales*. That all three texts were placed among the preliminary matter, while a page was left free at the rear of the book, suggests that the placing of these 'Ballads' was more deliberate. Blodgett ('William Thynne and his 1532 Edition', pp. 257–8) suggests that Hoccleve's ballad was a conscious evocation of the name of Henry V at this signal point in the text (one of the few 'political' resonances that he allows the edition).

4. Questions about the placing of individual poems are inevitably subsidiary to a wider debate about Thynne's inclusion of non-Chaucerian material generally. Here critics are divided into two camps; one assumes that the *Works* were intended as a collection of pieces by Chaucer and other writers in the manner of a medieval manuscript miscellany (exponents of this view include W. W. Skeat, *Chaucerian and Other Pieces*, especially, p. ix–x, and Skeat, *The Chaucer Canon, with a Discussion of the Works Associated with the Name of Chaucer* (Oxford, Clarendon Press, 1900), pp. 94–116: see the accounts of the fifteenth-century manuscript anthologies in A. S. G. Edwards, 'Fifteenth-Century Middle English Verse Author Collections', in Edwards, Gillespie, and Hanna, eds., *The English Medieval Book*, pp. 101–12; Julia Boffey and John J. Thompson, 'Anthologies and Miscellanies: Production and Choice of Texts', in Jeremy Griffiths and Derek Pearsall, eds., *Book Production and Publishing in Britain, 1375–1475* (Cambridge, 1989), pp. 279–315; and Julia Boffey and A. S. G. Edwards, 'Literary Texts', in Lotte Hellinga and J. B. Trapp, eds., *The Cambridge History of the Book in Britain: III: 1400–1557* (Cambridge, Cambridge University Press, 1999), pp. 555–75). The opposing camp sees the edition as intended to be specifically Chaucerian, and assumes that the apocryphal pieces were there because Thynne erroneously assumed them to be genuinely Chaucer's (see Yeager, 'Literary Theory', p. 148; Lounsbury, *Studies in Chaucer*, iii, pp. 265, 269, and 430; E. P. Hammond, *Chaucer: A Bibliographical Manual* (New York, 1908), pp. 116–18). For a measured discussion of the options, see Donaghey, 'William Thynne's Collected Edition', pp. 151–4.

5. See, for example, Edward Hall's claim that God had finally 'illumined the eyes of the King' to the state of the Church in 1529 (Hall, *Chronicle*, p. 765).

6. Is it when priests' teachings are no longer inspired by faith, or when faith is no longer placed in those teachings that these things will occur? Will Albion's confusion stem from clerical failings, or popular anticlericalism?

7. *LP* v 286.

8. Blodgett suggested that the earliest recorded reference to Chaucer as 'learned' occurs in the dedication to the 1532 *Works* (Blodgett, 'Willaim Thynne and his 1532 Edition', p. 255). But, see n. 12, below.

9. Yeager, 'Literary Theory', pp. 155–6. See also Donaghey, 'William Thynne's Collected Edition', pp. 159–63.

10. Brian Donaghey has concluded from the state of the frame of the title-pages that the *Romaunt of the Rose* section was printed first, followed by the *Canterbury Tales*. Sig. A and the preliminaries were printed last, as was common practice, after the final gathering and colophon (Donaghey, 'William Thynne's Collected edition', pp. 161–4).

11. Spurgeon, *Five Hundred Years*, p. xcv.

12. John Lydgate had, for example, praised Chaucer as a writer of 'sawes'—that is nuggets of wisdom and moral guidance—in his *Troy Book* (iii, 4237), and Thomas Hoccleve took up and magnified the claim, asking rhetorically of the dead poet in his *Regement of Princes*, 'Who was heir, in philosophie / To Aristotle in our tonge but thow?' (both cited from D. Brewer, ed., *Chaucer: The Critical Heritage* (2 vols, London, Routledge and Kegan Paul, 1978), pp. 63ff). Stephen Hawes spoke in *The Pastyme of Pleasure* (*c.* 1506) of Chaucer and Gower together as moral poets who

wrote 'our vyces to cleane' and to kindle 'our hertes with the fyry leames of moral vertue' (1320–3, cited in *ibid.*, p. 82).

13. Thomas Hoccleve had celebrated him unequivocally as 'the firste fyndere of our fair langage' (*Regement of Princes*, 4978), while John Lydgate's *Troy Book* contained a lengthy paean to the poet, 'For he owre Englishe gilte with his sawes, / Rude and boistrous first be olde dawes, / That was ful fer from al perfeccioun, / And but of litel reputatioun, / Til that he cam and thorug[h] his poetrie, / Gan our tonge firste to magnifie / And adourne it with his elloquence' (III, 4237–43). George Ashby's 'Active Policy of a Prince' (1470) similarly spoke of Chaucer, in company with Gower and Lydgate, as 'Primier poetes of this nacioun, / Embelysshing oure Englisshe t'endure algate, / Firste finders to oure consolacion / Off fresshe, douce Englisshe . . . and formacion / Of newe ballades, not used before, / By whome we all may have lernyng and lore' (Brewer, ed., *Critical Heritage*, I, p. 68 ff). The anonymous *Book of Curtesye*, printed by Caxton *c.* 1477, explicitly contrasted Chaucer's linguistic and stylistic qualities with Gower's moral authority (330–1) (cited in Brewer, ed., *Critical Heritage*, I, p. 72).

14. Leland, *Commentarie*, cited in the translation by T. Launsbury, *Studies in Chaucer*, I, pp. 133–4, and 141. Needless to say, the Geoffrey Chaucer of the historical records was neither a university student nor a legal groupie, although the knowledge of the law displayed in his poetry is extensive. Leland was evidently less convinced by Thynne and Tuke's take on Chaucer's religion, as he took the view that the poet had been a stern critic of the catholic clergy.

15. Although there is not time to do so here, it is interesting to speculate how reading the edition on the assumption that it was a contemporary *speculum principis* would affect one's reading of other familiar Chaucerian texts, not only the overtly exemplary works such as *The Monk's Tale*, *Melibee*, *Boece*, or the *Legend of Good Women* (the last two being Thynne and Tuke's additions to the canon), each of which offered further endorsement of the advocacy of moderation in personal and political conduct, but also works like *The Parliament of Fowls*, with its comic treatment of the rancorous and disruptive conduct of the seed fowl and other lesser birds (how might that have been read in the context of the current debates in the House of Commons?) or the ruminations on the parlous effects of rumour, gossip, and slander on a great man's reputation in the *House of Fame*.

16. *Works*, sig. cv, (*Riverside Chaucer*, lines 1760–6, 1773–6).

17. Seth Lerer, *Chaucer and His Readers*, passim.

18. Derek Pearsall, *The Life of Geoffrey Chaucer* (Oxford, Blackwell, 1992), p. 132. In the final book of Gower's *Confessio* (VIII, 2955), the goddess Venus instructs the narrator to tell Chaucer to write 'his testament of love' in preparation for his death. It would not have been unreasonable for Thynne and Tuke to have assumed that this was a knowing allusion on the part of Chaucer's close associate Gower to a work of the poet's already underway or completed, and to conclude that Usk's text, bearing precisely that title, was that work. For a similar suggestion, see Skeat, *Chaucerian and Other Pieces*, p. xxviii.

19. *Works*, sigs. cccxxxvii and (v). For an excellent modern edition of the *Testament*, see Thomas Usk, *The Testament of Love*, ed. R. Allen Shoaf (Kalamazoo, Medieval Institute Publications, 1998).

20. The relevant passages are at fol. cccxxvi, cccxxxi, cccxxxvi(v), and cccxlv(v).
21. Yeager, 'Literary Theory', p. 152 notes the way in which the placing of these final texts serves to balance the effect of the lighter love poems that precede them, thus giving a sense of gravity to the edition as a whole.
22. Scogan's ballad had been printed by Caxton along with Chaucer's *Parliament of Fowls* (the latter under the title *The Temple of Brass*) with both an *incipit* and *explicit* that made clear its non-Chaucerian provenance: 'Here next foloweth a tretyse / whiche John Skogan sente unto the lordes and gentil men of the kynges hows / exortyng them to lose no tyme in theyr yougthe / but to use vertues'; 'Thus endeth the traytye whiche John / Skogan sent to the lordes and esta / tes of the Kynges hous'. (Boyd, *Chaucer According to William Caxton*, pp. 19 and 24.)
23. The most notable example of this is probably *Melibee* in *The Canterbury Tales*, 'authentic' authorial responsibility for which is emphasized by Thynne and Tuke's decision to entitle it (rather than 'Sir Thopas') *The Tale of Chaucer*.
24. Chaucer himself had, in 1400, added this stanza to another poem, the 'Complaint Unto His purse', turning it into a begging poem to Henry IV. Thynne and Tuke print the 'Complaint Unto his Purse' separately on fol. ccclxxxii. *The Riverside Chaucer*, pp. 656; Pearsall, *Life of Geoffrey Chaucer*, p. 274.
25. The ballad was printed by Caxton in 1477 as part of a volume containing *The Parliament of Fowls*. Yeager ('Literary Theory', pp. 140–1) suggests that Thynne, taking his lead from Caxton, published it in the 1532 *Works* thinking it to be Chaucer's. Thynne and Tuke's attribution of it to Gower would, however, seem to argue against this suggestion.
26. Indeed, given that Constantine's sparing of the children was related in the Christian chronicles as the prelude to his miraculous recovery from leprosy, his conversion to Christianity, and the passing of *imperium* to the Church, the story may be even more pointedly anti-caesaropapist in intent. See H. L. Strack, *The Jew and Human Sacrifice: Human Blood and Jewish Ritual*, trans. H. Blanchamp (8th edn, London, 1909), p. 63.
27. Hall, *Chronicle*, p. 771; *Spanish Calendar* IV (ii) 590, p. 14 (*LP* v 40); 641, p. 72; 664 (*LP* v 148); 683; (*LP* v 216), 853 (*LP* v 563); 861; 897 (*LP* v 762); 898 (*LP* v 773); 915 (*LP* v 850); 922 (*LP* v 879); 972; 986 (*LP* v 1256); 987; 993 (*LP* v 1292); *LP* v 776; *State Papers* VII, 339 (*LP* v 792). *LP* v 616, 693, 695, *LP* v; 888, 923, 1013, 1059, 1092, 1449, 1552.
28. See above, pp. 70–1.
29. *LP* v 202.
30. *Spanish Calendar* IV (ii) 584. See also the 'intemperate and insolent' letter that he sent to the Pope at the same time (*Spanish Calendar* IV (ii) 588).
31. *Spanish Calendar* IV (ii) 664 (*LP* v 148). See also *Spanish Calendar* IV (ii) 648 (*LP* v 124);
32. *Spanish Calendar* IV (ii) 739 (*LP* v 286).
33. *LP* v 738. See also *Spanish Calendar* IV (ii) 897 (*LP* v 762); *LP* v 820.
34. *Spanish Calendar* IV (ii) 915 (*LP* v 850).
35. *Spanish Calendar* IV (ii) 980 (*LP* v 1202); 993 (*LP* v 1292).
36. See, for example, *LP* v 202, 488, 850, 1449, 1552. Throughout 1531 and 1532 preparations were also being made to strengthen the northern border against a

possible Scottish invasion—a prospect made all the more troubling by the execution of Rice ap Griffiths for treasonable dealings with the Scots in December 1531. See, for example, *LP* v 488, 593, 762, 883, 941; *Spanish Calendar* IV (ii) 907, and 989. For Griffiths, see *Spanish Calendar* IV (ii) 853 (*LP* v 563). The preparations would lead, ultimately, to the Proclamation of 26 October 1532 preparing for a general muster in the event of attack of all men north of the Trent aged between 16 and 60.

37. *Works*, fol. Ai(v). For Thynne's appreciation of Chaucer's 'copiousness', read as a humanist scholarly virtue, see Blodgett, 'William Thynne', p. 35.

38. For the publication of texts such as *I Playne Piers Which Cannot Flatter* (1547), *STC* 19903a; *Pyers Plowman's Exhortation unto the Lords, Knights, and Burgoyses of the Parlyamenthouse* (1550), *STC* 19905; and *A Godly Dyalogue and Disputacyon Betwene Pyers Plowman and a Popysh Preest* (1550), *STC* 19903, see, for example, King, *English Reformation Literature*, *passim*; John M. Bowers, 'Piers Plowman and the Police', *Yearbook of Langland Studies* 6 (1992), pp. 1–50; Sarah A. Kelen, 'Plowing the Past: "Piers Protestant" and the Authority of Medieval Literary History', *Yearbook of Langland Studies* 13 (1999), pp. 101–36; and James Simpson, 'Grace Abounding: Evangelical Centralization and the End of *Piers Plowman*', *Yearbook of Langland Studies* 14 (2000), pp. 49–73, especially, pp. 54–5.

39. For the *vatic* tradition in poetry, see, for example, James L. Kugel, ed., *Poetry and Prophecy: The Beginnings of a Literary Tradition* (Ithaca, New York University Press, 1990).

40. See Pearsall, *Life of Geoffrey Chaucer*, pp. 276 and 295 (where it is suggested that the relocation of the tomb was 'perhaps . . . a move to reclaim Chaucer, with his rosary, for the temporarily restored catholic ascendancy'). For a similar suggestion, see Theresa M. Krier, 'Receiving Chaucer in Renaissance England', in Krier, ed., *Refiguring Chaucer*, p. 18, fn. 16. For Brigham, see McKisack, *Medieval History in the Tudor Age*, p. 68. For the most recent treatment of these issues, see Thomas A. Prendergast, *Chaucer's Dead Body: From Corpse to Corpus* (London, Routledge, 2004), *passim*.

6. MOCKING THE THUNDER

1. All quotations from Heywood's interludes are from Richard Axton and Peter Happé, eds., *The Plays of John Heywood* (Cambridge, D. S. Brewer, 1991), but see also the version of *Weather* in Greg Walker, ed., *Medieval Drama: An Anthology* (Oxford, Blackwell, 2000).

2. See Walker, *Plays of Persuasion*, pp. 133–7, and *The Politics of Performance*, chapter 3.

3. The identification of particular stanzas not to be spoken in the King's absence reveals its intended audience. *Witty and Witless*, l.675ff. *Witty and Witless*, unlike the author's other interludes, was not printed in his lifetime.

4. That the royal stance was recognized outside the immediate court is clear from the account of events produced by one London citizen, who, noting the proposal to establish a joint committee of laymen and clergy to consider legislation on clerical jurisdiction noted that the body would contain equal numbers of laity and clergy 'and the king to be umpire'. J. A. Guy, 'The Political Context of *The Debellation*', in J. A. Guy, C. H. Miller and R. McGugan, eds., *The Complete Works of Thomas More*

Vol. 10: The Debellation of Salem and Bizance (New Haven, Yale University Press, 1987), p. lxiv. See also Hall, *Chronicle*, p. 766, and S. E. Lehmberg, *The Later Parliaments of Henry VIII* (Cambridge, Cambridge University Press, 1536–47), pp. 35ff.

5. From 1529–30 onwards it was generally accepted that some degree of ecclesiastical reform was both necessary and inevitable. On 6 December 1529 Henry told ambassador Chapuys that, although Luther had gone too far in doctrinal matters, his criticisms of clerical abuses had merit, and that he, Henry, hoped 'little by little to introduce reforms and put an end to scandal', *Spanish Calendar* IV (I) 224. During 1530 Bishop Stokesley was energetically putting such ideals into practice in the diocese of London, initiating investigations aimed at weeding out inadequate priests. S. Brigden, *London and the Reformation*, (Oxford, Oxford University Press, 1989), p. 62. Other conservative figures had also argued for ecclesiastical and monastic reform in the period, including John Colet, Cardinal Wolsey, John Longland, Bishop of Lincoln, and Thomas Starkey. See C. Harper-Bill, 'Dean Colet's Convocation Sermon and the Pre-Reformation Church in England', *History* 63 (1988), pp. 191–210; P. J. Gwyn, *The King's Cardinal: The Rise and Fall of Thomas Wolsey* (London, Barrie and Jenkin, 1990), pp. 265–353; M. Bowker, *The Henrician Reformation: The Diocese of Lincoln Under John Longland, 1521–1547* (Cambridge, Cambridge University Press, 1981), pp. 7, 17–28, 108–9; Thomas Starkey, *A Dialogue Between Pole and Lupset*, ed. T. F. Mayer, Camden Society, 4th Series, 37 (1989), pp. 103–4; R. Hoyle, 'The Origin of the Dissolution of the Monasteries', *Historical Journal* 38 (1995), pp. 275–305, especially 280–2.

6. BL Harleian MS 1703, ff. 108a–109, printed most helpfully in B.A. Milligan, ed., *John Heywood's Works and Miscellaneous Short Poems* (Urbana, Ill., University of Illinois Press, 1956), pp. 250–2.

7. BL Add. MS 15233, ff. 43a–43b.

8. BL Add. MS 15233, ff., 58a–59a.

9. BL Add. MS 15233, ff. 62b–63b.

10. BL Add. MS 15233, ff. 64a–64b.

11. BL Add. MS 15233, ff. 45a–45b. The possibility that the ballad was the work of Heywood's associate John Redford is raised by the attribution to him in this manuscript. Heywood is, however, given as the author in the slightly later collection BL MS Cotton Vespasian XXXV, fol. 141b.

12. J. Heywood, *The Spider and the Fly* (London, 1556), RSTC 13308, reprinted in J.S. Farmer, ed., *The Writings of John Heywood* (London, 1908), pp. 426 and 414–15.

13. The dating of the first performance has been a matter for argument, largely over internal evidence. David Bevington initially favoured a date in the mid-1520s (David Bevington, *Tudor Drama and Politics: A Critical Approach to Topical Meaning* (Cambridge Mass., Harvard University Press, 1968), pp. 64–70). Subsequently, Alistair Fox and I, working independently in the later 1980s, argued that it was written and performed in 1529–30. While interpreting the play quite differently, we each saw it as an immediate response to (and reflection upon) the fall from favour of Cardinal Thomas Wolsey, the shift in royal governmental style that followed, and the period of the Reformation Parliament. (Alistair Fox, *Politics and Literature in the Reigns of Henry VII and Henry VIII* (Oxford, Blackwell, 1989), pp. 252–4; Greg

Walker, *Plays of Persuasion: Drama and Politics at the Court of Henry VIII* (Cambridge, Cambridge University Press, 1991), pp. 133–68; Walker, *The Politics of Performance in Early Renaissance Drama* (Cambridge, Cambridge University Press, 1998), pp. 89–91 and following). More recently still Richard Axton and Peter Happé's edition of Heywood's plays appeared, suggesting persuasively that *Weather* may well have been performed as late as March 1533, and so might reflect not only those earlier events but also the crisis surrounding the Supremacy and Anne Boleyn's pregnancy. (Axton and Happé, *Plays*, Introduction. See also Lynn Forest-Hill, *Transgressive Language in Medieval English Drama: Signs of Challenge and Change* (Aldershot, Ashgate, 2000), pp. 135–6.)

14. John Skelton had used Jupiter as an analogue for Henry in a passing allusion in his satirical poem *Speak, Parrot* (1521), thus perhaps establishing a precedent (see John Scattergood, ed., *John Skelton: The Complete English Poems* (Harmondsworth, Penguin, 1983), p. 242, l.399 and p. 243, lines 405–10; and Walker, *Plays of Persuasion*, pp. 148–9). More generally, the god had been used as a symbol for what Vives called 'the majesty of kingship' (Juan Luis Vives, *On Education*, cited in T. W. Baldwin, *William Shakspere's Small Latine and Lesse Greeke* (2 vols, Urbana, University of Illinois Press, 1944), I, p. 194). More direct links between classical deity and Tudor sovereign will be identified in what follows.

15. Axton and Happé (*Plays*, p. 52) remain agnostic concerning the interlude's auspices, suggesting a performance before either the court or 'a coterie of like-minded Roman Catholics in the London household of a baron of the realm'. In a subsequent essay ('Laughter in Court: Four Tudor Comedies (1518–85) from Skelton to Lyly', in Roberta Mullini, ed., *For Laughs(?): Puzzling Laughter in Plays of the Tudor Age: Tudor Theatre/Collection Theta* VI (Bern, Peter Lang, 2002), pp. 111–27) Happé suggested 'it was more likely intended for a court performance, though there remains a possibility that it was meant to be given in the house of an eminent person who might have influenced court matters obliquely' (p. 111). What we know of Heywood's milieu and employment history, however, suggests strongly that a production in the royal household was intended.

16. Axton and Happé, *Plays*, p. 52.

17. For Heywood's use of Lucian in the play, see K. W. Cameron (*John Heywood's 'Play of the Weather'* (Raleigh, North Carolina, Thistle Press, 1941), pp. 20–6 and following. The inspiration for Jupiter's hearing of contradictory suits probably came from scenes in *Icaromenippus* and *The Double Indictment*. In the former, Menippus, having flown to heaven on wings taken one each from a vulture and an eagle, is allowed to witness Zeus listening to the contradictory prayers of mariners for north and south winds, of farmers for rain, and washer-men for sunshine, although the god explicitly rejects a number of the 'impious' prayers in this scene (see *Icaromenippus: or The Sky-man* in A. H. Harmon, ed. and trans., *Lucian*, Loeb Classical Library (8 vols., London, Heinemann, 1915), II, pp. 267–323, 311–12). In the latter a number of rival suitors appear before the god in person. Heywood may well have found further inspiration from other dialogues. In *The Double Indictment* and *Zeus Rants* (Harmon, ed., *Lucian*, II, pp. 90–169), the comic relationship between Zeus and Hermes is played upon, and the latter acts as his father's herald and court usher. The inconveniences and confusion caused by the contradictory claims and demands of philo-

sophers are also a regular theme of the dialogues (see, for example, *Icaromenippus*, pp. 277ff and *The Double Indictment*, in Harmon, *Lucian*, III, pp. 85–151; and Lyn Forest-Hill, 'Lucian's Satire of Philosophers in Heywood's *Play of the Weather*', *Medieval English Theatre*, 18 (1996), pp. 142–60, pp. 142–5). For a useful overview of Lucian's habitually irreverent treatment of the gods and its implications, see R. Bracht Branham, *Unruly Eloquence: Lucian and the Comedy of Tradition* (Cambridge, Mass., Harvard University Press, 1989), pp. 136–44; and Douglas Duncan, *Ben Jonson and the Lucianic Tradition* (Cambridge, Cambridge University Press, 1979), pp. 1–41.

18. Kenneth Muir and Patricia Thomson, eds., *The Collected Poems of Sir Thomas Wyatt* (Liverpool, Liverpool University Press, 1969), pp. 187–8.

19. Walker, *Plays of Persuasion*, pp. 154ff; Fox, *Politics and Literature*, p. 253.

20. Hall, *Chronicle*, pp. 764–5.

21. Might the 'fallen' 'father most ancient' (6 and 37) represent Wolsey, and Phoebe Henry's new consort Anne Boleyn? (Axton and Happé, *Plays*, pp. 51–2.) And, if we take this suggestion further, might Eolus and Phebus perhaps suggest the Dukes of Norfolk and Suffolk, each of whom had cause to distance themselves from both Wolsey and Anne while the Reformation parliament was in session? If this reading is correct, then perhaps the eclipsed Saturn's 'frosty mansion' might be, not Whitehall but Esher or the more northerly (and so more 'frosty'?) houses in the Cardinal's York archdiocese to which he was sent in internal exile after his fall in 1529. It might even suggest Leicester Abbey, Wolsey's final resting place, where he died of a (possibly deliberately self-induced) flux on his way back to London in 1531. Equally plausibly, one might take the allusion to be to Henry VIII's literal father, Henry VII. The context of the description, however, with its deliberate and arch references to its 'ancient' setting, would seem to militate in favour of a more conventional, classical frame of reference. For the classical and iconographic traditions behind the idea that Jupiter's benevolent aspect 'neutralised' the harmful effects of Saturn's malign influence, see Raymond Klibansky, Erwin Panofsky, and Fritz Saxl, *Saturn and Melancholy: Studies in the History of Natural Philosophy, Religion, and Art* (London, Thomas Nelson and Sons, 1964), pp. 140 and 271 ff. Even this tradition could be read in more than one way, however (see p. 112, below).

22. That events in the Olympian parliament and the suitors who appear in the play proper were supposed to be symptoms of the same disorder and provide a political lesson to the audience is made clear in Jupiter's statement that 'Such debate as from above ye have harde, / Suche debate beneth amonge your selfes ye se. / As long as heddes from temperaunce be deferd, / So longe the bodyes in dystemperaunce be.' (1132–5).

23. See Walker, *Plays of Persuasion*, pp. 138–42.

24. In this context both Cameron (*John Heywood's 'Play of the Weather'* p. 45), and Axton and Happé (p. 51) cite those clauses of the Eltham Ordinances of 1526 designed to restrict the access of 'boys and vile persons' to the area around the doors of the King's Chamber. We might also note the proclamation issued in 1533, within months of the putative date for the performance of *Weather*, which ordered 'all vagabonds, masterless folk, rascals, and other idle persons which have used to hang on, haunt, and follow the court' to depart within twenty-four hours or face imprisonment, and declared that

thereafter, no courtier or officer 'of what estate or degree he or they be of, shall suffer any of his or their servants to enter the king's gate but such as shall be like men to rest in good order, excluding from them in any wise all boys and rascals, upon pain of the king's grievous displeasure'. (Paul L. Hughes and James F. Larkin, eds,. *Tudor Royal Proclamations* (3 vols, New Haven, Yale University Press, 1964), I, pp. 211–12). The struggle to exclude undesirable classes and individuals from the innermost areas of the royal household was, however, a perennial feature of court life. The, so called, *Black Book* of Edward IV, a detailed series of ordinances covering every aspect of household service, instructed court officers to ensure that 'the rascals and hangars upon this court be sought out and avoided from every offices monthly' (a clear recognition of the intractability of the problem), and drew up a due process of examination and punishment for any household officers suspected of themselves being 'a thief or outrageous rioter in much haunting slanderous places, companies, and other' or those 'known for a common daily drunken man'. (See A. R. Myers, ed., *The Household of Edward IV: The Black Book and Ordinance of 1478* (Manchester, Manchester University Press, 1959), pp. 63 and 162–3).

25. See Walker, *Plays of Persuasion*, pp. 138–42.
26. Axton and Happé, *Plays*, pp. 11–13 and 26.
27. Ibid., p. 290.
28. Ibid., p. 290.
29. Ibid. *Plays*, p. 26ff. For the former, see, for example, lines 161, 786, 1123; for the latter, 244 and 342. If, as Axton and Happé suggest (see, for example, *Plays*, p. 30), Mery Report consciously alludes to the figure of Mercury/Hermes (the son of Zeus) in his costuming, the paternal relationship would be more literal (and incongruous), and might create a further visual 'pun', Mercury's staff or *caduceus* doubling as the Tudor household servant's rod of office.
30. Axton and Happé, *Plays*, p. 289 fn.
31. See Walker, *Plays of Persuasion*, pp. 143–4.
32. Branham, *Unruly Eloquence*, pp. 142–3.
33. More described Lucian as 'Very witty, but always decent, and no human vice escapes his censure and rebuke. He aims his blows so skilfully and judiciously that, though no satirist strikes nearer home, his victim does not resist the stinging impact, but cheerfully admits its force.' More, *Lucubrationes*, pp. 273–6, quoted in H. A. Mason, *Humanism and Poetry in the Early Tudor Period* (London, Routledge and Kegan Paul, 1959), pp. 67–8. For the satirist's influence more generally, see Christopher Robinson, *Lucian and His Influence in Europe* (London, Duckworth, 1979); C. P. Jones, *Culture and Society in Lucian* (Cambridge Mass., Harvard University Press, 1986), especially pp. 33–5; Duncan, *Ben Jonson and the Lucianic Tradition*, pp. 1–41; and Luca D'Ascia, 'Humanist Culture and Literary Invention in Ferrara at the Time of the Dossi', in Luisa Ciammitti, Steven F. Ostrow, and Salvatore Settis, eds., *Dosso's Fate: Painting and Court Culture in Renaissance Italy* (Los Angeles, The Getty Research Institute Publications, 1998), pp. 309–32.
34. Axton and Happé, *Plays*, pp. 52 and 298. See also Forest-Hill, 'Lucian's Satire', pp. 142–60.
35. For the relationship between Dosso's images and Alberti's text, see Luisa Ciammitti, 'Dosso as a Storyteller: Reflections on His Mythological Paintings', Ciammitti,

Ostrow, and Settis, eds., *Dosso's Fate*, pp. 83–113. I am very grateful to my colleague Dr Anne Marie D'Arcy for suggesting the similarity in scenarios of Heywood's interlude and Dosso's paintings.

36. Thomas Elyot, *The Book Named the Governor* (London, Thomas Berthelet, 1531), sig. Gii(v).

37. Heywood alludes to this characteristic Lucianic mode when he has Mery Report claim to be able to 'report a sad mater merely' (138).

38. See Mark Thornton Burnett, *Masters and Servants in English Renaissance Drama and Culture: Authority and Obedience* (Basingstoke, Macmillan Press Ltd, 1997), especially p. 80 and following. Burnett suggests (p. 81) that the trickster-servant character's 'pleasure in his own inventiveness', with other of his characteristics, mark a new departure in the dramaturgy of late-sixteenth and seventeenth-century England. But all the features of the figure that he describes seem present and well developed in Mery Report.

39. Frances van Keuren, ed., *Myth, Sexuality and Power: Images of Jupiter in Western Art*, *Archaeologia Transatlantica* XVI (Providence Rhode Island and Louvain-la-Neuve, 1998), p. xi.

40. Lactantius, *The Epitome of the Divine Institutes*, cap. 10, *Corpus scriptorum ecclesiasticorum latinorum* (Vienna, 1866–). The attitude towards Jupiter can be judged from the following rhetorical questions concerning him: 'Why, therefore, is he called best and greatest, since he both contaminated himself with filth, which is the part of one who is unjust and bad, and feared a greater than himself, which is the part of one who is weak and inferior?' (ibid.). The Sibylline Oracles took a similar line. See George Boas, *Primitivism and Related Ideas in the Middle Ages* (Baltimore, Johns Hopkins University Press, 1948), pp. 33–8.

41. H. S. Versnel, *Triumphus: An Inquiry into the Origin, Development, and Meaning of the Roman Triumph* (Leiden, E. J. Brill, 1970), especially pp. 1–6 and 56–93.

42. Axton and Happé, *Plays*, p. 288. It is just conceivable that Heywood is here indulging in an additional erudite reference, playing with the kind of objections raised by St Augustine concerning Jupiter's paradoxical nature with regard to time, he being supposedly both 'an eternal divinity' and the son of Saturn, who was taken by association between Chronus and Kronos to be Time itself. (Augustine, *De consensus evangelistarum*, lib I, cap. 23, in Migne, *Patrologia Latina*, XXXIV, pp. 1057ff, quoted and translated in George Boas, *Primitivism and Related Ideas*, pp. 196–7.) See also Klibansky, Panofsky, and Saxl, *Saturn and Melancholy*, pp. 162–3. For a useful discussion of the Kronos figure, see Erwin Panofsky, 'Father Time', in *Studies in Iconology: Humanistic Themes in the Arts of the Renaissance* (London, Harper and Row, 1962), pp. 69–94.

43. Alexandra F. Johnston, '"At the Still Point of the Turning World": Augustinian Roots of Medieval Dramaturgy', *European Medieval Drama* 2 (1998), pp. 1–19. For an alternative reading of the use of Latinate language in *Mankind*, see Janette Dillon, *Language and Stage in Medieval and Renaissance England* (Cambridge, Cambridge University Press, 1998), pp. 54–69.

44. For Herod's swans ('Agaynst jeauntis ongentill have we joined with ingendis [(siege) engines], / And swannys[th] at are swymmyng to oure swetnes schall be suapped.' (York, *Christ before Herod*, 14–15), see Walker, *Medieval Drama*, p. 112. For the

comparison between Jupiter and Herod, see Axton and Happé, *Plays*, p. 288 n. ('The antithesis and witty play on sound and sense [in the "hyely... lowly" pun] barely conceal a vaunt of absolute power that links Jupiter with the boasting tyrants of the miracle play stage').

45. Stephen May, 'Good Kings and Tyrants: A Reassessment of the Regal Figure on the Medieval Stage', *Medieval English Theatre* 5: 2 (1983), pp. 87–102.
46. *Statutes of the Realm*, III, 427ff.
47. An Act for the King's Highness to be Supreme Head of the Church of England and to have authority to reform and redress all errors, heresies, and abuses in the same; st. 26 Henry VIII, c I; *Statutes of the Realm*, III, 492. *EHD*, V, pp. 745–6.
48. 22 Henry VIII, *c*. 15, cited in G. R. Elton, *The Tudor Constitution: Documents and Commentary* (2nd edition, Cambridge, Cambridge University Press, 1982), pp. 346–7; and 26 Henry VIII, *c*.3, *Statutes of the Realm*, III, p. 493, cited in *EHD* V, pp. 746–7.
49. This qualifies the view that I advanced in *Plays of Persuasion*, pp. 144ff.
50. For Elton's claims, see G. R. Elton, *The Tudor Revolution in Government: Administrative Changes in the Reign of Henry VIII* (Cambridge, Cambridge University Press, 1953); Elton, *Reform and Renewal: Thomas Cromwell and the Common Weal* (Cambridge, Cambridge University Press, 1973); and Elton, *Policy and Police: The Enforcement of the Reformation in the Age of Thomas Cromwell* (Cambridge, Cambridge University Press, 1972). The language of these statutes is now linked more generally with the team of scholars and bureaucrats around Edward Fox that Henry established to provide documentary ammunition for the divorce campaign, and which went on to provide the theoretical basis of the Supremacy as well. See the arguments of Graham Nicholson summarized in Nicholson, 'The Act of Appeals and the English Reformation', in Claire Cross, David Loades, and J. J. Scarisbrick, eds., *Law and Government Under the Tudors* (Cambridge, Cambridge University Press, 1988), pp. 19–30.
51. For an analysis of Heywood's political strategy in these plays, see Walker, *The Politics of Performance*, pp. 51–75.

7. SIR THOMAS ELYOT AND THE KING'S GREAT MATTER

A small part of this chapter's discussion of Elyot's religion is taken from my essay, 'Dialogue, Resistance, and Accommodation: Conservative Literary Responses to the Henrician Reformation', originally published in N. Scott Amos, Andrew Pettegree, and Henk van Nierop, eds., *The Education of a Christian Society: Humanism and the Reformation in Britain and the Netherlands* (Aldershot, Ashgate, 1999), pp. 89–112. I am grateful to the publishers for permission to reproduce that material here.

1. For Elyot's own treatment of the idea, see his discussion of 'Opportunity' in *The Governor*, sigs. bv ff, and in *Pasquil the Plain*, Avii–viii(v).
2. *Spanish Calendar* IV (ii), 957.
3. Pearl Hogrefe, *The Life and Times of Sir Thomas Elyot, Englishman* (Ames, Iowa, Iowa State University Press, 1967), pp. 170–1.
4. *Spanish Calendar* IV (ii) 957.

5. Perhaps, as Stanford Lehmberg has suggested, Elyot saw himself as fulfilling a higher duty as a counsellor, and was trying to act as a mediator between King and Emperor, 'assuring each of the other's good intentions' (Stanford E. Lehmberg, *Sir Thomas Elyot: Tudor Humanist* (Austin, Texas, University of Texas Press, 1960), p. 108.): a suggestion to which we will return later in this section, and again in the section on the career of Sir Thomas Wyatt.

6. *Spanish Calendar* v (i), 8 (Elyot reputedly told Chapuys that he thought there were 'a large majority of good Christians, indignant at the way the Pope is treated in this country', who would, if sufficiently encouraged, vote in Parliament against the King's initiatives. See also, Henry Herbert Stephen Croft, ed., *The Boke Named The Governour, devised by Sir Thomas Elyot, Knight* (2 vol., London, Kegan Paul, Trench, and Co., 1883), I, p.xcvii.

7. Greg Walker, *Persuasive Fictions: Faction, Faith, and Political Culture in the Reign of Henry VIII* (Aldershot, 1995), pp. 29–30, and n. 38; J. A. Guy, *The Public Career of Sir Thomas More* (New Haven, 1986), p. 160. Elyot's willingness to engage directly in the battle over the 'divorce' may well have been still greater if one accepts Richard Rex's suggestion that he was the author of an anonymous defence of the Aragon marriage, the *Non esse neque divino, neque naturae iure prohibitum* (printed in 1531). Richard Rex, *The Theology of John Fisher* (Cambridge, 1991), p. 179 and fn. I am grateful to Dr Rex for bringing this point to my attention. Elyot's *Defence of Good Women* (1540) offered a covert eulogy of Katherine's virtue (see Walker, *Persuasive Fictions*, pp. 178–204).

8. Hogrefe, *Life and Times*, p. 37. For the biographical details that follow, see ibid., pp. 1–38; Lehmberg, *Sir Thomas Elyot*, pp. 1–35; Alistair Fox, 'Sir Thomas Elyot and the Humanist Dilemma', in Fox and J. A. Guy, *Reassessing the Henrician Age: Humanism, Politics, and Reform, 1500–1550* (Oxford, Basil Blackwell, 1986), pp. 52–73; K. J. Wilson, ed., 'The Letters of Sir Thomas Elyot', *Studies in Philology: Texts and Studies* 72 (5) (1976), Introduction.

9. Until 1530 Elyot's principal residence was at Long Combe near Oxford. In 1530 he moved to Carlton, Cambridgeshire, where he was based for the remainder of his life. Although he received no lands in the distribution of property following the dissolution of the smaller monasteries in 1536, he gained a parcel of manors attached to the abbey of Eynsham, Oxfordshire (one of the larger monastic houses), including the manor of Histon Eynsham, on 5 December 1539. For these properties he paid what seems the very favourable price of £437 15s 4d, plus an annual rent of £4 to the Court of Augmentations. For the details and the calculations, see Lehmberg, *Sir Thomas Elyot*, p. 158.

10. F. W. Conrad's excellent doctoral thesis on Elyot's political career dates his appointment to the Council to 4 May 1526, but the 'swearing in' conducted on that day may have been the result of a formalization of his role, or of a promotion from one post to another, rather than his first appearance at the Council table. See Frederick William Conrad, 'A Preservative Against Tyranny: The Political Theology of Sir Thomas Elyot (*c.* 1490–1546)', The Johns Hopkins University D.Phil. dissertation, 1988, pp. 6ff.

11. That Elyot had been forced to relinquish the office of clerk of the assize in order to take up his new role, and was (he claimed) never to receive the salary attached to the

Council post, were issues that rankled with him long after he left the job in 1529–30. Many of his letters to Cromwell during the next eight years dealt partly (and sometimes almost exclusively) with his financial losses during the 1520s and the recompense and rewards that he thought he was owed for his services. See Wilson, 'Letters', *passim*.

12. The recorder of this rumour was again Chapuys, in a despatch completed on 10 September 1531 (*Spanish Calendar* IV (ii) 239ff). There are difficulties with some of the details of this account, but there is no reason to doubt that Chapuys was reporting a genuine rumour.

13. *Spanish Calendar* IV (ii) 777, 786, 788; Lehmberg, *Sir Thomas Elyot*, pp. 95–6.

14. BL Cotton MS Vitellius B xxi f. 60; Lehmberg, *Sir Thomas Elyot*, pp. 96–7.

15. Scholars have differed over the likely success or otherwise of Elyot's mission. Alistair Fox ('Thomas Elyot and the Humanist Dilemma', p. 62) suggested that he might have been recalled as a result of his ineffectuality in the role; Lehmberg thought Elyot 'too bookish' to have made a good ambassador (Lehmberg, *Sir Thomas Elyot*, p. 102). Diarmaid MacCulloch, *Thomas Cranmer* (New Haven, Yale University Press, 1996), p. 69, suggests that he was recalled 'since Henry considered Elyot unsound on the question of the divorce' (a conclusion which raises the question of why he was sent in the first place.) And yet, as Lehmberg acknowledges, a letter of Augustine de Augustinis, written in April 1532, remarked that 'I have heard everyone [at the imperial court] say that there had been no one sent from our illustrious kingdom for many years who was more apt in doing things, more grave with princes, and also more accommodating to diverse nations' (Nicholas Pocock, *Records of the Reformation* (2 vols., Oxford, 1870), pp. 247–51, translated in Lehmberg, *Sir Thomas Elyot*, p. 102).

16. Wilson, 'Letters', pp. ix ff. Again scholars differ over the nature and possible effectiveness of the 'remonstrance'. Fox (Elyot and the Humanist Dilemma', p. 61) suggests that if he did remonstrate with the King, he 'cannot have expressed his objections very forcefully', given that he was invited to attend upon Anne Boleyn at her coronation (see next footnote). As Hogrefe suggests, however, the assignment as servitor to the new Queen and Archbishop Cranmer may well have been either a pointed humiliation for Elyot or a test of his willingness to acquiesce in the new dispensation (Hogrefe, *Life and Times*, p. 187).

17. In 1 June 1533 he was among those 'knights and gentlemen' appointed to serve at the Queen's board at Anne Boleyn's coronation (*LP* IV, 562). On 3 January 1540 he was one of the party that attended the King when he travelled to meet his latest bride, Anne of Cleves, at Blackheath. (*LP* XIV (ii) 572 (3.viii); xv 14 (p.6).)

18. Alistair Fox, 'Humanism and the Body Politic', in Fox and Guy, *Reassessing the Henrician Age*, pp. 34–51, p. 46.

19. See below, p. 177. That the goal of all learning should be to serve the commonwealth was, of course, a humanist commonplace, harking back to Plato and Aristotle. See, for example, Thomas Starkey's repeated declarations to that effect in his *Dialogue Between Pole and Lupset*. 'Little availeth virtue that is not published abroad to the profit of other... (for al such gifts of God and nature must ever be applied to the common profit and utility...)... and this is the end of civil life, or as me-seemeth, rather the true administration of the common weal' (Thomas Starkey, *A Dialogue*

Between Pole and Lupset, ed. T. F. Mayer, Camden Society, fourth series, 37 (London, Royal Historical Society, 1989), pp. 4 and 14, and see also p. 6).

20. *The Dictionary of Syr Thomas Elyot Knyght* (London, 1538), sig. av. The translation is Stanford Lehmberg's (Lehmberg, *Sir Thomas Elyot*, p. 10). This statement makes it hard to accept Lehmberg's resurrection of the claims of his earliest biographers that Elyot had studied for degrees in the Arts and Law at the University of Oxford between 1516 and 1523 (ibid., p. 12). For scepticism about the claim, see Croft, *The Governour*, p. xxxviii; and A. Fox, 'Elyot and the Humanist Dilemma', p. 54.

21. *The Bibliotheca Eliotae: Or Elyot's Library* (1542) was reprinted during Elyot's lifetime in 1545; *The Banquet of Sapience* was printed in ?1534, 1539, 1542, and 1545. In addition *The Governor* was printed in 1531 and reprinted in 1537, 1544, and 1546, *The Doctrinal of Princes* in *c.* 1533, *The Education or Bringing Up of Children c.* 1533–5; *Pasquil the Plain* in 1533 (twice) and 1540; *Of the Knowledge Which Maketh a Wise Man* in 1533 and 1534, *A Sweet and Devout Sermon of Saint Ciprian and The Rules of a Christian Life Made by Picus, Earl of Mirandula* in ?1534 and 1539, *The Castle of Health* in ?1536, 1539, 1545 (twice), and 1544, *The Defence of Good Women* in 1540 and 1545, and *A Preservative Against Death* in 1545. See Lehmberg, *Sir Thomas Elyot*, pp. 197–8.

22. William Roper, *The Lyfe of Sir Thomas Moore Knight*, ed. Elsie Vaughan Hitchcock, EETS, original series, 197 (Oxford, Oxford University Press, 1935), pp. 103ff; Thomas Stapleton, *Tres Thomae* (Douai, 1588), Part III, 52, translated in P. E. Hallett, ed., *The Life and Illustrious Martyrdom of Sir Thomas More* (London, 1928), p. 44; Lehmberg, *Sir Thomas Elyot*, pp. 15–16.

23. Wilson, 'Letters', pp. 26–8. As the letter is dated only 'the Vigil of Saint Thomas', Wilson suggests that it could have been written on either 6 March (the Vigil of St Thomas Aquinas) or 20 December (St Thomas the Apostle), and the fact that Elyot addressed Cromwell as 'Master Secretary' would seem to date the letter before his elevation to the office of Lord Privy Seal in July 1536. Hence he suggests a range of possible dates: 6 March 1534, 1535, or 1536, or 20 December 1534 or 1535. 'The Vigil of St Thomas' applied strictly must, however, refer to the Feast of St Thomas the Apostle, which is a First Class Feast and Vigil in the Proper of Saints, *Missa: 'Mihi Autem'*. St Thomas Aquinas had no proper vigil, 6 March being rather the Feast of Saints Perpetua and Felicity. We can thus reduce the range of possible dates for the letter to two, 20 December 1534 or 1535. I am to Anne Marie D'Arcy for her advice here.

24. More was arrested on 13 April 1534 and executed on Tower Hill on 6 July 1535. That Elyot had been the subject of doubts about his loyalty is seemingly confirmed by his suggestion, later in the letter that, 'Perchance natural simplicity not discretely ordered might cause men [to] suspect that I favoured hypocrisy: superstition and vanity [all evangelical tags for religious conservatism and pro-papal sympathies that had been adopted into the rhetoric of the Supremacy by 1534/5]. Notwithstanding, if ye might see my thoughts as God doth, ye should find a reformer of those things and not a favourer, if I might that I would, and that I [would] desire no less that my sovereign lord should prosper and be exalted in honour than any servant that he hath, as Christ knoweth' (Wilson, 'Letters', p. 27). Indeed, Elyot was to be the subject of such an accusation again in January 1537, when, in the aftermath of the Pilgrimage

of Grace, one John Perkins or Parkins, a common lawyer, denounced him to Cromwell as a favourer of abbots and conspirator against the Supremacy (see G. R. Elton, *Star Chamber Stories* (London, Methuen and Co., 1958), pp. 19–51). The letter of accusation was, as Lehmberg claims, 'incoherent and nearly illegible' (Lehmberg, *Sir Thomas Elyot*, p. 151), but the charges were not inconsequential. Parkins was no village paranoiac or eccentric; he was a member of the Inner Temple and the author of a hugely successful book on conveyancing written in French (*A Profitable Booke Treating of the Lawes of Englande*, published in French in 1528 and in its first English translation in 1555. It went through fifteen editions in the course of the sixteenth century. See Elton, *Star Chamber Stories*, p. 20 and Hogrefe, *Life and Times*, pp. 265–8). To be accused of conspiracy in the wake of the Pilgrimage, even by a known troublemaker, was no laughing matter. Reminding Cromwell of an occasion when he had warned Elyot, over supper, that 'he should not be superstitious, saying that your honourable lordship was not married to abbots', Parkins claimed that Elyot and the abbot of Eynsham, Oxfordshire, were near neighbours, and that they were 'marvellous familiar'. Elyot was also allegedly familiar with the abbot of Reading, who had spoken against the Supremacy, and he had also consorted with 'one Dr Holyman', who, in Parkins' view was 'no doubt...a privy fautor [supporter] to the Bishop of Rome'. Doubtless the accusations were, as the investigation into them concluded, 'light matters of malice', but there is at least a hint of plausibility to the claim that Elyot, given his imperial experience and sympathies, had told Dunstone that 'the imperator of Allmayn [the Emperor] did never speak of the bishop of Rome but he aveiled [removed] his bonnet'. Perhaps he was speaking rather more freely than was wise in what he thought was likeminded company. It may well have been, as Lehmberg suggests (Lehmberg, *Sir Thomas Elyot*, pp. 151–3), that Elyot needed Cromwell's intervention on his behalf to clear the matter up, and that this was the occasion over which the author thanked the minister for 'the honourable and gentle report to the king's Majesty on Wednesday last past in my favour' (Wilson, 'Letters', pp.30–32).

25. Wilson, 'Letters', pp. 30–2. Again the dating is provided by the recipient's elevation to Lord Privy Seal, as this time Elyot employs that title in addressing him.

26. *Bibliotheca Eliotae*, cited in Major, *Elyot and Renaissance Humanism*, p. 91. In Erasmus's *Adagia* it was glossed as follows: 'Pericles, when he was asked by a friend to swear a false oath in order to help him, replied: "It behoves me", he said, "to help my friends, but only up to the altars"...Plutarch...tells us that it is a proverb by which sometimes when we promote the advantages of our friends and comply with their wishes, it may seem right to depart from a just course of action, but only to the degree that we do violence to the godhead because of a friend: for in times past those who took oaths touched the altar with their hands' (Erasmus, *Opera Omnia*, ed. Jean Leclerc (10 vols., Leiden, 1703–6), III, II, x, p. 748 B–D, cited in translation in Wilson, 'Letters', p. 32 and Croft, *The Governour*, I, p. cxxxii.) As both Wilson and Croft point out, the Plutarch reference is to *Moralia*, '*De vitiose pudore*' (VII, 528c, p. 61).

27. Lehmberg, *Sir Thomas Elyot*, pp. 150–1; Conrad, 'A Preservative'. p. 116.

28. See, for example, Lehmberg, *Sir Thomas Elyot*, pp. 15–16 ('The whole explanation seems ungracious, a bit like some of More's own less fortunate comments on Wolsey

after the Cardinal fall'); and Major, *Elyot and Renaissance Humanism*, p. 96 ('even if we allow Elyot the advantage of all our major doubts, we can hardly suppress the feeling that his conduct in this great affair reveals a moral obliquity, a degree of opportunism, and a downright lack of judgement that little becomes the author of the idealist *Governor* and other works designed to educate Englishmen in the highest code of human behaviour'). For the contrary view ('if he was a coward, so are we all'), see Hogrefe, *Life and Times*, p. 274. In part at least, Major's disappointment with Elyot's conduct here stems from his exaggerated view of his closeness to More earlier. For, in Major's view, each of Elyot's dialogues of the early 1530s was written, to one degree or another, in defence of More's stance against the Supremacy (see, for example, Major, *Elyot and Renaissance Humanism*, pp. 97, 102, 106–8; and for similar views, see Hogrefe, *Life and Times*, pp. 201 and 213–14; and Fox, 'Sir Thomas Elyot and the Humanist Dilemma', pp. 64–5). Unless every reference in the texts to a good counsellor or philosopher is assumed to be a tacit allusion to More, however, it is hard to find any direct and personal comments concerning his position in these works. More's rehabilitation would no doubt have been a welcome by-product of the kind of governmental and personal *volte face* that Elyot was arguing for on the part of Henry VIII, but it does not seem to have been the principal object of his campaign.

29. BL Cotton MS Vitellius B XXI, ff 58–9. 'Although I had a chaplain', Elyot complained, 'yet could not I be suffered to have him to sing mass, but was constrained to hear their mass, which is but one in a church'. BL Cotton MS Vitellius B XXI, ff. 58–59; Wilson, 'Letters', p. 3. Describing the Nuremberg service in detail, Elyot noted that he left before the end, 'lest I should be partner in their communion'. Wilson ('Letters', p. 6) identifies the service as 'a modified version of Luther's *Formula Missae* (1523)', and so far from the most radical service available in continental protestant churches.

30. It is not, perhaps, surprising that Cromwell might suspect Elyot of not 'savouring' Scripture in the evangelical spirit. The attitude towards the biblical text in his printed works was reverential to a degree that many protestants might have found superstitious. Describing it as a holy relic that ought to be guarded from presumptuous readers (rather than laid open to all as the evangelicals claimed), *The Governor* suggested that believers should approach the non-narrative books of the Old Testament and the Gospels with great care. These books were 'To be reverently touched, as a celestial jewel or relic, having the chief interpreter of those books true and constant faith, and dreadfully to set hands thereon, remembering that Ozia, for putting his hand to the holy shrine, that was called *Archa federis* [sic], when it was brought by King David from the city of Saba, though it were wavering and in danger to fall, yet was he stricken of God, and fell dead immediately.' (Fi(v)) Elyot would return to the subject, and deploy the same analogy to Uzzah/Uzziah (2 Samuel 6/2 Kings 6: cf. 2 Chronicles: 16:20), in his final work, *The Preservative against Death*, in which he offered some sober advice to those seeking revelation in the biblical text. Do not, he warns, presume to understand everything that the Bible contains. Rather, 'humbly, therefore and simply read and hear holy scripture, not presuming that thou understandest every thing that thou dost read, which to other[s] seemeth dark...often times, if thou mayest, consult with them which be sincerely exercised therein, or with

the books of most ancient and catholic doctors. Or if thou mayest not easily or shortly come by the one or the other, cease to be curious, and commit all to God until it shall like him by some means to reveal it unto thee. Beware, draw not the understanding of scripture to thy affection; but slake thy affection before thou apply thy wit to make exposition. And always[s] think, that if any place of scripture seemeth to favour any carnal or worldly affection, or withdraw thee from charity, think then surely that thou dost misunderstand it, remembering what saint Paul sayeth: All scripture given by the inspiration of God is profitable to teach or reprove ... that the man of God may be perfect, prepared and ready to do all good works ... There be sundry places in scripture which do require both learning and a constant faith to be well understood. And that they which do lack both the one and the other do often times pervert it ... Without these leaders we ought reverently and fearfully to approach, lest we be stricken as Ozah was. (Div–Dv). (For a more explicitly exegetical notion of religious truth, see *The Banquet of Sapience*, sigs. Gii(v)–Giii: 'Let us not think that the gospel is in the words of scripture, but in the understanding, not in the skin, but in the marrow, not in the leaves of words, but in the deep roots of reason'.) For Elyot, it seems clear, the Bible was certainly the unique, divinely inspired text of infallible truth, but it had to be set alongside the other sources of revealed Truth available to the Christian community through Tradition and the *magisterium* of the Church. And like this other conduit of guidance and grace, the inspired writings carried as many dangers for the unwary as they did benefits for the wise.

31. Hogrefe, *Life and Times*, p. 274.
32. For dull friars, see, for example, *The Governor*, Li(v). The ways in which dancing between men and women might be used to symbolize marital harmony, he claims, are so commonly known 'that almost every friar limitor carrieth it written in his bosom', hence he will not labour the point for fear 'my book should be as fastidious or fulsome to the readers, as such merchant preachers be known to their customers'. On priestly luxury see *The Governor* Mvii(v)), where he suggests that he will leave a discussion of the fate awaiting gamblers in hell 'to divines, such as fear not to show their learning, or [fill] not their mouths so full with sweet meats or benefices that their tongues be not let to speak truth'.
33. Prerogative Court of Canterbury, Somerset House, MS 14 Alen, printed in Lehmberg, *Sir Thomas Elyot*, pp. 194–206. On the mass, Elyot praised it as an 'honourable ceremony' in *The Governor* (a. vi). On works, he commended his step-sister, Dame Susan Kingston (nee Fettiplace), who had become a nun in 1514, for 'her perseverance in virtue and works of true faith', in the prologue of his translation of *The Sweet and Devout Sermon of Holy Saint Cyprian of the Mortality of Man* (printed in 1534), which he dedicated to her, asking her to join her prayers with their 'two sisters religious' Dorothy and Elinor Fettiplace on his behalf. See Chapter 10 below.
34. In *The Banquet of Sapience* (1542), he had been still more unequivocal. In the section devoted to 'Alms-deed' he quoted the Book of Tobit (4:10) to the effect that 'alms delivereth thee from sin and from death, nor will suffer thy soul to enter in darkness' (Biv(v)). More tellingly, perhaps, he also devoted the section headed 'Faith' to an exposition of the importance of good works, quoting, *inter alia*, St Paul: 'They which believe in God, let them endeavour them to excel in good works'; and James 2: 26.

'Like as the body is dead, wherein is no spirit, so that faith is dead where there lack works' (Dii).

35. See T. F. Torrance, *The Doctrine of Grace in the Apostolic Fathers* (Edinburgh, Oliver and Boyd, 1948), and Alister E. McGrath, *Iustitia Dei: A History of the Christian Doctrine of Justification* (2nd edition, Cambridge, Cambridge University Press, 1998).

36. Similarly, in describing the reverence paid by the Romans to their gods, he states that 'this part of justice toward God in honouring him with convenient ceremonies is not to be condemned' (Yi(v)).

37. For More's sense that all heresy tended towards ultimate chaos, see Thomas More, *The Dialogue Concerning Heresies*, eds., Thomas C. Lawler, Richard C. Marius, and Germain Marc'hadour, The Yale Edition of the Complete Works of Saint Thomas More, vol. 6 (New Haven, Yale University Press, 1981), p. 369; and More, *The Confutation of Tyndale's Answer*, eds, Louis A. Schuster, Richard C. Marius, J. P. Lusardi, and R. J. Schoek, The Yale Edition, vol. 8 (New Haven, Yale University Press, 1973), pp. 59–60. In *Of The Knowledge that Maketh a Wise Man*, Elyot again attacked those evangelicals who sought to 'wrest' the scriptures to serve their private agenda: 'some do chiefly extol the study of holy scripture (as it is reason), but while they do wrest it to agree with their wills, ambition, or vainglory, of the most noble and devout learning they do endeavour them to make it servile and full of contention' (sig. Avi). Elyot's opinion of the reformer William Tyndale, that 'like as he is in wit moveable, semblably, so is his person uncertain to come by' (Wilson, 'Letters', p. 2), also resembles More's views in *The Dialogue Concerning Heresies* (1528/9).

38. In *Pasquil the Plain*, published in 1533, he painted a bleak picture of the effects of the Reformation in Germany, lamenting that, if only all counsellors of good will had spoken out at the time, then, 'Germany should not have kicked again[st] her mother. Emperors and princes should not have been in perpetual discord, often times laughed at as dissards [jesters], saints blasphemed and miracles reproved for jugglings [magic tricks], laws and statutes condemned, and officers little regarded.' (T. Elyot, *Pasquil the Plain* (London, 1533), RSTC 7672, sig. Bi (v)). Elyot's horror at the prospect of disorder is evident in the opening chapter of *The Governor*, where, in a passage that Shakespeare was to paraphrase in *Troilus and Cressida* (thereby launching many an essay on the Elizabethans' belief in a 'great chain of being') he asked, rhetorically, 'take away order from all things, what should then remain? Certes [certainly] nothing finally except some man would imagine eftsones, *Chaos*: which of some is expounded a confuse mixture. also, where there is any lack of order, needs must be perpetual conflict—whereof ensueth universal dissolution' (Aii(v)). 'Where all thing is common, there lacketh order: and where order lacketh, there all thing is odious and uncomely' (Av(v)).

39. PRO SP 1/75/81; printed in Wilson, 'Letters', pp. 16–17. For Elyot's religious position more generally, see Lehmberg, *Sir Thomas Elyot*, p. 103 and following.

40. See, for example, Wilson, 'Letters', pp. 16–17; MacCulloch, *Thomas Cranmer*, pp. 79–80; Fox, 'Sir Thomas Elyot and the Humanist Dilemma', p. 63.

41. Roper, *Life of More*, p. 31.

42. Ibid., p. 33.

43. *LP* IV 3140; Scarisbrick, *Henry VIII*, pp. 154–5; Ives, *Anne Boleyn*, p. 113.

44. Scarisbrick, *Henry VIII*, p. 155.
45. Hall, *Chronicle*, sig. CLXXX(v).
46. *LP* IV 6309; *Spanish Calendar* IV (i) 758; Scarisbrick, *Henry VIII*, p. 219.
47. *Spanish Calendar* IV (i) 460.
48. The Latin version of the pamphlet containing the favourable judgements was entitled the *Gravissiamae... Censurae* (printed in April 1531). The title of the English translation, printed in November 1531, gives a clear indication of its contents: *The Determinations of the most famous and excellent universities of Italy and France that it is so unlawful for a man to marry his brother's wife that the Pope hath no power to dispense therewith*.
49. See, for example, *The Glass of Truth* (1532), and Edward Fox's *De Vera Differentia* (1534).
50. Hall, *Chronicle*, sig. CLXXXVIII(v).
51. Christopher St German, *Doctor and Student*, eds. T. F. T. Plucknett and J. L. Barton, Seldon Society (London, 1974), p. 327. The importance of St German to the debates of this period is now far clearer thanks to the work of John Guy. See for example, J. A. Guy *Christopher St German on Chancery and Statute*, Seldon Society (London, 1985), esp. pp. 19–55; J. A. Guy, 'Introduction', in Guy, ed., *The Tudor Monarchy* (London, Arnold 1997); and Guy, *Tudor England* (Oxford, Oxford University Press, 1986), pp. 126–7.
52. Given that St German was heavily involved in drafting influential parliamentary bills aimed at disenfranchising the clergy at this time, as well as publishing anticlerical propaganda, his views carried considerable weight in government circles. For an excellent discussion of St German's role in these years, see John Guy, 'Thomas More and Christopher St German: The Battle of the Books', in Fox and Guy, *Reassessing the Henrician Age*, pp. 95–120.
53. The full title of the manuscript (BL Cotton MS Cleopatra E 6 fols. 16–135) was the '*Collectanea satis copiosa, ex sacris scriptis et authoribus Catholicis de regia et ecclesiastica potestate*'; see Nicholson, 'The Act of Appeals' for a full descriptive account of its content and use. For the work of the scholarly team that produced it (which at various points included in its ranks, Edward Fox, Nicolas de Burgo, John Stokesley, Thomas Cranmer, Edward Lee, and Stephen Gardiner), see also John Guy, 'Thomas Cromwell and the Intellectual Origins of the Henrician Revolution', in Guy, ed., *The Tudor Monarchy* (London, Arnold, 1997), pp. 213–32.
54. G. W. Bernard, 'The Pardon of the Clergy Reconsidered', *JEH* 37 (1986), pp. 258–82, p. 262.
55. See J. A. Guy, 'Henry VIII and The *Praemunire* Manoeuvres of 1530–31', *EHR* 384 (1982), pp. 481–503, p. 481. Guy argues here that Henry's motives in attacking the clergy were primarily financial. I follow the line advanced by Bernard ('Pardon of the Clergy') that they were rather political and aimed at intimidating the church over the divorce.
56. *Spanish Calendar* IV (i) 396, p. 673; IV (ii) 598, p. 27. *Praemunire*, Chapuys said, was an offence so obscure in nature, that it could be made to fit any crime Henry liked ('it rests on the imagination of the King, who comments and amplifies it at pleasure, connecting with it any cause he chooses'). *Spanish Calendar* IV (ii) 615 and 635; *LP* V 45 and 62.

57. Chapuys thought the qualification was little more than a figleaf to clerical honour, as in practice no-one would dare to suggest that anything Henry did was against 'the law of Christ' (*Spanish Calendar* IV (ii) 635, p. 63). Eric Ives has raised the possibility that the phrase itself was suggested by Cromwell as a 'Trojan horse' to circumvent clerical resistance (Ives, *Anne Boleyn* (Oxford, 1986), p. 187), but there is no direct evidence to support the claim.

58. Scarisbrick, *Henry VIII*, p. 276; C. Sturge, *Cuthbert Tunstal: Churchman, Scholar, Statesman, Administrator* (London, 1938), p. 192. Henry wrote an emollient explanation of his actions to Tunstal. There was nothing to fear in his new title, he claimed, because it did nothing more than clarify the powers that he already possessed. Yet in defining those powers, he revealed precisely why Tunstal and the other critics had felt the need to protest. According to Henry, the Crown already enjoyed authority over every aspect of clerical jurisdiction beyond the simple administration of the sacraments. '[Over] the persons of priests, their laws, their acts, and order of living... we... be indeed in this realm "*caput*" [head], and because there is no man above us here, [we] be indeed "*supremum caput*"', D. Wilkins, *Concilia Magnae Britanniae* (4 vols., London, 1737), III, p. 762; Scarisbrick, *Henry VIII*, pp. 278–9.

59. Scarisbrick, *Henry VIII*, p. 278.

60. St German, *Doctor and Student*, p. 327. See also Guy, 'Sir Thomas More and Christopher St German', p. 101.

8. *THE BOOK NAMED THE GOVERNOR*

1. Croft suggested that 'we must remember that Elyot's object was neither to construct an ideal form of government nor to teach rulers the arts of state-craft'; H. H. S. Croft, ed., *The Boke Named The Governour, devised by Sir Thomas Elyot, Knight* (2 vols., London, Kegan Paul, Trench, and Co., 1883), I, p. lxviii. The most recent restatement of this case is in James Simpson, *Reform and Cultural Revolution*, The Oxford English Literary History, vol. 2 (Oxford, Oxford University Press, 2002), pp. 238–9 ('Elyot's *Boke Named the Governour* need not detain us very long, since it is an educational rather than a political treatise'). For the suggestion that the work was Henrician propaganda, see L. C. Warren, *Humanistic Doctrines of the Prince from Petrarch to Sir Thomas Elyot* (Chicago, University of Chicago Press, 1939), pp. 99–100, and 105. Notable exceptions from the rule have been Pearl Hogrefe, who argued persuasively for the critical element implicit in part of Elyot's programme (Hogrefe, *Sir Thomas Elyot, Englishman*, pp. 136ff). John M. Major argued that 'there can be little doubt that most of what is addressed by him [Elyot] openly to magistrates and deputies, is at the same time addressed covertly to Henry VIII'. But he also denied that the work favoured the supremacy, or even addressed the political issues surrounding it, arguing that it does not contain, 'as far as I am aware, even a hint of the impending crisis, or anything that might honestly be used to support a plea for the King's spiritual as well as temporal domination'. (*Sir Thomas Elyot and Renaissance Humanism* (Lincoln, Nebraska, University of Nebraska Press, 1964), pp. 9 and 56–7 respectively.)

2. Lehmberg, *Sir Thomas Elyot*, pp. 36–7.

3. J. A. Guy, 'Tudor Monarchy and its Critiques', in Guy, ed., *The Tudor Monarchy* (London, Arnold, 1997), p. 78–109; see also Guy, 'The Henrician Age', in Guy, *Politics, Law, and Counsel in Tudor and Stuart England* (Aldershot, Ashgate/Variorum, 2000), pp. 13–46, especially 14–18.

4. Erasmus, *The Education of a Christian Prince*, trans. Neil M. Cheshire and Michael J. Heath, ed. Lisa Jardine (Cambridge, Cambridge University Press, 1997), p. 5. See Richard F. Hardin, 'The Literary Conventions of Erasmus's *Education of a Christian Prince*: Advice and Aphorism', *Renaissance Quarterly* 35 (1982), pp. 151–63.

5. 'The Godly Feast', in Desiderius Erasmus, *Colloquies*, ed., Craig R. Thompson, The Collected Works of Erasmus, vol. 39 (Toronto, University of Toronto Press, 1997), pp. 171–243, esp. 185. See also Quentin Skinner, *The Foundations of Modern Political Thought* (2 vols., Cambridge, Cambridge University Press, 1978), i, p. 24.

6. Erasmus, *The Education of a Christian Prince*, p. 5.

7. Erasmus, *The Education of a Christian Prince*, p. 10. On the need to instil a fear of tyranny in the young prince, see ibid., p. 26 ('The prince's tutor shall see that a hatred of the very words "despot" and "tyranny" are implanted in the future prince by frequent discourses against those names which are an abomination to the whole human race: Phalaris, Mezentius, Dionysius of Syracuse, Nero, Caligula, and Domitian, who wanted to be called "god" and "lord". On the other hand, any examples of good princes which make a strong contrast with the image of a tyrant should be eagerly put forward with frequent praise and commendation.' Elyot offers his own account of Erasmus's counsel-laden environment for the prince later in *The Governor*. He imagines an ideal royal palace in which virtually every object or surface upon which the prince's eyes might fall could be employed to offer an educational opportunity or a morally encouraging snippet of advice from the biblical or classical canon of wisdom literature: 'In like wise his plate and vessels would be engraved with histories, fables, or quick and wise sentences, comprehending good doctrine and counsels' (oiv).

8. Erasmus stressed the point on a number of occasions. 'where there is no power to select the prince, the man who is to educate the future prince must be selected with comparable care'. 'A country owes everything to a good prince; but it owes the prince himself to the one whose right counsel has made him what he is' (*The Education of a Christian Prince*, p. 6. See also pp. 64–5 and 91, and *The Panegyric for Archduke Philip of Austria*, in ibid., p. 131.)

9. A number of earlier texts had also followed the model established by Plato's *Republic* of combining aristocratic educational material with advice to princes, notably William Perrault's *De Eruditione Principium* (pre-1275), the fifth book of which concentrated on the education of noble children, and Pierre du Bois's *De Recuperatione Terrae Sanctae* (1305–7), which was dedicated to Edward I. I am grateful to Anne Marie D'Arcy for these references.

10. Major, *Elyot and Renaissance Humanism*, p. 6.

11. Baldesar Castiglione, *The Courtier* (Harmondsworth, Penguin, 1976), p. 284. See above, p. 8.

12. Erasmus, *The Education of a Christian Prince*, p. 64.

13. An example of the theory in action, allowing an alternative voice to be heard at court in the guise of good counsel, is provided by the work of Cardinal Reginald Pole.

When Pole produced his forthright attack on Henry and his religious policies in *De Unitate* (1536), he justified his stance by explicit reference to the theory of good counsel. Flattery, he said, and the refusal of his ministers to criticize him openly, have led Henry to his current madness, and now only harsh words would be able to bring him back to sanity. *LP* x 420, 426, 619. I am grateful to G. W. Bernard for suggesting this reference to me. Thomas Starkey's *Dialogue*, similarly offers itself as counsel to an affable prince, but actually proposes constitutional reforms that would strip him of virtually all of his powers. See Starkey, *Dialogue*, pp. 16–18, and below, p. 270 and note. For a more detailed discussion of Henry VIII and the politics of good counsel, see my *Persuasive Fictions: Faction, Faith, and Politics in the Reign of Henry VIII* (Aldershot, Ashgate, 1996), pp. 99–119.

14. D. R. Carlson, 'The Latin Writings of John Skelton', *Studies in Philology: Texts and Studies* 4 (1991), p. 39; Thomas More, *The History of King Richard III*, ed, Richard Sylvester, The Yale Edition of the Complete Works of Saint Thomas More, vol., 2 (New Haven, Yale University Press, 1963); Dermot Fenlon, 'Thomas More and Tyranny', *JEH* 32, (1981), pp. 453–7. See above, pp. 8–9.

15. F. M. Nichols, ed., *The Epistles of Erasmus* (2 vols., London, 1901), I, no. 210, p. 457. Plato's famous dictum, 'happy the state where either philosophers are kings or kings are philosophers' (Plato, *The Republic*, ed and trans, Paul Shorey, Loeb Classical Library (London, William Heinemann, 1955–6), II, 473d) was widely quoted and admired in the early-modern period. See, for example, Erasmus, *The Praise of Folly*, ed. and trans., Betty Radice, with introduction and notes by A. H. T. Levi (Harmondsworth, Penguin, 1971), pp. 97–8, and Thomas More, *Utopia*, ed. Richard Marius (London, J. M. Dent, 1994), p. 39.

16. See, for example, Fox, 'English Humanism and the Body Politic', in Fox and Guy, *Reassessing the Henrician Age*, pp. 34–51, p. 43. Elyot acknowledged the element of importation and domestication in his work himself, justifying the function of *The Governor* with the claim that 'like as the Romans translated the wisdom of *Grecia* in to their city, we may, if we list, bring the learnings and wisdoms of them both in to this realm of England, by the translation of their works' (Miv(v)). For Elyot's admiration for Erasmus's work, see sigs. Fii and ci(v). That the book was always intended as a guidebook for princes as well as noble readers is acknowledged explicitly at various points (see, for example, sigs Bvi; ci(v); Dii; Dv; and zvi(v)), as well as implicitly in the fact that almost all of the examples of good and bad conduct that it offers are those of emperors, kings, and princes.

17. Sig. Dv(v): 'I agree me, that some be good of natural inclination to goodness, but where good instruction and example is there added, the natural goodness must there with needs be amended and be more excellent'.

18. Elyot relates a similar tale at sigs. Piii(v)–Piv. For a fuller discussion of these themes, see Walker, *Persuasive Fictions*, pp. 99–119.

19. 'By these examples', Elyot concluded, 'appeareth now evidently what good cometh of affability or sufferance of speech, what most pernicious danger always ensueth to them that either do refuse counsel or prohibit liberty of speech, since that in liberty (as it hath been proved) is most perfect surety, according as it is remembered by Plutarch of Theopompus, king of Lacedemone, who, being demanded how a realm might be best and most surely kept, if (said he) the prince give to his friends liberty to

speak to him things that be just, and neglecteth not the wrongs that his subject[s] sustaineth' (Piv(v)).

20. Lehmberg, *Sir Thomas Elyot*, p. 91; Major, *Elyot and Renaissance Humanism*, p. 33.

21. Here I differ from the analysis in K. J. Wilson's excellent study of the dialogue form, *Incomplete Fictions: The Formation of the English Renaissance Dialogue* (Washington DC, The Catholic University of America Press, 1985), p. 86, where it is suggested that Elyot intended 'consultation' to mean simply the form of the Socratic dialogue, and 'counsel' to imply study.

22. The city of Athens, 'during the time that it was governed by those persons unto whom the people might have a familiar access, and boldly expound their griefs and damages, prosper[ed] marvellously, and during a long season reigned in honour and weal'. Only when it fell under the sway of the Thirty Tyrants who ruled through fear and repression did it suffer 'continual injuries' (Rvi–vi(v)).

23. See, for example, Fox, 'Elyot and the Humanist Dilemma', p. 56, and also K. J. Wilson, ed., 'The Letters of Sir Thomas Elyot', *Studies in Philology: Texts and Studies* 73, 5 (1976), pp. ix, x, xii, xv, and xvi.

24. There is, for example, at least a hint of overreaching in *The Governor's* assertion that those who 'excel other in the influence of understanding, ought to be set in a more high place than the residue, where they may see and also be seen, that, by the beams of their excellent wit, showed through the glass of authority other of inferior understanding may be directed to the way of virtue and commodious living. And unto men of such virtue, by the very equity appertaineth honour as their just reward and duty.' (A iv(v)) Lehmberg, *Sir Thomas Elyot*, p. 42, reads this statement as a justification of 'the existence of the nobility and gentry', but its stress on understanding as the key to pre-eminence suggests rather that Elyot has scholars and learned men in mind. If, like him, such men combined their wisdom with social elevation too, no doubt this was so much the better.

25. As Fox suggests ('Elyot and the Humanist Dilemma', p. 57) it seems likely that Elyot was well informed about events at the political centre, probably through his links with Cromwell.

26. Lehmberg, *Sir Thomas Elyot*, p. 37; Hogrefe, *Life and Times*, pp. 40–1.

27. See, for example, Croft, *Boke Named the Governour, passim*; Lehmberg, *Sir Thomas Elyot*, pp. 74–91; Major, *Elyot and Renaissance Humanism, passim*.

28. For tolerance, see Lviii ff and following.

29. Alistair Fox, for example, claims that *The Governor* set out to justify royal absolutism, but fell into self-contradiction when it came to describe the virtues of an ideal governor in the later sections of the book. There is, he argues, 'a basic contradiction between the unlimited power ascribed to the prince in the opening chapters, therefore, and the severe limitations imposed on that power by the virtues described in Book Three, which the prince, along with other inferior governors, is supposed to embody' (Fox, 'Sir Thomas Elyot and the Humanist Dilemma', pp. 56–7.)

30. Lehmberg, *Sir Thomas Elyot*, pp. 45–9. See for example Sir John Fortescue, *On the Nature of the Law of Nature*, in Shelley Lockwood, ed., *On the Laws and Governance of England* (Cambridge, Cambridge University Press, 1997), p. 135. Fortescue cites Thomas Aquinas's unfinished work *On Princely Government*, I.iii, for the idea that hereditary monarchy was the best of all forms of government, but princely tyranny

was the worst. See Quentin Skinner, *The Foundations of Modern Political Thought* (2 vols., Cambridge, Cambridge University Press, 1978), I, p. 54. There is, nonetheless, some discussion of tyranny in *The Governor*, as at sig. Bi and following, where the example of Roboaz, the son of King Solomon is described, 'who, being unlike to his father in wisdom, practised tyranny among his people' thus provoking the rebellion of nine of the tribes of Israel, a bloody civil war, and the eventual defeat of the Israelites by the Medes and the Babylonian captivity.

31. Lehmberg, *Sir Thomas Elyot*, pp. 45–9 ('In the opening chapters of *The Governor* there is much that would have pleased Elyot's sovereign, nothing at which he might have grumbled'), and p. 51 ('the praise of monarchy in *The Boke Named the Governour* stands as one of the earliest implicit justifications of the English reformation.')

32. The obvious source for this discussion of the best form of civil government is Books VIII and IX of Plato's *Republic*, which Elyot may have used directly or through the summary of Plato's arguments in a source that he was to draw upon explicitly later in the 1530s, Diogenes Laertius' *Lives of the Eminent Philosophers*. See Diogenes Laertius, *Lives of the Eminent Philosophers*, ed. and trans. R. D. Hicks, Loeb Classical Library (2 vols, London, William Heinemann, 1925), I, p. 349. For Elyot's use of this text, see the following chapter.

33. For the best-known uses of the sun and moon as a political image, see Innocent III's Letter to the Prefect Acerbus Falseronis and the nobles of Tuscany, *Sicut universitatis conditor*, PL 214, 337, translated in B. Tienney, *The Crisis of Church and State 1050–1300* (Englewood Cliffs, 1964), p. 132 and Dante, *Monarchia*, trans. P. Shaw (Cambridge, 1995), pp. 107–13. Within two years of its publication this part of *The Governor* would, whether Elyot intended it or not, take on still more strikingly 'anti-imperial' overtones. After the Act in Restraint of Appeals of 1533, with its confident assertion that 'this realm of England is an Empire, and so hath been accepted in the world, governed by one supreme head and king having all the dignity and royal estate of the imperial crown of the same, unto whom a body politic, compact of all sorts and degrees of people, divided in terms and by names of spirituality and temporality, be bounden and own to bear next to God a natural and humble obedience' (*EHD* V, p. 738), *The Governor's* bold opening gambit that 'a public weal is a body living, compact or made of sundry estates and degrees of men, which is disposed by order and equity and governed by the rule and moderation of reason' (Ai), could not but have appeared an implicit rejection of the Crown's claims. To assert that the realm was not a submissive empire, but 'a body living', governed not by a supreme sovereign head but by reason, and moderated by equity, offered a very different conception of the state to that advanced by the government. And while Elyot could not have known so far in advance of its passing what the preamble to the Appeals Act would claim, it is clear that the ideas that it would immortalize were being discussed at court much earlier. A draft bill circulating at the time of the Commons' Supplication in 1532, for example, claimed that the realm was 'but one body politic, living under the allegiance, obedience, tuition and defence of the King's royal majesty, being their alonely supreme, imperial head and sovereign, of whom all laws compulsory be to be made, executed within this realm, taking their vigour, soul, life, and effect next God only of his highness, and of none other, and to him

belongeth to make all laws, statutes and ordinances' (PRO SP 2/L ff. 78–80 (*LP* v 721(i)). See G. Nicholson, 'The Act of Appeals and the English Reformation', in Claire Cross, David Loades, and J. J. Scarisbrick, eds, *Law and Government Under the Tudors: Essays Presented to Sir Geoffrey Elton on his Retirement* (Cambridge, Cambridge University Press, 1988), pp. 19–30, p. 28; and G. Nicholson, 'The Nature and Function of Historical Argument in the Henrician Reformation', Cambridge University Ph.D. Dissertation, 1977, pp. 136–7. For the classical forebears of Elyot's organic conception of the state, see Philip George Neserius, 'Isocrates's Politics and Social Ideas', *International Journal of Ethics* 43 (1933), pp. 307–28; Felix Gilbert, 'The Humanist Concept of the Prince and the Prince of Machiavelli', *The Journal of Modern History* 11 (1939), pp. 449–83; and Major, *Elyot and Renaissance Humanism*, pp. 178–80. In a footnote Major suggests similarities between Elyot's formulation and that in the Appeals Act (ibid., p. 178). Thomas Aquinas's *On Princely Government* ii, iiv, and ii, and xiii, had similarly suggested that members of the body politic were guided towards the common good by reason

34. Citing Virgil's *Georgics*, Pliny, and Collumella as sources of profitable further reading on the subject, Elyot informs readers 'I suppose [those] who seriously beholdeth this example, and hath any commendable wit, shall thereof gather much matter to the forming of a public weal' (*Governor*, sig. Aviii).

35. John Trevisa, *On the Properties of Things*, ed. M. C. Seymour, *et al* (Oxford, Oxford University Press, 1975), 610/24–7.

36. Thomas Hoccleve, *The Regement of Princes*, ed. Charles R. Blyth (Kalamazoo, Western Michigan University Press, 1999), lines 3375–88.

37. *Mom and the Sothsegger*, lines 1031–7, in Helen Barr, ed., *The Piers Plowman Tradition* (London, Dent, 1993). I am very grateful to Professor John Scattergood of Trinity College Dublin for drawing this and the previous reference to my attention.

38. Erasmus, *Education of A Christian Prince*, pp. 12, 23, and 29–30. His source for his anti-tyrannical use of the analogy was, as he states, Seneca's *On Clemency*. Seneca, writing for the benefit of Nero, used the passage that Erasmus was to paraphrase to exemplify the notion that 'nothing can be imagined which is more becoming to a sovereign than clemency'. 'The most remarkable distinction [between kings and other bees] is [that] . . . bees are very fierce, and for their size are the most pugnacious of creatures, and leave their stings in the wounds which they make, but the king himself has no sting: nature does not wish him to be savage or to seek revenge at so dear a rate, and so has deprived him of his weapon and disarmed his rage. She has offered him as a pattern to great sovereigns.' (L. Anneaus Seneca, *Minor Dialogues*, trans. Aubrey Stewart, Loeb Classical Library (London, George Bell and Sons, 1900)). The same use of the analogy would later be made by Jean Bodin in *Les Six Livres de la République* (Paris, 1576), iv, p. 6. Thanks to Anne Marie D'Arcy for bringing these uses of the analogy to my attention.

39. Typically, Erasmus (*Education of a Christian Prince*, pp. 29 and 60ff) uses the principal bee's lack of a sting to enjoin upon the prince the virtues of a pacific foreign policy as well as clemency and a settled domestic administration. The other writers cited by Elyot, while noting the stingless nature of the 'principal bee', had put the analogy with human society to more martial and celebratory purposes. In the

Natural History, Pliny declared himself to be uncertain 'whether the king of bees alone hath no sting, and is armed only with majesty, or, whether Nature has bestowed a sting upon him, and denied him only the use thereof'. Yet he was nonetheless impressed by the creature's military prowess and leadership. 'For certain it is, that this great commander... does nothing with his sting, and yet a wonder it is to see how they all are ready to obey him. When he marches abroad, the whole army goes forth likewise, then they assemble together that they will not suffer him once to be seen... If he chances to be entrapped and surprised by the enemy, the whole army is sure withal to be taken with him. If he be defeated and slain, the field is lost. (Pliny, *The Natural History*, vol 3 Books VIII–XI, trans. H. Rackham, Loeb Classical Library (London, William Heinemann, 1989) XI, 17). Virgil's *Georgics*, while using the hive as a symbol for the well-ordered human society, similarly dwelt upon the military aspects of the royal bee's role, describing a conflict between two swarms in terms of a human battlefield. '[I]f they are gone forth to battle, for often high-swelling discord arises between two kings, and at once and after thou may foreknow the raging of the multitude and the hearts beating fast for war... then they muster hurriedly together with vibrating wings, and whet their stings on their beaks and brace their arms, and crowd in mingled mass round their king and close up to the royal tent, and with loud cries challenge the enemy... The monarchs move splendid-winged amid their ranks, and mighty passions stir in their tiny breasts, stubborn to the last not to retreat, till weight of the conqueror forces these or those to turn backward in flying rout.' (Virgil, *Eclogues, Georgics Aeneid I–IV*, ed. H. Rushton Fairclough Loeb Classics Edition (London, William Heinemann, 1932), IV, 67–87; 153–219). For the martial aspects of the bees' commonwealth idea, and Shakespeare's revision of it, see Andrew Gurr, 'Henry V and the Bees' Commonwealth', *Shakespeare Survey 30* (1977), pp. 61–72.

40. William Tyndale, *The Obedience of a Christian Man* (Marburg, 2nd edition, ?1535), sig. xxix–xxxiii.

41. Elsewhere in the book Elyot was equally assertive on the point that princely authority brought additional burdens of responsibility rather than liberation from constraint. Citing Erasmus, he declared that 'They [princes] shall not think how much honour they receive, but how much care and burden' (Nv(v)). See also sigs. Yv(v)–Yvi.

42. Elyot, *Dictionary*, (London, 1538), RSTC 7659 sig. Aii.

43. For accounts of the trial, see Hall, *Chronicle*, pp. 826–7; John Foxe, *Acts and Monuments*, v, pp. 229–34.

44. See Erasmus, *Letter to Jean Desmarez* in *The Education*, pp. 114–15 ('Those who believe panegyrics are nothing but flattery seem to be unaware of the purpose and aim of the extremely far-sighted men who invented this kind of composition, which consists in presenting princes with a pattern of goodness, in such a way as to reform bad rulers, improve the good, educate the boorish, reprove the erring, arouse the indolent, and cause even the hopelessly vicious to feel some inward stirrings of shame... [They] exhort rulers to honourable actions under cover of compliment.'). For an insightful discussion of the classical models of the panegyric, see H. A. Drake, *Constantine and the Bishops: The Politics of Intolerance* (Baltimore, The Johns Hopkins University Press, 2000), pp. 69ff. ('Lavish praise, when obviously not deserved, could signal an attempt to modify the ruler's behaviour.')

45. As the discussion below will indicate, Elyot includes a lengthy justification of his inclusion in the second edition of new sections on heretics and heresies 'justly condemned by the whole consent of all true Christian men' (Aii(v)), and a description of the 'benignity of principal governors' who had advanced honest men to office (Aiii). Even after the death of Cromwell and his own apparent disillusionment with the prospect of Henry's political redemption (see Chapter 11, below), Elyot was still, it seems, prepared to argue passionately for the preservation of traditional doctrines, as both this text, and his final published work, *The Preservative Against Death* (1545) demonstrate.

46. Hogrefe, *Sir Thomas Elyot*, p. 250.

47. St German, *Doctor and Student*, p. 327; Guy, 'Sir Thomas More and Christopher St German', p. 101; Wilson, 'Letters', pp. 2–5. We might also note in this context his declaration, following a list of his published writings in *The Image of Governance*, that 'in none of these works, I dare undertake, a man shall find any sentence against the commandments of God, the true catholic faith, or occasion to stir men to wanton devices' (aiii(v)).

48. Elyot sketched out some portion of this idea in *The Governor*. Glossing the Socratic dictum '*nosce teipsum*: know thy self', he declared that; 'a man knowing himself shall know that which is his own, and pertaineth to himself. But what is more his own than his soul? Or what thing more appertaineth to him than his body? His soul is undoubtedly and freely his own. And none other person may by any mean possess or claim it.'

49. Later Elyot revisits the story from another angle, suggesting that 'if the insolency and pride of Tarquin had not excluded kings out of the city, it had been the most perfect of all other' (Evii).

50. Read against the discussions of the role of the Roman Senate in a text such as Fortescue's *The Governance of England*, this passage might seem proto-absolutist in its intentions, but, as we shall see, Elyot's use of Parliament varied, like his line on royal authority, depending upon the issues at stake in each discussion. Fortescue declared that 'The Romans, whilst their council, called the senate, was great, got, through the wisdom of that council, the lordship of a great part of the world ... But after this, when ill-disposed emperors, such as Nero, Domitian, and others had slain a great part of the senators, and scorned the council of the senate, the estate of the Romans and their emperors began to fall down', and are now in such decay that 'the lordships of the emperor are not as great, as are the lordships of some one king, who, while the senate was whole, was subject to the emperor' (Fortescue, *On the Laws and Governance of England*, chapter 16, p. 117. Elsewhere in *The Governor*, Elyot took a similar line, arguing that 'as long as the senate continued or increased in the city of Rome, and retained their authority, which they received of Romulus ... they wonderfully prospered, and also augmented their empire over the more part of the world.' (gi–i(v)).

51. Sir John Fortescue, *On the Laws and Governance of England*, pp. xxiv and 83,

52. See, for example, Fortescue, *On the Nature of the Law of Nature*, in Lockwood, ed., *On the Laws and Governance of England*, p. 128: 'For in the kingdom of England the kings make not laws, nor impose subsidies on their subjects, without the consent of the three estates of the realm, and even the judges of that realm are all bound by their

oaths not to render judgement against the laws of the land, even if they should have the command of the prince to the contrary'. Similarly, Thomas More's epigram, 'What is the best form of Government?', argued that it was one in which the prince was counterbalanced by a powerful senate or parliament. See Thomas More, *The Latin Poems*, eds, Clarence H. Miller, Leicester Bradner, Charles A. Lynch, and Revilo P. Oliver, The Yale Edition of the Complete Works of Saint Thomas More, vol. 3(ii) (New Haven, Yale University Press, 1984), no. 198.

53. S. T. Bindoff, ed., *The History of Parliament: The House of Commons, 1509–1558* (3 vols., London, Secker and Warburg, 1982), II, pp. 96–8.

54. *Spanish Calendar* v (i) 8.

55. Guy, 'Intellectual Origins', p. 227.

56. See, for example, the very clear statements of the King's subservience to the law in *In Praise of the Laws of England*. 'A king ruling politically is not able to change the laws of the kingdom ... For the King of England is not able to change the laws of his kingdom at pleasure, for he rules his people with a government not only royal but also political ... he himself is not able to change the laws without the assent of his subjects, nor to burden an unwilling people with strange impositions, so that, ruled by laws that they themselves desire, they freely enjoy their goods, and are despoiled neither by their own king nor any others' (Fortescue, *In Praise of the Laws of England*, in Lockwood, ed., *On the Laws and Governance of England*, p. 17.) See also his discussion, later in the same work, of the maxim, 'what pleases the prince has the force of law': 'The laws of England do not sanction any such maxim, since the king of that land rules his people not only royally but also politically, and so he is bound by oath at his coronation to the observance of his laws' (ibid., p.48. and see also Fortescue, *On the Nature of the Law of Nature*, in ibid., pp. 128 and 135–6.)

57. See, for example, the account of how the emperor Alexander Severus, when he was advised that 'the Emperor was not bounden to observe his own laws', angrily replied, 'God forbade that ever I should devise any laws whereby my people should be compelled to do anything which I myself cannot tolerate' (yvi(v)). See Chapter 11 for a discussion of the role Alexander Severus was to play in Elyot's last political treatise, *The Image of Government*.

58. *The Governor*, sig. Pvi, describes the wrathful man, once noble of visage but now, 'by fury changed in to an horrible figure, his face infarced with rancour, his mouth foul and embossed ... not speaking but as a wild bull, roaring and braying out words despiteful and venomous ... forgetting learning, yea, forgetting all reason'.

59. Anon, *The Famous Victories of Henry The Fifth* (London, Thomas Creede, 1598), see especially sigs B3–B4.

60. Notably, when, elsewhere in *The Governor*, Elyot advises those with power to 'know the bounds of your authority' (yvi(v)), he again refers not to constitutional limits to their jurisdictions, but to personal, ethical constraints on their behaviour. Thus he concludes that they should 'speak or do nothing unworthy the immortality and most precious nature of your soul'. By the time that he came to write *The Image of Governance* in 1540, however, his opinions had shifted markedly on the subject. See Chapter 11, following.

61. The good man skilled in speech, *vir boni dicendi peritus* was described in Cicero's *De Oratore*, Book 1.

62. See, for example, sig. GV(v) ('It may not be denied, but that all laws be founden on the deepest part of reason and, as I suppose, no one law so much as our own'), and the long description of legal moots as training grounds in rhetoric that follows. But see also his implicit demands for reform of English legal practice in his comments on the obfuscatory qualities of Law French (GV(v)) and the glosses in contemporary legal textbooks (GViii). Elyot's brief discussion of contemporary legal training makes it clear just how far short of classical standards he thought it actually fell (see sigs Hi–iii(v)).

63. See, for example, the declaration in the Proheme to *Of the Knowledge Which Maketh a Wise Man* (1533), that Henry VIII had commended Elyot's courageous approach in *The Governor*, 'that I spared no estate in the rebuking of vice' (Aiii–iii(v)).

64. More, *Utopia*, p. 132 ('When I consider and weigh in my mind all these common-wealths which nowadays do flourish, so God help me, I can perceive nothing but a certain conspiracy of rich men procuring their own commodities under the name and title of the commonwealth'); Starkey, *Dialogue*, p. 56 ('princes, lords, bishops, and prelates . . . every one of them looketh chiefly to their own profit, pleasure, and commodity, and few there be which regard the wealth of the comminality, but under the pretence and colour thereof every one of them procureth their private and their singular weal').

65. Quentin Skinner notes that it was characteristic of the northern humanists generally that 'their basic demand was not so much for the reformation of institutions, but rather for a change of heart' (*Foundations of Modern Political Thought*, I, p. 228). Only to a modern reader who has come to see Machiavelli's *Prince* as a more practical and realistic view of political life would such an analysis seem strange or naïve, however. It is again vital to take into account the very different political contexts in which Machiavelli and Elyot were writing if one is to see the practicality of the latter's viewpoint. If the principal threat facing the state came from an invading French or Spanish army, intent upon annexing one's city and deposing its rulers, then advocating a return to Aristotelian principles of moderation and affability in personal and political life on the part of the ruler(s) might seem a curiously abstract and inappropriate response to the situation. If, however, the principal threat was a rancorous internal division seemingly provoked and exacerbated by the Prince's desire to intimidate the church for his own ends, then such a remedy might seem more pertinent and shrewd.

66. The contrast with Machiavelli's account of the political situation in *The Prince*, while clearly extreme, is not uninstructive. In his twelfth chapter Machiavelli asserted that 'the chief foundations on which all states rest' are 'good laws and good arms', and 'where there are good arms, there are bound to be good laws'. (Nicolo Machiavelli, *The Prince*, ed, Robert M. Adams (New York, W.W. Norton, 1992), p. 34.) In his account the prince 'should have no other object, no other subject of study than war, its rules and disciplines' (ibid., p. 40).

67. For this idea, see Erasmus, *Education of a Christian Prince*, pp. 5ff and 25, and Fortescue, *In Praise of the Laws of England*, pp. 53, 99, and xxx. ('The king is given for the kingdom, and not the kingdom for the sake of the king'), where Fortescue quotes the pseudo-Aquinas (i.e. Ptolemy of Lucca), *De Regimine Principium*, III, iii (in J. Perrier, ed., *Opuscula Necnon Opera Minora*, I: *Opera Philosophica*, (Paris, 1949).

See also Aristotle, *Politics*, 3.5.1 and 4.8.3. *The Governor*, working on the assumption that 'the power that is practised to the hurt of many, cannot continue' (Avii), sets out to describe a state that is both stable and beneficial to all. It is important to recall that *The Governor*'s initial defence of monarchy is presented as a discussion of how best to limit the adverse consequences of power misdirected into the wrong hands or misapplied by self-interested oligarchs or demagogues. At the root of Elyot's argument is the assertion that monarchy is the best system of government in a fallen world because it is the least harmful to the public weal. In this he follows the logic of his favourite classical political theorist, Isocrates, who suggested, in a passage in his *Nicocles, or The Cyprians* that Elyot followed closely here, that, of the three major systems of government: democracy, oligarchy, and monarchy, the last was to be most admired because it was milder in the administration of justice than the other two, allowed for a fairer system of appointments and rewards, and created a more experienced, stable and efficient administration, free from the tyranny of rule by cabal or the vagaries of capricious popular ballots. See *To Nicocles* 13–26, in George Norlin, ed. and trans., *Isocrates*, Loeb Classical Library (2nd ed., London, William Heinemann, 1954), I, pp. 85–91; and, for similar arguments, Isocrates' *Areopagiticum* 20 and following, in ibid., III, pp. 117ff. See also Philip George Neserius, 'Isocrates's Political and Social Ideas', *International Journal of Ethics* 43 (1933), pp. 307–28. For a pithy account of Machiavelli's reaction against this tradition, see Quentin Skinner, *Machiavelli: A Very Short Introduction* (Oxford, Oxford University Press, 2000), *passim*.

68. See, for example, Lehmberg, *Sir Thomas Elyot*, p. 115 ('Elyot was unwilling to criticise the King himself, and even critical comments about royal counsellors had to be veiled discreetly'). In the 'Proheme' to *The Governor*, Elyot had assured his royal dedicatee that he had not written 'of presumption to teach any person . . . But only to the intent that men which will be studious about the weal public may find the thing thereto expedient compendiously written'. (aii), and further, that 'where I commend herein any one virtue, or dispraise any one vice, I mean the general description of th'one and th'other without any other particular meaning to the reproach of any one person.' (aiii).

69. For what follows see Simon Thurley, *Whitehall Palace: An Architectural History of the Royal Apartments, 1240–1698* (New Haven, Yale University Press, 1999), pp. 37–41; and G. Rosser and S. Thurley, 'Whitehall Palace and King Street, Westminster: The Urban Cost of Princely Magnificence', *London Topographic Record* 26 (1990), pp. 57–77.

70. *Venetian Calendar*, 1527–33, 664; *Spanish Calendar* IV (ii) 720.

71. Hogrefe, *Life and Times*, p. 136.

72. Significantly, as we shall see Sir Thomas Wyatt was to translate the same sentiments at roughly the same time (see p. 297, below). Fortescue had cited verses to similar effect in his *On the Nature of the Law of Nature*, quoting Boethius's *Consolation of Philosophy*, III, v, as his source for the lines: 'For although the Indian land afar / Trembles at your laws, / And furthest Thule serves you, / Yet not to be able to banish black care, / Or put to flight wretched lamentations: / This is not power'. (Fortescue, *On the Laws and Governance of England*, p. 134). The conclusion that the good prince should not seek to test the full extent of his powers in exercising his will ('what

thou mayest do, delight not for to know'), but rather limit himself to those actions that accord with virtue and honour ('But rather what thing will become thee best') was at the heart of Elyot's political counsel for Henry VIII. It was, like so much else that he said, a commonplace of centuries of advice literature. But it was a commonplace precisely because it addressed an all-too-real political danger in a personal monarchy. Hence it was precisely this sentiment that Sir Thomas More left as his political legacy to Thomas Cromwell. According to his son-in-law and biographer, William Roper, More employed the same metaphor deployed by Erasmus in his colloquy 'The Godly Feast' to warn the future royal secretary of the dangers of the prince discovering the full extent of his powers. ' "Master Cromwell", quoth he, "You are now entered into the service of a most noble, wise, and liberal prince. If you will follow my poor advice, you shall, in your counsel giving unto his grace, ever tell him what he ought to do, but never what he is able to do. So shall you show yourself a true faithful servant and a right worthy counsellor. For if [a] Lion knew his own strength, hard were it for any man to rule him" ' (Roper, *Lyfe of Sir Thomas Moore*, pp. 56–7).

73. In the seventh of his *Letters*, he talks of the mistake of treating secondary matters as if they were of primary importance. See *Plato in Twelve Volumes*, VII; *Epistola*, ed and trans., R. G. Bury, Loeb Classical Library (London, William Heinemann, 1960), Letter VII: 330c.

74. *EHD* v 738. See pp. 116–17, above.

75. See the interrogatories put to Anne Boleyn's chaplain, John Skyp (discussed at pp. 256–7, below) for striking evidence of contemporaries' capacity to read texts in this way.

76. Skinner, *Foundations of Modern Political Thought*, I, p. 222.

77. Elyot refers at various times to the need 'to declare the fervent zeal that I have to my country, and that I desire only to employ that poor learning that I have gotten to the benefit thereof' (Bvii(v)); to 'my duty that I owe to my natural country, with my faith also of allegiance and other wherewith I am double bounden unto your majesty . . . thereby t'acquit me of my duties to God, your highness, and this my country' (aii); and 'the first fruits of my study'; and to the book as 'th'account that I have to render for that one little talent delivered to me, to employ (as I suppose) to the increase of virtue' (aii).

78. Skinner, *Foundations of Modern Political Thought*, I, p. 233. This was certainly the explicit motivation behind Starkey's *Dialogue*, in which medical metaphors for England's problems frequently dominate the discussion.

79. When Elyot did address texts explicitly to readers beyond the King or his circle of ministers, this was a distinct departure from the norm and done with distinct political aims in mind, as we shall see in what follows.

9.   TYRANNY AND THE CONSCIENCE OF MAN

1. The allusion would seem to be to the apocalyptic visions of imminent urban destruction in Habacuc 2: 9–12 ('[T]he stone shall cry out of the wall and the timber that is between the joints of the building shall answer. Woe to him that buildeth a town with blood, and prepareth a city by iniquity') and the prophetic utterance in Luke 19:

38–42. In the latter, Christ, having descended towards Jerusalem from the Mount of Olives, is told by the Pharisees to rebuke his disciples for praising him as 'the king who cometh in the name of the Lord'. He replies, 'I say to you that if these shall hold their peace, the stones will cry out.' 'And when he drew near, seeing the city, he wept over it, saying: If thou also hadst known, and that in this thy day, the things that are to thy peace: but now they are hidden from thy eyes.' He then proceeds to expel the moneychangers from the Temple.

2. For a detailed account of the origins of the *Pasquinade* and of Elyot's treatises on the 1530s more generally, see Frederick William Conrad, 'A Preservative Against Tyranny: The Political Theology of Sir Thomas Elyot (*c.* 1490–1546)', The Johns Hopkins University D.Phil. Dissertation, 1988, especially pp. 128–37; and Major, *Elyot and Renaissance Humanism*, p. 98. For a taste of the Italian *Pasquinades*, see Anne Reynolds, *Renaissance Humanism at the Court of Clement VII: Francesco Berni's Dialogue Against the Poets in Context* (New York, Garland, 1997).

3. Major, *Elyot and Renaissance Humanism*, p. 98; *LP* v (i) 658; vi, 299 (iii); *State Papers* vii 397.

4. Elyot, *Pasquil*, sig. Aii.

5. See Udall's *Floures of Latin Speaking* (1533), I.i.49–55.

6. Conrad, 'A Preservative Against Tyranny', p. 111 n.

7. Diarmaid MacCulloch, *Thomas Cranmer: A Life* (New Haven, Yale University Press, 1996), pp. 79–82; Alistair Fox, 'Sir Thomas Elyot and the Humanist Dilemma', p. 69; Pearl Hogrefe, *Life and Times*, p. 194. Conrad, 'A Preservative Against Tyranny', pp. 139–41, also explores the possibility that William Longland, Henry's official confessor during the 1520s and the man cited in some quarters as the original source of the King's 'scruple' concerning his marriage, might be Elyot's intended target.

8. MacCulloch, *Thomas Cranmer*, p. 82. See also the reference to the radical doctrine of predestination that Elyot also removed in the second edition, turning Pasquil's jibe 'since ye have such a pretty feat in seasoning, a likelihood ye be well seen in predestination' (ciii) into 'of likelihood ye be well seen in *constellations*' (my italics).

9. Given that in one strand of Roman mythology Harpocrates became god of silence because he was able to keep secret his knowledge of one of Venus' sexual affairs, Elyot's association of the character with Cranmer, the guardian of both the King's 'secret' love for Anne and his own secret marriage to Margaret, would have been all the more pointed to those in the know. In this tradition, the gift of a rose, presented to Haprocrates by Venus's son Cupid in reward for his discretion, gave birth to the term '*sub rosa*' as a marker of secrets. See, for example, the succinct account of this story in Henry Peacham, *The Truth of Our Times: Revealed out of one Mans Experience by Way of Essay* (London, 'N.O.' for James Becket, 1638), pp. 173–4, where it is stated that in taverns 'in many places, as well in *England* as the Low Countries, they have over their Tables a rose painted, and what is spoken under the Rose must not be revealed: the reason is this: the Rose being sacred to *Venus*, whose amorous and stolen sports that they might never be revealed, her son *Cupid* would needs dedicate to *Harpocrates*, the god of Silence'. See also Erasmus, '*Reddidit Harpocratem*' ('He imitates Harpocrates'), *Adage* IV.i.52, in *The Adages of Erasmus*, selected by William Baker (Toronto, University of Toronto Press, 2001), pp. 356–8 ('He Turned Him Into Harpocrates') for an erotically charged version of the proverbial use of Harpocrates' name as an emblem of silence. Elsewhere, however, Harpocrates'

silence was assumed to conceal vacuity rather than guilty secrets. It is possible that Elyot's lengthy report to the Duke of Norfolk quoted in the previous chapter contained an arch allusion to his fellow ambassador's behaviour in its half-humorous, half-censorious references to the openly flirtatious atmosphere in Nuremberg, and the fact that the clergy there chose the most attractive women of the city for their wives. See also *Spanish Calendar* v (i) 1047; MacCulloch, *Thomas Cranmer*, p. 86.

10. MacCulloch, *Thomas Cranmer*, pp. 76, 79, and 82–4.
11. Wilson, 'Letters', pp. 5–10.
12. Ibid., p. 8.
13. Ibid., p. 9.
14. Ibid., pp. 11–12.
15. Ibid., p. 14.
16. Ibid., p. 17.
17. In part at least, Harpocrates's position, and the response it elicits from Pasquil, revisits the debate between the narrator and the courtly flatterer Mum ('Silence') in the fourteenth-century alliterative poem *Mum and the Sothsegger*, a poem written in the aftermath of an earlier period in which a crisis of counsel had threatened the stability of the kingdom: the reign of Richard II. In this earlier work, Mum asserts that, at court, silence is safest, as 'who-so mellid muche more than hit nedeth / Shuld rather wynne weping watre thenne robes' and 'of "bable" cometh blame and of "be stille" never' (287–8 and 292), wheras the narrator charges him that therby 'thou suffris thy souvrayn to shame hym-self / There thou mightes amende hym many tyme and ofte' (273–4). See Helen Barr, ed., *The Piers Plowman Tradition* (London, Dent Everyman, 1993); and for a helpful reading of both *Mum* and *Pasquil*, Barr and Kate Ward-Perkins, ' "Spekyng for One's Sustenance": The Rhetoric of Counsel in *Mum and the Sothsegger*, Skelton's *Bowge of Court*, and Elyot's *Pasquil the Plain*' in Helen Cooper and Sally Mapstone, eds., *The Long Fifteenth Century: Essays for Douglas Gray* (Oxford, The Clarendon Press, 1997), pp. 249–72. I am very grateful to Professor John Scattergood and Anne Marie D'Arcy for suggesting these references.
18. Wilson, 'Letters', p. 17.
19. In order to make the political applicability of all this still clearer, Elyot would add a further case to the second edition of the text, published later in the same year. 'If thou be called to counsel, after thou hast either heard one reason before thee, or, at the least way, in the balance of thine own reason pondered the question, spare not to show thine advice, and to speak truly, remembering that God is not so far off, but that he can hear thee' (*Pasquil*, 2nd edition, sig. Eviii).
20. For an evocative account of the brethren and the evangelical circles in London at this time, see Susan Brigden, *London and the Reformation* (Oxford, Clarendon Press, 1989), pp. 1–215.
21. Note also his later assertion that 'the world is almost at an end; for after noon is turned to forenoon, virtue into vice, vice into virtue, devotion into hypocrisy, and in some places, men say, faith is turned into heresy' (Bv).
22. Lehmberg, *Thomas Elyot*, p. 117. Diarmaid MacCulloch (*Thomas Cranmer*, p. 80) thought that Pasquil 'was clearly an image of Elyot himself'; Pearl Hogrefe (*Life and Times*, p. 193) that 'Pasquil is Elyot himself'; and Alistair Fox ('Elyot and the Humanist Dilemma', p. 66) that he was 'his mouthpiece'.

23. Major, *Elyot and Renaissance Humanism*, p. 100.

24. Fox, 'Elyot and the Humanist Dilemma', p. 66, Barr and Ward-Perkins, 'Spekynge for One's Sustenance'. p. 258.

25. The point is well made by Alistair Fox: 'The fiction of *Pasquil the Plain* shows that even while Elyot was asserting this Hythlodaen stance, he was pointedly aware of the likely cost to his hopes of advancement of adopting it. His own remonstrance to the King had proved that waiting for the convenient time and place did not necessarily work; either that or . . . he had monumentally miscalculated the appropriateness of the occasion' (Fox, 'Elyot and the Humanist Dilemma', p. 67).

26. Hogrefe, *Life and Times*, p. 200. Gnatho's declaration to Pasquil, 'Peace, whoreson, he is also my lord's confessor' (Bv(v)) was replaced in the second edition with the conditional observation 'notwithstanding, for your silence ye might be a confessor', while the statement that a confessor should denounce the sins 'that he knoweth in his master' (Bvi) was replaced by the more general statement that a confessor should do so 'in him whom he hath in confession'. Likewise the later statement 'perdie, Gnatho named you to be your master's physician when he said ye were his confessor' (Dii) was replaced with 'the same is the office of a good confessor, where he perceiveth man's soul to be wounded with vicious affections . . .'

27. See below, pp. 200–1.

28. *Of the Knowledge*, sig. Aii–ii(v).

29. Hogrefe, *Life and Times*, p. 196.

30. The fact that Elyot makes no reference to Isocrates or Nicocles, the central 'characters' in *The Doctrinal of Princes*, while naming all the *dramatis personae* of *Pasquil* and *Of the Knowledge*, seems to confirm the suggestion that *The Doctrinal* had yet to appear at the time that this text was written, and so was the fourth of Elyot's overtly political texts to be published.

31. Diogenes Laertius, *Life of Plato*, III:18–19, in *Lives of the Eminent Philosophers*, ed. and trans., R. D. Hicks, Loeb Classical Library (2 vols, London, William Heinemann, 1925), I, p. 293–5. Elyot had cited the story in *The Governor* as an example of 'Magnanimity' or 'valiant courage' (*The Governor*, cvii(v)–cviii). Elyot does not seem to have used the fuller, but very different, account of Plato's Sicilian experiences to be found in a number of his *Letters*, especially Letter VII, which focuses on the philosopher's support for Dion and his political legacy. See Plato, *Epistola*, ed. and trans., R. G. Bury, Loeb Classical Library (London, William Heinemann, 1966). The story of Plato's relations with Dionysius was, however, almost proverbial as an example of the confrontation between philosophy and tyranny. See, for example, More, *Utopia*, p. 39, and Starkey, *Dialogue*, p. 15.

32. *Of the Knowledge*, sig. Pii–Pii(v).

33. On the conformity of inner and outer self, see, for example, sigs. Civ, Cvi(v). On the rule of reason, see sigs. H–K, *passim*, and especially Ji–i(v) On the need to exercise knowledge in action, see Nii, and Pi ff.

34. *Lives 2:17–18*, I, pp. 292–5.

35. See, for example, Fox, 'Sir Thomas Elyot and the Humanists' Dilemma', pp. 70–3; Major, *Elyot and Renaissance Humanism*, pp. 102ff.

36. *Lives 2:65–66*, I, pp. 194–5. For a more negative reading of the character of Aristippus in Elyot's dialogue, see Wilson, *Incomplete Fictions*, pp. 89–90, where he

is interpreted as 'a resistant, ill-equipped philosopher', who needs to be educated and redeemed by Plato's patient teachings. Wilson also argues, contrary to the line advanced here, that Elyot 'seems not to have known' Laertius's *Life of Aristippus*, or that 'at least he appropriates nothing of the Oscar Wilde-like character preserved in this biography' (ibid.).

37. *Lives 2:82*, I, pp. 210–11.
38. *Lives 2:73*, I, pp. 200–3.
39. *Lives 2:79*, I, pp. 206–7.
40. See, for example, *Lives 2:70*, I, pp. 198–9 ('In answer to one who remarked that he always saw philosophers at rich men's doors, he [Aristippus] said, "So too, physicians are in attendance on those who are sick, but no one for that reason would prefer being sick to being a physician.').
41. *Lives 2:81*, I, pp. 208–9.
42. *Lives 2:82*, I, pp. 210–11.
43. *Lives 2:78*, I, pp. 206–7.
44. *Lives 2:67*, I, pp. 196–7.
45. *Lives 3:36*, I, pp. 308–9. ('Plato was also on bad terms with Aristippus. At least in the dialogue *Of the Soul* he disparages him, saying that he was not present at the death of Socrates, though he was no farther off than Aegina. Again, they say that he showed a certain jealousy of Aeshines, because of his reputation with Dionysius, and that, when he arrived at the court, he was disparaged by Plato because of his poverty, but supported by Aristippus.')
46. *Lives 3:38*, I, pp. 310–11.
47. See *The Governor*, Mv(v)–Mvii(v).
48. *Lives 3:23*, I, pp. 296–9.
49. *Lives 3:23*, I, pp. 296–7.
50. Lehmberg, *Sir Thomas Elyot*, p. 115; Major, *Elyot and Renaissance Humanism*, pp. 11–12.
51. More than one critic has seen a direct allusion to Henry VIII in Plato's description of Dionysius as 'a man of quick and subtle wit, but therewith he was wonderful sensual, unstable, and wandering in sundry affections, Delighting sometime in voluptuous pleasures, another time in gathering of great treasure and riches, oftentimes resolved into a beastly rage and vengeable cruelty, About the public weal of his country alway remiss, in his own desires studious and diligent' (Nvi–vi(v)). (See, for example, Fox, 'Elyot and the Humanist Dilemma', pp. 70–1.) But, given that in the same passage he says of the King that he is 'a tyrant, that is to say commen to that dignity by usurpation and violence and not by just succession or lawful election' (Nvi), it would have been extraordinarily bold (not to say out of keeping with his other public statements) to have intended this as a literal portrait of his own King. Indeed the suggestion that Henry was a usurper would have placed Elyot in direct contravention of the terms of the Treason act of 1534. It is probably wiser to see this as a depiction of Dionysius in the mould of the traditional self-interested, capricious tyrant that is inflected to reflect certain similarities to Henry's case. Like Elyot's other portraits of Henrician bad kings it is intended as a warning of what he might become if he does not reform rather than as a picture of him as he actually is.
52. See, for example, sigs. Evii(v), Fvi, and Eviii.

53. Plato mocks Aristippus's desire for Lais the harlot ('in whom thou takest pleasure in fulfilling thy carnal appetite' (Ci(v))) and condemns his pursuit of pleasure ('thou art so nuzzled in carnal affections that thou keepest nothing in remembrance but only that which is commodious and pleasant' (G8)). See also CV and CVi(v). Wilson, *Incomplete Fictions*, pp. 89–90, argues for a more 'chivalrous' and 'patient' Plato here, who treats his adversary with 'courtesy and reinforcement', although the examples he cites suggest more the ironic condescension of a sardonic schoolmaster than true courtesy.

54. 'Now in good faith, though thou thyself hast a delicate mouth and thy taste distempered, yet I can thee thank: for now thou sayest truly' (Bvi(v)).

55. For similar instances of Aristippus's amiability, see Mvii, and Mviii. Major saw the allusion to 'six the best cities' as 'conclusive evidence' that the text was 'a veiled commentary' on Thomas More's resignation from the Chancellorship (Major, *Elyot and Renaissance Humanism*, p. 103). These are, Major claims, 'almost the very words' which, according to William Roper's biography of More, Charles V spoke to Elyot on the occasion of More's death in 1535. [I]f we had been master of such a servant', the Emperor is reported to have said, 'of whose doings ourself have had these many years no small experience, we would rather have lost the best city of our dominions than have lost such a worthy counsellor' (William Roper, *The Lyfe of Sir Thomas Moore, Knighte*, ed. E. V. Hitchcock, EETS, original series, 197 (Oxford, Oxford University Press, 1935), p. 104.). But the anecdote itself is notoriously suspect, as Elyot was not at the imperial court at the time of More's execution, nor at the time of his resignation, which has been suggested as an alternative occasion on which the remark could have been made. Major's further suggestion that the Emperor might have been pre-empting the possibility of More's later resignation (Major, *Elyot and Renaissance Humanism*, p. 93) seems a little too speculative for comfort. Moreover, the comparison of a good minister to a valuable city seems to have been a popular one. Certainly Elyot himself had used it, quite independently, earlier, attributing it in *The Governor* to King Xerxes of Persia as a comment on the worth of his commander Zopirus, who had cut off his own nose and ears to aid his King to a military victory. (His cited sources are Book III of Herodotus's *History*; and Plutarch's *Sayings of Kings and Commanders*, in *Moralia*, ed. and trans. F. C. Babbitt, *et al.*, Loeb Classical Library (London, William Heinemann, 1927–69), vol. III) (*The Governor*, sig. A ii(v))). The most likely explanation for Roper's use of the phrase is either that it, or something like it, was indeed said by Charles V after More's execution, but not to Elyot, and Roper simply confused the chronology and recorded Elyot as the recipient in error, or Elyot himself made up the story, putting a comparison which struck him as suitably grand and ennobling into the mouth of the Emperor in order to convey the admiration that true princes had for More's qualities, and claiming to have heard it himself to add veracity to the story. Either way, the coincidence of phrasing does not prove that Elyot wanted his readers to associate the Plato of his dialogue with More.

56. See sigs Oii and Oiv.

57. For similar sentiments, see *The Governor*, sig. Piii, where 'this worde Had I wist' is described as one 'which hath been ever of all wise men reproved'. In *The Education of a Christian Prince*, Erasmus had cited Scipio Africanus to the effect that 'I did not think' 'is not a fit expression for a wise man' (Erasmus, *Education*, p. 20, citing Valerius Maximus 7.2.2).

58. For Elyot's patriotism, see the Prologues to *The Governor, Of the Knowledge*, and *The Castle of Health*, and Lehmberg, *Sir Thomas Elyot*, pp. 40–1.

59. Diogenes' role in *Pasquil the Plain* will be considered in what follows. He makes a brief appearance in *Of the Knowledge* at sigs. cii–ii(v).

60. *Lives* 6:38, ii, pp. 40–1.

61. *Lives* 6:44, ii, pp. 44–5.

62. *Lives* 6:32, ii, pp. 34–5. For approving references to Alexander's statement, see, for example, Erasmus, *Education*, pp. 2–3.

63. *Lives* 6:24, ii, pp. 26–7, see also ibid. 6:32, ii, pp. 34–5 ('One day he shouted for men, and when people collected, hit out at them with his stick, saying, "It was men I called for, not scoundrels".'), and 6:60, pp. 62–3 ('Being asked what he had done to be called a hound [i.e. a cynic], he said, 'I fawn on those who give me anything, I yelp at those who refuse, and I set my teeth in rascals.'), and 6:39, pp. 40–1 ('When somebody declared that there is no such thing as motion, he got up and walked about').

64. See *Lives* 6:64, ii, pp. 66–7. ('He was going into a theatre, meeting face to face those who were coming out, and, being asked way, "This', he said, "is what I practise doing all my life." ')

65. See *Lives* 6:54, ii, pp. 56–7 ('When he was told that many people laughed at him, he made answer, "But I am not laughed down" '), and 6:58, pp. 60–1 (when told that 'most people' laughed at him, he said 'And so very likely do the asses at them; but as they don't care for the asses, so neither do I care for them').

66. See *Lives* 6:40, ii, p. 40–1 ('When Plato styled him a dog, "Quite true", he said, "for I come back again and again to those who have sold me" '), 6:43, pp. 44–5 ('Still he was loved by the Athenians. At all events, when a youngster broke up his tub, they gave the boy a flogging and presented Diogenes with another [tub]'), and 6:33, pp. 34–5 ('He described himself as a hound of the sort which all men praise, but no one, he added, of his admirers, dared go out hunting with him').

67. See *Lives* 6:26, ii, pp. 26–9 ('[O]ne day when Plato had invited to his house friends coming from Dionysius, Diogenes trampled upon his carpets and said, "I trample upon Plato's vainglory." Plato's reply was, "How much pride you expose to view, Diogenes, by seeming not to be proud." Others tell us that what Diogenes said was, "I trample upon the pride of Plato", who retorted, "Yes, Diogenes, with pride of another sort" ') and 6:53, pp. 54–5 ('As Plato was conversing about idea, and using the nouns "tablehood" and "cuphood", he [Diogenes] said, "table and cup I see, but your tablehood and cuphood, Plato, I can no wise see". "That's readily accounted for", said Plato, "for you have the eyes to see the visible table and cup, but not the understanding by which ideal tablehood and cuphood are discerned." ')

68. *Lives* 6:26 and 6:40, ii, pp. 28–9 and 42–3. See also 6:25, pp. 26–7 ('[At another] time he [Diogenes] was eating dried figs when he encountered Plato and offered him a share of them. When Plato took them and ate them, he said, "I said you might share them, not that you might eat them all up".')

69. See, for example, *Lives* 6:38, ii, pp. 38–41, 6:66, pp. 68–9 ('He [Diogenes] said that bad men obey their lusts as servants obey their masters.'), and 6:69, pp. 70–1 ('Being asked what was the most beautiful thing in the world, he replied, "Freedom of speech"').

70. *Lives* 6:54, II, pp. 54–5 ('On being asked by somebody, "What sort of man do you consider Diogenes to be?", "A Socrates gone mad", said he.')

71. *Lives* 2:78, I, pp. 206–7 and 6:30, II, pp. 30–3, and 6:26, II, pp. 26–7, respectively.

72. The two versions are at *Lives* 6:58, II, pp. 58–61 and 2:68, I, pp. 196–7 respectively. For another 'shared' anecdote, see *Lives* 6:32, II, pp. 34–5 ('Some one took [Diogenes] . . . into a magnificent house and warned him not to expectorate, whereupon, having cleared his throat, he discharged the phlegm into the man's face, being unable, he said, to find a meaner receptacle. Others father this upon Aristippus').

73. Note in this context Wilson's shrewd observations that 'Like the drama of our time [he was thinking particularly of Beckett and Stoppard], certain ancient and Renaissance dialogues offer representation of the striving of a divided mind toward resolution' rather than the clear exposition of an already settled argument or case; and that 'Elyot's finest eloquence rises from the well of his ambivalence, and this dialectic takes its most natural form in a dialogue concerning self-knowledge' (Wilson, *Incomplete Fictions*, pp. 15 and 77–8, respectively).

74. See, for example, *Lives* 2:72, I, pp. 200–1. ('He [Aristippus] was asked by some one in what way his son would be the better for being educated. He replied, "If nothing more that this, at all events, when in the theatre he will not sit down like a stone upon stone." ')

75. *Pasquil the Plain*, sig. Avi–vi(v).

76. Hogrefe, *Life and Times*, p. 275.

77. Fox has addressed these issues in a series of articles published in Fox and John Guy, *Reassessing the Henrician Age: Humanism, Politics, and Reform, 1500–1550* (Oxford, Basil Blackwell, 1986). See, for example, 'English Humanism and the Body Politic', in ibid., pp. 34–51, especially p. 46; and 'Sir Thomas Elyot and the Humanist Dilemma', in ibid, pp. 52–73, especially pp. 52–3. Although I differ from Fox on points of detail and the degree of pessimism and finality that Plato's conclusions mark in Elyot's thinking, I am greatly indebted to his arguments, and in particular his recognition of the attraction that Aristippus seem to exert upon Elyot. See 'Elyot and the Humanist Dilemma', p. 73. See also Hogrefe, *Life and Times*, p. 203, where it is suggested that, by the time that he wrote *Of the Knowledge*, Elyot had 'become hopeless about the ruler and has shifted his concern to the philosopher who is out of favour'.

78. The ambitious, experimental nature of the translation is attested to in Elyot's introductory address to his readers. 'I have translated out of Greek', he announced, 'not presuming to contend with them which have done the same in Latin, but to th'intent only that I would assay if our English tongue might receive the quick and proper sentences pronounced by the Greeks' (Aii-ii(v)). See also Lehmberg, *Sir Thomas Elyot*, p. 126; and Lillian Gottesman, ed., *Four Political Treatises . . . by Sir Thomas Elyot* (Gainesville, Florida, Scholars Facsimiles and Reprints, 1967), introduction.

79. George Norlin, ed and trans, *Isocrates*, Loeb Classical Library, (2nd edn, 3 vols., London, William Heinemann, 1954), I, p. xviii. All references to Isocrates's texts are to this edition.

80. For Isocrates' assertion of the morality of oratory, see his *Against the Sophists*, 21, in *Isocrates*, II, pp. 176–7, and the *Antidosis*, 275, in ibid., II, pp. 336ff. For his advocacy

of the life of retirement, see *Antidosis*, 150 and following, in *Isocrates*, III, pp. 270–1; for his justification of his own role as a counsellor outside government, see *To Philip*, 8 and following (in *Isocrates*, I, pp. 294–7), and *Panathenaicus*, 35 and following (ibid., I, pp. 395ff). For his patriotism and sense of his own responsibility to cure the ailments of the state, see *Panegyricus*, 18 and following (ibid., pp. 128ff), *On the Peace*, and the *Areopagiticus*, (ibid., III, p. 7–157), and the *Panathenaicus*, (ibid., III, pp. 372–84). For his criticisms of other teachers, see *Against the Sophists*, 9–10 (ibid., I, esp. p. 169) and *Antidosis*, 285 (ibid., I, esp. pp. 342–3) and the *Panegyricus*, 3–4 (ibid., I, pp. 120–3). For the need to apply wisdom, see, for example, the *Antidosis*, 75–6 (ibid., I, pp. 290–5). See also Philip George Neserius, 'Isocrates's Political and Social Ideas', *International Journal of Ethics* 43 (1933), pp. 307–28, esp. p. 314.

81. Lillian Gottesmann suggested, on the strength of the order in which Elyot listed his works in *The Image of Governance*, that *The Doctrinal* may have been the second of his works to be printed, dating it 'shortly after Elyot's return from the court of Charles V' in June 1532. Gottesmann, ed., *Four Political Treatises*, p. 1x.

82. Hogrefe, *Life and Times*, p. 314.

83. Indeed, critics have tended to see *The Doctrinal* as less specific and political in its intensions as Elyot's earlier treatises. Pearl Hogrefe thought 'Elyot was not making any special or conscious effort to influence Henry VIII in *The Doctrinal*', but added, 'of course, he probably penned any comment on government with the pious hope that it might have an influence on his beloved England', before concluding, 'But this particular work has nothing that is either timely or urgent' (Hogrefe, *Life and Times*, p. 235).

84. 'When public ordinances and institutions are not well founded, alter and change them. If possible originate for yourself what is best for your country, but, failing this, imitate what is good in other countries' (*To Nicocles*, 17, in *Isocrates*, I, p. 49).

10. FROM SUPREMACY TO TYRANNY, 1533–1540

1. For these events, see Brigden, *London and the Reformation*, pp. 188–224. For Frith and Hewet, see Hall, *Chronicle*, p. 816. For Elizabeth Barton, see Alan Neame, *The Holy Maid of Kent* (London, Hodder and Stoughton, 1971).

2. *LP* VI 807.

3. Elton, *Policy and Police*, pp. 222–6; *Spanish Calendar*, V, p. 58.

4. *LP* VII 522.

5. Elton, *Policy and Police*, pp. 227–9.

6. *Statutes of the Realm*, I, p. 508.

7. See *Spanish Calendar* v (i) p. 453; Roper, *Lyfe*, pp. 80–1, Hall, *Chronicle*, p. 817.

8. Brigden, *London and the Reformation*, p. 230; *LP* VIII 949, Hall, *Chronicle*, pp. 817–18. Even Hall was to concede of Fisher that 'this bishop was of very many men lamented, for he was reported to be a man of great learning and a man of very good life'. For More's jokes, see ibid., p. 817.

9. *Spanish Calendar* v (i) 179 (*LP* VIII 949).

10. Brigden, *London and The Reformation*, p. 241; Wriothesley, *Chronicle*, I, p. 30.

11. Unusually Elyot chose to add a precise date to the Preface on this occasion.

12. Hogrefe, *Life and Times*, pp. 209–12.

13. Indeed, other Bridgettines, such as Richard Whitford, were also highly critical of the Supremacy and the Boleyn marriage, suggesting that even at this stage Syon was a centre of conservative sentiment.

14. Thaschus Caecilius Cyprianus, *De Mortalitate*, Corpus Chistianorum Series Latina (Turnhout, 1953-) 3A, 15–32. Elyot deliberately widens the focus of the sermon from the specific issue of the plague signalled in the original title, *De Mortalitate* ('On the Mortality/Plague'), to a concern with death generally: 'Of mortality of man' as his title-page has it. Similarly, where the Latin text has reference to the attack of 'this disease' (*De Mortalitate*, 8, CCSL 3A 20, 108), Elyot substitutes 'this trouble' (Bvii–vii(v)). A similar motive seems to underlie another substantial change of emphasis in Elyot's otherwise very faithful translation, when he implies a more human source of tribulation than had been implicit in Cyprian's text, by replacing the latter's suggestion that the Christian soul travailed '*inter diaboli gladius*' ('among the devil's weapons') (*De Mortalitate*, 19, 70) with 'among the swords of people malicious' (Bv). For Cyprian's text in translation, see Cyprian, *Treatises*, The Fathers of the Church, vol. 36, ed. and trans. Roy J. Deferrari, *et al.* (Washington, The Catholic University of America Press, 1958).

15. See also Proverbs 17: 3; Wisdom 3: 6; and Zechariah 13: 9.

16. See sigs Biv(v)–v (rather than delighting to tarry among the lures of the Devil and 'the swords of people malicious', the Christian should embrace death and 'desire death setting thee forward to haste thee toward Christ').

17. See Bvii ('When they whom we do most favour or love do depart out of this world, we should rather be glad than sorry.')

18. The text is from Psalm 50:19. See also Tobit 2:1–3; 6.

19. See Cyprian, *De Mortalitate*, 4, 68, CCSL 3A, 19 ('*conpellaris iurare quod non licet*'). Perhaps significantly, he also tightens up the implied criticism of those whose resistance was more dramatic, but undertaken, he implies, more for show or self-indulgence than true conviction and humility. Where the Latin text states that the public assertion of courage 'is a wanton display when there is no danger. Struggle in adversity is the trial of [the] truth' (*De Mortalitate*, 23; 197–9: '*Delictata iactatio est, cum periculum non est: conflictatio in adversis probation est veritas*'), he has 'Boasting out of peril is pleasant, but resistance in adversity is the trial of truth' (civ–iv(v)), adding the implication that there is a degree of self-gratification to be gained from unnecessary posturing.

20. Hogrefe, *Life and Times*, p. 213.

21. Elyot's outward conformity can also be seen in his willingness to take part in Anne Boleyn's coronation in June 1533, when he acted as a Knight servitor to the new Queen and Archbishop Cranmer, a role that, given his feelings towards the latter, must have been particularly galling for him.

22. At some point between 1533 and 1535, 'in times vacant from business and other more serious study, as it were for my solace and recreation', he had also translated a short treatise by Plutarch on *The Education or Bringing Up of Children*. The work is dedicated to Elyot's sister, Margery Puttenham, in the hope that she will, 'endeavour yourself to adapt and form in my little nephews inclination to virtue and doctrine, according to my expectation' (Aii(v)). Having already drawn extensively from Plutarch's treatise in the educational chapters of *The Governor*, Elyot may well have been

working up copious notes into a coherent text rather than starting afresh with a new translation, but the achievement remains impressive at a time when he had many other irons in the fire. It also demonstrates how intensely Elyot's mind was focused at this time on the question of how to deploy his wisdom in the best interests of the state. For even in this most private and occasional publication, written, or so he claimed, 'for my pastime without much study or travail' (Aii(v)), he was to return to the dilemma that had so exercised him in *Of the Knowledge Which Maketh a Wise Man*: 'They been assured and perfect men which can mix politic wisdom with philosophy. And I dare affirm they do thereby obtain double commodity. That is to wit, they do lead their life to the common weal of their country, and also they do pass their time in studies of wisdom and virtue, with quietness of mind, never overflown with the waves of fortune' (Dii).

23. William G. Crane, *Wit and Rhetoric in the Renaissance: The Formal Basis of Elizabethan Prose* (Edinburgh, Edinburgh University Press, 1937), argued for Elyot's indebtedness to the *Polyanthea*, but Major (*Elyot and Renaissance Humanism*, pp. 18–19) rejected the claim, suggesting instead that the two writers drew upon a common pool of classical authors.

24. The passage quotes material from Proverbs 9:1–5, 1:20–7, and 8:14–18. It is interesting to note the markedly less powerful effect that the same lines produce in *The Governor*, sig. F viii(v), when they are cited as the words of Solomon rather than spoken directly in the narratorial voice.

25. Elyot is here quoting Proverbs 8:17–21.

26. Proverbs 12:15 and 13:20.

27. His sources are Proverbs 9:8 and 15:31. See also the maxim of Plato (cited at Ev-v(v)): 'Most happy is that public weal where either men studious of wisdom do reign, or where the king is studious of wisdom.'

28. The sources here are Cicero, *De Officiis*, I, 86–7; and Matthew 12:25–6. See also Cvi(v)): 'With concord small things grow to be great, with discord the most greatest things be brought unto nothing.'

29. See above, pp. 466–7, n. 24.

30. Proverbs 16:32 ('The patient man is better than the valiant: and he that ruleth his spirit than he that taketh cities'); Seneca, *De Ira* 2, 11; *De Clementia*, I, in *Seneca*, ed and tranls J. W. Basore, T. H. Corcoran, R. M. Gummere, and F. J. Miller, Loeb Classical Library (10 vols, London, William Heinemann, 1943), Book I. See many of the maxims to the same effect in *Banquet*, sigs. Bii–Bii(v) and Civ(v).

31. Gregory the Great, *Liber regulae pastoralis* (*The Book of Pastoral Care*), 9, PL 77.

32. Wisdom of Solomon 6:1–6.

33. Plutarch *The Precepts of Statecraft*, 20, in *Moralia*, ed. and trans. F. C. Babbitt, Loeb Classical Library (5 vol., London, William Heinemann, 1927–36), I, p. 253. The sentiments echo those in Erasmus' *Education of a Christian Prince*, p. 71: 'The prince should avoid all innovation as far as proven possible: for even if something is changed for the better, a novel situation is still disturbing in itself. Neither the structure of the state . . . nor long established laws may be changed without upheaval'.

34. The passage cited is from the *Commentary on Matthew* (*Commentariorum in Mattheum*, 5:1; CCSL 77). He follows this with further commentary on bishops' silence in the face of heresy (again a telling point given the association of Cranmer with

Harpocrates in *Pasquil the Plain*) drawn from Jerome's *Letter to Oceanus* (*Epistola as Oceanum* (*de vita clericorum*), letter 69, CSEL 54, 691ff ('Devout conversation, without communication, as much as by example it profiteth, by silence it hurteth. For with barking of dogs and staves of the shepherds, the raging wolves be let of their purpose.') Thanks to Anne Marie D'Arcy for this reference.

35. Ecclesiasticus/Sirach 7:21.
36. I Corinthians 7:27.
37. These events will be discussed in greater detail in Chapter 12. For various interpretations of the motives behind Anne's destruction, see, E. W. Ives, 'Faction and the Court of Henry VIII: The Fall of Anne Boleyn', *History* 57 (1972), pp. 169–88, and Ives, *Anne Boleyn* (Oxford, Basil Blackwell, 1986), pp. 335ff; G. W. Bernard, 'The Fall of Anne Boleyn', *E.H.R.* CVI (1991), pp. 584–610, reprinted in Bernard, *Power and Politics in Tudor England* (Aldershot, Ashgate, 2000), pp. 80–107; and Greg Walker, 'Rethinking the Fall of Anne Boleyn', *HJ* 45 (2002), pp. 1–29.
38. For these details, see Brigden, *London and the Reformation*, pp. 248–51; *LP* XI 576.
39. Elton, *Policy and Police*, p. 387.
40. *LP* VIII 771, 846; Brigden, *London and the Reformation*, p. 271.
41. Foxe, *Acts and Monuments*, v, p. 408.
42. *E.H.D.* v, pp. 814–16.
43. Foxe, *Acts and Monuments*, V, p. 505; *LP* XIV (i) 1108 and 1152; S. E. Lehmberg, *The Later Parliaments of Henry VIII, 1536–1547* (Cambridge, Cambridge University Press, 1977), p. 73.
44. *LP* XIV (i) 116; Lehmberg, *Later Parliaments*, p. 72; Brigden, *London and the Reformation*, p. 305.
45. Lehmberg, *Later Parliaments*, pp. 46, 83, and 85. When Parliament resumed, after two further prorogations, on 12 April 1540, Elyot's place had been taken by another local lawyer and administrator, Thomas Rudston.
46. I have written at length on possible political readings of this text elsewhere. (See Walker, *Persuasive Fictions: Faction, Faith, and Politics in the Reign of Henry VIII* (Aldershot, Scolar Press, 1996), pp. 178–204, so will not go into the arguments in detail here.)
47. Hall, *Chronicle*, p. 828.
48. Brigden, *London and the Reformation*, p. 318.

11,   THE APOTHEOSIS OF SIR THOMAS ELYOT

1. *The Image*, sig. aii. ('Albeit I could not so exactly perform mine enterprise as I might have done if the owner had not importunately called for his book, whereby I was constrained to leave some part of the work untranslated.')
2. The colophon is dated 1540, but the title-page carries the date 1541, thus suggesting that the text was printed over the Christmas and New Year of 1540–1.
3. See Uwe Baumann, 'Sir Thomas Elyot's *The Image of Governance*: A Humanist's *Speculum Principis* and a Literary Puzzle', in Dieter Stein and Rosanna Sornicola, eds., *The Virtues of Language: History in Language, Linguistics, and Texts* (Amsterdam, John Benjamins, 1998) [hereafter, '*The Image*'], pp. 177–99, especially 181–3. The essay is reprinted in slightly expanded form in Fritz-Wilhelm Neumann and Sabine

Schülting, eds., *Anglistentag, 1998: Proceedings of the Conference of the German Association of University Teachers of English*, xx (Trier, Wissenschaftlicher Verlag, 1999), pp. 181–98. Baumann's article draws upon two unpublished doctoral theses, N. N. Woolger, 'Sir Thomas Elyot's *The Image of Governance*, its Sources and Political Significance', Oxford University D.Phil Dissertation, 1970; and Robert C. Pinckert, 'Sir Thomas Elyot's *The Image of Governance* (1541): A Critical Edition', Columbia University Ph.D. dissertation, 1964. For similar doubts concerning the details of Elyot's story, see Hogrefe, *Life and Times*, pp. 320–1; and Lehmberg, *Sir Thomas Elyot*, 178–9. For the suggestion that the claims might be taken at face value, see Croft, ed., *The Governour*, i, pp. xcxlix–cl. Pinckert, 'A Critical Edition', pp. v–xii, makes a good case that *The Image* does fulfil Elyot's promise to provide the second volume promised in *The Governor*. I was able to obtain a copy of Dr Pinckert's thesis only after the completion of the first draft of this chapter, and so have acknowledged the principal points of similarity and difference in our arguments in the footnotes that follow.

4. Horace, *Ars Poetica*, 388, in *Satires, Epistles, and Ars Poetica*, ed. and trans., H. Rushton Fairclough, Loeb Classical Library, (London, William Heinemann, 1929).

5. The *Historia* would have been well known in humanist circles at this time, as it had been edited by Egnatius Johanne Baptista (Giovanni Battista Cipelli) and published twice by the Aldine Press in 1516 and 1519, and by Froben in Basle with amendments by Cipelli's pupil, Erasmus in 1518. See Pinckert, 'A Critical Edition', p. xliii, where it is argued on linguistic grounds that Elyot followed the Aldine edition rather than that with Erasmus's additions. Baumann argues ('*Image of Governance*', *passim*), that Elyot's citation of the spurious Encolpius/Eucolpius as his source indicates that he knew the *Historia* itself to be a forgery or hoax, and was consciously joining in the game of misappropriation of sources that he spotted in his source. I do not think that Elyot need necessarily to have seen through all the levels of deception perpetrated in his source, however, to have realized the potential in the text for his own ironic purposes. Certainly the fact that he cites Lampridius as the source for a number of the anecdotes related in *The Governor* (see, for example, DV(v) and PI–i(v)) would suggest that he thought him to be authentic at that time. See p. 255 below.

6. For a detailed discussion of the *Historia*, its sources and history, see the essays collected in Ronald Syme, *Historia Augusta Papers* (Oxford, Clarendon Press, 1983), esp. pp. 109 ff.

7. For the suggestion of 'blown up', see Baumann, '*The Image*', p. 192. For the idea that 'Encolpius' was the *Historia* author's comic invention, see Syme, *Historia Augusta Papers*, p. 103. It is just possible that the change to 'Eucolpius' was a printer's error as Pinckert at one point suggests ('A Critical Edition', p. xlviii), but given that the name appears spelled in the same way in Berthelet's edition of the *Bibliotheca Eliotae* (where Elyot mentions, s.v. Origen, 'the book which I translated out of Eucolpius and called it *The Image of Governance*') the printer would have had to have been both very persistent and very observant in the commission of his error.

8. Who these 'other' writers of Alexandrian biographies might have been is not clear. Although Elyot draws minor details from both Cassius Dio's *Roman History* and the *History of the Empire* by Herodian, his text differs markedly from these standard sources in both tone and emphases. Cf. Cassius Dio, *The Roman History*, ed. and trans,

E. Cary, *The Loeb Classical Library* (9 vols., London, William Heinemann, 1917), and E. H. Warmington, ed. and trans., *Herodian*, The Loeb Classical Library (2 vols., London, William Heinemann, 1970), II. See Pinckert, 'A Critical Edition', p. xxxvi, for similar conclusions.

9. Croft identified the existence of a Neapolitan family called Poderico and suggested that Elyot's importunate book-owner might have been one of their number (Croft, *The Governour*, I, pp. cxlix–cl). But it is more likely that this name too was another humanist literary joke, an allusion to the Neapolitan Lawyer Laurentius Pudericus, who wrote a commentary on the *Decretum*. See J. F. von Schulte, *Die Geschichte de Quellen und Literatur de Canonischen Rechts* (2 vols., Stuttgart, Verlag von Ferdinand Enke, 1875), II, p. 392. I owe this suggestion to Dr Anne Marie D'Arcy.

10. Lord Berners, ed., *The Golden Boke of Marcus Aurelius Emperour and Eloquent Oratour* (London, 1536), sig. Aiiii.

11. For the suggestion that *The Image* should be treated entirely seriously as an idealization of its subject and a *speculum principis*, see Pinckert, 'A Critical Edition', p. iv.

12. See, for example, Lehmberg, *Sir Thomas Elyot*, p. 179; Fox, 'Humanism and the Body Politic', pp. 45–6, Major, *Elyot and Renaissance Humanism*, p. 193, and Pinckert, 'A Critical Edition', pp. xxi, xxxvi, xliii, and lx.

13. Pinckert, 'A Critical Edition' draws out parallels between *The Image* and *Utopia*, but sees any irony implicit in the former as merely an embellishment to its serious idealizing purpose and not part of its overall design.

14. That Alexander's mother, Mamaea, was converted to Christianity by Origen was a claim that Elyot was to recall in the *Bibliotheca Eliotae* (s.v. Origen). Origen's persuasive speech to the royal mother and son was, seemingly, Elyot's own invention, despite his claim that it was drawn from the eyewitness experience of the author, Eucolpius. See Pinckert, 'A Critical Edition', p. 281.

15. See David Magie, ed., *The Scriptores Historiae Augustae*, Loeb Classical Library (3 vols., London, William Heinemann, 1924) (hereafter the *Historia*), 49:6, II, pp. 278–9. All references to the lives of Heliogabalus and Alexander Severus in the *Historia* are to this edition.

16. Again, the information is contained in the *Historia*, but Elyot (both here and at cii(v), where he repeats the anecdote) carefully prunes away additional information that might undercut the claim to Christian virtue. Here, no mention at all is made of the pagan images that the *Historia* says Alexander also kept in his closet, including those of the deified emperors, the Pythagorian philosopher and miracle-worker Apollonius of Tyana, and Orpheus (*Historia* 29:2–3, p. 234–5). At cii(v) he mentions Socrates and Apollonius but converts the pagan deities to 'other ancient and virtuous men'.

17. The *Historia* 51: 7–8, pp. 282–3, notes, 'He used often to exclaim what he had heard from someone, either a Jew or a Christian, and always remembered, and he also had it announced by a herald whenever he was disciplining anyone, "What you do not wish that a man should do to you, do not do to him." And so highly did he value this sentiment, that he had it written up in the palace and in public buildings.'

18. Elyot's version is a fairly literal translation of the account in *The Historia*, albeit he removed the reference to the emperor Hadrian's previous attempt to found a Christian temple, and the fact that his syncretic temples contained no images—a

timely omission given the current evangelical assault upon pilgrimage sites and the cult of the saints. See *Historia* 43: 6–7 pp. 266–7.

19. There are useful accounts of Cromwell's fall, and various interpretations of the motives behind it in Lacy Baldwin Smith, *Henry VIII: The Mask of Royalty* (London, Jonathan Cape, 1971), pp. 72ff; G. R. Elton, *Reform and Reformation: England, 1509–1558* (London, Edward Arnold, 1977), pp. 291–4; David Starkey, *The Reign of Henry VIII: Personalities and Politics* (London, George Philip, 1985), p. 121; G. W. Bernard, 'Elton's Cromwell', in Bernard, *Power and Politics in Tudor England*, pp. 108–28; R. B. Merriman, *The Life and Letters of Thomas Cromwell* (2 vols., Oxford, Clarendon Press, 1902), I, pp. 209ff. The details of what follows are drawn from these accounts and the specific documents and calendars cited.

20. *LP* xv 486.

21. *LP* xv 804, 847, and 926.

22. Cromwell's letters from the Tower reveal that Norfolk, Southampton, and the Lord Chancellor, Thomas, 1st baron Audley, were his chief interrogators; and Cromwell evidently saw them as his chief accusers and enemies. Merriman, *Life and Letters*, II, p. 268ff.

23. As the martyrologist John Foxe recorded the speech, Cromwell went on to ask those present 'to bear me record, I die in the Catholic Faith, not doubting in any Article of my Faith, nay, nor doubting in any Sacrament of the Church. Many have slandered me and reported that I have been a bearer of such as have maintained evil opinions, which is untrue. But I confess that, like as God by his holy Spirit doth instruct us in the Truth, so the Devil is ready to seduce us, and I have been seduced: but bear me witness that I die in the Catholic Faith of the holy Church, and I heartily desire you to pray for the King's grace that he may long live with you in health and prosperity, and that after him his son, Prince Edward, that goodly Imp, may long reign over you.' (Foxe, *Acts and Monuments*, II, p. 453. A similar, although not identical, speech is recorded in Hall, *Chronicle*, p. 839.) Cromwell had also maintained his innocence in a series of deeply moving letters written to the King from his cell in the Tower, in which he had hoped that God would 'reveal the truth to your Highness', adding 'mine accusers, your grace knoweth, God forgive them'. 'Should any faction or any affection to any point make me a traitor to your majesty', he declared, 'then all the devils in Hell confound me'. The King, whom he described as 'more like a dear Father, your majesty not offended, than a master', was not, however, moved. Having obtained from the letters the information he needed to aid his case for an annulment to the Cleves marriage, he consigned Cromwell to his fate, (Merriman, *Life and Letters*, II, pp. 264–5.)

24. Wilson, 'Letters', pp 1, 11, 30, and 36.

25. Pinckert, 'A Critical Edition', pp. lxvi–vii, also makes the connection between the cases of Turinus and Cromwell (see below, pp. 250–4), but assumes that Elyot's intention was to justify Henry's destruction of his former minister on the grounds of necessary severity.

26. While Norfolk was the third Howard Duke, both Audley and Southampton were first generation peers, ennobled in the past decade, like Cromwell, for service to the royal bureaucracy.

27. The detail is taken from the *Life* of Heliogabalus in the *Historia* (a section attributed, like the Biography of Alexander himself, to Lampridius). 'He took money for

honours and distinctions and power, selling them in person or through his slaves and those who served his lusts. He made appointments to the Senate without regard to age, property, or rank, and solely at the price of money, and he sold the positions of captain and tribune, legate and general, likewise procuratorships and posts in the Palace. And charioteers Protogenes and Cordius, originally his comrades in the chariot-race, he later made his associates in his daily life and actions.' (*Historia* 6: 1–2, pp. 116–17.)

28. See *Historia* 11: 1–2, pp. 128–9, 'He made his freedmen governors and legates, consuls and generals, and he brought disgrace on all offices of distinction by the appointment of base-born profligates.' See also the further details of low-born and vicious men appointed to high office in *Historia* 12: 1–4, pp. 130–1.

29. The story of Aurelius Zoticus, a former athlete from Smyrna, is also taken from the *Life* of Heliogabalus in the *Historia*, albeit the account there contains rather more details of his sexual relationship with the Emperor than is presented in *The Image*. See *Historia* 10: 1–5, pp. 126–7. 'During his [Heliogabalus'] reign Zoticus had such influence that all the chiefs of the palace-departments treated him as their master's consort. This same Zoticus, furthermore, was the kind to abuse such a degree of intimacy, for under false pretences, he sold all Heliogabalus' promises and favours, and so, as far as he could, he amassed enormous wealth. To some men he held out threats, and to others promises, lying to them all, and as he came out from the Emperor's presence, he would go up to each and say, 'In regard to you I said this', "in regard to you I was told that", and "in regard to you this action will be taken". That is the way of men of this kind, for, once admitted to too close an intimacy with a ruler, they sell information concerning his intentions, whether he be good or bad, and so, through the stupidity or the innocence of an emperor who does not detect their intrigues, batten on the shameless hawking of rumours. With this man Heliogabalus went through a nuptial ceremony and consummated a marriage, even having a bridal-matron and exclaiming, "Go to work, cook" [Zoticus's nickname was cook, as that had been his father's trade.]—and this at a time when Zoticus was ill.' Elyot's version may also have followed the abbreviated account of the story in Erasmus's *Adage*, '*Fumos vendere*' ('To Sell Smoke'), which similarly excises almost all of the overtly sexual material. See Erasmus, *Adages: Ii1 to Iv100*, trans. Margaret Mann Phillips with annotations by R. A. B. Mynors, The Collected Works of Erasmus, vol. 31 (Toronto, University of Toronto Press, 1982), Add I iii 41/ LB II 128D–129D, pp. 270–2.

30. In 1539 Cromwell, hitherto the archetypal Tudor bureaucrat, had been appointed titular head of the King's Privy Chamber, and in the following year he added the household office of Lord Great Chamberlain to his portfolio of roles. Hence, technically, at least, he became Henry's principal body servant as well as his chief minister and political confidante. (See Starkey, *Reign of Henry VIII*, p. 121.) Elyot's stress on the personal, household nature of the service performed by Zoticus and the other servants described in *The Image* would thus have increased their resemblance to Cromwell rather than reducing it. The association is made stronger because, like Erasmus, Elyot tones down the references to Zoticus's sexual relationship with his master, and adds the emphasis on his promising to pass on suits for favours ('Your matter or request shall come thus to pass') In Elyot's conception, Zoticus is primarily a patronage broker and a conduit for suits and requests.

31. There are hints in his letters and elsewhere that Elyot may have harboured some resentment at Cromwell's steady social elevation during the 1530s and the consequent distancing effect that it had on their relationship. It is interesting to consider the rather wistful remarks about his own absence from Cromwell's circle of friends at dinner in the Prologue to the 1539 edition of *The Castle of Health* (see Wilson, 'Letters', p. xviii), for example, or his talk of the 'many vain journeys' he had made in an attempt to find Cromwell at home to guests in his letter of 8 October 1534, or the similar comments in the letter of 2 July 1535 (see Wilson, 'Letters', pp. 24–5 and 30), in the light of the comments on the importance of equivalence of rank to real friendships in *The Governor*. There he had observed that 'it is seldom seen that friendship is between . . . him which is elevate in authority and another man of a very base estate or degree. Yea, and if they be both in an equal dignity, if they be desirous to climb, as they do ascend, so the friendship for the more part decayeth . . . And it is oftentimes seen that diverse which before they came in authority were of good and virtuous conditions being in their prosperity, were utterly changed, and despising their old friends, set all their study and pleasure on their new acquaintance' (siv). Still more pointed, perhaps, was the lament at sigs. xii–ii(v) over the decline in friendships in his own time. 'But alas such perverse constellation now reigneth over men that where some be aptly disposed to amity, and findeth one in similitude of study and manners equal to his expectation, and therefore kindleth a fervent love toward that person, putting all his joy and delight in the praise and advancement of him that he loveth, it happeneth that he which is loved, being promoted in honour, either of purpose neglecteth his friend, or else esteeming his mind with his fortune only, and not with the surety of friendship, hideth from him the secrets of his heart and either trusteth no man or else him whom prosperous fortune hath late brought in acquaintance.' Perhaps significantly, Elyot was to cite 'similitude of study and manners' as the bond that first drew he and Cromwell together in *c.* 1519, and had united them since (see his letter to Cromwell of 6 March 1536, in which he refers to the secretary as one 'whom I have always accounted one of my chosen friends, for the similitude of our studies which undoubtedly is the most perfect foundation of amity' (Wilson, 'Letters', p. 26)). The date for their first meeting is provided in the Latin dedicatory note inscribed on the flyleaf of a presentation copy of his *Dictionary*, now in the British Library (Wilson, 'Letters', pp. 34–5).

32. The *Historia* provides a similar account. 'When he began to play the part of emperor, his first act was to remove from their official posts and duties and from all connexion with the government all those judges whom that filthy creature [Heliogabalus] had raised from the lower class. Next he purified the senate and the equestrian order; then he purified the tribes [of free citizens] and the lists of those whose positions depended upon the privileges accorded to soldiers, and the Palace too, and all his own suite, dismissing from service at the court all the depraved and those of ill repute. And he permitted none save those who were needed to remain in the retinue of the Palace.' (*Historia* 16: 1–4, pp. 204–7.) The point obviously struck Elyot as important, as this was the second time that he had described these measures, having already done so at sigs. Bv–v(v). The stress on the significance of the adoption of imperial powers, and the allusion to flatterers were typically Elyotian additions, the former at least with a sharp contemporary edge.

33. The account of Turinus's offences in the *Historia* does not mention a desire to ingratiate and make himself indispensable to the emperor among his motives, and treats his case as only the most prominent of many similar ones. 'There were certain men that he [Alexander] always refused to see alone in the afternoon [when he was signing documents and attending to business] or, for that matter, in the morning hours, because he found out that they had said many things about him falsely, and chief among them was Verconius Turinus. For Turinus had been treated by him as an intimate friend, and all the while he had sold favours under false pretences, with the result that he had brought Alexander's rule into disrepute, for he made the Emperor seem a mere fool, whom he, Turinus, had completely in his power and could persuade to do anything, in this way he made all believe that the emperor did everything at his beck and call.' (*Historia* 35: 5–6, pp. 246–7.)

34. Erasmus concludes his version of the story, drawn largely from the *Historia*, with the declaration that Turinus's death was 'A horrible punishment, yet fitting for such heinous crimes'. *Adages*, p. 272.

35. Again, this scene and the speech that it provokes would seem to be Elyot's invention.

36. 'He caused Turinus immediately to be arrested, and openly in his presence to be accused, which was done by a great number, whom he had also deceived.' (Gi(v))

37. *Historia* 36: 2–3, pp. 246–9. 'Thereupon Alexander ordered him to be indicted, and when all the charges had been proved by witnesses, of whom some were present and saw what Turinus had received [in bribes] and others heard what he had promised, he [Alexander] issued instructions to bind him to a stake in the Forum Transitorium. Then he ordered a fire of straw and wet logs to be made and had him suffocated by the smoke, and all the while a herald cried aloud, "The seller of smoke is punished by smoke." And in order that it might not be thought that he was too cruel in his punishing one single offence, he made a careful investigation before sentencing Turinus, and found that when selling a decision in a law-suit he had often taken money from both parties, and that he had also accepted bribes from all who had obtained appointments to commands or provinces.'

38. Alexander's treatment of Turinus obviously impressed Erasmus, for in addition to retelling the story in '*Fumos vendere*', he also alluded to it elsewhere, albeit not without apparent anxiety about how the story would be received, in support of the idea that those who corrupt a prince's mind and reputation deserved as severe a punishment as those who stole his revenues. See Erasmus, *Education of a Christian Prince*, p. 56 (my italics): 'Since we have the death penalty (and that beyond all the laws of the ancients) for a thief who steals a bit of money that he has come across, it ought not to seem cruel to anyone if the ultimate penalty is invoked for someone who has tried to corrupt the best and most precious thing that the country possesses. *But the novelty of the idea may prevent its acceptance*, although the Roman emperor Alexander ordered a seller of empty promises called Thurinus to be bound to a stake and smoked to death by green logs set alight at his feet.' In his *Panegyric for Archduke Philip of Austria* (printed in ibid., p. 131) he cited the story again, this time with less apparent awkwardness. 'The emperor did deal with the related evil of those who make empty promises, through executing them ("smoke-sellers" they are called) by crucifixion, and by suffocation by smoke. An emperor worthy of immortal dominion, indeed ... I would call on you to emulate him. I would propose this

young man of your own age up to you for emulation, if you had not already embarked on that road on your own accord.' The political context in which Erasmus was writing was, however, very different to that under which Elyot wrote in 1540. And the more immediate experience of the effects of royal severity available to Elyot suggests why he should have seen the story so differently at that time.

39. Again the detail in the *Historia* was fortuitous, as one of Cromwell's earliest appointments was as Master of the King's Jewel House, the unofficial treasurer of the Household.

40. It is perhaps significant, when we try to gauge the potentially satirical intent behind this passage, that Sir Thomas Wyatt in his first satire identified among the hallmarks of courtly hypocrisy the capacity of flatterers to name 'cruelty' 'zeal of justice', and to claim 'tyranny / To be the right of a prince's reign'. See below, p. 307. Was Elyot consciously recalling Wyatt's formulation here?

41. *The Governor*, sig. Qvi.

42. '*Nam et Severus est appellatus a militibus ob austeritatem et in animadversibus asperior in quibusdam fuit*', *Historia* 25: 2, pp. 224–5. Elyot refers to the attribution on several occasions, noting, for example, that the Senate named Alexander 'Severus', 'which betokeneth constant or sharp in punishment' (Biii(v)), and that 'moreover for his great Austerity against the presumption and lightness of his soldiers and servants, he was named Severus, which betokeneth constant or sharp in punishment', or that it arose from his harsh punishment of a secretary, 'wherefore he was called Severus, which is as much as to say as sharp or rigorous' (fiii(v), and see also Yiv). Interestingly Elyot chooses to highlight the meaning 'severe', rather than 'just', its alternative sense: a sure sign of his critical purpose. The etymology assumed is, however, false, as the choice of epithet reflected Alexander's desire to assert his claims to kinship with his imperial predecessor Septimus Severus.

43. Pinckert, 'A Critical Edition', p. xliii, dismisses the idea that Elyot could have been greatly influenced by the *Libro Aureo*, but his argument rests on the assumption that Elyot's intentions were wholly serious and laudatory, whereas Guevara's were ironic and cynical, presenting his imperial subject, Marcus Aurelius as a jaded cynic rather than a stoical hero. But if Elyot is allowed also to be motivated by a critical intention, then he may well have found in Guevara's work precisely the inspiration he needed to return to Lampridius's *Life* (whether or not he believed that text itself to be authentic) as the source for his new project.

44. For a detailed account of Elyot's borrowing from the *Historia*, see Pinckert, 'A Critical Edition', pp. xxxiii–iv, and Appendix 1.

45. PRO SP1/103, ff 75–81, 75, 77–77(v), 77, and 80(v) respectively. I am very grateful to Professor G. W. Bernard for bringing this document to my attention and kindly providing a transcript of its contents.

46. The Emperor, we are told, sought out the company of writers and instructed them to celebrate everything that he did that was commendable, and 'suffering also them to reprove him when they seemed convenient' (Aii(v)). He was himself a scholar, a master of religious divination, and, like Henry VIII, a singer who 'wrote the lives of good princes in verses eloquently, and sang them unto the harp and organs right sweetly' (aii(v)). He would visit even the humblest of his servants, 'desiring them to tell to him freely what they thought of him, whom he would attentively hear. And

when he had heard them thoroughly, then as the thing was spoken of did require, he would diligently amend and correct it' (Aiii). There are parallel passages in the *Historia* 21: 1–2, pp. 214–15 and 26: 2–9, 230–3.

47. The same points are made in *Historia* 3: 5, pp. 182–5.

48. Fox, 'Humanism and the Body Politic', pp. 45–6.

49. The inspiration for some of these reforms can be found in the *Historia*. For the Conservatores, see *Historia* 32: 2–3, pp. 240–3; for Alexander's sumptuary laws and his views on dress codes in general, see *Historia* 27: 1–9, pp. 228–31 and 34: 3–4, 242–5. For the public baths, see *Historia* 24: 2–3, pp. 222–5. There are further details of the baths in the following chapter (*Historia* 25: 3–4, pp. 224–7). The education reforms (which show close similarities with some of the ideas expressed in *The Governor*), the anti-dicing regulations, and the reforms of the markets, seem to have been Elyot's own invention. For Elyot's views on dicing, see *The Governor* Fiv and Mv(v)–Mvii.

50. For Alexander's public works generally, see *Historia* 44: 6–9, pp. 268–9, 22: 4, 218–19, and 25: 4, 224–6 The libraries were seemingly Elyot's conception, as the *Historia*'s Alexander seemed to prefer to spend spare money on colossal statues of himself (*Historia* 25: 7–9pp. 226–7).

51. Elyot argued that when citizens were allowed to buy goods from the craftsmen who produced them to sell them on at market themselves, the producers were 'defrauded of the just price' for their labours. Citizens were thus banned from selling anything at market that they had not produced themselves. No explanation is offered as to why replacing a Roman middle-man with a stranger should necessarily improve the situation. Elyot's memory of anti-foreigner riots such as Evil May Day (1517) in London ought to have persuaded him that such a policy was fraught with difficulty. The first measures listed were taken from the *Historia* 21: 9, pp. 218–19; the ban on merchant adventuring was Elyot's own addition, perhaps inspired by the statement in the same list that 'In order to bring merchants to Rome of their own accord he bestowed the greatest privileges upon them' ('*negotiatoribus ut Roman volentes concurrerent, maximam immunitatem dedit*') (*Historia* 22: 1–2, pp. 218–19).

52. Lehmberg, *Sir Thomas Elyot*, p. 158.

53. The detail, as Pinckert notes ('A Critical Edition', p. 279) seems to have been imported from Valerius Maximus, *Memorable Doings and Sayings*, ed. and trans. D. R. Shackleton Bailey (2 vols., Cambridge, Mass., Harvard University Press, 2000), II, pp. 11 and 8.

54. Elyot omits or tones down those incidents that represent Alexander as a victim of others' malice, most notably Heliogabalus' attempts to kill him during the previous reign, which he makes markedly less of than does the *Historia* (see *Historia* 2: 4–5pp. 180–3), thus underplaying a rational motive for his frequently stated allusions to attempts to murder him. And the *Historia*'s careful explanation that his eventual murder was the result of a political plot rather than a general resentment of his severity among his troops (*Historia* 59: 5–6, pp. 298–9) is undercut by Elyot's bald statement that his soldiers in general 'would not suffer any longer his rigorous gravity' (sig. CC iv(v)) before the claim that his actual murders were conspiring to replace him with his successor Maximus (CC iv–iv(v)). Stories that stress the Emperor's personal and political modesty are also generally either omitted or toned down. Elyot does not

repeat, for example, the statement that 'he associated with his friends on such familiar terms that he would sit with them as equals, attend their banquets, have some of them as his own daily guests, even when they were not formally summoned' (*Historia* 4: 3, pp. 184–5). Similarly the statement that he treated with respect and reverence the Pontifices, the Board of Fifteen, and the Augurs (*Historia* 22: 6, pp. 218–19) are not used. Nor is the story that the Emperor purchased grain with his own money to feed the poor (*Historia* 21: 9, pp. 216–19). The lengthy eulogies and acclamations delivered by the Senate at his accession, and the lengthy analogy between him and Alexander the Great are also cut. In addition, the story (seemingly extrapolated from the reference in the *Historia* to Alexander's veneration for the Golden Rule of Luke's gospel) concerning his horror at being told by a counsellor that he was not bound to obey his own laws (*The Governor*, yvi(v): 'God forbid that ever I should devise any laws whereby my people should be compelled to do anything which I myself cannot tolerate') that Elyot had placed in *The Governor*, at a time when he was probably still thinking of using the Emperor as an example of good governorship, did not find its way into *The Image*.

55. See *Historia* 52: 1, pp. 282–3.
56. The anecdote is deployed in the *Historia*, but there it is used as an example of the Emperor's severity in the specific context of military discipline (*Historia* 53: 1–2, pp. 284–7), whereas Elyot uses it as an example of the Emperor's dealings with 'all..[e]states' (ʀii). Elyot's presentation of the offence for which the captains (the *Historia* has only the tribunes) were executed also seems to be understated, with the effect that Alexander's response seems more of an overreaction than it did in the *Historia*. Where Elyot describes the troops', actions as merely a 'commotion', the *Historia* calls it a mutiny, and has the tribunes executed for their connivance in that action (*Historia* 54: 7, pp. 288–9).
57. *Historia* 46: 3, pp. 270–3.
58. *Historia* 28: 3–4, pp. 232–3.
59. Elyot's ironic intentions here can be judged by comparing his unlikely picture of an always smiling and benign Severus with the original statement in the *Historia* that concerned purely the Emperor's capacity to work late at his papers without tiring or falling victim to inattention. 'Of course, if necessity demanded it, he would give his attention to public business even before dawn and continue at it up to an advanced hour, never growing weary or giving up in irritation or anger, but always was indeed a man of great sagacity and he could not be tricked, and whoever tried to impose on him by some sharp practice was always found out and punished' (*Historia* 29: 5–6, pp. 236–7).
60. What was in the *Historia* an account of righteous indignation and rage becomes in Elyot's hands an entirely literal, uncontrollable venting of bile of the sort that Skelton had depicted the eponymous hero of his Morality play *Magnificence* indulging in when he had fallen into tyranny under the influence of a pack of courtly vices (see John Scattergood, ed., *John Skelton: The Complete English Poems* (Harmondsworth, Penguin Books, 1983), pp. 188–9). The *Historia* account ran as follows. 'It is told, furthermore, by Septimus, who has given a good account of Alexander's life, that so great was his indignation at judges, who, although, not actually found guilty, yet laboured under the reputation of being dishonest, that, even if he merely chanced to

see them, he would vent all the bile of his anger in great perturbation of spirit and with his whole countenance aflame, so that he became unable to speak.' (*Historia* 27: 2–3, pp. 208–11.) That Elyot intended to see the contradiction between the claim to equanimity and Alexander's actual behaviour is further suggested by the fact that he included on the same page as the description of the venting of bile the statement that 'he was of such a wonderful discretion and soberness, that no report could bring him out of patience' (fiii).

61. See sig. Aiii(v).

62. The story may conceivably have been prompted by the statement in the *Historia* that 'He reduced the interest demanded by money-lenders to the rate of four per-cent— in this measure too looking out for the welfare of the poor. (*Historia* 26: 2–3, pp. 226–7.)

63. The story of the punishment itself is to be found in the *Historia* (see 23: 8, pp. 220–3), but the subsequent accusation of tyranny and Alexander's conversation with Ulpian seem to have been Elyot's own invention, added seemingly precisely to point up the cruelty of the punishment and what it suggests about the Emperor's character and methods.

64. For Machiavelli's advocacy of cruelty, see *The Prince*, ed. Adams, pp. 27ff.

65. See *The Governor*, Diii(v), where he cites 'The sweet writer Lactantius' as his source for the statement that 'of cunning cometh virtue and of virtue perfect felicity is only engendered' (Elyot suggests that his source is 'the first book to the emperor Constantine against the gentiles', but it is actually Book III, cap. 12), and *The Governor*, b v, where he cites Lactantius (Book III) as the source of the maxim, 'Thou must needs perish if thou know not what is to thy life profitable that thou mayest seek for it, and what is dangerous that thou mayest flee and eschew it'. See also the possible echo of *Divine Institutes*, Book IV, Chapter iii (in Alexander Roberts and James Donaldson, eds. and trans., *The Works of Lactantius* (2 vols., Edinburgh, T. and T. Clark, 1871), I, pp. 215–16) in Alexander's comments on the name and role of 'father' at sigs. zii–ii(v).

66. See, for example, Lactantius, *The Divine Institutes*, Book V, cap. xi (*Works*, I, p. 318) ('I saw in Bithynia the praefect [Ulpian was first *preafectus annonae* then *praefectus praetorio* under Alexander] wonderfully elated with joy, as though he had subdued some nation of barbarians, because one [Christian] who had resisted for two years with great spirit appeared at length to yield. They contend, therefore, that they may conquer and inflict exquisite pains on their bodies, and avoid nothing else but that the victims may not die under the torture'). See also T. Honore, *Ulpian* (Oxford, Oxford University Press, 1982).

67. See Fi–Fi(v).

68. There is, perhaps, a similar ironic intention behind the declaration in the Preface that '[this] book I do dedicate unto you noble lords, gentle knights, and other in the state of honour or worship, as being ready to be advanced to the governance under your prince' (aii(v)), the lords' eagerness to be advanced to a greater role in the governance of the realm having been a prime motive behind their hostility to Cromwell.

69. See, for example, John Skelton, 'Ware the Hauke', lines 216–18 ('Yet the Sowden [sultan] nor the Turke, / Wroght never such a work, / For to let their hawkys fly / In the church of Saynt Sophy'); and Collyn Clout, lines 429–30 ('What coude the

Turke do more / With all his false lore[?]'). See John Scattergood, ed, *John Skelton: The Complete English Poems* (Harmondsworth, Penguin, 1983).

70. See Fox, 'Renaissance Humanism and the Body Politic', p. 46.

71. In earlier passages the text had cited, with varying degrees of accuracy, Nero, Caligula, Domitian and Commodus as emperors who had been slain by their aggrieved subjects (Bii–ii(v)), and Heliogabalus' own predecessor Macrinus, who was also 'abandoned (or rather betrayed) of his own people, and slain with his son Diadumenus' (Aiii(v)).

72. The speech was Elyot's own invention. He had cited the same maxim in *The Governor/Of the Knowledge* a decade earlier. The 'he' who argued that fear was a greater safeguard than love may well have been Machiavelli, who made that claim in *The Prince*, ed. Adams, p. 46.

73. The description of Alexander's *consilium principis* in the *Historia* is rather different in both its details and emphases, suggesting a clearing house for administrative business reporting to the Emperor rather than the legislative and policy-making body imagined by Elyot. (*Historia* 15: 6, pp. 206–7 and 16: 1–3, pp. 206–9.) There is mention of a sixteen-strong aristocratic council in Herodian's account of the reign, but it is specifically stated to have been appointed by Alexander's mother, Mamaea, in order to advise the young emperor during his minority only. (Herodian, *Works*, II, pp. 78–81.)

74. Starkey began his programme of proposed reforms with a frank (and 'Lupset' fears, possibly treasonous) statement of the problem they faced. As 'Pole' informed his interlocutor, 'it is not unknown to you, master Lupset, how that our country hath been governed and ruled this many years under the state of princes which by their regal power and princely authority have judged all things pertaining to the state of our realm to hang only upon their (will and) fantasy, in so much that what so ever they ever have conceived or purposed in their minds, they thought by and by to have it put in effect without resistance to be made by any (private) man (or subject), or else by and by they (have) said (that) men should minish their (princely) authority.' Pole thus concludes that 'that country cannot be long well governed nor maintained with good policy where all is ruled by the will of one not chosen for election but cometh to it by natural succession.' His answer is to create a powerful and independent council, headed by the Constable of England, and a more robust parliament to balance and rein in the powers of the prince. Although he is quick to assert that Henry VIII himself is 'such a prince and of such wisdom that he may right well and justly be subject to no law', he suggests that his heir may prove less just, so 'to him must be joined a council (by common authority) not such as he will, but such as by the most part of the parliament shall (be) judged to be wise and mete thereunto'. This council, consisting of the greater lay lords, the bishop of London and archbishop of Canterbury, four judges, and four 'of the most wise citizens of London', 'should have authority of the whole parliament in such time as (the) parliament were dissolved', and their role would be explicitly to limit the king's capacity to follow his own desires and fall into tyranny. Likewise the newly enhanced office of Constable of England would be created 'to counterpoise the authority of the prince and temper the same, giving him authority to call a parliament in such case as the prince would run into any tyranny (of his own heady judgement)'. Starkey, *Dialogue*, pp. 67–8, 69, 111–13, and 121.

75. Starkey too had been much taken with the Roman offices of Censors and conservators of the state as a mechanism for reforming and policing civil society and checking the power of the prince and his officers. See, for example, *Dialogue*, p. 136, where Pole declares 'I would some man should be appointed in every great city and town the which should have none other cure nor charge but to see that all other officers diligently did execute their office and duty'. Such officers, he notes, were called 'censors' in ancient Rome, but he would rather see them termed 'conservators', because their role would be to conserve the state.

76. The equivalent passage in the *Historia* says only that Alexander 'appointed fourteen overseers of the city of Rome, chosen from among the ex-consuls, and these he commanded to hear city-cases in conjunction with the prefect of the city, giving orders that all of them, or at least a majority, should be present whenever the records were made.' (*Historia* 33: 1–2, pp. 240–1)

77. Pinckert, 'A Critical Edition', p. 269.

78. Desiderius Erasmus, 'The Godly Feast', in Thompson, ed., *Colloquies*, p. 58. See above, p. 142.

79. See pp. 147–50, above.

80. That there is an element of wish-fulfilment fantasy to this passage was also suggested by Pinckert, 'A Critical Edition', pp. lxxv–lxxvi.

81. See *The Governor*, Gv–Gvii, and p. 481, n. 62, above.

82. Perhaps Elyot had by this time decided to devote his leisure time to his last published text, the devotional work *A Preservative against Death* (published in 1545), and a second, now lost work, a history of England, the *De rebus memorabilibus Angliae*, that Roger Ascham claimed that he was working on at his death. (See *Toxophilus* (1545) in William Aldis Wright ed., *The English Works of Roger Ascham* (Cambridge, Cambridge University Press, 1904), p. 52; Lehmberg, *Sir Thomas Elyot*, pp. 181–2). See Croft, *The Governour*, I, p. clxxv for the suggestion that this text may have been the work listed as 'Sir Thomas Elyot, his chronicle of the description of Britain' among the sources of a seventeenth-century manuscript history of Chester.

83. As Pinckert shrewdly observes ('A Critical Edition', pp. lxxx–xi), Elyot may well have allowed himself one further piece of self-justification in relating as his final case study of an imperial subject, the story of one Marcus Geminus. Again the story was largely the product of Elyot's own imagination, and has striking similarities with his own history. For Geminus (the Latin form of 'Thomas'), a man 'having his principal pleasure in reading or writing' (Aa iii), was the victim of unjust accusations from his tenants and political enemies, who alleged that he was both dispossessing them of their lands and consorting with a known traitor, Ovinus Camillius. As Pinckert suggests, these accusations have more than a passing relevance to the accusations of treasonable associations with known or alleged opponents of the Royal Supremacy levelled against Elyot by John Perkins in 1537, and to an ongoing legal dispute that he was engaged in to oust a recalcitrant tenant, Gilbert Claydon, from lands attached to the manor of Carlton, that Elyot had bought from Cromwell in 1538. Thus the triumphant vindication of Geminus when, after an investigation his accusers are revealed to be lying in order to discredit him, again allows Elyot to enjoy the privileges of a 'maker of books' to discomfort his enemies.

12. SIR THOMAS WYATT: POETRY AND POLITICS

1. Kenneth Muir and Patricia Thomson, eds., *Collected Poems of Sir Thomas Wyatt* (Liverpool, Liverpool University Press, 1969), p. 238, poem number 236. Unless otherwise stated, all future references to Wyatt's poems are to this edition.

2. See Muir and Thomson, *Collected Poems*, p. 429. '*Rotta è l'alta colonna e 'l verde lauro / Che facean ombra al mio stanco pensero; / Perduto ho quel che ritrovar non spero / Dal borea a l'austro o dol mar indo al mauro. / Tolto m'hai, Morte, il mio doppio tesauro / Che mi fea viver lieto e gire altero; / E ristorar no 'l può terra nè impero, / Nè gemma orïental, nè forza d'auro. / Ma, se consentimento è di destino, / Che posso io piú se no aver l'alma trista, / Umidi gli occhi sempre e 'l viso chino? / Oh nostra vita ch'è sí bella in vista, / Com' perde agevolmente in un mattino / Quel che 'n molti anni a gran pen s'acquista!*' (Petrarch *Rime*, cclxix). H. A. Mason provides the following translation: 'Smashed is the tall column, smashed the green laurel / Which gave cooling shade to my weary thought; / Lost is that I do not expect to find again / From North to South, from East to Western sea. / Taken you have, Death, my two treasures from me, / Which made me glad to walk with a high head; / And bring them back to me can no land, no realm, / No Eastern jewel, no mountain of gold. / But if such is the will of destiny, / What else can I do more than to have a sorry mind, / Eyes ever dropping tears and head bent to ground? / This life of ours which seems so fine, / How easily in a brief morning you lose / That which was gathered together with great pains over many years.' (H. A. Mason, *Thomas Wyatt: A Literary Portrait* (Bristol, Bristol Classical Press, 1986), p. 245.)

3. Horace, *The Odes and Epodes*, ed. and trans., C. E. Bennett, Loeb Classical Library (London, William Heinemann, 1952), II, xvii, 3–4, p. 153.

4. The same vocabulary was deployed in another English translation of the same sonnet produced about the same time—perhaps an earlier essay at translation from Wyatt's pen. 'The precious pillar perished is and rent / That countenanced life and cheered the wearied mind.' See Mason, *A Literary Portrait*, pp. 245–6.

5. Again there is no hint of this sense of self-hatred and division in either Petrarch's text or the anonymous English translation. The anonymous English text reads: 'But if the cause proceed from the upper place, / What can I more than mourn that am constrained, / What woeful tears to wail that woeful case? / O brittle life, with face so fair ystained, / How easily lost thou art in a moment space / That many years with much ado attained' (Mason, *A Literary Portrait*, pp. 245–6).

6. For Wyatt's verisimilitude, see Chapter 17 below.

7. See, for example, Muir and Thomson, *Collected Poems*, p. 430: 'The only remark difficult to explain in personal terms is the self-hatred expressed in line 11. Wyatt certainly was not directly responsible for Cromwell's fall. It could be that the failure of his mission in Spain (1537–9) or his service in France (1539–40) in which he had to collaborate with Cromwell's enemy the Duke of Norfolk, made him feel that he had indirectly contributed to it.'

8. Alistair Fox, *Politics and Literature in the Reigns of Henry VII and Henry VIII* (Oxford, Basil Blackwell, 1989), p. 260.

9. R. B. Merriman, *The Life and Letters of Thomas Cromwell* (2 vols., Oxford, Clarendon Press, 1902), II, p. 135. See also Kenneth Muir, ed., *Life and Letters of Sir Thomas Wyatt* (Liverpool, Liverpool University Press, 1963), pp. 46–55.

10. B. L. MS Harleian 3362, f. 79, cited in Mason, *A Literary Portrait*, pp. 247–8. The text ends with the printer's name and the legend, 'God save the King', suggesting either that it is a draft for a printed text, or a copy of such a text. That Bishop Cox copied a version of the same text into his commonplace book suggests that it was indeed printed and circulated as it appears here, but that Hall chose to print a different version, whether because he had access to a different text, or because he chose to edit the details of the text he was using.

11. Corpus Christi College Cambridge MS 168. See Richard Harrier, *The Canon of Sir Thomas Wyatt's Poetry* (Cambridge, Mass., Harvard University Press, 1975), pp. 78–9; Stephen Merriam Foley, *Sir Thomas Wyatt*, Twayne English Authors Series (Boston, Twayne Publishers, 1990), pp. 42 and 117.

12. *Cronica del Rey Enrico Otavo de Ingaletera* (Madrid, 1887), translated in Martin A. Sharpe Hume, *Chronicle of King Henry VIII of England* (London, 1889), pp. 68–9. The poet's son, Thomas Wyatt the younger is another possible source for the chronicler's account.

13. For the biographical details here and in what follows, see Muir, *Life and Letters*, pp. 3ff; and D. M. Loades, ed., *The Papers of George Wyatt, Esquire of Boxley Abbey in the County of Kent, Son and Heir of Sir Thomas Wyatt the Younger*, Camden Society, 4th series, 5 (London, The Royal Historical Society, 1968), Introduction. See also Fox, *Politics and Literature*, pp. 259–60.

14. *LP* II, 2735; IV 6418.

15. *LP* IV 2037, 2075, 2875, 2931, 3011.

16. Loades, *Papers*, pp. 28–9. George Wyatt claimed that the image 'had relation to the history of Thesius set out in Plutarch's *Lives*, and others and here fitted to the affairs of the king with the Bishop of Rome and his enterprise of delivering himself, his people, and Realms from the servitude of the Romish Minos and Minotaur, Clement the seventh, composed of crafty subtleties and vain semblances of humanities, as also of menacing terror of his rearing bulls, wherewith he kept the world in awe . . .'

17. For the diplomatic context and the events surrounding the Sack of Rome, see J. J. Scarisbrick, *Henry VIII* (2nd edition, New Haven, Yale University Press, 1997), pp. 140–7; and Peter Gwyn, *The King's Cardinal: The Rise and Fall of Thomas Wolsey* (London, Barrie and Jenkin, 1990), pp. 530–7.

18. The psalmic verse had been cited by Pope Alexander III during the Investiture crisis of the thirteenth century. He had fled from Rome to Genoa disguised as a secular knight to escape the armies of Emperor Frederick II. On his arrival he was greeted by the ringing of the church bells and the acclamation 'Our soul is escaped like a bird out of the snare of the fowler.'

19. Loades, *Papers*, p. 28.

20. The text was printed in the following year by Richard Pynson. It was to be the only work of Wyatt's published in his own lifetime (Muir, *Life and Letters*, pp. 9–10). The text of *The Quiet of Mind* is printed in Muir and Thompson, *Collected Poems*, pp. 440–63.

21. Wyatt, *Quiet of Mind*, sigs. a vii(v)–a viii, printed in Muir and Thompson, *Collected Poems* pp. 445–6.

22. His friend and servant John Mason would commend Wyatt in his epitaph as one 'in whom, with knowledge of the world, and skill in war, were combined eloquence,

knowledge of the highest art, and acquaintance with various tongues, so that (the lot of few) he was both good in council and strenuous in action.' (*'in quo cum rerum usu ac rei militaris peritia, conjunctae erant facundia, honestissimarum artium scientia et variarum linguarum literatura: ut idem (quod paucis contigit) consilio bonus esset, et manu strenuus.'* (Muir, *Life and Letters*, p. 213)

23. *LP* IV 5978, 6490, 6751; V 838; VII 922.

24. *LP* VII 674.

25. *LP* VII 922 (p. 337); Muir, *Life and Letters*, p. 26.

26. *LP* IV 6418. Patricia Thomson has argued, plausibly, that, since there is no other record of a daughter named Elizabeth, when Wyatt concluded his second letter to his son in 1537 with 'Recommend me to my daughter Jane and my daughter Besse' he was referring not to his own children but to his new daughter in law, Jane, the daughter of Sir William Hawte, and *her* sister, Elizabeth Hawte. Patricia Thomson, *Sir Thomas Wyatt and His Background* (London, Routledge and Kegan Paul, 1964), p. 274.

27. Muir, *Life and Letters*, p. 37. See also *LP* XII (i), 637, 766; *LP* XVI 467; and *Spanish Calendar* VI (i), 155.

28. Muir, *Life and Letters*, pp. 40–1; E. W. Ives, *Anne Boleyn* (Oxford, Blackwell, 1986), pp. 82–6. Wyatt's grandson Sir George Wyatt, would later claim that the poet was struck first by Anne's looks, and 'after much more with her witty and graceful speech, his ear also had him chained unto her, so as finally his heart seemed to say, I could gladly yield to be tied to her for ever with the knot of love'. Muir, *Life and Letters*, p. 15.

29. For perhaps the best known of the stories, concerning a game of bowls between King and poet, in which each conspicuously produces a favour given to him by Anne to measure a disputed end, see Muir, *Life and Letters*, p. 48.

30. See *Spanish Chronicle*, p. 63; and Nicholas Harpsfield, *A Treatise on the Pretended Divorce Between Henry VIII and Catherine of Aragon*, ed. N. Pocock, Camden Society second series, XXI (London, Camden Society, 1878), p. 253.

31. Foley, *Sir Thomas Wyatt*, p. 51. In *Tottel's Miscellany* the poem itself is entitled, 'Of his love called Anna', and the line reads 'it is mine Anna', Hyder Edward Rollins, ed, *Tottel's Miscellany (1557–1587)* (2 vols., Cambridge, Mass, Harvard University Press, 1928), I, p. 211.

32. Having identified the occasion of the poem with some certainty, however, it is rather more difficult to say precisely what the text tells us about Wyatt's feelings. Is the speaker's derisive laughter directed towards Anne and prompted by the kind of misogynistic 'realisation' familiar in such poems that the woman upon whom he has devoted so much attention and 'service' is not worthy of his attentions after all? Or is it directed inwards, based perhaps upon a realization of his own naivety in pursuing a woman whom he now sees (to borrow a phrase from another of his lyrics of the same period) was 'Caesar's' all along?

33. Muir and Thompson, *Collected Poems*, p. 78.

34. That the poem was readily understood to be 'about' Anne at the time is evident from Sir George Wyatt's confident assertion that her 'usual words' were 'I am Caesar's all, let none else touch me'. Loades, *Papers*, p. 185. Petrarch's *Rime* reads: '*Una candida cerva sopra lerba / Verde mapparve con duo corna doro / Fra due riviere allambra dun alloro / Levandol sole a la stagione acerba. / Era sua vista si dolce suberba / Chi lasciai*

per seguirla ogni lavoro | Come lavaro chencercar tesoro | Con diletto laffanno disacerba. | Nessun mi tocchi al bel collo dintorno | Scritto avea di diamenti et di topaçi | Libera farmi al mio cesare parve. | Et eral sol gia volto al meçço giorno | Gliocchi meie stanchi di mirar non saçi | Quondido caddi nelacqua et ella sparv.' (quoted in Mason, *A Literary Portrait*, p. 135). Mason translates as follows: 'As the sun was rising in the bitter season, a white hind with two golden horns appeared to me in the shade of a laurel on the green grass between two streams. So pleasant-proud was its appearance that I left my work and, like a miser in whom the pleasure of hunting for treasure mitigates the inherent vexations, I followed the hunt. Round its fair neck was written in diamonds and topazes: "Let no man touch me for Caesar's will is that I remain free." The sun had reached midday when, my eyes weary but not satiated with gazing, I fell into the water and the hind disappeared.' (H. A. Mason, *Humanism and Poetry in the Early Tudor Period* (London, Routledge and Kegan Paul, 1959), p. 190).

35. Chapuys, the imperial ambassador, reported Suffolk's fury at his wife's relegation to second place at a banquet on 10 May 1530. The Duke's vengeful response was to inform Henry that Anne had once been 'intimate' with a gentleman of the court. Henry had, Chapuys reported, banished both Suffolk and the gentleman from court for a period. 'There is no reason to doubt', Muir suggests, 'that the gentleman in question was Thomas Wyatt'. (*Spanish Calendar*, IV (i) 421 and 535; Muir, *Life and Letters*, p. 22.)

36. For an account of the events surrounding Anne's fall, see Greg Walker, 'Rethinking the Fall of Anne Boleyn', *HJ*, 45 (2002), pp. 1–29.

37. *LP* x 865, 920.

38. It does not seem necessary to assume a factional explanation for Wyatt's release. For such suggestions see, for example, Susan Brigden, ' "The Shadow That You Know": Sir Thomas Wyatt and Sir Francis Bryan at Court and on Embassy', *HJ* 39 (1996), pp. 1–31, p. 5. For doubts about factional readings of Anne's fall, see, *inter alia*, Walker, 'Rethinking the Fall of Anne Boleyn', *passim*.

39. *LP* x 840.

40. In the Blage Manuscript (Trinity College Dublin Library MS 160) the poem is preceded by a Latin inscription, in which Wyatt's name ('Viat') is surrounded by the words: '*V. Innocentia*' (Innocence), '*Veritas*' (Truth), and '*Fides*' (Faith) and by a phrase '*Circumdederunt me inimici mei*' ('my enemies have surrounded me'), which is adapted from the Psalms 16:9: 'my enemies have surrounded my soul'. Whether this was written by Wyatt as a prophylactic charm against the accusations against him, and later transcribed into the Blage manuscript copy, or whether a later owner of the manuscript (possibly Blage himself) added it as posthumous testimony to the poet's innocence—an inverse equivalent, perhaps, of the accusatory *impressa* that Wyatt left on the wall of his Italian chamber, is unclear. For a sensitive reading of the poem, see Heale, *Wyatt, Surrey and Early Tudor Poetry*, pp. 124–5.

41. See, for example, Mason, *Humanism and Poetry*, p. 202; Thomson, *Wyatt and His Background*, p. 234.

42. Seneca, *Phaedra*, ed. and trans. Michael Coffey and Roland Mayer (Cambridge, Cambridge University Press, 1990), 1140. The translation is in Foley, *Sir Thomas Wyatt*, pp. 44–5.

43. Richard Harrier, for example, questions the attribution to Wyatt on stylistic grounds. Richard Harrier, *Canon of Sir Thomas Wyatt's Poetry*, p. 72.

44. Muir, *Life and Letters*, p. 35: 'We can see the change brought about by these events by comparing the two Holbein portraits—one of a handsome man in the prime of life, the other of a prematurely aged man. The fashionable courtier and writer of ballets was superseded by the hard-working diplomat, by the writer of satires and penitential psalms. He did not need the stern warnings of the King and the affectionate warnings of Cromwell to make him change his way of life.'

45. *LP* x 1131.

46. Wyatt's sense of guilt and desire for improvement do seem to have been genuine. In the following year he would describe his behaviour in the period prior to his imprisonment in very contrite terms in a letter to his son. 'And of myself I may be a near example unto you of my folly and unthriftiness that hath as I well deserved brought me into a thousand dangers and hazards, enmities, hatreds, prisonments, despites, and indignations, but that God hath of His goodness chastised me and not cast me clean out of His favour, which thing I can impute to nothing but to the goodness of my good father that I dare well say purchased with continual request of God His grace towards me more than I regarded or considered myself, and a little part to the small fear that I had of God in the most of my rage and the little delight that I had in mischief' (Muir, *Life and Letters*, pp. 39–40). There may, as Foley suggests, have been an element of calculation, of careful family choreography, behind the presentation of this image of a chastened and contrite Wyatt in both his own letters and those of his father (Foley, *Sir Thomas Wyatt*, pp. 11–12). But it would be too cynical to deny the poet all claim to sincerity, especially in this later text, where self-interest was not so obviously at stake.

47. Wyatt himself testifies to his service in the royal army. In his *Defence* of 1541, he recalled how he 'came out of the tower in the commotion time', and 'was appointed to go against the king's rebels, and did, until I was countermanded, as speedily and as well furnished as I was well able' (Muir, *Life and Letters*, p. 201).

13. TYRANNY CONDEMNED

1. Note, for example, the wry reflection on his own experiences during the month of May—traditionally dedicated to love and lovers—in 'You that in love find lucke and habundace' (Muir and Thompson 92): 'Let me remembre the happs most unhappy / That me betide in May most commonly. / As oon whome love list litil to avaunce. / Sephame [an astrologer] saide true that my nativitie / Mischaunced was with the ruler of the May: / He gest I prove of that the veritie. / In May my welth and eke my liff I say / Have stoude so oft in such perplexitie...' (6–13)

2. The debate over whether or how often Wyatt actually 'performed' his lyrics at court, either by reading them aloud or singing them accompanied by a lute, is a long and still unresolved one. For the case for musical performance, see C. S. Lewis, *English Literature in the Sixteenth Century* (Oxford, Oxford University Press, 1954), p. 230; Raymond Southall, *The Courtly Maker: An Essay on the Poetry of Wyatt and His Contemporaries* (Oxford, Basil Blackwell, 1964), pp. 9–11; for that against, see John Stevens, *Music and Poetry at the Early Tudor Court* (London, Methuen, 1961), pp. 112–13, Heale, *Wyatt and Surrey*, p. 82.

3. The same principle informed John Trevisa's early fifteenth-century English translation of Giles of Rome's *De Regimine Principium*: 'For he that wol be wise and kunnynge to governe and rule oer schal be wise and konnyng to governe and to rule hymself.' (D. C. Fowler, C. F. Briggs, and D. G. Rimly, eds., *The Governaunce of Kings and Princes: John of Trevisa's Middle English Translation of De Regimine Principium of Aegidius Romanus* (New York, Garland, 1997), p. 8, lines 118–20).

4. The relevant Boethian texts are, *Consolation of Philosophy* III, metrum 5, 6, and 3, respectively. See Boethius, *The Theological Tractates and The Consolation of Philosophy*, ed. and trans. H. F. Stewart, E. K. Rand, and S. J. Tester, Loeb Classical Library (London, William Heinemann, 1978).

5. John Scattergood, 'Thomas Wyatt's Epistolary Satires and the Comforts of Intertextuality', unpublished essay. I am very grateful to Professor Scattergood for the opportunity to read and cite this essay in advance of publication. For the contrary claim ('Wyatt's poetry is rarely bookish'), see Foly, *Sir Thomas Wyatt*, pp. 45–6.

6. Horace, *Satires, Epistles, and Ars Poetica*, ed. and trans. H. Rushton Fairclough, Loeb Classical Library (London, William Heinemann Ltd, London, 1932), ii, vi, and Seneca, *Ad Lucilium Epistolae Morales*, ed. and trans. Richard M. Gummere, Loeb Classical Library (3 vols., London, Heinemann, 1917), vii.

7. The relevant Latin text (*Thyestes*, 391ff) reads: '*Stet quicunque volet potens / Aulae culmine lubrico: / Me dulcis saturet quies / Obscuro positus loco / Leni perfruar otio / Nulla nota Quiritibus / Aetas per tacitum fluat. / Sic cum transierint mei / Nullo cum strepitu dies / Ignotus moritur sibi.*' (Muir and Thompson, p. 431). Mason's translation brings out the closeness with which Wyatt followed his source: 'Let anyone who wishes stand in power on the slippery roof of the court, let sweet quiet fill me full; let me be situated in a dim spot; there let me enjoy a life of luxurious ease. Let my life flow silently along unknown to the upper-class citizens of Rome, so that when my days have passed with no disturbance I may die like any old plebian. Death falls heavy on the man who, known too much by the world, dies unknown to himself.' (Mason, *A Literary Portrait*, pp. 236–7).

8. All references to Chaucer's works are, unless otherwise stated, to the texts printed in Larry Benson, ed., *The Riverside Chaucer* (Boston, Houghton Mifflin, 1987).

9. Mason, *A Literary Portrait*, pp. 259–60.

10. '*Sono in Provenza, ove quantunque pieni / Di malvagio voler ci sian glingegni / Lignoranza el timor pon loro i freni, / Che benche sian d'invidia & d'odio pregni / Sempre contro i miglior per veder poco / Son nel mezzo troncati i lor disegni. / Hor qui dunque mi sto, prendendo in gioco / Il lor breve saper, le lunghe voglie / Con le mie Muse in solitario loco.*' ('But I am in Provence, where, although the locals are full of malice, their evil efforts are kept within bounds by their ignorance and fear. Much as they are forever bursting with hatred and envy of their betters, their wicked plots are frustrated by their short-sightedness. So here I dwell in solitude with my Muses, mocking the yokels' lack of wit and slow desires.') The translation is again Mason's (*A Literary Portrait*, pp. 263 and 266).

11. As with much of Wyatt's more intensely felt poetry, the syntax here seems to reflect the tangled emotional response to his situation, making the precise sense of this passage potentially ambiguous. Does the clause describing the condition of the courtly man end with 'lookes' (5), 'cloke' (5), or 'lawe' (6)? If the latter, then it is

at court that the poet had to discipline his 'will and lust', and the point would seem to be that the liberties of the subject are unjustly restricted by the thraldom of royal service. If, on the other hand, 'wrappid within my cloke, / To will and lust lerning to set a lawe' is his current state, to be set against the thraldom of the court, then the hard lesson in self-discipline is a virtuous condition of rural retirement. The latter is, of course, the more plausible reading—and it was the sense of Alamnni's original text: '... *perch'amo, et colo / Piu di tutti altri il lito Provenzale, / Et perche qui cosi povero & solo, / Piu tosto chel seguir signori & Regi / Viva temprando il mio infinito duolo*', which Mason translates as 'I will tell you why I love the shore of Provence and prefer it above all others, and the reason why I had rather live in poverty and solitude moderating my endless grief there than follow the progresses of princes and kings' (Mason, *Literary Portrait*, p. 263). And both Wyatt and Surrey were to use the image of the man wrapped in his cloak as a figure of solitary virtue in other poems. But the ambiguity of the syntax, and the possibility that the phrase might convey precisely the reverse of its surface meaning to readers inclined to take it that way, effectively suggests the tension in the poet's own mind over the nature and value of his own association with the court.

12. Scattergood, 'Wyatt's Epsitolary Satires'.
13. Mason, *A Literary Portrait*, p. 263.
14. The very dark fabric known as 'black-a-lire' proverbially could not be dyed to take any other colour. Alamanni's text read, more prosaically, 'That is not to say that I am not fired from time to time with a love of glory. I refuse to join the liars' (Mason, *A Literary Portrait*, p. 264).
15. '*Non saprei piu ch'à gli immortali Dei / Rendere honor con le ginocchia inchine / À piu ingiusti che sian, fallaci & rei.*' Mason, *A Literary Portrait*, p. 261.
16. Muir, *Life and Letters*, p. 200; see Chapter 14 below.
17. Mason, *A Literary Portrait*, p. 265.
18. Ibid., pp. 262 and 264.
19. See, for example, Heale, *Wyatt, Surrey and Early Tudor Poetry*, p. 30; Simpson, *Reform and Cultural Revolution*, pp. 249–50. Colin Burrow, 'Horace at Home and Abroad: Wyatt and Sixteenth-Century Horatianism', in Charles Martindale, ed, *Horace Made New: Horatian Influences on British Writing from the Renaissance to the Twentieth Century* (Cambridge, Cambridge University Press, 1993), p. 36, is more critical of what he sees as the poet's 'self-censorship': 'Alamanni blazes about Brutus and the defenders of republican liberty, while Wyatt chooses a famous regulator of appetite to admire.'
20. Mason, *A Literary Portrait*, p. 277.
21. Elyot, *The Book Named the Governor*, ff 212–212(v)/sigs. di and v.
22. Elyot, *Governor*, fol. 223–223(v)/sig. eiiij and v.
23. Burrow, 'Horace at Home', p. 36.
24. See, for example, Fox, *Politics and Literature*, p. 270: 'In proclaiming the virtues of the mean estate, he [Wyatt] was making a virtue of necessity which makes one suspect that he may well have adopted this theme as much to bolster his bruised ego as from genuine conviction.'
25. As Robert Whittington observed in his adaptation of Seneca, published as *The Myrror or Glasse of Maners and Wysedome*, 'Our Seneca declared by a mervaylous exhortation

to Latin men what maner of *actes* shuld issue out of vertue' [my italics]. 'For he defyned [th]at all the frute of phylosophy resteth in action and practise' (*Myrror*, sig. Av). See Teresa Morgan, 'A Good Man Skilled in Politics: Quintilian's Political Theory', in Yun Lee Too and Niall Livingstone, eds, *Pedagogy and Power: Rhetorics of Classical Learning* (Cambridge, Cambridge University Press, 1998), pp. 245–62.

26. Stephen Greenblatt, *Renaissance Self-Fashioning*, pp. 127–9.

27. Fox, *Politics and Literature*, p. 270.

28. Burrow, 'Horace at Home', pp. 42–9; and Burrow, 'The Experience of Exclusion: Literature and Politics in the Reigns of Henry VII and Henry VIII', in David Wallace, ed., *The Cambridge History of Medieval English Literature* (Cambridge, Cambridge University Press, 1999), pp. 793–820.

29. *LP* x 908.

30. 'The Fable of the Two Mis' in *The Subtyl Historyes and Fables of Esope whiche were translated out of Frensshe in to Englysshe by Wyliam Caxton* (Westminster, Caxton, 1484); Robert Hennryson, 'The Taill of the Uponlandis Mous and the Burges Mous', in Hennryson, *Moral Fables*, ed. George D. Gopen (Notre Dame, Indiana, University of Notre Dame Press, 1987). That Wyatt was aware of Hennryson's text (presumably in manuscript as the earliest known printed version was not published until 1570) is suggested by the fact that he follows the Scottish poet in making the two mice sisters and having a cat and not a pack of dogs interrupt their courtly feast.

31. '*Modus agri non ita magnus, / hortus ubi et tecto vicinus jugis aquae fons / et paulum silvae super his foret. auctius atque / di melius fecere. bene est. nil amplus oro, / Maia nate, nisi ut propria haec mihi munera faxis*'. Horace, *Satire* II VI, 1–5, in Horace, *Satires*, pp. 210–11.

32. Horace, *Satires* ii, vi, 77.

33. Caxton, *Historyes and Fables of Esope*, fol. xxxvii.

34. Burrow, 'Horace at Home', pp. 27–49, p. 40.

35. Horace, *Satires* ii, vi, 100.

36. Burrow, 'Horace', p. 41.

37. See Mason, *A Literary Portrait*, p. 307.

38. William Langland, *The Vision of Piers Plowman: A Complete Edition of the B-Text*, ed. A. V. C. Schmidt (London, J. M. Dent and Sons, 1978).

39. See, for example, Mason, *A Literary Portrait*, pp. 307–8: 'There does not seem to be much point in the fable he has rendered so vividly...Nothing prepares us for the vicious close where Wyatt virtually curses "these wretched fools", for it is impossible to see where Wyatt was heading and what his "moral" amounted to'; and Jason Gleckman, 'Thomas Wyatt's Epistolary Satires: Parody and the Limitations of Rhetorical Humanism', *Texas Studies in Literature and Language* 43 (2001), pp. 29–45, p. 33: 'Instead of what we might expect at this point in a humanist diatribe—namely a plea...that the injustice reigning at court be terminated and flattery destroyed or at least exposed—Wyatt concludes with a subdued prayer.'

40. G. G. Ramses, ed. and trans. *Juvenal and Persius*, Loeb Classical Library (London, William Heinemann, 1918), pp. 346–7; Mason, *A Literary Portrait*, pp. 324–5.

41. Horace, *Odes*, ii, xvi, 9–12, pp. 148–9.

42. Wyatt, *The Quyete of Mynde* (London, Pynson, 1528), sig. bvii, printed in Muir and Thompson, *Collected Poems*, p. 452.

43. *The Quyete of Mynde*, sig. bvii(v), printed in Muir and Thompson, *Collected Poems*, p. 453.

44. Scattergood, 'Thomas Wyatt's Epsitolary Satires'. Boethius was imprisoned by Theoderic the Ostrogoth for asserting the role of the Senate in the Roman state. Boethius, *Theological Tractates*, pp. xi–xv.

45. *Boece*, II, Metrum viii, 1–9; *Works*, fol. CCLI(v). The source of the image of seeking grapes among brambles was Matthew 7:16: 'By their fruits you shall know them. Do men gather grapes of thorns, or figs of thistles?'

46. *Consolation* II, prose v: '*paucis enim minimisque natura contenta est*', which Chaucer had translated as: 'with ful fewe thynges and with ful litel thyngs nature hath her apayde', *Works*, fol. CCXLIV(v).

47. '*Quid igitur, o mortales extra petitis intra vos positam felicitatem?*', Boethius, *Consolation of Philosophy*, II, prose iv.

48. Persius had made a similar point about self-sufficiency in his Satire 1.7: '*nec te quaesiveris extra*' ('look to no one outside yourself'), *Juvenal and Persius*, pp. 316–17; Foley, *Sir Thomas Wyatt*, p. 59.

49. In *The Quiet of Minde* he had followed Bude's translation in claiming that 'fools let good things pass though they be present, and regard them not when they perish, so much doth their thoughts gape greedily after things to come. Contrariwise, men of wit with sharp remembrance, reducing themself to things that be present, make those things that yet are not to be at hand', Muir and Thomson, *Collected Poems*, p. 455, Mason, *A Literary Portrait*, p. 324.

50. Mason, *Humanism and Literature*, pp. 203–4; Heale, *Wyatt, Surrey, and Early Tudor Poetry*, p. 126.

51. See David Starkey, 'The Court: Castiglione's Ideal and Tudor Reality', *Journal of the Warburg and Courtauld Institutes* 45 (1982), pp. 232–9, for an astute reading of the relationship between the historical Sir Francis Bryan and the 'Bryan' of Wyatt's poem.

52. Burrow, 'Horace at Home', p. 43.

53. R. B. Merriman, ed, *Life and Letters of Thomas Cromwell* (2 vols, Oxford, Clarendon Press, 1902), II, p. 167. Cromwell to Wyatt, 19 January 1539.

54. Muir, *Life and Letters*, p. 86. Wyatt to Cromwell, 2 January 1539.

55. Merriman, *Life and Letters*, II, p. 161. Cromwell to Wyatt, 28 November 1538.

56. *LP* XIII (i) 981 (2); Brigden, 'The Shadow that you Know', pp. 5–6.

57. Muir, *Life and Letters*, p. 43.

58. Huntington Library Manuscripts, HL MS 183. Bryan cites the proverb 'A rollinge stone dothe never gather mosse' at line 156 of his poem, and talks of gifts and generosity at lines 53–4. For a detailed analysis of Bryan's poem and its sources, see Robert S. Kinsman, ' "The Proverbes of Salmon do Playnly Declare": A Sententious Poem on Wisdom and Governance, Ascribed to Sir Francis Bryan', *Huntington Library Quarterly*, 42 (1979), pp. 279–312.

59. The maxims were drawn, again via Elyot's *Banquet*, from, *inter alia*, Proverbs 13:16 and Ecclesiasticus 8:20.

60. Robert Whittington, *A frutefull worke of Lucius Anneus Senecae. Called the Myrrour of glasse of maners and wysedome* (London, William Middleton, 1547), sigs. AVi–AVi(v). Kinsman, 'The Proverbes of Salmon', p. 309.

61. Sir Francis Bryan, *A Dispraise of the Life of a Courtier, and a Commendacion of the life of the Labouryng Man* (London, Richard Grafton, 1548), sigs. av(v) and aii(v).

62. See, for example, Fox, *Politics and Literature*, p. 278; Muir and Thompson, *Collected Poems*, p. 432; Brigden, 'The Shadow that you Know', p. 1. For a rather different reading of the poem, see Christopher Z. Hobson, 'Country Mouse and Towny Mouse: Truth in Wyatt', *Texas Studies in Literature and Language* 39 (1997), pp. 230–58, pp. 237–8.

63. Brigden, 'The Shadow that you Know', pp. 1–2, citing an original suggestion of the biblical source in G. F. Nott, ed, *The Works of Henry Howard, earl of Surrey, and of Sir Thomas Wyatt* (reprint edition, 2 vols., New York, AMS, 1965), i, p. 359. Brigden does not state precisely what these ruinous secrets might have been, however: 'In his last poems to Bryan, Wyatt reminded him of secrets which a friend must keep: surely particular secrets, for secrets are the stock in trade of diplomats and courtiers, and Wyatt and Bryan shared many.' The Vulgate text reads rather differently: 'If thou hast opened a sad mouth, fear not, for there may be a reconciliation: except upbraiding, and reproach, and pride, and disclosing of secrets, or a treacherous wound; for in all these cases a friend will flee away.'

64. As Brigden notes ('The Shadow that you Know', p. 20), Wyatt used the image again in another poem that was possibly directed to Bryan ('The Flaming Sighes that Boile within my Breast', Muir and Thompson 238), where again the point is that scars remain after wounds have healed to witness to the damage done: 'The wounde, alas, happ in some other place / Ffrom whence no toole away the scarre can race' (13–14).

65. If there are biblical overtones to these lines, they are more likely to point towards Jeremiah 30:17ʟ: 'For I will close up thy scar, and will heal thee of thy wounds, saith the Lord. Because they have called thee, O Sion, an outcast'. The same issues of marginalization and slander are treated here, albeit from the prospect of healing rather than suffering. I owe this suggestion to Dr Anne Marie D'Arcy.

66. The subject of wounds and their healing arose again elsewhere in Bryan's text. At line 80 he wrote, 'The wounde oft renewed ys longe in the healinge', a maxim quoted in Elyot's chapter on 'Custom' ('The wound often renewed is hard to be healed'), taken from Isidore of Seville's *Soliloquiorum*. Kinsman, 'The Proverbs of Salmon', p. 289.

67. As Kinsman notes ('The Proverbs of Salmon', p. 287), the Bryan manuscript seems to read 'stabe' rather than 'scabe' here, raising the possibility that Bryan was translating the original Ciceronian word '*labes*' as a 'blow' ('stab') rather than a disease ('scab'). But as Bryan was, here as elsewhere, quoting from Elyot's text rather than Cicero directly, the word he was looking at was clearly 'scab', and scribal error is probably to blame for the variation.

68. Muir, *Life and Letters*, p. 193.

69. See Chapter 16, below.

70. Horace, *Satires*, v, v, *passim*.

71. Nott, *Works*, ii, p. 365; Mason, *A Literary Portrait*, p. 335.

72. Muir and Thompson, *Collected Poems*, p. 356, citing Ruth Hughes, ed., *The Arundel Harington Manuscript of Tudor Poetry* (2 vols., Columbus Ohio, Ohio State University Press, 1960).

73. Horace, *Satires*, ii. v, 75–6.

74. For Wyatt's conception of 'truth', see Kenneth J. E. Graham, 'The Performance of Conviction: Wyatt's Antirhetorical Plainness', *Style* 23 (1989), pp. 374–93; Thomas Greene, *The Light in Troy: Imitation and Discovery in Renaissance Poetry* (New Haven, Yale University Press, 1982), pp. 254–63; and Hobson, 'Country Mouse and Towny Mouse', pp. 230–58.

75. Muir, *Life and Letters*, p. 42. In his first letter to his son, written from Spain in 1537, Wyatt had commended 'wisdom, gentleness, soberness, desire to do good, friendliness to get the love of many, and truth above all the rest' as the essential attributes of a gentleman (Muir, *Life and Letters*, p. 38). In his second letter he declared, 'I have nothing to cry and call upon you for but honesty, honesty!' (Muir, *Life and Letters*, p. 41).

76. Bryan is here paraphrasing ideas from Elyot's Introduction to *The Banquet of Sapience*.

77. Similar sentiments litter the poem. 'I judge hym to be miserable that never kn[e]we myserye; / A covetous hart ys never sacyat with treasure.' (35–6); 'Ryches shall nothinge avayle when God will take vengeaunce, / Nor he that gathereth ryches with a tonge full of lyes: / Wronge goten goodes shall com to small substaunce. /A wise manes wyt ys all craft to dispise.' (121–4).

78. Starkey, 'The Court: Castiglione's Ideal and Tudor Reality', p. 235.

79. *LP* XIII (i) 981.

80. See, for example, Greenblatt, *Renaissance Self-Fashioning*, p. 135: 'His was a career of conniving, betrayal, politic marriage, sycophancy, and pandaring... More than one of the vices it [the poem] catalogues bears an uncanny resemblance to well-known incidents in Bryan's life'; and Starkey, 'The Court: Castiglione's Ideal and Tudor reality', pp. 135–6.

81. *LP* x 873.

82. Starkey, 'The Court: Castiglione's Ideal and Tudor reality', pp. 236–7.

83. Catherine Bates, ' "A Mild Admonisher": Sir Thomas Wyatt and Sixteenth-Century Satire', *The Huntington Library Quarterly* 56 (1993), pp. 248–9.

84. Horace drew attention to the incongruity by having Tiresias refer to Odysseus as '*doloso*' (a 'man of wiles') even as he chastises him for his naivety. Horace, *Satires*, II, v pp. 198–9.

85. As Burrow suggests ('Horace at Home', p. 45), Wyatt is here following the complex, self-subverting pose of Horace's second book of Satires, and indeed, adopts this ironic spirit here so successfully that he unsettles 'any sense that there might be a single posture emerging though the [text]'. 'Wyatt here arrives at a rapprochement with the idiom by undermining the stable certainties of his own "Horatian" ideals.' His is, as James Simpson suggests, an irony that 'undoes itself' (*Reform and Cultural Revolution*, p. 250); 'albeit the first law of irony states that two negatives do not make a positive, an undone irony remains anything but straightforward to read'. For these ideas see also the sensitive analysis of Wyatt's text in Bates, 'A Mild Admonisher', which was drawn to my attention after the completion of this chapter. I have referred to Bates' conclusions, where appropriate, in the footnotes.

86. Cromwell had a copy of the *Triomphi* in his possession in April 1530, which he intended to lend to Edmund Bonner (*LP* IV (iii) 6346), suggesting at very least that the text was known at court at this time.

87. For an argument along similar lines, see Hobson, 'Country Mouse and Towny Mouse', pp. 248–9.
88. The principal identifiable sources here are Romans 13:2 ('Therefore, he that resisteth the power resisteth the ordinance of God. And they that resist purchase to themselves damnation.') and Ephesians 6:5 ('Servants, be obedient to them that are your lords according to the flesh, with fear and trembling, in the simplicity of your heart, as to Christ.'). The other sentiments would seem to have been Bryan's own additions to the material in Elyot's *Banquet*.
89. *LP* XIII (ii) 270 and 277, Brigden, 'The Shadow that you Know', p. 18; Starkey, 'The Court: Castiglione's Ideal and Tudor Reality', p. 237.
90. *LP* XIII (i) 1405, 1451, 1455; (ii) 23, 280, and 77.
91. *LP* XIII (ii) 210, 243, 280, 312, 430, 1120, 1163, and 1280 (44 and 48b).
92. See, for example, *LP* XIII (i) 1382, 1346, 1350, 1377, 1383, 1509, for a tiny sample of the allegations and denunciations being reported and investigated in this period. For the wider picture, see G. R. Elton, *Policy and Police: The Enforcement of the Reformation in the Age of Thomas Cromwell* (Cambridge, Cambridge University Press, 1972), *passim*.

14. WYATT'S EMBASSY, TREASON, AND 'THE DEFENCE'

1. BL Harleian MS 282 fol. 79 ff.
2. R. B. Merriman, ed., *Life and Letters of Thomas Cromwell* (2 vols., Oxford, Clarendon Press, 1902), II, p. 92. Cromwell to Wyatt, 10 October 1537.
3. Muir, *Life and Letters*, pp. 45–6.
4. *LP* XIII (ii), 270. See also the subsequent letter of 15 October (*LP* XIII (ii) 615). Both letters are printed in full in Muir, *Life and Letters*, pp. 64ff. All references to the letters here are to the latter versions, unless otherwise stated.
5. Muir, *Life and Letters*, pp. 64–5.
6. *Spanish Calendar* v (ii) 225.
7. *LP* XIII (ii) 270; Muir, *Life and Letters*, pp. 66.
8. In his second embassy, in 1539–40, the reverse was the case, and Wyatt (possibly in a determined effort not to appear conciliatory) seemed almost wilfully to court contention with the Emperor, having on a number of occasions to be saved from fruitless confrontations by his more emollient fellow ambassadors. See, for example, Muir, *Life and Letters*, pp. 121–6, 129–30, 134–8.
9. Ibid., p. 60.
10. Ibid., p. 67.
11. Burrow, 'Horace at Home', p. 40.
12. Muir, *Life and Letters*, p. 198.
13. *State Papers*, I, p. 538 (*LP* XII (i) 479); *LP* XI 1271 and 894.
14. G. W. Bernard, 'The Piety of Henry VIII', in N. Scott Amos, Andrew Pettegree, and Henk van Nierop, eds., *The Education of a Christian Society: Humanism and the Reformation in Britain and the Netherlands* (Aldershot, Ashgate, 1999), pp. 62–88, and D. Knowles and T. Dart, 'Notes on a Bible of Evesham Abbey', *English Historical Review* 89 (1964), p. 776. I am grateful to G. W. Bernard for the latter reference.

15. See G. W. Bernard, *The Power of the Early Tudor Nobility: A Study of the Fourth and Fifth Earls of Shrewsbury* (Brighton, Harvester Press, 1985); and Bernard, ed., *The Tudor Nobility* (Manchester, Manchester University Press, 1992), pp. 1–48.

16. *LP* xv 954.

17. Sir Walter Raleigh, *Selected Writings*, ed. G. Hammond (Harmondsworth, Penguin, 1984), pp. 133–4. See above, p. 6.

18. *LP* xiii (ii) 348; 612 (2); Muir, *Life and Letters*, p. 183.

19. Muir, *Life and Letters*, p. 208.

20. BL MS Harleian 78, ff 7–15, printed in Muir, *Life and Letters*, p. 187–209, p. 188–9. This document is headed 'To the Judges after the Indictment and the Evidence'. It follows after the shorter statement headed 'A Declaration made by Sir Thomas Wyatt, Knight, of his Innocence being upon the false accusation of Doctor Bonarde, bishop of London, made (unto) the Council the year of Our Lord 15[41]' (BL MS Harleian 78, ff 5 and following, printed in Muir, *Life and Letters*, pp. 178–84). In what follows I shall quote from the printed text unless otherwise stated, referring to the shorter, earlier text as 'the Declaration' and the later longer one as 'the Defence'.

21. For this and what follows, see Muir, *Life and Letters*, pp. 175ff.

22. J. Kaulek, ed., *Correspondence Politique* (Paris, 1885), pp. 261–3, translated in Muir, *Life and Letters*, p. 176.

23. *Proceedings of the Privy Council* vii, p. 119, reprinted in Muir, *Life and Letters*, p. 177. The man instructed to put these orders into effect, Sir Richard Southwell, was also, as we shall see, to play a significant role in the destruction of Wyatt's friend and fellow poet Henry Howard, Earl of Surrey.

24. 'The Declaration', Muir, *Life and Letters*, p. 178.

25. In the Declaration he refers to one session: 'as I complained before your Lordships' (Muir, *Life and Letters*, p. 180), and clearly knew that Mason had been examined concerning their conversations and activities in Nice and Villa Franca.

26. Muir, *Life and Letters*, p. 179.

27. Ibid., pp. 179–80.

28. Ibid., p. 181.

29. In the Declaration Wyatt noted the impact of 'the examination of Mason' in renewing interest in his activities in Nice and Villa Franca.

30. Muir, *Life and Letters*, p. 181.

31. Ibid., p. 183.

32. Ibid., p. 184.

33. Ibid., p. 184.

34. *Spanish Calendar* vi (i) 155 (*LP* xvi 391). For the suggestion that Surrey may have been behind Catherine Howard's plea, see Sessions, 'Surrey's Wyatt', p. 172. That it was indeed the Queen's 'great and continual suite' that was the decisive factor is confirmed by the Privy Council's account of the matter cited below.

35. *State Papers*, viii, p. 546.

36. *LP* xvi 711; Muir, *Life and Letters*, p. 210.

37. Fox, *Literature and Politics*, pp. 279–80. See also Muir, *Life and Letters*, p. 210: 'We must assume that the rest of Wyatt's life was unhappy. He was separated from the woman he loved, and reunited with the wife he could not bring himself to forgive.'

38. Muir, *Life and Letters*, p. 209.

39. Muir, *Life and Letters*, p. 200.
40. Ibid., pp. 204–5.
41. An immediate and obvious point of contrast is provided by Cromwell's last letters to the King while he himself was in prison awaiting news of his fate. The fallen minister's version of the same plea was to declare that 'I do [ac]knowledge myself to have been a most miserable and wretched Sinner and that I have not towards God and your Highness behaved myself as I ought and Should have done. For the which mine offences to God while I live I shall continually call for his mercy and For mine offences to your grace which, God knoweth were never malicious nor wilful, and that I never thought treason to your Highness, your realm, or posterity so God help me either in word or deed, nevertheless prostrate at your majesty's [feet] in what thing soever I have offended I appeal to your Highness for Mercy, grace, and pardon as such wise as Shall be your pleasure.' (Merriman, *Life and Letters of Thomas Cromwell*, II, p. 267).
42. Muir, *Life and Letters*, p. 205.
43. Ibid., p. 205.
44. See, for example, Greenblatt, *Renaissance Self-Fashioning*, pp. 121–6.
45. See Quintilian, *The Orator's Education*, ed. and trans, Donald A. Russell, Loeb Classical Library (5 vols., London, Heinemann, 2001) 1, pr. 9–20; T. Morgan, 'A Good Man Skilled in Politics: Quintillian's Political Theory', in Y. L. Too and N. Livingstone, eds., *Pedagogy and Power: Rhetorics of Classical Latinity* (Cambridge, Cambridge University Press, 1998), pp. 245–62. For a more sceptical view, see L. Panizza, 'Lorenzo Valla's *De Vero Falsoque Bono*, Lactantius and Oratorical Scepticism', *Journal of the Warburg and Courtauld Institutes* 41 (1978), pp. 76–107. I am grateful to Dr Anne Marie D'Arcy for these references.
46. Muir, *Life and Letters*, p. 196.
47. Muir, *Life and Letters*, pp. 208–9. William Lord Dacres of Gillesland was arraigned for treason on 9 July 1534, but was subsequently acquitted of all charges by a jury of his peers.
48. Fox, *Politics and Literature*, p. 279.

15. PLEADING WITH POWER

1. Scholars differ over the dating of Wyatt's psalms, some arguing for 1536 others for 1541. The fact that Wyatt seems to draw upon the language of parts of Luther's *Ennaratio Psalmorum LI Miserere mei, Deus, et CXXX De Profundis... Clamavi... Adjecta est etiam Savonarolae Meditatio in Psalmum LI* (first published in Strasburg in 1538), would, however, as both Mason and Fox suggest, make the case for the later date the more compelling. It has also been suggested that the poet may have written the psalms while in prison in early 1541, but I would favour a later date, immediately following his release. Wyatt was otherwise occupied during his imprisonment, preparing the Declaration and Defence, and writing a number of shorter lyrics, which suggests he would have little time for the substantial endeavour that the *Paraphrase* represented. Moreover, the fact that he seems, as we shall see, to have consulted a wide range of printed books while working on the *Paraphrase*, borrowing phrases from some, and ideas from others, would argue that he had access to a substantial collection of books, if not a formal library, while he was working. Access to books was not, of course, impossible in the Tower, but access to a

collection of this size strongly suggests that he had the liberty to consult widely and to borrow freely from friends.

2. Fox, *Politics and Literature in the Reigns of Henry VII and Henry VIII* (Oxford Black-well, 1989), p. 284. See also p. 285.

3. For a more sceptical reading of the autobiographical element in the text, see Rivkah Zim, *English Metrical Psalms: Poetry as Praise and Prayer, 1535–1660* (Cambridge, Cambridge University Press, 1987), pp. 6–7 and 70–1.

4. The Vulgate text merely reads 'I have laboured in my groanings, every night I will wash my bed: I will water my couch with tears. / My eye is troubled with indignation: I have grown old amongst all my enemies. / Depart from them, all ye workers of iniquity: for the lord hath heard the voice of my weeping.' (Psalms 6: 7–9). Pietro Aretino, who provided Wyatt's principal model for this psalm, offered a more florid account of David's feelings for Bathsheba which is both more critical (in its admission of 'lasciviousness') and more distanced in its formality and conventionality than Wyatt's touching and affectionate lines. 'Mine enemies still persevere against me ... and now, having found out new snares against my repentance, evermore assemble themselves and make it their discourse in what manner I am to finish my days, taking me yet to be in hold of lasciviousness as are they, and I am really troubled at their whisperings, which they buzz in mine ears. One of them presenteth to mine eyes the rare image of her whole comely graces and beauty, on me have heaped more than many sins, another telleth me of her harmonious speech, how sweet it was, which now so bitterly resoundeth in mine ears ...' (Pietro Aretino, *I Sette Salmi*, translated into English by John Hawkins, as *Paraphrase upon the Seven Pentiential Psalmes of the Kingly Prophet, Translated out of Italian by I. H.* (London, 1635), pp. 24–5.)

5. The Vulgate text reads, 'But my enemies live, and are stronger than I; and they that hate me wrongfully are multiplied. / They that render evil for good, have detracted me, because I followed goodness' (Psalms 37: 20–1). Aretino dealt with the theme of untrustworthy aids and supporters, but unequivocally interpreted them as the mental and spiritual faculties of the speaker that desert him in the face of fear:

'My heart whose tears have paid thee (as one who is good is satisfied by the candid and sincere meaning of anyone) is troubled, contristated for that the faculties and the strength, columns, pillars of my soul, have abandoned me, utterly forsaken me, and I am miserably shaken with fear of my destruction, and utter loss, since that I find I am deprived of such sustentacles, such main supporters. Ah! hereon speak who will sensibly deliver their minds, who I say will, who is he and who would not fear to be deprived of such like associates, such companions? Fortitude and the virtues and faculties of the mind are the weapons wherewith the fallacies, the enticements, and snares of the world are overcome and brought to nought; herewith the adversaries of all good (I mean by adversaries the Devil and his fiends) are trodden under foot.'

(Hawkins, *Paraphrase*, pp. 80–1.)

6. Indeed Wyatt seems deliberately to have amended the text during composition to increase such implications, for, having initially followed Aretino's explicitly psycho-machian reading, writing 'Myn owne vertus wherin I sett my trust / As frendes most sure, sonest then did quaile', he changed this to the more ambivalent 'My frendes most

sure, wherein I sett most trust, / Myn own vertus sonest then did ffaile' Baron, 'Penitential Psalms', p. 283.

7. In the Authorized Version, the relevant Psalms are numbered 6, 32, 38, 102, 130, and 143.

8. H. A. Mason, ed., *Sir Thomas Wyatt: A Literary Portrait* (Bristol, Bristol Classical Press, 1986), p. 16.

9. Zim, *English Metrical Psalms*, pp. 81–2, and 85. See also the critical introduction to Desiderius Erasmus, *Expositions of the Psalms: The Collected Works of Erasmus*, vol. 63, ed. Dominic Baker-Smith, trans. and annotated by Michael J. Heath (Toronto, University of Toronto Press, 1997). For the flexibility of the psalms as polemical texts, see Michael P. Kuczynski, *Prophetic Song: The Psalms and Moral Discourse in Late Medieval England* (Philadelphia, University of Pennsylvania Press, 1995), pp. 6–9, where it is pointed out that they had been deployed in the course of the fifteenth century to justify both the active and the contemplative lives by advocates of those ideals.

10. Zim, *English Metrical Psalms*, p. 89.

11. Ibid., pp. 81–2.

12. Joannes Campensis, *Pslamorum omnium juxta Hebraicam veritatem paraphrastica interprtatio... Paraphrasis in concionem salomonis Ecclesiasticaie* (Lyon, 1532).

13. Pietro Aretino, *Lacrime del Peccatore ne i sette salmi della Penitenza di Davidde* (Venice, 1534). For a comprehensive analysis of Wyatt's sources, see Helen Valerie Baron, 'Sir Thomas Wyatt's Seven Penitential Psalms: A Study of Textual and Source Materials', University of Cambridge Ph.D. thesis, 1977. Charles A. Hutter has suggested that Wyatt was influenced by (even if he did not borrow directly from) Clemont Marot's translation of the psalms into French, and Luigi Alamanni's translation of the Penitential Psalms into Italian verse (the latter being, like Wyatt's psalms in *terza rima*). See Charles A. Hutter, 'English Metrical Paraphrases of the Psalms, 1500–1640', Northwestern University Ph.D. thesis, 1956, p. 23. See also Mason, *Literary Portrait*, p. 158 and 188, where the Italian rhetorician Jacopo Sadoleto's *Interpretatio in psalmium Miserere mei deus* (1525) is suggested as another source.

14. Kuczynski, *Prophetic Song*, pp. xx–xxi. As Kuczynski points out (p. 9), 'The Psalmist's double persona as both Christ and Ecclesia implies a double role for him as prophet. He is both a visionary poet and a moral reformer and teacher whose poetry can repair the damage done by original sin, thus making whole again Christ's corporate self.' See also Donald Davie, ed., *The Psalms in English* (Harmondsworth, Penguin, 1996), Introduction.

15. For the interweaving of the private and the public in the psalms more generally, see Kuczynski, *Prophetic Song*, p. xvii and following.

16. *Certayne Psalmes chosen out of the psalter of David, commonlye called thee vii penytentiall psalmes, drawen into Englysshe meter by Sir Thomas Wyat, Knyght* (London, Thomas Raynold and John Harrington, 1549, 'the first day of September').

17. Wyatt's holograph text is contained in BL Egerton MS 2711.

18. Alexandra Halasz, 'Wyatt's David' in Peter C. Herman, ed., *Rethinking the Henrician Era: Essays on Early Tudor Texts and Contexts* (Urbana and Chicago, University of Illinois Press, 1994), pp. 193–218, p. 194.

19. Greenblatt, *Renaissance Self-Fashioning*, pp. 116, 121; Foley, *Sir Thomas Wyatt*, p. 85, who notes, 'Wyatt's self-conscious insertion of a line of political or moral criticism in the Psalms; they address the scandal of Henry VIII and to some extent they inscribe the ideological disruption of the times upon the King, figuring it as moral depravity.'

20. The closeness to Aretino's text here is striking: 'Love, taking his stand in the eyes of Bersabe, to give laws to gentle and flexible spirits transformed himself in a glance cruelly piteous and, making through-pass to King David, first casting a mist before his eyes then after breathed into him passion and in a seeming sweet touch of his senses, had access, yea ingress to his very bones, and there dispersed his fire' (Hawkins, *Paraphrase*, p. 1).

21. Aretino has a more benevolent account of David's reaction: 'Nathan the Prophet deeply weighted his enormities, yet compassionating him, in plain terms laid before his understanding his injustice as well in murder as also in adultery contrary to his Maker's commands. The good old man, astonished with the punishments which heaven prepared for his sin, felt as well from his soul, heart, as also his sense, his desire, his fire, and his over-weaning delight, to forsake him, to depart, to vanish, even as heat from the limbs' (Hawkins, *Paraphrase*, pp. 2–3).

22. For such 'historical' readings of the psalms in Augustine's highly influential *Enarrationes* and subsequent medieval exegetical texts, see Kuckzynski, *Prophetic Song*, pp. xx, 21–2, 52, 55; Zim, *English Metrical Psalms*, p. 43. For an example of such an illustration, see Mason, *Literary Portrait*, p. 35.

23. Greenblatt, *Renaissance Self-Fashioning*, p. 123–5.

24. Zim, *English Metrical Psalms*, pp. 47–9.

25. Ibid., p. 47; Halasz, 'Wyatt's David', pp. 207–8.

26. Halasz, 'Wyatt's David', p. 214. For Henry VIII's use of a Davidic persona, see John King, 'Henry VIII as David' in Peter C. Herman, ed., *Rethinking the Henrician Era* (Urbana, University of Illinois Press, 1994), pp. 78–91; Pamela Tudor Craig, 'Henry VIII and King David', in D. Williams, ed., *Early Tudor England* (Woodbridge, D. S. Brewer, 1989), pp, 183–205; and Walker, *Persuasive Fictions*, pp. 80–2.

27. Zim, *English Metrical Psalms*, p. 47.

28. Halasz, 'Wyatt's David', p. 196.

29. Stephen Greenblatt, for example, describes the psalms as capturing 'the authentic voice of early English Protestantism, its mingled humility and militancy, its desire to submit without intermediary to God's will, and above all its inwardness'. (*Renaissance Self-Fashioning from More to Shakespeare* (Chicago, University of Chicago Press, 1980), p. 115). W. A. Sessions describes Wyatt as a 'reformed Christian' (Sessions, *Henry Howard, The Poet Earl of Surrey: A Life* (Oxford, Oxford University Press, 1999) [hereafter Sessions, *Henry Howard*], p. 256), and 'a strong Protestant' (Sessions, *Henry Howard, Earl of Surrey* (Boston, Twayne Publishers, 1986) [hereafter Sessions, *Surrey*], p. 102). Susan Brigden talks of his 'evangelical commitment' ('Henry Howard, Earl of Surrey, and the "Conjured League" ', *Historical Journal* 37 (1994), pp. 507–37, p. 514. Alistair Fox talks of the psalms, especially the one hundred and fifty-first, displaying an 'unmistakable Lutheran bias', (*Politics and Literature in the Reigns of Henry VII and Henry VIII* (Oxford, Basil Blackwell, 1989), p. 282), while H. A. Mason detects a progression within the psalm sequence

from a 'wholly catholic' position in Psalm 6, through Psalm 50, which he sees as 'orthodox' or 'looking both ways', to something 'more like a Lutheran position' in the later psalms. For Mason, Wyatt finally 'nailed his colours to the mast' in the lines concerning 'rightful penitence' in the prologue to Psalm 102 and the discussion of justification in the final lines of Psalm 51, making his 'conversion to the views of Luther and Tyndale' explicit. See Mason, *A Literary Portrait*, pp. 159–60 and 212. See also Mason, *Humanism and Poetry in the Early Tudor Period* (London, Routledge and Kegan Paul, 1959), p. 227, where it is stated more boldly that 'Wyatt was ... a Lutheran'. Few, however, would go as far as Horace Walpole, who claimed that 'Sir Thomas Wyatt may justly be said to have placed the key-stone of the reformation, which holds the whole fabric together' (*Miscellaneous Antiquities* (Strawberry Hill, 1772), p. 19). More guardedly Alexandra Halasz suggests that 'We may retrospectively identify Wyatt's concerns as protestant, but we must also acknowledge their historicity. Wyatt's strategic use of the figure marks a crisis, not a solution' ('Wyatt's David', p. 215); while Raymond Southall, *The Courtly Maker: An Essay on the Poetry of Wyatt and His Contemporaries* (Oxford, Basil Blackwell, 1964), p. 107, shrewdly cautions that to describe Wyatt as 'Protestant' is 'limiting' and anachronistic, as 'the term Protestant is not very meaningful at this date'.

30. *Certayne Psalmes*, sig. Aii(v).
31. Muir, *Life and Letters*, pp. 195–6.
32. Ibid., p. 204.
33. Ives, *Anne Boleyn*, pp. 91–2.
34. For differing views on the degree of Anne's personal commitment to the evangelical cause, see Ives, *Ann Boleyn*, pp. 302–3; and 'Anne Boleyn and the Early Reformation in England: The Contemporary Evidence', *HJ* 37 (1994), pp. 389–400; Maria Dowling, 'Anne Boleyn and Reform', *JEH*, 35 (1984), pp. 30–46; and G.W Bernard, 'Anne Boleyn's Religion', *HJ*, 36 (1993), pp. 1–20. For the biographical details about Elizabeth Darrell that follow, see Muir, *Life and Letters*, pp., 83–5; Fox, *Politics and Literature*, pp. 277–8, and *LP* v, p. 319; vii 135; x, 40, 87, 1134.
35. *LP* xiii (ii) 702, 766, 772.
36. Muir, *Life and Letters*, p. 211.
37. Baron, 'Sir Thomas Wyatt's Seven Penitential Psalms', pp. 238–40.
38. Brian Cummings, *The Literary Culture of the Reformation: Grammar and Grace* (Oxford, Oxford University Press, 2002), p. 225. Cummings notes that 'By 1540 the Psalms were swarming with Lutheran connotations', and, following Mason (*Humanism and Poetry*, pp. 213–16), suggests that 'the countervailing rhythm of the Lutheran Passive voice is heard' in the tortured syntax and logic of Wyatt's rendering of Psalm 31, 'but only as a faint echo amid the self-censoring burden of Henrician prohibition'.
39. That Wyatt uses the word 'coverth' here does not imply reformist sympathies. The orthodox English Primer published '*cum privilegio Regali*' by John Bydell for William Marshal in 1533 translated the same lines as 'Blessed is he whose ungodliness is forgiven and whose sins are covered.' (*The Prymer in Englyshe* (London, Fleet Street, 'at the sign of Our lady of Pity', John Bydell for Wyllyam Marshall, 1533). Sig. oviii. John Fisher preferred the still more Lutheran sounding, 'Blessed be they whose sins be hid and put out of knowledge' (*Meditations*, sig. cii).

40. Cummings, *Literary Culture and the Reformation*, p. 225.
41. Hawkins, *Paraphrase*, p. 36. Aretino, *I Sette Salmi*, sig. B4 ('*Obe Ati coloro le cui iniquita perdonna Iddio, lasciandole impunite, non perle opere della contritione, ne della penitentia, se ben senza esse le colpe nostre non hanno remissione ma per beneficio della gratia sua, la bonta della quale nel cor rintenerito riguarda, e per la compuntion sua move a ricoprirgli i peccati col lembo della misericordia*'.)
42. Mason, *A Literary Portrait*, p. 214.
43. The comparison was also made, briefly, in Elizabeth Heale's excellent survey, *Wyatt, Surrey, and Early Tudor Poetry* (Harlow, Longman, 1998). Heale concludes, 'If Wyatt's lines seem contorted and contradictory, then so, it must be said, was the bishops' formulation'. James Simpson has also recently pointed out that 'the acceptance of God's grace as the sole ground of justification before God was official doctrine' at this time, citing the Ten Articles of 1536. (See *Reform and Cultural Revolution: The Oxford English Literary History Volume 2: 1350–1547* (Oxford, Oxford University Press, 2002), pp. 323–5.) But Simpson concludes, rather differently to what follows here, that evangelical abjection before God played into the hands of royal absolutism: 'The many sixteenth century calls for absolute obedience to the royal will represent not only a political necessity but also the coherent result of an evangelical conception of divine grace whose overwhelming force etoliates the Church to the profit of the state. Wyatt may, as Surrey suggests, be registering protest against Henry in the *Penitential Psalms*, but the evangelical form of that protest equally neutralizes it, since evangelical theology, in Henrician England at any rate, played directly into royal hands' (see ibid, p. 328). The inability of David to influence his own spiritual destiny through his own deeds leaves him, Simpson suggests, wholly powerless before God, and so before the King who claims to stand in for God on earth. He stresses 'the sheer concentration of power and initiative in God's hands' and notes that 'It is God who gives the sinner power and voice to declare his unworthiness in the first place' (ibid., p. 324). But this underplays the rhetorical dimension to Wyatt's translation, the sense of the orator's voice at work in the text not merely stating a doctrinal position but actively seeking to negotiate its implications. There is in Wyatt's text, as we shall see, a sense in which the sinful David does not simply cry out to God but strikes up a conversation with him. The text thus becomes at times not simply a prayer, a plea to a distant and possibly unheeding God, but a speech for the defence, delivered to a God who is assumed to be both very present and very susceptible to persuasion. Wyatt argues, pleads, negotiates, and at times even comes close to lecturing his God, seeking to convince him not simply of the necessity of pardoning and redeeming David, but also of the advantages to God himself of His doing so. Thus, while the doctrinal positions that Wyatt describes may place the theoretical sinner—the universal human subject—in a position of abject impotence, the ways in which he deploys and *works* that doctrine in the course of the text reveal the actual and present sinner, the David whose voice we hear, as supremely *active* on his own behalf.
44. On Penance, the *Bishop's Book* declared that, 'The said sacrament was instituted by God in the New Testament as a thing so necessary for man's salvation that no man which after his baptism is fallen again and hath committed deadly sin can without the same be saved or attain everlasting life.' (*The Institution of a Christian Man*

(London, Thomas Berthelet, 1537), sig. ĸi/p. 37). A little later on the same page the point was made more explicitly; 'Item, that like as such men, which after baptism do fall again into sin, if they do not penance in this life shall undoubtedly be damned. Even so when so ever the same men shall convert them self from their naughty life and do such penance for the same as Christ requireth of them they shall without doubt attain remission of their sin and shall be saved.' Elsewhere the text is still more emphatic: 'Item, that these precepts and works of charity be necessary works to our salvation, and God necessarily requireth that every penitent man shall perform the same when so ever time, power, and occasion shall be ministered unto him so to do (*Institution*, p. 38(v)). See also ibid.: 'Item, that by penance and such good works of the same we shall not only obtain everlasting life but also we shall deserve remission or mitigation of the present pains and afflictions which we sustain here in this world, for Saint Paul sayeth that if we would correct and take punishment of ourselves in this world, we should not be so grievously corrected of God.'; and the statement at p. 24, glossing the Creed's reference to the Last Judgement, that 'at that day every man shall be called to make a straight account of his life, and shall be then finally judged even according to his own proper works, good or bad, done in his lifetime'.

45. *The Institution*, pp. 96–96(v). For the 10 Articles, see *EHD* v, pp. 801–2.
46. *The Institution*, p. 96(v).
47. *Institution*, p. 37(v); *EHD* v, p. 799.
48. For the contrary suggestion, that Wyatt rejects the stress on the three parts of penance that he found in sources such as Fisher's *Commentary*, see Baron, 'Sir Thomas Wyatt's Seven Penitential Psalms', p. 242.
49. As Mason notes, Wyatt seems to echo Fisher's stress on the overwhelming power of Original Sin here. Mason, *A Literary Portrait*, p. 195, citing Fisher, *Commentary*, p. 225 and 106.
50. Greenblatt, *Renaissance Self-Fashioning*, p. 115; Fox, *Politics and Literature*, pp. 282–3.
51. Mason, *A Literary Portrait*, pp. 162–3, quoting Luther's *Paraphrase*, 327/33.
52. Mason, *A Literary Portrait*, p. 163 and 188.
53. Ibid., p. 206. Mason cites Tyndale's discussion of the same point in his Prologue to *The Epistle of Paul to the Romans*: 'This word law may not be understood as it goeth with man's law, where the law is fulfilled with outward works only, though the heart be never so far off. But God judgeth the ground of the heart, yea and the thoughts and the secret movings of the mind, and therefore His law requireth the ground of the heart and love from the bottom thereof and is not content with the outward work only, but rebuketh those works most of all which spring not of love from the ground and low bottom of the heart, thought they appear outward never so honest and good, as Christ in the gospel rebuketh the Pharisees above all other that were open sinners, and calleth them hypocrites, that is to say simulars and painted sepulchres. Which Pharisees yet lived no man so pure, as pertaining to the outward deeds and works of the law.' But only in the polemical twist that he gives to the last sentence, does Tyndale depart from conventional catholic teaching on this point. It would be hard to find any sane individual supporting the contrary position that merely exterior obedience to the law was necessary to ensure salvation.

54. In Fisher's *Meditations* (*This Treatyse Conteynynge the fruyfull sayenges of Davyd the Kynge and Prophete in the seven Penetencyall Psalmes* (London, Wynkyn de Worde, 1524), the bishop states that 'almighty God hath ordained more even laws which be common both to poor and rich, he desireth none other sacrifice but such as ye poor may do as soon as ye rich, and, peradventure, more soon, for almighty God taketh more heed to ye good intent of ye mind than to ye greatness or valour of ye gift, which thing is showed in ye gospel of Mark [i.e. in the story of the widow's mite]' (sig. Miii(v)), and, 'Our prophet here remembreth another manner sacrifice which is most acceptable to God and is named ye very penance of man's soul...The sorrowful and penitent soul is chief sacrifice to God for purging of sins' (Miv). See also sig. ni(v): 'The sorrowful and penitent soul is chief sacrifice to God, and, blessed lord, thou shalt not despise a contrite heart, whosoever ordereth himself in this manner that by his inward sorrow may have a contrite heart, he is able and mete unto the high building in the heavenly city whose walls be not yet finished.'

55. Mason, *A Literary Portrait*, pp. 208–9. *Sancta admodum ac religiosa pietate refertissima expositio in quinquagesimum psalmum, cuius principium, Miserere mei Deus, secundum magnam misericordiam tuam.* (Paris, *Apud Simonem Colinaeum*, 1523), sig. d.ii(v), Mason's translation.

56. Mason, *A Literary Portrait*, p. 212, and *Humanism and Poetry*, p. 218.

57. 'By this word penance', Tyndale wrote, 'they make the people understand holy deeds of their enjoining with which they must make satisfaction unto God-ward for their sins. When all the Scripture preacheth that Christ hath made full satisfaction for our sins to God-ward and we must now be thankful to God again and kill the lusts of our flesh with holy works of God's enjoining and to take patiently all that God layeth on my back. And if I have hurt my neighbour, I am bound to shrive myself to him and to make him amends, if I have wherewith, or if not then to ask him forgiveness, and he is bound to forgive me. And as for their penance, the Scriptures know not of [it]. The Greek hath *metanoia* and *metanoite*, repentance and repent.' William Tyndale, *An Answere unto Sir Thomas Mores Dialoge made by Willyam Tindalle* (Antwerp, 1531), f.12.

58. *Institution*, p. 37. See above, pp. 364–5. Conforming closely to traditional catholic teaching on the nature of penance, the *Bishops' Book* explained that 'the sacrament of perfyte penance' was a process consisting in three distinct stages: Contrition, Confession, and Amendment of former life (the latter being glossed as 'the new obedient reconciliation unto the laws and will of God, that is to say, exterior acts and works of charity, according as they be commanded of God, which be called in Scripture, *fructus digni penitenciia*: the worldly fruits of penance'). Contrition, the first of these stages, was itself a two stage process. First the sinner must acknowledge his or her sins and God's anger with him or her resulting from them: 'That is to say, the penitent and contrite man must first knowledge the filthiness and abomination of his own sin (unto which knowledge he is brought by hearing and considering the will of God declared in His laws) and feeling and perceiving in his own conscience that God is angry and displeased with him for the same: he must also conceive not only great fear of God's displeasure towards him, considering he hath no works or merits of his own which he may worthily lay before God as sufficient satisfaction for his sins, which done, that afterward with this fear, shame, and sorrow must needs succeed and

be conjoined the second part, that is to wit, a certain faith, trust, and confidence of the mercy and goodness of God, whereby the penitent must conceive certain hope and faith that God will forgive him his sins and repute him justified . . . not for the worthiness of any merit or work done by the penitent but for the only merits of the blood and passion of our Saviour Jesu Christ.' [*Institution*, pp, 37–27(v).] The bishops were, however, careful to emphasize in a number of places the vital import- ance that good works had nonetheless in the process of Justification. Hence all teachers and preachers were instructed to declare unto those in their cure, 'That, although Christ and His death be the sufficient oblation, sacrifice, satisfaction, and recompense for the which God the Father forgiveth and remitteth to all sinners not only their sin but also eternal pain due for the same: yet all men truly penitent, contrite, and confessed must needs also bring forth the fruits of penance, that is to say, prayer, fasting, and alms deeds with much mourning and lamenting for their sins before committed. And they must also make restitution or satisfaction in will and deed to their neighbours in such things as they have done them wrong and injury in. And finally they must do all other good works of mercy and charity, and express their obedient will in the executing and fulfilling of God's commandment, outwardly when time, power, and occasion shall be ministered unto them, or else they shall never be saved. For this is the express precept and commandment of God: "Do you the worthy fruits of penance" [Luke, 3:8]'

59. Mason, *Humanism and Poetry*, pp. 218–19, suggests that Tyndale's Lutheran asser- tion that 'good works [are] outward signs and outward fruits of faith' (William Tyndale, *A Compendious Introduction unto the Pistle to the Romayns* (Worms, 1526), sig. AV) may be the inspiration for Wyatt's formulation. But the difference in terminology between the poet's 'sign or fruit' of 'rightful penitence' and Tyndale's 'fruits of faith' is crucial. While Wyatt seems to have consciously adopted an evangelical vocabulary in choosing to affirm 'penitence' over the more orthodox 'penance', the choice does not reveal any more significant adoption of Lutheran doctrine on the value of works *per se*, given that, unlike Luther and Tyndale, he chose to read 'penitence', as we have seen, as almost synonymous in meaning with the more orthodox term. Here again, he was following the *Bishops' Book* rather than Tyndale in terms of the doctrinal implications which he invested in the word. Good works, he insisted, were the fruits and signs of penitence, not of faith itself. As we shall see in Chapter 16, it was Surrey rather than Wyatt who was to follow the Tyndalian formulation in his psalm translations.

60. Mason, *A Literary Portrait*, p. 209, suggests similarities between Wyatt's David's repeated assertion that from God 'alone thus all our good proceeds' (line 508) and Luther's gloss in the *Enchiridion*, 'here too he attributes everything to the kindness of God and not to his own deserts and expectations'. But, as the discussion of Justifica- tion suggests, Wyatt has his David expound a Henrician theological position in which God was indeed the absolute and sufficient cause of Justification, but good works had a necessary role to play as well.

61. The text was printed simply as *An exposicyon after the Maner of a Contemplacyon upon the li Psalme / called miseremei Deus* ('Malborow', 1538).

62. For the contrary suggestion that Wyatt does advance solafideism here, see Fox, *Politics and Literature*, p. 285.

63. Luther, *Enchiridion*, 420/32, translated in Mason, *A Literary Portrait*, pp. 210.

64. See Greenblatt, *Renaissance Self-Fashioning*, p. 115, and Colin Burrow, 'The Experience of Exclusion: Literature and Politics in the Reigns of Henry VII and Henry VIII' in David Wallace, ed., *The Cambridge History of Medieval English Literature* (Cambridge, Cambridge University Press, 1999), pp. 793–820, p. 808: 'Wyatt's David repeatedly touches on the language of Protestant theology, and these moments can generate effects of fearful inwardness.'

65. Zim, *English Metrical Psalms*, pp. 29, 45–6, and 70; Greenblatt, *Renaissance Self-Fashioning*, p. 116.

66. Fisher, *Meditations*, p. 102/36.

67. As Zim notes (*English Metrical Psalms*, p. ix) the psalms themselves were not without their negotiative elements: 'The psalms assume not only that God listens, and sometimes hears, but also that God can be argued with and given orders'. But, as Halasz's work suggests ('Wyatt's David', p.205), the degree of persuasive rhetoric and coercive argument in Wyatt's text takes the theme to a new level of interest.

68. Muir, *Life and Letters*, p. 197.

69. Simpson, *Reform and Cultural Revolution*, p. 326.

70. Halasz, 'Wyatt's David', pp. 204–5.

71. Ibid., pp. 205.

72. As Mason points out (*A Literary Portrait*, p. 174), Campensis is probably Wyatt's source here: '*Redi quaescio Domine ad Solitam clementiam*' ('O, lord, I beseech thee, return to the kindness that thou was wont to have...'). The relevant passage in Aretino is far more supplicatory and desperate: 'Look again on my soul, my Lord, with the self same benign countenance with which thou favourably dost behold him, who by long penitence is more worthy than am I poor wretch... Surely I shall henceforth be more solicitous to serve thee than heretofore I have been, as having been slow, careless, and altogether dully sottish. O my lord, if without all fear and trembling, I might call upon thee, would'st thou not vouchsafe an answer to me?... Even now Lord give quiet to the soul, which with an adverse ye of enmity troubledly gazeth on the body, not without just cause of offence, for that through its inordinate appetites, the soul is even condemned to the everlasting punishments of Hell, and as for my body which daily, nightly, incessantly gnawed and worn by its conscience's affliction, soon will fall, soon become ashes, if thou be not to it its sustentacle, its strength, its full vigour, alas! My soul dying in such state, will go to a place which I have horror to name, yea to think of. // But if I die, my Lord, not being among the dead who can call thee to mind, how shall I make mention of thee? How shall I call on thy name?... Alas! yet what shall I say of my state, I shall die the death, I shall make my passage to Hell, and going thither, it being not allowed but otherwise decreed, that any there being love thee for that thou wilt not be beloved of such, how shall I publish and pray thy infinite goodness to them there abiding? Which who so should attempt to define or circumscribe, he should seem to prescribe an end to infinity' (Hawkins, *Paraphrase*, pp. 15–19).

73. For an interesting discussion of Wyatt's treatment of pride and humility, especially in Psalm 6, see Halasz, 'Wyatt's David', p. 202.

74. Ibid., p. 215.

16. 'WYATT RESTETH HERE'

1. *LP* xvii 71.
2. Muir, *Life and Letters*, pp. 211–15.
3. *An Excellent Epitaffe of Syr Thomas Wyat with two other compendious ditties wherin are touchyd and set forth the state of mannes lyfe* (London, John Herforde for Robert Toye, 1542), sigs. ai–i(v).
4. W. A. Sessions, 'Surrey's Wyatt: Autumn 1542 and the New Poet', in Peter C. Herman, ed., *Rethinking the Henrician Era: Essays on Early Tudor Texts and Contexts* (Chicago, University of Illinois Press, 1994), pp. 168–92, pp. 169–72, and 182.
5. John Leland, *Naeniae in mortem Thomae Viati equities incom parabilis Ioanne Lelando Antiquario Autore* (London, 1542).
6. For the echo of Surrey in Sidney, see Susan Brigden, 'Henry Howard, Earl of Surrey, and the "Conjured League" ', *HJ* 37 (1994), pp. 507–37, p. 537.
7. W. A. Sessions, *Henry Howard, the Poet Earl of Surrey: A Life* (Oxford, Oxford University Press, 1999) [hereafter, Sessions, *Henry Howard*], p. 27.
8. *LP* xxi (ii) 555 (i); Sessions, *Henry Howard*, p. 151.
9. Sessions, *Henry Howard*, p. 80.
10. *LP* xii (ii) 248; Sessions, *Henry Howard*, p. 129.
11. Unless otherwise stated, all references not quoted from original manuscripts or printed sources are taken from E. Jones, ed., *Henry Howard, Earl of Surrey: Poems* (Oxford, Clarendon Press, 1964), citing Jones's numbering (here J27).
12. For the biographical details in this and the following paragraph, see Sessions, *Henry Howard*, pp. 82ff; Brigden, 'Conjured League', *passim*; and Jones, ed., *Poems*, pp. xxviff.
13. W. A. Sessions, *Henry Howard, Earl of Surrey* (Boston, Twayne Publishers, 1986) [hereafter, Sessions, *Surrey*], pp. 13–14; Brigden, 'Conjured League', p. 511; *Spanish Calendar* viii, 226.
14. *LP* xxi (ii) 555 (4); Sessions, *Henry Howard*, pp. 333ff. As Brigden suggests ('Conjured League', p. 530), the decorative arch in the Scrots portrait seems also, through its display of the Brotherton and Woodstock arms, to allude overtly to Surrey's royal descent from Edward the Confessor and Edward III respectively.
15. In July 1546 Norfolk had rebuked his son's incautiousness, saying openly that 'I am glad my said son used himself humbly and repentantly [now], which I pray God he may often remember and not trust too much his own wit'. Bodleian Library Jesus MS 74, fol. 282; Brigden, 'Conjured League', p. 526.
16. Sessions, *Henry Howard*, p. 380. Surrey's father had famously declared in 1540, in response to the publication of the Great Bible in the previous year, 'I have never read Scripture nor ever will read it', and said that the world had never been the same since this 'new learning' had appeared. Ibid., pp. 12ff. In 1546, Blage had been convicted of having declared on 9 May, and within no less a place than St Paul's cathedral, that 'the sacrament of the altar did no good, neither to the quick nor the dead . . . [and] the good Lord's body could not in any means be minished ne impaired'. He was only spared from a heretic's death at the stake by Henry VIII's personal intervention. Sessions, *Henry Howard*, pp. 354 and 378–9; Brigden, 'Conjured League', pp. 521–2.

17. Sessions, *Henry Howard*, p. 382; *LP* xviii (i) 351; Brigden, 'Conjured League', p. 510.
18. Sessions, *Henry Howard*, p. 371.
19. *State Papers* i, p. 891; Brigden, 'Conjured League', p. 528; and Sessions, *Henry Howard*, pp. 389–91.
20. For this and the following paragraph, see Lord Herbert of Cherbury, *The Life and Raigne of King Henry the Eighth* (London, 1649), p. 739; Martin A. Sharpe Hulme, ed. and trans., *A Chronicle of King Henry VIII of England: Being a Contemporary Record of Some of the Principal Events of the Reigns of Henry VIII and Edward VI, Written in Spanish by an Unknown Hand* (London, 1889) [hereafter, *Spanish Chronicle*], pp. 146–8; Sessions, *Henry Howard*, pp. 406–9.
21. For the suggestion that the exchange with Blage may have been the occasion of this remark, see Brigden, 'Conjured League', p. 521.
22. *LP* xviii (i) 351; Brigden, 'Conjured League', p. 528; J. G. Nichols, ed., *The Chronicle of Grey Friars*, 53 (London, Camden Society, 1852), p. 52; *Spanish Chronicle*, p. 148; Sessions, *Henry Howard*, pp. 358, 361, and 406–9. The weakness of the evidence against Surrey quickly became notorious. Queen Mary's opening speech to her first parliament made overt reference to the case in its discussion of the need to repeal her father's statutes of treason 'by words'. 'And Henry Earl of Surrey... for such like words, and the poor crime of assuming somewhat into his coat of arms, was actually beheaded... [and] many honourable and noble persons and others of good reputation... for words only suffered shameful deaths, not accustomed to nobles'. John Strype, ed., *Ecclesiastical Memorials* (3 vols., Oxford, Oxford University Press, 1810–28), iii, i, p. 58. And in 1585 Surrey's grandson, Philip Howard, earl of Arundel, recalled how 'my grandfather was brought to his trial and condemned for such trifles as it amazed the standers by at the time, and it is ridiculous to this day to all that hear the same' (Sessions, *Henry Howard*, p. 390).
23. Sessions, *Surrey*, pp. 20–1; Brigden, 'Conjured League', pp. 531ff.
24. Elizabeth Heale, *Wyatt, Surrey and Early Tudor Poetry* (Harlow, Longman, 1998), pp. 26–7.
25. Not in Jones. The text is quoted from F. M. Padelford, ed., *The Poems of Henry Howard, Earl of Surrey* (2nd edn, Seattle, University of Washington Press, 1928), pp. 88–90.
26. See Sessions, *Henry Howard*, pp. 224–7, for an excellent reading of this poem.
27. Herbert, *Life and Raigne*, p. 563.
28. Brigden, 'Conjured League', pp. 51–4; Sessions, *Surrey*, p. 14. Surrey's attitude to the marriages proposed by his father seems to have been highly ambivalent. As his sister later testified, he suggested to her that she show some reluctance to marry when addressed on the subject by the King, and seek his advice, in the hope that he might become attracted to her himself and take her for a mistress, or even as his seventh wife. This suggestion evidently aroused particular ire on the King's part, for the relevant interrogatory was heavily amended in the royal hand. 'If a man compassing *with himself to govern the realm, do actually go about to rule the king*, and should for that purpose advise his daughter, or sister, to become his harlot, *thinking thereby to bring it to pass, and so would rule both father and son... what this importeth?*' (*State Papers* i, p. 891; Brigden, 'Conjured League', p. 528; Henry's amendments italicized).

29. T. Amyot, 'Transcript of an Original Manuscript Containing a Memorial from George Constantyne to Lord Thomas Cromwell', *Archaeologia* 23 (1831), pp. 50–78, p. 62. Even Constantyne, who reported Barlow's words and sought to refute them, felt obliged to concede his pride and youth, suggesting that 'experience will correct [them] well enough'.
30. Sessions, *Henry Howard*, p. 390.
31. G. W. Bernard, 'The Continuing Power of the Tudor Nobility', in Bernard, *Power and Politics in Tudor England* (Aldershot, Ashgate, 2000), pp. 20–50, expanding upon ideas in Bernard, *The Power of the Early Tudor Nobility: A Study of the Fourth and Fifth Earls of Shrewsbury* (Brighton, Harvester, 1985), and Bernard, ed., *The Tudor Nobility* (Manchester, Manchester University Press, 1992), pp. 1–48.
32. Sessions, *Henry Howard*, p. 21. James Simpson notes the 'suicidal quality' to Surrey's Wyatt poems, most obvious in the allusion to Pyramus and Thisbe in the final couplet of 'Dyverse thy deth doo dyverslye bemone', in which the poet imagines himself in like case to the lover who will fall upon his own sword rather than live without the beloved whom he mistakenly believes to have been killed (Simpson, *Reform and Cultural Revolution*, p. 123). And, if not perhaps actively suicidal, there is a sense in much of Surrey's most overtly political verse of death as a very real and tangible threat, a close companion in all his doings. There is a despair in Surrey's writing, a sense that the world has shown him the best that it can offer, and that he is now living out a version of the Last Days, peopled by monsters and beset by plagues. His best poetry, as Alistair Fox observes, 'is almost all memorial'. 'Whether he is remembering his own happy youth, the Tuscan ancestry of his Lady's 'worthy race', the virtues of Wyatt, his dead preceptor, or the deeds of Aeneas and his Trojan followers as he found them in Virgil's *Aeneid*' (Fox, *Politics and Literature*, pp. 286–7). It is memorial in a more literal, monolithic and sepulchral sense too. Wyatt's best work consists in large part of epitaphs, whether formal or otherwise, memorials for dead men of honour: Wyatt, Fitzroy, Thomas Clere, and for honour itself, sacrificed to or cowed by tyranny in the brutal world of Henry VIII's last years.
33. For an excellent account of Surrey's ambitions, see Sessions, *Henry Howard*, pp. 142ff.
34. Leland, *Naeniae*. As Sessions observes, the title *Naeniae* invests the collection with a monumental seriousness, drawing its inspiration from the description in Cicero's *De legibus*, 2:24: '*honoratum virorum laudes cantu ad tibicinem prosequantur cui nomen naenia*' ('The praises of honourable men sung by a flute-player follows, to which (we give) the name *naenia*'). Sessions, *Henry Howard*, p. 251 and footnote.
35. Leland, *Naeniae*, sig. Aiii(v).
36. '*Joannis Lelandi Antiquarii Carmen ad HENRICUM HOWARDUM Regnorum comitem juvenem tum nobilis. Tum doctissimum*', Leland, *Naeniae*, sig. Aii.
37. The translation is taken from Sessions, 'Surrey's Wyatt', p. 184.
38. BL Add. MS 36529, fol. 57 (printed as J29).
39. Burrow, 'The Experience of Exclusion', pp. 814–6.
40. See above, pp. 380–1, and Sessions, 'Surrey's Wyatt', p. 172.
41. Ibid., pp. 187–8.
42. Jones, ed., *Poems*, p. 124.
43. BL Add MS 36529, fol. 56(v) (J30); Patricia Thomson, ed., *Wyatt: The Critical Heritage* (London, Routledge and Kegan Paul, 1974), p. 29.

44. BL Egerton MS 2711, f. 85(v) (J31). Thomson, *Critical Heritage*, p. 28.
45. Sessions, *Surrey*, p. 104; and Brigden, 'Conjured League', p. 515. See also Heale, *Wyatt, Surrey and Early Tudor Poetry*, p. 176.
46. Brigden, 'Conjured League', p. 514.
47. As Sessions has noted, he was not averse to translating '*sapientia*' as 'grace' (Ecclesiastes 2, 55), thereby giving an evangelical slant to an otherwise orthodox statement; and in his paraphrase of the fifth chapter of Ecclesiastes, for example, he pointedly talked of prayer as 'fruit of faith' rather than of penitence, 'whereby God doth with sin dispense' (18–19).
48. See also the passage in his translation of Psalm 54 in which he talks of how the penitent sinner may 'With words of hott effect, that moveth from hert contryte / Such humble sute, O Lord, dothe perce Thy pacyent eare' (30–1).
49. The discussion of Justification in his version of chapter 5 of Ecclesiastes, for example, appears at first glance to be setting a radical agenda, rejecting the efficacy of outward vows and other good works in favour of inward contrition alone. (See Sessions, *Surrey*, pp. 106–7, and Brigden, 'Conjured League', pp. 514–15 for the suggestion that this passage 'breathe[s] the language of the reformers'.) But on closer inspection it is clear that, for all the 'hot effect' and passionate language, Surrey is only condemning hypocritical vows and utterances that are insincere. True oaths and vows made in good faith he praises as 'smoking sweetly':

> When that repentant teares hathe clensyd clere from ill
> The charged brest, and grace hath wrought therin amending will,
> With bold demands then may His mercy well assaile
> The speche man sayth, with owt the which request may not prevaile.
> More shall thy pennytent sighes His endles mercy please,
> Than their importune siuts whiche dreame that words Gods wrath appease.
> For contrit of fault is gladsome recompence,
> And praier fruicte of faythe, wherby God dothe with synne dyspense.
> As ferfull broken slepes spring from a restles hedde,
> By chattering of unholly lippis fruitles prayer bredde.
> In wast of wynde, I rede, vowe nought unto the Lord,
> For humble vowes fulfilled by grace right swetly smoks,
> But bost of such perfitnes, whose works suche fraude expresse,
> With fayned words and othes contract with God no gyle:
> Suche craft returns to thy nown harme, and doth thy self defile.
> And though the myst of sinne perswad suche error light
> Therby yet ar thy outward works all dampned in His syght.

> (4–20)

And elsewhere the statements on piety that he offers are hardly at odds with those of devout catholics such as More or Fisher, as, for example, when he discusses the mortification of the flesh in his paraphrase of Psalm 72 as, ' . . . the warr . . . that I by faythe mayntayne \ Against the fleshe, whose false effects my pure hert wold disdayne, \ For I am scourged still, that no offence have doon, \By wrathes children, and from my borth my chastesing begoon' (29–32). For the altar in Boulogne, see Brigden, 'Conjured League', p. 522.

50. Mishtooni Bose, 'Theorising *Latinitas*: Netter, Gascoigne and Fifteenth-Century Orthodoxy', paper delivered at the International Medieval Congress at the University of Leeds, July 2003. I am grateful to Dr Bose for permission to cite her formulation here.

51. That 'Wyatt's friends' was a group with some historical validity rather than simply a rhetorical construct devised by Surrey in his verses, is suggested by the small number of names that recur in accounts of Wyatt's own companions during his lifetime and in the ownership and transmission of manuscript copies of his works after his death. His son, Thomas Wyatt the younger, Surrey, Mason, Sir George Blage, John Harrington, John Mantell, John Poyntz, Sir Francis Bryan, each of these men had a role to play in receiving, copying, or circulating Wyatt's work during his lifetime or after his death, suggesting that there was indeed an informal 'Wyatt circle' at court in the 1540s.

52. Brigden, 'Conjured League', p. 507.

53. Brian Cummings, *The Literary Culture of the Reformation: Grammar and Grace* (Oxford, Oxford University Press, 2002), p. 224; Simpson, *Reform and Cultural Revolution*, p. 499; Brigden, 'Conjured League', p. 508.

54. Sessions, *Surrey*, pp. 103–4 suggests that the poet was thinking of his own plans for Mount Surrey here, but this would imply a degree of ironic self-criticism not otherwise very evident in Surrey's writings.

55. *Acts of the Privy Council* (1547–50), p. 191; Bodleian Library Rawlinson MS 781, fols. 34 and 197, all cited in Simon Thurley, *The Royal Palaces of Tudor England: Architecture and Court Life* (New Haven, Yale University Press, 1993). The King's size (in 1547 he was 55 inches in the waist, an inch for every year of his life (Sessions, *Henry Howard*, p. 111) and immobility were, seemingly, the subject of considerable indiscrete gossip and joking among the younger Howards. At Whitehall, special wheelchairs had been built to enable Henry to move around the palace, and the royal beds had been strengthened and enlarged to cope with his rapidly expanding frame. (Thurley, *Royal Palaces*, p. 60.) Surrey's brother, Lord Thomas III, is reported to have scoffed that 'the old King lived and moved by engines and art rather than nature' (BL Sloane MS 1523, f. 32(v); Cherbury, *Life and Raigne*, p. 563; Brigden, 'Conjured League', p. 510, fn 47.) Surrey's stress upon the corpulence of the tyrants he describes becomes readily explicable in the light of such evidence. For an unflattering caricature of the King's appearance at this time, see the Cornelis Matsys engraving printed in J. J. Scarisbrick, *Henry VIII* (2nd edn, New Haven, Yale University Press, 1997), plate 23 preceding p. 267; and Sessions, *Henry Howard*, pp. 238–9.

56. The King himself, rather than experience any obvious deathbed dark night of the soul, seems to have gone to his grave quietly confident of his own redemption. He is reported to have told his faithful Groom of the Stool, Sir Anthony Denny, that 'Yet is the mercy of Christ able to pardon me all my sins, though they were greater than they are.' Scarisbrick, *Henry VIII*, p. 495.

57. *LP* xvi, 589–90.

58. For a powerful account of Henry's last years, see Lacey Baldwin Smith, *Henry VIII: The Mask of Royalty* (London, Jonathan Cape, 1971). It would not seem too fanciful to see a reflection of the dramatic changes made to the English landscape through the dissolution of the monasteries and the conversion of their lands and houses to new

secular estates in the poet's reflection of the Vulgate's phrase 'a time to destroy: a time to build' (Ecclesiastes 3:3). 'Auncient walles to race (raze) is our unstable guyse, / And of their wetherbeten stones to buylde some new devyse. / New fanzes dayly spring, which vaade [fade] returning moo; / And now we practyse to optaine that strayt we must foregoo.' (11–14). Sessions, *Surrey*, p. 104.

59. Surrey's own failure to gain a place on the royal Council probably gave an added personal vitriol to this line. Fox, *Politics and Literature*, p. 294.

60. The relevant verses in the Vulgate read simply 'Better is a child that is poor and wise than a king that is old, who knoweth not to foresee for hereafter. Because out of prison and chains sometimes a man cometh forth to a kingdom, and another born king is consumes with poverty. I saw all men living that walk under the sun with the second young man who shall rise up in his place' (Ecclesiastes 4:13–15).

61. Sessions, *Henry Howard*, p. 378.

62. See, for example, his version of Psalm 87: 'My soule is fraughted full with greif of follies past; / My restles bodye doth consume and death approcheth fast; / Lyke them whose fatall threde Thy hand hath cut in twayne, / Of whome ther is no further brewte, which in their graves remayne.' (5–8); and 'Oh Lorde, Thow hast cast me hedling to please my fooe, / Into a pitt all botomeles, whear as I playne my wooe. / The burden of Thy wrath it doth me sore oppresse, / And sundrye stormes Thow hast me sent of terrour and distresse. / The faithfull frends ar fled and bannyshed from my sight, / And such as I have held full dere have sett my frendshipp light. / My duraunce doth perswade of fredom such dispaire / That, by the teares that bayne my brest, myne eye sight doth appaire.' (9–16)

63. 'They are covered with their iniquity and their wickedness. / Their iniquity hath come forth, as it were from fatness: they have passed into the affection of the heart' (Psalm 72:4–8). The source for lines 8–11 in particular is Joannes Campensis, *Psalmorum omnium Iuxta Hebraicam veritatem paraphrastica interpretatio...Paraphrasis in concionem Salomonis Ecclesiastae*: '*Tota enim vita non solum fortunata illis omnia fuerunt, sed et in morte illis accidere solet, ut aetate defecti sine longo cruciatu extinguantur, et palatia relinquant regia haeredibus suis. A molestis, quibus ex ipsa conditione homo fragilis obnoxius est: liberi esse videntur, nec sicut reliqui homines flagellis a malo deterrentur*', quoted in Jones, ed., *Poems*, p. 159.

64. A similar confidence underpins a passage in Ecclesiastes 5: 'Though wronge at tymes the right, and welthe eke nede oppresse, / Thinke not the hand of Justice slowe to followe the redress. / For such unrightius folke, as rule with out dredd, / By some abuse or secret lust He suffereth to be led.' (25–8). F. M. Padelford, ed., *The Poems of Henry Howard Earl of Surrey* (Seattle, University of Washington Press, 1928), p. 107.

65. Scarisbrick, *Henry VIII*, pp. 485–6; Sessions, *Henry Howard*, p. 111.

66. Jones cautiously concludes, 'It is tempting, but not necessary to see in this poem a covert allusion to Henry VIII.' Jones, ed., *Poems*, p. 127.

67. Jones, ed., *Poems*, p. 159; Sessions, *Surrey*, p. 113. Brigden suggests, interestingly, that, given that the text goes on to accuse 'Friowr, whose harme and tounge presents the wicked sort / Of those false wolves, with cootes which doo their ravin hyde' (42–3), the 'frendly foo' may have been one Dr John Fryer, a servant of Surrey's. Brigden, 'Conjured League', pp. 533ff.

68. Sessions, *Surrey*, p. 109.

69. Is it, perhaps, significant that Blage himself does not seem to have been the one to raise the argument as evidence in the court? Had a hastily despatched psalm done its work?
70. Brigden, 'Conjured League', p. 522.
71. Heale, *Wyatt, Surrey and Early Tudor Poetry*, pp. 180–1.
72. Brigden, 'Conjured League', p. 533.
73. BL Additional MS 36529 (printed as J34).
74. Heale, *Wyatt, Surrey and Early Tudor Poetry*, p. 122.
75. For the claim that this was Surrey's last work, see Henry Howard, Earl of Northampton, *Dutiful Defence of the Royal Regimen of Women*, dedicatory Epistle, cited in Jones, *Poems*, pp. 130–1.
76. Heale, *Wyatt, Surrey and Early Tudor Poetry*, pp. 183–4.
77. Ibid., p. 184.

17. WRITING UNDER TYRANNY

1. G. R. Elton, *The Tudor Revolution in Government: Administrative Changes in the Reign of Henry VIII* (Cambridge, Cambridge University Press, 1953).
2. In this way the Henrician poets and prose writers pre-empted a phenomenon that historians of ideas have tended to see as a development of the later sixteenth-century, the revival of classical republicanism. See J. G. A. Pocock, *The Machiavellian Moment: Florentine Political Thought and the Atlantic Republican Tradition* (Princeton, Princeton University Press, 1975); Markku Peltonen, *Classical Humanism and Republicanism in English Political Thought, 1570–1640* (Cambridge, Cambridge University Press, 1995), especially p. 4, where it is claimed that only in the 1550s did the idea of the humanist as merely a counsellor to princes make way for 'the Tacitean courtier in whom we encounter the first signs of a fully fledged conception of a political community as an association of active participants'.
3. Stephen Greenblatt's *Renaissance Self-Fashioning: From More to Shakespeare* (Chicago, University of Chicago Press, 1984) was obviously the seminal text here, but one of the earliest and most insightful of subsequent treatments was Alistair Fox's psychoanalytically driven study, *Politics and Literature in the Reigns of Henry VII and Henry VIII* (Oxford, Basil Blackwell, 1989)
4. James Simpson, *Reform and Cultural Revolution: The Oxford English Literary History*, vol. 2 (Oxford, Oxford University Press, 2002), p. 558.
5. Simpson, *Reform and Cultural Revolution*, p. 150.
6. Thomas Starkey, *A Dialogue Between Pole and Lupset*, ed. T. F. Mayer, Camden Society 5th series, 37 (London, Royal Historical Society, 1989), p. 166.
7. For this suggestion, see Hogrefe, *Sir Thomas Elyot*, p. 200.
8. Lerer, *Courtly Letters*, passim.
9. For a powerful account of Surrey's political vision and ambitions, see Sessions, *Henry Howard*, pp. 217ff.
10. George Puttenham, *The Arte of English Poesie (1589)*, Scolar Facsimile Edition (Menston, Scolar Press, 1968), p. 48.
11. Puttenham, *Arte of English Poesie*, p. 49.
12. Stephen Greenblatt, *Renaissance Self-Fashioning*, p. 156.

13. See, for example, Sergio Baldi, *Sir Thomas Wyatt*, trans. F. T. Prince (Harlow, Longman for the British Council, 1961), pp. 18–22.

14. See, for example, Heale, *Wyatt, Surrey and Early Tudor Poetry*, p. 3; Baldi, *Sir Thomas Wyatt*, p. 7; E. M. W. Tillyard, *The Poetry of Sir Thomas Wyatt: An Appreciation and a Study* (2nd edn, London, Chatto and Windus, 1949), p. 20; H. A. Mason, *Humanism and Poetry in the Early Tudor Period* (London, Routledge and Kegan Paul, 1959), pp. 190–91; Raymond Southall, *The Courtly Maker: An Essay on the Poetry of Wyatt and His Contemporaries* (Oxford, Basil Blackwell, 1964), pp. 114 and 128–9.

15. Sessions, *Henry Howard*, p. 132. See also Heale, *Wyatt, Surrey and Early Tudor Poetry*, p. 83.

16. Sessions, *Henry Howard*, p. 137.

17. Baldasar Castiglione, *The Courtier*, trans. Charles S. Singleton (New York, Doubleday and Co., 1959), p. 43, where *sprezzatura* is defined as: 'the true art' that 'does not seem to be art'.

18. See Hyder Edward Rollins, ed., *Tottel's Miscellany* (2 vols., Cambridge, Mass., Harvard University Press, 1928), vol. I. For perceptive accounts of the influence of the Miscellany on subsequent poetic activity in England, see Sessions, *Henry Howard*, pp. 116 and 274ff; and Sergio Baldi, *Sir Thomas Wyatt*, p. 5: 'Until 1579, when Spenser published his *Shepheardes Calendar*, *Tottel's Miscellany* remained almost the sole school of poetry for English writers, from it the poets of the first twenty years of Elizabeth's reign learnt not only the seriousness of which the new lyric poetry was capable, but also many new means of expression, valid for all kinds of verse…'

19. The *frottola* was a form of stanzaic lyric with a refrain, conventionally a tetrameter, rhyming ababcc. It was developed by Serafino de'Ciminelli dall'Aquila (1446–1500) at the Mantuan court, and first arrived in England with the Venetian Nicolo Sigurdino in *c.* 1515 (Heale, *Wyatt, Surrey and Early Tudor Poetry*, pp. 78–83; Sessions, *Henry Howard*, p. 29). Wyatt subsequently popularized its use in English in the 1530s. Serafino also devised the *strambotto*, an eight-line lyric rhyming abababcc, which Wyatt also domesticated. Poulter's Measure, the curious arrangement of lines of 12 and 14 syllables in rhyming couplets is, as Sessions observes, 'probably the most maligned of all meters in English', but it enjoyed a remarkable popularity in the sixteenth century, to the point where George Gascoigne could call it (not without a hint of condescension) 'the commonest sort of verse which we use now adays'. As Gascoigne explained, the name stemmed from its curious amalgam of syllables: 'I know not certainly how to name it, unless I should say it doth consist of Poulter's measure, which giveth xii [eggs] for one dozen and xiii for another'. G. Gascoigne, *Works*, ed., John W. Cunliffe (2 vols., Cambridge, Cambridge University Press, 1907–10), I, p. 472; Sessions, *Henry Howard*, p. 88.

20. For Wyatt's 'inwardness', see Raymond Southall, *The Courtly Maker* (Oxford, Basil Blackwell, 1964), p. 98ff; and Anne Ferry, *The 'Inward' Language: Sonnets of Wyatt, Surrey, Shakespeare, Donne* (Chicago, University of Chicago Press, 1983), Chapter 2.

21. Burrow, 'The Experience of Exclusion', pp. 815–16: ' "inwardness" in Surrey's verse… grows from a social milieu; it was usually prompted by the experience of being at odds with the rest of the world… He, like Wyatt, writes a poetry of selfhood which grows from an environment of accusation'. See also James Simpson's conclusion that 'the discursive features hailed as characteristic of Renaissance poetic practice

are in fact the product of the peculiarly repressive discursive conditions of the Henrician Court' (*Reform and Cultural Revolution*, p. 152); and Sessions, *Henry Howard*, pp. ix–x.

22. Heale, *Wyatt, Surrey and Early Tudor Poetry*, p. 86.
23. Ibid., p. 88.
24. Ibid., pp. 100–3.
25. *OED* sv 'Baffle'.
26. Thomas A. Hannen, 'The Humanism of Sir Thomas Wyatt', in Thomas O. Sloan and Raymond B. Waddington, eds., *The Rhetoric of Renaissance Poetry from Wyatt to Milton* (Berkeley, University of California Press, 1974), pp. 37–57, p. 43.
27. Heale, *Wyatt, Surrey and Early Tudor Poetry*, p. 105.
28. Foley, *Sir Thomas Wyatt*, p. 57.
29. Sessions, *Henry Howard*, p. 131.
30. Simpson, *Reform and Cultural Revolution*, pp. 134 and 127.
31. Sessions, *Henry Howard*, pp. 136–9.
32. Ibid., pp. 260ff.
33. *Legend of Good Women*, F-496–7.
34. Stephen Hawes, *The Pastime of Pleasure*, ed. William Edward Mead, EETS original series, 173 (London, Oxford University Press, 1928), 5408ff.
35. My sense of the peculiarity of Skelton and Hawes's poetic personae was reinforced by the stimulating discussion conducted in the 'The Past as Present: Medieval Traditions, Tudor Politics, and Tudor Poetics' session at the 2003 International Medieval Congress at the University of Leeds by Professors Tony Hasler, of Saint Louis University, Nancy Bradley Warren of Florida State University, and Robert Meyer-Lee of Rhodes College, the University of Notre Dame. I am grateful for the chance to develop these ideas here, and to record my indebtedness to their inspiration. Thanks in particular to Tony Hasler for allowing me to read a draft chapter of his unpublished study of Hawes's work.
36. Rollins, ed., *Tottel's Miscellany*, p. 2.

Index